**Springer Texts in Business and Economics**

Springer Texts in Business and Economics (STBE) delivers high-quality instructional content for undergraduates and graduates in all areas of Business/Management Science and Economics. The series is comprised of self-contained books with a broad and comprehensive coverage that are suitable for class as well as for individual self-study. All texts are authored by established experts in their fields and offer a solid methodological background, often accompanied by problems and exercises.

More information about this series at http://www.springer.com/series/10099

Parthasarathi Shome

# Taxation History, Theory, Law and Administration

Springer

Parthasarathi Shome
London School of Economics
London, UK
International Tax Research and Analysis Foundation
Bengaluru, India

ISSN 2192-4333 ISSN 2192-4341 (electronic)
Springer Texts in Business and Economics
ISBN 978-3-030-68213-2 ISBN 978-3-030-68214-9 (eBook)
https://doi.org/10.1007/978-3-030-68214-9



This Springer imprint is published by the registered company Springer Nature Switzerland AG.
The registered company address is: Gewerbestrasse 11, 6330 Cham, Switzerland

*To Dipti Shome, my mother, in loving memory*

*hostinato rigore*

—Leonardo da Vinci
1452–1519 A.D.
painter, architect, engineer and thinker
of the High Renaissance

# Preface

This book introduces taxation with a comprehensive approach. Usually, different aspects of taxation are taught in separate blocs—history, economic theory, law, and administration—in near-independent courses of instruction. With that demarcation, students are deprived of an understanding of taxation from beginning to end in an integrated approach, that is, through its many stages from conceptualisation to drawing up various tax laws, to its interpretation and administration, leave alone any historical experience of it. In this book, that opportunity is provided so that students and tax professionals specialised in particular areas can become familiar with all these aspects and their mastery over taxation can be all inclusive.

The text is written in a simple style so that the reader can move smoothly from one aspect to the next, the crux of the approach being to ensure a solid understanding of the subject matter from their pillars rather than being a reference book exclusively for research scholars. Selected references are cited that represent early discussion of an idea initiated by an established scholar which resulted in recognised theory. Those are relevant, historically or currently, and continue to play a crucial role in the subject of taxation. Others comprise references to readings on hypotheses that may not have been firmed up though they are on the forefront of international discussion and should not be missed. The progress of the chapters witnesses more involved analysis as the complexity of the topics itself increases. In this sense, the reader goes through pyramidic learning, from the simpler to the more involved, and to the still evolving.

This volume should be considered as a book in the direction of learning the first steps of taxation and its wide ramifications. After this stage, students would proceed further in undertaking studies at more advanced levels in taxation and possibly take their learning forward in more narrowly defined areas that have fascinated them in this book. That goal would be achieved if institutions too teach taxation in the wider canvas presented in this book under the same umbrella or course of study. In this sense, the book should be relevant and useful also to the tax-related professions during the process of their learning and training in taxation. Globally, possibly few books currently offer the cross-cutting coverage across fields that this book provides.

Having been trained in the theoretical aspects of taxation, I took up university teaching of tax economics—rather, public finance—for 7 years. I subsequently spent several years in a multilateral institution, and worked, in particular, on tax policy issues in many countries, for 17 years. Subsequently, I worked in two governments—6 years in an emerging economy and 3 years in an advanced economy—delving into their tax laws and tax administration, and assisting in the design and implementation of tax policy.

I faced the challenge of becoming familiar with the legal and administrative issues of taxation since I had been originally trained only in its economic aspects. I realised that there was no particular reason why I should not have been taught the missing aspects in a continuum during my student years. Writing a book on all aspects of taxation with an integrated scope took shape in my mind. A comment from my mother that I had begun my career as an academician and should I not write a book for students, combined with my desire to write a book on all aspects of taxation, pushed me towards writing this book on taxation for students—a textbook.

Examples cited in books that I learnt from as a student were usually from a Western perspective, sometimes beyond the comfort of a young Eastern student not too familiar with Western society or culture. In this book, I have corrected that deficiency somewhat. I have provided historical evidence taking India as a case study; nevertheless, any international student should find learning from this book helpful. There are many institutions in the West deeply involved in the study of Indian economic history and its public finances that should also find the context of this book useful. A relevant emerging economy context represents a crucial need and I have found that the modern student actually expects to be so informed. I have sought to fill that need.

To sum up, the book has been written with the objective that students achieve competence over the foundations of taxation and prevalent practices in an integrated way. It covers glimpses of taxation history, use of economic theory, basis of taxation law and prevalent taxes, emerging issues in international taxation, and the best structures and practices in tax administration. I have confined references to historically important treatises and selective recent works. This should enable the student to focus on the rudiments and master the material at hand, while those interested in pursuing the subject further could accomplish that through further enquiry into the depths of taxation. Note that the gender neutral pronoun "he" has been used throughout the book reflecting usual practice.

A word in conclusion. This book has been written during extraordinary global times, that of the Covid-19 pandemic. Taxation takes on an especially crucial role in that governments need significantly enhanced resources as their expenditure pressures have mounted. For success, a two-pronged approach is necessary. First, governments must win the confidence of taxpayers by treating them as stakeholders and customers so that their tax participation can improve even in these trying times. School children should also be taught about taxation and why they should pay taxes when they buy consumption items and earn incomes. Second, to buttress such an approach, governments should reveal through announcements and advertisements how taxpayer contributions are being used. Clearly, an altogether new approach to taxation will have to be developed and deployed by tax administrations in the unfolding and uncertain future.

I owe my appreciation to several people and institutions. Some have played important and direct roles in this endeavour of mine. Navneet Manohar contributed the India case studies of Chaps. 17, 19, and 27, and Appendix 1 and 2 of Chap. 20. Kunal Chakrabarti read the part on taxation history to ensure factual correctness and brought several scholarly works to my attention as did Shubhra Chakrabarti. Carlos Julio Moreno Leguizamon read those portions where I felt I needed a reader to ensure that they were balanced. My location at the tax law programme of the London School of Economics (LSE) was enabled by Philip Baker, and I received encouragement from Eduardo Baistrocchi and Ian Roxan. I appreciate the mutual cooperation I experienced there. The International Tax Research and Analysis Foundation (ITRAF) provided infrastructural support. Rohitash Chaudhary provided technical support of downloading information, converting my hand-drawn figures with appropriate software, and listing my abbreviations. I am grateful to the anonymous referees and to Irene Barrios-Kezic and Rocio Torregosa of Springer for taking me through the sometimes arduous process of publishing. Most of all, I remain ever indebted to my parents for their persistent and invaluable support throughout my education and beyond.

London, UK
Spring 2021

Parthasarathi Shome

# Contents

## Part III Tax Law

## Part IV Prevalent Taxes

**Part VII Ideal Tax Design**

# About the Author

**Parthasarathi Shome** is Visiting Senior Fellow at the London School of Economics; Chairman, International Tax Research and Analysis Foundation (ITRAF), India, www.parthoshome.com; and Member, Academic Board of Advanced Diploma in International Taxation (ADIT), London.

He served in the Government of India as Minister of State and Secretary between 2004 and 2015, as Chairman, Tax Administration Reform Commission (TARC), as Adviser to the Indian Finance Minister, and as Chairman, Expert Committee on GAAR (international tax avoidance), and other assignments.

Between 2008 and 2011, he was Chief Economist, Her Majesty's Revenue and Customs (HMRC), United Kingdom. He served as Director of two of India's frontline economic research institutions: International Council for Research on International Economic Relations (ICRIER), 2011–2013, and National Institute of Public Finance and Policy (NIPFP), 1995–1997.

He served at the IMF between 1983 and 2004 in various capacities including Chief of Tax Policy, the first Senior Economist in the Office of the Managing Director, and a diplomatic assignment as Director, IMF Singapore Institute. He has provided technical assistance in the fiscal field to 35 countries in Africa, Asia, Europe, and Latin America and drafted many related policy reports.

He rose to a tenured Professorship at the American University, Washington D.C., 1975–1983. His Ph.D. thesis on the incidence of the corporation income tax from Southern Methodist University, Dallas, 1975, fetched him the Jeanne S. Mattersdorf Award of the National Tax Association of America as "an outstanding student in the field of taxation and public finance". He received Brazil's highest civilian honour, *Commander of the Order of the Southern Cross*, for contributions to Brazilian tax reform, in 2000.

He is widely published in peer-reviewed journals including *IMF Staff Papers, Journal of Public Economics, National Tax Journal (US), Oxford Economic Papers, Oxford Review of Economic Policy, Public Finance*, and several others. He has written and edited books from Cambridge University Press, Lexis Nexis, Oakbridge, Orient Blackswan, Oxford University Press, Springer, Wolters Kluwer, and others. He continues to be a popularly invited speaker in conferences and seminars across the globe. He has published a professional memoir and a coffee table volume on Naïve Art in which he became interested during his global travels to 80 countries.

# Abbreviations

| | |
|---|---|
| AAAR | Appellate Authority for Advance Ruling |
| AAR | Authority for Advance Ruling |
| AB | Administrative Burden |
| AC | Accumulated Credit |
| AC | Average Cost |
| ADB | Asian Development Bank |
| ADR | Alternative Dispute Resolution |
| AHT | Agriculture Holdings Tax |
| ALP | Arm's Length Price |
| AMT | Alternate Minimum Tax |
| AO | Assessment Officer |
| AoA | Article of Association |
| AoPs | Association of Persons |
| AP | Average Product |
| APA | Advance Pricing Agreement |
| AR | Advance Ruling |
| ARA | Advance Ruling Authority |
| ATAD | Anti-Tax Avoidance Directive |
| AY | Assessment Year |
| B2B | Business-to-Business |
| B2C | Business-to-Consumer |
| BC | Before Christ |
| BCE | Before Common Era |
| BCTT | Banking Cash Transaction Tax |
| BEPS | Base Erosion and Profit Shifting |
| BRICS | Brazil, Russia, India, China, and South Africa |
| C2C | Consumer-to-Consumer |
| CA | Competent Authority |
| CbC | Country-by-Country |
| CBDT | Central Board of Direct Taxes |
| CBIC | Central Board of Indirect Taxes and Customs |
| CBIN | Common Business Identification Number |
| CC | Chief Commissioner |

| | |
|---|---|
| CC | Compliance Cost |
| CCC | Customer Communication Centre |
| CCC | Customs Co-operation Council |
| CCFT | Corporate Cash-Flow Tax |
| CCI | Constant Cost Industry |
| CCT | Common Customs Tariff |
| CENVAT | Central Value-Added Tax |
| CFCs | Chlorofluorocarbons |
| CFC | Controlled Foreign Company |
| CFO | Chief Financial Officer |
| CGE | Computable General Equilibrium |
| CGST | Central Goods and Services Tax |
| CGT | Capital Gains Taxes |
| CIC | Community Indifference Curves |
| CII | Cost Inflation Index |
| CIS | Commonwealth of Independent States |
| CIT | Corporate Income Tax |
| CMAA | Customs Mutual Administrative Agreement |
| CN | Combined Nomenclature |
| CoRA | Comparative Risk Assessment Initiative |
| CPC | Central Processing Centre |
| CPM | Cost Plus Method |
| CRM | Customer Relationship Manager |
| CRS | Common Reporting Standards |
| CSR | Corporate Social Responsibility |
| CST | Central Sales Tax |
| CT | Corporate Tax |
| CTA | Covered Tax Agreement |
| CTS | Corporate Tax Statistics |
| CTT | Commodities Transaction Tax |
| CUP | Comparable Uncontrolled Price Method |
| C-VAT | Consumption-Type VAT |
| CVD | Countervailing Duty |
| DANIDA | Danish International Development Agency |
| DCI | Decreasing Cost Industry |
| DDT | Dividend Distribution Tax |
| DFID | Department for International Development |
| DGFT | Directorate General of Foreign Trade |
| DL | Deadweight Loss |
| DPV | Discounted Present Value |
| DRI | Directorate of Revenue Intelligence |
| DRP | Dispute Resolution Panel |
| DST | Digital Services Tax |
| DTAA | Double Tax Avoidance Agreement |
| EBIT | Earnings Before Interest and Taxes |
| EBITDA | Earnings Before Interest, Taxes, Depreciation, and Amortisation |

| | |
|---|---|
| EC | Education Cess |
| EC | Empowered Committee |
| ECU | European Customs Union |
| EC-VAT | Empowered Committee of State Finance Ministers |
| EDI | Electronic Data Interchange |
| EDR | Early Dispute Resolution |
| EFS | Elasticities of Factor Substitution |
| EIC | East India Company |
| EL | Equalisation Levy |
| ESS | Electronically Supplied Services |
| EU | European Union |
| EWB | Electronic Way Bill |
| FAQ's | Frequently Asked Questions |
| FATCA | Foreign Account Tax Compliance Act |
| FBT | Fringe Benefits Tax |
| FC | Fixed Cost |
| FDI | Foreign Direct Investment |
| FF | Fully Funded |
| FHTP | Forum on Harmful Tax Practices |
| FII | Foreign Institutional Investor |
| FIU | Financial Intelligence Unit |
| FPI | Foreign Portfolio Investor |
| FTA | Forum on Tax Administration |
| FTC | Foreign Tax Credit |
| FTS | Fees for Technical Services |
| FTT | Financial Transaction Tax |
| FY | Financial Year |
| G20 | Group of 20 |
| GAAR | General Anti-Avoidance Rule |
| GATT | General Agreement on Trade and Tariffs |
| GDP | Gross Domestic Product |
| GOI | Government of India |
| GST | Goods and Services Tax |
| GSTN | Goods and Service Tax Network |
| HEC | Health and Education Cess |
| HIRE | Hiring Incentives to Restore Employment |
| HMRC | Her Majesty's Revenue and Customs |
| HRA | House Rent Allowance |
| HTVI | Hard-to-Value Intangibles |
| HUF | Hindu Undivided Family |
| ICAI | Indian Chartered Accountant Institute |
| ICAP | International Compliance Assurance Programme |
| ICEGATE | Indian Customs and Central Excise Electronic Commerce |
| ICI | Increasing Cost Industry |
| ICRIER | Indian Council for Research on International Economic Relations |

| | |
|---|---|
| ICT | Information and Communications Technology |
| IEO | Independent Evaluation Office |
| IF | Inclusive Framework |
| IGST | Integrated Goods and Services Tax |
| IIT | Indian Institute of Technology |
| IMF | International Monetary Fund |
| IOT | Internet of Things |
| IP | Intellectual Property |
| IPR | Intellectual Property Rights |
| IRS | Internal Revenue Service |
| ITA | Income-Tax Act |
| ITAT | Income Tax Appellate Tribunal |
| ITC | Input Tax Credit |
| ITeS | Information Technology Enabled Services |
| ITIC | International Tax and Investment Centre |
| ITR | International Tax Regime |
| I-VAT | Income-Type VAT |
| KAI | Knowledge, Analysis, Intelligence |
| KPIs | Key Performance Indicators |
| LAN | Local Area Network |
| LBS | Large Business Service |
| LDCs | Least Developed Countries |
| LIBOR | London Inter-Bank Offered Rate |
| LLP | Limited Liability Partnership |
| LoB | Limitation of Benefits |
| LTA | Leave Travel Allowance |
| LTCG | Long-Term Capital Gains |
| LTFP | Long-Term Fiscal Policy |
| LTU | Large Taxpayer Unit |
| M&E | Monitoring and Evaluation |
| MAP | Mutual Agreement Procedure |
| MAT | Minimum Alternate Tax |
| MC | Marginal Cost |
| MD | Managing Director |
| METR | Marginal Effective Tax Rate |
| MIDS | Madras Institute of Development Studies |
| MLI | Multilateral Instrument |
| MNE | Multinational Enterprise |
| MoA | Memorandum of Association |
| MODVAT | Modified Value Added Tax |
| MoU | Memoranda of Understanding |
| MP | Marginal Product |
| MRS | Marginal Rate of Substitution |
| MRT | Marginal Rate of Transformation |
| MRTS | Marginal Rate of Technical Substitution |
| MSME | Micro, Small, and Medium Enterprise |

| | |
|---|---|
| MVT | Motor Vehicle Taxation |
| NACIN | National Academy of Customs, Indirect Taxes and Narcotics |
| NADT | National Academy of Direct Taxes |
| NAFTA | North American Free Trade Agreement |
| NAMA | Non-Agricultural Market Access |
| NCMP | National Common Minimum Programme |
| NEC | National E-assessment Centre |
| NGO | Non-Governmental Organisation |
| NIC | National Insurance Contribution |
| NIPFP | National Institute of Public Finance and Policy |
| NPA | Non-Performing Asset |
| NTT | National Tax Tribunal |
| OECD | Organisation of Economic Co-operation and Development |
| OIT | Offshore Indirect Transfer Tax |
| OPTR | Observatory on the Protection of Taxpayers' Rights |
| OTS | Office of Tax Simplification |
| PAN | Permanent Account Number |
| PAYG | Pay-As-You-Go |
| PBR | Pre-Budget Review |
| PCC | Principal Chief Commissioner |
| PE | Permanent Establishment |
| PGT | Tax on Passengers and Goods |
| PIS | Passenger Information System |
| PIT | Personal Income Tax |
| PN | Participatory Note |
| POEM | Place of Effective Management |
| PoS | Place of Supply |
| PoW | Programme of Work |
| PP | Production Possibility |
| PPF | Public Provident Fund |
| PPP | Public–Private Partnership |
| PPT | Principal Purpose Test |
| PSM | Profit Split Method |
| PTC | Proforma Tax Credit |
| P-VAT | Production-Type VAT |
| PVE | Permanent Virtual Establishment |
| R&D | Research and Development |
| RBI | Reserve Bank of India |
| RCM | Reverse Charge Mechanism |
| REC | Regional E-assessment Centre |
| RIA | Regulatory Impact Assessment |
| RMD | Risk Management Division |
| RPM | Resale Price Method |
| RST | Retail Sales Tax |
| SAAR | Specific Anti-Avoidance Rules |
| SAFE FoS | Framework of Standards to Secure and Facilitate Global Trade |

| | |
|---|---|
| SC | Settlement Commission |
| SC | Surcharge |
| SCM | Standard Cost Model |
| SCN | Show Cause Notice |
| SCST | Scheduled Caste and Scheduled Tribe |
| SDLT | Stamp Duty Land Tax |
| SEP | Significant Economic Presence |
| SERPRO | Federal Data Processing Service |
| SEZ | Special Economic Zones |
| SFC | State Finance Commission |
| SGST | State Goods and Services Tax |
| SHEC | Secondary and Higher Education Cess |
| SLA | Service Level Agreement |
| SLOB | Simplified Limitation on Benefit |
| SMEs | Small and Medium-Sized Enterprises |
| SPV | Special Purpose Vehicle |
| STCG | Short-Term Capital Gains |
| STT | Security Transaction Tax |
| TARC | Tax Administration Reforms Commission |
| TAS | Tax Advocate Service |
| TBML | Trade-Based Money Laundering |
| TC | Total Cost |
| TCS | Tax Collected at Source |
| TDOTS | Tax Dispute Online Tracking System |
| TDRC | Taxpayer Dispute Resolution Centre |
| TDS | Tax Deducted at Source |
| TIN | Taxpayer Identification Number |
| TNMM | Transactional Net Margin Method |
| TP | Transfer Pricing |
| TPO | Transfer Pricing Officer |
| TRAQ | Tax Risk Assessment Questionnaire |
| TREAT | Tax Risk Evaluation and Assurance Tool |
| TRIPS | Trade-Related Aspects of Intellectual Property Rights |
| UA | Unified Approach |
| UK | United Kingdom |
| US | United States |
| USTR | U.S. Trade Representative |
| UTDT | Universidad Torcuato Di Tella |
| VAT | Value-Added Tax |
| WAN | Wide Area Network |
| WCO | World Customs Organization |
| WDV | Written-Down Value |
| WHO | World Health Organization |
| WHT | Withholding Tax |
| WTO | World Trade Organization |

# List of Figures

# List of Tables

# Introduction to Taxation

# 1

In this introductory chapter, students first get a snapshot of how markets work and what happens when a tax is introduced in the market. They will understand why governments impose taxes while, at the same time, what the modern principles are that should be borne in mind when introducing taxes. For example, some taxes may reallocate allocated economic resources, determined at the pre-tax market situation, more extensively than other taxes. Yet other taxes may hurt one group of economic agents such as labourers more than other agents such as capital owners by affecting their relative market prices. To the extent that such effects are known, they should be kept in mind when introducing taxes. From there, students will transit to the matter of tax design comprising a menu of taxes that typically forms a tax structure. The student will be introduced to a comprehensive list of taxes used commonly across countries.

Once a tax design has emerged, the entire structure has to be set in legal terms usually termed a tax code or tax statute. A tax code is used for implementing a tax legally by the tax administration on a taxpayer, and by legal experts and the judiciary if there are disputes in the interpretation of law. Thus, once tax economists complete the design of a tax system, tax law emerges as a crucial subsequent element. A capsule on the legal role is examined next in that it converts taxation theory based on economics into understandable and interpretable language that can be referred to for any subsequent action such as tax payment by taxpayer, tax assessment by tax administrator, tax argumentation by legal experts or tax judgements by the judiciary.

While tax design may be clear and tax law may be comprehensible, the transparency of its application depends crucially on the tax administration. This includes: (1) the methods by which taxpayers are assessed to pay tax, (2) the manner in which tax is collected, (3) the transparency with which a taxpayer may be audited or scrutinised, (4) the extent to which measures may or may not be applied—draconian or otherwise—to determine and control tax evasion, (5) the willingness of the tax administration to recognise any errors that may have been committed against an honest taxpayer, (6) whether there is overemphasis on a revenue objective, or (7) whether revenue is accepted as a reflection of the economic cycle. Experience



P. Shome, *Taxation History, Theory, Law and Administration*, Springer Texts in Business and Economics, https://doi.org/10.1007/978-3-030-68214-9_1

reveals that tax administrations across the world have tended to move in tandem in terms of their structure and practices though a few countries have not. Such administrative aspects will also be touched upon here.

Taxation across the world has a basis. There is a history of taxation in every country. Textbooks suffer a bias in presenting the history of taxation with almost exclusive citations from western history. Yet Indian history is replete with examples of the design and application of taxes. Here the student will go through a short history of Indian taxation from pre-history through modern-day history. This is a crucial aspect that any student should be familiar with, in particular, the knowledge of the extreme burdens that the ordinary citizen may have to suffer through the centuries.

Why is this important? When a student holds the office of a tax administrator, he should be fully aware of the background of taxation, and conduct himself with the utmost transparency and even compassion when facing a taxpayer. It should never be assumed that a taxpayer is a tax evader unless it is so proven. Investigations should be appropriate, without undertaking any roving enquiry against him. If evasion is proved, then of course action should be taken but, until then, no presumption should be made. Below we take up in greater detail the numerous aspects of taxation mentioned above.

## 1.1 Market Behaviour of Consumers and Producers

In a world without taxes, how are consumers and producers assumed to behave? Consumers behave in reflection of their preference—or utility—functions while producers depend on available technology and engineering to construct the trajectory of their costs and, thereby, their supply of outputs at given market prices of outputs. All consumers combine to generate market demand at different prices and all suppliers combine to generate market supply at given prices.

Equilibrium price and quantity occur where the demand and supply schedules—curves—intersect. This occurs for all commodities demanded and supplied. They are then grossed up to get a complete picture of the entire economy. Where marginal rates of substitution among consumers equal the marginal rates of transformation among producers, the economy is in equilibrium. Through figures and explanations, these foundational concepts will be elaborated in the chapters that follow.

## 1.2 Introduction of Taxes in Market Equilibrium

Governments impose taxes on consumption and incomes generated at the market equilibrium to finance public expenditure. But taxes distort the original market decisions as indicated above. If the tax is taken directly from consumers, they will modify their demand away from taxed goods and towards untaxed goods. This decision to shift demand is made entirely due to tax, rather than being based on their free market choice. If the tax is taken from producers or the owners of factors of production that go into making a commodity or good—investors, wage earners and owners of land—then they will also modify their production decisions and supply a different, post-tax supply in the market. Thus, the post-tax equilibrium in the market will tend to be quite different from the pre-tax equilibrium. And the relationship between the two will reflect various elasticities—or reactions—of substitution between commodities and across various factors of production.

The impact of taxation in shifting the original market equilibrium to another point results in an 'excess burden' caused by tax reflecting the fact that some of the consumer benefit—also termed surplus—is forever lost as a result of this shift. Some taxes are said to cause higher excess burden than others. The role of taxation in causing distortions that result in excess burden is illustrated with figures and explanations so the student knows right from the start the need for caution in introducing taxes.

## 1.3 Partial and General Tax Incidence

A tax may be collected from a firm or individual but its final burden, or what economists term 'tax incidence', may fall on another economic entity. Thus, a tax on consumers such as a selected excise on tobacco, alcohol or petroleum may have to be partially borne by producers if a high elasticity of demand drives away some consumption as a result of the tax. Looking just at the consumption market reveals the 'partial incidence' of a tax since it does not examine comprehensively how the markets for factors of production—in the supply chain—are affected.

A corporate income tax on the earnings of capital in the corporate sector, may be passed on from capital to other factors of production such as wage earners or landowners depending on the elasticities of substitution among these factors of production. When all resultant factor movements are completed after the tax is imposed, and a 'general equilibrium' of the economy is reached again, the final picture of 'general incidence'—which factors of production bear what proportion of the tax—is revealed.

If firms can pass on their tax burden irrespective of the taxes they face, then an explanation is needed as to why they spend time and financial resources in lobbying for their preferred tax structures. This practical side of the tax experience has to be juxtaposed on the more conceptual basis of tax and its incidence. Tax incidence coupled with actual patterns in firm behaviour will be examined in some detail since, moving away from the economic aspects, this area comprises a central point for practical aspects of taxation analysis comprising the concerns of tax law, accountancy and administration. Explanations and figures will be used.

## 1.4 Why Governments Impose Taxes

Nevertheless, all governments, with few exceptions, impose taxes. This is because governments need to supply certain goods and services that market decisions made by individuals cannot ensure. Sometimes there is also little private sector generated demand for them. Examples of such goods include goods that are indivisible, so that no consumer can be excluded even if he does not pay for it, and yet are considered essential for society. These are typically defence, law and order, education, public health, large infrastructure—dams, highways, waterways—and others. Therefore, they have to be provided by government through its budget allocation in which the issue of exclusion does not arise. It is presumed that the distortion caused by the collection of tax revenue will be overcompensated by the utility or satisfaction derived by society from consuming such public goods.

The rationale behind taxes and the provision of public goods will be delineated through figures and explanations.

## 1.5 Principles of Taxation

### 1.5.1 Traditional Concepts

Thus, taxes distort market prices of products and inputs, and distort consumer and producer behaviour. Nevertheless, as explained, governments have to collect taxes. It becomes imperative, therefore, to develop certain principles that have to be adhered to in order to minimise their distortionary ramifications as well as their other adverse effects. These principles are encased in a series of criteria that comprise, first, 'efficiency' or minimisation of market distortions.

Second, a tax could affect consumers and producers differently due to their different positions in the overall economy; thus taxes are usually inequitable. Therefore, they must be designed in such a way as to adhere as closely as possible to the 'equity' principle of taxation. Inequity caused by a tax may also be encountered among entities that were equally placed prior to the imposition of the tax. Or a tax may cause further inequity down the distribution scale. These concerns are termed 'horizontal' and 'vertical' equity, respectively.

Equity is achieved by designing 'progressive' taxes such as the individual income tax in which tax rates rise as the income of a taxpayer rises with the underlying premise that his 'ability to pay' tax increases with his income. This is because the extra satisfaction he receives from every additional rupee he earns, declines. This principle counters the 'benefit' principle which directs a tax to be collected from a taxpayer in reflection of the benefit he receives from a tax despite the possibility that, if the poor receive more benefit from a tax, they would have to pay more tax.

Third, a progressive tax supports the traditional principle, that of 'stabilisation' of the economy. Thus, an income tax whose rates rise with income will collect proportionately more revenue as incomes are rising during a period of boom. Such a tax is called an 'elastic' tax. It contrasts with a proportional tax such as the goods and services tax (GST) or value added tax (VAT) in which the tax rate remains the same. Care must be taken to ensure that progressivity does not put the taxpayer in a higher tax bracket when his 'nominal' income rises due to inflation though his 'real' income remains the same. Such a phenomenon has been called by different names such as 'bracket creep' or 'fiscal drag' and several countries have experienced it.

Selected aspects of the principles of taxation will be developed with figures and explanations in subsequent chapters.

### 1.5.2 Modern Principles

Several additional principles have been added over time for a good tax design. They include a tax's revenue productivity, administrative feasibility and international neutrality. These principles are usually not included in academic courses even though they are the most likely aspects of taxation that they will face immediately after entering the professional world. It is imperative that these aspects be integrated into modern learning.

A tax can be well designed in terms of the efficiency, equity and stabilisation principles, yet be somewhat wanting in terms of its revenue-generating capacity. In order to meet the need for revenue, a tax should be broad based, covering a lot of items in its base that would, in turn, enable its rate to be low. Again, a tax may be so selective or have so many built-in tax incentives that finding the right taxpayers or confining it to the right beneficiaries could become a difficult task for the tax administration. Administrative feasibility is therefore increasingly recognised as an important principle of taxation.

A very new aspect that has emerged and taken prime place in the concerns of tax authorities internationally is the fact that the same tax may turn out to fall on taxpayers in a non-neutral manner across the globe. It has been observed that selected global multinational enterprises (MNEs) have been able to take advantage of different cross-country corporate tax structures and pay insignificant overall corporate tax on their global profits, compared to other MNEs. This is termed 'tax avoidance' reflecting that it is legal as opposed to 'tax evasion' which is illegal. A modern principle of taxation needs to recognise that tax avoidance enabled by tax structures unintended by tax authorities should be curbed by achieving 'neutrality' in international taxation of MNEs across the globe. Neutrality in this context implies that MNEs in similar income positions should pay tax at comparable levels at the global level.

These emerging principles of taxation will be addressed in the following chapters through examples from the modern taxation literature.

## 1.6 Tax Legislation

A country's tax structure reflects the social philosophy of policymakers and an underlying theory, usually written and analysed by tax economists, that supports it. The theory is translated into law by lawyers and advocates who play an important role in both the writing of tax law and in its interpretation through the judicial system. The taxpayer is assisted by the accountancy profession to calculate the correct tax payment and in fulfilling appropriate procedures in filing tax returns. Tax administrators examine those tax returns and determine whether the tax payment can be accepted or if further tax needs to be demanded from the taxpayer. The taxpayer may contest the tax demand and raise the matter with the judiciary for final resolution. This progression from economists to lawyers to accountants to administrators to the judiciary does not receive attention in textbooks on taxation as an integrated chain but only in segmented sections that are considered together.

In the modern world, students need to familiarise themselves with how taxation actually performs from formulation to application to resolution. Filling this large gap will be a feature of this textbook.

### 1.6.1 Tax Assignment

Within a country, the rights to impose particular taxes are assigned to different levels of government. This is usually enshrined in a country's constitution. Thus, some taxes are levied at the central government level while others are levied at the state or local government level. Yet countries can be quite different. For example, the United States and Indian constitutions are different in assigning taxation powers to the central and state governments. US states are permitted to impose income tax over and above the central income tax, but this is disallowed in India. The United Kingdom is more 'unitary' or centralized than the United States or India in that its VAT is central while India's earlier VAT and current GST are levied at both levels.

India has undergone a churning as it has moved away from the early constitutional provisions regarding how various tax bases are assigned to different levels of government. Interestingly, services were not included in the list possibly reflecting that lack of existence of modern services in 1950 when the constitution was introduced. It began to tax selected services in 1994 using an unspecified 'residual' category in the tax assignment list that was assigned to the central government. Subsequently, it amended the constitution to subsume all goods and services under the GST, a rubric introduced in 2017 that covers both central and state governments.

A variety of recent experiences and changes, usually addressed under the term 'fiscal federalism', will be brought to the attention of the student in the context of the constitution as it applies to taxation.

### 1.6.2 Writing Tax Law

Once a country's tax design is formulated, it is the job of legal experts to set that in clear, comprehensible legal language in the form of tax legislation. When attempted in a consolidated form comprising various laws, it may be referred to as a tax code, for example a direct tax code that India has been grappling with for its income tax over the last decade. Or it may be a law, such as the GST Law of India that was passed in 2017. Tax legislation is usually detailed and complex. From a legal point of view, such detail is essential to ensure correctness or certainty of comprehension and interpretation, to ensure that persons should know whether they are, or not, subject to any tax on any income or transaction.

What is interesting is that an economist's view, after his work on tax design has been completed and set on the table, is that tax law should be simple, short and almost self-explanatory. The legal view can be observed to stand quite apart from this and, in real life, tax law is generally complex. Once legal experts get to work, the sheer volume of what is produced is enormous and may not always match the expectation of a tax theorist. The chapter on drafting tax law exposes the student how to actually carry out this task. In the ultimate analysis, it remains a challenge for the tax drafter to produce tax law that is simple, is able to deal with complexities and, yet, is comprehensible and successfully implementable.

## 1.7 Globally Prevalent Taxes

### 1.7.1 Categorising Taxes

After examining the approach to writing tax legislation, we shall analyse a menu of taxes that are usually found in the tax statutes of countries. And they are found in advanced and emerging economies alike. Taxes are often divided into 'direct and indirect', 'consumption and production', 'trade and domestic' or 'partial and general', with identifiable characteristics for each category. Nevertheless, sometimes there is confusion among the concepts and students have to be aware of their definitions and explanations.

Commonly identifiable taxes raise some questions. For example, why is income tax a direct tax while excises and the GST or VAT are indirect; why is the GST or VAT a consumption tax while excises are production taxes; why are customs duties and export taxes trade taxes while the property tax is domestic; or why are excises recommended to be selective while the income tax and VAT are recommended to be broad based. The discussion will inform the student of the circumstances under which a particular tax may be more suitable than others, and if some taxes are generally worse than others.

### 1.7.2 Survey of Taxes

The groupings of taxes that will be covered are as follows. Several new taxes and variations of familiar ones will also be covered.

#### 1.7.2.1 Individual Income Tax

- Payroll Tax
- Taxation of Interest and Dividends
- Taxation of Capital Gains Tax
- Wealth Tax
- Property Tax
- Estate, Inheritance and Gift Taxes
- Withholding Taxes/Tax Deducted at Source (TDS)
- Standard Deduction
- Exemptions and Allowances

#### 1.7.2.2 Corporate Income Tax

- Minimum Tax
- Methods of Presumptive Taxation
- Marginal Effective Tax Rate
- Taxation of Financial Sector
- Scheme of Taxation
- Income from Business or Profession
- Deductions Allowed from Business Income
- Expenditure on Scientific Research
- Amortisation of Certain Preliminary Expenses
- Deductions Allowed on Actual Payment
- Other Deductions from Business Income
- Deductions not Allowed from Business Income
- Maintenance and Audit of Accounts
- Presumptive Taxation Scheme
- Tax Incentives
- Accelerated Depreciation, Tax Holidays, Investment Allowance
- Special Economic Zones (SEZs)
- Minimum Alternate Tax (MAT)

#### 1.7.2.3 Consumption and Production Taxes

Retail Sales Tax (RST)
Value Added Tax (VAT)
Goods and Services Tax (GST)
Selective Excises
Stamp Duty

#### 1.7.2.4 Environment Taxes and User Charges

- Pigouvian Taxes and Substitutes
- Petroleum Tax
- User Charges
- Global Carbon Tax

#### 1.7.2.5 Taxation of International Trade

Customs Tariffs
Export Duties

#### 1.7.2.6 Innovative Taxes

Financial Transactions Tax
Securities Transactions Tax
Commodities Transactions Tax
Banking Cash Transactions Tax
Fringe Benefits Tax

First, the rationale, design, and best and worst characteristics of the menu of taxes will be delineated through explanations and figures where needed. Second, the historical background of some of the taxes that may help to place a tax in context will be mentioned so that the student can anchor his knowledge of taxation through the historicity that it entails. Third, the role and ramifications of tax incentives will be explained in detail. Other selected taxes and aspects of these taxes will also be addressed.

## 1.8 Global Experiences in Taxation

In the twentieth and twenty-first centuries, as countries have emerged, their use of certain taxes has increased while that of others has declined. Thus, customs duties on imports and taxes on exports, being easy to collect at a country's border, have been widely used in the early stage of economic development. At that stage, even selective excises targeted at quite a few items of domestic consumption or production were used since they could be conveniently collected at the factory gate.

As an economy becomes more developed, however, it depends more on general consumption taxes such as a GST or VAT and on income taxes that are likely to fall on all individuals and firms with an appropriate threshold to exclude low incomes and to make tax administration feasible. In addition, a few selective excises continue to remain, typically on conspicuous consumption such as luxuries—furs and yachts—demerit goods such as tobacco products and consumable alcohol, and non-renewable resources such as petroleum products.

In each country's experience, including advanced economies, the overall tax structure tends to worsen with taxpayer lobbying and policymakers' interventions with poor design changes. When this occurs, it is time to undertake fundamental tax reform as many countries attempt to do. Various country experiences reveal what comprises an ideal tax structure and what to eschew. A wide array of country experiences will be covered as various taxes are analysed in the following chapters.

## 1.9 Emerging Issues in International Taxation

The central concern of international taxation today is to limit global tax avoidance. Recently, global concern has focused on the tax behaviour of MNEs, in particular those in the services sector. Inability to tax has become a major constraint in technologically emerging sectors in the digital economy. In this backdrop, the two streams of study comprise, first, domestic law against tax avoidance and, second, international efforts at limiting perceived tax avoidance by MNEs. Perhaps it would not be an exaggeration to say that the global tax profession has not yet come to grips with the insufficiency of MNE tax contribution globally. An added challenge is that major countries have not arrived at a commonly shared view on the matter.

In this textbook, therefore, both aspects will be addressed in some detail. First, it will examine domestic law against egregious tax avoidance, usually termed specific and general anti-avoidance rules (SAAR and GAAR, respectively). Second, it will examine actions that were issued by the Organisation of Economic Cooperation and Development (OECD) to contain tax base erosion and profit shifting (BEPS) across the globe. Ongoing discussions based on recommendations by the United Nations and the OECD that are sometimes at variance will be addressed with the objective that the student is able to understand in simple terms, the nature and extent, the agreements and disagreements, in the ongoing international debate and discussion over the tax behaviour of MNEs.

## 1.10 Tax Administration: Principles and Practices

How a country's tax system written in the tax statute or code actually functions reflects how it is administered in the field. Tax administration is a subject that is occupying increasingly larger space in academic concern and research. Its inefficient application is agreed to adversely affect large taxpaying portions of a population.

There are many crucial elements in a successful tax administration. To begin, it must focus all its attention on its taxpayers, viewing them as customers rather than as mere citizens from whom tax is to be extracted. How should trade and business facilitation be set up for ease of tax compliance. Second, to buttress its customer focus as well as for administrative efficiency, how should a tax administration structure itself or formulate its rules of governance. What is the global experience in this?

Third, how does a tax administration conduct its 'people function' or its responsibilities towards its own staff. How should top officials conduct themselves in their dealings with lower level officers when facing the need to collect additional revenue in the face of low collections. Is a rational policy followed or are unjustifiable pressures applied to collect tax? Fourth, reflecting two sides of the coin—the tax officer and the taxpayer—it is only natural that the two may not see eye to eye in a tax demand to be met with a matching tax payment. The matter can be resolved in one of two ways, either an agreement is reached as to the right tax amount, or a dispute is recognised and filed to be resolved by higher levels of the administration or by the judiciary. This is usually called a dispute management process.

Fifth, how are key internal processes set up. That is, how summarised or detailed should a tax return be in its design to facilitate ease of tax compliance. How much tax is to be deducted from wages during the year, or advance tax is to be paid by a business owner so that the taxpayer is not burdened with too large a payment at the end of the year. What should the approach be for the tax administration regarding scrutiny and audit of a taxpayer in cases where tax payment is deemed to be incorrect. What should the process be of determining tax refunds; and how can briskness be assured. And when, and under what conditions, is a severe technique of survey, search and seizure justified?

Sixth, what should the role and use of information and communications technology (ICT) be as a facilitator in tax administration? What kinds of hardware and software are needed to be installed when financial resources pose a constraint for the administration. Can ICT be used to facilitate quick processing, assessment and refunds of tax for the majority of taxpayers who have uncomplicated returns, for example reporting incomes only from salary, interest and a single residence. ICT has become doubly important in the area of information exchange, not only across domestic departments but also among tax administrations globally with the objective of keeping international tax avoidance in check.

Finally, the role of research, and knowledge acquired therefrom, cannot be minimised for implementing meaningful improvements in tax administration. In India, very few tax officers are assigned for this function compared to other countries even, for example in East Asia. The work of such a function includes undertaking proper revenue projections over a changing business cycle for which a reliable economic model needs to be installed. If that is done, the rudimentary approach of just projecting revenue based on a pre-determined increase from the collection of the previous year, could be set aside. Another research function is to carry out impact assessment of every tax measure contemplated in a country's annual budget. Yet another function would be to estimate the potential number of taxpayers and hence an expansion of the taxpayer base projected from a carefully generated data set, rather than setting random targets in such an endeavour. Appropriate analytical methods exist and have to be employed for carrying out each of these, and many other, necessary research functions.

Such questions arise in all taxes, whether income taxes, GST or VAT, selective excises or customs. Given the similarities of functions on the direct and indirect tax side, more than fifty countries have introduced large taxpayer units (LTUs) or large business service (LBS) that combine common functions of both direct and indirect taxes under one roof for large taxpayers. Largeness is defined usually in terms of size of tax payment or business size. There are great advantages of the LTU structure and they were introduced in India in 2006. They then fell under wavering emphasis across different political regimes, and appear to languish today. Unless LTUs are given prominence and function well, the exchange of information and other common functions between the direct and indirect tax administrations are likely to suffer.

These and other tax administration functions and their reform have been covered in a series of reports of India's 2013–2015 Tax Administration Reform Commission (TARC). It represented the first full commission—as opposed to previous committees and task forces—that addressed tax administration reform exclusively. When considered in combination, volumes of the TARC Report represent the longest such treatise with the widest coverage in a line-up of global reports.

Elements of that report are being taught in selected Indian universities but the subject is not yet integrated into textbooks on taxation. In this textbook, that gap will be filled so that students of taxation can familiarise themselves with the vast field of tax administration in a capsule. Taking from global experiences and reflecting on that report, this textbook will address how a tax administration should be structured, how it may be improved and how tax evasion by the taxpayer should be addressed. The hallmarks of an ideal tax administration will thus be developed conceptually and illustrative examples will be provided.

## 1.11 Ideal Tax Design

In the final part, the textbook will draw up a quick review and checklist of what should comprise ideal tax design that a country should keep in mind as it moves forward in its tax reform formulation and implementation. While it is best that fundamental tax reform takes place as a comprehensive package in all aspects of the structure of tax policy, its drafting, and administrative reform, all as one massive consolidated effort, that is understandably not always practicable. Nevertheless, tax reform has to proceed in a steady and coordinated manner.

# Part I

# Selected History of Indian Taxation

# Taxation in Ancient India

# 2

## 2.1 Introduction

The earliest known references to good governance and taxation are found in the Indian epics, the *Ramayana* (the story of Rama) and the *Mahabharata* (the story of great India), that emerged and evolved over millennia in the domestic tradition, replete with guidance for governance based on appropriate taxation. These are the most significant civilisational texts of India and are among the earliest to engage in discourses of good governance, including taxation.

Later, Kautilya's *Arthashastra* (the science of economics), initiated towards the end of the Mauryan period,[1] laid down direct instructions for how to tax and govern. It is the *locus classicus* of the Brahmanical[2] idea of political economy in the form of a prescriptive text and merits close scrutiny.

Other religious philosophies including Buddhism and the early Greeks, also provided guidance based on reason. Thus, to the east, Lord Shang of China and, to the West, Plato, a philosopher in ancient Greece, provided such guidance, albeit founded on different tenets of governance, reflecting the mores of societies in which

---

[1]The Maurya period was between 320 and 185 BCE (before the common era). Kautilya's name is associated with the *Arthashastra* though its completion probably occurred over several centuries. See McClish and Olivelle (2012, pp. ix–xxxiii).

[2]Hindu society was divided into four main castes defined by occupations. Brahmanas or brahmins comprised the priestly class and the repository of knowledge of the epics and astronomical almanac. Kshatriyas were warriors and rulers. Vaisyas were providers of services such as medical practitioners, accountants, traders and others. Sudhras were menials such as washermen and street cleaners. Below the four-caste system existed a myriad subcastes that were considered untouchable including cremation operators, skinners of dead cattle, trappers for occupations such as snake charmers, monkey and bear dancers and others. Gandhi named the untouchables Harijans, or children of God, though they remained vulnerable and powerless. Post-independence, they formed themselves into political groups that have given them political freedom and a claim to public education and public sector jobs, not infrequently to the objection of caste-Hindus, though caste discrimination continues unabated in several geographical pockets.



P. Shome, *Taxation History, Theory, Law and Administration*, Springer Texts in Business and Economics, https://doi.org/10.1007/978-3-030-68214-9_2

they lived and functioned.[3] In this chapter, we take up selected examples of ancient historical evidence of governance and taxation to familiarise the student of taxation with this rare aspect of learning in taxation.

## 2.2 References in the *Ramayana* and *Mahabharata*

During *Ramrajya* or the reign of Rama, as recounted in the *Ramayana*, people are known not to know dishonesty or untruth. Rama, the virtuous, godlike king[4] is reported to have represented his people with a clear set of rules for kingship. The seven books in the *Ramayana* of the *muni*, or sage, Valmiki contain multiple dimensions of life and governance including 'philosophy, spirituality, politics, economics, sociology, culture, literature, language, poetry, (and) technology'.[5] When Rama leaves for the forest and assigns Bharata,[6] his brother, to govern in his absence, he implores Bharata to take the responsibilities of the art and craft of governance. On fiscal prudence, he instructs

> O, Bharata! I hope your income is abundant and your expenditure, minimum. . . I hope your treasure does not reach undeserving people. I hope you are regularly giving your army the daily provisions and suitable salary without any delay. . . I hope that you seek to conciliate by gifts, a loving mind and polite words, the aged, the children and the foremost physicians. . . Are you cherishing all those who live by agriculture and cattle rearing, O, dear brother, . . . providing them what they need and abstaining from what they fear? All the citizens are indeed to be protected by the king through his righteousness.[7]

The popular understanding of the *Mahabharata*[8] is as an epic of sacrifice and war, of which the *Bhagwat Gita*, or the Song of God, is the most universally familiar. In it, He (Krishna) relates to man (Arjuna) the craft of war and the justification to conduct it under certain circumstances. However, as the longest known epic produced by humankind of which the *Gita* is a miniscule component, the *Mahabharata* constitutes eighteen *parvas* or books spanning major facets of societal governance including taxation.

---

[3]Religions founded in rural societies, that grew subsequent to the visions revealed to a single founder, for example, the Christian Bible, the Sikh Guru Granth Sahib and Islam's Quran, and others, in combination, have comprised a set of insights through the manner of living, interacting, taxing, administering, and dying in those early societies.

[4]Rama is described as Vishnu, the god, in bravery, benevolence and justice, and attractive like the full moon. He equals the earth in perseverance but is like the conflagration fire in his wrath.

[5]See Muniapan and Satpathy (2010, p. 645).

[6]Note that Bharata also describes ancient India.

[7]Muniapan and Satpathy, op. cit., pp. 651–659.

[8]Or, the Greatness of India.

A contemporary of Chandragupta II Vikramaditya,[9] was Kalidasa. Kalidasa wrote a play called *Abhignanshakuntalam*, based on an episode in the *Adiparva*, or earlier epoch, of the *Mahabharata*. Kalidasa mentions a six percent tax that could have existed in the earlier era or it may have reflected Kalidasa's contemporary reality.[10] The tax revenue was to be used, as a responsibility of the king, for the pursuance of the common good, that is the provision of basic amenities and security.[11] The point to note is how far back in India's history, taxation is found to have had a designated role in improving societal welfare.

The *Rajdharma*, or kingship and statehood, of the *Mahabharata*, focuses on *Shantiparvam* relating to peaceful existence, and is spread over one hundred and thirty chapters. It comprises the counsel of Bhishma, great-uncle of the cousins Pandavas and Kauravas, the two main contender families in the epic, the latter winning the battle over the former at Kurukshetra. Bhishma's counsel could be viewed as a treatise for post-conflict government formation and its functioning, with details of the roles and responsibilities of a dutiful king in the sphere of state activity.[12] In terms of economic progress, the king should encourage the development of commerce and industry, impose appropriate taxes within prescribed limits of income, institute penalties for tax evasion, and ensure the welfare of his subjects.

In carrying out his responsibilities, the king should be advised by a five-member council, with particular attributes and characteristics, while there should be a thirty-seven member cabinet comprising different castes with commensurate expertise and portfolios. The king should be vigilant and may have to engage in espionage to contain the activities of enemies and to assess the moods of his subjects.

The king should be firm but, unless *Rajdharma* was practised genuinely, 'the *Mahabharata* explicitly sanctions revolt against a king who is oppressive or fails in his function of protection, saying that such a ruler is no king at all, and should be killed like a mad dog,'[13] Anarchy should be prevented at any cost. Indeed, a kingless state might even invite an invading king to avert such a possibility.

---

[9]Vikramaditya was an emperor of the Gupta dynasty who ruled towards the end of the fourth century CE.

[10]There is no exact means of knowing or reconstructing the history of such a remote past. Historians, therefore, tend to take recourse to expressions such as probably, it appears as if, it might have been, and so on.

[11]See Sharma (2008).

[12]See Sharma (2003).

[13]See Basham (1967, pp. 88–89), in Sharma (2003).

## 2.3 Kautilya

### 2.3.1 Manu and Kautilya

To cite other examples from the early epoch, taxation finds its references in *Manu Smriti* reputed to have been composed over centuries between the second century BCE and the second century CE. Manu speaks of a variety of tax measures that the king could take according to the *Shastras* and advises that taxes should relate to the income and expenditure of the subject. He says,

> As the calf and the bee take their food little by little, even so must the king draw from his realm moderate, annual taxes.

The prevalence and necessity of taxation is recorded by Kalidasa in the *Raghuvansha* when he says thus of King Dileepa,

> It was only for the good of his subjects that he collected taxes from them, just as the Sun draws moisture from the Earth to give it back a thousand-fold.[14]

Kautilya's *Arthashastra* is agreed by most historians to have developed over centuries. Though some scholars have recently doubted whether it represented the description of any actual state, it remains a highly analysed treatise on the statecraft of a centralised and bureaucratic state. The crux of the treatise was to link the power of the state to governance. Its central objective was internal peace, with economic wealth and military power assuming a prime of place.[15]

The essential elements of the *Mahabharata*'s *Shantiparvam* are also found in the *Arthashastra*, with two crucial differences. First, the latter is not a work of political philosophy while the former could be perceived to be so.[16] Second, the latter does not sanction or recommend the removal of the king, leave alone in a forbidding manner suggested in the former. Instead, the king is described in the latter as a servant of the state who should have no personal preference.[17]

In the *Arthashastra*, the ruler was the embodiment of the state, diligent, and a just and efficient administrator. Kautilya emphasised economic and financial discipline in running the state in an efficient and fruitful manner. He says,

[14]Directorate of Income Tax (2012, p. 1).

[15]Nevertheless, Kautilya—translated as the crooked one—did not refrain from recommending extreme solutions including war or internecine taking of life where preservation of the kingdom was concerned.

[16]See Niaz (2008).

[17]See Sharma (2005).

> A wise Chancellor is one who collects revenue so as to increase income and reduce expenditure. He shall take remedial measures if income diminishes and expenditure increases.[18]

Although taxes on land were the largest source of revenue, the efficient operation of state-owned businesses, the promotion of domestic and international trade, anti-corruption measures and strict accounting procedures, merited the sovereign's attention. The ruler and his servants should have sound factual knowledge of the economic assets controlled by the state. They must also have the means to punish violations of taxation discipline with fines, confiscations and imprisonment. This pressure extended to a host of indirect taxes on leisure activities, such as liquor and gambling, as well as service charges for irrigation, transport and technical support. Royal monopolies over mines were particularly critical for non-tax revenue.

Kautilya not only lists the best taxes but also cautions against heavy tax burdens and ruthless tax administration practices whose relevance has not disappeared even in modern times. Thus,

> Financial discipline was to be maintained through budgeting, accounting, auditing and espionage, with senior officers held personally liable for any major discrepancies. . . .The ruler (should) reward upright financial administrators who increase the revenues without resorting to heavy-handed or arbitrary measures. . . .A country can indefinitely sustain a moderate level of taxation. . . .An overly high level of taxation destroys the basis of future productivity, deprives people of their subsistence and provokes rebellion, thereby making the state vulnerable to external pressure. (Thus) laxity in financial administration breeds chaos and disintegration of the country.[19]

Kautilya's emphasis on domestic management rather than on foreign diplomacy revealed his apparent conviction that the existence of a state depended more on its internal dynamics and economic equilibrium than on external influences. The relevance of his writings carries on intact as the imperatives of economic and financial discipline and of political stability reverberate across the globe today.

### 2.3.2 Kautilya, Plato and Lord Shang

The need for firmness in statecraft is pervasive in historical texts. With overarching ramifications for fiscal federalism, Lord Shang,[20] who lived during the era of the Warring States[21] when decentralisation to feudal heads was occurring, cautions in his book,

---

[18]See *Arthashastra*, Book 2, Chap. 6, Verse 28. See Shome (2002).

[19]See Niaz (2008), op. cit., pp. 5–6.

[20]See Shang Yang (390–338 BCE) was an important statesman of the State of Qin during the Warring States period of Chinese history.

[21]475–221 BCE. See *Encyclopaedia Britannica*.

> 'Benevolence and righteousness are not sufficient for governing the empire,'

while Plato, in *Laws*,[22] indicates,

> 'For that state in which the law is subject and has no authority, I perceive to be on the way to ruin'.[23]

The basis for Plato's position is that increasing political stimulation of man's wants beyond his capacity to supply them has generated forms of disorder. Wants generated by political means are bound to outstrip a community's economic capacity to satisfy such wants and hence must give rise to increasing frustration of man's expectations. This ascendance of political over economic want generation, together with the disorder which comes in its wake, may be numbered among the progeny of the two Peloponnesian wars which sundered the world of European civilisation and polity between 1914 and 1945.[24] Its relevance has taken on a sharp edge of reality in the twenty-first century, as if foreseen by Spengler while placing it in historical context.

Interestingly, while Kautilya wrote over a large, expansive and consolidating land empire, Plato's world reflected the concerns of small seafaring city states, and Sheng's comprised the preoccupations with unfolding federalism. These early thinkers from across the known world all found common solace in ultimately emphasising the need for, if not praising, the incipient importance of authority, severe if called for, the non-application of which would result in anarchy, possibly the ultimate sin that a society could commit. In this sense, they seemed to have come close to Webster's[25] description that governance is government while, at the same time, attaching important responsibilities to the ruler. Expectedly, Webster does not, however, provide conditions for the authority's ouster unlike the recommendations in the *Mahabharata*.

### 2.3.3 Mauryas and Kautilya

Therefore, *Mahajanapada* or a system of state politics based on Aryan clan dominance existed for centuries. There were some sixteen components of this system that, interestingly, formed the political context of both the *Ramayana* and the *Mahabharata*. Control over the Ganges valley was subsequently won by the rulers of Magadha (543–491 BCE), where large tributaries of the Ganges join. Around 360 BCE, Nanda's conquests broke the *Mahajanapada* system, he himself having had a Shudhra (lower caste) mother.

---

[22]360 BCE. See *Internet Classics Archive*, MIT. http://classics.mit.edu/Plato/laws.html.

[23]See Spengler (1969, p. 450).

[24]See Spengler (1969), op. cit., p. 451.

[25]See Webster's II (1984).

Following that, the Mauryan state was founded by Chandragupta Maurya in 320 BCE in Pataliputra (today's Patna) in the same area. The military interventions of Alexander of Greece and the ensuing turmoil led to the further demise of *Mahajanapada*. The firm establishment of the Mauryan kingdom emerged, together with the undeniable advent of Buddhism and Jainism.[26] Chandragupta, whose master and advisor was Kautilya, ushered in an era of trade with various regions, and engendered fundamental changes in the societies and cultures that had taken root in all parts of the area. Indeed, the student is entitled henceforward to call this geographical area 'India': a distinctive land and people with enviable achievements and products.

After Alexander's death in 323 BCE, Chandragupta assumed sovereignty south of the Hindu Kush range in 305 BCE, over a territory as large as the one commanded by the Mughals two millennia later. Magasthenes, a Greek observer, described Pataliputra as one of the world's great cities while citing the existence of caste-like divisions in society. Bindusara, Chandragupta's son, conquered southern territories. Ashoka, his son, who ruled between 270 and 230 BCE, left inscriptions on rock faces and pillars found along trade routes.

From the spread of his rock edicts, it has been surmised that Ashoka commanded a stretch of 1500 miles from Lampaka in the northwest to Karnataka in the south, and 1200 miles from Girnar on the Arabian Sea to Orissa in the east. A road network criss-crossed the massive region, from Bengal to Taxila at the Hindu Kush, and from the Ganges–Jamuna confluence to the Arabian Sea. From an economic standpoint, he established centres synonymous with the ethics of Buddhism that suited commercial, conservative and a profit orientation of the merchant. Brahman-mediated sacrifices were considered profligate by thrifty accountants of Buddhist inclination.

### 2.3.4 Mauryan Revenue and Taxation Systems

Authors have concluded from the descriptions by Megasthenes that the financial base of the imperial system was income from land revenue and, to some extent, from trade. Two domestic taxes were levied, one on the amount of land cultivated, and the other on the produce from land. Taxes on foreign and domestic trade were also levied. Following Kautilya's guidance for a strong administration, and the gradual expansion of the agrarian economy, administration was sharpened with revenue collection in mind. Roads improved communication with local administrations and became the channels of exchange and trade.

Tax exemptions were given to certain occupational groups of which there were seven: philosophers, magistrates, councillors, soldiers, artisans, farmers and herdsmen. The first group comprised priests, monks and religious teachers who

[26]This historical king himself converted to Jainism towards the end of his life, abdicated to Bindusara, his son, in 297 BCE, and travelled to the south as a renunciate, dying in the ascetic Jain manner of slow starvation.

were exempt from tax and the only group that could marry into other groups, thus clarifying caste divisions.

Every five years, there was a central audit of local administrations. Fines were the common punitive levy while capital punishment was not banned. At the village level, the headman, accountant and tax collector, all had identified roles. Some officers performed both assessment and judicial duties in rural areas. Government expenditure comprised public works. Some observers have claimed that there was oppression by the Mauryas. Others have indicated that this could have occurred during the reigns of Chandragupta and Bindusara but unlikely during Ashoka's, though these matters remain mainly speculations.

The decline of the Mauryas came as the economy weakened and a presumed population of 50 million became increasingly challenging to support. The empire's silver currency weakened with time. Around 185 BCE, a brahman general seized power and established the Shunga dynasty. He reintroduced horse sacrifice in contradiction with Ashoka's edict against animal sacrifice, and caste formation took an increasing stronghold. Hierarchies of royalty re-entered the northern Indian ethos and nomenclature, though stability remained elusive due to itinerant attacks from Alexander's successors whose interest in India's wealth had ceased to wane.

### 2.3.5 Gupta Revenue and Taxation Systems

The Gupta empire which lasted 250 years between 300 and 500 CE, representing a re-emergence of Brahmanism, also provides ample evidence of governance and taxation systems. Chandragupta I and his son Samudragupta unified almost all of the Gangetic valley and ruled with a strong and well organised government in a rich and populous region of India. Buddhism faded from the courts but existed in monasteries. Fa-hsien, a Chinese traveller, left detailed accounts of the reign of Chandragupta II. Pataliputra was a major town and Magadha a major district.

Ownership of land and land-based revenue comprised the mainstay of finance. Over centuries, Brihaspati, Gautama, Manu, Narada and others had elaborated on acceptable rules of possession and ownership and they were incorporated during the Gupta period. Wealth acquisition without distinction of caste included inheritance, gifts of affection and dowry of a wife. Three exclusive rights to wealth were listed respectively for three caste groups: Brahmins from alms, sacrifices and instructing a pupil, Kshatriyas from taxes, conquests and fines on wrongdoers and Vaisyas from tillage, tending cows and commerce.

Certain wealth and wealth extraction belonged exclusively to the king. They included treasures, mines and mineral deposits and, most interestingly, the digging of salt, the latter playing a crucial role in India's independence movement (see Chap. 5). Treasures found by brahmanas were assigned to them. If found by lower castes, treasures belonged to the king.

Megasthenes, the Greek chronicler, reported that the 'second caste' (ostensibly the Vaisyas) devoted the whole of their time to tillage, paid a tribute to the king because all India was the property of the crown, and no private person was permitted to own land. They also paid into the royal treasury a fourth part of the produce of the soil. The tax represented rent in return for tenancy.

The Guptas maintained the power to accord rights over villages to religious bodies. Fiscal exemptions for grants made are recorded in many Gupta and post-Gupta inscriptions. Nowhere is it stated, however, that there was a right to dispossess peasants through confiscation though, of course, they could be evicted if they did not pay their dues. Land measurement units were used, some of which are understood and used even now. The smallest measurement was the *angula* (middle finger), or 3/4 inch. Twenty-four *angulas* made a hasta (hand). Larger units were the *dhanu* (bow) and *danda* (rod), the latter being four hastas.

Taxation existed from the earliest Vedic times and the Guptas sharpened it. In the Rig Vedic period,[27] people paid tribute to the king since a full treasury was considered essential and the root and basis of kingship. Advisors Gautama and Narada both laid down that taxation was to be levied in return for the king's protection. It was felt that the subjects of every state ought to contribute towards the support of the government, as nearly as possible, in proportion to their respective abilities; that is in proportion to the revenue which they respectively enjoy under the protection of the state.

Nevertheless, taxation should not be oppressive, advised Kamandaka, another detailer, to the King,

> Just as cows are at one time to be tended and nourished and at other times to be milked, so are the subjects to be helped at one time with provisions and money, and at other times to be taxed. Again, a florist both tends and sprinkles water on his plants and cuts off flowers from them.[28]

Kalidasa stated that the king should receive one-sixth of the earnings of *asramas* or retreats, while different castes should pay according to their respective capacities to provide for *vrittih* (subsistence allowance) of the king. Narada corroborated Kalidasa. Manu added an innovation in the form of progressivity, indicating that tax should be one-sixth, one-eighth or one-tenth of crops reflecting fertility of the soil. Sukraniti of a later period, recommended more severe taxation, rising from one-sixth in barren and rocky areas, to one-fourth, one-third and even half, in rain-fed and irrigated locations. In short, one-sixth would be merely a baseline while tax incidence would steadily increase. And this occurred throughout the first millennium AD. There is some evidence that there may have been commutation of land tax for payment in cash over crop, though there is a lack of concrete evidence of this aspect.

The prevalent term, *bhoga-bhaga kara* may be transliterated even today as enjoyment of the share of the tax. *Bhoga* was the king's one-sixth share, over which were *bali* mentioned in the *Arthashastra* that would include several other

---

[27]The Vedas comprise the Rigveda, Samaveda, Yajurveda and Atharvaveda. https://byjus.com/free-ias-prep/types-vedas/ The Rigveda is the oldest known Vedic Sanskrit text (1800–1100 BCE).

[28]See Maity (1957, p. 53).

taxes and royal dues including *vishti* or obliged labour, and dairy produce. Cows for milk, or bullocks for cultivation or drawing state carts, could be temporarily extracted by the king with the aid of visiting *chata-bhatas*, or officers who were partly police and partly military. They, "possibly collecting oppressive extra impositions.... were hated by villagers for their cruelty and greed".[29] *Pranaya*, or emergency tax, was also imposed when required, for example when building a dam.

Indirect taxes—those on production and consumption in modern terms—also featured in the tax structure. *Klipta* or *kliptika* represented purchase tax or sales tax. Tolls and customs also played important roles. *Sulka*, mentioned in *Atharvaveda*, a very early treatise, comprised fees at the ferries, and tolls at military and police stations. Brahmanas were exempted from paying ferry duty. *Sulka* has also been viewed as a levy on merchants in fortified towns, as inferred from the *Arthashastra*. Reflecting the prosperity of the Gupta period and the significant incidence of inland and foreign trade, a superintendency of customs was prominent that, among other responsibilities, carried out valuation for customs purposes. Fines were imposed at eight times the amount evaded.

Scholars of the period have concluded, therefore, that the one-sixth mark was probably a threshold above which actual tax incidence lay, indicating a degree of oppression in the implementation of taxation. Evidence exists that, to curtail such oppression by preferred societal groups, the king cautioned donees not to receive further donations from taxpayers who had already paid tax to the treasury.

## 2.4 Southern Brahmanic Kingdoms

Apart from the northern Indian kingdoms and empires, southern Indian kingdoms were also advanced and established their own land-based revenue systems spanning millennia beginning from the BCE era. While direct references or descriptions of their tax systems are rare, the types of royal grants for temple building and to privileged groups such as the brahmanas gave a hint of the role and manner of governance. The influence of India's Brahmanic kingdoms on Southeast Asian royalty and their governance has also been established from archaeological excavations in Bali, Java, Malaysia, Thailand and Vietnam between the fourth and sixth centuries BCE, and going to the fourth century CE during the reign of the Pallava dynasty. The evidence lies in the form of stone tablets and inscriptional evidence in Tamil and Sanskrit that there was an important regional commercial network that existed for centuries. Later millennia document the actual structure and implementation of taxation, based significantly on land.

Among the influential dynasties should be included the Satavahana Andhras, Chedis of Kalinga or today's Orissa, Cheras, Pandyas, early Cholas, Pallavas and later Cholas of today's Tamilnadu, Chalukyas of today's Karnataka and Perumals and Namboodiris of today's Kerala. Later, spreading over many of these regions,

[29]See Maity (1957), op. cit., p. 60.

appeared the Vijayanagara state, perhaps the most powerful state in southern Indian history. While their revenue systems reflected land as the main base, bowing to brevity, instances of land and taxation policy of the Chola kings and the Vijayanagara dynasty are provided below.

### 2.4.1 Chola Taxation and Land Policy

The later Cholas ruled during 985–1044 CE. A well-developed Chola administration (*puravuvari*) existed for revenue collection. It comprised offices with defined functions and features including accountant supervisor, tax register and its entries and accounts, writer of palm leaf records and royal stamp. Copper plate inscriptions show 50 villages that were granted to brahmanas, the names, titles and villages of revenue officers, and names of secretariat officers and executors of local administrations, totalling more than 40. Thus, a fairly well-established bureaucracy functioned in the Chola regime. Officers of the judiciary were brahmanas who maintained grandiose official titles pre-fixed by the king's name. Established by Rajaraja I, the system continued until the end of Chola rule.

Rajaraja I introduced a standard measure though Rajendra subsequently modified it. While moving towards centralisation and away from local kinship arrangements, Chola inscriptions reveal tax imposition or exemption and land grants with a certain logic or explanation as discerned from 27 terms in 10 inscriptions. Some terms appear in a particular period of Chola rule but not in others. Yet seven terms appear during the entire period representing the main taxes that comprised an established principle in the revenue system that remained invariant during the long Chola rule.[30]

Among the seven continuing terms, two were land taxes on landowners and cultivators, the Cholas being heavily dependent on agrarian cultivation and production of rice and other crops. Double crop cultivation was encouraged. Acquired treasure from conquests was spent on irrigation to improve the land. Labour was obliged to work for the maintenance of irrigation facilities and desilting of tanks, sluices and riverbeds. Other terms related to levies on merchants and artisans whose frequency increased during the last phase of Chola rule.

Changes in the landholding system occurred during the Chola period. In the early period, land was individually held by the brahmanas and by astrologers and dancers who performed special services. Otherwise land was held by the localities. Landholders were separated from the cultivators. Individual landholding became more prevalent in later Chola rule during the thirteenth century reigns of Rajaraja III and Rajendra III.

Like the Pallavas, the middle Cholas gave away land to high officials for lifetime holding in the fertile Kaveri delta, ultimately leading to land transfers among individuals. Inscriptions recorded land transfer between individual owners, and

[30]Chola rule was between 846 and 1279 CE. The revenue system was established primarily by Rajaraja I during the 1100s.

five recorded the transfer by 39 persons of an entire village. Another inscription relates the sale of a village by one individual who had inherited it from an ancestor who, in turn, had bought the land in a government auction. The state tried to control such land transfers but it was not fully successful. The inscriptions reveal an increase of non-brahmana sellers or donors and a decrease of brahmanas.

### 2.4.2 Taxation in Vijayanagara

By late fifteenth century, the state was divided into big territories called *rajyam* and administered by *nayaka* or members of the royal family, with the help of *adhikari* or junior officers. Senior officers were *mantri*, *pradani*, *rajyam karta* and so on. Considerable evidence of taxation methods exists. The system of progressive taxation perhaps owes its origin to emperor Krishnadevaraya of Vijayanagara, who maintained that taxes should not be levied at flat rates; rather, the amount of tax levied must depend on the income of the farmer.[31]

One inscription relates the plight of the people as a result of a poll tax imposed by the *adhikarigal* who put up its collection for competitive bidding, leading to a revolt. Other inscriptions relate the distress of the people caused by revenue farming in the fourteenth and fifteenth centuries. Fifteenth century inscriptions record tax remissions granted by the nayakas in response to appeals. In the sixteenth century, tax concessions were given to artisans and merchants to encourage trade and industry. Taxation had its ups and downs and the populations appear to have suffered considerably during certain periods and in particular regions, including in the Tamil speaking south.

Moving forward, we shall see that Akbar, the Mughal, collected one-third of the produce as revenue though the cost of collection was quite high. During the British period, Indian states collected two-fifths of the revenue complemented by additional extractions. Therefore, those systems were considerably more extractive and, as we will find in Chaps. 3, 4 and 5, they had significant deleterious ramifications on the individual taxpayer—the farmer and the merchant.

## References

Basham, A.L. 1967. *The Wonder that Was India*. New Delhi: Rupa and Co. (reprinted in 1995).

Directorate of Income Tax. 2012. *150 Years of Income Tax*. New Delhi: Government of India.

Encyclopaedia Britannica. n.d. India-Magadhan Ascendancy. Accessed August 15, 2020 https://www.britannica.com/place/India/The-Shunga-kingdom.

Maity, S.K. 1957. *Economic Life of Northern India in the Gupta Period (Cir. A. D. 300–500)*. Calcutta: World Press Private Ltd.

McClish, Mark, and Patrick Olivelle. 2012. Introduction. In *In Arthasastra—Selections from the Classic Indian Work on Statecraft*. Cambridge: Hackett Publishing Company Inc.

[31]Directorate of Income Tax (2012, p. 2).

Muniapan, Balakrishnan, and Biswajit Satpathy. 2010. The Relevance of *Valmiki Ramayan* in Developing Managerial Effectiveness. *International Journal of Indian Culture and Business Management* 3 (6): 645–668.
Niaz, Ilhan. 2008. Kautilya's *Arthashastra* and Governance as an Element of State Power. *The Institute of Strategic Studies* 28 (2): 1–16.
Sharma, Sanjeev K. 2003. Good Governance in Ancient India: Remembering Kingship in *Shantiparvam* in Mahabharat. *Journal of Political Science and Public Administration* 6 (1): 109–123.
———. 2005. Indian Idea of Good Governance: Revisiting Kautilya's *Arthashastra*. *Dynamics of Administration* 17 (1–2): 8–19.
———. 2008. Spheres of Public Governance in Ancient India: Reflections on *Abhignanshakuntalam* of Kalidasa. *Journal of Political Studies* 2 (1): 6–16.
Shome, Parthasarathi. 2002. *India's Fiscal Matters*. New Delhi: Oxford University Press.
Spengler, Joseph J. 1969. Kautilya, Plato, Lord Sheng: Comparative Political Economy. *Proceedings of the American Philosophical Society* 113 (6): 450–457.
Webster's II. 1984. *New Riverside University Dictionary*. Boston: Houghton Mifflin Company.

# 3 Taxation Under the Mughals

## 3.1 Introduction

The Mughals reigned in India from 1526 when Babur, the first Mughal, defeated Ibrahim Lodi of Delhi in Panipat. The Mughals continued until 1858 when, under Bahadur Shah, the last Mughal's unwilling leadership, a coalition of forces from Indian states fought for their independence, and were defeated by the British. Shah was banished to Rangoon in 1862. There are many scholarly studies on taxation during Mughal rule over three centuries from which a summary of impositions and conclusions therefrom may be drawn.

In a nutshell, for the Mughals, 'taxation (was) justified as the monarch's reward for the government and protection of his subjects'.[1] Land comprised the main tax base, along with a few other taxes including import and export duties, and tributes from states controlled by the Mughals. In this chapter, we look at revenue systems under emperors Akbar and Aurangzeb who were, respectively, the most effective and most controversial Mughal rulers.

Accordingly, an array of scholarly works on their administrations and on other aspects of their reigns are widely available. Indian history emphasizes the imposition of *jizya*, a progressive income tax on non-Muslims with an exemption for minimum wagers. Akbar, the third Mughal, was uncomfortable with religious segregation and abolished it. Aurangzeb, the sixth Mughal and great-grandson of Akbar, reinstated *jizya*. In what follows, we shall find that the Mughal revenue administrations had a lot to offer to a scholar of taxation, beyond *jizya*.

[1]See Grapperhaus (1998, p. 141).



P. Shome, *Taxation History, Theory, Law and Administration*, Springer Texts in Business and Economics, https://doi.org/10.1007/978-3-030-68214-9_3

## 3.2 Revenue Administration Under Akbar

Babur's grandson Akbar, who reigned between 1556 and 1605, was deemed the Great Moghul due to his egalitarian approach to religions, the expansion of the boundaries of his empire, and his administrative skills, among other cited qualities. A study of the Akbar administration's taxation regime reveals a comprehensive, complex and relatively fair system of taxation that applied over a vast area comprising eight provinces (*subas*) created in 1580 that extended from Afghanistan in the west to Bengal in the east and Gujarat in the south. By 1586, the *bigha*, a unit of measurement of land, was redefined and made about 12 percent larger than before. It is interesting that to this day the same unit is followed under the same name, in many parts of India.

Akbar's was a standardized land revenue system. Three-quarters of government revenue was extracted from land—hence the enunciation of the term land revenue. Scholars have analysed what proportion of the agricultural produce was drawn from the producer in different provinces across the land.[2] Other taxes made up the rest, in particular from urban areas.

Assessment of how much revenue was to be collected was based on the application of standard rates, fixed annually, to be paid in cash. The rates are derived according to the area planted with each crop including wheat, barley, gram, bajra, jowar, sugarcane, mustard and indigo. However, in the initial four years after the provinces were created, the same rates were applied in most of them. Hence, the underlying assumption by officials who set the rates must have been that the same prices and uniform productivity prevailed across these vast expanses. Subsequently, the rates began to vary and, by the tenth year, rates were also reduced across the board, and were given a range of maximum and minimum rates. In other words, the rate structure became more complex, possibly recognising different prices and varying yields in different provinces. Even within a province, rates became considerably varied.

Over time, the rate structure became more equitable albeit at the cost of even greater complexity. In the Agra circle—part of a province—the rates for a variety of crops[3], calculated in terms of value of yield, ranged from 32.45 percent (for mash and shamakh) to 51–53.2 percent (for arzan and gram). The average was 38 percent for *kharif* (summer) and 44 percent for *rabi* (winter) crops.[4] This indicates that tax rates were set on the basis of detailed background calculations yielding a range and variety of rates. Nevertheless, they were very high by today's standards. There was

---

[2]An exhaustive analysis has been carried out by Moosvi (2015, pp. 97–153). There she mentions other authors including W H Moreland, R P Tripathi, Irfan Habib and others.

[3]Rabi crops reported were wheat, barley, gram, lentil, arzan, mustard, peas and fenugreek, while kharif crops were mung, mash, moth, jowar, shamakh, kodron, sesamum, bajra and lobiya.

[4]The agricultural crop year in India is July–June. The cropping seasons are *kharif* and *rabi* reflecting the monsoons. *Kharif* is July–October during the south-west monsoon and *rabi* is October–March during winter's north-east monsoon. Crops grown during Marc-June are summer crops. See *Arthapedia*. www.arthapedia.in.

not as wide a variation in the range of rates in other areas as Agra where the rates were also the highest.[5]

There were some taxes other than land revenue, the ratio varying from area to area, for example in the Agra rural environs (*haveli pargana*), the share of other taxes to land revenue was 10 percent while, in the town of Agra, it was 24 percent. The average share was about 14 percent. Since Agra was the largest urban city in the Mughal empire, its share of urban taxes was probably the highest. In Gujarat and Bengal also, evidence of taxes other than land revenue exists.

Despite the setting of various rates, statistical evidence reveals that actual collection was, on average, about 70 percent of set rates. There was considerable variation in revenue incidence (*jama*), ranging from 93 percent to 55 percent within and around the vast Delhi area on both sides of the Yamuna. The highest revenue incidence was along the Delhi–Lahore route that had considerable economic activity. Another area with high incidence was Gujarat reflecting different reasons including a higher tax demand from the authorities compared to northern India.

Revenue incidence was lower in the Uttar Pradesh region, sometimes falling to less than half of claimed revenue, including in Meerut, Awadh, Bahraich, Baran and elsewhere, a deficiency that continues to the present day. It partly reflected high expenditure—collection costs—of region *zamindars*. Overall, an inverse relation could be deciphered: high expenditure of *zamindars* as a percent of *jama* implied low net incidence of revenue collected.

Unfortunately, the Akbar administration did not undertake measurement of land in Bengal, Bihar and some other areas. Hence gross cropped area estimates are not available, no satisfactory assessment data exist and revenue incidence inferences cannot be satisfactorily calculated. However, information exists that prices in Bengal and Bihar remained characteristically low. Hence revenue incidence must have been low other than in more commercially oriented regions around the Hugli River.

Interestingly, the monarch was not the only beneficiary of revenue. There are calculations for the seventeenth century revealing the share of *zamindars*, or collectors on behalf of the monarch, as being fixed at 10 percent of collection. But if they were keeping for themselves as high as 25 percent prior to the Mughal administration, Akbar allowed its continuance, for example in Gujarat. Revenue collectors (*karori*) were allowed 20 percent as cost of collection. Other officials together kept about 7 percent—including the *pargana chaudhuri* or local tax collector (2.5), village headman (2.5), record keeper (1.0) and village accountant (1.0). Thus, 37 percent of total revenue was the normal cost of revenue collection.

On the whole, whether it was Bengal, Gujarat or Rajasthan, quite an array of reasons could explain a relatively low revenue incidence in some of these regions. They included large leakages caused by *zamindars*' shares, especially where they were strong such as the Gond *zamindars*. Yet another reason was the lack of administrative control in certain areas such as tracts of forests or hills. Thus, similar

[5]However, Ajmer and Lahore that had higher rates than Agra for cotton and indigo.

challenges in tax administration existed five hundred centuries back as are prevalent today.

## 3.3 Revenue Administration of Aurangzeb

Aurangzeb, a great-grandson of Akbar, reigned between 1658 and 1707. He remains controversial due primarily to his reinstatement of *jizya* reflecting his particular interpretation of Islam, standing apart from the practices of Jahangir or Shah Jahan, his grandfather and father, respectively. He also manifested an enormous amount of cruelty towards his own family. In pursuit of consolidating his power to rule, he killed his four brothers and imprisoned his father in 1658 who subsequently breathed his last in prison in 1666. Once on the throne, he revealed a penchant for military campaigns against Hindu and Muslim potentates alike, including Shivaji of the Marathas and Sikandar Shah of Bijapur, as well as Sikhs, Rajputs and Jats in the north, and Ahoms in the east, as well as various other groups.

In the second half of his reign, Aurangzeb faced serious challenges in countering rebellion by Akbar, his son. He receded to Persia, but later returned in pursuit of continuing his military campaigns. Possibly his nemesis was a belligerent policy towards the Deccan that he remained intent on annexing but, after which, any barrier between the Mughals and Marathas was effectively removed, resulting in continuing skirmishes and rebellion.

Aurangzeb nevertheless was a comprehensive administrator and has been recognised as one of the ablest of Mughals. Nevertheless, his tax collection methods were punitive.

> .... the slightest weakness of the imperial authority could give cause for rebellions... order was therefore maintained, i.e., the taxes were collected with a rod of iron, with the assistance of the army.[6]

Historical experience, therefore, confirms the supremacy of power in the practice of tax collection. Nevertheless, when crops failed, lower output led to contraction in cultivated area, flight of the peasantry, and declines in real revenue.

Rank holders, or Mansabdars, comprised civil servants who were given a choice in the manner of receipt of emoluments. Their remuneration could take two forms, salary plus fringe benefits or the allotment of a jagir or land area from which tax could be collected which was, however, shared with the monarch. The jagir system of compensation was preferred by and large by the ruler.

Problems arose from the manner of implementation. For example, though Aurangzeb abolished an existing road toll, the *jagirdars* refused not to collect it. There were orders or *farman* sent out by the administration of Aurangzeb that the distribution of remissions—or reductions from revenue collection—after

[6]Grapperhaus (1998), op. cit., p. 138.

calamities should not be left to *chaudhuris* or other officials since the benefits would not reach the small peasants. Also, that the *diwan*, or subordinate ruler, 'should not let these officials meet him in private, which implies awareness of collusion between them and the revenue officials'. Thus, the prevalence of corruption in tax administration is not a phenomenon exclusive to the modern era.

## 3.4 Moghul Taxation after Aurangzeb

The British East India Company that began to operate in India as the Mughals declined in power obtained from the Moghul Emperor, as early as 1717, the right to trade in salt, opium, tobacco and betel nut without paying customs duties.[7] In other words, even before the British took over the administration of India completely, they were exempted from paying tax.

By the 1720s, governors of the Mughal emperor were increasingly assuming self-governance. Consequently, the transfer of revenues to the emperor receded. However, Murshid Quli Khan, a converted Brahmin slave, and Governor of Bengal, remained loyal, sending half a million pounds annually in revenue to Delhi. He was,

> Notorious for the harshness of his tax-collecting regime. Defaulters among the local gentry would be summoned to.... the capital Murshidabad, and there confined without food and drink. In winter, the Governor would order them to be stripped naked and doused with cold water, then....suspend the *zamindars* by the heels, and bastinado (beat) them with a switch....throw (them) into a pit....filled with human excrement in such a state of putrefaction as to be full of worms, and the stench was so offensive....(and) oblige them to wear long leather drawers, filled with live cats.[8]

The conduits used by Khan for sending revenue collected to the emperor were Jagath Seth or Bankers of the World, a family of Marwari Oswal Jain financiers from Nagar, Jodhpur, whose name as a hereditary distinction, had been conferred in 1722 by the emperor himself. The family controlled minting as well as the collection and transfer of revenues and, accordingly, exercised immense power. Their wealth was documented to be enormous by Company commentators and historians alike.[9] Indeed, between 1718 and 1730, the Company itself had borrowed an average of 400,000 rupees per annum from the Jagath Seth group. No wonder comments such as 'the greatest shroff and banker in the known world' and 'a greater banker than all in Lombard Street (banking district of London) joined together', were made by Robert Orme and Captain Fenwick, respectively, on the affairs of Bengal circa 1747–1748.

[7]See Mukerjee (2010, p. xvi).

[8]See Dalrymple (2019, p. 34), quoting Allah (1788). See also Mukherjee (2009).

[9]See Dalrymple (2019), op. cit., p. 34.

As the power of the Company and, subsequently, the British monarch, came into place, perhaps tax imposition and collection took a more onerous turn. This is what we turn to next.

## References

Allah, Salim. 1788. *A Narrative of the Transactions in Bengal: During the Soobahdaries of Azeem-us-Shan, Jaffar Khan, Shuja Khan, Sirafraz Khan and Alyvardy Khan*. Translated by Gladwin F. Calcutta: Press of Stuart & Cooper.

Dalrymple, William. 2019. *The Anarchy—The Relentless Rise of the East India Company*. London: Bloomsbury Publishing.

Grapperhaus, Ferdinand H.M. 1998. Taxation in the Empire of the Great Moghuls. In *Tax Tales from the Second Millennium*, 109–158. Amsterdam: International Bureau of Fiscal Documentation (IBFD).

Moosvi, Shireen. 2015. *The Economy of the Mughal Empire c. 1595*. New Delhi: Oxford University Press. (first edition 1987).

Mukerjee, Madhusree. 2010. *Churchill's Secret War—The British Empire and The Ravaging of India During World War I*. New Delhi: Tranquebar Press, Westland Ltd.

Mukherjee, Tilottama. 2009. The Co-ordinating State and Economy: The Nizamat in Eighteenth-Century Bengal. *Modern Asian Studies* 43 (2): 389–436.

# Taxation in Early British Period

# 4

## 4.1 Introduction

The tax pressure imposed by the British in India is proverbial. There is no way to go around it. While it became worse through time during British rule, it was heavy and detrimental to productivity right from the start. In this chapter, we recount that early period of British taxation in India.

The date that indisputably established Britain's governance into India was 23 June 1757, when Robert Clive defeated a young and wayward Siraj-ud-Daulah, the Nawab of Bengal, at Plassey, by conspiring with the latter's general, Mir Jafar. Soon, however, Clive replaced Mir Jafar with Mir Qasim, his brother-in-law, who was then subjected to heavy payments as a reward for his elevation. And the impositions began.

## 4.2 Extractions by Robert Clive

Despite fighting on the side of the British, Mir Qasim had to pay the Calcutta Council comprising senior local British officers, 200,000 British £, as compensation for the support he received in ascending the throne. In addition, future revenues from the prosperous districts of Midnapore, Burdwan and Chittagong would go to the Company. To begin,

> The Council put the task of collecting taxes up for auction, ceding it to whoever promised the greatest returns for each of the contract's three years. Thus, numberless harpies were let loose to plunder, whom the spoil of a miserable people enabled to complete their first year's payment.[1]

[1]See Mukerjee (2010), pp. xvii–xviii.



P. Shome, *Taxation History, Theory, Law and Administration*, Springer Texts in Business and Economics, https://doi.org/10.1007/978-3-030-68214-9_4

Mir Qasim was also dextrous in collecting taxes. He opened the account books of Bihar maintained by Raja Ram Narain, the ruler of Patna. His tax collectors examined soldiers' pay and matched it against the number of soldiers. Narain was accused and imprisoned, confiscating 15 lakh rupees[2] and jewels from his personal wealth. Nevertheless, Mir Qasim struggled to pay reparations to the British and doubled pre-Plassey tax levels, successfully raising 30 million rupees.[3] The collection went directly to London.

The burden on the peasantry was incalculable and even towns in Bengal began to empty out. Nonetheless, even Mir Qasim eventually complained that traders were being forced to sell at a quarter the correct price and tyranny prevailed over the common man and the trader. This led to war, he fled and died in poverty. Ironically, Mir Jafar was reinstated at a cost to him of 500,000 British £. After Mir Jafar's death in 1765, his son was installed on the throne at the cost of 230,000 British £.

The same year, Clive extracted from the Mughal emperor the *diwani* or the right to collect tax from Bengal, Bihar and Orissa that he estimated to yield 1,650,900 British £ per annum after transferring 272,000 British £ to the Mughal emperor in Delhi per annum. This enabled him to pass on the right to the Company of taxing 20 million people. These contributions helped him to acquire a seat in the British parliament. However, for Bengal, Bihar and Orissa,

> The assumption of the "*Diwani* was an unmitigated catastrophe. The Nawab was no longer able to provide even a modicum of protection for his people: tax collectors . . . plundered the peasantry to raise funds from the land, and no one felt the least bit responsible for the wellbeing of the ordinary cultivator.[4]

India's British colonial period continued to sharpen and tighten taxation beyond any justifiable degree. High taxation and a famine in 1769 ruined Bengal.

> Company tax collectors were guilty of . . . 'shaking of the pagoda tree', what today would be described as major human rights violations committed in the process of gathering taxes. Bengal's wealth rapidly drained into Britain, while its prosperous weavers and artisans were coerced 'like so many slaves' by their new masters.[5]

> This fine country which flourished (even) under the most despotic and arbitrary government, is now verging towards ruin.[6]

[2]£ 20 million today.

[3]£ 390 million today.

[4]See Dalrymple (2019), pp. 206–210.

[5]See Dalrymple (2019), op. cit., p. xxviii.

[6]See Dalrymple (2019), op. cit., p. 210, quoting Richard Becher who recorded in 1769.

## 4.3 Attitude of Warren Hastings

By mid-1770, the region had experienced deficit rainfall for 3 years. The population was suffering deeply. To alleviate the suffering, Shitab Rai, the new governor of Patna, imported grain from Benaras where prices were lower. Many could not afford to buy even at the lower prices; so, Rai began gathering them in separate enclosures for Hindus and Muslims and distributed food and small coins.

Unfortunately, this policy was not contemplated or applied in Bengal. Though the English and the Dutch attempted to emulate Rai, essentially

> Company efforts to alleviate the famine were contemptible even though half the labouring and working people had died by June 1770. Nor did it make seed or credit available. Instead, anxious to maintain their revenues at a time of low production . . ., the Company, in one of the greatest failures of corporate responsibility in history, rigorously enforced tax collection and in some cases even increased revenue assessments by 10 per cent.[7]

> Within five years, Bengal became India's poorest province. The directors (of the Company) in London expected enormous profits as they owed His Majesty's Government an annual payment of 400,000 British £; so the Company proceeded to collect agricultural taxes . . . . No longer were taxes a portion of the harvest to be paid in kind; (based) on the principle that all land belonged to the state . . . fixed the tax at specific monetary level, now called rent to be paid in silver even when a crop failed.[8]

Tax collectors were so oppressive that Bolts, a cloth merchant, wrote that 'farmers were often necessitated to sell their children in order to pay their rents, or otherwise obliged to fly the country'. Becher, an administrator, commented, 'Am I really quietly to stand by and see them commit the vilest acts of oppression, without being able to tender the aggrieved redress? The creatures of our government enrich themselves at the people's expense, nay even their ruin.'

But Warren Hastings commented regarding tax collections, 'violently kept up to their former standards', and, in February 1771, the Calcutta Council reported to the directors in London that,

> notwithstanding the great severity of the late famine, and the great reduction of people thereby, some increase (in revenue) has been made.[9]

## 4.4 Lord Cornwallis' Permanent Settlement

By the end of the eighteenth century when British atrocities were accepted above reproach, Lord Charles Cornwallis, the Viceroy or head of government, introduced changes in land laws and taxation. A Permanent Settlement was introduced in 1793

[7] See Dalrymple (2019), op. cit., p. 219.
[8] See Mukerjee (2010), op. cit., p. xviii.
[9] See Dalrymple (2019), op. cit., p. 220.

in which absolute rights were given to *zamindars* provided they paid a pre-designated land tax fixed in perpetuity. Unless they paid punctually, the land would be sold to someone else, and the occurrence of that was not rare. Indeed, many old estates were split up, with employees of earlier owners buying up the rights.

'In the ensuing decades, draconian tax assessments led to nearly 50 percent of estates changing hands'.[10] From the Company's viewpoint, Cornwallis's changes were fruitful in that they brought in more revenue, and with greater regularity. And a new, pro-British Bengali banking and trading class emerged also as wealthy landowners who managed their local responsibility to the satisfaction of their British masters.[11]

The conditions were not confined to the Bengal region alone. Extractions of land rent and natural calamity led to a series of famines in India. The Madras region had famines in 1783, 1792, 1807, 1813, 1823, 1834 and 1854 but they attracted little comment from London. An influential scholar, 'James Mill argued that poverty rather than wealth was India's intrinsic and unvarying condition.'[12]

A significant explanation of the spread and hold of British presence across India as well as those of other colonial powers such as the French, the Portuguese and the Danes reflects, to no small extent, the self-indulgent autocracy that ruled over many parts of India. In Bengal, additionally it had been the intra-familial treachery encountered by Siraj-ud-Daulah that provided the impetus. Such treachery continued through subsequent ascensions to the throne that enabled the British to extract additional monumental cash. Thus, changing alliances was not rare among Indian rulers to be gainfully taken advantage of by the British whose target remained steadfast from the very beginning of their rule.

> For the colonial administration the most important objectives with regard to the functioning of the Indian economy were: (i) to maintain the Indian market for British manufactures; (ii) to ensure the remittance on government account to meet the disbursements in Britain; and (iii) to ensure the remittance of returns on British investment in India.[13]

Even as far away as America, the patriots there referred to the Company's atrocities in increasing Bengal's burden. In 1780, American patriots had turned on the British king, an outcome of the Company's attempts to sell its tea in the American colonies and collect tax on it for their English masters. It was feared that the Company would let loose on the 13 colonies of America just as it had done in Bengal. They dumped 90,000 pounds of tea into the sea worth 9659 £, aptly termed the Boston Tea Party after the event. John Dickinson, a patriot writer, described the tea as 'accursed trash', elaborating,

---

[10]See Dalrymple (2019), op. cit., p. 328.

[11]See Dalrymple (2019), op. cit., p. 329.

[12]See Mukerjee (2010), op. cit., p. xxiv.

[13]See Sen (1992), p. 137.

> This 'almost bankrupt Company, having been occupied in 'corrupting their Country', and wreaking 'the most unparalleled Barbarities, Extortions and Monopolies' in Bengal, now wished to do the same in America. 'But thank GOD, we are not Sea Poys, or Marattas .... Beware of the East India Company'.[14]

The tea tax could be never imposed as British forces met their final defeat at the hands of George Washington at Yorktown, culminating in British surrender to America in October the following year.

## 4.5 Unbearable Revenue Burden of the 1800s

Thus, it is not surprising that, over the following century, by 'the 1850's, the land revenue increased at a lower rate than prices, but the lag was more than compensated by an enormous absolute and relative increase in indirect taxation'.[15] Overall policy effects of deindustrialisation[16] and steep rise in agricultural indebtedness with stagnated agricultural wages, comprised non-tax factors that exacerbated the depleted human condition in India. Some studies have shown that real wages declined significantly between Akbar's reign and the end of the nineteenth century, that is well into the British period.[17] Indeed, per capita income declined over the three centuries 1600–1900,[18] and the structure of GDP also remained unchanging. Under such stagnant conditions, extraction of taxes must have overburdened all producers—agricultural and non-agricultural—in the economy.

The excruciating burden on India's poor of indirect means of taxing, including diversion of production to Britain, continued until India's independence. Even during severe production shortfalls in agriculture such as between 1860 and 1880 caused by famines and resulting in shortages in supply, resulting in famine and death, marketed surplus was attempted to be maintained 'in part (through) compulsory extraction in the form of land revenue, rent and interest'.[19] Neither did agricultural exports diminish on a significant scale, rupturing deeply any balance between population and food availability. And agriculture was not alone. Any industry that was allowed to grow—yarn, jute textiles, plantations and coal—were 'chosen fields of investment of British India ... and the first two were export-oriented'.[20]

Resultantly, growing accumulation of India's reserves transferred and held in Britain—Gold Standard Reserve—implied 'lost opportunities for reduction of taxes,

[14]See Dalrymple (2019), op. cit., p. 258.

[15]See Moosvi (2008), p. 24.

[16]The period 1840–1900 experienced import value of cloth increasing rapidly compared to that of yarn, revealing that cloth had to be imported rather than be produced in India from imported yarn (Table 1.18, Moosvi (2008), op. cit., p. 27).

[17]See Mukerjee (2010), op. cit., p. 58.

[18]See Moosvi (2008), op. cit., p. 33.

[19]See Sen (1992), op. cit., p. 136.

[20]See Sen (1992), op. cit., p. 136.

or of immediate reduction of external debt' though India was paying higher interest on this debt compared to the interest it was earning from Britain on its reserves. Despite this, Britain's Royal Commission refused to recommend 'any upward limit on the accumulation in this reserve, and the reserve to import ratio went on rising'.[21] This was one important reason why taxes were not reduced.

Having traversed the tale of taxation during the first British period in India, we now proceed to examine how taxation transpired leading on to India's independence.

## References


Dalrymple, William. 2019. *The Anarchy—The Relentless Rise of the East India Company*. London: Bloomsbury Publishing.

Moosvi, Shireen. 2008. *People, Taxation and Trade in Mughal India*. New Delhi: Oxford University Press. (2010 paperback edition).

Mukerjee, Madhusree. 2010. *Churchill's Secret War—The British Empire and The Ravaging of India During World War II*. New Delhi: Tranquebar Press, Westland Ltd.

Sen, Nabendu. 1992. *India in the International Economy 1853-1913*. Calcutta: Orient Longman Ltd.


[21] See Sen (1992), op. cit., p. 149.

# Taxation in Pre-Independence Period: The Salt Tax

5

## 5.1 Introduction

Mohandas Karamchand Gandhi, or Mahatma[1] Gandhi, is commonly recognised as the leader who delivered India's independence on 15 August 1947 from the British Raj.[2] Nevertheless, it was a fractious achievement in that Gandhi and the All India National Congress, or Congress, a party comprising a large segment of politicians from across India, and of which he was a part, had to accept the partition of continental India to gain independence.

Partition was preferred by Muhammad Ali Jinnah, the head of the Muslim League party. It carved out significant portions with a Muslim majority, as well as a few Hindu majority enclaves, to form Pakistan, a new country. Pakistan was given independence on 14 August 1947. In this chapter, we address the role of taxation in India's independence movement.[3]

## 5.2 Tax Resistance as an Instrument

Despite this unanticipated outcome, it is noteworthy that Gandhi used tax resistance and tax revolt as instruments in the independence movement. To understand how tax or non-payment of it was used by Gandhi, a few historical events are essential to be recounted.

[1] A term first used by Rabindranath Tagore, a friend of Gandhi's, and the only Indian Nobel laureate for literature to this day.

[2] Raj may be conveniently translated to mean rule or reign.

[3] This textbook names only two Indians who were directly associated with their use of the salt tax as an instrument of protest. It should not be interpreted as an oversight. Indeed, India's independence was the outcome of the efforts and sufferings, including paying the ultimate price, of hundreds, if not thousands of Indians, as well as the sacrifices of some Britishers who were sympathetic to the cause.



P. Shome, *Taxation History, Theory, Law and Administration*, Springer Texts in Business and Economics, https://doi.org/10.1007/978-3-030-68214-9_5

At a December 1916 meeting of the Congress, a peasant from a remote village in Bihar, appeared, seeking Gandhi's help.

> They were indigo growers from Champaran on the marshes of Nepal who worked under almost feudal conditions as sharecroppers for the English planters. When the indigo market declined because of the invention of aniline dyes, the planters sought to compensate themselves by demanding cash instead of indigo from the peasants; they established a reign of terror to ensure that there would be little defaulting. This situation had lasted for years, and the local lawyers had drawn profit from the peasants' attempt to obtain redress, without achieving anything on their behalf.[4]

Several English authors have written on the Champaran matter. Woodcock was not the only English author who reported on Champaran.

> Here white settlers had taken possession of much land and forced their Indian tenants to grow indigo for their factories, where a dye was made from the plant. The Indian tenants were little better than slaves, taxed by the landlords—mostly white men—for every conceivable reason. The landlord taxed every home and every marriage and even levied special taxes to pay for their own hunting or holidays.[5]

While these accounts do not represent the worst atrocities of British colonial rule in India, they give a snapshot to the student of the vicissitudes of daily life experienced by the peasantry as a result of the widely prevalent behaviours of the colonists.

Gandhi not only proceeded to Bihar in 1917 but recruited Rajendra Prasad, later India's first President, and other lawyers, and entered the concerned area. When the police asked them to leave, he did not, and went to prison for it. The lawyers courted arrest but the Lieutenant Governor of Bihar dropped the proceedings. An enquiry that followed obliged the planters to return most of the money they had extorted from the peasants. This was one of Gandhi's first *satyagraha*, or civil disobedience or non-violent protest movement, in India.

## 5.3 Deprivation of Indians

The condition of Indians had deteriorated to an extent that, unable to accept the tortuous conditions any longer, small but potent revolutionary groups had begun to appear in Bengal, Punjab and other areas. In July 1918 a commission under Justice Rowlatt recommended heavy penalties and secret trial without appeal for possessing any seditious document as per official interpretation. A Rowlatt Bill was accordingly introduced in March 1919 but it was never applied. Ironically, the anti-sedition law has been invoked in post-independence India.

By the end of 1920, Gandhi was the undisputed leader of Congress. By late 1921, *Swaraj*, or full independence, became the objective of the Congress and Gandhi

[4]Woodcock (1972, p. 51) of 1974 edition.

[5]Reynolds (1959, p. 97).

moved into the next phase of *satyagraha*. The Prince of Wales was arriving in Bombay—today's Mumbai. He proposed a mass refusal to pay taxes in Bardoli, a district in Gujarat. But in February 1922, policemen fired into a crowd of demonstrators who then turned on the policemen. They took refuge in the city hall which was set on fire. Some policemen died. Gandhi disapproved of this, fasted for five days in penance, and postponed the planned civil disobedience against paying taxes in Bardoli.

At that stage, immediate *Swaraj* became untenable in Gandhi's mind, though he remained convinced that 'non-violence (was) made of sterner stuff than armies'. Nevertheless, it left several Indian groups including those from Punjab dissatisfied with Gandhi's decision since they felt that independence was within reach but was sacrificed by Gandhi for reasons they could not fathom.[6] And the leaders were in any event sent to jail. Gandhi was sentenced to six years though he was released from jail in Poona in January 1924 for acute appendicitis surgery.

## 5.4 Unsustainability of British Rule

While putting scores of Indian leaders and volunteers in jail at the same time, the British increasingly began to question the sustainability of their rule in India. Gandhi himself went through a period of repose and reflection until, in October 1927, Lord Edward Irwin, the Viceroy, summoned him and others to Delhi to inform the group that Sir John Simon would head a commission to report on the possibility of constitutional changes, however, without any Indian representative in it.

To Gandhi and his group, it revealed a clear denial of any possibility of *Swaraj*. When the commission arrived on 3 February 1928, parties including the Muslim League and the Hindu Mahasabha boycotted it. Gandhi contemplated reinventing the Bardoli strike, originally planned seven years earlier. He said,

> My ambition is much higher than independence. Through the deliverance of India, I seek to deliver the so-called weaker races from the crushing heels of western exploitation in which England is the greater partner.

With this, Gandhi laid explicit his objective to destroy the entire imperial system. The Bardoli tax strike that followed embodied *satyagraha*, and was the first fully successful civil disobedience. Some 84,000 peasants of the area remained firm in their resolve not to pay taxes for six months. Then, after a national *hartal* or strike was called in their support, the government gave in, formed an enquiry commission, reduced taxes the peasants had demanded and compensated losses for the seizure of goods.

[6]And it remains a matter of speculation whether India would have been divided if it gained independence in the early 1920s.

On 26 January 1930—later commemorated annually as the Republic Day of independent India beginning 1950—Gandhi published an *Indian Declaration of Independence* in which he declared,

> The British government of India has not only deprived the Indian people of their freedom but has based itself on the exploitation of the masses, and has ruined India economically, politically, culturally and spiritually. We believe, therefore, that India must sever the British connection and attain *Purna Swaraj*, or Complete Independence.

## 5.5 Salt Tax as an Instrument

Gandhi next picked the salt tax, a tax whose burden over almost two centuries had been especially heavy on the poor who could not make salt without paying tax on it. Gandhi knew that, given that a salt tax had been a factor in the French Revolution, if India's salt tax was widely revealed to the general British public, they would be struck by the raw and cruel nature of the British administration in India. On 12 March 1930, he set out from his *ashram* or retreat, Sabarmati, in Gujarat with 79 volunteer men and women, and walked to Dandi on the sea, some 241 miles away. On 6 April, Gandhi picked up a fragment of salt without paying tax on it. In between, India and the world saw the march in newspapers, on newsreels, and heard about it on the radio. The reaction all over India was electric. People began to manufacture salt everywhere without paying tax. Officials began to resign, the army—Garhwali Rifles in Peshawar—refused to fire on demonstrators.

On the same day as Gandhi picked up salt in Dandi, a western outpost of India, a salt march also took place from Tamluk, an ancient town in the eastern backwaters of Midnapore. Midnapore was the district where the East India Company had been given its original exclusive rights over the production, manufacturing, taxing and trade in several commodities including salt. Until the early eighteenth century, Midnapore had supplied salt to eastern India and Nepal. But the monopoly of Britain over salt had converted it to an importer of salt from England. The excessive burden of the salt tax had continued for two centuries.

Thousands of protesters marched from Tamluk under the leadership of Sushil Dhara, a Congress youth. Their goal too was to walk to the sea and make salt. Sixty-five rebels calling themselves the Indian Republican Army, seized a police armoury in Chittagong in what is now Bangladesh whereupon they came under the firepower of the authorities. But every villager was making salt at home, uncaring of the law. The resultant police atrocities in anticipation of a rebellion being provoked, was a deliberate strategy of James Peddie, District Magistrate, whose view was,

> As long as they remain non-violent it is very difficult for us. If they become violent, we can crush it in a day.

Later, Peddie confessed that he 'felt small' about the affair. In April 1931, he was shot dead by a revolutionary in Midnapore.

The salt movement quickly spread across India. Khan Abdul Ghaffar Khan, who was later called the Frontier Gandhi as a result of his crucial role in the North West Frontier region, led non-violent protests, refusing to pay taxes. Khan set up an administration of the city until the Gurkha regiment arrived to put down the protests. But Hindu soldiers from a regiment from the Himalayan foothills refused to participate in the ensuing mayhem. Police brutally attacked the non-violent march causing two hundred deaths, thousands wounded and 60,000 arrests. At the cost, or because, of casualties all across India, the world came to see the shocking spectacle first hand as reported by the American and British Press. Nevertheless, Gandhi and other leaders were imprisoned.

In its climax, there were 100,000 prisoners. Lord Irwin, the Viceroy, realised that a dialogue was necessary. Gandhi was released from prison on 25 January 1931. On 26 January, one year after Gandhi's *Declaration of Independence*, Irwin released all leaders and a pact between Gandhi and him was drawn up. Salt could be manufactured along coastal areas and for personal use without tax; non-violent prisoners would be released. And Gandhi would represent Congress at Roundtable Talks in London comprising the next stage of forming a constitutional government in India. This pact with the Viceroy was not understood or appreciated by Gandhi's colleagues though they had to agree to it. Though Gandhi's presence in London gave England the opportunity to glance at India's struggles in colonial rule, Gandhi did not meet success, returning to India to see repression in full throttle.

Interpreting the emotions of Gandhi's colleagues, Reynolds (1959) commented that, though he 'persuaded most of the other Congress leaders to agree to it.... explaining Gandhi was always difficult'. Though some Congress leaders were opposed to the pact, Gandhi's view was that what mattered to the Indian masses should be the route that the leaders should pursue. And that was what he was pursuing in terminating the movement. It is true that Gandhi stopped further *satyagraha* after the salt march in favour of the pact, but Woodcock (1972) has been of the opinion that the march against the salt tax was among the last nails on the British colonial coffin that was to come not too long thereafter.

## 5.6 Gandhi–Irwin Pact

Winston Churchill was so incensed with the Gandhi–Irwin pact that he said to a conservative association in February 1931,

> It is alarming and also nauseating to see Mr. Gandhi, a seditious Middle Temple lawyer, now posing as a *fakir*[7] of a type well-known in the East, striding half-naked up the steps of the Viceregal palace, while he is still organising and conducting a defiant campaign of civil disobedience, to parley on equal terms with the representative of the King-Emperor....For the British Raj to abandon its responsibilities would be an 'act of cowardice, desertion and

[7] A *fakir* is a mendicant.

dishonour, as well as a hideous act of self-mutilation, astounding to every nation in the world'.[8]

Churchill would continue to write in this tone in subsequent years.

The authorities' actions continued with brutality culminating, on April 13, with Brigadier General Michael O'Dwyer's order to fire—by Gurkha and Pathan soldiers—into unarmed peaceful demonstrators, killing 379 people and wounding 1100. This massacre in the Jalianwallah Bagh area of Amritsar in a walled public garden from where there was only a narrow escape route, once again exposed the brute force underlying British rule. Dwyer's atrocities continued for months. Charles Andrews, an English friend of Gandhi's and admired in India, wrote a report of those atrocities; but the government report did not reveal certain people who were protected. Gandhi and other leaders were shocked at the inaction of the government. On 21 May, 2500 volunteers again marched to the Dharasana Salt Works.

In September, Gandhi went to London at the invitation of the British government though he returned without results, and called for continuation of civil disobedience. Gandhi was rearrested on 4 January 1932 and, within four months 80,000 protesters were jailed. To add salt to their wounds, the salt tax was increased, yielding a record revenue of 102 million rupees. Churchill commented that the Government of India had finally 'begun to act sensibly. I always said how easy it would be to crush Gandhi and the Congress'.[9]

## 5.7 Small, Earmarked Tax[10]

During 1932, Midnapore refused to pay a small earmarked tax for maintenance of the village chowkidar, also a police informer. Police, comprising personnel from northwest India,[11] were sent to keep the law. 'In lieu of the tax of a few rupees, they confiscated cattle and jewellery worth thousands. The government also imposed a punitive tax to fund these police outposts'.[12] Also, in this period, the global Great Depression witnessed a significant drop in farm incomes. Nevertheless, taxes were increased under the presumption that farmers had accumulated jewellery and land in the previous decade. But with the drop in prices, farmers could not pay full tax. Moneylenders extracted the families' gold jewellery which was then melted down and a booty of 3.4 billion rupees (£ 255 million) was sent to London in support of the English currency.

[8]Mukerjee (2010), op. cit., pp. 26–27.

[9]Mukerjee (2010), op. cit., p. 27.

[10]An earmarked tax is one whose revenue is assigned to pre-identified, specific expenditures.

[11]British colonial policy was based on what is now famous as its 'divide and rule' policy, employed not only in India, but in Malaysia/Singapore between Malays and Chinese, in Ireland between Catholics and Protestants, in Rwanda between Hutus and Tutsis, and other colonies.

[12]Mukerjee (2010), op. cit., p. 28.

Thus, widely available evidence has revealed that the British extracted what they wished with little standard or guidance in what they imposed. There is no doubt that the Indian taxpayers suffered immensely through the unfolding of taxation history but tax terrorism may have reached its peak under their rule. This continued until the very end but there was excitement in the air despite War-related shortages in food, cloth and electricity. Dhara wrote, 'the people were realising that the era of the British was coming to an end.... we began to fan the flames....in the hope of uniting them all into one gigantic conflagration'.[13]

## 5.8 Gleaning from the History of Taxation

Rules of governance supported by guidance for taxation and government expenditure have been documented since the beginning of the written record. So, what can be concluded from this survey of early practices in taxation? It may be concluded that religions, based both on reason or on revelation, were quintessentially founded on matters of governance. A sweep of history reveals a central emphasis on authority in decision making, buttressed by a cabinet, clearly charted taxation systems, a forceful army and, if necessary, the use of espionage for the success of government and, surrounding it, a recognition of justice, fairness and equanimity towards farmers and the vulnerable. Strong punishment was usually to await a ruler and the ruling class if governance failed due to negligence or defeatism.

Keeping in mind the time machine of Man and ideas, how has taxation featured in the modern era of conquests? There is no doubt that tax terrorism played an intrinsic part in India's struggles through some of the Mughal periods and even more so during the British Raj. Eventually, Gandhi, supported by the efforts of many others, led India to its independence from its previous, extremely repressive occupiers.

Post-independence India passed tax laws that resembled those of advanced economies, for example its 1961 Income Tax Act that began to be implemented from 1962. Since then the Act has gone through many fundamental changes in structure and rules. Similarly, selected indirect taxes were introduced on domestic production and consumption, and on the import of goods at the central government level.

And, in addition to what India could learn from international sources, its constitution—carefully delineated by Bhimrao Ramji Ambedkar, the father of the Indian Constitution—made provisions for taxation powers among all levels—central and state—of government since India became a fiscal federal state with distinguishable powers to tax at different levels of government. Thus, states were assigned the sale of goods as their tax base. Only in the 2000s, the earlier indirect tax structure was improved and re-assigned in steps, first as a value added tax (VAT) in 2006, followed by a Goods and Services Tax (GST) in 2017. We shall learn the modern tenets of taxation as well as the system of prevailing taxes later in this textbook.

[13]Mukerjee (2010), op. cit., p. 31.

## 5.9 Impact of Indian Society

One question that arises in a discriminating student's mind is why India suffered so much with foreign rule from the West for so many centuries without strong revolts other than centuries apart. Were Indians not brave in battle, or inventive in strategy to stave off or win attacks? Or could it be that their internecine divisions had been a significant constraint?

We know from the citations of India's ancient texts that proper governance was well articulated by the ancestors. Then what was the main impediment that worked in India's disfavour? For example, could the Laws of Manu that separated one group from another, so that Indians were not free to perceive themselves as one society but, rather, in exclusive and hierarchical clusters by birth, have had anything to do with the outcomes?

Two readings, Dutt (1898) and Rao (2009), one old, one contemporary, among various others that are available, may be used to ponder this matter. Another interesting treatise is by Roy (2013) on explanations found in military history to get an inkling of how the British organised themselves vis a vis their Indian counterparts that would ultimately lead to the now familiar outcomes.

In short couplets in erudite and attractive English, Dutt translates a small segment of the *Mahabharata*, the longest epic ever written, by Vyasa Muni, compiler of the Vedas. It narrates Indian philosophy in its expanse and rudiments through the story of an internecine war circa 1300 BC. In addition, India's caste distinctions emerge as an element that existed even in those ancient times.

The fact that such caste distinctions continued with insuperable strength even at India's independence is discussed in Rao's treatise in which he convincingly argues that its virulence would have continued to discriminate as during pre-independence had it not been for its conversion to a powerful political force in India's post-independence political system under the rubric Scheduled Caste and Scheduled Tribe (SC and ST, respectively) uncluttered by Hindu hierarchy and the establishment of rights of its own.

Analysts have observed that the British Army in India grew from a mere colonial police force into one of the world's largest 'volunteer' armies, which saw service around the globe where its 'practical experience in counter-insurgency' was used such as in Greece and Indonesia.[14] The word 'volunteer' leaves a bitter taste in that large segments of working class Indians chose to join the British army over its various Indian counterparts. Whether this reflected better pay, better treatment, better leadership or any other factor, the clue could perhaps include the existence and continuance of India's divisions—caste, class, regional, religious—that fell into

[14]Of course, we have already seen how it all began with the Battle of Plassey in 1757 in which Robert Clive, the British leader, defeated Siraj-ud-Daulah, the Nawab of Bengal with a larger army, due to his own traitorous general.

British laps rather than for the British following 'any deliberate policy of Indianisation'.[15]

Most strikingly, however, such separation in society does not seem to be an exclusive characteristic of Indian society. In a book just published, Wilkerson (2020) compares America, India and Nazi Germany where their world was shaped by caste—and how their 'rigid, arbitrary hierarchies still divide us today. She unearths eight pillars that connect caste systems across civilisations, and demonstrates how our own era of intensifying conflict and upheaval has arisen as a consequence of caste'.[16] Thus, the discerning student must anchor his studies on the fundamentals of society; then the analysis, policymaking and implementation will become much easier to define and chart. With this background, we are now ready to dive headlong into further learning of taxation—its theory, its transformation into law, and its application and administration.

## References

Dutt, Romesh. 1898. *Mahabharata—The Epic of Ancient India*. 1st ed. Calcutta: J.M. Dent and Co.

Mukerjee, Madhusree. 2010. *Churchill's Secret War—The British Empire and The Ravaging of India During World War II*. New Delhi: Tranquebar Press, Westland Ltd.

Rao, Anupama. 2009. *The Caste Question—Dalits and the Politics of Modern India*. New Delhi: Permanent Black, Ranikhet / Orient Blackswan.

Reynolds, Reginald. 1959. *The True Book About Mahatma Gandhi*. London: Frederick Muller Ltd.

Roy, Kaushik. 2013. *Army in British India: From Colonial Warfare to Total War, 1857–1947*. London: Bloomsbury.

Wilkerson, Isabel. 2020. *Caste—The Lies that Divide Us*. UK: Penguin Random House.

Woodcock, George. 1972. *Gandhi*. London: Fontana/Collins.

[15]Roy (2013), Synopsis.

[16]Wilkerson (2020), inner leaf description of book.

# Part II

# Theory of Taxation

# 6 Principles of Taxation

## 6.1 Introduction

Having traversed the history of taxation, let us delve into its modern premises and concepts. Right at the start, it is pertinent to note the comments of legal scholars,

> Much of the material is economic in formulation ... because there has been too little participation by ... legal scholars in the debates.[1]

Taxes are often assessed in terms of their economic benefits and costs. Their benefits are that they finance government expenditures needed for commodities and services that the free market cannot provide such as economic infrastructure, public health and education, national security and war and emergency services during periods of calamity or epidemics.[2] The market is said to fail in the provision of such public goods because individuals who do not pay for them cannot be excluded from their consumption. When the government provides such goods, however, the question of exclusion does not arise in most cases.[3]

In emerging economies and advanced economies alike, public resources may also be utilised for socio-economic protection of the weak and vulnerable such as meals and shelter for the poor. In many economies, health and education are provided by the public sector even though they may also be provided by the private sector. Such economies ensure that a minimum level of those services is guaranteed for all

[1] See Tiley and Loutzenhiser (2012), p. 7.

[2] This textbook focuses on a full range of taxation aspects exclusively. When only tax policy aspects are considered with public expenditure considerations under one umbrella that field is usually referred to as public finance. A recent treatise by Tanzi (2020a) takes the public finance approach.

[3] See Browning and Browning (1994), Chap. 2, for an elaboration of the nature of public goods, and how a free-rider problem emerges when citizens do not pay for public services they consume, but cannot be excluded from consumption because of the composite nature of such goods. Buchanan and Flowers (1987), Chap. 4, describe them as collective goods and services or indivisible goods.



P. Shome, *Taxation History, Theory, Law and Administration*, Springer Texts in Business and Economics, https://doi.org/10.1007/978-3-030-68214-9_6

citizens irrespective of their payment capacity. These comprise the classical objectives of raising revenue.

But taxes also have costs of various kinds, the first among them being the impact they have in distorting the preferences of consumers in the market that get expressed in the form of tax-driven changes in their demand. In turn, this affects the production decisions made in the pre-tax situation in the supply side of the market. These outcomes of a tax are viewed as its quintessential ramifications in moving the market away from the pre-tax equilibrium between consumers and producers and, instead, landing the market in a sub-optimal post-tax position.

It would be an error to view taxes as a mere means of obtaining revenue. In the final analysis, it may represent 'the most pervasive and privileged exercise of the police power of the state'.[4] It determines different ways for some people to become richer and others poorer through unequal taxation under specific intentions. A widely prevalent example across the globe is the use of legislation and subordinate legislation or rules to provide tax incentives that tend to cut back tax contributions from particular groups of privileged taxpayers. This worsens the position of other taxpayers who are not given similar incentives.

Governments should thus exercise the power of taxation and its unequal imposition with great perspicacity. They cannot just tax away as they please. They must also keep in mind the role of the voting constituents. That is why, in India and other emerging economies, there was a strong movement in the 1990s to privatise services that had traditionally belonged to the government sector.[5] The totality of such considerations and the extent of need for public resources lead to a configuration and commensurate choice of a tax system.[6] The study of the principles of taxation that should lie behind the design of a tax structure comprises the subject matter of this chapter.

## 6.2 Seven Principles of Taxation

With the development of concepts underlying taxation, it came to be agreed over time that tax design should have theoretical underpinnings in the form of certain principles of taxation. Many of these were mentioned in a well-known 1978 report chaired by James Meade in the United Kingdom.[7] However, even earlier, many authors had developed this whole area of discussion.

[4]See Tiley and Loutzenhiser (2012), op. cit., p. 10.

[5]Policies such as privatisation of public sector enterprises, reducing conspicuous expenditure in education such as subsiding higher education while primary education was being deprived, and many others were characteristically discouraged in International Monetary Fund (IMF) assisted economic reform programmes when these countries approached the Fund for loans to restructure their economies. Usually that reflected inefficiencies in the public sector that typified its condition at a moment when they usually approached the Fund.

[6]See Levi (1988).

[7]See Meade (1978).

Among the many costs of taxation, the first usually mentioned is the distortions that it causes in consumer choices that comprise the foundation of the market economy. This, in turn, affects decision-making by producers who react to the post-tax consumption decisions by reallocating productive resources away from the original market allocation of resources. This is termed the allocative inefficiency of resources caused by taxation.[8] Such distortions can have macro effects on savings and investment of the economy.

An inefficient tax could be a good revenue-raiser in the short run but will be detrimental for economic growth in the medium term and, in turn, for tax revenue. Contemporary models of economic growth have linked long-run growth to present and future tax measures and to expectations of future events. They suggest that the detrimental growth effects of taxation could be permanent rather than temporary.[9] The tax treatment of capital income affects capital accumulation and growth. Changes in the after-tax interest rate, prompted by capital income taxation, could have dynamic effects such that savings may no longer be represented as a stable function of the return on capital.[10]

The welfare cost of capital taxation can turn out to be high in a dynamic context. As theories of growth incorporate the effects of technological change, human capital accumulation and similar growth-inducing factors, newer insights are being obtained on the ramifications of taxation for economic growth. Therefore, here too, the solution must lie in the realm of a simple tax system, one that minimises detrimental effects on the long run growth potential of the economy.[11]

A related concern in structuring taxes has been to maintain neutrality across taxpayers. Narrowing the dispersion in taxation is usually agreed to promote such neutrality. In the 1970s–1990s, a general consumption tax on all goods and services—a Value Added Tax (VAT) or a Goods and Services Tax (GST)—became popular across the world, and in India. This tax subjects all taxpayers to the same tax rates without categorising them by too many criteria that have little to do with the nature of the tax itself.

The second well-known negative effect of taxation is that it could have regressive effects on the distribution of income if the tax does not fall proportionately on taxpayers. In fact, a poorly designed tax could fall more heavily on lower-income groups than higher-income groups. This difficulty has to be countered with progressive tax rates, that is tax rates should increase as incomes rise. However, if the tax is not on income but say on consumption, then the problem of regressivity remains such as in VAT or GST.[12]

---

[8]A seminal early treatise on the anatomy of distortions caused by taxation was by Harberger (1974).

[9]See Xu (1994).

[10]See Tanzi (1991).

[11]See Jones et al. (1993).

[12]See Chap. 2 of Musgrave (1959) who is historically linked to enunciating the equity aspects of taxation and formulating its rules.

The third effect is on taxation's probable influence on the stabilisation or destabilisation of an economy. A progressive tax rate structure is counter-cyclical in that, more tax is taken out automatically as the economic cycle is on the upswing. And less tax is taken out during a downswing. This stabilises the economy. A regressive rate structure, on the other hand, is pro-cyclical which destabilises the economy. Most of these principles are well-known in the present day though, during the formulation and implementation of tax policy, governments often fail to adhere to the fundamentals of these principles. Governments' role should be, instead, to exercise great care and perspicuity in exercising their taxing powers.

After the first three principles enunciated above, additional principles, with a tax administration perspective, feature as new principles emanating from the interests of other stakeholders in the tax system. For example, revenue productivity of a system of taxes is important for tax administrators. Thus, fourth, any tax administration would be interested in a buoyant tax structure that has a built-in ability to be revenue productive during both affluent years through the income tax and during deflation through a VAT or GST.

Fifth, the scope of a tax should be clear. Clarity of taxation law and the ease of tax compliance are important to taxpayers.[13] If, despite the good intentions of tax designers, the tax law is cumbersome and hard to interpret, the tax system loses its edge and could end in litigation and, the worse is the law, the longer is the litigation process likely to be.[14]

Sixth, simplicity and the associated ease of taxpayer compliance have increasingly come to be recognised to comprise 'customer focus' of a tax administration, and an important tenet in tax design.[15] In fact, the 'ease of paying taxes' has been included as a component of the World Bank's cross-country 'ease of doing business' index.[16] This principle is also known as the ease of 'tax compliance'. Often, in an attempt to reduce the cost of a tax administration, a taxpayer, or even the taxpayer's employer, is expected to take on more responsibilities to comply with the tax law. This simply implies a transfer of burden from the government to the taxpayer, increasing the latter's financial cost, time costs and psychological costs. The cost of compliance, as a result, could rise several times. Such changes result in far higher burdens on small business than on multinational enterprises (MNEs).[17]

Last, and no less important, are a tax administration's transparency, incorruptibility and impartial application of taxation law—the tax statute or code—even as subordinate legislation or administrative rules that can override legislative intent,

[13]See Baker and Pistone (2015).

[14]See TARC (2014), First Report, Chap. V, "Dispute Management," on litigation in particular.

[15]Tanzi (2020b) has elaborated on the matter of simplicity versus complexity in public finance as a whole.

[16]See World Bank (2016).

[17]Reviews based in the United Kingdom have revealed this unequal burden, for example by Shaw et al. (2010).

are minimised.[18] This is an issue in many emerging economies and, unless their tax administrations leave archaic administrative practices behind, revenue collection would continue to reflect not the condition of the economy but the coercion of a taxpayer by the tax administration. That is why this remains possibly the greatest challenge in emerging economy tax reform.

But advanced economies are not completely above board either. Several books have been written by ex-tax administration and finance ministry officials recounting poor prevalent practices.[19] They usually reflect high costs to comply with an increasingly complex tax structure and authoritarian behaviour of the tax administration. Thus, all countries have to, in one way or another, focus on being transparent with the taxpayer so that the latter can trust the tax officer and comply with the tax law willingly.

## 6.3 Conflicts Among Principles of Taxation

It is not uncommon for various principles to conflict with one another which could pose a challenge to carry out tax reform with clarity and without conflicts.[20] An inefficient tax that can be revenue productive in the short term could impinge upon economic growth and thus lead to revenue stagnation in the medium term. Indulgence in taxing capital gains appropriately would lead to inequity across income sources, yet adverse tax treatment of capital income could slow down capital accumulation and economic growth. It is this fear that had led to a long period of accommodation to the taxation of returns to capital of MNEs.[21]

MNEs became used to the lack of symmetry in tax laws across nation states that led to widely prevalent tax arbitrage in how they structured their businesses across the world so that they could minimise their global tax payments. For example, taxpayer A may have to pay tax in year 1 but B, its 'closely related party' such as a subsidiary, may be able to take a deduction for it in another country in year 2. Depending on whether the tax rates are different, here there could be an opportunity for 'tax arbitrage', and A and B together could minimise their global tax payment.

Thus, MNEs organise their tax matters to minimise tax payments globally through complex tax avoidance (which is legal)—to be separated from tax evasion (which is illegal). This has led many tax administrations to attempt to stem revenue

[18]See TARC (2015), Fourth Report.

[19]See Graetz (2008) and Rossotti (2005) for example. Graetz was Deputy Assistant Secretary and Assistant to the Secretary of the US Treasury (Finance Ministry) between 1990 and 1992. And Rossotti was IRS Commissioner or the top tax administration official of the United States between 1997 and 2002. Both have expressed considerable criticism of the US tax system from policy and administration perspectives, respectively.

[20]An early discussion of such conflicts appears in Messere (1993), Chap. 1, Sect. C.

[21]An array of legal experts, economists and tax administrators has considered a list of related issues in Shome (2016).

depletion through specific and general anti-avoidance rules. They may also use retrospective taxation. Retrospectivity implies that, even if a law is passed today, it may be applied from an earlier date. Retrospectivity in tax law can have significant deleterious effects on the continuity of a business environment, and lead to lower investment. It may be useful to elaborate on its probable ramifications.

An investor has to have a business model that would guide him to decide how much resources he should invest in a project. He makes this decision reflecting, from his standpoint, a known tax risk that reflects his attitude—aversion, neutrality or preference—towards risk. Uncertainty takes the matter one step beyond risk. It removes the possibility for the existence of a risk-based business model. Why does this occur? An explanation follows.

If, say after 5 years of his investment decision, the government declares that the tax law has now been changed but will be applied from 5 years prior to the present day. Then the basis of his investment crumbles. It is as if the government informs him today in time t that the law in time $t - 5$ was actually quite different from what had been written down as law in $t - 5$. This manner of retrospectivity in taxation becomes untenable for business decision-making. Yet certain tax jurisdictions have tended to use this unjustifiable route through redefined legal interpretation of the law with the objective of capturing revenue already lost.

MNEs have explicably complained that retrospective legislation leads to an uncertain—as opposed to merely risky—environment thus leading them to scale back investments in such jurisdictions.[22] Reflecting the high mobility of international capital, such withdrawal can be brisk. Lower investment leads to lower economic growth and, therefore, to lower tax revenue collection. And, as already indicated, the deleterious effects on growth could be near permanent, rather than merely transitory.

In this way many of the principles of taxation could conflict with others; in this case, it is between the objective of the tax administrator whose objective is to collect revenue and the taxpayer who desires simplicity and assurance of stability in tax law. Thus, in enacting tax laws, a careful balance has to be struck among the various principles.

[22]This manner of distinguishing uncertainty from risk explained here is not usually found in the literature where the terms have been commonly used interchangeably. For example, to quote Atkinson and Stiglitz (2015), 'Uncertainty is a feature of any economy, and attitudes towards risk-taking are likely to play an important role in determining economic performance' (p. 97) . . . 'draws attention to the need to consider the kind of risky event that we have in mind—whether . . . it is uncertainty surrounding technology, due to cyclical variations, etc.' (p. 99). Here risk and uncertainty appear to carry the same meaning.

## 6.4 Does Tax Reform Last?

A package containing a restructured tax system is usually termed 'tax reform'. Many countries attempt it after a gap of some years, sometimes with an incoming government. However, what is termed reform may be flawed. First, the term itself is used by authors in a variety of ways.[23] Some have expressed their view that reform must comprise fundamental improvements in the tax system; others seem to refer to any change as reform provided it is viewed by a group—say a ruling political party—as an improvement.

The middle view is that it is not practical to expect an entire tax system to be replaced by a fundamentally improved new system. An example would be India's income tax code that has gone through many attempts at reform without success, or Brazil's VAT structure encompassing all—central, state and municipal—levels of government. Hence those in the middle are generally of the view that any package of improvements that can be introduced without expecting the entire structure to be reformed is the practical reality of tax reform.

Second, the concept of tax reform varies across tax professions. Economists tend to emphasise the efficiency criterion, remaining critical of a structure that has too many tax incentives. Some economists believe that achieving equity using expenditure policies is superior to a tax structure that attempts to promote equity. Legal experts tend to focus on the sharpness or clarity of law. If it is not, they take as a worthy challenge, intelligent interpretation of the law, to be finally resolved by the judiciary. And a tax administrator's best tax structure is one that is most revenue productive. Those groups were brought together for intrinsic dialogue and analysis.

Thus, it sometimes appears as if there is a glass wall between the tax economist and the tax administrator. Differences between a legal expert and a tax administrator in the interpretation of the law also emerge, reflecting differences in professional perceptions. Perceiving these gaps, and then to bridge them, remains a crucial challenge in policymaking for the wider taxation profession.[24] Nevertheless, sometimes a collection of legal experts, economists and tax administrators have come together to consider issues that are, in the final analysis, in their mutual interest to resolve.[25]

Even if it is argued that those differences are not terribly important, a source of the ephemeral nature of tax reform emerges from an empirical observation that, after about 5 years of undertaking reform, country authorities face new challenges to the edifice that begins to crack. First, those who are adversely affected, even if marginally, begin to lobby, often steadily and strongly, for reinstatement of their privileges, usually for sector-specific tax incentives, tax holidays, accelerated depreciation, lowered GST or VAT rates for individual commodity classifications and so

[23]For example, Bernardi et al. (2006), Mintz and Chen (2011), Focanti et al. (2013), Gimenez and Rodriguez (2016), Alm and Sheffrin (2016), or Ruiz et al. (2017) to name a few.

[24]See Shome (2013) where those groups were brought together for intrinsic dialogue and analysis.

[25]See Footnote 21.

on. Thus, those who complain rightly about the adverse effects on them of retrospective taxation, now can very well lobby for incentives favourable to them as a means to compensate against the impact of one adverse policy with a beneficial one.

Second, in most democracies there is likely to be a change in government in 4, 5 or 6 years. The new administration characteristically likes to put its own stamp on public policy including or, in particular, tax policy. Relatedly, third, the usage of the term 'reform' in 'tax reform' has possibly become too loose in modern professional usage. Any change could be termed 'reform' and successive governments attempt to rapidly change what their predecessors have done though, by a mere check of definition or consistency, none of these changes would be called reform by a serious taxation expert. In fact, there is constant justification made for 'change' for which tax administrations have even set up full and expansive departments. This renders a rather amusing interpretation that tax policy or tax administration reform may exist under perennial change and, therefore, never achieve a stable equilibrium.

To conclude, with the ever longer global reach and internationalisation of taxation, a country's tax structure gets affected by movements in global thought regarding international taxation. Such changes in thought and positions could emanate in multilateral institutions as well as in changing trading blocs. Thus, the life of a prevailing global trend in tax reform can be cut short by blowing international crosswinds that fail to adhere to established and well-grounded principles of taxation.

## References

Alm, James, and Steven M. Sheffrin. 2016. What Drives State Tax Reforms? *Public Finance Review* 45 (4): 443–457.

Atkinson, Anthony B., and Joseph E. Stiglitz. 2015. *Lectures on Public Economics*, revised ed. Lecture 4: Taxation and Risk-Taking. New Jersey: Princeton University Press.

Baker, Philip, and Pasquale Pistone. 2015. The Practical Protection of Taxpayers' Fundamental Rights. Congress of the *International Fiscal Association*, Basel, August. Cahiers de droit fiscal international, vol. 100B. The Hague: Sdu Uitgevers.

Bernardi, Luigi, Angela Fraschini, and Parthasarthi Shome, eds. 2006. *Tax Systems and Tax Reforms in South and East Asia*. Oxford: Routledge.

Browning, Edgar K., and Jacquelene M. Browning. 1994. *Public Finance and the Price System*. 4th ed. New York: Macmillan Publishing Company.

Buchanan, James M., and Marilyn R. Flowers. 1987. *The Public Finances—An Introductory Textbook*. 6th ed. Homewood: Richard Irwin Inc.

Focanti, Diego, Mark Hallerberg, and Carlos Scartascini. 2013. *Tax Reforms in Latin America in an Era of Democracy*. IDB Working Paper Series, No. IDB-WP-457.

Gimenez, Eduardo L., and Miguel Rodriguez. 2016. *Optimality of Relaxing Revenue-Neutral Restrictions in Green Tax Reforms*. Governance and Economics Research Network (GEN), GEN Working Paper A 2016–5. https://doi.org/10.13140/RG.2.1.4969.5121.

Graetz, Michael J. 2008. *100 Million Unnecessary Return: A Simple, Fair, and Competitive Tax Plan for the United States*. New Haven: Yale University Press.

Harberger, Arnold C. 1974. *Taxation and Welfare*. Chicago: University of Chicago Press.

Jones, Larry E., Rodolfo E. Manuelli, and Peter E. Rossi. 1993. Optimal Taxation in Models of Endogenous Growth. *Journal of Political Economy* 101 (3): 485–517.

Levi, Margaret. 1988. *Of Rule and Revenue*. Berkeley and Los Angeles: University of California Press.

Meade, James. 1978. *The Structure and Reform of Direct Taxation*. London: Allen and Unwin.

Messere, Ken. 1993. *Tax Policy in OECD Countries: Choices and Conflicts*. Amsterdam: IBFD Publications BV.

Mintz, Jack, and Duanjie Chen. 2011. Federal-Provincial Business Tax Reforms: A Growth Agenda with Competitive Rates and a Neutral Treatment of Business Activities. *SSRN Electronic Journal* 4 (1). https://ssrn.com/abstract=1920860 or https://doi.org/10.2139/ssrn.1920860.

Musgrave, Richard A. 1959. *The Theory of Public Finance: The Study of Public Economy*. New York: McGraw-Hill Book Co.

Rossotti, Charles O. 2005. *Many Unhappy Returns*. Harvard: HBS Press.

Ruiz, Sandra V Lizarazo, Adrian Peralta-Alva, and Damien Puy. 2017. *Macroeconomic and Distributional Effects of Personal Income Tax Reforms: A Heterogenous Agent Model Approach for the US*. IMF Working Paper, WP/17/192. https://www.imf.org/en/Publications/WP/Issues/2017/09/01/Macroeconomic-and-Distributional-Effects-of-Personal-Income-Tax-Reforms-A-Heterogenous-Agent-45147. Accessed 8 May 2020.

Shaw, Jonathan, Joel Slemrod, and John Whiting. 2010. Administration and Compliance. In *Dimensions of Tax Design: Mirrlees Review*, ed. Stuart Adam et al., 1100–1162. Oxford: Oxford University Press.

Shome, Parthasarathi, ed. 2013. *Indian Tax Administration: A Dialogue*. New Delhi: Orient Blackswan.

———, ed. 2016. *Base Erosion and Profit Shifting (BEPS): The Global Taxation Agenda*. Gurgaon: Wolters Kluwer.

Tanzi, Vito. 1991. The Fisher Effect and the Term Structure of Interest Rates. *Osaka Economic Papers* 40: 86–98.

———. 2020a. *Advanced Introduction to Public Finance*. Cheltenham: Edward Elgar Publishing Limited.

———. 2020b. *The Economics of Government: Complexity and the Practice of Public Finance*. Oxford: Oxford University Press.

Tax Administration Reform Commission (TARC). 2014. *Tax Administration Reform in India: Spirit, Purpose and Empowerment (First Report)*. New Delhi: Government of India.

———. 2015. *Tax Administration Reform in India: Spirit, Purpose and Empowerment (Fourth Report)*. New Delhi: Government of India.

Tiley, John, and Glen Loutzenhiser. 2012. *Tax Law*. Oxford: Hart Publishing.

World Bank. 2016. *Doing Business—2017: Equal Opportunity for All*. https://www.doingbusiness.org/en/reports/global-reports/doing-business-2017. Accessed 8 May 2020.

Xu, Bin. 1994. *Tax Policy Implications in Endogenous Growth Models*. IMF Working Paper No. 94/38. https://ssrn.com/abstract=883491. Accessed 8 May 2020.

# Market Behaviour of Consumers and Producers

# 7

## 7.1 Introduction

In a world without taxes, how consumers and producers are assumed to behave in a perfectly competitive economy is addressed in this chapter. Consumers express their demands for products in the marketplace reflected in their 'utility functions'. Producers use engineering technology and associated costs to construct factories and warehouses that comprise their fixed cost for their production structure. They also use machinery, raw materials and labour and obtain their input prices from the market. They combine fixed cost with the variable costs, the former remaining constant and the latter varying with the quantity they choose to produce. In turn, that determines their supply in the market revealing how much they will supply at each price faced by their product.

Thus, all consumers combine to generate varying market demands at different market prices and all suppliers combine to generate changing market supplies at different market prices. An equilibrium price–quantity combination occurs where the schedules or curves of market demand and supply of a commodity intersect. At the equilibrium, the 'marginal rates of substitution' (MRS) among consumers equal the 'marginal rates of transformation' (MRT) among producers.[1] These foundational concepts of market equilibrium are elaborated through figures and explanations in this chapter. Following that, the impact of taxation on the market can be comprehended.

## 7.2 Consumer Theory in Market Economics

Each consumer in a market economy has a utility function and a budget constraint. The former expresses his shape and scale of satisfaction (1) as he switches from, or substitutes, one commodity to another; and (2) as his income, with which he can

[1]These concepts are developed in Sects. 7.4 and 7.5.



P. Shome, *Taxation History, Theory, Law and Administration*, Springer Texts in Business and Economics, https://doi.org/10.1007/978-3-030-68214-9_7

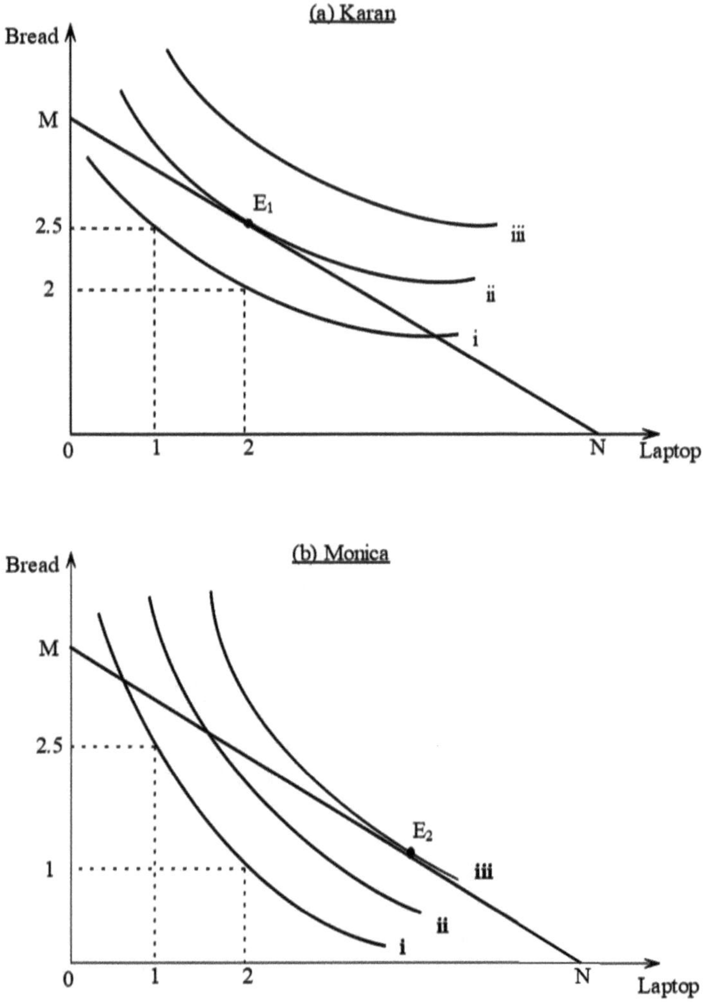


**Fig. 7.1** Consumers in a (2 × 2) Framework

purchase these goods, increases or decreases. For simplicity, let us assume that there are two goods in the market from which he can select different combinations of the goods. Let us say they are Laptop and Bread. This is a convenient approach to take for economic theory has shown that, under certain circumstances, the two commodity framework can be extended to a finite number of commodities for the same conclusions to emerge. Similarly, let us assume two individuals Karan and Monica so that our framework, to begin with, is a (2 × 2) model.

Figure 7.1 (a) shows the utility curves of Karan. As one moves along each curve, one commodity is substituted for another, but the utility or satisfaction derived by Karan from the changing combination remains the same. He thus remains indifferent among all choices along each curve. Thus, this curve is called an 'indifference' curve. Note that they are convex in shape towards 0, the origin, though rather flattish compared to Monica's indifference curves. This indicates that Karan is willing to give up less Bread for every 1 unit of Laptop compared to Monica. Thus, to remain at the same level of utility *i*, Karan is willing to give up 0.5 units of Bread while Monica's utility curvature reveals that she is willing to give up 1.5 units of Bread for every 1 unit of Laptop.

Karan then is a Bread preferer compared to Monica who is a Laptop preferer. Each consumer has a different set of utility curves whose shape reveals their individual preference in consumption. In Fig. 7.1, as they go up the utility scale, say from *i* to *ii* to *iii* and beyond, their satisfaction increases. Traditional economics only describes this kind of variation in choice and does not offer any opinion regarding which bent of mind may be better. We use this traditional framework and set of assumptions to move ahead to learn how taxation affects consumer and production behaviour.

Let us assume Karan and Monica each has exactly the same budget, say Rupees 1000. This is portrayed as a budget 'constraint' since neither can spend more. This is shown in Fig. 7.1 by the straight line *MN* representing the Rs. 1000 that each one can spend on a combination of the two commodities. They cannot choose a point above that line. The line is exactly the same for both since it reflects, given their market prices, what combinations of Bread and Laptop can be obtained with Rs. 1000. Thus, *M* is 1000 divided by the unit market price of Bread and *N* is 1000 divided by the unit market price of Laptop.

It becomes apparent that Karan maximises his satisfaction level at $E_1$, his equilibrium point, while Monica maximises her satisfaction level at $E_2$. Note that if either chose any other point to the left or right on their budget constraints, their satisfaction level would be lower than what they achieve at $E_1$ and $E_2$ respectively, which are therefore called their equilibrium choices. To go to the full market from here, one has to scale up all individuals which we shall examine as we move further on.[2]

## 7.3 Cost and Production

Figure 7.2 elaborates on the producer's perspective. Figure 7.2 (a) depicts the total cost (TC) of producing a Laptop. The shape of the TC curve is given by the state of technology that is available for this commodity. That technology yields a total product schedule which, when multiplied by the market price of Laptop, yields the TC curve. In this sense, total product and total cost are dual concepts.[3] Returning to the TC curve, the distance 01 shows the fixed cost (FC) for the producer even if he produces zero. This signifies his cost of a factory for processing and packing Laptops

[2]See Watson and Getz (1993), Chap. 6, on elaboration of indifference curves.

[3]See Hadar (1974), Chaps. 2 and 3 for the correspondence between the two.

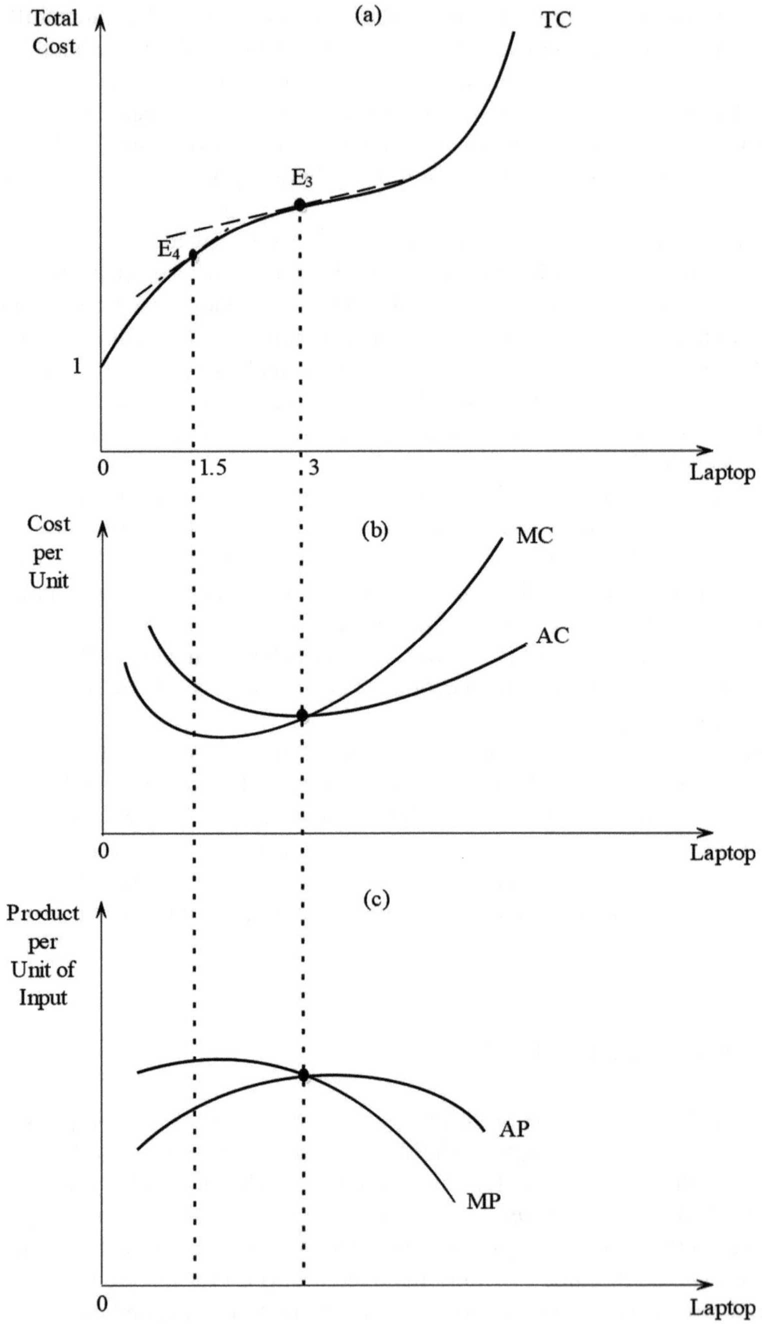


**Fig. 7.2** Cost and product of a firm

and, once he has made this fixed investment, it remains constant irrespective of how many he produces.

The producer increases his production of Laptop unit by unit (shown on the horizontal axis). The fixed cost of investment is getting distributed among more and more units produced. In the beginning, he gets more than proportionate returns as he adds variable inputs of labour and machines to his fixed investment in the warehouse so that there are increasing returns to every unit of his cost of production. Thus, though his total cost of production increases (shown on the vertical axis), it increases at a decreasing rate. In graphical terms, the cost does not increase in a straight line (or proportionately) but in a concave manner, that is less than proportionately until he reaches $E_3$.

After point $E_3$, his costs rise more than proportionately to his production, the reason being that a 'law of diminishing returns' sets in. In this range, his production has already reached a certain size and, comparably, the size of his warehouse—which is represented in the fixed cost—gets too congested for labour to work efficiently in it or for machines to be accommodated with sufficient space. After $E_3$, therefore, the total cost increases more than proportionately because those advantages do not continue. Therefore, $E_3$ is a point of 'inflexion' where the curvature of the total cost curve reverses. The complete TC curve is therefore known to possess an inverted-S shape.

The discerning student may point out that a fixed warehouse can be explained only in the short run. Surely its size can be increased in the long run. That is indeed correct. Nevertheless, the TC curve continues to possess an inverted-S shape. This is justified through the assumption that, in the long run, it is possible to introduce more intensive specialization in the use of factors of production and more efficient organisation of the productive process. Thus, when the firm's plant size is enlarged, not only does the scale of operations reach larger dimensions but it also results in increasing returns. This is referred to as 'economies of scale'.[4]

After $E_3$, the situation reverses and 'diseconomies of scale' set in. This results in an inverted S-shape of the TC curve in the long run. Thus, both in the short run and in the long run, total cost has an inverted S-shape.

Figure 7.2 (b) reveals how the behaviour of total cost translates to per unit costs. The average cost (AC)—total cost divided by the number of units produced—goes down as long as economies of scale are realised; after that AC begins to increase. Thus, AC is minimised at 3 units of supply.

However, there is another concept called marginal cost (MC) that shows how the producer's cost increases as every unit is produced incrementally. Like AC, MC—the cost to produce each additional unit—also decreases in the early stage of production for the same reason, but MC is minimised earlier at 1.5 units of supply.

To understand why, note that a crucial difference between AC and MC is that FC is built into AC but MC is calculated while ignoring FC. Thus, MC is not affected by FC though AC is. Reflecting the technologically given shape of TC, therefore, at the

[4]See Hadar (1974), op. cit., Chap. 4, for further details.

start, MC begins to decline but reaches its minimum at $E_4$ after which every additional unit of supply costs a bit more, thereby giving rise to a positively sloped MC schedule after $E_4$. However, AC—which incorporates the FC component—continues to decline until $E_3$ after which it begins to rise.

To recapitulate, MC reaches its minimum point at $E_4$. AC continues to decline even after $E_4$ though MC begins to rise. MC then intersects AC from below at $E_3$, the latter's minimum point. Both AC and MC are called U- or cup-shaped curves. What is sometimes missed is that the facts—the production technology as well as the market price of the Laptop—are given to the producer. Hence there has been no decision-making, so to speak, up to this point on his part.[5]

Finally, Fig. 7.2 (c) depicts the cap-shaped average product (AP) and marginal product (MP) curves. They are simply the dual reflections of the AC and MC curves. They are useful at the stage when each commodity's product curves have to be assimilated into a national production possibility frontier. We will return to that in Sect. 7.4 when we consider the economy as a whole.

## 7.4 Market Demand and Supply

From the indifference curves of Monica in Fig. 7.1, we can infer that, while she selects $E_2$ as her equilibrium combination of Laptop and Bread, she will change that point to some other choice if the price of either of the two commodities changes. Thus, if Bread becomes cheaper, her budget constraint will become steeper since, now, more Bread is available for the same amount of Laptop at the marketplace. Accordingly, her new equilibrium will move to the left from $E_2$.

Thus, we can conclude that, as the price of a commodity declines, in general, the consumer will tend to buy more of it. That is why a demand curve is downward sloping. Such demand curves are shown in Fig. 7.3. The steepness of her two demand curves reflects her different nature of preferences for Laptop and Bread.

We have already seen that Monica prefers Laptop to Bread relative to Karan. Therefore, Monica would be willing to give up fewer Laptops for the same unit price increase than Karan would. To put it another way, as the price of the Laptop rises, Monica would be willing to switch less easily from demanding Laptop compared to Karan. If that is so, Monica's demand curve for Laptops will be steeper than that of Karan. This is termed as Monica's demand for Laptop being more 'inelastic' than Karan's. The opposite is the case for Bread. Figure 7.3 (a) and (b) depict this variation.

If we imagine Monica and Karan to comprise the entire economy, we can derive the market demand for Laptops by aggregating their demand curves horizontally. That gives us the market demand—the summation of their two demands—curve at each market price.[6] Of course, we can increase the number of consumers by

[5]See Hadar (1974), op. cit., Chap. 4, and Henderson and Quandt (1980), Chap. 3, for elaborations.
[6]Note that the term price always refers to a price per unit of supply.

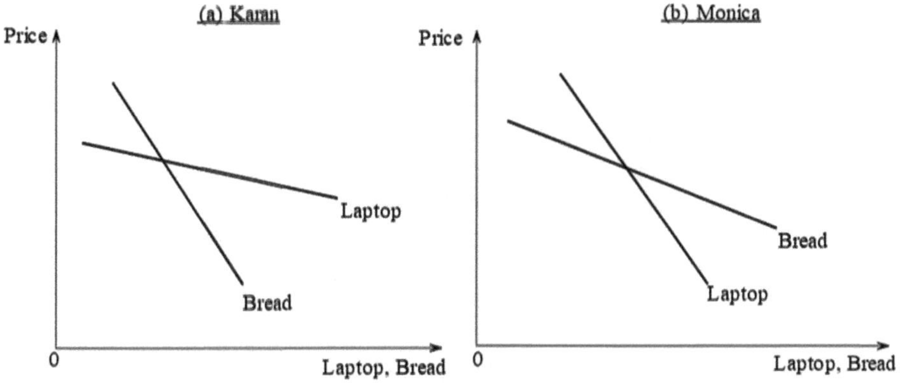


**Fig. 7.3** Demand curves

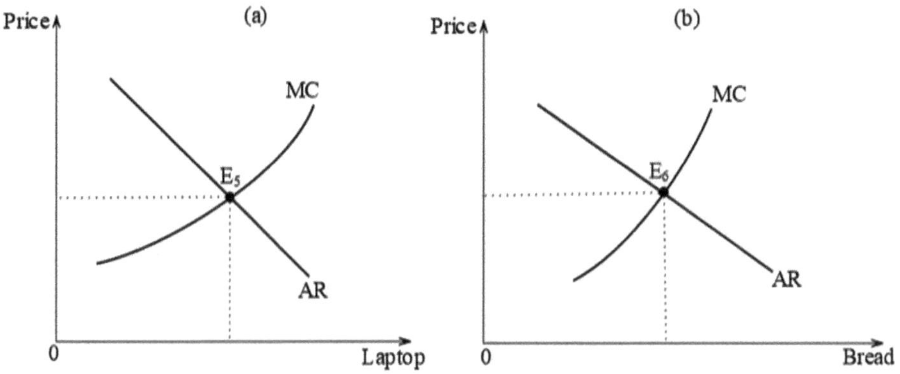


**Fig. 7.4** Market equilibrium

horizontal summation of demand by each of them at every price of Laptop. Similarly, we can derive the market demand curve for Bread.

We can also generate market supply curves for both commodities. A supplier is assumed to supply the market on an incremental basis, that is whether the last unit he sells brings an income higher than it cost him to produce that unit. And this is given by MC where the MC curve shows how much his cost is to produce his last unit. Therefore, it is rational that his MC curve becomes his market supply curve. In essence, it is the upward sloping component of the MC curve. He will supply more, the higher is the price that he can receive per unit. The steepness reflects the type of technology behind the TC curve in the background.

On the other hand, the amount the supplier will actually earn per unit is determined by the number of units he sells multiplied by their average revenue or price. Therefore, the AR curve becomes the market demand curve.

Market equilibrium occurs where the market demand curve and the market supply curve intersect. This is shown for Laptop and Bread in Fig. 7.4. Some interesting characteristics are embedded in them. First, since the elasticity of demand for a commodity varies among consumers—for example it is more elastic for Laptop for Karan than for Monica—one may assume that it is not unlikely that, when aggregated, the variation in elasticity will get diminished. This will happen for all commodities. Thus, first, the difference in the steepness of the market AR curve in Fig. 7.4 (a) for Laptop lies somewhere between the elasticities individually for Monica and Karan. The same is the case for Bread.

Nevertheless, second, overwhelming that averaging effect, overall, the market demand curve for one commodity may be less elastic than for the other. The Laptop still turns out to be less elastic with a slightly steeper market demand curve than the market demand curve for Bread. This is because, at the market level, Laptop is likely to turn out to be inelastically demanded if it is more of a necessity than Bread which may have more alternatives such as Idli or Paratha. Hence the latter's market demand may be expected to be more elastic and, therefore, be represented by a flatter—more elastic—curve than that of a Laptop.

$E_5$ and $E_6$ are the market equilibria for Laptop and Bread, respectively, the dotted lines indicating their equilibrium market supplies and prices per unit.

## 7.5 Scaling Up the Economy

Just as every individual has a budget constraint, any economy as a whole has a budget constraint reflecting its overall resource availability. It has to produce Laptop and Bread within that constraint. As a result, an economy has a bounded curve called the production possibility curve (PP) showing all the production combinations that it can achieve. Figure 7.5 (a) depicts this.

When all the resources of the economy are used to produce Bread, $0P_1$ is produced. If instead, all resources are used to produce Laptop, $0P_2$ is produced. In between, the PP curve is concave towards 0, the origin, for a reason. Nearer the $P_1$

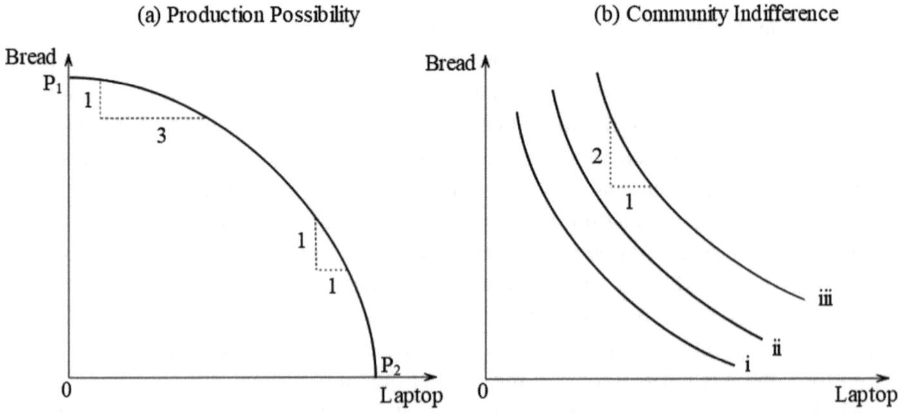


**Fig. 7.5** Economy curves

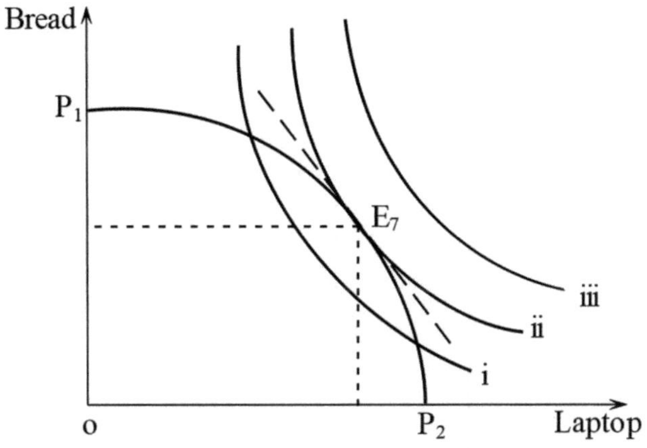


**Fig. 7.6** Economy's equilibrium

point, by giving up 1 unit of Bread, the economy can produce 3 units of Laptop. Nearer the $P_2$ point, resources used to produce 1 unit of Bread can produce only 1 unit of Laptop. This is because, near $P_1$, resources that are better suited to produce Laptops are being diverted to produce Bread which is therefore being produced inefficiently. Instead, for every Bread foregone, a high amount of Laptop could be produced at this point.

On the other hand, near $P_2$, less Bread is produced; hence resources that are better suited for Bread production are being utilised for Laptop production. They are not suited to producing Laptop. Thus, giving up resources producing 1 unit of Bread can yield only 1 unit of Laptop. The rate at which one commodity can be substituted for another in the production process is called the MRT. Near the upper end the MRT is 1/3. Near the lower end it is 1/1. Note that the MRT continually changes along a PP curve.

Figure 7.5 (b) shows how preferences of the community at large are manifested. Just as an individual's indifference map, the community indifference curves (CIC) comprise curves convex towards 0, the origin, that give higher satisfaction to the community as they rise from *i* to *ii* to *iii* and beyond. The rate at which the community is willing to substitute one commodity for another at any point along any CIC is called the MRS at that point. Thus, the MRS on CIC *iii* at the curvature shown is 2/1. And MRS changes along *iii*, as well as along *i* and *ii*. Also note that indifference curves can never touch one another since at every point, *iii* must represent higher satisfaction than *ii*, *ii* higher than *i*, and so on.

The community—made up of all its individuals—wants to be able to reach as high a CIC as possible but is limited by its PP curve, which represents its maximum production constrained by its resource availability (Fig. 7.6). The economy's equilibrium occurs at $E_7$, where the PP curve just touches CIC *ii*. The dotted tangent line touches both these curves and its slope represents the MRT and the MRS at the level of the economy. Thus, at equilibrium, MRT = MRS. All is well since the community has maximised its satisfaction or utility at CIC *ii*, while adhering to its production possibilities that its budget constraint has allowed. The horizontal and vertical dotted

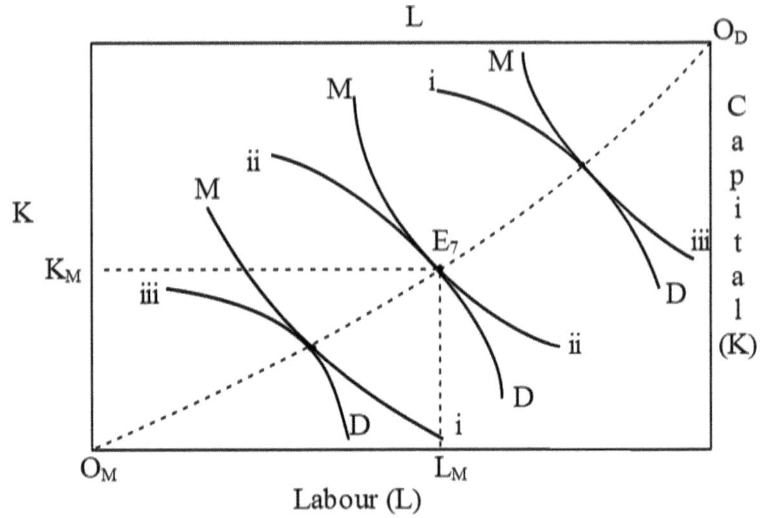


**Fig. 7.7** Limited resources

lines, when measured from 0, the origin, show how much Laptop and Bread the economy has chosen to produce and consume.

## 7.6 Limited Resources

We have used the term resources in deriving the PP curve; hence it is important to understand its role. In a simple world that we are working with, one can imagine the two main resources being labour and capital, both of which are available to the economy in limited amounts.[7] These limited resources account for the bounded nature of the PP curve which shows the two commodities, Laptop and Bread, that are produced. Let us now elaborate on the role of labour ($L$) and capital ($K$) for illustrative purposes.[8]

Figure 7.7 is a box that depicts the total labour and capital, the two finite resources in the economy. They have to be allocated between the production of Laptop and Bread. Labour $L$ is measured along the horizontal axis and capital $K$ along the vertical axis. From the southwest origin $O_M$ for Bread, its convex production possibilities spread out from *Mi* to *Mii* to *Miii*. Each curve, say *Mi*, depicts different combinations of labour and capital that can produce the same amount of Bread.

[7]There are other resources such as land and modern economics has used others such as technology. Here we refrain from including them since we are using a simple framework to understand the basics of a market economy based on which we will be able to proceed to taxation.

[8]Income tax is one that taxes returns to labour and capital as well as other income sources such as land. We will go into further details in Chap. 15.

Hence the curve is called an isoquant.[9] With more labour and capital, higher isoquants, *Mii*, *Miii* and so on, can be achieved. The same occurs for Laptop from *Di* to *Dii* to *Diii*.

The rate at which labour and capital can be substituted to produce Bread is the marginal rate of technical substitution (MRTS) between labour and capital for the production of Bread, similar to the concept explained in Fig. 7.5 (a). The only difference is the word 'technical' which is added to acknowledge that the substitution is taking place between two factors of production.[10] Similarly shaped are the isoquants for Laptop.

The $M$ and $D$ isoquants are tangential to each other along the dotted diagonal line referred to as the 'contract' curve. This corresponds to the PP curve in Fig. 7.6. Only, in Fig. 7.7, we are able to show how labour and capital, the factors of production, combine to give rise to PP. On which point the economy ends up reflects the underlying community preferences depicted in Fig. 7.6. We can say that the equilibrium point $E_7$ in Fig. 7.7 corresponds to the equilibrium point $E_7$ in Fig. 7.6.

The only difference between the two is that Fig. 7.6 pertains to community consumption and the economy's production of Laptop and Bread, whereas Fig. 7.7 pertains to the economy's production of Laptop and Bread, together with how the economy's factors of production, labour and capital, are distributed into the production of Laptop and Bread. Thus, Fig. 7.7 demonstrates that $(L_M, K_M)$ are the amounts of labour and capital used to produce Bread, while $(L - L_M)$ and $(K - K_M)$ are the amounts of labour and capital used to produce Laptop. In this sense Fig. 7.7 explains the production details that underlie Fig. 7.6.

To conclude, therefore, we have learnt that the economy's maximum satisfaction or utility from consumption is achieved at level ii, the highest CIC that can be reached given its budget constraint. $E_7$ shows both how much Laptop and Bread are produced in equilibrium, and also how the available amounts of labour and capital are allocated in that equilibrium production of Laptop and Bread.

We now have a pretty comprehensive impression of a market economy, beginning with individual consumers and producers and examining behind the scenes, so to speak, how factors of production are used to produce the commodities demanded. Since they were two each in number, they are referred to comprise a $(2 \times 2 \times 2)$ economy, the results of which can be expanded to an $(m \times n \times k)$ economy with comparable outcomes for equilibria in product and factor markets.

As we superimpose the actual world on this rudimentary economy, the outcomes become more complex. The real world could comprise a producer who is not a perfect competitor who has to take all prices in product and factor markets as given to him, as we assumed so far, but a monopolist who can influence the prices at which he sells his product. Or, instead of the demand curve intersecting the supply curve where the latter is rising, it could do so where costs are still decreasing. In that case,

[9]See Henderson and Quandt (1980), op. cit., for detailed illustration of this concept.

[10]See Varian (2010), Chaps. 3 and 32 and Pindyck and Rubinfeld (2013), Chaps. 3 and 6 for the development of these concepts.

producers' outcomes get altered. We will learn about the decreasing cost case in Chap. 9, Sect. 9.4.

And, importantly, the market could be interfered with by a tax or a slew of taxes thereby distorting consumer preferences or production decisions. Yet taxation has become a fact of life of the citizen and that is what this book is all about. And a tax does not always have a simple dimension; it may be quite complicated in its structure and effects. The number of resources may also pose issues to contend with. Thus, say there is a third factor of production, land, which is used significantly in one sector only, say Bread, but not for Laptop. In such a case, the impact of a tax may not be easily generalizable. We shall take up such a case in Chap. 9, Sect. 9.8.

Nevertheless, knowledge of the pure market is not only useful but also essential to fully understand how to design taxes and assess their ramifications for the economy at large, in particular on the efficiency of resource allocation.

The objective of this chapter was, therefore, to convey the underlying framework of a market economy that buttresses taxation theory and its application.

## References

Hadar, Josef. 1974. *Elementary Theory of Microeconomic Behavior*. 2nd ed. Boston: Addison-Wesley Publishing Company.

Henderson, James M., and Richard E. Quandt. 1980. *Microeconomic Theory: Mathematical Approach*. 3rd ed. New York: McGraw Hill Book Co.

Pindyck, Robert S., and Daniel L. Rubinfeld. 2013. *Microeconomic Theory and Application*. 8th ed. Upper Saddle River: Pearson Education.

Varian, Hal R. 2010. *Intermediate Microeconomics: A Modern Approach*. 8th ed. New York: W Norton & Co.

Watson, Donald Stevenson, and Malcolm Getz. 1993. *Price Theory and Its Uses*. 5th ed. Lanham, Maryland: University Press of America.

# Introduction of a Tax in the Market

# 8

## 8.1 Introduction

Reflecting their need for public expenditure, governments impose taxes on the production or consumption or incomes (or on some or all of them) that prevail at the market equilibrium. But taxes distort the original market decisions underlying the equilibrium. If a tax is taken directly from consumers, they will modify their demand away from taxed goods and towards untaxed, or lesser taxed, goods, and this decision is made entirely due to the tax. Therefore, their pre-tax, free-market choice gets distorted and a new post-tax choice emerges. If the tax is taken from producers or the factors of production—comprising investors, wage earners and owners of land—that go into making a product, then they will also modify their decisions to produce and supply, and a different, post-tax supply will be established in the market.

Thus, the post-tax equilibrium in the market will be different from the pre-tax equilibrium. And the relationship between the two will reflect how consumers, producers and owners of factors of production react to the tax that has been imposed. These reactions depend on various elasticities of substitution between products, and elasticities of factor substitution across various factors of production.

The impact of taxation in moving the original market equilibrium to another point results in an 'excess burden' of tax reflecting the fact that some of the consumer utility or satisfaction is lost forever as a result of the tax. Some taxes cause more excess burden than others. The role of taxation in causing distortions that result in excess burden will be elaborated through figures and explanations so the reader is aware right from the start of the need for caution in introducing taxes. These matters are the subject of analysis in this chapter.



P. Shome, *Taxation History, Theory, Law and Administration*, Springer Texts in Business and Economics, https://doi.org/10.1007/978-3-030-68214-9_8

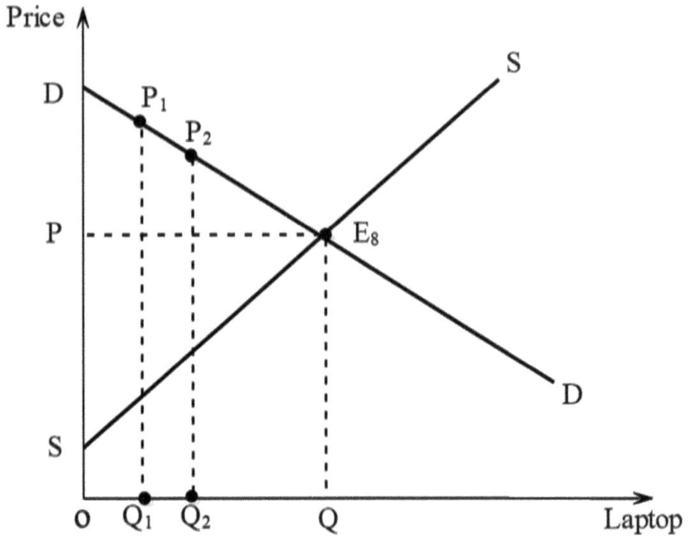


**Fig. 8.1** Consumer and producer surplus

## 8.2 Consumer and Producer Surplus

Figure 8.1 shows that pre-tax market equilibrium occurs at $E_8$, the intersection of the demand curve DD and supply curve SS, and $Q$ is the number of units sold at unit price $P$. Consumers pay an amount in rupees represented by the rectangle $E_8POQ$, or the equilibrium price per unit multiplied by the equilibrium quantity sold. That is exactly the amount also received by producers.

Now let us consider what consumers would have been willing to pay if they were offered Laptop in the market unit by unit. This may be observed from DD, the demand curve. Thus, for the first unit $Q_1$, they would be willing to pay $P_1$, for $Q_2$ the second unit, they would be willing to pay a slightly lower price $P_2$ per unit,[1] and so on. Thus, they would be willing to pay $P$ for the $Q$th unit. And if they had proceeded to buy unit by unit until they purchased the $Q$th unit, they would have had to spend the amount represented by the area $DE_8QO$. Therefore, the difference between this area and the amount they actually pay in the market is the triangular area $DE_8P$. This triangular area is called the 'consumer surplus' in the sense that consumers would have been willing to pay that extra amount for $OQ$ but do not actually have to pay it.

[1] Since they possess the first unit, they had already derived some satisfaction from it, hence would be willing to pay marginally less for the second unit. This is referred to as diminishing marginal utility. This argument carries forward for each additional unit they buy, resulting in the downward sloping demand curve for Laptop. The same is the case for every commodity except that the steepness of the slope could differ reflecting the nature of their demand. See also Chap. 10, Sect. 10.2.

It is easy to work out conceptually that a similar 'producer surplus' is represented by the triangular area $SE_8P$. Thus, both consumers and producers are said to derive a surplus or a certain extra benefit over and above the rupee amount that is exchanged between them. Their total surplus is the triangle $DE_8S$, the sum of the two surpluses. This is an essential characteristic of the pure market economy.[2]

## 8.3 Introduction of a Tax on Supply

Recall that it is the relative price between Laptop and Bread prior to the imposition of any tax that expresses equilibrium decision-making by consumers and producers of both commodities. If a tax is now levied on Laptop and not on Bread, that alters the relative price between the two commodities and would be termed distortionary. It is so called in the sense that the relationship between their two prices is now different from what it was prior to the levy of the tax.

This kind of tax is called a selective excise whose use tax experts prefer to keep to a minimum because of the distortions in the market allocation of resources that it causes. Excises are usually justified, however, as appropriate levies on luxuries, non-renewable resources such as petroleum products, or goods detrimental to health such as tobacco products and consumable alcohol. We shall learn more about selective excises in Chap. 21, Sect. 21.9, and Chap. 22, Sect. 22.4. Here we will simply use a tax on Laptop as a convenient example to demonstrate how a tax, even if simple, introduces distortions in the efficiency of market functioning.

Figure 8.2 shows what happens to the market equilibrium and to the surpluses when $T$, a tax per unit supply of Laptop, is imposed. To begin, the cost per unit of supply goes up; therefore, the supply curve shifts up by the distance $T$ at every point of the supply curve. Consequently, the pre-tax equilibrium $E_8$ shifts to a post-tax equilibrium $E_9$. If you compare Fig. 8.2 with Fig. 8.1, you will notice that, at $E_9$, the equilibrium quantity has decreased from $Q$ to $Q_T$ and the equilibrium price has increased from $P$ to $P_T$.

This implies that, overall, the tax has led to a reduction in quantity sold in the market and increased its unit price. Note further that the combined area of consumer and producer surplus has decreased from $DE_8S$ to $DE_9S_T$, and so has each surplus. Clearly, the tax has made both consumers and producers lose a degree of satisfaction due to the partial loss of their surpluses.

Figure 8.3 shows what government collects in the form of revenue from the tax. Consumers pay the rectangle $P_TE_9Q_TO$ to the suppliers. The suppliers keep rectangle $P_SRQ_TO$, and have to pass on $P_TE_9RP_S$ to government. Thus, what the government takes is the per unit tax $E_9R$ ($= T = P_T - P_S$) multiplied by the post-tax quantity $OQ_T$. This amount is $P_TE_9RP_S$. The overall outcome is that government extracts

[2]See Harberger (1974), Chap. 1.

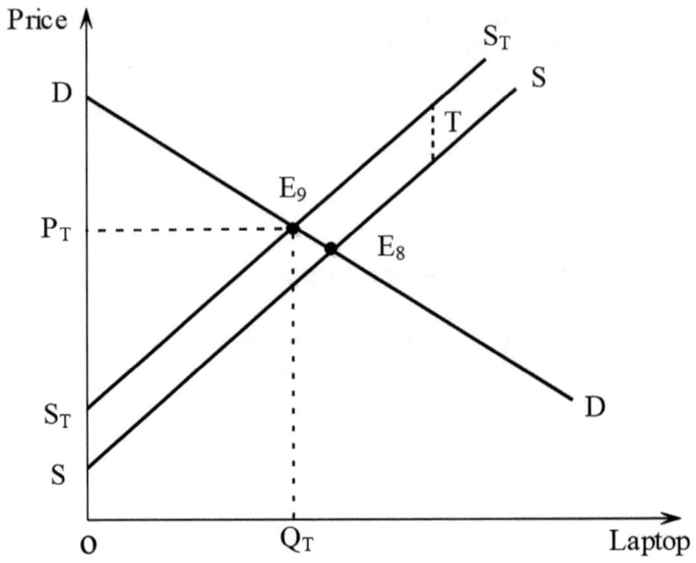


**Fig. 8.2** Tax on supply

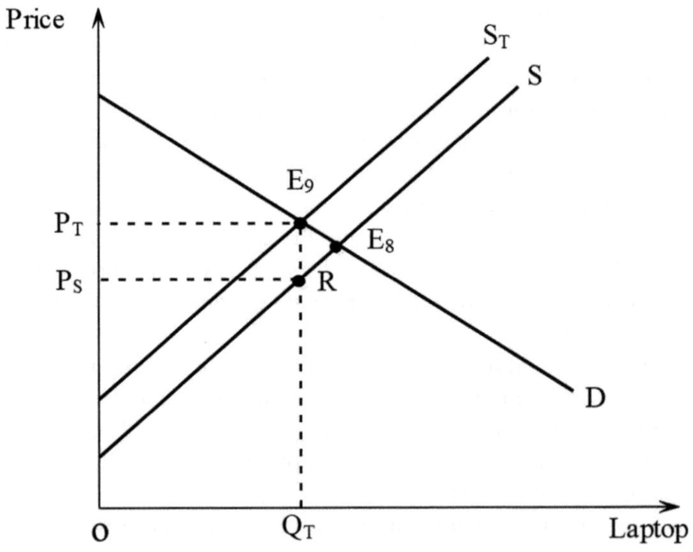


**Fig. 8.3** Government revenue

revenue from the market, consumers pay a higher market price, and suppliers take back less as their post-tax income compared to before the tax was imposed.[3]

[3]See Herber (1983), Chap. 7.

An important aspect to be noted is that the small triangle $E_9E_8R$ is an area that is forever lost for it does not appear in either the post-tax consumer surplus, or the post-tax producer surplus or as government revenue. This loss in surplus is not recoverable and, in this sense, is termed a 'deadweight loss' or 'excess burden' due to the tax.[4]

This loss can perhaps only be justified if we assume that government is obliged to provide certain public services that the private sector cannot provide such as national defence or police, large public infrastructure such as highways, irrigation or electricity-producing dams. If government acquires more resources than needed for its justifiable functions, then society has to take measures to reset such erroneous policy.

An increasingly controversial area of study is the provision of public education, nutrition and health in particular because of their low quality, and leakage from the public coffers. What is increasingly pondered is whether private sector provision—with government subsidies provided to disadvantaged students—would better achieve the objective of providing such services at reasonable cost to all.

On the other hand, many jurisdictions across the globe, including the local administration of the city of Delhi in India, have demonstrated that high-quality education could be provided by the public sector. Countries such as Mauritius and Colombia also have good public sector provision of health. Therefore, it is not necessarily correct that public sector provision is always bad. But society has to keep a careful watch on corruption and deterioration of good systems over time.

## References

Harberger, Arnold C. 1974. *Taxation and Welfare*. Chicago: University of Chicago Press.
Herber, Bernard P. 1983. *Modern Public Finance*. 5th ed. Homewood: Richard D. Irwin Inc.

[4]All taxes suffer from causing such deadweight loss other than a 'lumpsum' tax that is levied on all individuals and extracts a fixed absolute amount from every taxpayer so that no one's pre-tax behaviour changes in the post-tax situation in relation to anyone else.

# 9 Incidence of a Tax

## 9.1 Introduction

A tax may be levied on a firm or individual but its final burden, or what economists term 'incidence' may be shared also by another economic entity. Thus, a tax on the supply of Laptops may be shifted partially to consumers if their demand is less than fully elastic. This is referred to as the 'partial incidence' of a tax which we shall study in this chapter. If it is even slightly inelastic due to a Laptop possessing the attributes of being a necessity rather than a mere luxury, he will share the tax incidence with the supplier. Elasticity is soon to be described below.

The supplier of Laptop may pass on some of the burden to the labour that he hires, in other words, to the inputs he uses in his production. When all actors in the production process—inputs and output—are considered together, the final distribution of the burden of the tax among them is called 'general incidence' of a tax. We shall also examine this concept.

## 9.2 Partial Incidence of a Tax

Here we analyse tax incidence from the supply and demand of Laptop, or only the product market. In other words, we do not examine how the markets for factors of production are also affected.

An interesting question to ask is, if a tax $T$ is imposed on supply and collected from suppliers in the first instance by government, is this total tax amount what the suppliers finally bear, or can, and do, they pass on some of the burden of T to their consumers? Fig. 9.1 delineates this point. Note that the very fact that the supplier can increase the market price from $E_8$ to $E_9$ as a result of the tax, indicates that a part of the tax has to be borne by consumers. Of $E_8V$, the total tax per unit ($= E_9R$ in Fig. 8.3), $E_8U$ is borne by consumers and UV is borne by suppliers. Thus, even



P. Shome, *Taxation History, Theory, Law and Administration*, Springer Texts in Business and Economics, https://doi.org/10.1007/978-3-030-68214-9_9

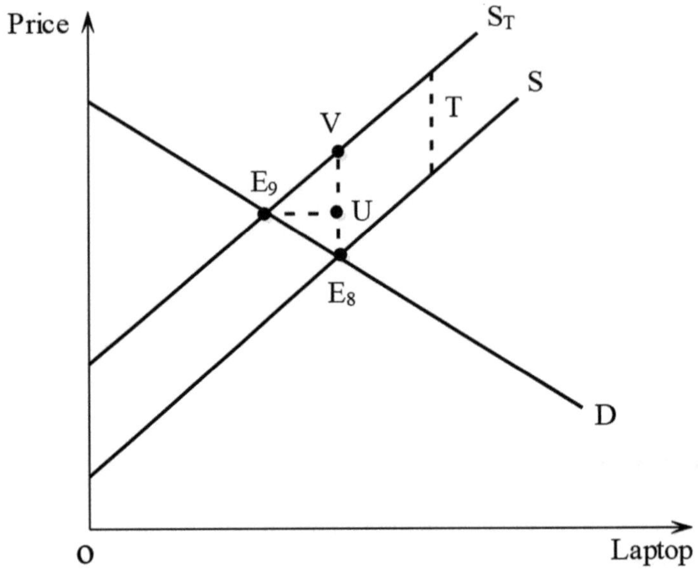


**Fig. 9.1** Partial incidence of tax

though the tax appears to be imposed on market supply, its burden is shared by both suppliers and consumers. This is called 'forward shifting' of a tax.[1]

It is also be called partial incidence or absolute incidence of a tax since it has focussed only on one market, that of Laptop. If as a result of the tax, the supplier also curtails the wages of his labourers, or shifts to a smaller factory or warehouse thus using less land, that would be called 'backward shifting' of the tax.

Thus, the incidence is a much wider concept that could comprise many markets with many products and many factors of production. When the entire economy is represented in an incidence analysis, it is termed the general incidence of a tax or of a structure of taxes (since such models can incorporate and simultaneously analyse a multitude of taxes). Such analysis is termed 'multi-person, multi-sector, multi-factor, general equilibrium' incidence models.

## 9.3 Role of Elasticity

An essential element in shifting theory is how exactly the burden of a tax is shared. Fig. 9.1 shows the burden on consumers as $UE_8$ and that on suppliers as $VU$. Is this division fixed or can it change under different circumstances? The answer is that it depends on how 'elastic' the demand and supply for Laptops are. You can imagine that if demand were less elastic, then the demand curve would be steeper. In that case

[1]See Herber (1983), Chap. 8, for an analysis of incidence under a market monopoly, that is where there is just one seller in the market, as opposed to a perfectly competitive market being used here.

$E_9$, the post-tax intersection between market demand and supply, would lie further to the right.

This would in turn imply that the price rise for consumers would be greater than $UE_8$ so that they would bear more of the tax $T$. The supplier in turn would bear less of the tax since the total tax, $VE_8$ (the same as $T$), remains the same. A similar exercise can be carried out by varying the elasticity of supply.

It is therefore quite important to understand elasticity conceptually. The formula for elasticity $E_{p,q}$ may be depicted as:

$$E_{p,q} = \frac{(\Delta p/p)}{(\Delta q/q)}.$$

Referring to our example of a tax on supply, the denominator denotes how a particular quantity $q$ responds to an exogenous introduction of a tax in the background. That change in quantity is $\Delta q$. That trigger or $\Delta q$ leads to a price change $\Delta p$ from the original price $p$. When $\Delta p$ is divided by the original price $p$, it becomes a percent change. Similarly, when $\Delta q$ is divided by $q$, that too becomes a percent change. When these two elements are divided by each other, a pure number without any unit of measurement is obtained. That is $E$, the elasticity.

Elasticity is a pure number and denotes the reaction of a dependent variable (price in this case) consequent to a change in an independent variable (quantity in this case). Indeed, you can experiment with figures of the demand and supply curves with different elasticities and examine where, in each case, the post-tax equilibrium occurs. You should then be able to realise that the more elastic the demand is, the less is its share of $T$, the tax. And, the more elastic supply is, the more is the share of $T$, the tax, that can be shifted to demand.

In the next section, we will explore selected scenarios of different industry cost conditions that are associated with different elasticities of supply, and examine how the same tax affects them differently.

## 9.4 Varying Supply Conditions of Products

The nature of supply elasticities varies according to the market structure of supply. It is useful to think of this in terms of: (a) a constant cost industry (CCI), (b) an increasing cost industry (ICI) and (c) a decreasing cost industry (DCI). CCI is one in which the average cost, AC, of production does not change as production increases. ICI is one in which AC increases; and (c) DCI is one in which AC decreases. Such variation could occur since producers could experience zero, negative or positive economies of scale, in turn reflecting the engineering that underlies production technology that determines their cost conditions (see Chap. 7, Sect. 7.3).

Let us go behind this more carefully. In the case of CCI (Fig. 9.2 (a)), note that $S$, the supply curve, becomes perfectly elastic or horizontal. This is because the average cost never changes in such an industry so that at $P$, a pre-tax price, the industry can supply any amount in the market. When a tax $T$ per unit is imposed on Laptop, the

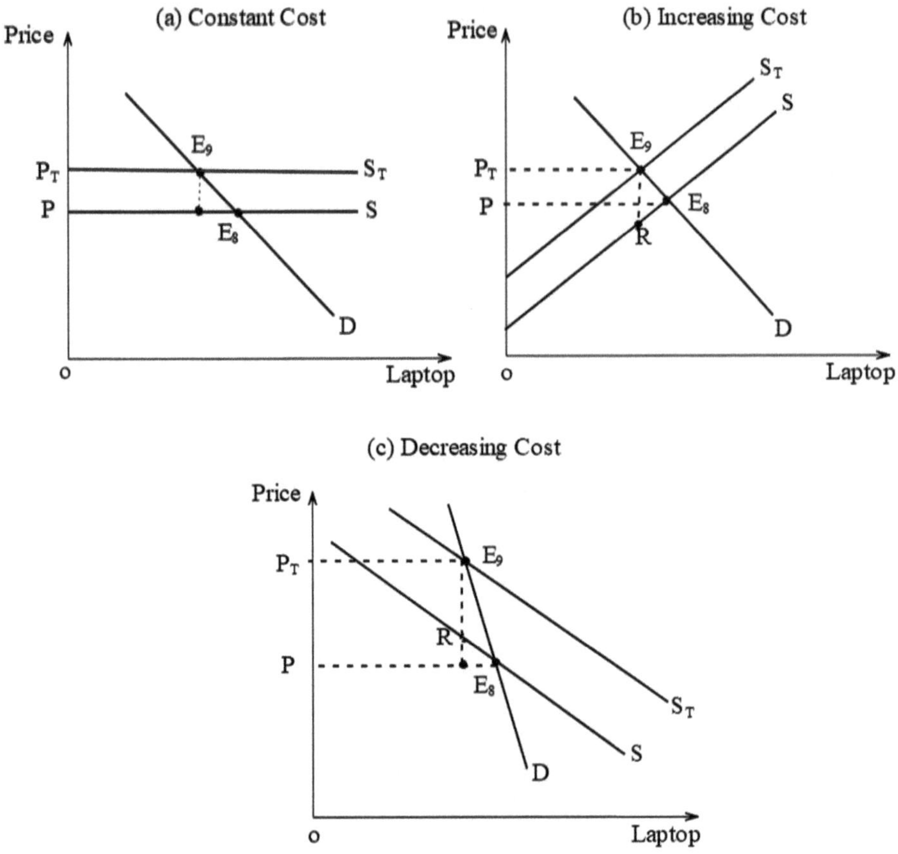


**Fig. 9.2** Cost conditions of industry

*S* curve shifts up by the amount of tax *T*. And the price increase for the consumer, $P_T - P$, equals the full amount of tax. Thus, there is complete forward shifting of the tax to consumers.

This is explained by the fact that, given the totally elastic supply curve, suppliers will not tolerate any decrease in the post-tax price they receive. If forced to do so, they would shift with their resources to some other industry. Hence the tax burden is shifted completely to consumers who are obliged to bear its full incidence.

In the case of ICI (Fig. 9.2 (b)), the tax again increases the unit cost of production so the post-tax supply curve shifts up. It was explained in Chap. 7, Sect. 7.3 that, given the state of technology, both marginal cost and average cost of production begin to increase after a certain amount of production has been reached. This tends to occur as factory space gets congested in the short run, or the advantages of emerging technology and management wear thin in the longer run.

Therefore, the supply curve is usually depicted as upward rising. This was reflected in the upward rising supply curve in Figs. 8.1 to 9.1. From Fig. 9.2

(b) we see that, in the ICC case, the tax ($E_9R$) must be shared between consumer and supplier, the increase in the consumer price being $P_T - P$. Thus, there is partial forward shifting in the case of ICC.

An interesting case is that of DCI (Fig. 9.2(c)). Decreasing cost can occur when the demand curve intersects the supply curve rather near the left-hand margin, implying that the intersection occurs prior to the supply curve begins to rise (in contrast to Fig. 9.2 (b)). This implies that demand is small so that it intersects supply even before producers have been able to increase production to a point where diminishing returns have set in or economies of scale have been exhausted, a matter we considered in Chap. 7, Sect. 7.3. In such a case a tax $T$ on supply would represent a situation where producers will scale back their production to such an extent that the price rise $P_T - P$ will be larger than the tax ($E_9R$) itself.

An example of DCI may be helpful here. In a remote rural or hill area where the population is likely to be significantly more sparse than in the plains or urban areas, the demand may be relatively small for phones. Hence the demand curve would lie closer to the vertical axis. In such a thinly populated area the low demand would intersect cost curves where they are still downward sloping, in other words, not quite economical for producers to supply the market.

The imposition of a sudden tax would make them cut back production and supply, and, in addition, they would pass on more than the full amount of the tax $E_9R$ to consumers in the form of a higher-than-tax price increase of $P_T - P$. Otherwise operations would be unviable for them under the thin demand situation. Hence there is higher than 100 percent forward shifting in the case of DCI. In such a case, the government would have to subsidise supply rather than tax it if it does not want consumers to bear too heavy a burden of the tax. The subsidy could, for example be in the form of providing towers or other infrastructure that the phone company would otherwise bear under ordinary circumstances.

## 9.5 Supply Conditions of Factors of Production

Suppliers of final products can not only shift the burden of a tax on them 'forward' to consumers but also shift it 'backward' to the owners of 'factors of production' or resources such as labour and land who sell these resources to the producers or capital owners. The higher is the elasticity of a factor supply—that is the ease with which factor owners can increase or decrease their supply depending on the remuneration they receive—the more protected is that factor's owner from sharing the burden of a tax that is levied on the producer. This is because, if the producer tries to shift the tax burden backward to the factor owner, the latter can curtail his factor supply more easily.

By contrast, the more inelastic the factor supply is, the tax on a producer can be shifted backward on the factor owner more easily since the latter cannot easily pull back his factor supply. It is easy to depict demand and supply curves in a factor market with two possibilities—high and low elasticity of factor supply—and then to impose a tax on the demander of the factor (who is the producer of the final product) to compare and contrast how the backward shifting would vary in the two cases.

## 9.6 Shifting Varies with the Type and Base of Tax

Classification of taxes segregates them into two broad categories. If the intention of tax design is for the burden to remain primarily at its impact point, then it is termed a 'direct tax'. If it is expected that the burden is likely to be shifted, then it is termed an 'indirect tax'.

The mechanism of tax shifting is through market transactions. Reflecting that direct tax is less adaptable to market transactions than an indirect tax, the latter is more likely to be shifted than the former. Put another way, market transactions are generally further removed from the taxable event in the case of a direct tax such as an individual income tax. This is not so for an indirect tax such as a selective excise where the tax is levied on a market transaction enabling the tax to be passed on or shifted forward to another market agent.

A 'broad based tax' is more easily shifted than a 'narrow based tax'. Take a 'selective excise tax' on furs. The taxed consumer can easily switch his demand and substitute it with, say an alpaca sweater. Here the demand is elastic. Or, if there is a toll on entering a highway, drivers may substitute it by taking untaxed, narrower roads, a phenomenon not unknown, for example in India. At least it may take quite some time for drivers to accept the toll and opt for the highway.

Instead, if the tax is on most consumption items at a general tax rate such as in the case of a GST or VAT, the consumer is unlikely to find an untaxed item to buy as a substitute. Here the demand is less elastic. Hence the consumer is likely to bear the tax burden rather than escape it through switching between consumption items.

## 9.7 Shifting at Varying Levels of Government

Most country constitutions specify what taxes different levels of government—national or central, state or provincial, local or municipal—can levy. The widest geographical area comprises the nation-state itself. A central government tax can therefore be expected to stay at the first impacted economic agent since he is unlikely to be able to move elsewhere other than abroad. With a state government tax, there is some possibility of sellers to shift a tax forward to buyers provided the latter cannot move out of the state too easily. A tax imposed at the local government level has to be sensitive to the fact that a taxed person may move out of the locality. Therefore, property tax rates, levied typically at the local government level, should not be uncompetitive with other localities.

To summarise, therefore, in a partial equilibrium context, the extent of tax shifting depends on a number of conditions, namely: (i) the type of market structure, (ii) nature of long-run industry costs, (iii) price elasticities of output demand and factor supply, (iv) type of tax, (v) width of tax base and (vi) the level of government at which a tax is imposed. Thus, though the tax revenue collected at the initial impact point appears to burden only that economic agent from whom the tax is collected, in reality, its burden is likely to be shifted forward and backward, its final distribution determined by the six aspects listed above. However, note that the incidence analysis we surveyed in this chapter focused on a single product market comprising its consumers and producers and, effectively, the markets for factors of production associated with that product. In this sense, our incidence analysis was limited or partial.

Nevertheless, partial equilibrium tax incidence analysis is helpful for analytical purposes. To begin, recall that *T*, the tax we introduced, led to a change in the absolute price of the product essentially ignoring how the post-tax price related to other prices in the economy. This is a practical method that can more easily convey the essence of tax incidence. This is often the context adopted by other branches of the taxation profession in which the impact on the taxed product at the collection point is considered as the sole or primary tax burden.

One of the objectives of this textbook, however, is to convey to students that the collection point of a tax is distinct from the final distribution of the tax burden. And general equilibrium analysis is necessary to convey this reality. We will describe it next.

## 9.8 General Equilibrium Incidence of Taxes

### 9.8.1 The Economic Incidence of the Corporate Income Tax

The incidence of the corporate income tax has been intensively researched regarding its 'legal' incidence or 'statutory' incidence, that is, who the tax is initially collected from. However, though the company remits the tax to government, ultimately, the burden may be passed on to its workers, or capital owners in the economy as a whole, or workers in general, or a combination of them. This may be called the long run or 'economic' incidence of a tax. Harberger (1962) divided the US economy into two sectors—corporate and non-corporate—with both sectors employing capital and labour, with perfect mobility of the factors of production between the corporate and non-corporate sectors,[2] and carried out corporate tax incidence analysis in such a framework comprising the entire economy.

The corporate income tax is a tax on the return to capital employed in the corporate sector, that is a tax on a factor of production, capital, that is imposed only in one sector. Harberger applied parameters from the United States around 1958, and found that, for several reasonable sets of demand and factor substitution elasticities,[3] the corporate income tax was borne by the owners of capital in the economy as a whole rather than by corporate capital, from which the tax is collected,

[2]See Krelove (1995) for further discussions.

[3]Elasticities are explained further in Sect. 9.9 and Appendix 9.1.

alone. His results also disproved a prevalent belief that the tax was shifted to labour. An application of the model to corporate taxation in India and in East Asian countries also indicated that capital bears almost all of the tax, depending on the value of the elasticity of substitution in the non-corporate sector.[4]

Subsequently, the model was modified to check on its robustness. If its simple assumptions are modified in particular ways, then the outcomes also get affected. For example, a third factor—land—was introduced in the non-corporate sector (since it comprised mainly real estate and agriculture) and it was found that some of Harberger's conclusions get modified reflecting the simplicity of assumptions in the Harberger model.[5] Others solved for a more disaggregated model of the economy, adding more sectors, and found that Harberger's incidence results were only approximately maintained.[6]

Another critique has been that, since interest expense is deductible in determining the tax base, only equity-financed capital is taxed. Corporate tax would not change the cost of debt-financed capital, and would not lead to the resource reallocations determined by Harberger. Provisions in corporate tax law, for example the type of tax incentives, also determine its incidence. The 1986 corporate tax reform in the United States reduced a tax incentive known as tax credit for investment while, at the same time, reducing the corporate tax rate. This had a neutralising effect among all new taxpayers due to the removal of the incentive and, therefore, any discrimination between those who could use the incentive and those who could not. Further all taxpayers gained from the lower corporate tax rate.[7]

### 9.8.2 Frameworks of Incidence Models

The simplest economy-wide model as we have discussed earlier is a 2 × 1 × 2 model where there are two consumers Karan and Monica, one product Laptop, and two factors of production labour and capital. For a general equilibrium framework that we discussed in the previous section, we have to introduce at least two products, Laptop and Bread, to arrive at a 2 × 2 × 2 version that, in turn, could be blown up to an (m × n × k) model. As soon as we move from one product to two, we are in a two-sector framework, concerned with the 'relative price' between the two products and not the 'absolute price' of any one of them.[8]

[4]See Shome (1978) for the Indian case study and Shome (1985) for the East Asian case study.

[5]See Shome (1981).

[6]See Shoven and Whalley (1972) for their pioneering work.

[7]Note that, since the corporate tax rate was reduced, the tax burden also declined on previously invested corporate capital, making them gainers from the reform.

[8]Atkinson and Stiglitz (1980), Lecture 6, elaborates on this concept.

### 9.8.3 Taxing Product Laptop

A tax on Laptop alone will increase its post-tax price and thus the relative price of Laptops will rise vis a vis Bread. In turn, the tax will adversely affect demand for the factors of production that are utilised in its production; but it will affect the price of that factor more which is used more intensively in the production of Laptop. If this is capital as opposed to labour, the relative price of capital will decline vis a vis the price of labour. Thus, the ratio of capital to labour used in both the product sectors will change. If the relative demand for capital falls in comparison to that of labour, capital's remuneration would also decline compared to that of labour. At this point, the final incidence of the original tax on Laptops is revealed in the form of which factor of production bears more of the burden of that tax.

The important matter is that, in general, equilibrium analysis, we do not speak of the impact of a tax on an individual product or consumer. We always analyse it in relative terms in reflection of what occurs across the economy, taking into account how incidence falls on all factors of production. This is the most important element in understanding the difference between partial and general equilibrium analysis of tax incidence.

Our point of reference for the framework is Fig. 7.7. Before any tax is imposed, production equilibrium for Bread and Laptop is at $E_7$. One can easily view from the isoquants how much Laptop and how much Bread are produced at $E_7$. The capital and labour utilised for Bread production at $E_7$ are $K_M$ and $L_M$, respectively. The capital and labour that go into the production of Laptop at $E_7$ are $K_D = K - K_M$ and $L_D = L - L_M$, respectively.

### 9.8.4 Taxing Factor Capital in Capital-Intensive Sector

Let us now use a slightly more complex example than a tax on the product Laptop. Let us assume that a corporate income tax (CIT) is levied on companies i.e. on the earnings of capital in the corporate sector, but not on the earnings of capital used in the non-corporate sector. Assuming that Laptop is produced by a company though Bread is produced by a non-corporate entity, the tax is, therefore, imposed on the income of corporate capital owners or $K_D$ alone (and not on $K$ or $K_M$).

CIT is collected in the first instance from the owners of $K_D$. But that is not the final resting place of the tax burden of CIT once we consider the chain of events that are set forth after the tax is collected. To begin, the price of Laptop, the corporate good, rises in relation to that of Bread, the non-corporate good. There is an immediate reaction of Laptop producers to reduce production due to the tax so that resources or factors begin to move out of Laptop towards Bread.

### 9.8.5 Expulsion of Resources from Taxed Sector

At this point, a very important assumption needs to be made. Let us assume that Laptop uses capital more intensively per unit of labour than does Bread. This is termed as follows: Laptop is relatively more capital intensive in its use of technology than is Bread.

Further, as capital moves out of Laptop, note that it carries with it labour as well, in a ratio of $K_D / L_D$. But $K_D / L_D$ is greater than $K_M / L_M$. So, the demand for capital will be relatively less by the Bread producer at the pre-tax price for capital, so he will absorb the $K_D$ advancing towards his sector only if $K_D$ is willing to be absorbed at a lower price compared to its pre-tax price. In turn, since capital $K$ can flow freely between the two sectors, the rental or per unit income of capital $K$ as a whole, will decline compared to the income of $L$ as a whole.

This is exacerbated by the fact that the Bread producer, if he is to absorb all of the capital emerging from the Laptop sector, would want more labour than is leaving the Laptop sector. This is because, to recall, the labour/capital ratio is higher in the Bread sector than in the Laptop sector. In the first instance, therefore, the rental of capital declines relative to the wage rate in the economy as a whole.

Thus, the corporate income tax—a tax imposed on that portion of capital, which is used exclusively in the Laptop sector—has two outcomes after all factor movements are completed and a general equilibrium is reinstated in the post-tax economy. The outcomes comprise a two-pronged change in relative prices. First, the price of the Laptop increases relative to that of Bread reflecting a lower post-tax production and supply of Laptop and higher production and supply of Bread.

Referring to Fig. 7.6, $E_7$ moves leftward on the production possibility curve. In turn, this implies that a community indifference curve lower than ii is reached by society at the post-tax equilibrium. Then why would society acquiesce to being taxed? The answer, as we specified earlier, is that the revenue that government collects will presumably be used for useful purposes of producing various 'public goods' that would allow society to again reach ii, and perhaps iii.

The second outcome is that the price of capital declines relative to that of labour throughout the economy reflecting the reduced demand for capital relative to that of labour. Therefore, capital, the taxed factor of production, even though taxed only in its use in one sector, loses in income relative to that of labour. In this sense, note that though the impact point of CIT is $K_D$, that is CIT is collected from the income of $K_D$ alone, the long-run incidence of CIT, in our example, is on $K$ as a whole.

## 9.9 Elasticities of Factor Substitution

Elasticity—or the percentage reaction of a variable to a percentage change in another variable—comprises a backbone of economic analysis of the impact of a tax change or of its introduction on economy-wide responses from producers, owners of factors and consumers.[9]

In relative terms, how much percentage gain does the economy's wage rate make compared to the economy's rental of capital. This depends on the relative 'elasticities of factor substitution' (EFS). EFS is the rate at which labour can be substituted by capital in the Bread sector, say EFSM. If EFSM is high, capital can be more easily absorbed in the Bread sector than if EFSM is low. In that case, capital coming out of the Laptop industry will be more easily absorbed by the Bread sector. In turn, the rental of capital will decline less relative to the wage rate and capital will suffer less compared to the case in which EFSM is low.

My final question to ponder is, if firms can pass on the burden of a tax that is initially collected from them, then why do they spend time and financial resources in lobbying for their preferred tax structures. The answer that may be gleaned from the corporate sector is that they cannot pass on all their burden forward and backward, and must genuinely believe that the burden, or a significant part of it, has to be borne by themselves. This practical side of the tax experience has to be juxtaposed on the more conceptual basis of tax incidence that we just covered. We shall address aspects as we analyse corporate tax behaviour in Chaps. 18, 19, 20, 27, 28, 29, 30 and 31.

## Appendix 9.1: Method of Elasticity Calculations

### Elasticity of a Tax System

Now that we have become familiar with the concept of elasticity, this Appendix takes the opportunity to make a digression and examines how the elasticity concept is used to assess tax revenue response to growth in the GDP of an economy. Elasticity is estimated with a log-linear equation, which simply means the percentage response in the dependent variable such as tax revenue to a percentage change in the explanatory or independent variable such as the Gross Domestic Product (GDP) of an economy.

The above response is usually called the 'buoyancy' of a tax system. If we cleanse the data of any tax revenue that has been collected from discretionary tax measures that the government announces in its central budget, then we get a tax revenue series that represents only the automatic response of the prevalent tax structure to GDP—or economic—growth. In the elasticity formula introduced in Sect. 9.1, p would

[9] See Appendix Table 9.1 for how the concept of elasticity may be used in an analysis of revenue productivity of tax systems.

represent the tax revenue series, and q would represent the GDP series. When we estimate the coefficient of response of the former to the latter, we obtain the elasticity of a tax system.

## Deconstructing Elasticity

The elasticity formula can be de-constructed if we view it as a product of two underlying elasticities:

$$\text{Elasticity of a tax with respect to GDP} = \text{Elasticity of a tax with respect to its appropriate base} \times \text{Elasticity of the base with respect to GDP}$$

First, it is of primary importance to define the base as closely as possible to the source from which a tax is collected. For example, corporate income tax is collected from corporate profits. GST or VAT is collected from the consumption of goods and services. But taxes involve exclusions, exemptions and deductions. As a result, data on broad categories of bases obtainable directly from the national accounts have to be modified by including approximations of the elements that cause tax base erosion. That yields usable proxy bases for the theoretically correct bases. Usually, despite taking all possible actions to cleanse a data series, estimates of the elasticity of tax systems may be somewhat imprecise.

Nevertheless, appropriate substitutions may be made in order to improve the elasticity estimates so that meaningful policy conclusions could be drawn. For example, if agriculture falls virtually outside the income tax net, the GDP of agriculture should be removed from the income tax base. Thus, the elasticity of an income tax on wages should use as its base, domestic wages and salaries–net of agricultural wages. Appropriate definitions for such bases for major taxes appear in the Appendix Table 9.1.

Second, the most commonly used method of elasticity estimation[10] has its shortcomings. While the numerator in the tax-to-base elasticity—the tax revenue series in question—is adjusted for discretionary changes in both the tax base and the tax rates, the denominator—the base itself—is not adjusted for the impact it undergoes due to any of the discretionary measures. Not even the discretionary measures with respect to the tax base are incorporated directly as an addition or subtraction to the base and, its consequences, in turn, are not applied to the tax revenue series.

Discretionary measures taken on tax rates are assumed not to affect the tax base, either through the natural reactions of taxpayers to the resulting changes in relative prices or through a change in the degree of evasion or of administrative efficiency. For example, a significant increase in the import tariff could affect taxable imports, which is the tax base, adversely; unless this is taken into account, the potential yield

[10]See Prest (1962).

**Table 9.1** Method of elasticity calculations

| | Proxy Tax Base[a] | Tax-to-Base Buoyancy b1[b] | Adjusted Tax-to-Base Elasticity b2[c] | Base-to-GDP Elasticity b3[d] | Overall buoyancy (b1) × (b3) | Overall elasticity (b2) × (b3) | Weights[f] |
|---|---|---|---|---|---|---|---|
| Personal income tax | Personal income net of agricultural value added | | | | | | |
| Wage income | Domestic (net of agricultural) wages and salaries | | | | | | |
| Interest income | Interest paid to households | | | | | | |
| Other | Income from property (net of farm rent) plus professional and unincorporated enterprise income received by households | | | | | | |
| Corporate income tax | Corporate profits | | | | | | |
| Excise duties | Consumption of all components | | | | | | |
| Soft drinks | Consumption of non-alcoholic beverages | | | | | | |
| Spirits | Consumption of alcoholic beverages | | | | | | |
| Petroleum | Consumption of fuel and related products (e.g. electricity) | | | | | | |
| Tobacco | Consumption of tobacco and tobacco products | | | | | | |
| General sales tax | Value added of domestic goods and services | | | | | | |

(continued)

**Table 9.1** (continued)

| | Proxy Tax Base[a] | Tax-to-Base Buoyancy b1[b] | Adjusted Tax-to-Base Elasticity b2[c] | Base-to-GDP Elasticity b3[d] | Overall buoyancy (b1) × (b3) | Overall elasticity (b2) × (b3) | Weights[f] |
|---|---|---|---|---|---|---|---|
| Import-based taxes | cif value of dutiable imports | | | | | | |
| Import duties[e] | | | | | | | |
| Total | | | | | | | |

Source: Author's exposition

[a]The proxy tax bases should be closely related to the actual coverage of the various taxes. The bases described here would tend to approximate the commonly found coverages in representative tax laws

[b]b1: log (tax) = a1 + b1 log (base)

[c]b2: log (tax adjusted for discretionary changes) = a2 + b2 log (base)

[d]b3: log (base) = a3 + b3 log (GDP)

[e]Often import duties on oil and non-oil imports are strongly differentiated. Further, the behaviour of these two categories of imports may be quite distinct over time. It may, then, be helpful to estimate the elasticities of oil and non-oil imports separately

[f]Weights used for the calculation of the weighted buoyancy and elasticity of the taxes as a whole should be the shares in overall tax revenue collected from the categories under consideration

from the increased duty rates would tend to be overestimated. Similarly, a large increase in income tax rates, especially in the upper-income brackets, could increase the occurrence of tax avoidance or evasion, again adversely affecting the income tax base.

All attempts at elasticity estimates to date ignore these elements. When using elasticity estimates for policy conclusions, therefore, one needs to bear their shortcomings in mind.

## Elasticity of Tax Structure

Discretionary measures usually take the form of tax increases rather than tax base expansions; as a result, they contribute little to enhancing the revenue elasticity of the tax system. In fact, a close examination of discretionary measures often reveals that many of the measures in the income tax area erode the tax base and, therefore, its revenue elasticity is reduced. Also, the structures of customs duties and selective excises, which often account for significant portions of tax revenue in several African and some Asian countries, use rate changes rather than base expansion in making discretionary changes. Finally, unchanging patterns of consumption and production may explain to a good extent why elasticity is difficult to raise.

## Improving Tax Elasticity

Despite the various limitations to increasing the elasticity of developing country tax systems, it is obvious that any improvement in tax elasticity would have to come from a sustained expansion of the tax base. This would entail an expansion of coverage, that is minimising tax incentives that erode the base, a sustained effort in enhancing the taxpayer base, a regular modification in the tax rates to adjust for inflation, possibly a conversion from specific to ad valorem rates wherever feasible, as well as a reasonable degree of progressivity in the system as a whole.

## References


Atkinson, Anthony B., and Joseph E. Stiglitz. 1980. *Lectures on Public Economics*. New York: Mc-Graw Hill Book Co.

Harberger, Arnold C. 1962. The Incidence of the Corporation Income Tax. *Journal of Political Economy* 70: 215–240.

Herber, Bernard P. 1983. *Modern Public Finance*. 5th ed. Homewood: Richard D. Irwin Inc.

Krelove, Russell. 1995. General Equilibrium Incidence of Taxes. In *Tax Policy Handbook*, ed. Parthasarathi Shome, 39–45. Washington, DC: IMF.

Prest, A.R. 1962. The Sensitivity of the Yield of Personal Income Tax in the United Kingdom. *Economic Journal* 72: 576–596.

Shome, Parthasarathi. 1978. The Incidence of the Corporation Tax in India: A General Equilibrium Analysis. *Oxford Economic Papers* 30: 64–73.

———. 1981. The General Equilibrium Theory and Concepts of Tax Incidence in the Presence of Third or More Factors. *Public Finance* 36 (1): 22–38.

———. 1985. Is the Corporate Tax Shifted? Empirical Evidence from ASEAN. *Public Finance Quarterly* 13: 21–46.

Shoven, John B., and John Whalley. 1972. A General Equilibrium Calculation of the Effects of Differential Taxation of Income from Capital in the U.S. *Journal of Public Economics* 1: 281–321.

# Equity Effects of Taxation 10

## 10.1 Introduction

Entities equally placed prior to the imposition of a tax may find themselves to be unequally affected by the imposition of the tax. Thus, a tax could be inequitable across different consumers and producers in the economy, that is, it may suffer from 'horizontal inequity'. Also, a tax may exacerbate the inequity that already exists in the income distribution in the economy. This indicates that the tax suffers from 'vertical inequity'. The design of taxes should prevent worsening the prevailing distribution of income in the population.

There are alternative criteria behind how taxes are imposed. One is the benefit principle, that is, a tax should be collected from a taxpayer in reflection of the benefit he derives from a public service. It does not recognise equity as a principle but has certain advantages such as transparency. Another method is taxing according to the ability to pay of a taxpayer that results in higher taxation as incomes rise. Yet another method is optimal taxation that emphasises the efficiency criterion with built-in subsidies for the poor primarily through the expenditure side of the budget. This chapter considers these principles and concludes that the ability to pay criterion is the most widely used.

## 10.2 Equity and Progressivity

Equity is extended by designing 'progressive' taxes such as an individual income tax structure in which tax rates rise as the income of a taxpayer rises with the underlying premise that his 'ability to pay' tax increases as income rises, since the extra satisfaction he receives from every additional rupee he earns, declines.

Figure 10.1 explains the principle. In Fig. 10.1a, the first unit of income gives an individual L1 extent of satisfaction or utility. The second equal unit of income gives him an M2 extent of utility or a smaller extent than the first unit of income. As he earns additional units of income, he gets less utility than from the previous unit. This



P. Shome, *Taxation History, Theory, Law and Administration*, Springer Texts in Business and Economics, https://doi.org/10.1007/978-3-030-68214-9_10

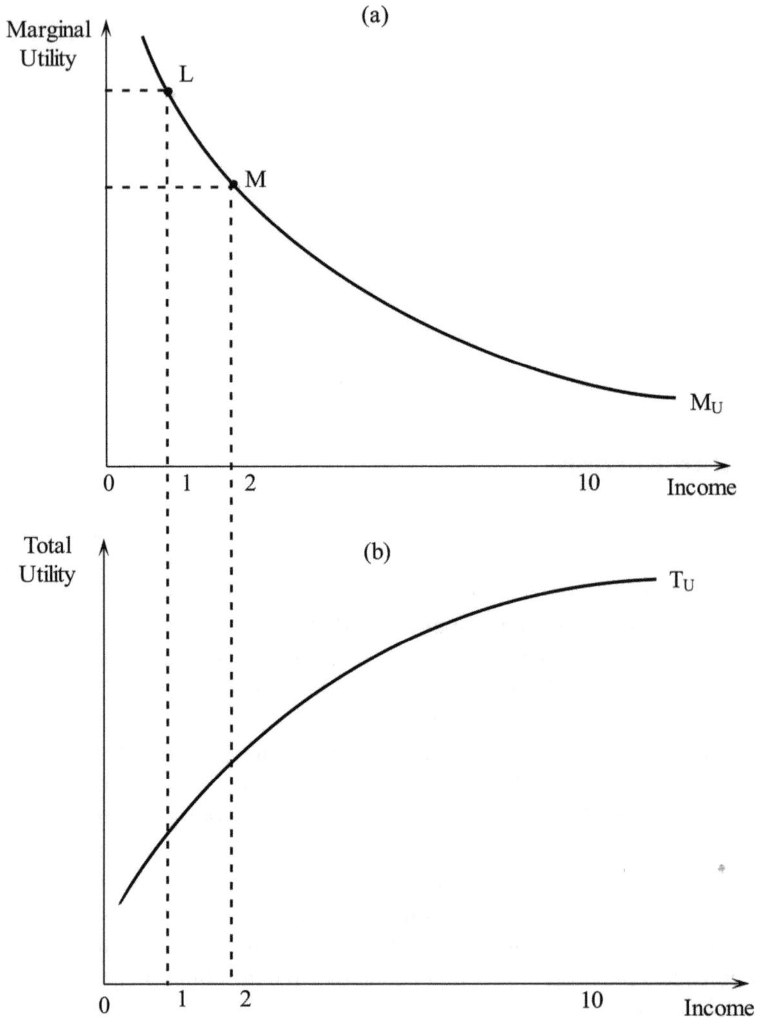


**Fig. 10.1** Utility of income

phenomenon is referred to as the 'declining marginal utility of income' $M_U$. It is convex to the origin O. This can be extended to a comparison of two persons, poor and rich. The poorer person may be expected to derive more utility from a third unit of income if he is earning only 2 units, compared to the utility derived by a richer person from an eleventh unit if he is already earning 10 units. This is based on the assumption that the eleventh unit must give less additional utility compared to what the third additional unit does (even when we compare two different persons).

A declining marginal utility of income schedule which is convex to the origin is reflected in a total utility of income schedule $T_U$ which is rising, though at a declining

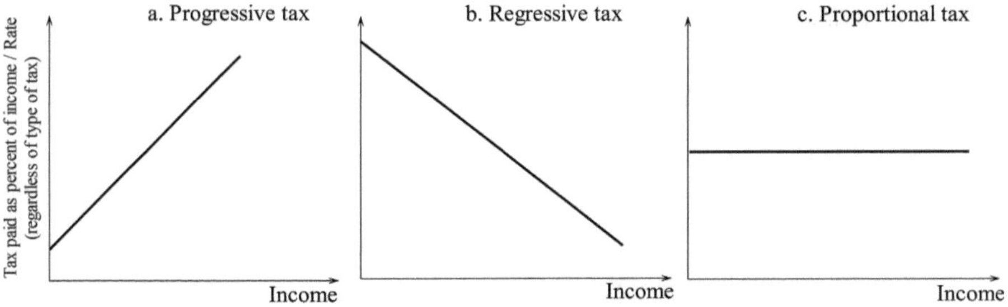


**Fig. 10.2** Various tax base–rate relationships in distributional equity terms

rate, as shown in Fig. 10.1b. This is because any extra utility—with each additional unit of income—declines, so that $T_U$ takes on that particular shape.

This pattern of declining marginal utility as income increases translates to a higher ability to pay tax by the richer person while maintaining the same sacrifice of utility as the poorer person. Thus, it may be observed from the diagrammatic scheme of Fig. 10.1 that, if the richer person is earning 10 units of income, even if 8 units are taken away from him as tax, and he would arrive at 2 units of post-tax income, he would still have the same utility—marginal and total—as the poorer person who earns 2 units of income. Thus, there is space to tax the richer person even while equalising the utility of the rich with that of the poor. It is, therefore, justified to tax the rich more than the poor, or to have a 'progressive tax' rate structure as incomes rise. Figure 10.2a–c depict the tax rate structures that result in terms of distributional equity.

Figure 10.2a shows a progressive rate structure inasmuch as the tax rate measured on the vertical axis goes up as income, measured on the horizontal axis, rises. But, even if the legal or 'statutory' structure of an income tax may appear to be progressive, there may be many tax incentives favouring the rich and wealthy, so that the 'effective' tax rates may be 'regressive' as shown in Fig. 10.2b. In this case, the tax rate, in practical terms, declines as incomes rise. Finally, as shown in Fig. 10.2c, if the tax rate remains constant as a proportion of income, then it is a 'proportional' tax structure.

To illustrate, the corporation income tax in India, which is supposed to be proportional or slightly progressive as per the law, had effectively become somewhat regressive. This was due to the nature of tax exemptions of various types in the overall tax structure. The effective tax rate curve had become U-shaped as shown in Fig. 10.3, that is, as corporate profits increased, the effective tax rate decreased.

Only as profits increased to very high levels—mainly comprising financial sector profits—did the effective tax rate curve rise slightly, thus giving it a U-shape. This reflected a plethora of incentives that only large corporations could benefit from. In India's 2006 annual budget, the problem was mitigated somewhat by abolishing the surcharge[1] component of the corporate income tax for small corporations while

[1]An additional charge that was being imposed on the calculation of the tax itself.

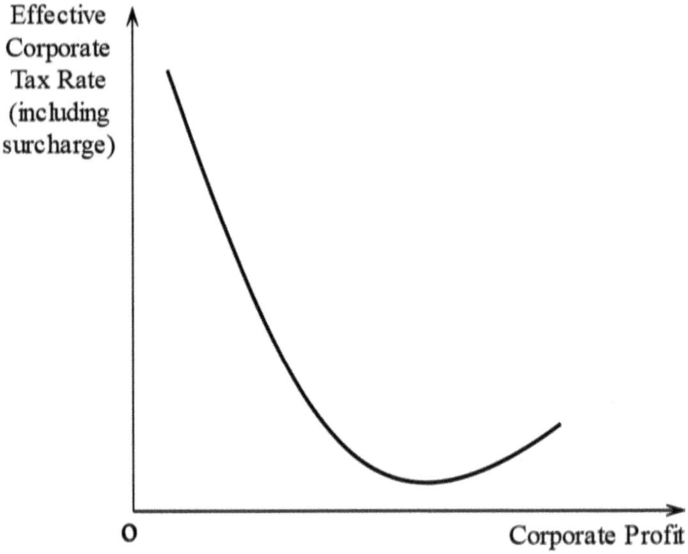


**Fig. 10.3** Regressivity in corporate income tax (India—Pre-2006 Union Budget)

keeping it in place for large corporations. This reduced the element of regressivity to the overall corporate tax structure.

## 10.3 Tax and Distribution

In the context of equity, a question that is asked is whether a tax structure, after it is changed, has improved or worsened the distribution of income across income classes. This is depicted through a diagrammatic scheme known as the Lorenz Curve, named after the person who first specified it. Figure 10.4 demonstrates it. The box diagram measures the percentage of population along the horizontal axis and the percentage of income along the vertical axis. The diagonal depicts exactly equal income distribution of the population, the first 1% of the population receiving 1% of national income, the first 50% receiving 50% (at point C), and so on. But no country has actually achieved such a state even among those who made unsuccessful and cruel attempts to do so such as the Soviet Union, Communist China or the Khmer Rouge of Cambodia during different periods of their history in the twentieth century.

In actuality, pre-tax income distribution is likely to lie away from the diagonal such as the solid bulging line. Given its convexity, it may be observed that the first 50% earns only 20% (point A) and, as we move up the curve, it is obvious that the richer income groups earn greater proportions. Now, if we consider a tax that is progressive, the post-tax distribution becomes more equitable as represented by the dotted line (still convex). After tax, the income of the first 50% is 35% of the total

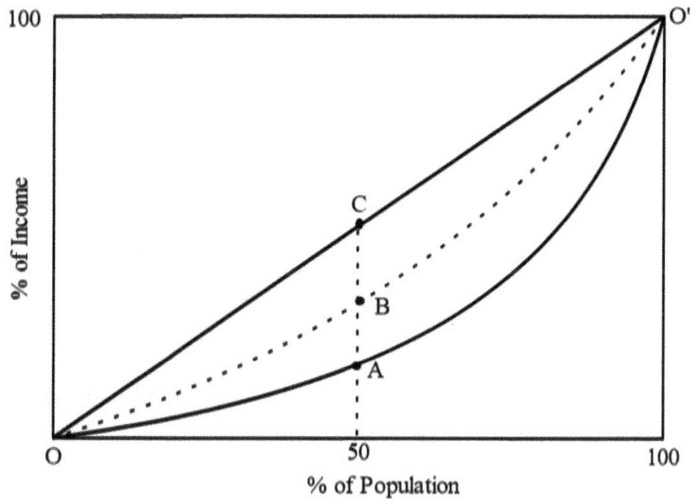


**Fig. 10.4** Lorenz curve of income distribution

(point B). Thus, the closer the Lorenz or income distribution curve is to the straight-line diagonal, the more equal the income distribution is in the population. Yet it is true that, if the tax structure is too progressive, that could discourage work effort of labour or the utilisation of capital by capital owners. Perspicacity is, therefore, of the essence in finding the best progressive tax rate structure for a taxpaying population.

## 10.4 Regressive Effect of Consumption Tax

It is not just the statutory specification of the income tax and its effective distributional outcomes that may be different as depicted in Fig. 10.3. The GST or VAT may be designed as a fixed-rate tax but, in effect, they may tend to turn out to be regressive. Being a tax on consumption rather than on saving and, given that consumption is a higher proportion of a low-income budget compared to that of a high-income budget, the GST or VAT tends to fall on a wider tax base for the poor than for the rich. Hence, these taxes are deemed to be regressive in effect.

The regressivity of consumption taxes may be further exacerbated unless they are designed appropriately. Usually, in structuring a GST or VAT, items consumed by low-income groups are exempt from taxation. Thus, items of cheaper varieties of clothing and footwear as well as unprocessed food including vegetables, fish and meats, and bakery products such as loaves of bread would be typically exempted from the tax. But it is not enough to assume that consumption patterns are similar across the globe.

Let us take an example, that of South Africa when the VAT was being designed for its introduction in 1990–1991. In the initial design, unprocessed food products such as the ones listed above were planned to be exempted. But this author's research investigation found that the poor and vulnerable were not able to consume fresh vegetables or bread in a significant way and, instead, were obliged to buy canned and pre-packaged products from corner shops. Fresh food was likely to be consumed more by the rich in proportion to their budgets. This was because, at that time, South Africa was racially segregated, the blacks being legislated to live in 'Homelands' that were basically arid and barren hinterland where little fresh produce could be grown or agriculture fruitfully undertaken.

The inhabitants of Homelands had little option but to consume canned and pre-packaged products. When this was pointed out to researchers in the country, they took the matter into account in structuring the VAT to reflect the particular consumption pattern of South Africa. Soon South Africa experienced a regime change under the leadership of Nelson Mandela so that the races—black, mixed, Indian, white—could thenceforth mingle legally. This is why economics and its branches, including taxation, are a social—and not a physical—science in which human aspects combine to play a key role.

## 10.5 Benefit Principle of Taxation

Recall that a person pays a tax by foregoing his personal purchasing power in anticipation of receiving government-provided goods and services. The 'benefit' principle directs a tax to be collected from a taxpayer in reflection of the extent of benefit he receives from paying a tax. Thus, taxpayers pay directly for the public good or service received by them. This could, in principle, lead to regressivity if the poorer benefit more than the rich from a particular tax. Thus, it could be viewed as countering the ability to pay principle in its essential elements.

Equity under the benefit principle may, however, be viewed differently. First, payment and receipt by a purchaser of a public good provided under this principle may be 'voluntary' just as he is free to purchase, or not, from the private market. Second, the extent of payment is related to the benefit received which could, in turn, reflect how much it cost the government to supply it just as in the case of a private sector supplier.

In practice, the use of the benefit principle is difficult since the nature of public goods—that of 'collective consumption'—often restricts it from excluding non-payers from consuming them. Examples are national defence and police force that maintain security and law and order in society; everyone effectively 'buys' or consumes them even if they did not care to pay for them. On the other hand, examples of other government provisions that may be subjected to the benefit principle are parks, health centres and schools. Therefore, the benefit principle can be applied to a relatively narrow base of public provision and, therefore, it never became a widely applied criterion for taxation or for achieving equity in the distribution of tax burdens.

Rather, the use of the benefit principle is limited to 'user charges' for entrance to government maintained state and national parks, zoological gardens, archaeological sites, museums and the like. Another use is in the form of 'earmarked taxes' where

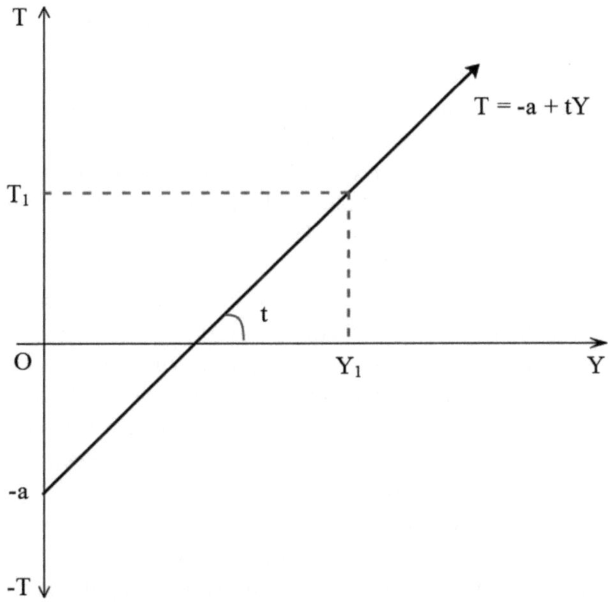


**Fig. 10.5** Effect of optimal taxation

the revenue collected from individuals is used for specific objectives, the benefit from which accrue to the same group of individuals. Examples are government-provided pensions, and unemployment and medical insurance. To conclude, one advantage of using the benefit principle is that it connects the tax and expenditure sides of government activity directly. It is transparent and is more easily amenable to monitoring and evaluation (M&E) of government tax and expenditure implementation which has become increasingly important in justifying public projects.

## 10.6 Optimal Taxation

The proponents of the optimality approach have attempted to combine efficiency and equity aspects.[2] To begin, its premise is that a progressive income tax causes non-neutrality in the work–leisure choice of taxpayers. This forces a reallocation of their pre-tax choices between work and leisure and results in an 'excess burden' on the taxpayers. On the other hand, the revenue gathered, if effectively transferred through government expenditures to lower-income groups, will lead to a distributional gain enjoyed by the latter.

To illustrate with a simple case, Fig. 10.5 depicts an income tax schedule as a straight line

[2] Atkinson and Stiglitz (1980), Lecture 14, develop this aspect. Several other authors have also discussed and debated optimal taxation.

$$T = -a + tY$$

where $T$ is tax revenue and $Y$ is pre-tax income, while $a$ and $t$ are tax-related parameters. Since a goes into the negative portion of the vertical axis, the distance $-a0$ shows that, when income $Y$ is zero, an individual pays negative tax $-a0$. In other words, he receives $-a0$ as a guaranteed minimum payment from the government. And $t$ is the tax 'rate' so that, when $t$ (a rate) is multiplied by $Y$ (a magnitude), it yields a magnitude again. Thus, at income $Y_1$, the tax revenue collected is $T_1$. Note that if $a = 0$, then $tY = T$.

The more society is averse to inequality or poverty, the higher will be the angle $t$ and the income tax schedule will rotate backward (become more steep). But if the schedule becomes too steep, taxpayers will become averse to work and increasingly prefer more leisure, which is the outcome of the elasticity of his labour supply. Thus, as indicated before, striking the right balance between distributional concerns and probable deleterious allocative outcomes between work and leisure is crucial in arriving at an optimal tax rate.

Two conclusions that can be drawn from the above 'linear' analysis of optimal taxation are: (1) distributional concerns of a government tend to result in a negative tax (or subsidy) for some of the (poor) population; and (2) an optimal tax rate imposed on the non-poor has to be found keeping their work–leisure trade-off in mind, in a way that revenue collected should suffice for income transfers to the poor.

The more progressive a tax structure is, the higher is the excess burden on the upper-income groups. On the other hand, as the transfer to lower-income groups increases, their gain in marginal utility decreases (as they move rightward along their decreasing marginal utility curve as shown in Fig. 10.1a). Thus, the optimal rate structure of income tax is bound to be determined at the point where the rising excess burden curve of upper-income groups (who pay more in tax in the net) cross the declining marginal utility curve of lower-income groups (who receive net distributional gains from transfers). This intersection point is termed the 'social optimum'.

Though conceptually it cannot be easily faulted, a critique of the optimal taxation approach has been its placing allocation (or efficiency) considerations on equal footing as distributional (or equity) considerations. In a sense, it sets aside any supremacy of the ability to pay principle of taxation, that is, of vertical equity among taxpayers. This is necessarily so since distributional considerations are attempted to be resolved through the expenditure side of the government's budget rather than through taxation.

Nevertheless, it has to be recognised that, as the theory of taxation principles progressed, taxation experts tended to emphasise the efficacy of achieving distributional goals through expenditure instruments rather than through taxation. One important reason for this is that expenditure allocation can be carried out directly from the budget and monitored and evaluated whereas the distributional incidence of taxation can at best be a matter of heuristic analysis and conclusions drawn therefrom.

Finally, a further complicating aspect of optimal taxation has to be considered. If we recognise that there are variations in professional skills among economic agents, then we have to accept that there will be differences in work–leisure behaviour as a result of a tax. Thus, ideally, there is likely to be a range of optimal tax rates across such variations of taxpayers. And, as skills are acquired over time, that range will also change—converge or diverge—in number. Further, such changes in optimal tax rates could be frequent. It is not surprising, therefore, that country income tax systems opt for an income tax structure that reflects the ability to pay rather than optimality per se.

## Reference

Atkinson, Anthony B., and Joseph E. Stiglitz. 1980. *Lectures on Public Economics*. New York: Mc-Graw Hill Book Co.

# Tax and Stabilisation of the Economy 11

## 11.1 Introduction

One of the government's roles is to maintain aggregate demand in the economy which is consistent with stability in employment. When the economy is in recession, government should bolster it by taxing less; and, when the economy's demand outpaces supply, government should cut the excess demand back by taxing more. This is called counter-cyclical tax policy. A progressive tax structure achieves this objective and is called an automatic stabiliser.[1] The objective of this chapter is to examine the economic stabilisation capability of a tax structure.

Relatedly, it examines the concepts of 'buoyancy' and 'elasticity' of tax structures that measure the revenue response to rises in income. It analyses the impact of progressivity of taxes in an inflationary environment when nominal incomes rise, though real incomes may not. Nevertheless, higher nominal incomes would drag taxpayers to higher tax brackets. This phenomenon is termed 'bracket creep' or 'fiscal drag'. To alleviate it, some inflation adjustment in tax payments is called for. On the other hand, during inflationary times, any slowness or lags in revenue collection deplete the real value of revenue collected. Tax administrations should structure revenue flows to guard against it. These aspects are considered in this chapter.

## 11.2 Buoyancy and Elasticity

To begin, we extend the concept of elasticity that we are familiar with, in order to explain the above-mentioned government role. Using the personal income tax as an example,

[1] Singer (1976) goes into some detail of this concept in Chap. 8.

 
P. Shome, *Taxation History, Theory, Law and Administration*, Springer Texts in Business and Economics, https://doi.org/10.1007/978-3-030-68214-9_11

$$E_R = \frac{\Delta R/R_0}{\Delta Y/Y_0},$$

where $E_R$ is the elasticity of tax revenue with respect to income,[2] and $R$ is tax revenue, $Y$ is income, and 0 is the base year. If tax revenue responds more than proportionately to a change in income, such a response is represented by $E_R > 1$.[3] Generalising, if tax revenue grows at a faster (or slower) rate than the growth in income, then the relationship is 'buoyant' (or not buoyant). Its value depends on the progressivity of the tax rate structure and the responsiveness of the tax base to changes in income. Let us deconstruct these components.[4]

First, let us define $t$ as the ratio of $R$, the tax revenue yield, and $B$, the tax base as defined in law. If the tax rate structure specified in the tax code is progressive, then $t$ rises as the tax base increases. In that case, $t$ is the average tax rate that reflects the statutory progressive tax rate schedule. $B$, the tax base, is the taxable income comprising wages, property value, and other gross incomes. In elasticity terms,

$$E_t = \frac{\Delta t/t_0}{\Delta B/B_0},$$

where $E_t$ is the elasticity of $t$, the average tax rate, with respect to changes in $B$, the tax base.

Second, $E_B$, the elasticity of $B$, the tax base, with respect to $Y$, income, is to be considered,

$$E_B = \frac{\Delta B/B_0}{\Delta Y/Y_0},$$

The value of $E_B$ reflects the responsiveness of $B$, the tax base, to changes in income $Y$. $E_B$ does not depend on the progressivity or regressivity of the tax rate structure. The literature explains how the two concepts combine to explain the elasticity of $R$:

> Let us assume that cyclical fluctuations in profits exceed those of total income, while fluctuations in wage income fall short thereof. The value of $E_B$ in this case exceeds 1 for a tax on profits and falls short of 1 for a tax on wages.[5]

The value of $E_R$ is given by,

[2]If the entire economy is being considered, income may be construed as national income.

[3]Musgrave (1959) and Herber (1975) elaborate on this elasticity concept in Chaps. 21 and 24, respectively.

[4]Musgrave (1959), op. cit., introduced the two components in Chap. 21.

[5]Musgrave (1959), op. cit., p. 507.

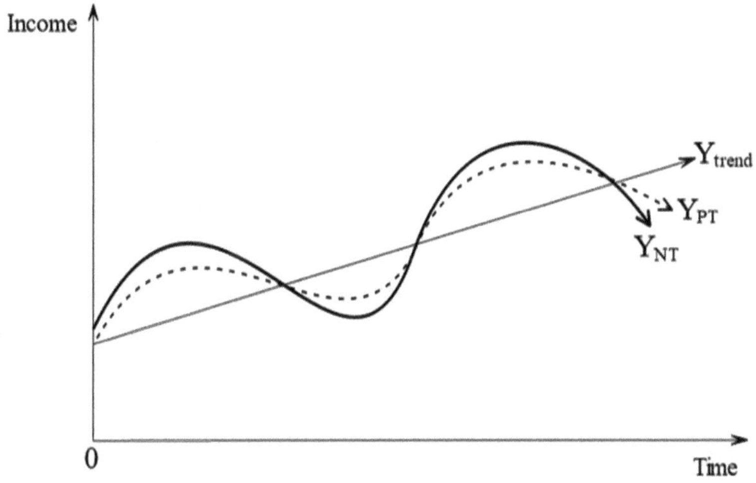


**Fig. 11.1** Progressive tax stabiliser

$$E_R = \left(1 + E_t \frac{B_1}{B_0}\right) E_B = E_B + E_t E_B \frac{B_1}{B_0},$$

From this elaborated expression of $E_R$ one can perceive that it is an expression underlying which are both $E_t$ and $E_B$.

$E_t > 1$ holds for a progressive income tax structure. A GST or VAT, on the other hand, will tend to have $E_t < 1$ since, under these consumption taxes, $t$ is usually proportional and $\Delta B/\Delta Y$ shrinks as $Y$ increases.[6]

Figure 11.1 depicts the automatic stabilizer diagrammatically. The vertical axis measures national income and the horizontal axis shows time, with 0 as the base year. The straight-line $Y_{\text{trend}}$ shows national income as a 'trend' that averages out the actual cyclical pattern (solid line) $Y_{\text{NT}}$ experienced by the economy. $Y_{\text{NT}}$ is simply the national income turnouts with no income tax.[7]

Now if a progressive income tax is imposed on this economy by designing a rate structure that possesses higher tax rates as incomes go up,[8] then the swings of $Y_{\text{NT}}$ around the trend $Y_{\text{trend}}$ are dampened to yield the post-tax income pattern (dotted line) $Y_{\text{PT}}$. The crux is that this happens automatically due to the way the tax rates have been structured and is achieved without the need for any discretionary tax measure to be introduced to reduce or contain the cycles.

The outcome is that, during a recession, as incomes decline, the applicable tax rates also decline automatically, leaving proportionately more incomes in the hands

[6]Only a lumpsum tax will have $E_R = 0$. This is because, as Herber (1975), op. cit., explains, it is a tax on a 'person as a person', and not upon his income, wealth or commodity purchases (p. 568). Its aggregate is not related to the movements in income.

[7]$Y_{\text{trend}}$ is derived by statistically minimizing its distance—both above and below—from $Y_{\text{NT}}$.

[8]See Chap. 10, Sect. 10.2, to revisit the technical concept of a progressive income tax.

of the taxpayers. Diagrammatically, this brings $Y_{PT}$ closer to $Y_{trend}$, than was $Y_{NT}$. Most governments, therefore, legislate a degree of progressivity in their income tax statutes.

It should be kept in mind that the corporate income tax on corporate income is usually set as a proportional tax, the rates remaining constant with changes in income. But corporate income is a cyclically volatile component of national income. This could result in its elasticity to be above unity. This was observed after a very positive phase in corporate revenue during 2004–2008 when India's economy was booming. Corporate revenue grew more than proportionately to income registering an elasticity well above unity.[9] After the 2008 global economic crash, however, income tax revenue growth, in particular from the corporate income tax, declined though the decline was proportionately somewhat less than in the case of the rest of the global economy.

Global taxation trends reveal that the progressivity in income tax structures has been scaled back since the 1980s in much of the world, and certainly since the mid-1990s in India. Thus, presently, the structures of income tax and their changes reflect less concern regarding the achievement of macroeconomic stabilisation, and greater concern for containing their potential detrimental effects on the efficiency of resource allocation and, presumably, on economic growth.

## 11.3 Progressivity During Inflation

Progressivity in the tax structure could have beneficial equity characteristics as explained in Chap. 10. However, there has to be a careful follow-up to avoid unintended effects of a progressive tax structure as time unfolds. One example is an unintended rise in effective tax rates in an inflationary environment for all, or some, income groups. Termed 'bracket creep' or 'fiscal drag', it can occur because inflation tends to raise nominal incomes, though real incomes may remain the same.[10] And since income tax brackets are expressed in nominal terms, income earners may enter upper-income tax brackets as nominal incomes rise. Now higher marginal tax rates would apply to them though their real incomes have not changed.

On the opposite side, in the 1980s and 1990s, many countries reduced the top marginal income tax rates as an incentive for higher productivity and economic activity. This was known as 'supply side' reform.

In the 1980s, Botswana, a country in southern Africa, had seven marginal individual income tax rates. Keeping both supply-side considerations and fiscal drag in mind, Botswana decreased the top marginal rate from 65 per cent to 60 per

[9]In India, the central government's tax/GDP ratio has been around 10 per cent, with slightly higher collection from commodity taxes (higher than 5 per cent) than income taxes (less than 5 per cent). The years 2004-08 were a golden age for the rate of growth of tax revenue growth in real terms and income tax collection surpassed that of commodity taxes.

[10]Nominal incomes are in currency (Rupee) terms while real incomes are incomes after adjustment for inflation.

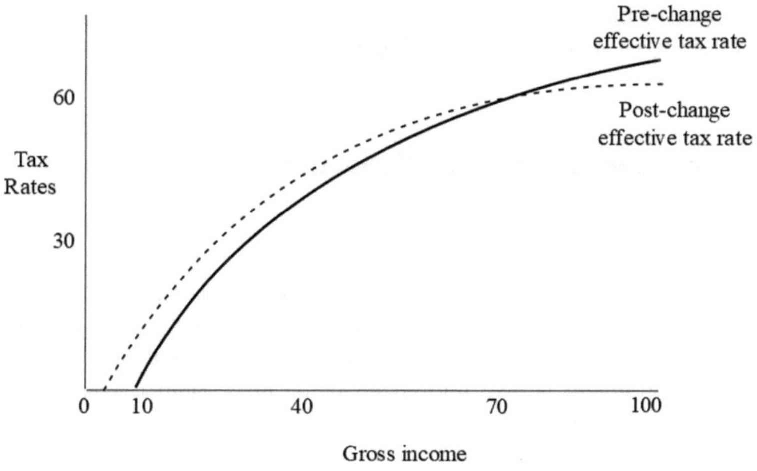


**Fig. 11.2** Effect of fiscal drag on tax rates

cent, while maintaining the next rates of 60 per cent and 50 per cent. Thus, the change favoured the top incomes while maintaining the status quo for middle incomes in terms of tax rates. It was found that the outcome was an unintended distributional impact in favour of the top income groups.

It can be seen from Fig. 11.2 that, after the change, the effective tax rates for higher income groups went down while those for lower groups went up. Why did this occur when the statutory tax rates for most of the middle income had remained the same? This reflected less than comprehensive correction for fiscal drag. Thus, the rate reduction overwhelmed the fiscal drag effect for upper incomes. But, since there was no tax rate reduction for middle incomes, inflation led to fiscal drag for them. It is important, therefore, to check on the effective tax rates from time to time for unintended underlying phenomena that may be occurring if left unattended. Of course, the anomaly was advised to be corrected in Botswana.

In practice, any aspect in the income tax structure that is set in nominal terms including tax reliefs gets affected by inflation, usually adversely. Thus, standard deductions and personal exemptions and tax credits, if set in nominal terms, also suffer an erosion in value unless corrected for inflation from time to time. The problem is that, though governments may adjust them for inflation periodically, they may do so with a lag in time. In between, taxpayers suffer an unintended loss in real incomes while governments enjoy an unanticipated windfall in real value of revenue.

To avoid bracket creep, one alternative would be to index income tax brackets to inflation in order to avoid taxpayers getting pushed into higher tax brackets even when their nominal incomes have not changed. In economies that are prone to experiencing high inflation, however, there is a danger that any knowledge or practice of automatic inflation adjustment can, by itself, tend to exacerbate inflation reflecting such inflationary expectations. This is where judicious timing for modifications in the tax rate structure becomes important for ensure appropriate treatment of taxpayers to maintain neutrality in effective tax rates.

## 11.4 Time Lags in Revenue Collection[11]

There is an obverse side to the problem of fiscal drag. This comprises the possible loss in the value of tax revenue collection in real terms in times of inflation, if there is a significant time lag between income earned and revenue collected. This problem occurs in particular in countries where inflation is traditionally high such as in Latin America. Of course, the problem does not occur if the lags in the collection of taxes are short. The problem is also minimized if the tax system is elastic so that, as nominal incomes rise with inflation, taxpayers are pushed up to higher tax brackets. This tends to mitigate the real revenue loss caused by any time lag in tax collection.

To study the effects of collection lags, assume that the rate of inflation is given, and that the elasticity of the tax system is unitary.[12] Then, first, the longer is the lag in the collection of taxes, the greater will be the inflation-induced real reduction in the tax revenues received by government. Second, given a particular lag in the collection of taxes, the higher is the rate of inflation, the lower will be the real value of the tax revenue collected. Third, there could be gains to be reaped by switching from one tax to another with different collection lags. Thus, a country experiencing prolonged inflation could replace an income tax with a VAT or GST which has a shorter collection lag, and benefit from gain in real value of tax revenue collected.[13]

Thus, the elasticity aspect matters mainly for the personal income tax, and may be compensated for by the existence of other taxes such as GST, VAT or property tax which, if levied at specific rates, are likely to have an elasticity of less than unity. Therefore, for a developing country or an emerging economy where inflation is a concern, a tax system with unitary elasticity for the tax system as a whole—comprising taxes on income and consumption—may be envisaged as a solution that may keep in check both bracket creep as well as any declining value of real revenue due to collection lags.

One development that has occurred over the past several decades is that more tax administrations have introduced mechanisms for collecting tax on income as income is being earned during a year, rather than waiting for the end of a financial year.

[11]See Tanzi (1977) analysed this issue for Argentina. Other countries that have suffered high inflation with deleterious ramification on tax revenue include Bolivia, Brazil, Nicaragua, Peru and Venezuela, among others. The problem appeared in the 1980s and appears from time to time to the present day.

[12]This assumption is needed because if the elasticity is, higher than one, then as we argued earlier, the effect of collection lag can be mitigated.

[13]Once elasticity is not unitary, the results on total real tax revenue as a result of changes in the rate of inflation become more complex. But they still indicate how lags reduce the real value of each revenue rupee collected compared with the real value of a tax liability of a rupee at the time when it accrues—in other words, in relation to what real revenue would be in a lagless world.

Thus, income tax is subjected to advance tax payments, and many other sources of income are subjected to tax deduction at source (TDS), for example from interest income on bank interest, or withholding taxes if the income is being transferred abroad. And GST and VAT are subjected to tax collection every quarter of the year. Such measures have mitigated any loss in the real value of tax revenue collection.

However, those measures have increased the compliance cost of paying taxes for employers and employees transferring, to a significant extent, the burden of tax collection that should be borne by government, to the private sector. Such practices of governments should, therefore, be regularly monitored and evaluated by regulatory agencies, the audit branch of government, or oversight committees of parliament. Unfortunately, not all emerging or developing economies allocate adequate public resources for those functions.

## References

Herber, Bernard P. 1975. *Modern Public Finance*. 3rd ed. Homewood: Richard D. Irwin Inc.

Musgrave, Richard A. 1959. *The Theory of Public Finance: The Study of Public Economy*, International student edition. New York: McGraw-Hill Book Co.

Singer, Neil M. 1976. *Public Microeconomics—An Introduction to Government Finance*. 2nd ed. Boston: Little Brown and Company.

Tanzi, Vito. 1977. Inflation, Lags in Collection, and the Real Value of Tax Revenue. *IMF Economic Review* 24: 154–167.

# Part III

# Tax Law

# Tax Assignment and Revenue Sharing 12

## 12.1 Introduction

A decentralised economy comprises different levels of government with independent fiscal powers. A crucial issue is the design of appropriate assignment of taxes and expenditures to different levels of government. The rationale for decentralising fiscal responsibility derives from the premise that the welfare generated by providing public goods and services is maximised by reflecting, as closely as possible, the preferences revealed by the population at the subnational levels of government.[1] Accordingly, governments that comprise several levels assign different expenditure responsibilities to each level.

Tax assignment also follows a stratification of objectives. A central government function is achieving appropriate redistribution which should be assigned to it since, otherwise, people bearing any resultant burden of local redistribution policies would emigrate to another state or province or local jurisdiction. The central government must also remain ultimately responsible for overall macroeconomic stabilisation since local attempts at stabilisation policies would have spillover effects across jurisdictions. Subnational—state and local—governments, on the other hand, are assigned taxes that do not adversely affect the efficiency of resource allocation. The mix of tax and expenditure responsibilities of different levels of government is referred to as fiscal federalism. This chapter focuses on the taxation side of fiscal federalism.

[1] An early proponent of this hypothesis to bring in the supremacy of consumption preferences at local levels of government was Tiebout (1956).

 
P. Shome, *Taxation History, Theory, Law and Administration*, Springer Texts in Business and Economics, https://doi.org/10.1007/978-3-030-68214-9_12

## 12.2 Fiscal Federalism and Tax Assignment

Reflecting global experiences of large fiscally federal countries such as Argentina, Brazil, Canada, India, and the United States, the assignment of taxes to lower levels of government appears to follow a pattern. At the level of states or provinces, GST, VAT and RST taxes have comprised a primary source of tax revenue.

Customs duties and selective excises are assigned to the central government level since customs duties are collected at points of entry to the country while excises, if they were assigned to the states, would benefit only particular states that manufacture them to the exclusion of others.

Even though the income tax is usually assigned to the central government level, some early economists[2] suggested assigning it to the states or provinces. Indeed, the United States assigns it to both levels, with the states 'piggybacking' or structuring their own income taxes on the basic structure of the federal—or central—income tax. The state-level income taxes are, however, levied at much lower rates.

Indeed, in general, while the tax rates could be left to local taxing powers, the tax base should be determined at the central level. This is because the base involves who would be taxed and who would not, with concomitant distributional consequences. Thus, differences in base across jurisdictions would not maintain neutrality in equity. A national-level government may need to use revenue sharing and grants to achieve an objective of income redistribution across states. Its objective in that case should be to compare each state's ratio of total revenue generated to the quantum of services needed by it and attempt to bridge the gap across states based on stipulated criteria.

A good local tax is one whose burden cannot be exported by the local jurisdiction elsewhere. Thus, governments at the municipal, county, council (or *panchayat* in India) level are likely to be assigned user charges, fees and taxes on selected local services such as laundry and restaurants. Land and property taxes also satisfy this criterion and are, therefore, assigned to the local government level.

## 12.3 Ability to Borrow by Subnational Governments

Where state and local governments possess the ability to borrow relatively freely, without oversight from the central government, it has led to impediments in fiscal stabilisation and high inflation. Recent experience has revealed this problem in Latin America, for example, Venezuela over a period of four decades since the 1980s. Instead, a competent role of central government through grants and revenue sharing from central tax revenue in financing subnational governments has helped keep such potential extravagance in check. Indeed, they may receive grants that are earmarked (block grants) for particular projects.

This translates to saying that lower-level governments should be responsible for all appropriate expenditure functions, and upper-level governments should ensure

[2]See, for example, Musgrave (1959).

the adequacy of funds. Thus, the idea that a vertical imbalance in the mix of revenue collection and expenditure responsibilities is somehow to be changed towards greater balance may not always work out. Australia, India and the United Kingdom represent this approach of vertical imbalance between the centre and subnational governments.[3] Others such as Argentina, Brazil, China and the United States follow a pattern in which the latter collect substantial revenue; and some may even pass some of it upstream to the former.[4]

To this day, the ability to borrow by subnational governments remains a contentious issue since, as explained, it could have adverse ramifications for the consolidated fiscal deficit. The United States has had the experience of financing local infrastructure projects for over a century through bonds issued by local governments. In India, selected local governments were rated by rating agencies for the issue of bonds but they never took hold. The central government has been quite opposed to it for fear that it could result in a constitutional right of subnational governments to issue paper with a potential for high inflation. Nevertheless, states have managed to subvert this limitation in recent years. Even though they cannot borrow independently if they have accumulated debt to the central government, states have mobilised funds by borrowing through public enterprises owned or managed by them.

## 12.4 Revenue Sharing Among Levels of Governments

With the progress of decentralisation, more central government revenue is being subjected to revenue sharing. This may be the right policy direction, but it can have unwarranted implications for economic stabilisation unless the central government, after transfers, cuts back its own—including administration—expenditures. This has proved a difficult task in some Latin American countries, such as Colombia, where decentralisation and increased revenue sharing have led to significantly higher central deficits in recent years. Even in India, where decentralisation has been associated with higher economic growth, it has also led to higher fiscal deficit.[5] It is therefore important to recognise that, while tax assignment and revenue sharing reform can be carried out *pari passu* with expenditure assignment reform, caution is needed to ensure that the central government does not become a 'lender of first resort' for subnational governments.

It is important, therefore, to have stable systems for determining the revenue sharing formulae. India's institution of a Finance Commission has provided this

[3]Shome (2002) took India's 14 major states in an empirical study over two decades up to the late 1990s. He found that decentralisation of both developmental and non-developmental expenditure, financed through greater transfers from the central to state governments, led to higher economic growth.

[4]See De Mello and Barenstein (2001).

[5]As already indicated, an empirical study by Shome (2002), op. cit., arrived at this conclusion.

stability. It forms quinquennially, recommends how, and how much, central revenue is to be distributed among the states and disbands. Its temporary nature has lent it credibility and efficiency, and the record is that parliament has always accepted its recommendations. The lack of such a stable, constitutionally guaranteed framework has obliged the federal or central governments in Argentina and Brazil to enter, time and again, into protracted negotiations with the provinces or states to arrive at temporary 'pacts', often to be abrogated before their legal termination and giving rise to new rounds of negotiations.

## 12.5 GST or VAT in a Decentralised Economy

Chapters 21, 22, 23, and 24 will cover taxes on consumption such as the GST or VAT and others in some detail. Nevertheless, we mention them here in the context of a decentralised economy since there are particular issues that constrain the operation of a GST or VAT when assigned to more than one level of government. Some fiscally decentralised countries have introduced such a VAT. In the mid-1960s, Brazil introduced the earliest VAT on a comprehensive goods-cum-services base at the level of the states complemented by a narrow-based VAT on industrial products at the central government level.[6] Municipalities complement the structure by taxing local services. CONFAZ, a committee of state-level finance ministers, meets every quarter with the chairmanship of a central government officer, to modify the VAT structure where needed and settle disputes. While Brazil's composite VAT has been the major revenue earner in the panoply of taxes, its structure became complex over time and reforming it has proved difficult.[7]

Canada introduced a provincial-cum-central VAT in the mid-1990s, but not all provinces participate in it.[8] The European Union (EU) has been operating a temporary VAT whose design is not final. Argentina has researched and considered the feasibility of a provincial VAT, but actual progress on the matter has been slow. Considerable research exists in the United States, but the possibility of introduction of a state-level VAT is poor, reflecting the autonomy and safeguarding by the states of their own fiscal powers.

The Indian states laboured for a decade under an Empowered Committee (EC) of their finance ministers to reform a distortionary state-level sales tax regime. After a series of postponements, in 2003 the EC agreed to discuss the possibility of a VAT at the state level.[9] A state-level VAT was finally introduced in India in April 2005 with

[6]The prevailing decentralisation of revenues reflects a legal framework for tax assignment and revenue sharing drawn up in Brazil's 1988 Constitution. The constitutional assignment of income taxes to the federal—or central—level conforms to the same framework.

[7]Silvani and dos Santos (1996) and Shome (2002), op. cit., Chap. 3, and others, discuss the case of Brazil.

[8]See Bird and Smart (2014) for a discussion of the Canadian case.

[9]Bagchi (1997) carried out an initial analysis setting out a possible framework. A detailed analysis is also found in Shome (2002), op. cit., Chap. 3.

cooperation from the central government in the form of a guarantee for monetary compensation for 3 years to states that might lose revenue from the VAT's introduction.

In the context of tax assignment, what is it that makes a state-level VAT difficult to operate? The difficulty comes from two interrelated premises: (1) since the VAT is a tax on consumption, the operational structure should ensure that its incidence falls on the final consumer; and, therefore, (2) when a good is produced in a state and the VAT is collected by the tax administration of that producing state, there has to be a mechanism for the revenue collection to be transferred from the producing state to the exchequer of the state in which the good is consumed. The transfer would ensure what is termed the 'destination principle' in the context of a state-level VAT. The mechanism through which such a transfer would take place is not easy to design. Countries have usually tended to use the origin principle in which the producing state simply keeps the tax revenue it collects on the sale of the goods. This has been the case in Brazil and the European Union, as well as in India earlier when its states operated their sales taxes.

Several methods were proposed in international discussions of which some became more popular due to their practicality.[10] In practice, in any VAT tax return, there would be two columns, one for intrastate transactions and one for inter-state transactions. The former would be controlled by the tax administrations of the individual states. The latter would be taxed at a common rate by all the states. The net VAT payable on inter-state transactions would be remitted by every taxpayer to an overarching all-state administration or to the central tax administration. The revenue collected from inter-state transactions would be distributed to the states according to the consumption size of the states, on a rolling basis or at the end of a predesignated period.[11] Interestingly, in its GST, a comprehensive tax on goods and services applicable to both the central and state governments introduced in 2017, India's Goods and Service Tax Network (GSTN) mechanism uses this framework for collection and distribution of tax revenue from inter-state trade.

## 12.6 Tax Harmonisation

In recent years, certain countries with their independent tax systems have come together and decided to function as a group with commonly designed regulatory and taxation standards. Such an eminently identifiable group is the EU. They have drawn up guidelines regarding their VATs under the Sixth Directive, and harmonisation of their corporate income taxes. The newly formed Commonwealth of Independent States (CIS)[12] of the former Soviet Union also harmonised their tax systems

[10]See Versano (1999) for initial suggestions later adopted by implementing countries.

[11]This is one example of the 'clearing house' mechanism that could be operated by the states themselves or by the central government.

[12]The CIS was formed in December 1991 by the former Soviet republics other than the Baltic states of Estonia, Latvia and Lithuania. Georgia joined in 1993.

including scaling back customs tariffs, providing relief from double taxation in the corporate income tax and personal income tax, and ensuring a harmonised VAT. Comparable issues assumed importance in the 1990s for MERCOSUL, the Andean Pact and other groupings among Latin American countries. Research analyses found common statistical trends emanating from the tax systems of countries across Latin America from the 1990s.

Why have countries tended to harmonise their tax systems? Growing economic integration within the EU, for example, increased the need to harmonise capital income taxes since, unless they were similar across countries, capital being a mobile factor of production, would be encouraged to move across national boundaries. Harmonisation was to be based on a common tax base and a statutory minimum tax rate.[13] Indeed, at one point, indications were that an EU-wide corporate tax may be in the offing.[14] Similarly, the integration of personal and corporate taxes for the alleviation of the problem of double taxation within a harmonised tax system was an issue that was considered in the EU.[15]

Thus, there was considerable progress in several areas of harmonisation across the world at least in being analysed and proposed, if not always achieved.

## 12.7 Tax Assignment and Revenue Sharing in India

India's constitution has made provisions along the lines of the 1935 Government of India Act pertaining to the distribution of tax and non-tax revenues, the ability to borrow, and provisions for grants-in-aid from the Union, or central government, to state governments. The objective is the equitable distribution of financial resources among the centre and states, rather than dividing resources into two specific components. An explanation of the arrangement was given by the Supreme Court as:

> Sources of revenue which have been allocated to the Union are not meant entirely for the purposes of the Union but have to be distributed according to the principles laid down by Parliamentary legislation as contemplated by the Articles aforesaid. Thus, all the taxes and duties levied by the Union ... do not form part of the Consolidated Fund of India but many of these taxes and duties are distributed amongst the States and form part of the Consolidated Fund of the States. Even those taxes and duties which constitute the Consolidated Fund of India may be used for the purposes of supplementing the revenues of the States in accordance with their needs. The question of distribution of the aforesaid taxes and duties amongst the States and the principles governing them, as also the principles governing grants-in-aid ... are matters which have to be decided by a high-powered Finance Commission, which is a responsible body designated to determine those matters in an objective way ... The Constitution makers realised the fact that those sources of revenue allocated to the States may not be sufficient for their purposes and that the Government of India would have to subsidise their welfare activities ... Realising the limitations on the financial resources of the

[13]See Tanzi and Bovenberg (1990) on this issue.

[14]See European Community News (1992).

[15]See de le Fuente and Gardner (1990) on this issue.

> States and the growing needs of the community in a welfare State, the Constitution has made . . . specific provisions empowering Parliament to set aside as portion of its revenues . . . for the benefit of the States, not in stated proportions but according to their needs . . . The resources of the Union Government are not meant exclusively for the benefit of the Union activities . . . In other words, the Union and the States together form one organic whole for the purposes of utilisation of the resources of territories of India as a whole.[16]

### 12.7.1 Tax Assignment in India

The constitution differentiates between the power to 'levy' a tax and the power to 'appropriate tax proceeds' so levied, and are not identical. The former—power to legislate—is assigned to both centre and states through specific Entries in the Union (or centre) and State Legislative Lists in Schedule VII (Union List, State List, Concurrent List). Thus, for example, while states can levy estate duty on agricultural lands, only the central government has the same power for non-agricultural land. Again, states can levy tax on agricultural income, while the centre can levy tax on non-agricultural income.

Taxes on international trade—imports and exports—are Union subjects, and also taxes on sales in the course of inter-state trade since no state can legitimately levy a tax that would involve any other state. Residuary powers to legislate on a tax base not specified in the above-mentioned Lists are also with the centre. For example, a gift tax and an expenditure tax were assigned to the centre on the basis of residuary powers. Using residuary powers, when the centre also started taxing selected services in the 1994—which were never mentioned in any of the Lists—negotiations were initiated with the state-level EC regarding how they may be better assigned among the centre and states in the future.

The power to impose taxes on sale or purchase of goods (other than newspapers) belongs to states. The states' powers are, however, subject to certain limitations. For example, in their taxing power on profession, trade, calling or employment, the total amount imposable on any person was limited to a finite sum, more like a fee for a profession—so that they do not impinge upon the centre's income tax.

The 101st Amendment of the Constitution Act, 2016, was enacted to introduce the Goods and Services Tax (GST) from 1 July 2017. The GST replaced the above-described tax assignment of indirect taxes—sales tax/VAT and other small taxes of the states, the tax on inter-state trade, and central excise duties or CENVAT together with the service tax of the centre—to formulate a consolidated fiscal federal tax on all goods and services comprising both the central government and the states. We shall examine the GST in detail in Chap. 24.

[16] Supreme Court 870 (1971), 1 SCJ 14. Quoted from Basu (2020), Chap. 25, p. 369.

### 12.7.2 Revenue Sharing and Comparable Arrangements

Since a state's revenue collection may not suffice its expenditure needs, the constitution makes special provisions:

(1) Some duties are leviable by the centre but collected and appropriated by states such as stamp duty on bills of exchange and selected excise duties on medicinal and toilet preparations containing alcohol.
(2) Some duties are levied and collected by the centre but assigned by the centre to those states where they have been collected such as duties on succession to property, taxes on freight and railway fares, taxes on the stock exchange, taxes on sales and advertisement in newspapers, taxes on inter-state trade and commerce.
(3) Some duties are levied and collected by the centre but the revenue is distributed between the centre and states such as taxes on non-agricultural income, and selected excise duties in the Union List.[17]

Selected non-tax revenue such as from railways, post and telegraph, broadcasting, currency and mint, and public sector commercial and industrial undertakings—collected by the central government, are also shared with states. States also have their own non-tax revenue sources such as from forests, their own irrigation and commercial enterprises—electricity, road transport and industrial undertakings—soap, sandalwood, iron and steel, paper, milk supply, deep-sea fishing and silk—which vary with states.

Parliament may also enact grants-in-aid for particular states such as the north-eastern states reflecting the promotion of tribal areas or other objectives.

Articles 270, 273, 275 and 280 of the constitution ask for recommendations on the percentage of net proceeds of central taxes that should be distributed to states, and the formula for distribution of the transfer among the states. To list:

(1) The distribution between Union and states of the net proceeds of taxes which are to be, or maybe, divided between them under this chapter and the allocation between the states of the respective shares of such proceeds
(2) The principles which should govern the grants-in-aid of the revenues of the states out of the Consolidation Fund of India
(3) The measures needed to augment the consolidated fund of a state to supplement the resources of the *panchayats* in the states[18]
(4) The measures needed to augment the consolidated fund of a state to supplement the resources of the municipalities in the state[19]

[17]For an exhaustive list, refer Basu (2020), op. cit., Chap. 25, pp. 370–373.

[18]Inserted by the Constitution (73rd Amendment) Act, 1992, w.e.f. 24 April 1993. *Panchayats* are rural counties.

[19]Inserted by the Constitution (74th Amendment) Act, 1992, w.e.f. 1 July 1993.

(5) Any other matter referred to the Finance Commission by the President of India in the interest of sound finance

From the first Finance Commission constituted in 1951 to the 14th constituted in 2013, each made recommendations which Parliament essentially accepted. As a result, the current revenue sharing arrangements between the centre and states comprises a devolution of 42% of central taxes to states. The recommendations of the 15th Finance Commission modified the share slightly in reflection of the conversion of a state into centrally administered territories.

### 12.7.3 Local Government Responsibilities

So far, we have talked about the centre and the states. An additional development occurred through the 73rd and 74th Amendments to the Indian Constitution for fiscal responsibility of local level—municipal and *panchayat*—governments.

While centre–state fiscal relations and a related delivery mechanism developed long ago, no separate provisions existed for local government until 1993, even though local self-government had functioned for millennia. Provisions for *panchayat*-level institutions in the constitution had not, however, resulted in their functioning being universally effective. Similarly, urban municipal bodies needed clarification and strengthening of their functions and scope. The 73rd and 74th Amendments, 1992, respectively, designated 27 functions for *panchayats* and 18 for municipalities. These amendments obliged states to pass requisite legislation to empower local governments.

State-level finance commissions were formed to recommend the best ways to identify resources for carrying out these functions by local government, through own tax effort and/or through transfers from upper-level government. Articles of the same Amendments therefore stipulated the formation and functions of state-level finance commissions (SFCs), in line with the practice of the national Finance Commission. Several reports were subsequently tabled in respective state legislative assemblies[20] though implementation has progressed at varying speed.

In general, for 'own' resources, the recommendations favoured removing the 'octroi' tax prevailing at that time, which was a tax levied on the entry of vehicles by municipalities and administered through physical controls that was extremely distortionary for the efficient functioning of municipalities with deleterious negative externalities on transport costs and, in a chain effect, on the economy as a whole. Some municipalities had already moved away from physical control to financial control but the problem of high costs of the movement of goods persisted. With the

[20]A total 28 of 29 states set up SFCs. Three small north-eastern states, Meghalaya, Mizoram and Nagaland, were exempted from constituting SFCs. However, Nagaland constituted its first SFC in August 2008 and Mizoram in September 2011. Telangana, the newest state formed out of Andhra Pradesh in June 2014 constituted its first SFC in December 2017. See Gupta and Chakraborty (2019).

introduction of the GST, the octroi and entry tax were abolished and their revenue intake was built into the GST rates.

Local governments have favoured revising and stepping up the use of property tax as well as improving the design of user charges and cost recovery from public utilities. The process, however, has not always been smooth because the judiciary usually has been unsympathetic to levying property tax based on market value of a property.[21] Nevertheless, reliance on the property tax has become quite common among well-administered local governments in India.

While local governments are doing their part in raising their own resources, upper-level governments, as mentioned above, carry mandates to do their best to not only hand over charge for the enumerated expenditure responsibilities to their local counterparts but also to ensure resource availability for carrying out those responsibilities. The transfer of resources has been relatively slow in several municipalities that remain dependent on such transfers from the state, resulting in tensions in state-local government financial relations.

Having examined the rationale for tax assignment and revenue sharing and global practices followed by India's arrangements for all its tax and non-tax revenue sources based on its constitution, we shall now proceed to examine the manner of setting and drafting tax law.

## References

Bagchi, Amaresh. 1997. A State Level VAT? Harmonizing Sales Taxes: A Comparison of India and Canada. In *Value-Added Tax in India*, ed. Parthasarathi Shome. New Delhi: Centax Publications Pvt Ltd.

Basu, Durga Das. 2020. *Introduction to the Constitution of India*. 24th ed. Gurgaon: Lexis Nexis.

Bird, Richard Miller, and Michael Smart. 2014. VAT in a Federal System: Lessons from Canada. *Public Budgeting & Finance* 34(4): 38–60. https://ssrn.com/abstract=2534198 or https://doi.org/10.1111/pbaf.12052.

De Mello, Luiz, and Matias Barenstein. 2001. *Fiscal Decentralisation and Governance: A Cross-Country Analysis*. IMF Working Paper WP/01/71. https://www.imf.org/external/pubs/ft/wp/2001/wp0171.pdf. Accessed 18 Nov 2020.

European Community News. 1992. *Tax Notes International* 4 (13), March.

de le Fuente, Angelo, and Edward Gardner. 1990. *Corporate Tax Harmonization and Capital Allocation in the European Community*. Working Paper No. WP/90/103. Washington, DC: International Monetary Fund (IMF).

Government of Karnataka. 2001. *Report of the Tax Reform Commission*. Bangalore: Government of Karnataka.

Gupta, Manish, and Pinaki Chakraborty. 2019. *State Finance Commissions: How Successful Have They Been in Empowering Local Governments?* NIPFP Working Paper No. 263. https://www.nipfp.org.in/media/medialibrary/2019/05/WP_263_2019.pdf. Accessed 18 Nov 2020.

Musgrave, Richard A. 1959. *The Theory of Public Finance: The Study of Public Economy*. New York: McGraw-Hill Book Co.

[21]The report of the Government of Karnataka (2001) is a voluminous and well-articulated report at the state level of the then prevailing system of taxation in the state and recommendations for needed reform.

Shome, Parthasarathi. 2002. *India's Fiscal Matters*. New Delhi: Oxford University Press.

Silvani, Carlos, and Paulo dos Santos. 1996. Administrative Aspects of Brazil's Consumption Tax Reform. *International VAT Monitor* 7: 123–132.

Tanzi, Vito, and A. Lans Bovenberg. 1990. Is There a Need for Harmonizing Capital Income Taxes Within EC Countries? In *Reforming Capital Income Taxation*, ed. Horst Siebert, 171–197. Tübingen: Mohr-Paul Siebeck.

Tiebout, Charles M. 1956. A Pure Theory of Local Expenditures. *Journal of Political Economy* 64: 416–424. https://www.jstor.org/stable/1826343.

Versano, Ricardo. 1999. Subnational Taxation and the Treatment of Interstate Trade in Brazil: Problems and a Proposed Solution. In *Decentralisation and Accountability of the Public Sector*. Annual World Bank Conference Volume on Development in Latin America and the Caribbean. Valdivia: World Bank.

# Tax Legislation 13

## 13.1 Introduction

Once tax economists have deliberated on a tax matter and taken a view, they tend to take little continuing interest in the formulation or interpretation of subsequent law. Though the intensity of this separation is possibly diminishing with time, this textbook attempts to provide a bridge between the two learning experiences. This chapter illustrates the process of introducing tax law, who designs it, who writes it and who ensures that it adheres to the rule of law. In broad terms, it could be said that tax law is made by the legislature, implemented by the executive, and interpreted by the judiciary.

If tax law is not designed well, for example if retrospective taxation is introduced to suit a government's will, taxpayers are bound to express dissatisfaction eventually and, if the judiciary is unbiased, the courts are likely to interpret the law in the taxpayers' favour, with taxpayer rights and charters increasingly appearing in tax statutes. On the other hand, if taxpayers, in particular MNEs, indulge in sustained tax avoidance by taking advantage of loopholes available in different tax statutes across the world, global authorities will intervene and install cumbersome reporting requirements and mechanisms for the exchange of information amongst themselves.

These aspects, together with a comprehensive cross-country experience of tax legislation and a short recounting of India's pre- and post-independence legislative history of taxation comprise the areas of taxation that are covered in this chapter.

## 13.2 Policy Effect on Complexity

It is not too uncommon for government committees to observe that a tax code or statute has become too complicated and to recommend simplification. In the United Kingdom, in its Interim Report on Tax Legislation, 1995, the Tax Law Review Committee of the Institute of Fiscal Studies commented that 'tax law had become lengthy, complex and impenetrable (and that) the Inland Revenue (should) prepare a



P. Shome, *Taxation History, Theory, Law and Administration*, Springer Texts in Business and Economics, https://doi.org/10.1007/978-3-030-68214-9_13

report on tax simplification'. In 2010, United Kingdom established a recommendatory Office of Tax Simplification (OTS) in its continuing effort to reduce complexities for individual and corporate taxpayers. In India, various government-appointed committees have done so over the years, such as the Ninth and Tenth Five-Year Plan Taxation Task Forces, as well as the Tax Administration Reform Commission (TARC) of 2015,[1] and this is only a partial list.

As the scribing of tax law progressed, one aspect that assumed importance was the purpose of the legislation. Hence, the profession developed the practice of seeking guidance on interpretation and permitted reference to relevant material in formulating and interpreting the law. Expectedly, any treatise on the principles of tax law is replete with references to case law seeking justification for a position being taken on a particular point. This is rather different from the economic theory of taxation which, as it develops, tends to stand on its own, learning from the past but essentially discarding earlier edifices.

A reality of tax law is that it can become subject to the ideological bent of a prevailing regime. When a new government takes over, it tends to bring with it a penchant for introducing new tax legislation almost as a stamp of its existence. But often there is some dithering since there is little learning incorporated from existing work of previous administrations and, sometimes, an inability to take action is observed within the typical short period of a regime before the next elections.

Thus, through successive governments, India has been unable to introduce a new Direct Tax Code. A GST Law was introduced in 2017 in a hurry, suffering from a lack of comprehensive preparation and errors in its design. Such a law may become difficult to administer by the tax officer or comply with by the taxpayer. Similarly, the UK tax administration completed a Next Steps Report in 2011, indicating 2017 as the year of final implementation of its recommendations, but the political system failed to follow up, with the OTS suggesting that the plan should be better administered or suspended. Thus, 'tax is often seen as an ephemeral area: as a part of law devoid of principle and subject to the whims of politicians'.[2]

## 13.3 Process of Introducing Law

While tax theory is quintessential to be incorporated in tax law and rules, the law is the primary expression of the social and political setting in the background. Accordingly, the process of converting an intended tax structure through drafting of tax law is no easy task. In advanced economies such as the United States or United Kingdom, hundreds of tax officers may research and write those laws, rendering it

[1]These were chaired by Parthasarathi Shome. Before Shome, other committees had been chaired earlier by Raja Chelliah and Vijay Kelkar, as well as by others before them.

[2]See Lee (2013), p. 13.

into a complex process and outcome. On the other hand, in emerging economies such as India, less than twenty staff may be responsible for doing so.[3]

The process of scribing may be slow reflecting political interference, which tends to stall the consideration and passing of new legislation. This occurs, in particular, for major tax reforms such as an income tax code or comprehensive consumption tax reform such as a GST law. Resultantly, changes in legislation may come as a series of discretionary changes in the annual budgets of government more than as all-encompassing comprehensive reform with a promise of continuance. Thus, it is important for systems to focus as much on the process of reform than just the articulation of the tax structure itself.[4]

The need for new tax legislation may emerge from the overall tax structure becoming complex with time as tax incentives and preferences erode the tax base, result in inequity and steal its capacity to stabilise the economy. Therefore, in addition to the small coterie of tax officers who design tax laws every budget period, there should be continuous reviews of tax laws that could be carried out by a committee of experts comprising various areas of tax expertise. It is important to maintain a close dialogue with the parliament's finance committee so that, if a major reform package is drafted, parliament is already aware of the matter.

The private sector chambers of commerce and industry should be taken into confidence through surveys and direct contact since they would know best where taxes are posing the worst problems. The UK tax administration,[5] has a practice of regular consultations with stakeholders at different levels through official contact. India introduced a Tax Forum during 2013–2014 for such consultation geared directly to solving stakeholder issues in different economic sectors but subsequently the regularity of the Forum suffered. However, private sector participants should not be allowed to press the administration to change aspects of the law that they do not like merely because it may be inconvenient for them. This kind of pressure is real and should be rejected.

The continual review and cross-country comparisons of domestic tax law should indicate where domestic law is good and where bad, help avoid potential problems and result in an overall good law. Some emerging economies including India, Indonesia, Nigeria, South Africa and others have tended to eschew advice from multilateral institutions though this may be short-sighted since it may be a good source of information on prevalent international practice without having to suffer high financial costs. That knowledge could help minimise the frequency of change in domestic tax law that leads to instability in business decision-making and lower economic growth.

[3]Shome (2012), Chap. 2, provides details of the differences in staff allocation between the United Kingdom and India.

[4]Thuronyi (1996), Chap. 1, provides a detailed analysis of process.

[5]Her Majesty's Revenue and Customs (HMRC).

## 13.4 Who Writes Tax Law

Once the desired structure of taxes is pinned down, tax lawyers should pen actual legislative language in contrast to many emerging economies where career tax officers are assigned that task. The benefit of lawyers doing it is that they can more easily ensure the tax legislation's adherence to other branches of the legal system such as the constitution, commercial law or banking law with which tax law is entwined and has to function on a daily basis. In communication with tax administrators, lawyers should also formulate the language of 'subordinate law' or rules, that are stipulated for application to taxpayers. Needless to say, coordination with the theorists is important in ensuring that the objectives of the tax structure are not lost in drafting of the law.

Since lack of close coordination could lead to unintended and confusing tax law, it may be worthwhile to place theory and law under one large unit of the tax administration. This is the case in the United Kingdom where, after the consolidation of direct and indirect tax branches under one umbrella, 400 officers worked in the directorate of Knowledge, Analysis, Intelligence (KAI) in 2010, tasked to carry out the formulation of both tax design and law. By contrast, in India, 20–30 officers have performed this task. They examine the theory and write the law which is then sent for approval to the Ministry of Law whose attention is also demanded from various other branches of government.

The language of tax law can be deficient and confusing, in particular, if law ministry officers are not kept informed or involved until the last moment and pressure is applied to finish the work urgently. This has admittedly resulted in India's tax laws suffering from a lack of clarity at various points, thus resulting in the highest rate of litigation from the stage of appeals made at the tax administration level right through to the judiciary and ending at the Supreme Court. Such a situation should be avoided at all cost and, if it exists, should be eradicated with urgency.

After consultations with the parliamentary finance committee, once a draft tax law is ready at the ministry of finance, it has to clear 'line' ministries and then sent it to the cabinet. After that it is sent to parliament for its consideration and for passing of the law. It should presumably have been discussed with the private sector industry and tax professionals though this is not always comprehensively carried out. If so, members of parliament are lobbied to legislate changes desired by the private sector. Thus, prior consultation with private sector stakeholders is always desirable.[6]

[6]We have considered whether tax reform holds steady in the medium to long term in Chap. 6, Sect. 6.4.

## 13.5 Tax per Rule of Law

### 13.5.1 Constitutional Requirements

By the mid-nineteenth century in the Western world, a legal framework had emerged for drafting tax law. It enabled the framing of taxes with significant revenue generating capacity to be implemented during and after the First World War. Its characteristics were: (1) a tax must be lawfully enacted,[7] (2) it must be applied impartially and (3) tax revenue has to be spent for legal public—not private—expenditure. Further, (4) tax law has to reflect the constitution, adhere to civil law and maintain whatever fiscal federal framework exists in the country, and (5) be adjudicated by the judiciary.

A constitution could require that taxes should have a legal basis under the constitution itself, or it may allow the legislature to delegate the authority to pass tax law. Or there could be a midway position in that, while allowing the legislature to pass law, it may be required to function under an enabling law specified in the constitution. A mix of the definitions of taxpayer, taxable event, tax base, tax rates and rules of administration may be, or may not be, specified in the constitution.

As we saw in Chap. 12, taxpayer, tax base and several related matters are variously specified in the Indian Constitution. Even some rules to administer are specified such as the function of collection and revenue distribution among levels of government. While the United Kingdom does not have a constitution, it adheres to the principle of legality that was specified, in 1628, in a Petition of Rights. It elaborated that, 'no man ... (can) ... make ... tax or such like charge without common consent by act of Parliament'. Usually, tax law has effect for one budget year in that parliament must consent to government's levy of taxes annually. In India, this occurs in the annual budgetary process in parliament and state legislatures.

The rule of law requires neutrality to be maintained, that is all taxpayers to be treated equally. This may be achieved as follows: (1) the tax administration must send a notice to a taxpayer of any impending action to be taken, (2) a taxpayer must be allowed the same due process as is allowed to the tax authority during litigation and (3) the tax administration cannot go beyond the applicable interpretation of the law. These tenets of fair play may be at odds with those of the public order which can occur if there is a misstatement by the administration based on facts presented by the taxpayer. If subsequently, the error becomes apparent, the administration is duty bound to implement the correct interpretation reflecting public order—rather than its earlier intimation to the taxpayer—to ensure fair play. In the United States, a taxpayer's penalty is abated if a tax officer has advised a taxpayer wrongly. In France too an earlier favourable interpretation to tax law given by the tax administration may be used by a taxpayer in contesting a tax assessment. But most countries are less accommodating to the taxpayer.

---

[7]Vanistendael (1996) in Thuronyi (1996), op. cit., Chap. 2, has elaborated on the legal framework for taxation.

### 13.5.2 Taxpayers' Rights

The Observatory on the Protection of Taxpayers' Rights (OPTR) issued a report in 2018[8] that surveyed 42 countries regarding the state of protection of taxpayers' rights in raising awareness of the connection between human rights and taxation, the legal framework and jurisprudence on the matter, and creating and maintaining a database on the compliance of minimum standards. It examined how developments have been monitored regarding the effective implementation of legal procedures in domestic law, and safeguards and guarantees associated with taxpayers' rights. It presented a comparison by jurisdiction of the compliance of minimum standards and best practices and encouraged an annual exercise thereof. It is the most comprehensive account of the issue that exists in the taxation literature.

In writing tax law, or through an administrative declaration, some countries have lent importance to recognising the rights of taxpayers. Several countries have published such rights in the form of charters. In essence, charters act more as a reminder that taxpayers cannot be arbitrarily or adversely treated without cause by the tax administration. There is a split between countries as to whether a charter is legally binding or is an aspirational document.[9] They may or may not carry legal validation but, if they do, they possess the same legal backing as provisions in tax administration law. Countries that do not have charters also attach importance to taxpayers' rights and taxpayers there would tend to have similar rights.[10]

Among countries of the Council of Europe,[11] some national constitutions give reassurance that a tax may be struck down as being discriminatory or disproportionate. Germany has indeed done so in the past. The Constitutional Council of France rules on whether a proposed tax or a tax rate is excessive. Some have tended to link taxpayers' rights to human rights. The European Convention on Human Rights, enforced by a court in Strasbourg, could pressure governments politically to change their law. In the United Kingdom too, if a taxpayer puts forward that an investigation, assessment or tax charge infringes on his rights, he could find success in appealing it in which case the tax charge and the investigation would end.[12]

In the United States, the Taxpayer Bill of Rights itself has no built-in enforcement mechanism. However, there is right to privacy as a statutory right to due process in tax payment.[13] Thus, a taxpayer can approach an administrative appeals officer for a hearing if he feels there is opportunity to balance his legitimate interest against the

[8]See Baker et al. (2019).

[9]See Baker (2016), p. 598.

[10]See OECD (2003), p. 6.

[11]Founded on 5 May 1949 by 10 countries, currently the Council of Europe (CoE), based in Strasbourg, France, includes virtually the entire European continent, with 47 members. It seeks to develop throughout Europe, common democratic principles based on the European Convention on Human Rights and other reference texts on the protection of individuals.

[12]See Baker (2016), op. cit.

[13]Olson (2016) says, 'As an IRS employee, if I violate [section] 6103, I could be terminated from employment. That is in the law. It is not coming from the Taxpayer Bill of Rights. It is coming from

government's interest in collecting tax. Next, the taxpayer can go to the Tax Court for an examination of the administration's decision. Admitting that the tax administration had been wrong is considered tantamount to abuse of discretion. The court could also remand the matter back to the administration for a closer examination so that the latter gets another chance to get it right.

The 2018 OTPR Report mentioned above covers various aspects in the context of taxpayers' rights in India, including the framework for tax legislation, administration practice and guidance for taxpayers and institutional framework for protecting taxpayers' rights including an Ombudsman.[14] Many of these aspects will be covered in some detail in Part VI of this textbook, which covers tax administration.

### 13.5.3 Taxpayers' Charters

A taxpayers' charter has been described as a 'a short, accessible statement of the basic rights [and obligations] of taxpayers in dealing with the tax authorities'.[15] Charters do not provide additional rights or obligations to the legislation itself. They attempt to 'reflect the country's own policy and legislative environment and administrative practices and culture'.[16]

Even countries without a taxpayers' charter attach importance to taxpayers' rights and, in practice, taxpayers in such countries have rights similar to those found in formal taxpayers' charter statements.

India's central government finance minister, in her annual Budget speech for the financial year 2020-2021, announced the need for the creation of a trust-based tax environment, revealing that a taxpayers' charter was planned to be included in the income-tax law. She elaborated that,

> Any tax system requires trust between taxpayers and the administration. This will be possible only when taxpayer's rights are clearly enumerated. Towards this end, and with the objective of enhancing the efficiency of the delivery system of the Income Tax Department, I propose to amend the provisions of the Income Tax Act to mandate the Central Board of Direct Taxes (CBDT) to adopt a Taxpayers' Charter.[17]

A citizens' charter already existed as a part of the tax administration's mission statement, though it had no legislative backing and no consequences in case of

the statutory provision in the Internal Revenue Code and the sanctions there, but it gives teeth to this right to confidentiality', p. 600.

[14]It also addresses identification of taxpayers, issuance of tax returns and communication with taxpayers, tax assessments and enforcement, review and appeal, and confidentiality thereof.

[15]By Philip Baker, quoted in Young (2017).

[16]See OECD (2003), op. cit., p. 6.

[17]Indian Parliament, 1 February 2020.

non-compliance. The Budget statement gave it statutory force, though actual implementation of the charter is awaited at the point of writing.[18]

Several countries have well-developed histories of taxpayer charters and the establishment of commensurate rights. What is expected in a charter is a clarification of the fundamental rights of taxpayers that have to be respected by the tax administration. In Canada, France, Ireland and South Africa, charters explain that the rights include confidentiality, secrecy and privacy of information submitted, and protection under common law. The UK charter does not list such rights and, instead, elaborates on mutual responsibilities between taxpayer and tax officer. The US IRS[19] attempts to convey taxpayer rights through publicity. Despite the variation, charters should attempt to be clear on enforceable taxpayers' rights that complement the implementation of the tax system from the tax administration's viewpoint.

## 13.6 Tax Administration Angle

### 13.6.1 Exchange of Information

A particular issue has emerged in the matter of taxpayer rights with the internationalisation of tax.[20] In the context of the Base Erosion and Profit Shifting (BEPS) project of the OECD, actions have been recommended for the exchange of information among tax authorities across nations to ensure that decisions on taxability are based on full information available to all tax authorities internationally. Exchange of information, whether on request, spontaneous or automatic, is about achieving global tax co-operation among tax administrations through high standards of tax transparency and information sharing.

Ease of taxpayer compliance complemented by taxpayer rights are viewed as important criteria for the effectiveness of a tax system based on simplicity and transparency.[21] In their enthusiasm to tax taxpayers effectively, therefore, a question arises whether tax administrations would be able to protect and ensure taxpayers' rights. Baker (2016) commented,

> Khincha and others have raised the issue of taxpayers' rights in the context of international exchange of information. They go beyond taxpayer rights in exchange of information and present a cogent argument for greater respect for taxpayers' rights. Many people believe that protection of taxpayers' rights was the 16th missing Action Point in the BEPS project. It was a vital issue which the OECD and the countries engaged in the BEPS project should not have ignored; the fact that it was not included as an Action Point speaks volumes about the need to

[18]Butani (2020) provides additional details.

[19]Internal Revenue Service.

[20]Khincha et al. (2018) in Shome (2018), Chap. 9, discuss taxpayer rights in the context of international exchange of information.

[21]See Baker and Pistone (2015); and Shome (2018), Chap. 1, p. 1.

reconsider the international tax architecture to ensure that bodies with a specific human rights agenda play a greater role in the development of rules of international taxation.[22]

### 13.6.2 Retroactive Application of Law

Even though we have mentioned the deleterious impact of retrospective application of tax law on business decisions in Chap. 6, Sect. 6.3 and shall revisit it in some detail in Chap. 28, Sect. 28.4, in the context of tax avoidance, it would be useful to review country experiences here in the context of taxpayers' rights and to draw out the difference in usage between 'retroactivity' and 'retrospectivity'. 'Nominal retroactive application' may be defined as a situation 'that affects tax liability that has been fixed before the date on which the new law is passed'. Those experts who find a reason to justify retroactivity in selected circumstances tend to argue that, by definition, 'virtually every change in tax law has an effect on existing investments'. Nevertheless, the possibility of 'grandfathering' of existing investments should not be overlooked when passing retroactive law since grandfathering deserves consideration as an aspect of taxpayers' rights.

While some countries have enshrined the principle of non-retroactivity in their civil code as the ordinary rule to be applied, the United States and United Kingdom have used retroactivity in their tax laws. Therefore, it is not considered a legally binding principle, for example where technical corrections in law are to be made. The US Supreme Court has given the opinion that, retroactive application is permitted by the constitution as long as it 'is rationally related to a legitimate legislative purpose'. The United Kingdom has also used retroactive application to benefit the government, for example to disallow deductions for certain losses from tax shelters.

The French constitutional court, on the other hand, has ruled that 'penal' application of retroactivity will not be permitted. The German constitutional court relates the matter to the 'Rule of Law' regarding legal security and public trust. It makes a nuanced distinction between retroactivity from retrospectivity. The former affects transactions already closed in the past. The latter affects legal positions that have not yet been closed. More retrospective laws are permitted than retroactive. Usually, however, tax laws are prospective and provide protection from both retroactivity (transactions completed) and retrospectivity (transactions in progress) to taxpayers.

[22]Foreword by Baker in Shome (2018), op. cit., referred to Khincha et al. in Chap. 9 on taxpayers' rights.

## 13.7 Distribution of Power to Make, Apply and Interpret Tax Law

Lawmaking is usually carried out by the legislature, implementation of law by the executive branch or administration, and judicial pronouncements on the application of law by the judiciary.

### 13.7.1 Making and Implementing Tax Law

It is usual for the legislature not only to have the power to pass tax law. However, specific provisions in tax law may also contain particular types of administrative acts. Nevertheless, the tax administration usually has the power to pass subordinate laws or regulations—ordinances, decrees, orders, rules—that complement the law and carry a firmness that the law by itself may not possess. As long as regulations are not contrary to law, they have the force of law and are binding on both taxpayer and government.

The rules that administrations devise comprise, among others, the design and changes in tax returns, their frequency of filing, the withholding of taxes and at what rates, and stipulations regarding which entity is responsible for withholding taxes. When applying the law, an administration also has to interpret it; this necessarily involves some discretion, for example in examining and ruling on tax assessments and picking selected tax returns for audit or scrutiny. Because of the possibility of moral hazard on the part of tax officers, some tax administrations have introduced rules regarding the maximum length of time allowable for completing assessments, or exact criteria for picking up scrutiny cases and completing them. This minimises discretion allowed in the hands of the administration. Indeed, it should be considered an aspect that should be recognised in taxpayer charters.

The wide array of practices across countries reflects the structure of their constitutional law and administration and what is permitted within, and by, them. Civil law countries of Europe are typically different from common law countries that separate the making and application of law. In the former, usually there is a constitutional delegation of tax lawmaking power to the executive branch, though an act of parliament must specify rules that would define such power. In common law countries, delegation is by statute.

For example, the US Treasury (or ministry of finance) issues tax regulations in conformity with the Administrative Procedure Act. There the Congress (or parliament) remains uninvolved. Similarly, in the United Kingdom, the executive branch may issue such legislation that remains within delegated power. Otherwise, the judiciary may strike it down. The regulations themselves are voluminous though tax law is bigger.

### 13.7.2 Interpreting Tax Law

Implementation of tax law usually rests with the executive branch and, accordingly, its interpretation as well. It, therefore, issues subordinate law or rules and regulations, and circulars including for clarifications of law. Subordinate law must not conflict with statutory law. Courts are the final arbiter of tax law; they interpret tax law and adjudicate disputes between the tax administration and the taxpayer. However, judicial interpretation may vary in their admission whether an interpretative issue even exists, or in ascertaining legislative intent in a law. Some judiciaries use more, others less, legislative history, in concluding on a point.

The final determination is whether a taxpayer owes tax to the exchequer. For this, it is useful to distinguish 'common law' from 'civil law' countries. The former, such as Australia, Canada and the United States, emphasise examination of facts combined with legal reasoning, while the latter emphasise the exact word of law or rule while limiting the use of legal reasoning. Yet, the former also possess detailed statutory provisions that are used in the interpretation of law. Thus, a mix of facts and legal rules help arrive at the conclusion of an individual case.

The facts comprise legal, rather than physical, facts, being of the nature of a company, sales contract or perhaps an inheritance. Legal reasoning puts such facts in order, thus making them subject to the application of rules. On that basis, it arrives at a clear conclusion on tax owed by the taxpayer, rather than at a mere reconciliation with him. In doing so, three elements are important: (1) are tax laws to be interpreted strictly or in a wider sense through analogy or resemblance between two cases, (2) is the legal form of a transaction more important than its substance or content and (3) is tax law to be interpreted in an economic sense that may not be applicable in other areas of law; in other words, does tax law have a different perspective that brings it closer to economic and social objectives and the principles behind them.

The determination of tax owed has to ultimately contend with such competing interpretations. They boil down to two ways of interpreting tax law: (1) 'legality' which emphasises clarity of language and stipulates that tax should not be imposed where the language of the law is not clear. And (2) the other term may be called 'effectivity' which emphasises the intention of the law and eschews possibilities of circumvention through tax avoidance. It, therefore, draws on the principle of equality to be extended to all taxpayers without any one taxpayer benefiting more than others from the same tax law.

Though the emphasis varies across countries between the two rubrics, increasingly, tax authorities across the world are converging towards effectivity in their attempts to address what they view as egregious tax avoidance by MNEs which operate in many nations across the globe, yet minimise the sum total of their tax contributions from their global income generation. MNEs may view their practices as achieving 'tax efficiency' through appropriate management and successful financial operations.

But tax authorities have tended to view this as unacceptable tax behaviour, and subject MNEs to a 'business purpose test' to examine if the intention of a business structure is genuine and comprises the production of a good or service, or is it merely an artificial structure or arrangement among related business enterprises to avoid tax globally. Accordingly, many countries have introduced general anti-abuse provisions in tax law. We shall examine both sides of this global phenomenon in greater detail in Chaps. 28 and 29.

## 13.8 Evolution in India[23]

The separation of power among the branches—legislative, executive, judiciary—is practised strictly in India. Its evolution can be tracked over centuries.

### 13.8.1 Pre-independence Law

Traversing its development in India's history, India uses common law, based on recorded judicial precedents, that arrived with the East India Company (EIC) in the 1700s. The EIC established 'Mayor's Courts' in Madras, Bombay and Calcutta (now Chennai, Mumbai and Kolkata, respectively) by a charter from King George I in 1726. After its victory in the Battle of Plassey in 1757,[24] the EIC expanded its judicial functions and, by 1772, the EIC's courts expanded out to steadily replace the prevailing Mughal legal system. The earlier prevailing customary law in India continued to exist side by side in some domestic matters though it receded somewhat into the background. Nevertheless, perhaps even today India could be said to enjoy 'organic law' as a consequence of the common law system having been juxtaposed on its customary law.

Following the First War of Independence in 1857, which was not successful for India, the EIC ceded its territories to the British Crown. Supreme courts replaced mayoral courts and were initially barred to Indian practitioners.[25] These courts were converted to high courts through an Indian High Courts Act passed in the British parliament in 1862. Functions such as the operations of lower courts, and the enrolment of law practitioners, were deputed to the respective high courts.

An Indian Penal Code was drafted, enacted and brought into force by 1862 with Thomas Babington Macaulay as chairman of a Law Commission. A Code of Criminal Procedure was also drafted by the same commission, and other statutes and codes such as the Evidence Act (1872) and Contracts Act (1872). The Privy Council was the highest court of appeal, with the House of Lords adjudicating cases in the name of the British sovereign in her capacity as Empress of India.

---

[23]Bar Council of India, http://www.barcouncilofindia.org/about/about-the-legal-profession/legal-education-in-the-united-kingdom/

[24]See Chap. 4, Sects. 4.1 and 4.2, for details of this period.

[25]Right of audience was limited to members of English, Irish and Scottish professional bodies, later redressed through a Legal Practitioners Act.

### 13.8.2 Post-independence Law

B. R. Ambedkar was the recognised formulator of independent India's constitution. The founding fathers devoted considerable energy to design a constitution of globally exemplary scope, breadth and detail. A country's constitution sets the tone and direction a society chooses to take. Turning its direction towards social concerns and seeking to empower the weakest members of society, India's constitution guides the executive, legislative and judicial functions of Indian society. In essence, having inherited a common law system,[26] India fine-tuned it for Indian conditions in the form of its carefully crafted constitution that was subsequently buttressed by judicial pronouncements and legislative action.[27] Codification of laws made Indian law uniform throughout the country and fostered legal unity in its fundamental laws.

The judiciary is invested with the power to ensure that all organs of the constitution act within their respective constitutional limits. It is also the sole interpreter of the constitution and the sole arbiter in all constitutional disputes. The legal hierarchy places the supreme court at the apex. It adjudicates constitutional issues and also acts as the final court of appeal. It also exercises constitutional powers to issue writs in cases adjudicating infringements of fundamental rights guaranteed by the constitution. Indeed, the signature theme of the constitution, as pointed out by the supreme court, being social justice, Indian courts must keep those constitutional values in mind while administering justice.

Judicial independence being a core characteristic of the Indian constitution, the courts jealously guard against any encroachment by the executive or legislative branches. The appointment of judges to high courts and the supreme court is decided by judges through interpretative constitutional provisions. Independence of the judiciary is also reflected through the practice of the doctrine of judicial review of legislative and executive acts.[28] To provide an example, recently, the Indian judiciary was quick to react when it perceived the executive as stepping on its delegated powers. Reflecting the accumulation of litigation cases attracting international criticism for some years and, at the behest of the country's finance minister, in October 2003, the President of India promulgated a National Tax Tribunal (NTT) Ordinance to be set up under Article 323B of the constitution.[29]

On 6 December 2004, an NTT Bill was introduced in parliament to overcome the pendency of cases at the high courts amidst conflicting views regarding the legitimacy of the matter. As per the Act, the NTT would adjudicate and ensure speedy disposal of disputes over levy, assessment, collection and enforcement of direct taxes, as well as the determination of customs duty rates, central excise rates and valuation of goods, and service tax matters with an objective and outcome of

[26]See Syam (2014).

[27]See Nagar (2015).

[28]See Srikrishna (2008) for details.

[29]The background of the NTT Act has been described in detail in KPMG (2014).

reduction of tax arrears. Any appeal would be taken up by the supreme court, bypassing the high courts. The NTT Act was passed in 2005 but, before an NTT could be set up, several petitions were filed challenging it and the NTT Act languished for years from being implemented.

On 25 September 2014, a five-judge constitution bench of the supreme court headed by the chief justice of India held that the NTT Act was unconstitutional since several aspects of it violated constitutional norms. Justice Nariman in particular commented that the NTT Act was a departure made by parliament allowing tribunals to decide legal matters that had historically been decided by superior constitutional courts, taking away the power of judicial review from the high courts.

The underlying rationale for stoppage was the separation of powers between the judiciary and the executive in matters of jurisprudence. What emerges from the experience with the NTT Act is that the government cannot avoid taking a cooperative approach involving all stakeholders when proceeding with matters that overlap across different branches of allocated powers of governance. The fallout is that pendency in courts and tax arrears continue other than for occasional reductions from sporadic decisions by the executive to cut back its own appeals in particular circumstances such as when pending cases pertain to matters that were already decided in some court.

In the final analysis, India's delineation and practice in law, and tax law, have been rich and voluminous in the issuance of courts' opinions, and continue to raise the curiosity of the legal systems prevalent in advanced economies, and providing a good example to many emerging economy legal systems as well.

## References

Baker, Philip. 2016. The View from Vienna. Conversations: Jeffrey Owens, Nina Olson, and Philip Baker. Reprinted from *Tax Notes International* 81(7): 595–600. http://www.fieldtax.com/wp-content/uploads/2016/02/Conversations-Jeffrey-Owens-Nina-Olsen-and-Philip-Baker.pdf.

Baker, Philip, and Pasquale Pistone. 2015. The Practical Protection of Taxpayers' Fundamental Rights. Congress of the *International Fiscal Association,* Basel, August. Cahiers de droit fiscal international, vol. 100B. The Hague: Sdu Uitgevers.

Baker, Philip, Pasquale Pistone, and Carlos E. Weffe. 2019. *The 2018 General Report on the Practical Protection of Taxpayers' Rights*. IBFD Observatory on the Protection of Taxpayers' Rights. https://www.ibfd.org/sites/ibfd.org/files/content/pdf/2018%20OPTR%20General%20Report%20%28Final%29%20%28002%29.pdf. Accessed 14 Oct 2020.

Butani, Mukesh. 2020. Taxpayer's Charter Brings Focus on Taxpayers' Rights: What It Must Include. *Financial Express*, February 11.

Khincha, H. Padamchand, Neha P. Khincha, and Priya Kothari. 2018. Taxpayer Rights in International Exchange of Information. In *Challenges in Domestic & International Taxation-Emerging Indian Experience*, ed. Parthasarathi Shome, 269–301. Gurugram: OakBridge Publishing Pvt. Ltd.

KPMG. 2014. Supreme Court Strikes Down Constitutional Validity of the National Tax Tribunal Act. *KPMG Flash News*. https://home.kpmg/content/dam/kpmg/pdf/2014/10/SCstrikes-down-National-Tax-Tribunal-Act.pdf. Accessed 14 Oct 2020.

Lee, Natalie. 2013. *Revenue Law: Principles and Practice*. 31st ed. Haywards Heath: Bloomsbury.

Nagar, Raghav. 2015. *What Is Common Law? Does It Apply in India?* iPleaders. https://blog.ipleaders.in/common-law-apply-india/. Accessed 14 Oct 2020.

OECD. 2003. Taxpayers' Rights and Obligations—Practice Note. *Tax Guidance Series*. https://www.oecd.org/tax/administration/Taxpayers'_Rights_and_Obligations-Practice_Note.pdf. Accessed 14 Oct 2020.

Olson, Nina. 2016. The View from Vienna. Conversations: Jeffrey Owens, Nina Olson, and Philip Baker. Reprinted from *Tax Notes International* 81(7): 595–600. http://www.fieldtax.com/wp-content/uploads/2016/02/Conversations-Jeffrey-Owens-Nina-Olsen-and-Philip-Baker.pdf.

Shome, Parthasarathi. 2012. *Tax Shastra: Administrative Reforms in India, United Kingdom and Brazil*. New Delhi: Business Standard Books.

———, ed. 2018. *Challenges in Domestic & International Taxation-Emerging Indian Experience*. Gurugram: OakBridge Publishing Pvt. Ltd.

Srikrishna, B. N. 2008. The Indian Legal System. *International Journal of Legal Information* 36 (2): 242–244. http://scholarship.law.cornell.edu/ijli/vol36/iss2/8.

Syam, Piyali. 2014. What Is the Difference Between Common Law and Civil Law? https://onlinelaw.wustl.edu/blog/common-law-vs-civil-law/. Accessed 14 Oct 2020.

Thuronyi, Victor, ed. 1996. *Tax Law Design and Drafting*. Vol. 1. Washington, DC: IMF.

Vanistendael, Frans. 1996. Legal Framework for Taxation. In *Tax Law Design and Drafting*, ed. Victor Thuronyi, vol. 1. Washington, DC: IMF.

Young, Ian. 2017. Taxpayer Rights and the Role of a Taxpayers' Charter. *Tax Notes*. https://info.taxnotes.com/conferencepapers_the_role_of_a_taxpayers_charter_0818. Accessed 14 Oct 2020.

# Drafting Tax Law

# 14

## 14.1 Introduction

Drafting tax law falls within the specialisation of drafting any law. In the case of tax law, particular factual considerations of how to organise sections, the type of language to be used that is comprehensible to the tax community, considerations of how simple the law should be to read without sacrificing necessary detail, and more normative considerations regarding whether the law has achieved effectiveness in conveying the proper message to taxpayers and tax officers alike, all come into play in determining its usability domestically and quotability in the international sphere. Given the prevalence of some cross-country variation in definitions, there is little doubt that a domestic legislative drafting style with suitable definitions is preferred over blindly borrowing from international quarters. This is notwithstanding the awareness with which globally available styles have to be mastered by a drafter of any tax law. We consider some of these matters in this chapter.[1]

## 14.2 Effectiveness

In drafting tax law, the beginning point has to be the reflection of intended policy in the law. The drafter has to give credence to the policy behind the law and arrive at an understanding of the clarity to be achieved in its interpretation and implementation for taxpayers, tax officers and the courts. It could safely be stated that, clarity becomes increasingly crucial as the complexity of a particular section or sub-section increases. Taking the example of a tax incentive in the form of a capital allowance in the United Kingdom,

[1]Thuronyi (1996), Chap. 3, considers issues and specifications of drafting tax law mainly from advanced country practices. However, it is useful for emerging economies as well.



P. Shome, *Taxation History, Theory, Law and Administration*, Springer Texts in Business and Economics, https://doi.org/10.1007/978-3-030-68214-9_14

> Part 4A (sections 393A-393 W) was added by FA 2001 to give capital allowances for expenditure on converting or renovating qualifying business premises into flats. The scheme must be seen in the context of other fiscal incentives to assist urban regeneration—brown land.[2] This regime applies in respect of expenditure incurred prior to April 2013.
>
> Unlike the allowances for hotels, this is not fitted into the structure of the industrial buildings allowance but is free-standing. However, the industrial buildings allowance is clearly the model for this, as is shown by the use of the concept of the relevant interest. The writing-down allowance of 100%. There are also rules for calculating balancing adjustments. The allowance is given in calculating the profits of the claimant's property business relating to the flat; if there is no such business, one is deemed to exist.
>
> The relief is meant to be precisely targeted, so no allowance may be claimed for expenditure on acquiring the land, extending the building, developing adjacent land or providing furniture or chattels. The construction of the building being converted must have been completed before 1980. The legislation is silent on the effect of building works since then, but one could say that such a building would not qualify since it had not been 'completed'. The building must have the ground floor authorised for business use; it must have not more than four storeys above the ground floor (ignoring attics) and it must appear that the storey above the ground floor were originally intended for use as a dwelling. There are also detailed rules about which flats qualify. So the flat must be suitable for letting as a dwelling, held for short-term letting (not more than five years), have not more than four rooms (as defined) and not be a high value flat.[3]

The fact that the above quotation refers to a single tax incentive yet is complex in the way it filters down to a narrow base must have required an adept drafter to maintain clarity despite its complexity. If the drafting produced an outcome that was incomprehensible, perhaps that could in itself have led to a rethinking of the policy. This is explained below.

Policy could of course meander—in particular in democracies where government, and then the legislation, have their inputs, followed by lobbying by different interested parties who may play a paramount role—even as the drafting proceeds. The drafter has to keep vigil as to whether and, if so, how, to modify the draft accordingly. In other words, the drafter has to 'test the waters' as to whether a change is required or not. Usually, that guidance will be provided by a finance minister if competent but, if not, the drafter may have to find his own way by seeking guidance from, and keeping in touch with, various top-level stakeholders. If the drafting process can be completed with all this in mind, tax law is likely to have achieved a good degree of effectiveness.

Policy also could undergo changes by the drafting process itself. As the language of law is pinned down, the tax policy behind it comes into sharper focus. Therefore, even as the drafter comes to understand the reasons behind the policy and pens it in the draft, the policymaker may realise that the write-up has revealed that tweaking of the policy itself may be needed and, accordingly, may take the opportunity to make modifications. Therefore, the final language emanates from a process of mutuality between policymaker and drafter.

[2] As opposed to green—or undeveloped—land.

[3] See Tiley and Glen (2012), pp. 185–86.

It is not just the law but subordinate law—rules and regulations—that also has to be incorporated. The application and implementation of the former being supported by the latter, it is the drafter's responsibility to see that there is no ambiguity between them. The certainty that the absence of ambiguity produces, ensures effectiveness of the law combined with subordinate law. Most country experiences reveal at least some remaining ambiguity. For example, in 2006, India introduced a Fringe Benefits Tax (FBT) on a comprehensive list of fringe benefits given to an employee.[4] The application of the list produced ambiguities and there was blame cast on the law and on the tax officer for alleged erroneous interpretation. It generated so much continued unpopularity that the tax was repealed in 2009.

Drafting varies by classification of country practices. In general, civil law countries use rather detailed law but eschew incorporation of detailed rules. Broad principles are emphasised instead, leaving the application of those principles to the judgement of courts. Common law countries tend to draft every possible eventuality, with courts confining themselves to a narrow reading of the provisions. While leaving more or less discretion in the hands of the judiciary may reflect a societal view, it is difficult to conclude which approach produces more effectiveness.

## 14.3 Relation Between Law, Subordinate Law and Explanations

Tax laws are accompanied by rules and regulations, and explanatory material. The intention is for them to provide, together, robust understanding and operationality for taxpayers, tax officers and judges. Law has the force of legislative backing. Regulations sometimes possess the force of law but not in every jurisdiction. Explanations provide support without force of law. The combination of the three protects the main law from becoming too cumbersome. But, to achieve sufficiency in the law and not to scale it back too much, careful guidance is needed by the drafter to place different aspects in the most appropriate of the three categories. We have already seen that civil law and common law countries differ somewhat but the need for clear categorisation[5] nevertheless plays an important role in the actual practice by all stakeholders in both groups of countries.

Maintaining cohesion and effectiveness can be ensured in different ways. It may be presumed that the law is logically sequenced. It follows that regulations should be similarly arranged to make them user friendly. Explanations should be attached to either of them as needed. Unsurprisingly, this is not followed in some countries, especially where the law has aged and there is some reluctance to enter into

[4]It was payable by an employer at the rate of 30% which was the maximum marginal rate of the individual income tax. It was not deductible in computing the employer's income. See Chap. 26, Sect. 26.4, for a full discussion of FBT.

[5]Because of the rush to legislate a tax, there may be some pressure by policymakers to leave unresolved issues to subordinate law under the presumption that they could be introduced later. However, this needs to be resisted since correct fitting of issues into the three categories is essential for effectiveness and confidence in the law.

fundamental reform of the draft. In such cases, the tendency is to add on rules and explanations with a simple reference to connect with the law; however, severe challenges may continue in linking different portions of the documents.[6]

## 14.4 Terminology and Drafting

### 14.4.1 Cross-Country Variation in Definitions

Challenges in using legal tax terminology comprise, among others, variations in meaning of the same term in the same language across countries. This gets more unclear when similar terms are used in different languages. Though they are civil law countries, a 'legal person' in France and Spain includes companies and partnerships but, in Germany, it only includes companies.[7] In the United States, it is determined in tax law or code rather than in civil law. What in common law countries is referred to as 'tax policy' is referred to in civil law countries as 'fiscal policy'. Transliterated words may also cause confusion; 'tax' in English may appear as 'tribute' in some European languages, the latter word having a rather different connotation in English.

Terms such as 'employee' or 'independent contractor' also differ in scope. In common law countries, its use reflects the extent of control by an employer. In civil law countries, the labour code tends to determine it. In both sets of countries, directors are excluded from being employees for tax purposes.

The definition of 'property' is usually derived from civil law but may be differently defined across countries. 'Real' property in common law countries is not identical to 'immovable' property in civil law countries. Such variations can pose challenges in the familiarisation of tax law for practitioners who operate in multiple jurisdictions across the MNE world. Needless to say, the above are just a few examples of the variation in the meaning of terms and any practitioner has to be cautious not to fall into the trap of erroneous use.

Usually, there are so many definitions in a tax law that careful attention has to be given to where to place them—at the beginning, at the end, or as they arise in the course of the narrative. Modern tax statutes tend to place definitions in a special section at the end. Those in the definitions section are likely to be rather lengthy. Therefore, it may be considered to include short definitions in footnotes which may facilitate cross-referencing.

Unclear definitions of classifications could lead to heavy burdens on the taxpayer. For example,

[6]In such a case, professionals who know how to successfully connect different sections must be quickly identified and employed to redress the problem. Contrary to the belief that may prevail, such professionals usually can be found and brought into such assignments for writing the law on a selective basis. It is the sitting bureaucracy that may, however, stand in the way.

[7]Of course, in their own languages.

> If the classification assumed by the (related) parties is later found to have been wrong, the tax and national insurance contribution (NIC) treatment throughout the relationship will have to be revised. Where self-employed status is reclassified as employment, this can cause severe problems for the (newly designated) employer who will be primarily responsible . . . . for any unpaid income tax and employees' NICs but will have difficulties recovering that from the (possibly former) worker, as well as having the extra cost of employers' NICs.[8]

However, there is no hard and fast rule to enhance convenience and the drafter has to essentially find his way in the matter with appropriate guidance along the way.

### 14.4.2 Drafting

Language must be simple and understandable rather than archaic and verbose since the readership is likely to be one of the largest among all official documents of government. Authorities should attempt to move away from inherited language that has little relevance in the prevailing domestic context. A few indications are provided.

1. The overuse of 'shall' should be carefully pondered where 'must' would suffice lest 'shall' should get devalued.
2. The word 'any' should be used with care especially in instances where 'a' or 'an' would suffice.
3. The word 'where' is more complicated than 'if'. For example, 'where a trust has been approved' is likely to imply 'in the case', or, 'if'. Thus using 'if' would be preferable and 'where' should be reserved for use to indicate location.
4. Often the phrase 'is deemed' is found. Simpler language would be to use 'is treated as'.
5. To convey assurance, active voice directly asking a taxpayer to perform a task such as 'a taxpayer should file a return' is better than using passive voice as in 'a return should be filed'.
6. Use of the singular is more specific, such as 'a taxpayer is required to' rather than 'taxpayers are required to' since the latter could impart a broader scope, nevertheless with the possibility of some exception or exemption perhaps.
7. A parenthesis should be short. If it is too long, the sense of what is outside it may get lost. In that case, the matter in the parenthesis may be to put in a footnote.
8. Cross-referencing footnotes is common in tax law. However, this should not occur to such an extent that a practitioner is reduced to shifting from one page to another page in a volume of the law, or to another volume or yet another, possibly having to get back to the beginning volume. Such instances are not unknown despite their posing severe challenges to convenient use. Indeed, it diminishes the usability of a tax statute.

[8] See Lee (2013), p. 175, who wrote it in the context of UK income tax.

9. The use of provisos could be tricky. The phrase 'provided that' when added a second time narrows down the original stipulation further which could cause confusion and misunderstanding. It is better to divide such statements into two. Thus, 'an employer may deduct 125% of the cost of employees provided that he employs more than ten employees in that business unit' is fine. But an add-on phrase in a run-on sentence such as 'and provided that no other benefit was received by the employer based on his employees being from the scheduled castes or scheduled tribes (SC/ST) community' causes confusion.

The confusion could arise due to possible misinterpretation. For example, if SC/ST employees number <10, would the employer still be cut out of the general employment benefit if his total employee size (SC/ST plus non-SC/ST) exceeded 10? Thus, it would be better to have the second proviso as a second full sentence which would clarify the two provisos separately.

10. The word 'means' is exhaustive while the word 'includes' is partial. Thus, 'a person means' indicates that, whoever is not included in its associated list is *not* a 'person', whereas 'a person includes' is not an exclusive list in that some entities not in its associated list could also be a 'person'. These terms should, therefore, not be used synonymously.
11. Sometimes the phrases 'mentioned in', described in', 'referred to in' or 'contemplated in', may be found in the same law though they mean essentially the same thing. Other such duplication of phrases occurs in tax codes. It would be helpful for the reader to find one rather than three or four phrases to mean the same thing in the same law even though that may seem repetitious.[9]
12. Indian law continues to use complex Latin phrases in tax matters. Learning law in non-phonetic English is already a burden to many Indian students with vernacular backgrounds. It is advisable not to require them to learn phrases from another ancient and archaic Western language. There is no particular reason why they should not be replaced with simple English.

Reflecting that tax law drafting is a specialist's task, it is not surprising that occasional tensions between a country's tax administration and its law branch on the one hand, and the ministry of finance (or treasury) on the other hand, become visible in cross-country tax formulation experience. An example of the tension in bearing the responsibility of drafting tax law became apparent in Australia when the tax legislation function moved from the former to the latter in 2002. The treasury subsequently proposed 'principle-based drafting' that would better ensure a plain, non-technical style of drafting that would reflect the 'intuitive or obvious in the intent and context' of a law.

[9]Arguably, the English language tends to use repetitions to ensure specificity in meaning, sometimes in conflictive pattern of use in some European languages such as Spanish that appear to avoid repetition.

That presumption was not sympathetically assessed by tax experts who expressed a view that,

> Legal drafting is more complex. It requires phrasing, where each word will be interpreted extensively as to its particular and general meaning and specifically in the context of the sentence, the surrounding sections, the surrounding sections, like sections throughout the Act, its meaning and legal principle, decisions of the courts, both locally and internationally, and in the surrounding materials.
>
> To take a policy statement designed for another purpose—by its very nature, political instant and transient—and to use it to deliver law that must, by its nature, be apolitical, consistent and timeless, is to undermine the purpose of legislation.[10]

Indeed, the perceived tendency of a ministry of finance to take over the drafting of tax law in its own brief should be avoided. The better policy to be followed is for it to closely monitor whether tax law being drafted by the tax administration reflects the policy intent behind the law, yet leave the actual drafting to the branches that possess expertise in drafting. Obviously, for this to be successful, a co-operative, rather than an adversarial, approach between the two branches is imperative.

## 14.5 Best Characteristics

To conclude, tax law drafting is a complex task. One aspect that must be kept in mind is the achievement of brevity. A short tax statute is likely to be frequently referred to for popular use in contrast to a tome meant to be picked up only by a few. Second, the structure of sentences has to be consistent in the use of number, voice, punctuation, parentheses, phrases and footnotes. Third, the organisation must be simple in section headings, and the way they are numbered and sequenced. If there are several volumes, they must be rationally distributed.

No justifiable complexity should be sacrificed of course. Nevertheless, brevity, simplicity and organisation remain the paramount objectives to be achieved in drafting tax law.

## References

Bentley, Duncan. 2004. Tax law drafting: The principled method. *Revenue Law Journal* 14 (1), Article 1. https://rlj.scholasticahq.com/article/6651-tax-law-drafting-the-principled-method.

Lee, Natalie. 2013. *Revenue Law: Principles and Practice*. 31st ed. Haywards Heath: Bloomsbury.

Thuronyi, Victor, ed. 1996. *Tax Law Design and Drafting*. Vol. 1. Washington, DC: IMF.

Tiley, John, and Loutzenhiser Glen. 2012. *Tax Law*. Oxford: Hart Publishing.

[10]See Bentley (2004), p. 3.

# Part IV

# Prevalent Taxes

# Income Taxes—Design and Evidence 15

## 15.1 Introduction

The design of the income tax is embedded in defining its base—what deductions, allowances or credits are allowed—how rates are structured—the degree of its progressivity, as well as how, in addition, payroll taxes are based—on a pay as you go (PAYG) or a fully funded (FF) basis, among many other design considerations. Many countries use a withholding mechanism—tax deduction at source (TDS)—to facilitate tax compliance such as on interest and dividend incomes which are then deducted from the annual income tax returns.

Taxing wealth in various ways has been a historically important aspect of taxation though its implementation receded in quality and many countries removed it. Now, in an environment of impinging financial constraints, the necessity of bringing the tax back to a practical use has entered the academic discussion. Taxes on inheritance, gifts and estates had also reigned in tax statutes though, reflecting their relatively poor revenue performance over the years due to possibly high rates, some countries scaled them back though most countries continue to have them in various forms.

Other taxes have included a minimum tax on the well-off, and a presumptive tax on the hard-to-tax taxpayer not only in advanced economies such as the 'forfeit' system in France but, in particular, in developing economies based on the observed standard of living for an individual or, for a small factory owner, his floor space, number of employees and electricity use. India used presumptive taxation in the form of a flat tax on small businesses.

At the local level, the most prevalent tax across the globe is the property tax. Some countries have taken time to structure an appropriate property tax for want of a cadastral survey though, now, it is common to find it at least in large cities in emerging economies as well. The design and related aspects of income and wealth taxes and the property tax, and variations thereof, are considered in this chapter.



P. Shome, *Taxation History, Theory, Law and Administration*, Springer Texts in Business and Economics, https://doi.org/10.1007/978-3-030-68214-9_15

## 15.2 Individual or Personal Income Tax

### 15.2.1 Income and Taxable Income

It would not be an exaggeration to say that the longest debate in taxation theory has pertained to the concept and design of the income tax—both personal and corporate.[1] The Schanz-Haig-Simons definition of income is the sum of the market value of the rights exercised in consumption and the change in the total value of property rights between the beginning and the end of the period in question. On this basis, the definition of comprehensive income equals consumption plus the net wealth accumulated during the period, the inclusion of net wealth lending the term 'comprehensive' to the definition.

Optimal income taxation considers both efficiency and equity aspects of the tax and the trade-off between them as we saw in Chap. 10, Sect. 10.6. The optimal degree of income tax progressivity under alternative theories of distributive justice is based on the distribution of pre-tax income, the government's objective to maximize social welfare using the income tax and the disincentive effects or efficiency costs of individual work effort from the tax. While these factors lie at the base of many individual or personal income tax structures, their actual structures often also reflect principles other than just efficiency or equity as we saw in Chap. 6, Sect. 6.2.

The actual determination of taxable income has to recognize that an individual's income may have different sources including wages and salaries, interest, income from investment or dividends and business income. These incomes may be pooled together and be subject to one tax rate structure (global, comprehensive or pooled basis). Or different tax schedules may apply to each source (schedular basis). In case of the latter, the characterization of an income as business or some other category will determine the tax burden. Further, special rules for the accounting of tax apply to business income. For example, the structure of business income taxation specifies when, during a taxable year, a tax becomes due. These and other characteristics of its structure make business income taxation more complex than taxation of income from other sources. Taxes on business income will be elaborated in Chap. 18.

As income tax gets globalized, another aspect of taxation of an individual that has assumed some prominence is the residential status of that person in a country. This is important as taxpayers have become increasingly mobile and tend to move across international boundaries for income generating activities. Also, the income of an individual may result from cross-border economic activities such as overseas investment. Such income may be taxed in the country where the income is earned (referred to as the source country) or where the individual receiving the income normally resides (referred to as the country of residence).

Residence taxation of income is based on the principle that governments provide public services to people in the country where they live and they should contribute

[1] The early writings of G. Von Schanz (1896) and R. M. Haig (1921) and, later, H.C. Simons (1938) have survived in the annals of that debate.

towards such public services. On the other hand, source taxation is based on the principle that the country that provides the opportunity to generate income or profits should have the right to tax it. While the former premise generally taxes all incomes of a taxpayer irrespective of its source, the latter taxes all incomes that are sourced in the country claiming the taxation rights. In designing a tax system, it is necessary to specify the criteria when an individual is considered a resident of the country for tax purposes and also for inclusion of an income in the tax base of the resident individual.

### 15.2.2 Designing the Income Tax[2]

#### 15.2.2.1 Deductions, Allowances and Credits

The personal income tax may, as indicated, be global or scheduler, that is the same rate structure may apply to all income sources (global) or different rates may apply to different sources (schedular). Schedular taxes may apply to income sources such as pension income, capital gains, partnership income, individual proprietors' income, farm income, fringe benefits and others. Or they may be absorbed at one rate within an overall progressive rate structure.

'Taxable income'—derived after 'preferences' such as allowable deductions, exemptions and credits are removed from income—the nature of inflation adjustment to the tax base, the tax rate structure and the number of income brackets—known as the tax schedule—as well as the taxable unit—household or individual—comprise the overall tax structure. Such adjustments to income to derive taxable income are sometimes called tax reliefs that are available to all taxpayers. For example, pension contributions are an example found in most tax structures. While tax structures are likely to differ across countries, global experience shows that, during periods when exchange of ideas and experiences takes place, country tax structures have tended to move towards convergence.

Under some tax systems, deductions may comprise a standard deduction while in others, deductions may be itemised. Sometimes the taxpayer may have the option of selecting the arrangement that benefits him more. The standard deduction may be different for different taxpayer characteristics such as single, married, senior citizen by age group and so on. Itemised deductions have to be itemised may comprise unreimbursed employee business expenses, charitable contributions, education-related expenses, pension contributions, life insurance contributions, personal and mortgage interest payments, medical and dental expenses, taxes paid to other levels of national government or foreign governments, social security tax payments and casualty or theft losses. Itemised deductions tend to benefit taxpayers in higher tax brackets because they are more likely to incur expenses that are allowed to be itemised. Both standard and itemized deductions reduce the tax base thus bringing down the applicable marginal tax rate.

[2]See Stotsky (1995).

The menu of itemised deductions develops over time. Taxes that are paid to other governments are usually allowed to be deducted to protect a taxpayer from double taxation. But in some countries receiving a refund on this account may be difficult on account of fears of the tax administration that the taxpayer may be asking for a 'foreign tax credit' without having paid tax elsewhere. Increasingly, however, the growing prevalence of information exchange across tax administrations should alleviate such obstacles.

A menu of deductions for domestic expenses is usually available. Allowing a deduction for unreimbursed employee business expenses reflects the argument that income should be measured net of expenses incurred in earning it. Similarly, deductions for charitable contributions, educational expenses, pension contributions and life insurance contributions assume that they encourage and increase these socio-economically beneficial activities. Underlying elasticities of demand for these activities when their price (tax) is reduced determines how much such an itemised deduction will increase their quantity.

A common deduction to encourage home ownership is for mortgage interest on the first home owned. Some countries may allow a deduction for mortgage interest for a second home owned by a taxpayer while, at the same time, taxing any actual or 'imputed' income from that home whether the home is rented out or not. Some countries have occasionally allowed deductions for interest on personal loans though they are not encouraged by tax experts since they encourage consumption over savings.

Some expense deductions are justifiable since such expenses erode the ability to pay. For example, in countries that have inadequate, or do not have, government-provided health systems, a deduction for medical and dental expenses is justified. Social security contributions are sometimes partially deductible to encourage retirement savings but that should be taxed when social security benefits are received as income and consumed. Similarly, losses due to casualty or theft reduce the ability to pay involuntarily and at least a partial deduction may be justifiable.

Thresholds may apply on deductions, either up to a maximum amount, or if they exceed a minimum amount. A threshold may be based on gross or taxable income. The use of thresholds reflects administrative reasons so that tax officers do not have to assess small amounts of deductions. Or they may reflect revenue reasons by imposing a limit to some deductions such as a proportion of gross or taxable income. Thus, the design of thresholds affects marginal tax rates of taxpayers.

Some emerging economies have eliminated standard deductions and use itemised deductions though they may subsequently reinstate standard deductions for ease of implementation. Thus, there is no strict preference between the two as the better policy. Most countries use both.

Some countries allow personal exemptions as per family size. Exemptions, like deductions, reduce the tax by applicable marginal tax rate multiplied by the exemption amount. It is possible to convert personal exemptions to a tax credit which reduces the tax amount by the same nominal amount irrespective of the taxpayer's marginal tax rate; this enhances progressivity.

After computing tax on taxable income, the individual taxpayer may be allowed to claim certain tax credits. These credits vary but are often designed to provide tax relief to low-income households, married couples or both. Credits are also frequently allowed for taxes paid to other countries on foreign source income that is also subject to domestic tax. These credits are typically non-refundable, that is they cannot be claimed by taxpayers with no positive tax liability. If they are made refundable, they require an able tax administration to deter tax evasion.

#### 15.2.2.2 How Much Progressivity Is Desirable?

Most tax experts would agree that, over the past three to four decades, the income tax structure has lost its redistributive emphasis if not intent. Nevertheless, among all taxes that comprise the overall tax system, an element of progressivity remains in the personal income tax as the last vestige of the equity objective. However, too much progressivity tends to exacerbate tax evasion and accompanying challenges to tax administration, as well as to emigration of professional labour to countries with lower progressivity.

The definition of progressivity itself has varied. Reflecting the distribution of taxes, one measure may yield high progressivity, but the incidence of the tax may fall on just a few, for example the richest decile of income earners. Therefore, the tax collected from them may not yield much. Another progressivity measure—based on the after-tax distribution of income across all deciles—may conclude otherwise, that the first tax structure does not possess progressivity in a comprehensive sense. This is because even as the tax structure may have withdrawn revenue from the top decile, the relative positions of other deciles may not have changed.

We may reach varying conclusions on the equity effects of the same tax structure when progressivity is differently measured. The resultant debate on the appropriate measure of progressivity has not yielded a definitive conceptual preference. Added to this, due to the detrimental effects of progressivity on efficiency generally agreed upon by experts, it may be concluded that it is judicious to limit the steepness of progressivity. Countries that experimented with highly progressive rates also experienced high tax evasion and flight of capital.

## 15.3 Payroll Tax

A tax on the payroll is generally earmarked for supporting social insurance programmes, such as social security and insurance for health, unemployment and disability. Ideally, the tax is taken from the payroll of salary earners or employees, together with pre-determined contributions from employers. The revenue is destined for benefiting them through appropriate transfers. This relationship makes the tax unlike other taxes whose revenue accrues to the general budget.

### 15.3.1 PAYG Versus FF Systems

Social insurance systems may be financed on either a pay-as-you-go (PAYG) or a funded principle. Under the PAYG system, current workers effectively transfer resources to current beneficiaries with government as the conduit. Under the fully funded (FF) system, the contribution of each taxpayer is accumulated in an individual reserve account to cover his own future benefits. Payroll tax structures tend to be simple, with no exemptions from gross wages, and the tax is levied as a flat percentage of an employee's gross wages up to a limit (thereby often attracting the criticism that it is regressive) and at a single rate, though the rates are different for employee and employer contributions. Variations are found in the way a payroll tax is actually structured by countries.

The final incidence of the employer component of a payroll tax is generally perceived to be passed on by employers (capital owners) to the employees (wage and salary earners), though the extent to which this occurs depends on the elasticities of demand and supply of the factors of production as was explained in Chap. 9, Sect. 9.5. Again, if the final incidence is on employees, the tax could be perceived as doubly regressive. Despite this, governments see fit to impose the tax to ensure that a minimum social insurance coverage is maintained in society for contingencies and retirement. And governments choose to impose it as a tax based on the benefit principle rather than one that is financed from the general budget.

In developed economies with an ageing population, PAYG tends to lead to a rapid growth in current and future liabilities. This has resulted in an increasing burden on the working population, especially as declines in the growth of productivity have tended to stagnate the tax base. Reflecting the implicit nature of PAYG systems as inter-generational social contracts,[3] developed economies were confident in using PAYG as long as the growths of their economies and, commensurately, of their working populations, were robust. Recently, as populations have aged and growth rates have strained, there has been considerable discussion on the rationale for shifting over time to an FF system to ensure future viability of social insurance benefits. On the other hand, in developing economies with a vast labour pool, PAYG should be more viable. Yet developing countries in Asia have by and large opted for an FF system. Countries such as Singapore, Malaysia, India and Sri Lanka have operated individual account-based provident funds.

[3]Social contracts refer to the conceptual arrangement between society and the working population underlying a PAYG system. Today's earning generation pays a payroll tax in the expectation that they will receive benefits in the future from payments or contributions made by workers of subsequent generations.

### 15.3.2 Country Experiences

While PAYG tends to build up small, if any, surpluses, an FF system comprises a combination of contractual savings[4] and insurance coverage and has the potential to mobilize significant resources. Historically, the provident funds of Asian economies have done so, and governments, such as in India and Sri Lanka, typically legislated a requirement that the surpluses of these funds be invested mainly in government securities. Though it could be argued favourably that the funds were being used for financing economic development, nevertheless, government securities typically yield low rates of return even though they may be riskless.

Indeed, provident fund investments may not be entirely riskless either. In Singapore, provident fund contributions are allowed to be withdrawn after a specified period by contributors for purchasing either government-built or private housing. This has enabled 85 per cent of the population to purchase property. Early studies typically assessed this to be a perspicacious development policy. Later there emerged a different view, however, that retirees may be wealthy in terms of the valuation of their assets, but were cash-poor and tended to have insufficient retirement insurance coverage. There was also a continuing worry of the possible decline in property values brought on by the contagion effects of a number of global recessions. Thus, provident funds have attracted critical attention in terms of their opportunity costs.

It is worth mentioning Chile's experience with privatizing its social security system, which is now based on individual accounts. Due to a careful investment policy, at first it experienced continuing, stable and high returns but privatization has not been a panacea for solving all problems relating to the use of payroll taxes. Investment of the funds, managed by a private body, has been open to the volatility of the international capital markets, with no underlying guarantee by the government that a minimum coverage would be provided if investments did not yield the expected returns. In sum, privatized systems can meet only limited objectives even if they may steer clear of the type of challenges brought on by population changes in the PAYG system.

The need for payroll taxes continues to hold. The basis—a PAYG or FF system—has to be selected according to the particular needs of a society. Both systems have advantages and disadvantages, and both have come under stress and strains. Therefore, the system must be designed carefully to reflect the needs of that particular society. Privatization is not necessarily a solution to every systemic difficulty. Problems may need to be solved by appropriately modifying existing systems.

---

[4]Individuals save in designated accounts with contributions into those accounts also made by government.

## 15.4 Wealth Taxation

### 15.4.1 Alternative Means of Taxing the Well-Off

We are by now familiar with the issue of taxing the well-off in the context of the personal income tax. The taxation of high-income individuals is an issue of how to achieve equity and, more particularly, vertical equity. The marginal tax rate structure of the income tax is one method of achieving that objective. However, the achievement of vertical equity has to be based on better utilization of other taxes as well, such as property taxes, non-wage taxes, surcharge or surtax[5] on the super-rich and minimum income taxes. Such taxes should also add to horizontal equity by pooling together more effectively various sources of income at any particular income level.[6]

Following the Haig-Simons tradition, as we saw, equity is evaluated on the basis of ability to pay, which is operationalized by using a measure of comprehensive income. Such evaluation could be attempted through other approaches that modify the original concept by, for example (1) examining the net benefits to a taxpayer by bringing in the expenditure side of the budget and assessing vertical equity in that context, (2) assessing vertical equity over a lifetime and finding that taxes may be more progressive than might appear by looking at any single year or limited period and (3) recognizing wealth—the present value of the income stream—as a better measure of the ability to pay on which vertical equity should be assessed.

### 15.4.2 A Minimum Tax

There are some alternative tax bases on incomes that can be easier to administer than the usually more complex income tax. They could also offer a more equitable base for the taxation of high income earners.

The concern that self-employed business owners and professionals who can be classified as well-off—as well as some companies—typically escape appropriate taxation, led some Latin American countries to impose a minimum tax on them. The usual base of the tax was gross assets, with a tax rate that varied between 1–2 per cent. Mexico was quite successful in using this tax to raise revenue from the targeted taxpayers. More countries could design and implement a minimum tax on gross assets to raise the revenue-raising capacity of the income tax. Some policy experts have cautioned against its possible deleterious long-run effects on asset growth and, therefore, on economic growth. If that is a fear, the tax could be conceived as a bridge towards enhancing equity.

---

[5]A rate that is imposed on the highest marginal income tax rate.

[6]It is not possible to achieve vertical equity without having designed a tax system that is horizontally equitable. The concern over high income earners relates at least in part to the tax treatment of high wage and salary earners versus the professionals who could flexibly manage their 'benefits packages'. There has been some success in recent years toward taxation of non-wage fringe benefits.

Other bases for a minimum tax can be net worth or physical assets, but their bases tend to be narrow and require higher tax rates to generate the same revenue. In sectors in which assets may not be large, such as services, gross receipts may be used as the base. India's minimum tax applies to companies and its base is defined as their book profits in yet another variation and comprises the subject matter of Chap. 20.

Over the last decades, OECD countries have used variations of gross income as an alternative base for a minimum income tax. The decline in their high marginal tax rates attracted considerable attention because of their almost universal nature. Perhaps to recapture some of the top income earners who escaped adequate taxation—mainly because of wide-ranging allowances—schedular minimum taxes were increasingly being imposed on them.[7] In 1986, Denmark introduced a 12 per cent supplementary tax on 'personal income' (roughly, gross income minus income from capital) applicable above a threshold. In 1989, Norway adopted the 'top tax'—so termed since it was applicable at very high incomes—at 8.5 per cent on gross income.

In its 1986 Tax Reform Act, the United States introduced an alternative minimum tax. Higher-income taxpayers were required to pay the greater of 21 per cent of their gross income or the normal rate applied to their taxable income. Canada has similar provisions.

### 15.4.3 Presumptive Taxation

In the presumptive methods for income tax, the government may assign a presumed income to taxpayers on the basis of their standard of living, the value of the houses in which they live, and the value of the cars they drive, among other criteria. The tax authorities may also try to estimate, for example the value added of a business on the basis of sales statistics or on the basis of other criteria (number of employees, floor space, electricity use). In France, presumptive taxation—the forfeit system—has had a long history. While presumptive taxation is not generally considered for the taxation of the well-off, it could presumably play a useful role in the prevailing global environment of tax avoidance. However, if applied to high income levels, it would have to be carefully designed and justified in order to be accepted at the legislative stage.

[7] A schedular tax structure uses different tax rates for different sources of income, instead of pooling all sources and applying a single rate structure.

### 15.4.4 The Case of India

#### 15.4.4.1 Rs. 1400 Flat Tax[8]

In 1992 a flat tax of Rs. 1400 was introduced under section 115K of the Income Tax Act on small businesses but repealed in the Union Budget of 1997.[9] It was voluntary to opt for the scheme.[10] It taxed retail traders under an explicit presumption of taxable income earned at 7 per cent of the existing turnover threshold of Rs. 0.5 million (that is, at Rs. 35,000). A trader was not taxed below this threshold. At the prevailing income tax rates, this worked out to a tax liability of Rs. 1400. Subsequently, it simply became fixed and flat at Rs. 1400. It was expected that taxpayers would opt for it despite possible higher tax to be paid because of a lower compliance burden since they would not be subjected to the conventional assessment process.

The stipulated income was steadily raised from its initial level of Rs. 35,000 to keep pace with increases in the taxable income threshold, to Rs. 47,000 in 1995. The occupational coverage of the scheme was also widened. Income up to Rs. 5000 from financial assets or sources such as manufacturing not covered by section 115K, was taxed at 20 per cent. Higher income from such sources was not eligible for the scheme. The turnover ceiling was increased from Rs. 0.5 million to Rs. 0.6 million in the central government's annual 1995 budget.

A difficulty with the scheme was less the small numbers opting for it, than the lack of any reference point on the basis of which compliance could be enforced other than through conventional accounts-based self-declaration. It failed to help generate any listing of potential assessees.[11] Essentially, the tax called for voluntary compliance that did not fructify in the medium term as revealed in its poor revenue yield. The general conclusion was that it pursued the small when the big continued to evade the tax net. Its abolition was not surprising therefore.

#### 15.4.4.2 Tax on Agriculture Holdings

In 1972, a committee of the Indian government[12] was asked to analyse the possibilities of taxing agricultural wealth and income to raise resources for development, reduce economic disparities, and use existing resources more efficiently. The committee recommended replacing the states' land revenue levy with a progressive schedular agricultural holdings tax (AHT) on agricultural income. Its base would include income from livestock, fisheries, poultry and dairy farming. The recommendations were not accepted by the states. The state of Haryana implemented a tax but its version was quite different from the structure recommended by the committee.

[8]See Rajaraman (1996), Chap. 11.

[9]Average exchange rate in 1991-1992, £ 1 = Rs. 43.51 (Rs. 1400 = £ 32.18).

[10]See Government of India (1997), Appendix II.

[11]The same challenge existed in similar voluntary schemes introduced later for construction contractors and truck owners introduced in 1994 (Sections 44 AD and AE).

[12]Taxation of Agricultural Wealth and Income (commonly referred to as the Raj Committee).

## 15.5 Capital Taxes—Capital Gains and Interest

Between the well-off and the less well-off, the former receive a higher proportion of income from capital than from labour. Thus, it is important to bring capital income comprehensively into the tax net. To this end, the well-off tend to be taxed not only on the basis of their ownership of property, but also when they dispose of their property either through gifts, sales or bequests. Capital gains commonly comprise a source of income that is taxed with the equity objective. Capital is, however, more mobile than labour, adding to the ability of the well-off to move out of a high-tax environment in an increasingly globalised world. Consequently, capital gains tend to be taxed at lower rates than are other sources of income. Adequate taxation of capital is not a straightforward proposition unless appropriately harmonised and based on international exchange of information among tax authorities.

The well-off also account for a high proportion of interest-yielding savings. Thus, the taxation of interest should be carefully designed, for example through a withholding tax or tax deduction at source (TDS) (See Sect. 15.8). However, if it is a 'final' tax that is not required to be aggregated with other incomes in the annual income tax return, it could imply that it will be taxed at a lower rate than at the potential marginal rate for aggregate income. That would be deleterious for maintaining equity.

Further, withholding taxes only on selected interest-bearing deposits might result in some distortion in the particular forms in which savings are maintained that, in turn, could distort the allocation of resources. Such efficiency considerations have to be borne in mind together with equity objectives when designing a system of taxing interest from different sources. Taxation of interest and capital gains is considered in some detail in Chap. 16.

## 15.6 Property Tax

### 15.6.1 Rationale

Property is a heterogeneous entity comprising real, financial and hybrid components and each one demands different considerations for identifying the tax base and applying respective tax rates. In this section, we consider real property.[13] Historically, taxes on land and other property have featured among the oldest forms of

[13]Intangible property comprises life interests and annuities, personal effects, businesses and shares, as well as bequests of these items in the form of gift or inheritance. Taxing the value—rather than the income—of this category of property has yielded little revenue in developing countries, tending in fact to clutter the tax system. Even in advanced economies, they have given rise to other challenges such as 'generation-skipping', whereby bequests are made only to grandchildren to minimize the estate duty on bequests. Or, as in the United Kingdom, tax design may direct the bequest to be completed seven years before demise so that, in essence, there has to be assumed predictability of one's death. Such round-about, if not convoluted, tax design is best avoided.

taxation. They have been justified on grounds of both the benefit and the ability-to-pay principles since government provides benefits in the form of law and order enabling the maintenance of property rights, while the ownership of property indicates the ability to pay. Forms of property taxation include taxes based on rental value, capital value or land value.

Property tax is usually assigned to the local—urban municipal and rural village[14]—level. A good local tax is one whose burden cannot be exported elsewhere from a local jurisdiction. The property tax fits this bill well. To the extent that a local government provides law and order and maintains property rights, revenue from the tax is earmarked for such expenditures at the local level. Concerns for national security are expectedly assigned to higher level government.

But there are practical problems associated with the tax that has to be transcended. First, an accurate assessment of 'fair market rental' or 'fair market value' is often difficult, since they are usually based on elusive concepts such as income generation capacity, or on the value of comparable properties, or whether it is owner occupied or not. Second, voluntary assessments of property value tend to be declared at lower than market value thereby depleting the tax base. Third, while a low, flat tax rate is better in terms of tax compliance and is easier to administer, if assessments of value are low, it would necessarily result in a high tax rate. Fourth, to mitigate the problem, even progressive tax rates may be stipulated but there would be clustering of declared value under each threshold.

Fifth, the lack of adequate cadastral surveys has been given as a lagging application of a meaningful tax on property in many developing economies. However, this argument may have been somewhat exaggerated. To arrive at a practical solution, it may have to be accepted that older properties built earlier than a beginning date would have to remain under a low presumptive rate structure—perhaps beginning with a zero rate—in a manner comparable to excluding certain taxpayers below a threshold for the income tax or the GST. But it should be applied without exception for other cohorts of property owners.

The treatment of land and agriculture deserves separate mention because of the special treatment commonly accorded to this sector for tax purposes. While land revenue based on the size of property or produce from land, comprised the oldest source of revenue from a property-based tax, the importance of tax based on agriculture or land area has declined in terms of revenue since it is likely to fail to keep up with land value adequately and is likely to be inelastic in inflationary times. In addition, agricultural property tends to be given special consideration in its valuation for taxation to subsidize 'a way of life'. For example, the market value of agricultural property may be stipulated at a small proportion of market value, and differential consideration may be accorded if the property is inherited as opposed to being received as a gift or transfer. Some countries exempt agricultural property altogether.

[14]*Panchayat* is the village level in India.

Such special treatments could lead to a rupture in horizontal and vertical equity. What is needed is to examine the situation of those who receive special treatment and the extent to which the removal of such treatment would affect their cash flow adversely enough to affect basic livelihoods. The maintenance of comparable treatment for tax purposes for both agricultural and non-agricultural land also needs consideration. To the extent that non-agricultural business properties or their transfers are not taxed, it could be argued that commercial agricultural property should also not be taxed. The maintenance of neutrality in this sensitive area of taxation assumes great importance in advanced and developing economies alike.

### 15.6.2 Country Experiences

A review of country experiences reveals an array of global practices. In the United States, rural and urban local governments fund themselves and have been relatively successful in using the property tax as their primary source of revenue. Indeed, those that cannot, tend to languish in terms of quality of publicly provided schools or country roads. In Brazil, urban localities collect their own property tax, while the federal government collects it for rural counties. Many urban municipal corporations, especially large ones such as the city of Sao Paulo have been quite successful in their efforts. The success reflects reasonable tax rates—0.5 per cent to 0.7 per cent—on a tax base that uses sales value. In a modern economy such as Sao Paulo, the real estate market is organized enough to report correct sales value for registration purposes that can in turn be used for the tax base.

In general, Latin American experience shows relatively low use of property taxation despite their middle-income status, with higher-level governments finding a solution through expenditure sharing with lower-level governments. Comparatively, selected Asian countries have used this tax more intensively by undertaking reform in this area. For example, Taiwan made early progress by successfully implementing a tax on the increases in property values. Singapore and Korea also made steady progress by placing property taxes with local jurisdictions, introducing strong legislation and using robust implementation methods. Thailand initiated cadastral surveys of urban areas for reforming property taxation. Though progress had been slow, the pace picked up with urban modernisation.

Property taxation should not be relegated to being merely a long-term issue. Countries with urban cadastral surveys can implement the tax seriously by realistically updating the assessed values of properties, for example using a construction sector price index. Those countries that do not have an urban cadastral survey could start with the capital city and extend it to smaller cities. Surveys could be based on property values in blocks of cities and towns and the tax imposed at a very low tax rate to obviate overtaxing. As far as rural properties are concerned, property registrations tend to exist in several countries that could be used as an information base for taxation.

### 15.6.3 The Case of India

In India, the determination of property values and rates recommended by tax experts and accepted by the executive branch of municipal governments were not universally accepted by the judiciary in the early stages of reform in the 1980s. It preferred grandfathering the base and tax rate structure reflecting the absence of cadastral surveys in older parts of the cities.

More recently, city governments such as Bangalore, Chennai, Kolkata and others have computerised valuation and tax returns and offered discounts for early payment. Such actions have revived the role and adequacy of the property tax in various urban areas which has become a crucial source of financing the maintenance of urban economic infrastructure and urban renewal projects. Admittedly, upper-level governments may not always have adequate financing for transfers to municipalities and *panchayats* for requisite purposes despite the requirement to do so as per the 73rd and 74th Amendments to the Indian Constitution, as mentioned in Chap. 12, Sect. 12.7. In such a scenario, the importance of revenue from property taxation cannot be exaggerated.

## 15.7 Estate, Inheritance and Gift Taxes

### 15.7.1 Rationale and Challenges

There are three types of taxes in this category:

(1) Estate taxes are levied on the estate of a deceased person.
(2) Inheritance taxes are levied on those who receive the property of a deceased person.
(3) Gift taxes are levied either on the donor or donee for a property that is transferred before death.[15]

The inheritance tax reflects a social as well as an economic philosophy.[16] The objectives of the tax include limiting one's right to transfer accumulated wealth at one's death or on bequests acquired without 'own effort'. It establishes a final point to capture accumulated capital stock as a tax base while reducing disincentives for saving and investment during one's lifetime.

A gift tax typically generates little revenue. Its base is often eroded by large exemptions and undervaluation. Tax avoidance is practiced by 'generation skipping' whereby a bequest is left to grandchildren to minimize the number of times an estate

[15]These categories appear in McGee (2004).

[16]Historically, it was more common for the United States, United Kingdom and Commonwealth countries to apply estate taxes, whereas European countries applied inheritance taxes. See Musgrave and Musgrave (1989) for details.

changes hand. Rates can be progressive with three or four rates found in several countries. This tends to lead to parcelling of estates. Valuation problems arise from the heterogeneity of properties such as life insurance, annuities, personal effects and shares that are not easy to bring to a common denominator of measurement. A further issue is the timing of valuation, which has to be determined as the fair market value at the date of transfer or the date of death.

### 15.7.2 The Case of India

In India, the Inheritance and Estate Tax was abolished with effect from 1985. Inheritances have not been taxed since. Gifts were originally taxed under the Gift Tax Act of 1958. It was a donor-based tax in which gifts were taxed in the hands of the donor at a flat rate of 30 per cent with a basic exemption of Rs. 30,000. The Gift Tax Act was also repealed with effect from October 1998. Neither the donor nor the recipient was required to pay tax after that on gifts given or received.[17] Taxation of gifts was reintroduced in the 2004 central government budget with effect from 1 April 2005. Its objective was tax base expansion. The second Gift Tax was donee-based rather than donor-based, that is income from gifts was taxable in the hands of the recipient. To quote,

> Initially, only individuals and Hindu Undivided Families (HUFs) were covered within the ambit of taxation under the Income Tax Act concerning gifts. The scope has widened enough to cover all 'persons'[18] who are in receipt of specified gifts above the prescribed threshold limits. Exemptions have been carved out for certain specified categories of persons / recipients from the purview of taxation from gifts. Companies under certain specified schemes of reorganization too have been exempted from the above incidence of tax.[19]

## 15.8 Withholding Taxes or Tax Deduction at Source

### 15.8.1 Rationale and Practice

If the 1960s and 1970s firmed up the conceptual basis of taxation in the Haig-Simon tradition, the late 1980s (and its subsequent continuation) began to question the feasibility and some of the administrative challenges of the tax structures that emerged from purist objectives of equity, efficiency and stabilisation. Those objectives based on equal tax treatment of equals (horizontal equity) and unequal tax treatment of unequal (vertical equity) as well as of neutral treatment of different economic activities, generally led to a basis of taxation of all income sources of a

[17]See Vasal (2019).

[18]For tax purposes, 'person' includes an individual, HUF, company, firm, an association of persons, a body of individuals, a local authority, an artificial juridical person and others.

[19]See Vasal (2019), op. cit.

taxpayer on which the same progressive rate structure was applied. In other words, all sources of income were to be grouped together irrespective of source, that is globalized, and taxed under the same progressive rate schedule, assuring equity as well as stabilization over the business cycle.

In its implementation, global taxation had to depend on self-declaration of many sources of income. Even after the collection of tax, auditing turned out to be cumbersome and often infeasible. Slowly, withholding taxes (at the source of income) at low rates began to be introduced. Though not final taxes (whose rates, as reflected in the overall progressive tax structure, were higher), withholding taxes assured a minimum tax contribution from various income sources from the formal sector including wages, interest and dividends.

More recently, withholding taxes have been levied at higher rates and as final taxes, mainly for administrative reasons. Conceptually correct global taxation seems to have given way to a more administratively feasible means of taxing major sources of income. An opinion seems to have formed that withholding taxes are able to subject many sources of income—such as not only wages, interest and dividends, but also stock market transactions, payments to small suppliers, foreign remittances and others—to taxation. It was concluded that a wider application of schedular withholding taxes as final taxes could be more revenue productive compared to when such incomes were aggregated in tax returns with all sources of income and a progressive tax structure was applied. In short, withholding, rather than tax returns based on aggregated incomes was increasingly perceived as a better revenue raiser and easier to administer.

Today, withholding as a form of final taxation has become popular for an increasing number of sources of income not only in India but also in many Latin American countries. In such a scenario, a taxpayer would file a return only if a refund is elicited by him. Four important ramifications of final withholding taxes are: (1) tax systems have become more scheduler, that is different sources of income are subjected to different final tax rates; (2) this could have imparted some regressivity to the overall tax structure; (3) the tax withholder or deductor is performing a free service for the government that has to be carried out correctly though often there is no compensation for carrying out this function and (4) administrative feasibility may have taken precedence over a tradition-based design of tax systems.

### 15.8.2 TDS in India

Tax Deduction at Source (TDS) in India has comprised more than a third of income tax collections over recent years. The incomes covered under TDS include salaries, fees for professional or technical services, interest, dividends, rent from real estate, capital gains of non-residents and commissions from insurance and sale of lottery tickets. Winnings from lotteries, horse racing and crossword puzzles are subject to TDS. The repurchase value of mutual funds and government financial instruments, and withdrawal from designated savings schemes for which income tax deduction has been availed are also subject to TDS. Many of them have been applicable since the early 1970s and continue to the present day.[20]

## References

Government of India. 1997. *Tax Policy for the Ninth Five Year Plan (1997–98 to 2001–02)*. Report of the Working Group on Tax Policy. New Delhi: Centax Publications.

McGee, R.W. 2004. Estate, Gift and Inheritance Taxes. In *The Philosophy of Taxation and Public Finance*, 241–243. Boston: Springer.

Musgrave, Richard A., and Peggy B. Musgrave. 1989. *Public Finance in Theory and Practice*. 5th ed. New York: McGraw-Hill.

Rajaraman, Indira. 1996. Presumptive Taxation and Governance. In *Fiscal Policy, Public Policy and Governance*, ed. Parthasarathi Shome, 128–168. New Delhi: National Institute of Public Finance and Policy (NIPFP).

Shome, Parthasarathi, Pawan K. Aggarwal, and Kanwarjit Singh. 1996. Tax Evasion and Tax Administration: A Focus on Tax Deduction at Source. In *Fiscal Policy, Public Policy and Governance*, ed. Parthasarathi Shome, 128–168. New Delhi: NIPFP.

Simons, Henry Calvert. 1938. *Personal Income Taxation: The Definition of Income as a Problem of Fiscal Policy*. Chicago: University of Chicago Press.

Stotsky, Janet. 1995. The Base of the Personal Income Tax. In *Tax Policy Handbook*, ed. Parthasarathi Shome, 121–124. Washington, DC: IMF.

Vasal, Vikas. 2019. How Are Gifts Taxed in India? *Livemint* January 10. https://www.livemint.com/Money/jQoWpAhQxEZOA0KvMnfFkJ/How-are-gifts-taxed-in-India.html.

[20]See Shome et al. (1996), Chap. 10, for an early account of TDS in India.

# 16 Taxation of Income from Interest, Dividends and Capital Gains

## 16.1 Introduction

Interest earnings and dividends earned are comparable for tax purposes in that the taxation of interest and dividends is usually viewed as taxing nothing other than ordinary income. Dividends and interest on selected types of savings may be taxed less than individual income to encourage capital investment and savings. However, such incentives cause inefficiencies by encouraging taxpayers to invest and save in lower-taxed segments that could effectively favour higher-income taxpayers since they tend to have higher capital income.

On the payments side, interest payments may be fully or partially deductible, while dividends paid out may be partly deductible or may not be recognized in the calculation of taxable profits. Tax treatment of earnings that are retained by businesses and do not comprise dividend payments are usually treated differently for tax purposes. Selected country experiences are illustrative.

Taxing capital gains is subject to greater debate and discussion. It is a complex area of income tax design; hence some countries choose to tax it in a scheduler manner, that is independently of the regular income tax schedule. Its rationale, concept and design structure deserve particular attention.[1] These perspectives on the taxation of interest, dividends and capital gains are examined in this chapter.

[1] See Stotsky (1995).



P. Shome, *Taxation History, Theory, Law and Administration*, Springer Texts in Business and Economics, https://doi.org/10.1007/978-3-030-68214-9_16

## 16.2 Issues in the Taxation of Interest

### 16.2.1 Limiting Interest Deduction

Taxation of interest has to be considered not only from the viewpoint of savers but also from the side of borrowers, that is whether and, to what extent, a company's creditors are allowed to deduct such payments from income calculations. But if interest paid on debt by companies is treated for tax purposes more favourably than the tax treatment of dividends they payout, then companies have an incentive to disguise such dividend payments as interest. Thus, interest deductions may be subject to a limit or other restrictions.

Such limits may take different forms. A deduction for loan interest payments may be allowed only if one or more conditions of the following are satisfied: (i) the loan has been incurred for taxable business purposes, (ii) the loan is not from a shareholder, (iii) the loan interest is not considered excessive in light of the company's overall size and nature, (iv) interest is not too high compared to equity investment in the company, a problem termed 'thin capitalization' or others. Thin capitalization occurs, for example when subsidiaries appear to lend too much to a parent company to thin out its taxable income. Also, (v) a subsidiary should appear to pay too much interest to a parent against bank or other guarantees that the latter provides the former.[2]

### 16.2.2 Country Experiences

Countries vary in their approach to address thin capitalization. Belgium and Italy judge it on a case-by-case basis. Australia, Canada, the United States, Spain, France and Japan specify the maximum debt/equity ratio allowable for deduction of interest, for example 1.5:1. Many countries have introduced similar provisions to limit what authorities perceive as tax avoidance.

## 16.3 Taxation of Dividends

### 16.3.1 Dividends Versus Retained Earnings

The theoretical premise of tax incidence would lead one to expect that any tax charged on dividends, whether collected from companies or from dividend earners, must be borne eventually by the latter. An alternative view, however, is that, if collected from a company, the dividend tax may get capitalized in the market value of the company's shares and thus lower its asset value. Indian company executives argued along these lines against a Dividend Distribution Tax (DDT) that was

[2]See King (1995a).

collected from companies, until it was abolished in the central government's annual budget 2020.

In addition, a tax such as the DDT would encourage companies to retain their earnings—making it the preferred source of equity finance for new investment—rather than to give out dividends. If that is so, equity finance in the form of retained earnings will be less costly than the issue of new equity to finance new investments. Further, under a DDT due to higher retained earnings, a company's preference for debt over equity should also diminish.

### 16.3.2 Country Experiences

The treatment of dividends paid by a company varies widely. In Greece, for example dividend payments are deductible in full, on a par with interest payments. In Iceland, Spain and Sweden, a proportion of dividends is deductible from taxable profits. However, in most cases, the payment of dividends does not affect a company's taxable income.

Some form of alleviation from double taxation is needed. Thus, a dividend deduction is one way to alleviate double taxation of distributed profits for, otherwise, the same profits would be effectively taxed in the hands of both companies paying out dividends and dividend recipients. However, other methods are also available to alleviate double taxation. For example, the corporate tax paid on distributed profits could be credited against the shareholder's liability to pay tax on dividends received.

## 16.4 Taxation of Capital Gains

### 16.4.1 Rationale and Concept

A capital gain tax reflects the principle of equity or ability to pay. Conceptually, the definition of comprehensive income should include capital gains on real property and on financial assets such as stocks and shares. However, a question that may be raised is that capital gains comprise changes in the value of capital sources and should be distinguished from capital income which is a flow from those capital sources. This view implies that capital gains are not income and should be taxed differently. In practical terms, there are concerns that a tax on capital gains that is merged with a progressive income tax could have detrimental effects on investment.

Theoretically, capital gains should be taxed as they 'accrue'. In that case, valuation should be done on a continuing basis, as capital acquires additional value but is held on to, and not sold. That would require valuation to be made at appropriate market prices, of all assets of each individual or business, at the end of every period. This would be a formidable, perhaps impossible, task. In addition, taxing capital gains on an accruals basis may result in severe liquidity problems for the individual or business concerned who would need to pay tax without actually having realized any gains. Thus, there is a tendency to tax capital gains when they are realized with the disposal of an asset. Further, if taxed at the point of realization of gains, the generation of cash could more smoothly help meet any tax liability.

Further complexity in capital gains taxation is that the nominally measured capital gains between the acquisition and disposal of capital are a distorted reflection of the real value—after accounting for inflation—of gains that should be ideally included in a comprehensive measure of income and taxed. Thus, a different tax regime may be more appropriate for capital gains than for income.

That does not solve the problem, however. If the tax treatment of income and capital gains is allowed to differ, issues of interpretation may arise as to whether a gain in business value is income or a capital gain. For example, should gains made because of exchange rate changes be treated as income or capital gains, especially if they are not taxable until realized? As a result of such factors, capital gains typically have tax schedules with their own tax rates, thresholds, inflation adjustment, holding periods to 'lock in' investment and rollover provisions. To bring in even more complexity, some countries may treat some gains, for tax purposes, as capital gains under a separate capital gains tax, but other gains as income under the regular income tax.[3]

Thus, capital gains have usually been treated under special provisions in the tax statutes. Some components are often exempted or taxed at lower rates. Gains from owner-occupied residences and government securities tend to be exempted. On the other hand, if gains are made on the sale of assets that were depreciated earlier, the tax system might 'recapture' the depreciation allowances already taken and tax the capital gains as ordinary income.

### 16.4.2 Criteria and Design of Structure

Special provisions are usually incorporated in the tax law when capital gains are taxed at the time of realization. They could be different or similar to those found in the normal income tax.[4] The most common special provisions that are found are:

#### 16.4.2.1 Chargeable Gains

Those arising on the disposal of real property and financial assets, such as company shares.

#### 16.4.2.2 When a Tax Charge Arises

Realisation for tax purposes occurs at the disposal of an asset. However, 'deemed' realisation may also be included, for example transfers through a gift or bequest at death.

[3] See King (1995b).

[4] As in Ireland, Italy and the United Kingdom, among OECD countries.

#### 16.4.2.3 Tax Rates

Usually, rates of capital gains tax are different from those of ordinary income tax.

#### 16.4.2.4 Holding Period Criteria

In many countries, long-term capital gains on assets held for longer periods are more favourably treated than short-term gains because the latter may be interpreted as 'speculative' gains. Some countries may exempt long-term gains altogether, such as India.

#### 16.4.2.5 Capital Losses

Realized capital losses can usually be offset against gains in the same year. Sometimes if they cannot be offset in one year, losses may be allowed to be carried forward or backward. Capital losses may also be allowed to be offset against other forms of income. Such provisions vary by country.

#### 16.4.2.6 Threshold

Realized capital gains of individuals are usually taxed above a certain threshold that may be specified as annual or lifetime. Reflecting where the threshold is set, a lower effective tax rate may result in capital gains than for income. One reason for a threshold is administrative convenience including high cost of assessing capital gains on small assets.[5]

#### 16.4.2.7 Inflation Adjustment

Many countries allow an inflation adjustment from the date of acquisition to sale in their capital gains provisions. A specified inflation index has to be used. This should bring the capital gains from the nominal value to a real value. In practice, inflation adjustment or indexation may give rise to adversarial positions taken between the tax administration and taxpayer due to lower revenue intake after such adjustment.

### 16.4.3 Impact on Taxpayer Behaviour

One consideration of capital gains being taxed at the time of realization is that it can 'lock in' the investor by discouraging him from disposing of the asset and thereby generating a tax charge. However, the tax only gets postponed rather than getting eliminated. The effect gets exacerbated if the taxpayer holds onto the asset until retirement or death, passing any tax to the inheritor. Indeed, the law may exempt the spouse, widow or widower from paying any tax.

Second, allowing generous rollover provisions reduce the effective capital gains tax rate versus income tax, thus worsening the efficiency and equity considerations

[5]Countries that have a 'self-assessment' system such as the United States tend not to apply such a threshold.

of the tax structure, causing adverse reaction to tax, and worsening taxpayer behaviour.

Third, inflation adjustment provisions counter other provisions that exist for countering inflation such as reduced rates for all realised gains, or long-term gains from assets, or partial inclusion of gains in total taxable income.

### 16.4.4 Country Experiences

Individual and corporate income sides are both relevant for capital gains taxation. In the larger OECD economies, a major part of individuals' capital gains comprises gains on company shares, and these gains could compete with dividends earned by individuals as returns from their ownership of corporate equity.

The United States provisions date from 1913 with several subsequent changes. Japan's provisions for long-term capital gains date back to 1946, Denmark's to 1958, Sweden, Portugal, and the United Kingdom's to the 1960s; Canada, France, Ireland and Spain's to the 1970s; and Australia's to the 1980s. In most cases, provisions for short-term capital gains were introduced prior to the provisions for long-term gains.

To conclude, it is clear that countries have a variety of tax treatments for the capital gains or losses that can arise on many different kinds of assets or liabilities. In comparing different countries' tax systems, therefore, not only should their provisions for capital gains taxation be examined, but also how they distinguish capital gains and ordinary income, and what overlap may exist between them in the tax law.

## References

King, John R. 1995a. Debt and Equity Financing. In *Tax Policy Handbook*, ed. Parthasarathi Shome, 158–161. Washington, DC: IMF.

———. 1995b. Taxation of Capital Gains. In *Tax Policy Handbook*, ed. Parthasarathi Shome, 155–158. Washington, DC: IMF.

Stotsky, Janet. 1995. The Base of the Personal Income Tax. In *Tax Policy Handbook*, ed. Parthasarathi Shome, 121–124. Washington, DC: IMF.

# 17 Taxation of Individual Income—India Case Study

## 17.1 Introduction

India's individual or personal income tax has become complex over the years. It comprises various elements and branches thereof including the taxation of payroll or salaries, interest, dividends and capital gains, estate and wealth tax, inheritance and gifts. Some have been repealed. Several of them are linked to other taxes. For example, the tax on dividends has been linked to a tax on securities transactions, and the wealth tax was linked to a minimum tax though at present the wealth tax stands abolished. There also were components of presumptive tax on agricultural holdings several of which have not survived.

Thus, many income-oriented taxes have been experimented with over the decades since the Income-tax Act was introduced in 1961 and implemented from 1962. Several of those experiments did not last, for example, attempts to tax fringe benefits through a tax specifically on them, and a tax on bank transactions to control the black economy had to be repealed reflecting popular demand. In the 2000s, several attempts to reform the income tax into a consolidated direct tax code have not succeeded, more often than not due to the inaction of successive governments. The hope for reform survives, however, in the present day.

## 17.2 Tax on Payroll

The income for tax purposes in India is divided into various heads, one of them being the 'Income under the head Salaries'. Salary income under the Income-tax Act is a broad concept, which includes every kind of payment made by an employer to the employee, including monetary as well as non-monetary facilities. It is defined in the tax law to include wages, allowances, perquisites and retirement benefits such as annuity, pension, gratuity and other similar payments. Commission, fees, benefits or profits in addition to salary, advance salary and leave salary are all included in the salary income. For any payment to be charged to tax as salary income, the existence

 
P. Shome, *Taxation History, Theory, Law and Administration*, Springer Texts in Business and Economics, https://doi.org/10.1007/978-3-030-68214-9_17

of an employer–employee relationship between the people involved is a requisite. The employment can be full-time or part-time.

Salary income is chargeable to tax on 'due basis' or 'receipt basis' whichever is earlier. Once the employee accrues the salary, the liability to pay tax on the same arises. Thus, income from salary taxable during the year consists of the following:

(1) Salary due from the employer (including any former employer) to the taxpayer during the financial year, whether paid or not
(2) Salary paid by the employer (including any former employer) to the taxpayer during the financial year before it became due
(3) Arrear of salary paid by the employer (including any former employer) to the taxpayer during the financial year, if not charged to tax in any earlier year

The law allows for certain allowances and deductions out of the gross salary income to arrive at the net taxable salary income. Further, if the employee pays any professional tax, the same is directly reduced from the salary. Similarly, allowances for house rent (HRA) and leave travel (LTA) are exempt from salary income up to a certain level. These are first included in the gross salary and then deducted at the appropriate level. Exemption of a certain amount concerning perquisites is also allowed from gross salary income.

The place of accrual of the salary is a relevant factor for the taxation of salary income in cross-border situations. In general, salary accrues where the services are rendered even if it is paid outside India. Salary paid by a foreign government to its employee serving in India is taxable under the head Salaries. However, if a citizen of India renders services outside India and receives salary from the Indian government, it would be taxable as salary deemed to have accrued in India.

In the case of tax-free salary paid by an employer to the employee, the income from salary along with the tax thereupon will form part of the income from salary chargeable to the employee. Remuneration, bonus or commission received by a partner from the firm is not taxable under the head Salaries; rather, it would be taxable under the head Business or Profession.

The Indian tax law provides that every employer who is paying salary income to the employee is required to deduct tax from the salary income if it exceeds the basic exemption limit for tax. Therefore, every employer deducts tax at source (TDS) from the employee's salary before crediting the same to the employee's account. The rate of TDS on salary income is not prescribed in the law and depends on the income tax slabs applicable on the taxable income of the employee. The employer is required to calculate the tax liability on the average rate of income tax, which may be defined as the total tax liability divided by the total income of an employee. To arrive at total tax liability for deducting tax on salary, the employer should take into account the tax-saving investments made by the employee.

## 17.3 Taxation of Interest

Interest income in India is taxed under the residuary head of Income from Other Sources. Interest income is added to other incomes of the individual including salary, professional income and capital gains, and tax is paid on the aggregate income at the applicable rate. Interest accumulated in the savings bank account as well as fixed and recurring deposits of individuals is taxable under the head Income from Other Sources. Banks do not apply TDS on savings bank interest, but interest on fixed and recurring deposits attract TDS at the rate prescribed under the law. Tax is deducted on interest income on an accrual basis even though it may not have been paid. Banks are required to deduct tax when interest income from deposits held in all the bank branches put together for an individual is more than Rs. 40,000 in a year.[1]

A 10% rate of TDS for interest payments is generally applied. However, the account holder has to pre-submit to the bank his Permanent Account Number (PAN) which is India's tax identification number. Unless the bank has his PAN, it applies a 20% TDS rate. The law also provides that if the total income of a taxpayer, including interest income, is below the given taxable limit, the taxpayer can avoid TDS on his interest income by submitting a prescribed form[2] to the bank requesting them not to deduct any TDS. These forms must be submitted to the banks at the beginning of the financial year.

The Indian tax law also provides for a specific deduction for interest earned up to Rs 10,000 in a financial year. This deduction is allowed to a resident individual of age 60 years or less on interest income earned from a savings account with a bank, a post office, or a co-operative society carrying on banking business. Resident individuals of more than 60 years of age are allowed a deduction of Rs. 50,000 per annum on both savings and fixed deposit interest. In addition, certain types of interest income such as the interest earned on deposits in India's Public Provident Fund (PPF) account is exempt from tax. The PPF scheme is a long-term investment option that offers tax-free interest and returns on the amount invested.[3] In other words, all deposits made in the PPF are deductible under Section 80C of the Income-tax Act. Furthermore, the accumulated amount and interest thereon are also exempt from tax at the time of withdrawal.

[1]Prior to FY 2019–2020, this threshold was Rs. 10,000. Rupees 100 are UK £ 1 approximately.

[2]Form 15G and Form 15H.

[3]India has opted for no taxation of savings for retirement as they are made, invested or withdrawn for retirement consumption, under an Exempt-Exempt-Exempt (EEE) philosophy of taxation of retirement savings.

## 17.4 Taxation of Dividends

Dividend taxation policy in India has been subject to many changes over the years. Dividend taxation before the financial year (FY) 1958–1959[4] was based on the 'tax imputation method'[5] and dividends were taxed only once in the hands of shareholders. However, the process of grossing up dividend income for shareholders was complicated due to various incentives provided to corporations in the tax system. This single taxation of dividends at the shareholder level was abolished in FY 1959–1960; instead, corporate earnings distributed as dividends were taxed twice, first in the form of corporate tax on earnings, and then as dividend income taxed in the hands of shareholders.

In FY 1997–1998, a dividend distribution tax (DDT) was proposed whereby a 10% tax was levied on corporations distributing dividends out of taxable profit. The dividend income received by shareholders was made exempt from tax. Since there was no tax unless dividends were distributed, DDT indirectly encouraged firms to retain profits to use them for future investments. The introduction of DDT also shifted the responsibility of paying tax on dividends from a larger pool of individual investors to a smaller pool of corporations; therefore, collection of taxes on dividend income became easier for the tax administration.

The system, however, resulted in double taxation at the corporate level for a corporation distributing dividends to its shareholders, as the same profits were subject to the corporate tax and after payment, to the DDT. Further, since DDT was applicable at the corporate level, all shareholders, irrespective of their income category, got taxed at the single DDT rate. This benefited those shareholders who were in higher tax slabs compared to the DDT rate, which was initially 10%, later increased to 12% in 2003, and to 15% in 2007. The 2014 central government budget made a provision to ensure that DDT was deducted from the gross amount paid. From 2016, in addition to DDT paid by the corporations, tax at the rate of 10% of the gross amount of dividends was levied on the recipients of dividends, receiving in excess of Rs 1 million per annum. This in a way resulted in triple taxation of the dividend income, namely, the corporate tax, the DDT and the additional 10% tax on certain recipients.

At the time the DDT was introduced, the tax collection system was perhaps not too efficient so that the collection mechanism under the DDT regime provided a method to overcome any revenue loss by indirectly taxing shareholders at the hands of corporations. However, with time and with the introduction of ICT in banks and in the tax administration, the gaps in the tax collection system have improved.

---

[4]The financial year is 1 April to 31 March.

[5]A dividend imputation tax system aims to avoid double taxation by giving a credit for income tax paid at the corporate level to tax-resident shareholders which they can then use to either offset their own income tax liability or obtain a refund (under certain circumstances) of the income tax paid by the company. On a theoretical level, imputation credits effectively treat company tax payments as a prepayment of shareholder taxation. (Deloitte 2014)

DDT was abolished in India's 2020 central government budget and dividend income from shares and mutual funds became taxable in the hands of the recipient at the applicable income tax rates. Further, it was also provided that tax would be subjected to TDS at a 10% rate if dividends exceeded Rs 5000 in a financial year. All dividend payments are now taxable in the hands of the individual shareholder at his maximum marginal tax rate. Thus, the effective taxation of individuals on dividend income will increase. There is likely to be some impact on corporations also. On account of the removal of their DDT liability, they may pay out higher dividends to their shareholders since they will have more surplus funds for disposal.

## 17.5 Taxation of Capital Gains

Individuals invest in different assets based on their risk appetite and expectations of returns on investment. The assets can be broadly classified into two categories—physical assets such as gold and real estate; and financial assets such as equity, debt and mutual funds. Profits made from the sale or transfer of such capital assets are known as capital gains.

In the Indian tax law, a capital asset is defined as any kind of property held by an individual, such as buildings, lands, bonds, equities, debentures and jewellery. It excludes stock-in-trade, agricultural land and certain specified bonds. Any profit or gain arising from the sale of such capital assets is deemed as capital gains and is charged to tax under the head Capital Gains. The Income-tax Act provides a separate scheme for computation on income under the head Capital Gains. The tax depends on two factors: first, the nature of the capital asset and, second, the period for which it has been held.

The profits arising from the sale of capital assets are classified as Short-Term Capital Gains (STCG) or Long-Term Capital Gains (LTCG) depending on the period for which the capital asset has been held. In general, if a capital asset is held for a period <36 months, the profits arising from its sale are treated as STCG. If held for 36 months or longer, they are categorised as LTCG. However, in the case of listed equity shares and equity-oriented mutual funds,[6] a holding period of 12 months or more qualifies as 'long-term'. From FY 2017–2018, the holding criteria of 36 months was reduced to 24 months for immovable property. This change is, however, not applicable to movable property.

Agricultural land in rural areas in India is not considered a capital asset and therefore, no capital gains tax is charged on its sale. Further, long-term gains arising from the sale of a capital asset are exempt under Sections 54 and 54F of the Income-tax Act if they are invested in the purchase or construction of a house property subject to certain conditions. In addition, Section 54EC provides for the deduction of

[6]Equity-oriented mutual funds are those where the amount invested in equity and equity-related instruments is more than 65%, whereas those holding <65% of corpus in equity are called debt-oriented mutual funds.

long-term capital gains from the income tax base, if such gains are invested in certain long-term bonds issued by government agencies such as the National Highways Authority and the Rural Electrification Corporation. The maximum limit for investing the long-term capital gains in such 54EC bonds is Rs. 5 million.[7]

While STCG arising from the sale of capital assets, such as property, gold and bonds are included in the total income and taxed as per the individual income tax slab rates, LTCG on the sale of capital assets are taxed at 20% (on property and gold) and 10% (on bonds). LTCG on listed equity shares and equity-oriented mutual funds were tax exempted on the condition that the Security Transaction Tax (STT) was paid on such transactions.[8] However, in 2019, the tax on LTCG on equities was reintroduced and any realised gain from equities over and above Rs. 0.1 million in a financial year became chargeable to tax at the rate of 10%. The STCG on listed securities is, however, taxed at a flat 15%. Both short- and long-term capital gains from debt funds are taxed. The STCG on debt mutual funds are added to the income and taxed as per an individual's income tax slab. LTCG on debt mutual funds are taxed at 20% with indexation and 10% without indexation.[9]

The profit on the transfer of capital assets is computed by reducing the cost of acquisition of the capital asset from the total sale consideration. In the case of short-term capital gains from the transfer of capital assets, the cost of acquisition along with other incidental expenses are deducted from the total sale price of the asset. Such incidental expenses include the expenditure that is incurred wholly and exclusively in the transfer of the asset, for example, brokerage or commission in the case of real property. In the case of a transfer of shares or equity, expenses incurred for such transfer, such as broker's commission or demat account fee, may be deducted from the sale proceeds for calculating capital gains. However, payment of STT is not allowed as a deductible expense.

[7]A unit of lakh is often used in India. 1 lakh equals 0.1 million.

[8]STT is a form of financial transaction tax levied on every purchase and sale of securities listed on the recognised stock exchanges in India. STT was introduced in 2004 and is governed by Securities Transaction Tax Act (STT Act). This Act lists the securities transactions on which STT is leviable. The rate of STT is based on the type of security traded and whether the transaction is a purchase or a sale of securities. At the time of introduction of STT, a new section 10(38) was also introduced in the Income-tax Act to exempt income from long-term capital gains of taxpayers who incur STT.

[9]Commodities Transaction Tax (CTT) is a tax similar to STT, levied on transactions made on the domestic commodity derivatives exchanges. CTT was first introduced in 2008–2009 but withdrawn as commodity markets were considered nascent. CTT was reintroduced in 2013–2014. CTT was reintroduced though only on non-agricultural commodity futures at 0.01%. Losses from such transactions can be set off against income from other sources as for STT. In 2015, a revised list of 61 commodities was notified including certain commodities where trading was not taking place. In 2016, transactions in foreign exchange in a recognised international financial centre were exempt from CTT.

Both STT and CTT were conceived to discourage excessive speculation that could be detrimental to market fundamentals. The two taxes together ensure that there is no tax or regulatory arbitrage between the two. Security exchanges and commodity exchanges have been entrusted to collect STT and CTT, respectively, on behalf of the government. See Abraham (2016).

In the case of LTCG, the indexed cost of acquisition along with other incidental expenses is deducted from the total sale consideration realised for the transfer of capital asset for computation of the taxable capital gains. In this case, the indexed cost of acquisition is the cost of acquisition adjusted for inflation and is calculated by applying the Cost Inflation Index (CII) to the purchase price of the asset.

When the sale consideration from a transfer of capital asset is less than its cost of acquisition (whether indexed or not) and expenses on transfer, it results in a capital loss instead of a capital gain. However, the law does not allow any loss under the head Capital Gains to be set off against income from any other head. It can only be set off with income under the head Capital Gains. Long-term capital loss can be set off only against other LTCG, but short-term capital losses are allowed to be set off against both LTCG and STCG.

The law also allows carrying forward of capital loss to future years if the same is not set off against capital gains income in the same year. Both short-term and long-term capital loss can be carried forward for 8 financial years immediately following the financial year in which the loss was first computed.

If a long-term capital loss is incurred on selling shares or equity mutual fund units after 31.3.2018 then the same can be set off against any LTCG, as profits/gains on long-term shares or equity funds are now taxable in excess of Rs. 0.1 million.[10] These losses can also be carried forward for setting off in later years up to 8 years. Prior to 31.03.2018, there was no tax on long-term gains on shares and equity funds; therefore, long-term loss on shares and equity funds were considered as a dead loss, and the same was not allowed to be set off or carried forward.

## 17.6 Wealth Taxation

### 17.6.1 Minimum Tax

A tax on wealth tax is usually imposed on the richer section of the society with the intention of bringing parity amongst the taxpayers. In India, the wealth tax was introduced in 1957 through the Wealth-tax Act, 1957, and eventually abolished in 2015. The 1957 Act was revised in 1993 on the recommendations of a government-appointed committee, which recommended levy of a wealth tax only on such items of wealth that could be regarded as unproductive or such other items whose possession could legitimately be discouraged in social interest. Therefore, only a few specified assets were taken into account for the purpose of computation of taxable net wealth. The wealth tax was, however, abolished in the 2015 central government budget (effective FY 2015–2016) as the cost incurred for collecting the tax exceeded its benefits.

Wealth tax, prior to its abolition, was chargeable on individuals, Hindu Undivided Families (HUFs) and companies based on their residential status. While

[10] This amendment was announced in the central government's 2018 budget.

resident Indians were subject to wealth tax on their global assets, non-residents were taxed on their assets held in India. The basic threshold for chargeability of wealth tax was Rs. 3 million, that is, if the total net wealth on the valuation date (last date of the previous year being March 31) exceeded Rs. 3 million. The tax was leviable at a 1% rate on the amount in excess of this threshold.

The scheme of computation of wealth tax provided for computation of the total net wealth of the taxpayer liable to wealth tax as under:

Total Net Wealth $=$ Value of Assets belonging to the assessee on the valuation date $(+)$ Deemed wealth$(-)$Exempt Assets$(-)$Debts incurred in relation to the assets

The assets chargeable to wealth tax defined in the Wealth-tax Act included any building or land appurtenant thereto whether used for residential/other purposes. However, certain productive real assets such as house allotted by a company to its employee to be used exclusively for residential purposes, house forming part of the stock in trade or occupied for business/professional purpose, property in the nature of commercial establishment or complex, etc. were not included in the definition.

Other forms of assets liable to the wealth tax included motorcars (other than those used for running them on hire or those held as stock in trade); jewellery, bullion, furniture, utensils or other articles made fully/partly of gold, silver, platinum or such precious metals; yachts, boats and aircrafts other than those used for a commercial purpose; urban land situated in the specified area, with certain exclusions; and cash in hand in excess of Rs. 50,000. The wealth-tax law also defined certain deemed assets, which did not legally belong to the individual but were clubbed as his assets for computing his net wealth. These included assets transferred to spouse otherwise than in connection with an agreement to live apart, assets transferred to a person or Association of Persons (AoPs) for the immediate or deferred benefit of assessee or spouse, etc.

Assets exempt from wealth tax and not considered part of wealth for the computation of taxable wealth included items such as property held under trust/for the purpose of charitable/religious purposes and a house or part of house or plot of land not exceeding 50 square metres in area. Debts incurred in relation to the assets were also reduced to arrive at the net taxable wealth of the taxpayer.

The actual collections from the levy of wealth tax were quite nominal, for example, in FY 2011–2012 total collection was less than Rs. 0.8 billion. The number of wealth tax assessees in FY 2011–2012 was only 0.12 million. However, the levy of wealth tax created a significant compliance burden on the taxpayers and administrative burden on the tax administration. The taxpayers were required to get their assets valued every year as per the provisions of the wealth tax rules and for certain assets like jewellery, a valuation report from a registered valuer was required. Tracking of unproductive assets such as jewellery or luxury cars was nevertheless difficult for the tax administration and there was a general belief that many taxpayers under-reported or under-valued their assets.

The almost stagnant collection from wealth tax over the years and disproportionate compliance burden on the taxpayers and administrative burden on the department resulted in its final removal. The loss of revenue to the government on this account was compensated by an additional surcharge levied on high income earning taxpayers. Furthermore, information pertaining to assets, which was hitherto furnished by taxpayers in their wealth tax return, was made part of the income tax return.[11]

## 17.7 Presumptive Tax

### 17.7.1 Rs. 1400 Flat Tax[12]

In 1992, a flat tax of Rs. 1400 was introduced under Section 115 K of the Income-tax Act on small businesses but repealed in the Union Budget of 1997. It was voluntary to opt for the scheme. It taxed retail traders under an explicit presumption of taxable income earned at 7% of the existing turnover threshold of 0.5 million (that is, Rs 35,000, below which a trader was not taxed). At the prevailing income tax rates, this worked out to a tax liability of Rs. 1400. Subsequently, the presumption with respect to turnover was dropped, and the applicability of the scheme was directly stipulated at that level of taxable income at which income tax payable worked out to Rs. 1400. It was expected that taxpayers would opt for it due to a lower compliance burden, despite the possibility that Rs. 1400 may work out to be a higher tax compared to the tax resulting from a conventional assessment stream.

The stipulated income was raised from its initial level of Rs. 35,000 to keep pace with increases in the taxable income threshold, to Rs 47,000 in 1995. The occupational coverage of the scheme was also widened. Income up to Rs. 5000 from financial assets or sources such as manufacturing not covered by Section 115 K was taxed at 20%. Higher incomes from such sources were not eligible for the scheme.

A difficulty with the scheme was not the small taxpayer numbers opting for it, but with the lack of any reference point on the basis of which compliance could be enforced other than through conventional accounts-based self-declaration. In other words, it failed to help generate any listing of potential assessees.[13] Essentially, the tax called for voluntary compliance that did not manifest in the medium term as revealed in its poor revenue yield. It was believed that the scheme pursued the small when the many of the big continued to evade the tax net.

[11]The rationalisation of various taxes does raise a question, however, whether wealth could be asked to be reported in a tax return intended exclusively for the income tax. Indeed, there are other assets that are also asked to be reported in the income tax return such as the Schedule FA for foreign assets.

[12]See Rajaraman (1996), Chap. 11.

[13]The same challenge existed in similar voluntary schemes for construction contractors and truck owners introduced in 1994 (Sections 44 AD and AE).

#### 17.7.1.1 Tax on Agriculture Holdings

In 1972, a Committee on Taxation of Agricultural Wealth and Income (the Raj Committee) was asked to analyse the possibilities of taxing agricultural wealth and income to raise resources for development, reduce economic disparities and use existing resources more efficiently. The committee recommended replacing the states' land revenue levy with a progressive schedular agricultural holdings tax (AHT) on agricultural income. Its base would include income from livestock, fisheries, poultry and dairy farming. The recommendations were not accepted by the states. Haryana implemented a version quite different from the system recommended by the committee.

## 17.8 Property Tax

In India, the determination of property values and rates recommended by tax experts and accepted by the executive branch of municipal governments was not universally accepted by the judiciary in the early stages of reform in the 1980s. It preferred grandfathering the base and tax rate structure reflecting the absence of cadastral surveys in older parts of the cities.

More recently, city governments such as Bangalore, Kolkata and others have computerised valuation and tax returns and offered discounts for early payment. Such actions have revived the role and adequacy of the property tax in various urban areas which has become a crucial source of financing the maintenance of urban economic infrastructure and urban renewal projects. Admittedly, upper-level governments may not always have adequate financing for transfers to municipalities and *panchayats* for requisite purposes despite the requirement to do so as per the 73rd and 74th Amendments to the Indian Constitution, as mentioned in Chap.12, Sect. 12.7.

## 17.9 Estate, Inheritance and Gift Taxes

In India, the Inheritance or Estate Tax was abolished with effect from 1985. Inheritances have not been taxed since. Gifts were originally taxed under the Gift Tax Act of 1958. It was a donor-based tax in which gifts were taxed in the hands of the donor at a flat rate of 30% with a basic exemption of Rs. 30,000. The Gift Tax Act was also repealed with effect from October 1998. Neither the donor nor the recipient was required to pay tax any longer on gifts given or received.[14]

Removal of the Gift Tax resulted in freer transfer of movable and immovable property. Nevertheless, it could not eradicate tax planning, for example the fragmentation of transfers due to the threshold under which there was no tax, and through other means. This could be viewed as legitimate tax mitigation by potential

[14]See Vasal (2019).

taxpayers; nevertheless, taxation of gifts was reintroduced in the Finance Act (No. 2) 2004, with effect from 1 April 2005 to curb what was viewed as tax avoidance by policymakers. The second Gift Tax was donee-based rather than donor-based, that is, income from gifts was taxable in the hands of the recipient. To quote:

> Initially, only individuals and HUFs were covered within the ambit of taxation under the Income Tax Act concerning gifts. The scope has widened enough to cover all 'persons'[15] who are in receipt of specified gifts above the prescribed threshold limits. Exemptions have been carved out for certain specified categories of persons/recipients from the purview of taxation from gifts. Companies under certain specified schemes of reorganization too have been exempted from the above incidence of tax.[16]

## References

Abraham, Rosemary K. 2016. *Commodities Transaction Tax.* Arthapedia. http://www.arthapedia.in/index.php?title=Commodities_Transaction_Tax_(CTT). Accessed 29 Oct 2020.

Deloitte. 2014. Franking Credits—Who Is Right? https://www2.deloitte.com/content/dam/Deloitte/au/Documents/finance/deloitte-au-fas-infrastructure-series-franking-credits-2014.pdf. Accessed 29 Oct 2020.

Rajaraman, Indira. 1996. Presumptive Taxation and Governance. In *Fiscal Policy, Public Policy and Governance*, ed. Parthasarathi Shome, 128–168. New Delhi: National Institute of Public Finance and Policy (NIPFP).

Vasal, Vikas. 2019. *How Are Gifts Taxed in India?* Livemint. https://www.livemint.com/Money/jQoWpAhQxEZOA0KvMnfFkJ/How-are-gifts-taxed-in-India.html. Accessed 29 Oct 2020.

[15]For tax purposes, 'person' includes an individual, HUF, company, firm, an association of persons, a body of individuals, a local authority, an artificial juridical person, and others.

[16]See Vasal (2019), op. cit.

# Corporate Income Tax—Design and Evidence

# 18

## 18.1 Introduction

The corporate income tax has become increasingly complex across the globe. This reflects the complexity in measuring business income, divergence of tax law from accounting law, designing rules to depreciate capital assets or make inflation adjustments to ensure a correct tax base. The financial sector has particular characteristics that render it difficult to be taxed in a congruent manner with other sectors, so that special rules are needed to tax it.

Narrowing of tax base has led countries to legislate different minimum taxes to avert revenue depletion from tax incentives and tax avoidance. Incentives distort equilibrium resource allocation in the economy. Protecting the tax base from becoming too distorted by measuring the marginal effective tax rate becomes a necessity so that subsequent corrective structural improvements can be made.

Other considerations include the relationship between corporate and individual income taxes. Some countries attempt to integrate them. However, most countries tax individuals and corporations separately. Countries have considered alternatives to taxing corporate income such as taxing their cash flow, though the narrowness of the cash-flow tax base has obviated its introduction anywhere.

Therefore, as the business operations of a corporation become more complex with time, the determination of its taxable income also assumes greater complexity. An elaboration of some of these considerations is the subject matter of this chapter.

## 18.2 Taxable Unit, Valuation and Determination of Base

The taxable unit for the corporate income tax reflects the characteristics of the structure of a company or business. In this context, a business is a commercial or industrial activity of an independent nature undertaken for profit. The valuation of assets and liabilities determines its taxable income. First, valuation may use different criteria including economic value, original cost, market value, value to the owner,



P. Shome, *Taxation History, Theory, Law and Administration*, Springer Texts in Business and Economics, https://doi.org/10.1007/978-3-030-68214-9_18

replacement cost or others. Second, assets and liabilities may be designated in nominal or real terms. An incorrect inflation adjustment will measure profits erroneously. Third, cash or accrual basis will affect taxable income as they define the timing of income generation differently.

Fourth, the rules on how to depreciate different assets over their useful lives (the typical methods being the straight-line, declining-balance methods and accelerated depreciation), how to value inventories (the typical methods being last-in-first-out, first-in-first-out and period-average methods), and how to treat exchange rate changes when business assets are designated in a foreign currency, will have implications for a company's balance sheet and income statement. Fifth, the rules on the carry-forward or carry-backward of losses will affect taxable profits and, in association, risk-taking.

A sixth aspect—treatment and provisioning of loan losses—has risen in importance, especially as global economic crises have been appearing with regular frequency—the East Asian crisis of 1997–1998, the global economic crisis of 2007–2009 and the 2020 economic collapse led by a pandemic. This issue pertains, particularly to banks. Receipts associated with the risk of making loans are part of interest receipts and take place through the life of a loan, while loan losses may be concentrated in particular periods, reflecting the nature of business.

As opposed to financial assets, the current value of loans and consumer credit cannot be easily ascertained when disposed of. Some loans may become worthless and uncollectable before maturity. There is some argument, therefore, that it is judicious to allow a tax deduction for setting aside provisions for loan losses on the basis of transparent rules since the tax treatment of provisioning is expected to affect the profile of bank loans and risk-taking by business. Two methods have been used. The charge-off method expends a bad debt only as it becomes wholly or partially worthless. The reserve method sets up a reserve account as an allowance against the eventuality of a bad debt, while all receivables are recorded at face value until they become worthless.

## 18.3 Business and Taxable Income

### 18.3.1 Measuring Business Income in Company Accounts

There are two statements that elaborate the financial position of a business: (1) the balance sheet that shows the business's assets and liabilities at the end of the accounting period, and (2) the income statement or 'profit and loss account' which shows its revenues and expenditures between two consecutive balance sheet dates.[1]

[1] See King (1995) for an elaboration of the concepts.

The net worth of the business is the difference between its assets and liabilities as shown in its balance sheet.[2] The entries are made in the two accounts as a 'double entry'. This implies that the change in the net worth between two balance sheet dates is equal to the amount of profit earned in the interim period shown in the profit and loss account.[3]

Two matters that are crucial are, first, the specification of when an income—or revenue—and an expenditure, are said to arise for the income calculation. Income is measured on an 'accruals' basis, that is as the income arises.[4] Sales revenues are recorded when goods are supplied or an invoice is issued, rather than when cash is received against the invoice. Expenses include the value of assets used up against revenue receipts of the period. Because a capital asset may be used over several periods, its expense has to be spread out over a number of periods during which it is used.

The second matter comprises the valuation of assets in the balance sheet. Business accounts are constructed reflecting the underlying principle of 'value to the owner'.[5] Let us consider the following. There is a series of net earnings that the owner of the asset expects to receive from using it over its life term. When he discounts the series that has a yield from the present day into the future, he receives its 'discounted present value' (DPV). The asset owner will sell the asset only if its current market value exceeds DPV. The higher of the two is called the 'economic value' to him, of the asset. The principle of 'value to the owner' mentioned above would then imply that an asset should be currently valued at the lower of its replacement cost today and its economic value as explained.

In practice, however, accounting systems use simpler methods. For example, they may start with an asset's historical cost and allow for depreciation or amortisation as it appears in the profit and loss account. Some countries experiencing high inflation such as in Latin America may additionally allow an inflation adjustment from the date of acquisition of the asset. Using historical cost may be more transparent than other valuation methods such as replacement cost or value to the owner.

### 18.3.2 Tax Laws and Accounting Practice

Thus, in practical terms income tax laws tend to veer from the concept of comprehensive income but use a definition resembling the 'generally accepted accounting practice' definition that is found in the accounting law or similar practice from an

[2]The balance sheet classifies assets and liabilities as 'monetary' and 'nonmonetary'. The former includes values fixed in nominal terms such as cash, accounts receivable and payable, and borrowing. Examples of the latter include land and buildings, plant and equipment, inventories, and investments in subsidiaries or the shares of other companies.

[3]This equality holds after accounting for the profits distributed to shareholders.

[4]Except for small businesses which may be allowed a simpler treatment.

[5]See Edwards et al. (1987).

existing company act. The relationship between tax law and accounting practice is not congruent. Some countries have achieved substantial uniformity between the two. In others, tax and financial accounting are quite independent. In Germany, company accounts must conform to specific provisions in income tax law. Usually, however, for income tax purposes, accounting prescriptions in the income tax law override published company accounts if there is a conflict, in the calculation of tax liabilities of a business.

### 18.3.3 Country Practices

Most emerging countries have modernised and sharpened their comprehensive financial accounting rules from their past under colonial rule. A different situation occurs in most transition economies where financial accounting rules were designed to adhere to a centrally planned economic structure; thus, they have been undergoing rapid reform which has reduced conceptual conflicts. Nevertheless, the reform of their accounting laws is not sufficient for income tax purposes. Further, usually there are no judicial precedents that could be reliably cited or used. It may be anticipated, therefore, that their tax laws will increasingly specify and clarify accounting rules for income tax purposes—including characterisation and timing rules that were incomplete in their previous laws.[6]

## 18.4 Cash Flow as Tax Base

### 18.4.1 Concepts

Corporate tax legislation is based on a profits base which has become increasingly challenging to define. Further, a tax on profits is subject to wide fluctuations depending on the varying fortunes of companies. As a result, the flow of revenues to the exchequer is disrupted and government has to resort to ad hoc discretionary revenue measures. Such changes in tax laws build up adverse expectations that have a dampening effect on investment. Consequently, some economists have suggested that the complexity of the corporate income tax base be reduced by taxing the company's cash flow instead. As a concept, the base of a cash-flow tax would be relatively simple, comprising:

(all receipts) minus (current plus capital expenditures) per period.
or a variation of it.

By contrast, ideally the corporate income tax base should be:

---

[6]See Burns and Krever (1998), Chap. 16, Vol. 2.

(sales receipts from goods and services, financial incomes, and accrued capital gains) minus (wages, economic depreciation, inventory costs, and real interest), which is more difficult to measure.

Instead, in cash-flow taxation, measurement problems essentially disappear since the concept of economic costing is not used; for example there is no role for capital gains or depreciation in its calculation.

Three variants of cash flow have been suggested as a base for a corporate cash-flow tax (CCFT):

The first is the real (R) base in which the tax base is the net real transactions (the difference between sales and purchases of real goods and services). Here, immediate expensing of capital outlays is allowed, but deductions for interest payments are not.

The second is the real plus financial (RF) base in which the tax base includes, in addition to the R-base, non-equity financial transactions (the difference between borrowing and lending). Here, borrowing and interest received are taxable, while retirement of debt and interest payments are deductible.

The third is the shareholder (S) base in which the net flow from the corporation to shareholders (dividends plus purchases of shares minus issuance of new shares) is taxed. The third variant, so to speak, treats the government as a silent partner in any investment in the sense that a tax occurs only when a net flow to shareholders occurs from which government takes a cut.

The CCFT avoids grappling with the definition of economic depreciation, measuring capital gains, valuing inventories or adjusting for inflation. The three variants have relative advantages and disadvantages. The non-deductibility of interest from the R-base eliminates incentives for debt financing. Its exclusion of financial transactions obviates any need for inflation adjustment. Yet the inclusion of financial transactions gives the RF-base the advantage of a larger base. The S-base is claimed to be administratively simple, but it could lead to prohibitive tax rates due to the narrow tax base implied.

Nevertheless, whichever variant is used, the disadvantage of the cash-flow tax remains the narrowness of its tax base, however, defined, so that the revenue-neutral rate is much higher than the corporate income tax rate. Other problems include an uneven tax profile of a company caused by immediate capital expensing; transitional problems as a result of eliminating interest deductions, leading to windfall losses for indebted firms; and, in practical terms, the fact that the cash-flow tax is not creditable against the corporate income tax payable by foreign investors in their home countries which, at this point in time, makes it impractical in the prevailing backdrop of global taxation.

### 18.4.2 Country Experiences

In practice, no country has introduced the CCFT to replace the corporate income tax, though a few, such as Mexico, base the taxation of small entrepreneurs or the agricultural sector on the cash flow of businesses. Argentina proposed legislation on a modified cash-flow tax, and other Latin American countries also considered it seriously, in the hope that it would perform better than the income tax whose revenues had remained stagnant. However, to date the tax remain unimplemented internationally.

More recently, the United States discussed the cash-flow tax. The Speaker of the US House of Representatives proposed a 'blueprint' in 2016 that combined reduced individual income tax rates with a destination-based cash flow type business tax applicable to businesses. It had several problems in that it was incompatible with the US's obligations with the World Trade Organization (WTO), and was incompatible with the US's tax treaties. Tax experts also pointed out that it would not eliminate tax base erosion and profit shifting abroad (BEPS) that it was hoped to address.[7] The proposed tax rates were low enough to lead to a less progressive tax system and to large revenue losses. While there would be an increasing incentive for US firms to operate in the United States since it would appear as a tax haven while encouraging foreign operators to shift their profits out due to its adverse implications on foreign tax credit in their own countries. Thus, there was broad agreement that changes should be made within the US corporate income tax system itself rather than bringing in cash-flow tax elements.

The Trump administration itself published a one page 'tax reform' outline in 2017 deleting both the cash flow element and the destination-based element of the House blueprint. These changes removed some of the latter's anomalies though, nevertheless, the former would create significant implications for European foreign direct investment (FDI) into the United States and for US FDI into Europe. Eventually, the CIT rate was reduced to 21 percent compared to the EU average of 20.9 per cent.[8] Nevertheless, the controlled foreign company (CFC) rules[9] remained weaker in the United States which encouraged profit shifting from the United States to the EU.[10] This experience should comprise a major lesson for a student of corporate tax reform regarding what may pass off 'reform'. The use of this term has become lose and carries little meaning in the prevailing global tax environment.[11]

[7]See Avi-Yonah and Clausing (2017) for details of the Hose of Representatives package.

[8]See KPMG (2020).

[9]See Chap. 28, Sect. 28.2.11, for the definition of CFCs.

[10]See Avi-Yonah and Mazzoni (2017) for details of the Trump administration package.

[11]See Shome (2018) for a discussion of the fallacies that appear in the use of the term 'reform' since it has become common to use it even when there is little visible element of meaningful reform in a tax package.

## 18.5 Minimum Tax

A more popular tax among tax authorities to complement corporate tax revenue is a minimum tax based on a variety of alternate bases than corporate profits. We examine how the usual corporate tax base tends to get eroded over time and what alternative solutions have been used among tax structures across the world.

### 18.5.1 Erosion of Tax Base

Countries use tax incentives to stimulate domestic and foreign investments in preferred economic activities. They comprise tax rate reductions for priority sectors, tax holidays for a certain number of years, and allowances with fast write-off of investment expenditure such as accelerated depreciation or investment tax credits that allow an investment expense to reduce tax liability. Tax incentives are common despite existing evidence that non-tax factors such as economic and political stability supported by adequate infrastructure and a well-trained or trainable labour force, as well as the existence of natural resources, are likely to be more important in determining the level of investment. Among tax factors, dependability regarding the continuation of a tax structure and a low overall level of taxation are likely to be more attractive to investment than differential tax incentives for selective sectors.

Additionally, tax incentives have efficiency costs since they change the equilibrium allocation of resources. The question is whether the distortions are overwhelmed by any beneficial impact of the re-allocation of resources. However, at least initially, they erode the tax base, create an opportunity for 'tax planning', and tend to benefit short-term investments (for example, during a tax holiday period). Also, only those investors gain who are already earning profits against which a tax incentive may be taken. They also make monitoring and, therefore, tax administration, more difficult. A common experience in emerging economies that use tax incentives widely is that they become an instrument for tax planning, tax avoidance and tax evasion. They have also been observed to enable corruption in the bureaucracy where officials possess the power to dispense incentives.

Nevertheless, tax incentives tend to become wider in scope and much too complicated with time, cluttering the tax system with tax deferrals and exclusions and affecting tax compliance adversely. No matter how streamlined at the outset, the corporate tax acquires many special concessions and provisions over time because the corporate sector constitutes a focused interest group with financial clout and dispensable funds for lobbying. A secondary interest group tends to develop in the form of tax planners skilled in the art of tax minimisation within the framework of what is legally permissible. Profit-making zero tax companies are a worldwide phenomenon.

Revenues also get subdued because of generous depreciation allowances in certain industries that require heavy capital investment, such as mining and oil exploration. Further, those and other sectors may be allowed accelerated rates of depreciation to encourage investment in machinery based on their written down value. Depreciation rates should be determined on the basis of estimated replacement cost that is related to the economic life of the asset and the inflationary increase in the cost of the asset over its life cycle. For administrative ease, however, most assets are lumped together as a block and depreciation is allowed at a general rate. In effect, the depreciation is neither related to the true economic life of the asset nor to the asset-specific inflation in the cost of the asset. Hence error occurs on the generous side, that is depreciation allowance becomes too generous—often substantially greater than the allowance under commercial accounting, resulting in an erosion of the tax base—thus exacerbating the existence of low tax, or zero tax, companies.

Excessive depreciation allowance also results in overcapitalisation. It encourages mergers and amalgamations often not justified on economic grounds. To the extent depreciation allowance provides a tax shield, it distorts private investment behaviour. This is because, if other heads of income and expenditure are not allowed similar accelerated adjustment, inequity is generated between sectors with differences in the intensity of machinery use such as between manufacturing and services.

In some countries, during the 1970s–1980s, the authorities tended to compensate revenue depletion with a higher headline corporate tax rate which led to inequity across companies—those cushioned through incentives and those not so protected. Further, there were efficiency effects because, the higher was the headline rate of tax, the greater was the distortion in business decisions. Therefore, it became increasingly recognised that there was a need to restrict such adverse consequences without sacrificing simplicity. International tax advisers strongly advised against tax incentives. Once cross-country tax authorities began to recognise the reality of little tax revenue collection from capital-intensive activities, many increasingly felt the need to step back from incurring high 'tax expenditures'.[12] Those that did so in Asia and Latin America were able to stem revenue erosion from the deleterious effects of poor tax policy design as well as tax planning by taxpayers.

### 18.5.2 Introduction of a Minimum Alternate Tax

An indirect approach to taxation through presumptive means may succeed where a direct attempt to expunge special concessions may fail. It becomes useful to legislate a Minimum Alternate Tax (MAT) to ensure that businesses or individuals with economic income are obliged to contribute to the exchequer. By improving tax contribution, a MAT enables movement closer to the original intention of the law. A MAT set at the average tax liability line across taxpayers (which is generally lower than the marginal rate of tax) enables to keep the marginal tax rate low. It thus improves efficiency by minimising distortions while improving equity by requiring

[12]'Tax expenditures' is the term used to indicate the loss in tax revenue as a result of tax incentives. The United States initiated an annual calculation, followed by other countries including India.

all companies to pay near the average tax rate and helping eliminate the existence of zero tax companies.

### 18.5.3 International Experience with MAT

A variety of economic bases and methods of calculation has been used to provide presumption of income. For example, certain presumptions are based exclusively on the taxpayers' net wealth or on the value of the assets used in the business. Others are based on the gross receipts of the enterprise. Still others are based on visible signs of wealth.

#### 18.5.3.1 Gross Receipts or Sales-Based MAT

One variation of presumptive taxation that may be used in lieu of the corporate tax on net profits is a tax on gross receipts or sales. Such a tax avoids the difficulties of using sophisticated concepts such as depreciation in calculating net profit. The tax has been found to be effective in terms of revenue yield and ease of administration. Francophone African countries have been pioneers in the establishment of minimum corporate income taxes based on sales or turnover. The tax can be credited against the regular corporate tax, but no refunds may be allowed if the minimum tax exceeds the corporate tax. Sales or turnover is the most easily measurable financial variable for a business and can be made conveniently available to the tax administration. Also, the service sector may have low gross assets but high sales, and a turnover-based MAT may be appropriate for it.

A minimum tax based on gross receipts is equivalent to a simple presumption of income. For example, if the corporate tax rate in a country that applies this system is equal to 40 per cent of net profits and the minimum tax is equal to 1 per cent of gross receipts, authorities are effectively acting as if all corporations earn a minimum net taxable income equal to 2.5 per cent of their gross receipts. As an example, from Latin America, in 1983 Colombia established a general presumption of net income based on gross receipts, applicable to all taxpayers, individual and corporate, except those whose main sources of income were wages and salaries. The law presumed that net income amounts to at least 2 per cent of gross receipts.

The presumptive tax based on gross receipts has the objective of improving taxpayer compliance. In many developing countries, concealment of gross receipts is a favoured method of tax evasion. Presumptions of income based on gross receipts thus affect taxpayers who cannot easily conceal gross receipts, for example middle to large corporations. However, there are associated challenges since all corporations with the same reported turnover pay the same tax. Corporations with genuine losses are treated in the same manner as corporations that artificially reduce their profits by such methods as manipulating transfer prices. Smaller enterprises that have previously concealed a portion of their gross receipts can feel free to continue to do so if the probability to be audited remains low. Thus, the introduction of a presumption of net income based on turnover is of little consequence to them since it would have little material effect on their tax contribution.

#### 18.5.3.2 Wealth-Based MAT

The income tax legislation of several countries includes presumptions of income based on visible signs of wealth. These presumptions apply to individuals. In some countries such as Brazil and Peru, the tax administration is empowered, in somewhat general terms, to presume income higher than those reported by taxpayers on the basis of visible signs of wealth. It is left to the administration to decide which signs of wealth to use and what level of income to attach to them. In other countries including France, Italy and several francophone African countries, presumption based on visible signs of wealth is carefully specified in income tax law. The signs of wealth that must be considered are described and each is assigned an income equivalent. Such signs of wealth usually include the taxpayer's main and secondary residences, the number of domestic servants, automobiles, yachts, private planes and racehorses.

In practice, presumptions based on visible signs of wealth have proved difficult to apply. When they are established in general terms, tax administrators are hard pressed to decide which signs of wealth to use as a basis for the presumption and how to establish the income equivalent of each. In those countries in which both the signs of wealth and their income equivalent have been specified in the statute, the inflexibility of the provisions may lead to ostensible unfairness. Recognising these problems, tax administrations tend to apply these presumptions cautiously and only when additional assessments cannot be supported by regular means. One of the areas in which such presumptions have proved useful is in supporting assessments on illegal incomes, such as those derived from racketeering and drug trafficking.

#### 18.5.3.3 Income-Based MAT

In North America and Europe, some countries such as the United States, Canada, Denmark and Norway have a MAT based on alternative deductions from income. In the United States, the MAT is computed by making certain adjustments by adding back selected tax preferences to income. Generally, this results in fewer deductions than a calculation based on the regular income tax schedule. India bases its MAT on a particular definition of net worth. This version, however, suffers from base erosion since it is easier for businesses to manipulate net worth because of a list of allowable deductions. We will examine the Indian MAT in greater detail in Chap. 20.

#### 18.5.3.4 Assets-Based MAT

An assets-based MAT can use fixed assets or gross assets as base. A fixed asset-based MAT would include land and plant and equipment as its base, but this would discriminate against certain forms of assets and, in particular, against heavy industry, such as shipbuilding and oil exploration which are generally encouraged through generous incentives. Therefore, fixed assets have not been a popular base for the MAT.

A MAT based on gross assets is appealing since economic income could be expected to bear a systematic relationship to assets. Ideally, the base should include cash and securities, receivables, inventories, land and other fixed assets at a depreciated value and intangible assets at an amortised value. The MAT liability is ideally designed to be roughly equal to a taxpayer's income tax liability. If a taxpayer is assumed to earn, say, a 6 per cent return on assets and the corporate income tax rate is 35 per cent, a 2.1 per cent MAT ($35 \times 6/100$) is the equivalent. In the long run, the tax administration may expect to receive the equivalent of 2.1 per cent of gross assets in corporate tax revenues. For this, the MAT should be designed to allow carry forward or backward for several years, with set off allowed against the taxpayer's income tax liability.

This is the same as saying that industries that cannot earn 6 per cent on their gross assets must eventually shift capital to a more productive economic activity that yields a 6 per cent return. This is not feasible in some countries, given their labour laws that prohibit capital owners from closing operations without the government's permission and, instead, requiring them to pay wages even when running at a loss. Economists vary in their views regarding labour market efficiency. Some have been of the view that trade union generated wage rates have enhanced worker welfare. Others have been of the view that the workforce is better-off in the long run where wages are market determined and more are employed. Obviously, it is a political economy choice: either to make labour laws more market friendly or to continue with constrained, higher wage rates at the cost of lower employment.

Several Latin American countries, including Argentina, Colombia, Mexico and Venezuela, have adopted minimum taxes based on a fixed percentage of the gross assets of a business at some point in their recent taxation history.[13] The economic rationale for the gross assets based minimum tax is that investors can expect ex ante to earn a specified average rate of return on their assets. A minimum asset-based levy on corporations or individuals with offset against actual income tax involves presumption by definition since it, as a minimum, carries an efficiency criterion.

A presumptive levy on a company earning rates of return on assets below the minimum presumed, implies an implicit tax on income actuals at a rate higher than the prevailing corporate income tax rate. The implicit tax would increase, the greater is the performance shortfall. In Bolivia, such a tax replaced for a time the corporate income tax, that is it was an exclusive presumption. The tax base varies from gross assets in Argentina to net assets (assets minus debts) in Colombia. The Mexican tax takes a middle position whereby certain debts are deductible. Latin American countries have in general used the MAT as a revenue earner over and above achieving better equity and efficiency in their tax systems.

Some researchers in Brazil have concluded that the MAT was good for improving investment since it would not adversely affect the performance of high-risk, high-return firms.[14] If a MAT has a broad base and a low rate, the interplay of business uncertainty with the MAT tends to play a decisive role in the usefulness of the MAT. Uncertainty over the rate of return is much more likely to be affected by macroeconomic uncertainty, such as from a fiscal imbalance, than by the introduction of a MAT. High-risk firms tend to be high rate-of-return firms, and the latter element

[13]See McLees (1991).

[14]See Estache and Van Wijnbergen (1992).

reduces the impact of a MAT. Thus, a concern that MAT would discriminate against the most innovative but riskiest firms was unwarranted according to this view. Instead, a MAT, etched in a simple tax law, can be an appealing short cut to good revenue intake without affecting efficiency adversely.

Some experts have considered the tax to be unfair because the ex post return will differ from what was originally anticipated by the taxpayer. Moreover, the tax may discourage risky investments under circumstances where it denies the taxpayer the benefits of loss offset[15] in countries that have a large number of sick public sector companies, and institutional and structural rigidities in the economy disallow factory closure or free exit. In particular, public sector companies may be cash strapped and any policy towards their privatisation could be held back. Thus, while a MAT clearly gives a revenue advantage to the tax authorities, its possible deleterious impact on the smooth functioning of the economy cannot be minimised.

## 18.6 Other Methods of Presumptive Taxation

Many developing countries use an array of presumptive methods of taxation—other than the MAT—to ensure revenue performance of the corporate income tax. Presumptive taxation supplements and simplifies available tax administration instruments in generating revenue by helping reduce audit time and cost. Often, they are used to tax small businesses which, in certain economic environments, may represent the majority of enterprises. Such taxpayers may be excused from filing a standard tax declaration and opt for a presumptive method instead.

If used judiciously, presumptive taxation may broaden the tax base by increasing the number of taxpayers and their tax payments. Even if the revenue per taxpayer turns out to be low, it may have spillover benefits in facilitating the movement of small taxpayers from the informal to the formal sector and as a source of information to combat tax evasion. Nevertheless, caution needs to be taken in using presumptive methods. It carries the danger of harassment and extortion of taxpayers by unscrupulous tax officers, and the use of punitive presumptive tax rates to push small taxpayers into self-assessment may backfire by causing taxpayers to go underground.[16]

There are several different ways to levy a presumptive tax. Estimated income, assets, turnover or external indicators of income are all alternatives. The level of economic sophistication influences the choice of presumptive tax methods. A simple approach is to levy a lumpsum tax on all businesses. A more sophisticated approach involves a census of taxpayers and a determination of average profit margins, using objective factors differentiated by activity, based on which presumptive schemes

[15]As explained earlier, this can be mitigated by allowing loss carry forward and background for a generous number of years.

[16]See Shome (1993) who argues that small taxpayers have the potential to generate twenty per cent of total tax revenue if approached and garnered appropriately.

would be developed. Such methods could use indices of profitability, which vary by activity, to determine the taxpayers' incomes.

Nevertheless, such a detailed approach has been criticised because using selected factors to gauge income may move the tax away from approximating a general tax on income. The general principle should be to set the presumptive rate close to the rate on average or normal income. The marginal tax rate on income above this average income being zero, it would avoid the negative incentives associated with high marginal tax rates.

Assessment may be either on an individual or a collective basis. Under the latter, individual taxpayers cannot contest the levy, so that tax administration is simplified. Under the former, taxpayers may be required to submit certain annual figures based on which the administration could assess their net income by applying cost-to-profit ratios. Under the latter approach, taxpayers could also negotiate tax liability and appeal an assessment through the judicial system.

## 18.7 Marginal Effective Tax Rate

The Marginal Effective Tax Rate (METR) represents, in a way, the sum of the distortions created by a corporate income tax. The METR is also defined as the difference between the before-tax rate of return on a marginal investment and the after-tax rate of return on the savings that are used to finance that same marginal unit of investment. Many tax factors affect the METR. These include income tax laws that have an impact on financing operations—debt versus equity—of a firm; whether tax deductions for depreciation compare with true economic depreciation; and the after-tax returns to individual savers who are the suppliers of loanable funds.

Inflation is a non-tax factor that undermines the ability of a firm to recover the real economic cost of using its capital, though this should be weighed against the benefit from any decline in the real value of debt due to inflation. Thus, without indexation, inflation can either increase or decrease the true economic cost of investment. The direction in which inflation will affect the METR is not possible to deduce theoretically, given the two opposite forces at work. METRs tend to vary widely across capital assets and sectors reflecting, for example any favourable tax treatment for investment in preferred sectors such as agriculture, forestry and fishery versus more generous depreciation allowances in manufacturing and service industries.

## 18.8 Integration of Personal and Corporate Income Tax

The issue of integration arises, first, when there is an incentive for an income earner to shift between the two forms of organisation—corporate and individual business—in order to minimise taxation. It is for this reason that the top marginal personal income tax rate is often attempted to be set at the same rate as the corporate income tax rate.

Further, it is sometimes argued that corporations are essentially a conduit through which income flows to individuals and, as such, corporations should perhaps not be taxed at all except as a withholding mechanism for the personal income tax. Since a corporation is merely a legal entity, the rationale for the corporate income tax is that it is easier to tax a corporate entity in the organised sector than taxing an individual, the ultimate income earner, who represents the correct tax collection point. This premise aims at eliminating any double taxation in individual cum corporate income.

Some types of income, such as dividends, are taxed twice, once at the corporate level before they are distributed to individuals, and a second time as individual income. To avoid such double taxation, full or partial relief may be given at either the corporate or the individual level. Indeed, double taxation in the income tax could be thought of conceptually as cascading that occurs in the case of domestic consumption taxation.[17] Various forms may be devised to eliminate or reduce the extent of double taxation. Several countries have adopted at least partly integrated income tax systems.

The 'classical' system, however, prefers not to integrate the two taxes. This is based on several grounds, including the genuine conviction in certain quarters that individuals and corporations are distinct taxable entities. But the philosophical position tends to be complemented by the relative ease of administering a classical system, the possible revenue loss as a result of integration, and a lack of definitive empirical proof that integration would lead to better corporate performance or fewer bankruptcies. Country experiences reveal the adoption of partially integrated or classical systems.[18]

A handful of countries have adhered to the classical system of non-integration, for example the United States. The United States introduced the corporate income tax in 1909 and it was seen as an excise tax that was being imposed on the privilege of the enjoyment of limited liability. Defenders of the classical system argue that it is difficult to establish any direct connection between the benefits enjoyed by corporations in the form of limited liability and the income of a company and, therefore, there is a conceptual argument for corporations to be taxed independent of income.

The United Kingdom too follows a classical system. Expectedly, several Commonwealth countries have classical systems. Any discussion of a shift to integration, as mentioned above, fails to move forward due to the fear of possible revenue loss. The likely favourable effect in the medium term on economic activity and growth with a concomitant positive impact on tax revenue gets lost in the prevailing position.

[17]See Chap. 21, Sect. 21.3, and Chap. 24, Sect. 24.4, for the concept of cascading and how it can occur.

[18]See Chua and King (1995) who weigh the pros and cons of integration and present possible models describing the mechanics of integration.

## 18.9 Taxation of the Financial Sector

In the case of income taxation, the measurement of income of financial institutions relates to the timing of income. They provide services that have an explicit time dimension. The possibility of future receipts or payments is a part of their business activities. A corporate income tax typically applies to business income as it accrues. Yet banks have to set aside funds for bad loans and insurance companies for future payments on policies. Governments often require them to set aside minimum funds that may not necessarily match, and will probably fall below, their actual payment needs. Thus, the extent of tax deductibility becomes an issue. Another problem arises from the intertwined nature of investment and other services provided by financial institutions. Taxpayers typically owe tax on investment income net of costs while costs of services not related to investment income are not deductible. To the extent that financial institutions are not able to separate the two cost components, there may be an understatement of taxable income.

Another problem relates to the separation of return 'on' capital from return 'of' capital. Essentially, the fact that a deposit represents liability and not income, needs to be recognised in the calculation of taxable income. An insurance company's income is derived from premium payments by the insured and investment income. Premium payments may represent both a payment for services and a 'deposit' for investment. Only the former should comprise income since the other component must be returned. In practice, it may be difficult to fully separate the two. In the case of banks, however, deposits can be identified more clearly.

The overall outcome is that the corporate income tax as it exists today in most countries is a complex tax when weighed against how much revenue it fetches and how much manpower and financial resources the tax administration has to allocate for the function. Corporate tax reform, therefore, comprises repeated efforts by tax administrations across the world especially, perhaps, among advanced economies, albeit, often not with much success.

## References


Avi-Yonah, Reuven S., and Kimberly Clausing. 2017. Problems with Destination Based Corporate Taxes and the Ryan Blueprint, University of Michigan Law School. *Columbia Journal of Tax Law* 8 (2): 229–255. https://repository.law.umich.edu/cgi/viewcontent.cgi?article=2846&context=articles.

Avi-Yonah, Reuven S., and Gianluca Mazzoni. 2017. *The Trump Tax Reform Plan: Implications for Europe*. University of Michigan Law & Econ Research Paper No. 17-009, University of Michigan Public Law Research Paper No. 559. https://ssrn.com/abstract=2977370 or https://doi.org/10.2139/ssrn.2977370.

Burns, Lee, and Rick Krever. 1998. Taxation of Income from Business and Investment. In *Tax Law Design and Drafting*, ed. Victor Thuronyi, vol. 2. Washington, DC: IMF.

Chua, Dale, and John R. King. 1995. The Mechanics of Integration. In *Tax Policy Handbook*, ed. Parthasarathi Shome, 151–155. Washington, DC: IMF.

Edwards, Jeremy S.S., John A. Kay, and Colin P. Mayer. 1987. *The Economic Analysis of Accounting Profitability*. Oxford: Clarendon Press.

Estache, Antonio, and Sweder Van Wijnbergen. 1992. *Evaluating the Minimum Asset Tax on Corporations: An Option Pricing Approach*. CEPR Discussion Paper 684. London: Centre for Economic Policy Research.

King, John R. 1995. The Concepts of Business Income and Taxable Income. In *Tax Policy Handbook*, ed. Parthasarathi Shome, 134–136. Washington, DC: IMF.

KPMG. 2020. Corporate Tax Rates Table. https://home.kpmg/xx/en/home/services/tax/tax-tools-and-resources/tax-rates-online/corporate-tax-rates-table.html. Accessed 30 Aug 2020.

McLees, John A. 1991. Fine Tuning the Mexico Assets Tax. *Tax Notes International* 3: 117–120.

Shome, Parthasarathi. 1993. *Taxation of High Income Earners*. IMF Paper on Policy Analysis and Assessment, PPAA/93/19. Washington, DC: IMF. https://www.elibrary.imf.org/doc/IMF003/07344-9781451964578/07344-9781451964578/Other_formats/Source_PDF/07344-9781455235582.pdf.

———. 2018. *Contours and Conflicts in Tax Design: Principles and International Practice*. London School of Economics, LSE Legal Studies Working Paper No. 11/2018. https://ssrn.com/abstract=3199902.

# Corporate Income Tax—India Case Study 19

## 19.1 Introduction

A body corporate is an entity that is a separate and independent legal person from its shareholders. Corporate tax is paid on the net profit made from business by the body corporates that are liable to tax under the Indian income tax law. The income of corporations is taxed at a specific rate prescribed under the Income-tax Act (the law).

Indian as well as foreign companies are liable to pay corporate tax. An Indian company is one which is registered under the Indian Companies Act and also includes corporations established under central or provincial acts. A domestic company includes private as well as public companies. A foreign company is one which is incorporated under the laws of any foreign country.

Companies are taxed on the basis of their residential status. A company is said to be a resident for tax purposes and is liable to tax under the Indian tax law if it is incorporated in India or its place of effective management (POEM) is in India during the relevant fiscal year. POEM means a place where key management and commercial decisions that are necessary for the conduct of business are made in substance.

While a resident company is taxed on its global income, the non-resident company is taxed on Indian income with an Indian nexus that is accrued or received in India. The scope of Indian income is defined under the law. These matters are addressed in this chapter. Deductions, amortisation, maintenance of accounts and audits and presumptive taxation are also examined.

## 19.2 Scheme of Taxation

The tax laws in India provide for taxation of corporate entities as a separate person; and specific income tax return forms for companies are prescribed under the law. The income of a company is classified under different heads of income such as profits earned from the business, capital gains, income from real property and income from other sources such as dividend, interest and others. The aggregate of income under

 
P. Shome, *Taxation History, Theory, Law and Administration*, Springer Texts in Business and Economics, https://doi.org/10.1007/978-3-030-68214-9_19

all the heads after adjustment of intra-head and inter-head set-off of losses and the brought forward losses, if any, is charged to tax as per the rates specified under the law.

The main component of income of a corporate entity is its business income, which arises on account of its business activities. To arrive at the business income, the real nature of transactions needs to be ascertained from general accounting and commercial principles and not merely on the basis of entries made by the company in its books of account. The business income in a company's accounts is measured by reducing from the aggregate receipts the allowable expenses recorded in the books of account. The law allows only certain deductions to be made from the gross receipts to arrive at the business income for tax purposes. Certain adjustments are also required to be made based on the method of accounting while determining the net business income of the company.

The gross receipts reflected in the profit and loss of a company may include capital as well as revenue receipts. The revenue receipts are included in the taxable business profits while the capital receipts are not taxable. Certain revenue receipts may also be specifically exempt under the tax laws. Further, any sum chargeable to tax under capital gains is excluded from the head, business income. The charge to tax is not on gross profits, but on net profits and gains from the business. These profits are computed after allowing all expenses reflecting the ordinal principles of accountancy, unless the law specifically disallows such expenses.

In case a company carries on one business with several branches then the net profits of the business of that company is computed by pooling together the profits earned in all the branches. Similarly, if the entity carries on several businesses, then the profit of each business has to be computed separately and the tax is chargeable on the aggregate of all the businesses carried on by the company and not on every business separately.

## 19.3 Income from Business or Profession

The Indian tax law provides for a specific head of income, namely, Income from Business or Profession, under which income of corporates and businesses, as well as professionals, is taxed. The law provides for a wide definition of business which includes any trade, commerce or manufacture, or any venture in the nature of trade, commerce or manufacture. The definition of profession, which is also inclusive, may be referred to as an occupation requiring either purely intellectual skill or, if manual skill, such skill controlled by the intellectual skill of the operator. Profession includes any vocation which may be referred to as an occupation requiring predominantly manual skills.

Section 28 of the Income-tax Act is the charging section for income under the head business or profession. It specifies that the income chargeable under this head shall be the profits and gains of any business or profession which was carried on by the assessee at any time during the year. The business income also includes certain compensation receipts as well as non-compete payments.[1] The aggregate of all taxable business receipts is reduced by the allowable deductions to arrive at the business income liable to tax under the income tax laws.

## 19.4 Deductions Allowed from Business Income

Income from business under Section 28 of the Income-tax Act is computed after allowing the deductions provided under the law. Generally, any expenditure is allowed as deduction from the business income in the year in which the expenditure is incurred. Any expenditure before set-up of the business or after discontinuance of the business is not allowable. The initial burden to prove that a particular deduction is admissible lies with the taxpayer. The deduction is admissible on the ground of commercial expediency even though there may not be any legal liability to incur any particular expenditure.

The expenditure incurred to earn the income is allowed as deduction but, as a general principle, any expenditure incurred in earning income that is exempted is not allowable as deduction. Further, capital loss such as that arising due to depreciation in the value of an investment is not deductible. Trading loss is, however, allowed. The entries in the books of account may be relevant, but not the determinative factor to decide the admissibility of a claim.

The law provides for allowance of expenses in respect of assets deployed for the business, for example rent, and taxes in respect of the premises used for the purposes of business or profession are allowable. Also, the amount paid on account of current repairs, that is repairs that are attended to when the need for them arises and which are not allowed to be accumulated, is allowable as deduction. For computing business profits, most of the capital expenditure is not allowed as deduction as benefits of this kind of expenditure are distributed over a long period of time and allowing deduction for the same out of income of any one period would not reflect the correct taxable income. Further, the fixed assets deployed for business are subject to wear and tear and obsolescence and they have to be replaced over a period of time.

The concept of depreciation allowance under the tax law, which is a notional expenditure at a fixed rate on the actual cost of the assets, takes care of such expenses, which occur over a period of time. The deduction on account of depreciation gives the true picture of the profits of business of the entity. For the purposes of depreciation under the law, the assets are classified as tangible and intangible assets.

The rates of depreciation of different classes of assets are provided in the depreciation schedule under the Income-tax Rules. The depreciation is allowable as a fixed percentage of the Written Down Value (WDV) of the block of assets as per

[1]Non-compete payments refer to 'any sum received or receivable under an agreement for not sharing any know how, patent, copyright, trade mark, licence, franchise or any other business or commercial right of similar nature or information or technique likely to assist in the manufacture or processing of goods or provision for services and is chargeable to tax as business income' (Taxmann 2016–17).

the Rules. The block of assets is defined in the law and means a class of assets comprising tangible assets which include building, machinery, plant and furniture, and intangible assets which include know-how, patent, copyright, trademark, licence or any other business or commercial rights of a similar nature.

Ownership of the asset is a prerequisite for claiming depreciation allowance. Thus, depreciation allowance can only be allowed if the taxpayer is the owner of the asset, wholly or partly. Further, depreciation is allowable only if the asset is used for the purpose of the business or profession during the relevant financial year, though usage throughout the year is not necessary.

## 19.5 Expenditure on Scientific Research

'Scientific research' as defined in the law means any activity for the extension of knowledge in the fields of natural or applied science including agriculture, animal husbandry or fisheries. The references to scientific research expenditure include all expenditure incurred for pursuing, or the provision of facilities for pursuing scientific research, but does not include expenditure incurred for acquisition of rights in, or arising out of scientific research. The law provides for weighted deduction for certain expenditure incurred on scientific research related to the business. For example, the amount paid by an assessee to a research association (which has the object of undertaking scientific research); or the amount paid to a university, college or other institution to be used for scientific research, entails a weighted deduction at the rate of 175% of the amount paid. Similarly, the amount paid to a research association (which has the object of undertaking research in social science or statistical research); also amount paid to a university, college or other institution to be used for research in social science or statistical research entails a deduction of 125% of the amount paid. Further, the amount paid to a designated national laboratory or university or Indian Institute of Technology (IIT), an advanced institute of higher learning in engineering with several branches all over India, with a specific direction that the sum shall be used for scientific research undertaken under an approved programme, entails a 200% deduction. Further, where a company, engaged in the business of biotechnology, or business of manufacture or production of any article incurs expenditure on scientific research on approved in-house research and development facility, a 200% deduction of such expenditure is allowed.

## 19.6 Amortisation of Certain Preliminary Expenses

Normally any expenditure incurred before the commencement of business is not allowable as deduction under the law. However, Section 35D makes a departure from it and specifically provides for amortisation of expenditure in respect of some preliminary expenses, and such expenditure is allowed as deduction in instalments over a period of time. This deduction is available to an Indian company or any other resident taxpayer and includes expenditure on preparation of feasibility report or conducting a market survey for any business. In case of companies, preliminary expenses may include legal fees for drafting of Memorandum of Association (MoA) or Article of Association (AoA), fee for registering the company, printing and advertisement of prospectus for public subscription of shares etc. Deduction on such specified expenses is allowable in five equal instalments beginning from the year when business has commenced or production has commenced in the new unit, as the case may be.

## 19.7 Deductions Allowed on Actual Payment

India's Supreme Court has in its judgment[2] held that any statutory liability was allowable in the year in which it had arisen even if the liability was disputed by the taxpayer. Similarly, the deduction on account of Provident Fund, Superannuation Fund and other pension funds was allowable on the basis of provision alone. As such, many instances came to light where, even if the actual contribution to the funds were delayed, the deductions for such payments were allowed in the year of provision. To ensure that such statutory payments were not delayed, a Section 43B was inserted in the law with effect from 1st April 1984.

This is a restrictive provision, which allows for certain deductions only on the basis of actual payment either during the relevant financial year or within the due date of the filing of the return of income of the relevant year. The expenditure covered by this section should be allowable as per normal accounting principles and other provisions of the law, and the section cannot make any non-deductible expenditure as deductible.[3] Therefore this section has an overriding effect and applies to a deduction otherwise allowable. The items of expenditure covered under this section include tax, duty, cess or fee payable under any law; contribution to the funds maintained for the welfare of the employees like Provident Fund, Superannuation Fund & Gratuity Fund; bonus or commission payable by the employer to the employees; and interest on loans and advances from scheduled banks and cooperative banks.

[2]In the case of Kedarnath Jute Mfg. Co. Ltd. vs. CIT. 83 ITR 363 (1971).

[3]The expenditure under this section, although allowed on payment basis, should be otherwise allowable under the provisions of the law. For example, expenditure such as interest payment or PF payment should not be allowed only because it is covered under this section. It should be first allowable under the head of business income based on it being an expenditure incurred for earning the income. The condition of actual payment being made is above the basic condition of allowability of expenditure.

## 19.8 Other Deductions from Business Income

Section 36 of the Income-tax Act lists out the deductions that are allowed for computation of business income of the taxpayer. These include the premium paid in respect of insurance against risk of damage or destruction of stocks or stores used for purposes of business or profession, health of employees, keyman insurance policy premium for a partner of a firm, directors of company and other key personnel. Bonus and commission paid to employees are also allowed as a deduction if they would not have been paid as dividends or profits.

The section also provides for deduction of interest on borrowed capital on payment basis. Further, the number of bad debts written off from the books of account can be claimed as deduction if the bad debt is incidental to the business and had been taken into account while computing the income[4]. However, this shall not include any provision created for the same. Provision for bad debts in case of banks and certain financial institutions such as scheduled banks, primary agriculture credit society, primary cooperative agriculture bank, and rural development bank is allowed as a deduction subject to a specified limit.

The deductions under Section 36 also include profit from an eligible business transferred to a special reserve created by certain entities such as housing finance companies capped at a maximum prescribed limit. But if the amount transferred to this reserve is withdrawn, the same is treated as business income in the year of withdrawal. The deductions also include expenses incurred by a company for the purpose of promoting family planning among employees.

Further, the amount paid as Securities Transaction Tax (STT) on taxable security transactions is allowed as a deduction provided the income from which the tax was extracted was included as business income, and these transactions had been entered into in the course of business. This implies that dealers in stock markets and businesses who undertake trading are eligible for this deduction. Similarly, the amount paid as Commodities Transaction Tax (CTT) on taxable commodity transactions is allowed as deduction provided the income relating to this tax had been included as business income. This deduction is for commodity brokers and dealers.[5]

Section 37 provides for a general deduction out of business income provided the expenditure incurred is not covered under any other specific provision. The general principle for allowability of such expenditure is that the same should have been laid out or expended wholly and exclusively for the purposes of the business. The expenditure should have been incurred in the previous year and should be in respect of the business, the profits of which are to be computed and assessed. The

[4]Note that debts are primarily receivables and on accrual basis included in the income. This implies that only those debts, if declared bad, can be allowed as a deduction if earlier they were included in the income on accrual basis. Thus, the deduction for bad debts written off can be allowed only if it had been included in the business income.

[5]For descriptions of STT and CTT, see Chap. 17, Sect. 17.5.

expenditure claimed should not be in the nature of capital expenditure or in the nature of personal expenses. Further, any outgoing with the right of the taxpayer to receive it back cannot be claimed as deduction under this general provision.

The law further stipulates that any expenditure with respect to a purpose, which is an offence or prohibited by law, is not allowable. Finance Act 2014 introduced an explanation to the section specifying that any expenditure on the activities relating to corporate social responsibility referred to in Section 135 of the Companies Act, 2013, shall not be deemed to be for the purposes of business or profession and, therefore, does not comprise an allowable deduction under the Income-tax Act.

Expenditure of an earlier year, which is ascertained during the current year, is allowable in the current year. Further, in case the taxpayer follows a cash system of accounting, actual payment is necessary to be incurred. However, for mercantile or accrual system of accounting, the expenditure can be claimed as deduction on both paid or payable basis.

## 19.9 Deductions Not Allowed from Business Income

The explanation for why capital expenditure is generally deductible even though it may be for the purpose of business lies in the very nature of a capital expenditure, which connotes permanency. The acquisition of an asset is intended to be of lasting value and represents expenditure which gives rise to the benefit of enduring value. Capital expenditure must result in an expansion in the source of income through an expansion or addition to the profit-making apparatus.

Expenditure for acquisition of know-how, patent, copyright or trademark, useful for a substantially long period is also capital in nature. If the expenditure is incurred merely in facilitating the conduct of the business more efficiently without changing the fixed assets, it is revenue expenditure even if the benefit is extended through years. The nature of the expenditure in most cases, however, has to be decided based on the facts and circumstances of the case.

Personal expenditures such as expenses incurred for the maintenance of the family and on the maintenance of car, telephone and other amenities used for personal purposes are also not allowed as a deduction from business income, even though sometimes they are debited in the books of account of the company.

Capital loss is not allowable as deduction out of business income. However, trading losses are allowed as deduction, provided the loss is real and not notional, that is it should have actually arisen and not merely anticipated, and it must arise from carrying out a business operation, or must be incidental to that. Moreover, to claim a loss from business income, there should not be any specific prohibition in the law against the deductibility of such loss.

## 19.10 Maintenance and Audit of Accounts

The taxpayer under consideration being a firm or company, its true business income is determined on the basis of books of accounts maintained in the regular course of business. The law specifically provides for maintenance of accounts by certain persons engaged in business or profession. Section 44AA of the Act provides that the persons engaged in certain professions, such as legal, medical, engineering, accountancy, film artist and so on, shall maintain such books of account and documents as to enable the computation of their total income as per the Act. The maintenance of books of account is compulsory in case the turnover is above a certain threshold. Failure to maintain books of account attracts penalty under the law.

The law mandates audit of accounts in specified cases to arrive at true business income of the taxpayer. Section 44AB provides that the following persons are required to get their accounts audited:

- Those carrying on business when total sales or turnover or gross receipts exceeds Rs. 10 million.[6]
- Those carrying on profession with gross receipts exceeding Rs. 5 million.
- Those engaged in specific businesses referred in Sections 44AE (plying, hiring and leasing of goods carriages), 44BB (exploration of mineral oil) and 44BBB (foreign companies engaged in the business of civil construction in certain turnkey projects) that are taxed on a presumptive basis, when income shown by the assessee is lower than what is presumed on the basis of those sections.
- Those engaged in businesses referred in Section 44AD when income shown by the assessee is lower than what is presumed in the said section, and income of the assessee is above the maximum exemption limit.

Failure to get the books of accounts audited as per the relevant provisions may attract penalty under the law.

## 19.11 Presumptive Taxation Scheme

To give relief to small taxpayers from the tedious work of maintenance of books of accounts and getting them audited, the law provides for presumptive taxation under Sections 44AD, 44ADA and 44AE of the Act. Any person adopting the presumptive

[6]Rs. 10 million equals approximately UK £ 0.1 million. With effect from Assessment Year 2020–2021 (Financial Year 2019–2020), the threshold limit for tax audit under Section 44AB (a) for a person carrying on business has been increased from Rs. 10 million to Rs. 50 million in cases where the aggregate cash receipts and aggregate cash payments made during the year does not exceed 5 per cent of total receipt and total payment, respectively. In other words, more than 95 per cent of the business transactions should be carried out through banking channels in order to avoid tax audit.

taxation scheme can declare income at a prescribed rate and does not require to maintain books of account.

The presumptive taxation under Section 44AD can be availed by a resident individual, Hindu Undivided Family (HUF) and partnership firm engaged in any business other than those of plying, hiring or leasing of goods carriages. Certain persons such as those carrying on profession as referred to in Section 44AA, carrying on any agency business or earning income in the nature of commission or brokerage are not allowed to avail presumptive taxation scheme under this section. To avail the scheme, the total turnover or gross receipts for the year should not exceed Rs. 20 million. The presumptive income computed at the rate of 8 per cent[7] of the turnover or gross receipts of the eligible business is the final taxable income and no further expenses are allowed. A person opting for this presumptive scheme is required to follow the same scheme for the next five years.

Section 44AE of the Act provides for presumptive taxation for small taxpayers engaged in the business of plying, hiring or leasing of goods carriages and is applicable to every person including an individual, HUF, firm and company. The presumptive income under this section, which is applicable to a taxpayer owning 10 or lesser number of goods vehicles, is computed at the rate of Rs. 1000 per ton or Rs. 7500 per goods vehicle per month. The income computed on presumptive basis is the final and no further expenses are allowed.

The presumptive taxation under Section 44ADA is applicable to resident individuals, HUFs and partnership firms engaged in specified profession such as legal, medical, engineering or architectural, accountancy, technical consultancy, interior decoration or any other profession notified by the Central Board of Direct Taxes (CBDT). The benefit of this section can be availed only by those specified professionals whose annual gross receipts are under Rs. 5 million. The income of a person opting for taxation under this scheme is computed at the rate of 50% of the gross receipts of the profession. The balance 50% is deemed to have been allowed towards all the business expenses and no further expenses are allowed. A person can, however, declare income at lower rate, that is less than 50%, and if he does so, then he is required to maintain the books of account and has to get them audited as per the relevant provisions of the law.

## Reference

Taxmann. 2016–17. *Taxation of Non-compete Fees and Exclusivity Rights in Case of Profession.* https://www.taxmann.com/budget-2016-17/budget/samd313/memorandum.aspx. Accessed 23 Sep 2020.

[7]To promote digital transactions and to encourage small unorganized business accept digital payments, Section 44AD has been amended with effect from the assessment year 2017–2018 to provide that income shall be computed at the rate of 6% instead of 8% if the turnover/gross receipt is received by account payee cheque or account payee bank draft or by use of electronic clearing system through a bank account or through prescribed electronic modes.

# 20 Minimum Alternate Tax—India Case Study

## 20.1 Introduction

India's corporation income tax has been beset with tax incentives that reduce the tax base, adversely affect neutrality in the tax system and reallocate resources between industry sectors and commerce. They also reduce revenue collection as is evident in the government's annual calculations of revenue loss from tax incentives in its annual budget, an exercise that began in 2006. Continuing depletion of the revenue base generated an early interest in a minimum alternate tax (MAT) in India. In this chapter, we study the emergence, trajectory and behaviour of the Indian MAT. MAT was introduced in 1987, while an AMT was introduced in 2012 on entities other than companies.

The MAT itself underwent many changes including removal and rate changes. Its time series relationship with the corporation income tax is estimated and analysed. While the chapter shows in some detail how the Indian MAT has to be calculated by a taxpayer, it also proposes an alternative MAT base that combines a stock and a flow concept, that is an asset and an income combination. That would amplify the minimum revenue contribution behind a MAT by closing possible gaps that enable taxpayers to minimise their revenue contribution to the corporation income tax.

## 20.2 Emergence and Trajectory of Indian MAT

An Advisory Group on Tax Policy and Tax Administration for the Tenth Five Year Plan[1] found that, in Assessment Year (AY) 2000–2001,[2] in a sample of 1816 companies, 1293 profit-making companies had a final tax liability of 25.95 per

[1]See Government of India (2001).

[2]In India, AY follows one year after a financial year (FY) since the former denotes the year when tax assessments are carried out.



P. Shome, *Taxation History, Theory, Law and Administration*, Springer Texts in Business and Economics, https://doi.org/10.1007/978-3-030-68214-9_20

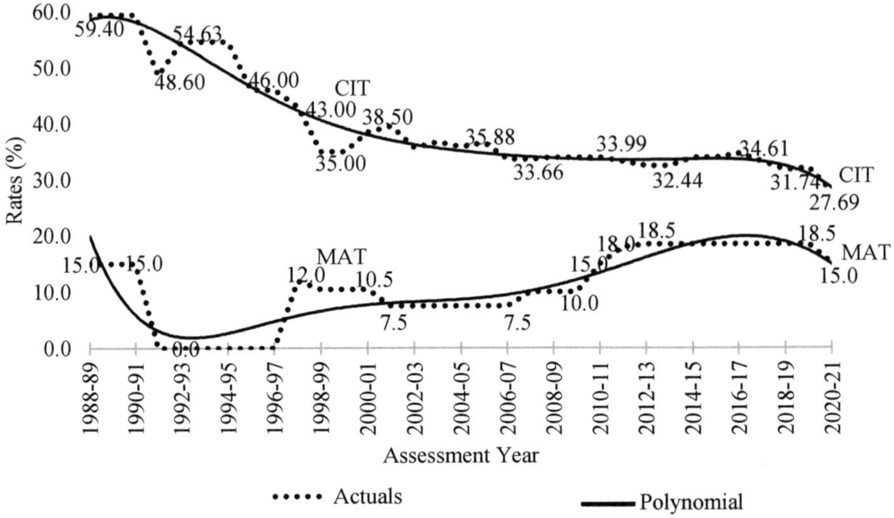


**Fig. 20.1** CIT-MAT: Rates over time. (Source: Author's calculations)

cent of the profits before tax in contrast to a statutory corporate tax rate of 38.5 per cent. Consequently, a minimum tax contribution against the corporate income tax has been used to improve the effective tax rate, the argument being attractive from both a revenue and a neutrality point of view.

A Minimum Alternate Tax (MAT) was first introduced as Section 115J within the scheme of the corporation income tax by Finance Act, 1987, and has, since then, played an important role as an instrument to ensure revenue collection. It should therefore be studied with a focus on its positive and negative elements while playing its role. Appendix 1 demonstrates the method of calculating the current MAT.

An Alternate Minimum Tax (AMT) with a different scope was also introduced in 2012 (see Appendix 2). Essentially, while the MAT is applicable to an assessee which is a company, the AMT is applicable to persons other than a company. The MAT is computed on the book profit, that is net profits as per books after making specified adjustments. The AMT is computed on the adjusted total income, that is total income as increased by specified deductions that are disallowed under the AMT. In what follows, this chapter will elaborate further on these aspects.

Note that the prevailing MAT has arrived at its current structure after a long journey over time. To reveal that journey, Fig. 20.1 illustrates the trajectories of both corporation income tax (CIT) and MAT rates from AY 1988–1989 to date[3], revealing the variability of both over time. The CIT rates shown include a surcharge and

[3]Finance Act, 1987, would be applicable from FY 1987–1988 or AY 1988–1989.

cess levied on the CIT rate, thus making the composite CIT rate different from the specified headline rate.[4]

Against a background of a 50 per cent CIT rate, the MAT rate at its appearance was fixed at 15 per cent of book profit. Book profit was defined as commercial profits subject to specified adjustments as explained in Appendix Table 20.2. However, after a brief life, the provision was deleted in Finance Act, 1990, ostensibly for the reason that a large number of incentives including the earlier prevailing investment allowance had already been withdrawn from the statute, thereby diminishing the necessity for a minimum tax.[5]

With the withdrawal of the MAT in 1990, the phenomenon of zero tax companies continued and, in 1996, the MAT was re-introduced at a rate of 12 percent through Section 115JA through Finance Act, 1996. The base was larger than the one in the erstwhile provision inasmuch as profits comprising foreign exchange earnings were not exempted. However, under pressure from business interest groups, they were exempted in the subsequent year. In addition, a provision was introduced for carry forward, comprising:

> a set off of (the excess of MAT liability over 'actual' liability) against (any excess of 'actual' liability over MAT liability) in the subsequent five years.

The law on MAT was again amended by Finance Act, 2000 through a new Section 115JB, which provided for a minimum tax of 7.5 per cent of book profit in the background of the then prevailing CIT rate of 38.5 per cent. Section 115JB made a conceptual departure from Section 115JA for the tax. In Section 115JA, if the total income of an assessee company was $<30$ per cent of its book profit, the tax base would comprise 30 per cent of such book profit. On the other hand, Section 115JB provided that, where the income tax payable on the company's total income was $<7.5$ per cent of its book profit, the tax payable would be 7.5 per cent of such book profit. Also, once the tax liability was determined on that basis, it would be increased by the surcharge.

These changes, together with an increase in the dividend distribution tax (DDT) through the 2000 central government budget from 10 per cent to 20 per cent, would alter the calculation of the Advisory Group's sample analysis mentioned above, to yield an increase in the effective tax rate to 28.15 per cent of profits before tax.

The rate of MAT remained at 7.5 per cent of book profits up to AY 2006–2007. The MAT was increased to 10 per cent while the CIT rate was reduced to 33.66 per cent in AY 2007–2008. The MAT rate was increased to 15 per cent in AY 2010–2011. It was increased further to 18 per cent in AY 2011–2012, and again to 18.5 per cent in AY 2012–2013. It remained at that rate until AY 2019–2020, and was reduced to 15 per cent from AY 2020–2021. This was done against a

[4]One convenience from the central government's point of view is that revenue from these surcharges does not have to be shared with state governments.

[5]See Government of India (1997) for a full discussion of the evolution of the early MAT.

considerable reduction in the main CIT rate, which was reduced to an average of 27.69 per cent (Fig. 20.1).[6]

What becomes clear from the above-described account elaborated through Appendix Table 20.3 is the volatility with which both CIT and MAT structures have been changed. This experience is further elaborated below.

## 20.3 Relationship Between CIT and MAT Rates

Since the MAT is a tax presumably imposed to collect unintended lost revenue from the CIT, it should be expected that when the CIT rate rises, so should the MAT rate, and vice versa. For example, when the CIT rate declines, the government should expect a lower revenue by leaving more resources in the hands of taxpayers. Accordingly, a lower MAT would be sufficient to garner close to the new, lower, expected CIT revenue. Nevertheless, as Fig. 20.1 reveals, as the CIT rates fell over time, the MAT rate increased by and large (except in the most recent years). This indicates an approach of collecting revenue in an indirect way, thereby defeating the objective of reducing the headline CIT rate to encourage industry.

The relationship between the CIT and MAT rates becomes clearer through a regression to test whether the CIT rate has any ramifications for the MAT rate. This is shown in Table 20.1, revealing a coefficient of −0.32, that is, almost one-third of a change in the MAT rate may be explained through a change in the CIT rate and that relationship is negative. And, as explained in the footnotes to Table 20.1, the estimate is robust so that it can be safely concluded that, as the CIT rate has declined over the years, the MAT rate has been increased possibly to stall some of the anticipated revenue loss, contrary to correct tax policy as already explained.

Unfortunately, the MAT suffers from additional structural defects. As already indicated, the increase in the average rate of MAT over the years has gone contrary to the decrease in the CIT rate. Further, the expansion of its coverage of Special Economic Zones (SEZ) has, in effect, abrogated any 'grandfathering' of tax incentives[7] in the application of MAT. This is because, though the broadening of coverage could perhaps be justified legally, SEZs, which came into being through the 2006 SEZ Act, were covered under the MAT retrospectively from 1 April 2012 that, in turn, led to uncertainty in the productive industrial sector in terms of past and future business plans. This has gone against the concept of a 'social contract' generally understood to prevail between the taxpayer and government.[8]

[6]Appendix Table 20.3 shows the details of rate differences for various categories.

[7]Grandfathering would assure that a change in tax law will come into effect only after the stipulated length of period of applicability of a tax incentive has expired.

[8]See Chap. 6, Sect. 6.3, Chap. 13, Sect. 13.6 and Chap. 28, Sect. 28.4, to revisit the deleterious ramifications of retrospective tax law.

**Table 20.1** MAT-CIT regression results

| | Independent variable: CIT | |
|---|---|---|
| Dependent variable: MAT | *c* | *b* |
| Coefficients[a] | 23.80 | −0.32 |
| 95 % Confidence Interval[b] | [14.95 32.65] | [−0.54 −0.11] |
| Standard error[c] | 4.35 | 0.11 |
| *t*-statistic[d] | 5.48 | −3.02 |
| *p*-value[e] | 0.00 | 0.00 |
| *R*-square[f] | 0.22 | |

Source: Author's calculations

Linear Regression Equation: MAT = $c + b$. CIT

[a]Coefficient for an independent variable measures the effect that variable has on the dependent variable, and its sign (positive or negative) gives the direction of the effect

[b]95% confidence interval of a coefficient gives a range within which the coefficient value falls. We can be 95% confident that the coefficient value falls within the shown range

[c]Standard error (standard deviation) is a measure of the coefficient's precision

[d]t-statistic = (coefficient/standard error). The larger the t-statistic, the more accurate the coefficient

[e]$p$ indicates probability of (un)reliability. $p \leq 0.05$ implies that the coefficient is statistically significant

[f]$R$-squared indicates the fraction (of variation) of the dependent variable accounted for by independent variables used in the regression estimation

## 20.4 Widening of MAT Base

A better designed MAT could curb some of the limitations that MAT has experienced over the years. Below, an alternative for broadening the MAT base is proposed, combining net worth with dividends distributed, and moving away from the prevailing MAT base of book profits. It is taken from an existing proposal from two decades back but not yet taken up by successive governments.

### 20.4.1 Defining the MAT Base

Rather than taking policy action only by increasing the MAT rate and intermittent expansion in the base at the margin, the above-mentioned Advisory Group recommended a considerable widening of the MAT base by using a mix of stock and flow concepts. This was because, experience revealed that, book profit, despite the definition in the statute, was being manipulated insofar as it was amenable to accounting practices. It recommended that the MAT base should provide a plausible estimate of the taxable capacity of the company, reflected comprehensively in the ability to earn, and allowing it to successfully average out its ability to pay over time.

The base to which the minimum tax would apply must, therefore, be something other than reported commercial profits. For example, total assets, fixed assets, total sales or net worth are possible alternatives. Of these, net worth was conceptually the closest to that of income, but was narrow in base and subject to possible manipulation. And it was argued that a minimum tax based on sales would discriminate against services while one based on total assets would work against heavy industry including steel and aluminium, and the financial sector including banks.

The variability of any one measure as a MAT base on its effects across sectors suggested that the definition of the base should be widened. A combination of both stock and flow components could comprise such a measure, one option being a combination of gross assets and sales/turnover. If this was not immediately feasible, a second-best option for the base could be a combination of a percentage of net worth plus a percentage of the dividend distributed. This combination could be argued to be both economically efficient and equitable. It would be efficient as in the case of the gross assets tax due to its link to the minimum presumed rate of return on the owner's capital. That is, the greater is the performance shortfall of a company, the greater is the excess of the implicit tax rate on actual income over the prevailing corporate tax rate. Second, it was equitable in that there would be little likelihood of a company escaping tax in comparison with other companies.

### 20.4.2 Neutrality of Wider MAT Base

The MAT could be allowed to be carried forward for set off against future liability in excess of the minimum tax. If the design provides for offset against MAT payable in years other than the current year, it serves three functions. First, it provides protection against the charge that the levy is unrelated to the ability to pay. Second, it mitigates the severity of the levy since it would provide relief in difficult business years. Third, it provides an incentive for the accurate reporting of returns even in years where actuals exceed the minimum threshold because of the feature of averaging over the years. Therefore, the method is also inter-temporally efficient.

The Advisory Group's proposed base would be efficient since, first, it would be neutral between retained earnings and dividend distribution. To the extent dividends are distributed, they suffer a higher rate of tax in the year of distribution. In the proposed base, if the company chose to retain its earnings it would still end up paying tax on it since it would result in an accretion to net worth. Even though the tax on net worth could be low, the discounted future liability would be almost equivalent to the current liability on dividends. Thus, both consumption and unproductive savings would be penalised.

In general, since depreciation is an allowable deduction in the computation of taxable income, the company benefits from the tax shield that depreciation provides. Given the higher use of capital assets in manufacturing and, therefore, claim for depreciation, compared to the services sector, there is an inherent bias in favour of manufacturing over services. One consequence of the proposed MAT base was that it would ameliorate this bias since the benefit from the tax shield would either be distributed or retained within the company and both would suffer taxation.

The combined measure of stock and flow as a base would be substantially unaffected by inflation. To the extent that the value of net worth is eroded by inflation, the real tax loss is partly compensated by the capital gains tax paid by shareholders. Further, if the assets are revalued periodically, the increase in their value is reflected in an increase in the net worth. If a company chooses otherwise, it will end up paying a substantially larger liability on liquidation.

### 20.4.3 Proposed Alternate MAT Structure

The DDT was abolished for both company and mutual funds through the 2020 central government budget, with a proposal to adopt the classical system instead, wherein dividends are taxed in the hands of the recipients at their applicable slab rates and companies are no longer required to pay DDT. However, TDS will be deducted from dividend recipients on such dividend incomes in excess of Rs. 5,000 per annum at the rate of 10 per cent.[9]

The MAT could be reconstituted as a tax equal to the aggregate of 0.75 per cent of adjusted net worth and 10 per cent of the dividend distributed. The adjusted net worth for tax purposes would be the capital employed by the company. The definition of capital employed would be the same as in s 80J of the Income-tax Act. It would be the average of capital employed as on the first day and the last day of the previous year.[10] As demonstrated by the Advisory Group, the MAT base broadening would lead to additional MAT revenue over and above improving efficiency and equity of the corporation income tax.

An administrative point that affects the acceptability of the MAT is that of its effect on foreign tax credit. This should be corrected when the MAT is reformed. To facilitate MNEs to avail of tax credit in their country of origin, the income tax paid by the company should be allowed to be credited against the MAT liability (rather than the other way around). Correct policy should not suffer merely due to revenue considerations. However, no refund should be granted if the MAT liability is less than the income tax liability.

## Appendix 1: Computation of Minimum Alternate Tax[11]

If the income tax payable on the total income of an assessee, being a company, as computed under the Act for AY 2020–2021[12] or later is less than 15 per cent of the book profit of a company, such book profit shall be deemed to be the total income of the assessee, and the tax payable by the assessee on such total income shall be the amount of income tax at the rate of 15 per cent[13]. SEZs are also covered under MAT

[9]See Agarwal (2020).

[10]This definition of adjusted net worth is administratively attractive.

[11]This is a simplified table for the purpose of broad understanding. For exact provisions for MAT computation, Section 115JB of the Income tax Act, 1961 may be referred to. See Taxguru (2005).

[12]An assessment year AY follows a financial year FY. Thus AY 2020–2021 refers to FY 2019–2020.

[13]Prior to the insertion of the proviso in sub-section (1) of Section 115JB by the Taxation Laws (Amendment) Act w.e.f. 1-4-2020 (i.e., A.Y. 2020–2021 onwards), the rate of MAT was 18.5% for A.Y. 2012–2013 onwards.

from 2012. For a unit located in an international financial services centre [referred to in clause (q) of Section 2 of the Special Economic Zones Act, 2005 (28 of 2005)] deriving its income solely in convertible foreign exchange, MAT shall be applicable at the rate of 9 per cent.

**Table 20.2** Computation of book profit

| | |
|---|---|
| **Net profit** | *Net profit as per the profit and loss account for the relevant previous year in accordance with the provisions of Schedule III to the Companies Act, 2013 (18 of 2013)*[a] |
| **Increase:** [b] | |
| (a)[c] | Amount of income tax paid or payable and the provision therefore |
| (b) | Amounts carried to any reserves, by whatever name called, other than a 'reserve' specified under s 33AC (for shipping business) |
| (c) | Amounts set aside to provisions made for meeting liabilities other than ascertained liabilities |
| (d) | Amount by way of provision for losses of subsidiary companies |
| (e) | Amounts of dividends paid or proposed |
| (f) | Amounts of expenditure relatable to exempt income [any income to which Section 10 (other than the provisions contained in clause (38) thereof) or Section 11 or Section 12 apply] |
| (fa) | Amounts of expenditure relatable to income, being share of the assessee in the income of an association of persons or body of individuals on which no income tax is payable [Section 86] |
| (fb)[d] | Amounts of expenditure relatable to income accruing or arising to an assessee, being a foreign company, from (A) the capital gains arising on transactions in securities; or (B) the interest, royalty or fees for technical services chargeable to tax at the rate or rates specified in Chapter XII, if the income tax payable thereon in accordance with the provisions of the Act, other than the provisions of this chapter, is at a rate <15.0% |
| (fc) | Amount representing notional loss on transfer of a capital asset, being share of a special purpose vehicle, to a business trust in exchange of units allotted by the trust referred to in clause (xvii) of s 47 or the amount representing notional loss resulting from any change in carrying amount of said units or the amount of loss on transfer of units referred to in clause (xvii) of Section 47 |
| (fd) | Amounts of expenditure relatable to income by way of royalty in respect of patent chargeable to tax under Section 115BBF |
| (g) | Amount of depreciation |
| (h) | Amount of deferred tax and the provision therefor |
| (i) | Amounts set aside as provision for diminution in the value of any asset |
| (j) | Amount standing in revaluation reserve relating to revalued asset on the retirement or disposal of such asset |
| (k) | Amount of gain on transfer of units referred to in clause (xvii) of Section 47 computed by taking into account the cost of the shares exchanged with units referred to in the said clause or the carrying amount of the shares at the time of exchange where such shares are carried at a value other than the cost through statement of profit and loss, as the case may be |

(continued)

**Table 20.2** (continued)

| **Reduce:** | |
|---|---|
| (i) | Amount withdrawn from any reserve or provision, if any such amount is credited to the profit and loss account |
| (ii) | Amount of exempt income<br>[to which any of the provisions of Section 10 {other than the provisions contained in clause (38)} thereof or Section 11 or Section 12 apply, if any such amount is credited to the profit and loss account] |
| (iia) | Amount of depreciation debited to the profit and loss account (excluding the depreciation on account of revaluation of assets) |
| (iib) | Amount withdrawn from revaluation reserve and credited to the profit and loss account, to the extent it does not exceed the amount of depreciation on account of revaluation of assets |
| (iic) | Amount of income, being the share of the assessee in the income of an association of persons or body of individuals, on which no income tax is payable in accordance with the provisions of Section 86, if any, such amount is credited to the statement of profit and loss |
| (iid)[d] | Amount of income accruing or arising to an assessee, being a foreign company, from (A) the capital gains arising on transactions in securities; or (B) the interest, royalty or fees for technical services chargeable to tax at the rate or rates specified in Chapter XII, if such income is credited to the statement of profit and loss and the income tax payable thereon in accordance with the provisions of this Act, other than the provisions of this chapter, is at a rate $<15.0\%$ |
| (iie) | Amount representing,—(A) notional gain on transfer of a capital asset, being share of a special purpose vehicle to a business trust in exchange of units allotted by that trust referred to in clause (xvii) of Section 47; or (B) notional gain resulting from any change in carrying amount of said units; or (C) gain on transfer of units referred to in clause (xvii) of Section 47, if any, credited to the statement of profit and loss |
| (iif) | Amount of loss on transfer of units referred to in clause (xvii) of Section 47 computed by taking into account the cost of the shares exchanged with units referred to in the said clause or the carrying amount of the shares at the time of exchange where such shares are carried at a value other than the cost through statement of profit and loss, as the case may be |
| (iig) | Amount of income by way of royalty in respect of patent chargeable to tax under Section 115BBF |
| (iih)[e] | Aggregate amount of unabsorbed depreciation and loss brought forward in case of a—<br>(A) company, and its subsidiary and the subsidiary of such subsidiary, where, the Tribunal, on an application moved by the Central Government under Section 241 of the Companies Act, 2013 (18 of 2013) has suspended the Board of Directors of such company and has appointed new directors who are nominated by the Central Government under Section 242 of the said Act<br>(B) company against whom an application for corporate insolvency resolution process has been admitted by the Adjudicating Authority under Section 7 or Section 9 or Section 10 of the Insolvency and Bankruptcy Code, 2016 (31 of 2016) |
| (iii) | Amount of loss brought forward or unabsorbed depreciation, whichever is less as per books of account[b] |
| (iv) to (vi) | Profits eligible for deduction under Sections 80HHC/80HHE/80HHF—Omitted |

(continued)

**Table 20.2** (continued)

| | |
|---|---|
| (vii) | Amount of profits of sick industrial company |
| (viii) | Amount of deferred tax, if any such amount is credited to the profit and loss account |

The provisions are not applicable to: (A) A foreign company (i) resident of a country with which India has a DTAA and the assessee does not have a permanent establishment in India in accordance with the provisions of such agreement, or (ii) resident of a country with which India does not have a DTAA and the company is not required to seek registration under any law relating to companies. (B) A foreign company, where its total income comprises solely of profits and gains from business referred to in Section 44B (shipping) or Section 44BB (exploration etc. of mineral oils) or Section 44BBA (operation of aircraft) or Section 44BBB (civil construction etc. in turnkey power projects) and such income has been offered to tax at the presumptive rates specified in those sections. (C) Any income accruing or arising to a company from life insurance business referred to in Section 115B. (D) A person who has exercised the option referred to under Section 115BAA or Section 115BAB

[a]A company to which second proviso to subsection (1) of Section 129 of the Companies Act, 2013 is applicable may prepare its statement of profit and loss account and compute net profit in accordance with the provisions of the Act governing the company. Further, such company, for the assessment years 2011–2012 and earlier, has an option to prepare its statement of profit and loss for the relevant previous year either in accordance with the provisions of Schedule III to the Companies Act, 2013 (18 of 2013) or in accordance with the provisions of the Act governing such company

[b]Items (a) to (i) are increased to book profit if same are debited to P&L account and (j) if same is not credited to P&L account

[c]For the purposes of clause (a), the amount of income tax shall include—(i) Any tax on distributed profits under Section 115-O or on distributed income under Section 115R. (ii) Any interest charged under this Act. (iii) Surcharge, if any, as levied by the Central Acts from time to time. (iv) Education Cess on income tax, if any, as levied by the Central Acts from time to time. (v) Secondary and Higher Education Cess on income tax, if any, as levied by the Central Acts from time to time

[d]For these provisions, the expression 'securities' shall have the same meaning as assigned to it in clause (h) of Section 2 of the Securities Contracts (Regulation) Act, 1956 (42 of 1956)

[e]This clause has been substituted for the existing clause (iih) of Explanation 1 to subsection (2) of Section 115JB by the Finance (No. 2) Act, 2019, w.e.f. 1-4-2020. For the purposes of this clause (iih)—(i) 'Adjudicating Authority' shall have the meaning assigned to it in clause (1) of Section 5 of the Insolvency and Bankruptcy Code, 2016 (31 of 2016). (ii) 'Tribunal' shall have the meaning assigned to it in clause (90) of Section 2 of the Companies Act, 2013 (18 of 2013). (iii) A company shall be a subsidiary of another company, if such other company holds more than half in the nominal value of equity share capital of the company. (iv) 'loss' shall not include depreciation

## Appendix 2: Alternate Minimum Tax

An Alternate Minimum Tax (AMT) was levied in India under Chapter XII-BA of the Income-tax Act on limited liability partnerships (LLPs) from 1st April 2012. Effective 1st April 2013, AMT was extended to any person other than a company, who claimed deduction in respect of income (other than cooperative societies) under the heading '*C.-Deductions in respect of certain incomes*' in Chapter VIA of the Act such as:

- Newly established industrial undertakings or hotel business in backward areas [Section 80HH].
- Newly established small-scale industrial undertakings in certain areas [Section 80HHA].
- Industrial undertakings after a certain date etc. [Section 80I].
- Industrial undertakings or enterprises engaged in infrastructure development etc. [Section 80IA].
- An undertaking or enterprise engaged in development of Special Economic Zone [Section 80IAB].
- Start-up engaged in specified business [Section 80IAC].
- Certain industrial undertakings other than infrastructure development undertakings [Section 80IB].
- Housing projects [s 80IBA].
- Certain undertakings or enterprises in certain special category States [Section 80IC].
- Business of hotels and convention centres in a specified area [Section 80ID].
- Certain undertakings in North-Eastern States [Section 80IE].
- From business of collecting and processing of biodegradable waste [Section 80JJA].
- Employment of new employees [Section 80JJAA].
- Certain incomes of offshore Banking Units and International Financial Services Centre [Section 80LA].
- Certain inter-corporate dividends [Section 80M].
- Royalties etc., from certain foreign enterprises [Section 80-O].
- Certain income of Producer Companies [Section 80PA].
- The business of publication of books [Section 80Q].
- Professional income of authors of textbooks in Indian languages [Section 80QQA].
- Royalty income etc., of authors of certain books other than textbooks [Section 80QQB].
- Remuneration from certain foreign sources in the case of professors, teachers etc. [Section 80R].
- Professional income from foreign sources in certain cases [Section 80RR].
- Remuneration received for services rendered outside India [Section 80RRA].
- Royalty on patents [Section 80RRB].

AMT is also applicable to deduction claimed in respect of newly established Units in Special Economic Zones [Section 10AA] or deduction claimed in respect of expenditure on specified business [Section 35AD] as reduced by the allowable depreciation under Section 32.

Under the provisions of AMT, where the regular income tax payable for a previous year by a person (other than a company) is less than the AMT payable for the previous year, the adjusted total income becomes the taxable income. Adjusted total income is the total income of the person as increased by any of the abovementioned deductions claimed by the assessee and AMT is the amount of tax computed on adjusted total income at a rate of 18.5 per cent. For a unit located in an International Financial Services Centre that derives its income solely in convertible foreign exchange, the rate for AMT is 9 per cent.

AMT does not apply to individuals, HUFs, association of persons, body of individuals (whether incorporated or not) or artificial juridical persons, if the adjusted total income of such person does not exceed Rs. 20 lakhs. With effect from 1st April 2021 the provisions of AMT shall not be applicable to any person who has exercised the option referred to in Sections 115BAC or 115BAD.

The credit for AMT paid by a person is allowed to the extent of the excess of the AMT paid over the regular income tax payable of that year. No interest is, however, payable on the tax credit allowed. The credit for tax paid can be taken up to fifteen assessment years immediately succeeding the assessment year for which the credit becomes allowable.

**Table 20.3** India CIT and MAT: rate changes over time

| AY | CIT (%)—Headline rate plus Surcharge (SC) and Cess | MAT (%) |
|---|---|---|
| 1988–1991 | 54.00 = Widely held, 50% + 8% SC<br>(SC applies on CIT rate)<br>64.80 = Closely held, 60% + 8% SC<br>59.40 = Average | 15 |
| 1991–1992 | 43.20 = Widely held, 40% + 8% SC<br>54.00 = Closely held, 50% + 8% SC<br>48.60 = Average | NA[a] |
| 1992–1995 | 51.75 = Widely held, 45% + 15% SC<br>57.50 = Closely held, 50% + 15% SC<br>54.63 = Average | Same |
| 1995–1997 | 46.00 = 40% + 15% SC[b] | Same |
| 1997–1998 | 43.00 = 40% + 7.5% SC[c] | 12 |
| 1998–2000 | 35.00[d] | 10.5[e] |
| 2000–2001 | 38.50 = 35% + 10% SC[f] | Same |
| 2001–2002 | 39.55 = 35% + 10% SC + 3% SC[g] | 7.5[h] |
| 2002–2003 | 35.70 = 35% + 2% SC[i] | Same |
| 2003–2004 | 36.75 = 35% + 5% SC[j] | Same |
| 2004–2005 | 35.88 = 35% + 2.5% SC | Same |
| 2005–2006 | 36.60 = 35% + 2.5% SC + 2% EC[k] | Same |
| 2006–2007 | 33.66 = 30% + 10% SC + 2% EC | Same |
| 2007–2008 | Same | 10.0 |
| 2008–2010 | 33.99 = 30% + 10% SC + 2% EC + 1% SHEC[l] | Same |
| 2010–2011 | Same | 15.0 |
| 2011–2012 | 33.22 = 30% + 7.5% SC[m] + 2% EC + 1% SHEC | 18.0 |
| 2012–2014 | 32.44 = 30% + 5% SC + 2% EC + 1% SHEC | 18.5 |
| 2014–2016 | 33.99 = 30% + 10% SC + 2% EC + 1% SHEC | 18.5 |
| 2016–2017 | 34.61 = 30% + 12% SC + 2% EC + 1% SHEC | Same |

(continued)

**Table 20.3** (continued)

| AY | CIT (%)—Headline rate plus Surcharge (SC) and Cess | MAT (%) |
|---|---|---|
| 2017–2018 | 31.96 = 29% + 7% SC + 2% EC + 1% SHEC<br>(total turnover < Rs. 5 crore in FY 2014–2015)<br>33.06 = 30% + 7% SC + 2% EC + 1% SHEC<br>(Rs. 1 crore < total income < Rs. 10 crore)<br>34.61 = 30% + 12% SC + 2% EC + 1% SHEC<br>(total income > Rs. 10 crore)<br>33.21 = Average | Same |
| 2018–2019 | 27.55 = 25% + 7% SC + 2% EC + 1% SHEC<br>(total turnover < Rs. 50 crore in FY 2015–2016)<br>Second two rates remained the same<br>31.21 = Average | Same |
| 2019–2020 | 27.82 = 25% + 7% SC + 4% HEC[n]<br>(total turnover < Rs. 250 crore in FY 2016–2017)<br>33.38 = 30% + 7% SC + 4% HEC<br>(Rs. 1 crore < total income < Rs. 10 crore)<br>34.94 = 30% + 12% SC + 4% HEC<br>(total income > Rs. 10 crore)<br>32.05 = Average | Same |
| 2020–2021 | Same rates, but total turnover condition for first slab changed:<br>(total turnover <Rs. 400 crore in FY 2017–2018)<br>**Special taxation regime introduced:**<br>25.17 = 22% + 10% SC + 4% HEC<br>(Existing manufacturing companies opted for s115BAA)<br>17.16 = 15% + 10% SC + 4% HEC<br>(New manufacturing companies opted for s 115BAB)[p]<br>27.69 = Average | 15.0 |
| 2021–2022 | Same except total turnover condition:<br>(total turnover < Rs. 400 crore in FY 2018–2019)<br>**Special taxation regime:** Same<br>27.69 =Average | Same |

Source: Central government budgets (1987–1988 to 2020–2021); and Income Tax Department information

Note: A company in which the public is not substantially invested is referred to as a 'closely held company', otherwise, it is referred to as a 'widely held company'

[a]NA = Not applicable. Union Budget 1990–1991 proposed to discontinue MAT from AY 1991–1992

[b]Budget 1994–1995 removed the distinction between the tax rates for widely held and closely held domestic companies and lowered both rates to a single headline rate of 40%

[c]Surcharge was reduced from 15 to 7.5% in Union Budget 1996–1997

[d]Budget 1997–1998 abolished the Surcharge of 7.5 and 35% of corporate tax rate was proposed on domestic companies

[e]Budget 1997–1998 proposed that companies would have to pay MAT of 10.5 % on its book profits

[f]Surcharge of 10% was reimposed in Budget 1999–2000

[g]Surcharge of 1% on corporates towards the National Calamity Contingency Fund and an additional 2% on all tax payers for the Gujarat Earthquake relief. Surcharge was first discussed in Budget 2001–2002 although it was imposed during FY 2000–2001 (AY 2001–2002)

[h]The new provision in Finance Bill 1999 provided that all companies having book profits under the Companies Act, prepared in accordance with Part-II and -III of Schedule-VI to the Companies Act, shall be liable to pay a MAT at a lower rate of 7.5%, as against the existed MAT rate of 10.5% of the book profits

[i]Budget 2001–2002 proposed to remove all surcharges payable by corporates and non-corporates except the surcharge of 2 % for relief to quake hit areas of Gujarat
[j]Budget 2002–2003 proposed to impose a surcharge of 5% across-the-board on all categories of taxpayers, except individuals and Hindu Undivided Families having total income up to Rs 60,000. The 2% surcharge imposed in FY 2001–2002 in the wake of the Gujarat Earthquake was abolished
[k]Budget 2004–2005 proposed to levy education cess (EC) of 2% on income tax, corporation tax, excise duties, customs duties and service tax. EC (0.72) = [35 + (35 * 0.025)] * 0.02
[l]Budget 2007–2008 proposed to levy an additional secondary and higher education cess (SHEC) of 1% on all taxes. SHEC (0.33) = [30 + (30 * 0.1)] * 0.01
[m]Budget 2010–2011 proposed to reduce the surcharge from 10 to 7.5% on domestic companies and increased the rate of MAT from 15 to 18% of book profits
[n]Budget 2018–2019 replaced the 3% education cess by a 4% Health and Education Cess (HEC). HEC (1.07) = [25 + (25 * 0.07)] * 0.04
[o]The Government of India has introduced the Taxation (Amendment) Ordinance 2019 on 20th September 2019
[p]Domestic company who has opted for a special taxation regime under Section 115BAA and Section 115BAB is exempted from provision of MAT

## References


Agarwal, Rahul. 2020. Dividend Distribution Tax: Will Abolished DDT Benefit You If Your Income Is High? *Financial Express*, May 1.

Government of India. 1997. *Tax Policy for the Ninth Five Year Plan (1997-98 to 2001-02)*, Report of the Working Group on Tax Policy. New Delhi: Centax Publications.

———. 2001. *Report of the Advisory Group on Tax Policy and Tax Administration for the Tenth Plan*. New Delhi: Planning Commission.

Taxguru. 2005. Guidance Note on Audit Under Section 115JB of the Income Tax Act, 1961. https://taxguru.in/income-tax/guidance-note-audit-section-115jb-income-tax-act-1961.html. Accessed 5 Oct 2020.

# Consumption and Production Taxes 21

## 21.1 Introduction

In indirect taxation, two types of taxes are prevalent. The first is to tax commodities selectively. These are called selective excises such as on 'demerit' goods like alcoholic beverages and tobacco products as well as on non-renewable resources like petroleum products.[1] Countries tend to have selective excises also on luxury items such as furs, yachts, highly priced cars and so on. Because they are usually collected at the factory gate, they are, therefore, referred to as production taxes.

Since excises are selective, they are narrowly based, and their rates tend to be higher than the rates associated with widely based consumption taxes that have evolved over the years including the sales tax, especially at the retail level (RST), value-added tax (VAT), goods and services tax (GST) and variations thereof.

The RST is imposed at the level of the retailer. Different commodities may have different tax rates and the tax must be collected correctly from each item sold. This is difficult to manage especially in an emerging economy, though the United States uses an RST at the state level. The GST or VAT collects revenue not just at the retail stage but also at every earlier stage of production and distribution while giving appropriate credit for taxes paid in earlier stages thereby minimising 'tax on tax' or cascading. Thus, if the retail stage is missed, tax is nevertheless collected in earlier stages.

Several developing countries that introduced the VAT initially introduced it at the level of supply of goods without including the supply of services.[2] It could perhaps be said that the inclusion of services with goods in the VAT base broadens the coverage to all items supplied in the economy and renders the tax, in essence, to a GST. Such a base is prevalent in most advanced economies of Europe that have introduced a VAT. New Zealand, Canada and India term their equivalent taxes a

[1] See Cnossen (2005) and Cnossen (2010) for discussions on selective excises.

[2] See Due (1988) for a coverage of indirect taxation in developing countries in the early years.



P. Shome, *Taxation History, Theory, Law and Administration*, Springer Texts in Business and Economics, https://doi.org/10.1007/978-3-030-68214-9_21

GST. In all of them, ideally, cascading should be eliminated, though some cascading remains in most structures as caused by exemptions that result in cascading and erode the base. These taxes on production and consumption are the subject matter of this chapter.

## 21.2 Comparing RST, GST and VAT

### 21.2.1 General Characteristics

For RST to be successful, the tax rate software has to be embedded in every shop's till. In a computerised society, that is not a big challenge. Individual states in the United States impose their own RSTs at different rates, and a few of them do not have an RST at all since they have alternative revenue sources such as oil and insurance products. In many developing economies, an RST is not feasible since many retailers are 'corner shops' that may be issuing handwritten, rather than machine-generated, receipts. Comprehensive revenue collection poses serious challenges in such environments.

In a GST or VAT, a supplier or seller collects revenue from his purchasers at the given GST or VAT rate. He is also given an 'input tax credit' (ITC) for the taxes he pays on his purchases. Thus, he passes the difference between debit (his collection) and credit (his payments) to the government. A primary benefit of this mechanism, as will be elaborated later, is the eradication of any tax 'cascading', or, any tax paid in an earlier stage of production getting embedded in the output price set at a subsequent stage.

And, because of the debit–credit mechanism along the production–distribution chain embedded in the GST or VAT, the revenue it generates from collection along the entire chain equals the revenue collected by the RST which is collected only at the final retail point. Many developing and developed countries alike have moved from a sales tax levied at a single stage—retail or wholesale—of distribution, to a GST or VAT, mainly for reasons of the latter's ability to collect tax at all stages. Thus, if an earlier stage is missed, the revenue loss can be made up in a subsequent stage, thereby easing the challenges of tax administration.

### 21.2.2 Equivalence of GST or VAT, and RST

In an RST, tax is collected at the retail level, and the revenue is equal to the retail price of the product multiplied by the tax rate. In an equal-rate GST or VAT, the total revenue yield from collection along the chain of production and distribution is the same. Table 21.1 illustrates this with the example of a laptop. Say, each tax is 12%. The pre-tax price of the laptop is Rs. 30,000. If an RST of 12% is charged, the government receives Rs. 3600 in revenue and the consumer pays Rs. 33,600 for the laptop. The same result occurs with a GST or VAT. But the tax is collected at four

**Table 21.1** Equivalence of RST with VAT/GST (Pre-tax price of product Laptop is Rs. 30,000)

| Product cycle stage | VAT (12%) Before tax | Tax | After tax | RST (12%) Before tax | Tax | After tax |
|---|---|---|---|---|---|---|
| *Mining* | | | | | | |
| Sales | 6000 | 720 | 6720 | 6000 | 0 | 6000 |
| Purchase[a] | 0 | 0 | 0 | 0 | 0 | 0 |
| Tax to government | | **720** | | | **0** | |
| *Manufacturing* | | | | | | |
| Sales | 12,000 | 1440 | 13,440 | 12,000 | 0 | 12,000 |
| Purchase | 6000 | 720 | 6720 | 6000 | 0 | 6000 |
| Tax to government | | **720** | | | **0** | |
| *Wholesale* | | | | | | |
| Sales | 18,000 | 2160 | 20,160 | 18,000 | 0 | 18,000 |
| Purchase | 12,000 | 1440 | 13,440 | 12,000 | 0 | 12,000 |
| Tax to government | | **720** | | | **0** | |
| *Retail* | | | | | | |
| Sales | 30,000 | 3600 | 33,600 | 30,000 | 3600 | 33,600 |
| Purchase | 18,000 | 2160 | 20,160 | 18,000 | 0 | 18,000 |
| Tax to government | | **1440** | | | **0** | |
| Final, after tax retail Price of laptop | | | 33,600 | | | 33,600 |
| Total tax collected | | 3600 | | | 3600 | |

Source: Author's calculations

[a]The assumption of zero purchases at the first stage does not affect the result. The assumption is made solely to simplify the example

Bold numbers show the tax paid at each stage of production and distribution under both VAT and GST

stages: Rs. 720 at each of the mining, manufacturing and wholesale stages and Rs. 1440 at the retail stage.[3]

The crucial difference is that the RST attempts to collect the full revenue at the retail stage which is the final consumer stage in the entire chain, while the GST or VAT collects it also at previous stages of the chain. The deduction or credit that the GST or VAT allows on purchases ensures that those purchases (that had been taxed at the previous stage in the chain) are not taxed again. Therefore, there is no repetition in the taxation of any component of that value; rather, only the 'value-added' is taxed at every stage. Hence, the phenomenon of 'tax cascading' which will be explained in what follows is avoided. If appropriately designed, therefore, a GST or VAT is efficient and equivalent to an RST. As already described, the advantage of the former over the latter is, however, that it is collected at various stages so that, if the retail stage is missed, the tax would have been collected at least at some earlier stage thereby suffering lower revenue loss.

[3]See Carlson (1980) for a comparable explanation.

## 21.3 Tax Cascading

### 21.3.1 The Concept

Some countries that introduced the VAT preferred to initially opt for a 'production'--type rather than a 'consumption'-type VAT mainly for considerations of revenue protection. The production-type VAT typically does not allow ITC to be given for capital goods purchases or allows it only in stages. This leads to cascading, that is, as explained above, the VAT itself may be taxed at a subsequent stage of the chain. This is because the tax base calculation at every stage of production fails to exclude all the taxes that had been paid in earlier stages of the production chain.

An extreme example of a tax that causes cascading is one on the turnover of a product that gets taxed at every stage without any ITC. Under such a tax, every sales transaction is taxed, possibly at different stage-specific or transaction-specific rates. Thus, say, a tax of x percent is imposed on the sale of rubber, and a tax of y percent is imposed on the sale of tyres, without any possibility of ITC. The value of the rubber and the tax paid on it are both incorporated into the tax base of tyres. In other words, there is a 'tax on tax'. This is cascading in taxation parlance.

Once tax cascading occurs, it is likely to cascade further as the chain moves forward, since the already cascaded value gets taxed repeatedly along the chain. Further, say, the tyre wholesaler is subject to a tax of z percent, without a provision of ITC, when he buys the tyres from the manufacturer. This results in even additional cascading in the distribution portion of the supply chain.

It is easy to surmise that the effective embedded tax rate of a cascading tax by the time the taxed commodity or service reaches the final consumer is likely to be higher than the nominal rate that appears to apply when the consumer makes his purchase. The cascaded tax rate, therefore, frequently remains hidden from the consumer.

Even if a commodity or service is exempted from tax at the retail stage, the retail price would include tax elements stemming from the tax imposed at earlier stages of the chain without ITC. Take the case of agricultural products some of which may be exempt from tax. But if inputs such as tractors and machinery are not exempt, then the tax paid on them by the farmer is likely to be embedded in the price at which he supplies his agricultural product in the market. The purchaser of the exempted agricultural product imagines that there is no tax on the item he is purchasing, thus remaining uninformed that there is indeed a tax element embedded in the price he pays.

Therefore, a market price does not necessarily reveal the pure cost of production but may be vitiated by embedded tax that has cascaded into its price. And the embedded tax may be different for different goods and services reflecting the different nature and extent of exemptions for different products along the chain. Market prices, therefore, represent a distorted picture from those that would prevail if there were no exemptions.[4]

[4]See Zee (1995) for a detailed illustration of the technical aspects of cascading.

### 21.3.2 Types of VAT or GST

For fear of revenue depletion, some countries first introduced the VAT as a production-type (P-VAT) or an income-type (I-VAT) rather than a consumption-type (C-VAT). The P-VAT does not allow ITC for tax paid on capital goods purchases. The I-VAT allows ITC to be spread over some years such as in the form of a depreciation rate. Both lead to cascading, though to different degrees.

Only the C-VAT allows full credit for capital goods purchases and does not suffer from cascading. In its initial phase, India allowed ITC for capital goods purchases over 2 years and as such was closer in its structure to the I-VAT.[5] It was referred to as a Modified VAT or MODVAT that operated at the central government level.

The definitions of the three bases could be specified as follows:

$$\text{Base of P} - \text{VAT} = \text{GDP} - G_W = C + I + G_C + (M - X).$$

$$\text{Base of I} - \text{VAT} = \text{GDP} - G_W - D = C + (I - D) + G_C + (M - X).$$

$$\text{Base of C} - \text{VAT} = \text{GDP} - G_W - I = C + G_C + (M - X).$$

where,
GDP is a country's Gross Domestic Product.
$G_W$ is the wages government pays out.
C is private sector consumption.
$G_C$ is government consumption.
I is investment.
D is depreciation of the investment.
M is imports.
X is exports.

If eradication of cascading is a central characteristic of a GST or VAT, the formulae illustrate that only the C-VAT is the correct structure for a GST or VAT. This is because the P-VAT includes investment in its base and the I-VAT includes (investment—depreciation) in its base, thereby leading to cascading.

## 21.4 Elements That Influence Cascading

The extent of cascading depends on the ratio of taxed to untaxed inputs, the number of stages in the production–distribution chain, the number of rates, elasticities of demand and supply and the manner of calculating the tax.

[5] Specifically, complete ITC was allowed in the first year of introduction but was spread over 2 years from the second year reflecting revenue fears.

### 21.4.1 Ratio of Taxed to Untaxed Inputs

The lower are the taxes on inputs in the chain of production and distribution, the less is the extent of cascading and, therefore, of input taxes getting into the output price. For example, if, in the agriculture sector, tractors and machinery are exempted, there is no input tax to cascade. And the final agricultural product will be supplied at a market price without embedded input tax in it. ITC is no longer an issue. This occurs in several developing countries. Relatedly, the agricultural product may be exempted but, additionally, it may be allowed ITC on its unexempted inputs. This phenomenon is known as 'zero rating' a commodity under GST or VAT.

Importantly, when a commodity is exported, it is also zero rated in order to ensure that it is competitive with similar commodities from other countries when entering the international market. Likewise, a GST or VAT is imposed on an import at the point of entry at the customs point in order to ensure that a domestically produced commodity—which has been subject to tax—remains competitive with an imported commodity in the domestic market.

Whether a commodity is zero rated or exempted affects the extent of cascading, and also the amount of revenue collected by the government. To recount, if a commodity is zero rated, then the tax on output is zero but ITC is also given for taxes that have been paid on inputs.[6] However, if it is exempted, output is not taxed but neither is ITC allowed on inputs.

### 21.4.2 Number of Stages in Production–Distribution Chain

The higher is the number of production and distribution stages that a commodity undergoes before it is offered at the retail stage, the higher is the number of possibilities for a GST or VAT to get embedded in the final retail price.

### 21.4.3 Number of Rates

Multiple rates in a GST or VAT make the tax difficult to administer, robbing it of the simplicity of the debit–credit method of calculating tax. With multiple rates, it is not uncommon for an input to have a higher tax rate than that on its output. Therefore, ITC cannot be taken fully, leading to unutilised ITC stacking up over time. ITC has to be utilised in future years against the same or other outputs. However, some countries have been known not to allow ITC to be taken against any output other than in which the input has been directly used. Such constraints lead, in reaction, to tax dodging as well as over-cautious and time-consuming scrutiny by tax officers.

[6]In this case the producer has to file a return with the tax administration to receive back the tax he had paid on his inputs.

## 21.5 Incidence Analysis

From tax incidence analysis that we are familiar with, how much of a tax a supplier can shift to a purchaser depends on various demand and supply elasticities of associated outputs and inputs. To begin, a tax is likely to affect both the price and quantity demanded of the taxed commodity, with impacts also on associated commodities even if they are untaxed. And then there are the supply elasticities that affect the outcome. The ultimate extent to which the tax is shifted cannot be determined until a complete general equilibrium analysis is undertaken.[7]

Nevertheless, in most policy analyses of the economic impact of indirect taxes, it is not uncommon to adopt a partial equilibrium focus, in which case, it is appropriate to assume that a complete forward shifting of an indirect tax will take place in the first instance. Thus, in GST or VAT analysis, under forward shifting with full ITC—no cascading—the tax is shifted forward fully by the supplier who collects the full tax revenue from the purchaser.

## 21.6 Calculation of Tax

The calculation of net tax liability may be of two kinds. The first is the 'credit method' which stipulates that GST or VAT revenue is the gross tax liability minus taxes already paid on purchases. The second method is the 'subtraction method' which involves subtracting the cost from gross income, and calculating tax on net income.

Using one or the other method leads to different tax calculations reflecting exemptions and zero rating along the production–distribution chain. Most countries use the credit method.

The final cascading outcome in a theoretical sense is, therefore, the result of the above-mentioned characteristics of a GST or VAT and the calculation of tax depends on the method utilised to calculate tax liability.

## 21.7 Estimating the VAT Base

In the case of a C-VAT, the potential GST or VAT revenue may be calculated by beginning with its GDP estimate and applying the formula for a GST or VAT shown above. This is because GDP is the summation of the value added in the domestic production of each good and service in the economy. However, in reality, as was explained above, the base of the VAT is unlikely to equal the GDP due to different exemptions and exclusions of selected outputs and inputs from the tax base. Therefore, the estimation of the tax base becomes relatively complex.

[7]See Chap. 9, Sect. 9.8.

A formula that is dependable in estimating the VAT base is as follows:[8]

Estimated Net Potential VAT = [(Estimated Potential Gross VAT = Gross Output x Effective VAT Rate[9]) – (VAT Credit for Intermediate Consumption) + (VAT Credit on Purchases of Exempted Products) + (VAT on Imports) – (VAT Credit for Exports)]

The theoretical calculation of GST or VAT revenue is made on the basis of a country's input–output table that shows what inputs are consumed by each sector of the economy. Some developing countries have a wide range of rate variation for sectors.[10] Once GST or VAT revenue potential is obtained for each such sector, a summation gives the potential revenue for the economy as a whole.

When this is compared with actual GST or VAT collection from the data available from the tax returns at the tax administration, then an estimate of GST or VAT evasion is obtained. Indeed, GST or VAT, evasion can be calculated for each sector if the information based on tax returns can be successfully separated into each sector.

## 21.8 Taxation of the Financial Sector

In the case of GST or VAT, its base should, in principle, include financial services. It is possible, in general, to measure value-added by adding profit, wages, rent, and interest or, alternatively, by taking the difference between investment income and the cost of funds. The use of invoices under the GST or VAT requires that tax liability be attributed to each transaction. This is not possible for the banking sector, however, since financial services provided by banks do not have specific charges attached to them. Charges result from differences in interest rates charged and paid.

In the insurance sector, value added in non-investment insurance is measured by the 'loading charge'—earnings of the insurer over and above payments of claims. Value added is not properly measured by the value of premiums or claims since this includes the component of premiums that is a redistribution from one policyholder to another. Again, value added has to be measured as the loading charge, eliminating the savings component. It is, therefore, not easy to tax financial institutions under the GST or VAT. They are, therefore, often exempted.

[8]For ease of exposition, only the term VAT is being used in the formula, but refers to both GST and VAT.

[9]Weighted average of the rate of tax for each sector.

[10]One such example could be separate tax rates for mining; beverages; tobacco; textiles; wood and furniture; paper and printing; chemicals, rubber, and plastic; petroleum products; processed minerals and non-metallic goods; machinery and equipment; transport equipment; miscellaneous manufacturing; electricity, gas and water; banks, insurance, and services; communications (electronic and others); personal services; and retail trade, though the entire structure may be called VAT because ITC is given, even if selectively.

The OECD countries exempt intermediary functions while taxing selected activities such as check printing, safety deposit rental and foreign exchange transactions. Israel is one country to have attempted to apply a comprehensive base deriving it by adding different value-added components. India has opted for a presumptive method of calculating GST bases for different components of the financial sector.

## 21.9 Excise Taxation

### 21.9.1 Elasticity Considerations

Traditionally, selective excises have been favoured in addition to an RST or VAT or GST to tax the consumption of 'demerit' goods such as tobacco, alcohol and gasoline.[11] Their elasticities of demand tend to be low at least in the short run, since it is not easy for consumers to change their consumption habits. Thus, a high tax rate or a tax increase could be used to generate high amounts of revenue since consumption does not diminish significantly.

Excises should be used selectively in order not to burden the consumers of other goods with low elasticities of demand, such as necessities. Thus, it is incorrect to view all goods with a low elasticity of demand as good for excises to be imposed. Rather, the other face of selective excises is the possibility, or even the desirability, of imposing them on luxuries that may have high elasticities of demand but nevertheless may not be adequately taxed under a low-rated general consumption tax such as VAT or GST. An excise on such items improves vertical equity. Therefore, it is not true that no commodity with a high elasticity of demand should be subjected to a selective excise.[12] Nevertheless, caution is needed not to proliferate the number of excises to meet a variety of objectives that may be understandable in their individual roles but may make the tax structure overtly complicated and challenging to administer.

### 21.9.2 Negative Externalities

Alcoholic and tobacco products are said to lead not only to addiction but also to possible health hazards that are said to have negative 'external effects' on society, that is, not only on the consumers but on those around them, such as cancer caused by secondary smoke. High taxation of such products has positive effects by making resources available for associated medical treatment, and for illuminating

[11]These excises may account for two-thirds of excise revenue in developing countries. Other excises that are found are on soft drinks, textiles, cement, sugar and gambling.

[12]These arguments have been made by Cnossen (1991) who argued that excise taxes may be systematically used to achieve greater progressivity in indirect taxation.

consumers, particularly the young, about the health hazards, when there is still time to change their habits as opposed to adults whose habits may have become more grounded.[13]

Heavy motor vehicle use also has negative externalities since it causes air, water and noise pollution, and congestion on highways and city centres. Local jurisdictions could reduce those effects by earmarking the revenue collected from such excises for the supply of appropriate public goods such as good roads, cleaning the environment and purification of water.

### 21.9.3 Nature of Rates

Some practical issues arise in the design of excise taxes—for example, should they be levied on production or on consumption, or at ad valorem rates (based on percentage) or specific rates (based on quantity). Production excises are easier to collect than excises at the consumption level. Administrative activity pertaining to the collection of tax can be carried out at the factory gate. And, the number of taxpayers—being factory owners rather than retailers—should not be too high, thus facilitating tax administration and minimising tax evasion.

Regarding the type of rates, ad valorem rates are considered better than specific rates since there is no revenue depletion with inflation with ad valorem rates. On the other hand, specific rates allow 'counting the boxes', that is to say, for example, cases of beer or cartons of cigarettes are easier to count and impose a tax on, than collecting off a retailer's shelf. The choice depends on country experience and preference and whether the method in practice is leading to challenges that need to be confronted. No pressure should be put by international technical advisers on developing countries to pick one method over the other reflecting their innate beliefs.

## References

Carlson, George N. 1980. *Value-added Tax: European Experience and Lessons for the United States*. Washington, DC: Office of Tax Analysis, Department of the Treasury.

Cnossen, Sijbren. 1991. The Extended Excise Tax System. In *The Jamaican Tax Reform*, ed. Roy W. Bahl, 537–556. Cambridge: Lincoln Institute of Land Policy.

———, ed. 2005. *Theory and Practice of Excise Taxation: Smoking, Drinking, Gambling, Polluting, and Driving*. 1st ed. Published to Oxford Scholarship Online. https://doi.org/10.1093/0199278598.001.0001.

———. 2010. *The Economics of Excise Taxation*. Working Paper 10–18. Atlanta: Andrew Young School of Policy Studies, Georgia State University. https://icepp.gsu.edu/files/2015/03/ispwp1018.pdf.

Due, John F. 1988. *Indirect Taxation in Developing Economies*. Rev. ed. Baltimore: Johns Hopkins University Press.

[13]See McCarten and Stotsky (1995) and Grossman et al. (1993).

Grossman, Michael, Jody L. Sindelar, John Mullahy, and Richard Anderson. 1993. Policy Watch: Alcohol and Cigarette Taxes. *Journal of Economic Perspectives* 7: 211–221.
McCarten, William J., and Janet Stotsky. 1995. Excise Taxes. In *Tax Policy Handbook*, ed. Parthasarathi Shome, 100–103. Washington, DC: IMF.
Zee, Howell H. 1995. Tax Cascading: Concept and Measurement. In *Tax Policy Handbook*, ed. Parthasarathi Shome, 75–79. Washington, DC: IMF.

# Environment Taxes and User Charges 22

## 22.1 Introduction

Despite the proverbial efficiency of a perfectly competitive market, the market can fail and does so under specific circumstances. It occurs when the social cost of producing and supplying certain commodities does not get reflected in market pricing, thus resulting in excessive market supply and consumption. It emanates, for example from pollution caused by production, and the actual cost of clearing the pollution is not factored into the market price of the product. This phenomenon is referred to as social cost or 'negative externalities' that do not get captured in market prices.

Correct pricing should 'internalize' or enclose all social costs of production and supply. However, this was considered economically impractical to do so until recently when irretrievable proof began to emerge that the atmosphere is being damaged through greenhouse effects alarmingly punching holes in the earth's ozone layer and leading to increased global temperatures or 'climate change'. Such deleterious effects will have significant inter-generational ramifications for posterity who will inherit a damaged earth from its present inhabitants.

Corrective measures to alleviate the challenge include regulation, user charges, permits and taxes that attempt to equate, at the margin,[1] the social cost of a supply with its social benefits. There are relative advantages and disadvantages to using them. Particular taxes have been considered to mitigate global pollution though not yet with final success. As the atmosphere becomes increasingly recognised as a global resource and, reflecting the rise in the use of mineral resources such as coal and petroleum products, the most prominent instrument that has been considered is possibly a global tax on carbon emissions. These and related issues comprise the subject matter of this chapter.

[1]See Chap. 7, Sect. 7.4, where a firm's supply is explained as its marginal cost curve.



P. Shome, *Taxation History, Theory, Law and Administration*, Springer Texts in Business and Economics, https://doi.org/10.1007/978-3-030-68214-9_22

## 22.2 Rationale for Environment Taxes

### 22.2.1 Market Failure and Erroneous Policy

An environment tax may be imposed for reasons pertaining to arresting the deterioration, or maintenance, or improvement, of the environment. Its extent reflects whether, and how much, society considers its benefit to be in comparison with its cost. For example, that reflects the cost to society of not eliminating the level of pollution from smoke emanating from a factory, so that cost is not included in the market price of cement, the factory's output. Only when the pollution is recognised to exist and the cost of eliminating it is included in the cost calculation, can resources be generated to eliminate the level of pollution emanating from the factory. As explained, such pollution is termed the negative external cost of factory production.

Taxes may also be imposed by government to change relative prices such that the prices of goods that cause environmental damage rise relative to those that do not. By using taxes, the demand for the former would decline. Further, the tax revenue could be used for implementing measures to eliminate the pollution from factory emissions.

However, most countries are unable or unwilling to internalise the full social cost of pollution since, for centuries, economies have been perceived to have advanced in reflection of private market costs alone, exclusive of any social costs they may have caused. Indeed, society's recognition of the importance of the environment over the span of history has been exclusively a matter of indigenous societies and not of market-oriented models driven by capital accumulation and growth. Even today, by and large, societies consider it economically impractical to intervene comprehensively to price production in a socially non-injurious manner.

Thus, in certain cases, markets fail to generate an equilibrium at which society's marginal social benefit curve equals its marginal social cost of a productive activity. For example, if forest rights or water rights along a river are not properly defined to include society's rights in them, overuse by the private sector is likely to result. Examples are the last tracts of vast forest cover and rainforest in Brazil and Indonesia. Some of the successive governments of Brazil have argued that today's advanced economies also had forest cover at one time but later levelled them to gain land for cultivation. Therefore, Brazil should be able to uncover its forests as well. Such arguments skirt the prevailing reality of environmental deterioration with deleterious consequences in Brazil as well as globally.

The failure to use microeconomic policy to change relative prices to make it costlier for excessive use of polluting inputs also causes environmental damage. Paradoxically, excessive use, say of chemical fertilisers, may be brought on by government subsidies. For example, India's overuse of chemical fertilisers since its 1960s-70s Green Revolution has poisoned the soil of entire districts and possibly caused diseases including arthritis, deformation and cancer in the contiguous populations.[2] Such 'external' costs were not included in agricultural market prices, or taxes raised on market supply that could have yielded revenue for government for the alleviation of the negative external effects.

### 22.2.2 Corrective Instruments

Where it is not possible to work through prices, quantitative measures may be employed. First, helpful measures include appropriate regulation, especially in forest management, and tradable permits for containing waste emissions. Second, land reform including clear definition of property rights can help allocate costs on polluters. Third, where the policy itself has caused environmental damage such as encouragement of the use of chemical fertilisers or resettlement of populations to accommodate deforestation for logging, construction or other purposes, what is needed is the removal of such policies.

Third, if setting tax rates is a challenging task, then government may issue tradable permits the total of which would reflect the maximum pollution to be permitted from the concerned polluting source. These permits can then be traded in the market for purchase and sale by factories reflecting how much they are willing to cut back the pollution they are causing versus continuing to maintain their market supply as before. The United States has operated such a market based in Chicago for many years.

### 22.2.3 Tax Policy Objectives

The revenues collected from environment taxes are usually earmarked to achieve related goals such as to help clean up downtown pollution, smoke emission from factories, downstream river pollution and sedimentation or modernizing garbage collection and processing. Therefore, like any tax, they are not linked to an individual taxpayer's benefit. Rather, if earmarked, they are linked to the alleviation of a selected aspect of environmental degradation that may benefit the country, a region, a city or a particular sector such as cleaning up air travel.

Environment taxes are said to provide a 'double dividend'. Say an additional rupee of revenue is raised by increasing the rate of an environment tax while lowering collection of a rupee from other taxes. While overall government revenue remains unperturbed, the environment tax gives an additional external social benefit by buttressing the clean-up of the environment. Yet, care should be taken that the revenue collected does not exceed the revenue that would be sufficient to achieve the

[2] Waste emission from factories into its rivers has also been a major challenge for a highly and densely population such as India.

environmental objective.[3] Such taxes could be legislated to possess a large base such as for a global carbon tax. We will address this tax in Sect. 22.6.

## 22.3 Pigouvian Taxes and Substitutes

Continuing with our example of factory emission, a 'Pigouvian tax'[4] is typically levied on units of smoke emission generated by the factory. Since it addresses the damage caused—a quantity—rather than the price of the activity, its tax rate is specific rather than ad valorem. It would be levied such that the rate of tax per unit is set where the marginal social cost equals the marginal social benefit. Thus, a Pigouvian tax uses to directly affect market produced economic activities in an attempt to reduce environmental damage efficiently. Instead, regulatory mechanisms tend to prohibit the pollution causing activity itself, albeit above a ceiling. The main challenge with a Pigouvian tax is the difficulty of determining the marginal social cost for linking it to the tax rate to be correctly set.

As a result of the practical limitations of a Pigouvian tax, other taxes have been designed that can be more easily structured, for example unit taxes levied on the use of inputs causing emissions or on consumption goods that cause environmental damage, without being too preoccupied with the quantity of damage caused. In other words, such taxes affect relative prices but are not levied directly on emission damage or environmental damage.

Such a tax should be levied on a tax base—such as inputs or final goods—that has an identifiable relationship to the environmental damage. If that relationship is not strong, the effectiveness of the tax in alleviating the problem will be weak. One such tax is a tax on petroleum.

## 22.4 Taxation of Mineral and Petroleum Resources

The taxation of mineral resources deserves special consideration. One way of addressing the issue is to treat it as a tax on the return on mineral resources when treated as capital assets. Government is perceived to have a dual role: it is a sovereign taxing power as well as a resource owner. As the sovereign tax authority, it will impose the same tax arrangements that apply to economic activities in general. Here it would impose a selective excise and GST or VAT. As the resource owner, it will seek a return on its resource assets. Here it can use a resource rent tax. The taxation

[3]See Nellor (1995), Chap. III, for details on environmental taxes and user charges.

[4]It is named after Pigou (1920), a British economist who first enunciated it. He elaborated on Alfred Marshall's concept of 'externalities', defined as 'the costs imposed or benefits conferred on others that are not accounted for by the person who creates these costs or benefits. Pigou argued that negative externalities (costs imposed) should be offset by a tax, while positive externalities should be offset by a subsidy'. See https://www.britannica.com/biography/Arthur-Cecil-Pigou.

of mineral and petroleum resources, especially as they have arisen in practical queries and design of tax systems, is the subject of a rich literature.

Petroleum use is not the only cause of the emission of pollutants by vehicles because the associated pollution also reflects the vehicle's operating efficiency, driving speed and road quality. Regulations such as the use of catalytic converters to reduce emissions may be more efficient in reducing pollution than a petroleum tax. Yet most countries use petroleum taxes to no small extent with an environmental objective but also because collection of revenue is easy from the oil industry directly or at the petrol pump.

Urban areas may be more environmentally challenged than semi-urban or rural areas and the same petroleum tax would not meet those differences. Further, congestion may be worse during particular times of the day. A petroleum tax cannot differentiate such differences either. Regulatory restrictions could address the challenge better, for example in Singapore, by imposing high marginal costs of vehicle use during congestion hours, or banning it altogether during specific hours. Such systems are dependent on computer software since a registered vehicle's entry needs to be automatically logged, the charges recorded and subsequently billed and revenue collected.

## 22.5 User Charges

User charges for providing public services are designed on the basis of the benefit principle, that is charging in accordance to the benefit received by the user of a public service. They may be collected as a toll from the user of a highway, or for receiving a passport, or entering a public park, or similar services for which the beneficiary can be identified. Adequate identification of the user and measurement of the intensity of use, comprise the design of correct structure of the charges.

The structure of a user charge can be quite complex, involving the speed with which a service is received, the length of travel on a toll road, the weight of vehicle that is travelling or, in other cases, the length of time to be spent in a public park, the rapidity with which a passport is issued, and so on. Sometimes, authorities may differentiate the country of citizenship when entering a museum or national monument, though that does not obviously distinguish between the benefits received. Similarly, the entrance fee to an archaeological site may be set at a higher level for a foreigner from an advanced economy, than for a domestic citizen. The rationale of some emerging economies is to replicate the price setting for similarly provided goods and services in advanced economies.

### 22.5.1 Advantages

User charges are quite different from the objective and design of a tax. They are not linked to taxes which do not possess any direct link to any particularly identifiable goods and services provided by the public sector.[5] Some have argued that user charges have advantages over taxes under certain circumstances. First, they adhere to the rationing mechanism of a market in that a good or service is provided only to consumers who pay for it directly. If appropriately priced, they could be compared to the private costs of providing a good or service. This, in turn, is useful in decisions relating to the future allocation of resources. However, critics question a government's ability to price goods or services correctly. They further argue that, unless differentially priced for different categories of users—rich and poor—user charges would not comprise a fair solution in the presence of unequal income distribution in the economy.[6]

Second, user charges are conceptually linked to different government perceptions of an economic activity. If fairness indicates that a public sector provided commodity or service should be paid for by the beneficiary, then a user charge is appropriate. If the ability to pay is the determining factor for fairness in a particular case, then a tax is appropriate. Third, if administration costs of a user charge are prohibitive, for example toll collection at different highway points, in particular in countries where such systems tend to break down due to unpredictable electric supply or lack of computer software, then the collection of user fees for highways could be accomplished indirectly through taxation of petrol at petrol stations. Connectedly, fourth, user charges remain essentially outside the political, parliamentary or budgetary processes that tend to be affected by interest groups and lobbies. Therefore, many of them can be introduced and operated by the executive branch of government.

Fifth, user charges could feature where governments prefer to keep some expenditures outside the budgets so that they do not suffer when there is a general expenditure cutback. In fiscal federal countries where central government budgetary revenues may have to be shared with sub-national governments such as in India, user charges shield the central government from having to share revenues therefrom.

Sixth, user charges are helpful in a situation where a decreasing cost industry is functioning. To recall, such firms exhibit decreasing average costs over the relevant scale of production, mainly due to large fixed costs compared to variable costs, for example telecommunication towers that have a high fixed cost contrasted with the smaller variable cost of providing telephone services to, say, a small farming community. Efficient pricing requires setting the price at marginal cost. But as average costs are declining (since marginal costs are lower than average costs), this pricing rule would lead to a price that would be lower than average cost. At this price, the firm would make a loss.[7]

It is not unusual for the supplier of such a product to be a 'natural monopolist' who possesses the power to set prices such that he is assured of a profit. But that could not only lead to setting price higher than most farmers could afford. It could also lead to a lower than optimal provision of telephone services in that community.

[5]See Richardson (1993).

[6]See Bird and Miller (1990).

[7]See Chap. 9, Sect. 9.4, Fig. 9.2c.

Government provision could improve the dearth of telephone services in such a scenario. It could impose a user charge set at only the level of marginal cost but, since such pricing would represent a loss, government would need to provide the difference from the general budget.[8]

### 22.5.2 Caveats

There are, however, critics of the solution of government provision. They argue that government production cannot be expected to occur at low cost and competitive prices or be reflective of technology advances that already exist in the domain of the private sector's knowledge that a monopolist would be more likely to avail. Such critics, therefore, prefer government to simply subsidise private production rather than itself provide the service.

Second, in some developing and emerging economies, governments have a tendency to provide a commodity or service that is not characterised by natural monopoly conditions. They are generally recognised in most other countries for provision by the private sector. One example is the airline industry. However, though there is a general view in advanced economies that, for overall economic efficiency, provision of such goods is better carried out by the private sector and that, therefore, any such public sector provision should be privatised, there is occasion to be cautious about blind adoption of privatisation.

For example, in India, the nationalised airlines provide services to far-flung corners of the geographically extensive country—in what could be called a positive externality—that a commercial airline would usually not provide; hence there is a role for public sector provision. Nevertheless, this is not clear-cut since government may suffer from significant financial loss from the operations of such a protected industry for successful long-term budgetary allocation. In India, examples of such sectors are airlines, petroleum, coal, steel, where the financial burden on government has been high; yet, public sector provision has tended to edge out private sector provision. Many other emerging economies suffer from comparable syndromes such as Brazil, South Africa, Venezuela, just to name a few. Under such circumstances, questions of the provision of those goods and services, whether through the private or public sector, becomes a dilemma for policymakers.

Third, there may be some blurring between user charges and taxes. The importance of any difference or similarity should not be overemphasised when the objective is to fund and provide an essential public service. The distinction that the former is used to fund specific programmes or agencies, while the latter are subsumed in government's general revenues, cannot always be clearly distinguished. An example of this was given above in the use of highway tolls versus taxing at petrol stations since both user charge and earmarked tax may have the same objective. If revenue from the user charge is not protected for earmarked use but

[8] See Bell (1995), Chap. III.

used for some unrelated objective, say a lottery for funding flood relief, then their distinguishing features cease to exist.

## 22.6 Global Carbon Tax

Combustion of fossil fuels is linked to the emission of carbon dioxide and sustained global warming. The challenge of global warming has assumed extraordinary importance as the world has undergone a rapid economic and technological change at the turn of the twentieth century and continues to do so in the new millennium. Many problems such as carbon emissions, mining, fracking, deep-sea trawling and resource exploitation, and polar resource exploitation have crossed national boundaries with transnational ramifications.

To meet some of the challenges posed by such activities, global sources of funding are being searched and appropriate designs contemplated and debated. The quantum and nature of resources available through multilateral financial institutional lending have been criticised as being inadequate to redress the challenge. Additionally, there are difficulties in expanding the traditional bases of tax revenue that are thinning out, for example that of the corporation income tax at the international level. Therefore, alternative bases need to be identified.

There is a growing consensus that a global tax designed and its revenue be earmarked for the global objective of stabilising the environment, not only for the current but also for future generations. Here we discuss such a possibility. A carbon tax of the Pigouvian variety can be levied on the units of carbon dioxide emission. And the revenue obtained from the tax needs to be used to facilitate the reduction of combustion and emission through appropriate market pricing and subsidies. We will consider the efficiency of such a tax in its design and effects, weighed against the feasibility of reaching an international agreement and the practicality of effective implementation.

The list of possibilities includes a carbon tax, user charges or taxes on international transport, as well as tradable or marketable permits. It is found that not all feasible national instruments are necessarily suitable for global use. A carbon tax is likely to fare best as a global tax and, in order for such a policy to be successful, a case is made for the imposition of a minimum global carbon tax.

### 22.6.1 Design of Global Carbon Tax

As discussed before, environmental degradation can cause factor depletion with respect to both capital and labour. This may be beneficially illustrated with the help of a diagrammatic scheme, the objective being to demonstrate how constraining influences such as environmental degradation could diminish the productivity of factors of production such as labour and capital in future generations. Schemata to illustrate the constraining influence of a global factor is presented in the Appendix 1 to this chapter.

### 22.6.2 Intra- and Inter-generational Perspectives

Population, technology and resources have been called the 'master variables' connected with a complex inter-relationship and resulting in an international tension between growth and development and also between the North and the South.[9] The North–South debate could (partially) be seen as an intra-generational one. Although multinationals, mainly from the North, carry technology, trade and investment to the South, they have distributive and allocational, as well as global and domestic, ramifications. Their investment tends to cause environmental degradation unless checked. Poverty and population growth are affected adversely by environmental degradation. In its turn, the North argues that poverty and population growth cause environmental degradation. This exacerbates the world's economic polarisation, and may necessitate a decision-making authority or at least a minimum degree of oversight at the global level.[10]

The rise of global politics on environmental issues has involved inter-disciplinary research and reflects a genuine interest in global sustainable development in balance with the biosphere as a whole. This has immediate inter-generational implications.[11] Past generations have bequeathed to the present generation an endowment reflecting the fruits of the former's efforts through trial and error and learning by doing. Thus, there is a backward indebtedness of the latter toward the former. A social contract represented by a social security transfer mechanism is inadequate for reaching sufficiently back into the past to repay this debt. Perhaps an alternative mechanism is for the present to ensure and safeguard its received gift of endowment for the future.

Most environmental threats (for example, global warming and depletion of forest cover) are not likely to affect us but our immediate descendants.[12] There is no particular reason, therefore, for a human being, or even for a particular country, to take unilateral action.[13] Commitment at a global level for equity with future generations, therefore, emerges as a distinct necessity. Global taxes comprise an important vehicle for the realisation of that commitment.

[9]See Choucri and North (1993). Their argument has carried intact to the present day.

[10]See Davidian (1994).

[11]See Brown Weiss (1993), and Rothenberg (1993).

[12]If there is no abatement of environmental degradation, damages from climate change would be relatively small for the next 50 years. It would accelerate thereafter.

[13]Indeed, non-governmental organizations (NGOs) formed by interested parties in their individual capacities often seem to do more than their governments. For the role that cooperatives and local governments have been playing, see Singh (1994).

### 22.6.3 The Atmosphere as an Illustration of a Global Resource

Examples of a global resource may be found in sea, land or air. The oceans are a common example of an international common property resource. Ships ply on the high seas and nation states bury refuse of various sorts in their beds. The quality of seas and oceans as a resource is thus degraded by chemical and nuclear wastes, and also by oil spills and atomic explosions. If and when any compensations are made for accidents, they tend to be small compared to their social cost. Further, payments made and received tend to be confined within individual countries, reflecting international norms regarding the prerogatives of state sovereignty, though some cross-country compensation has also taken place. Thus, first, marginal social costs of environmental degradation do not get fully reflected when such degradation occurs and, second, it is safe to say that it is generally not treated as a cutting-edge global issue in international politics.

Similarly, focusing on land on a global scale, the continent of Antarctica is an example of an abundant common property resource. Though the 1959 Antarctic Treaty has been praised by some[14] for the research coordination it has generated as the central component of international cooperation, the stakes already made out by individual countries for the eventual exploitation of the continent's natural resources again reveal individual motives of nation states, which conflict with truly global notions of inter- and intra-generational equity.

The common property resource that is most often discussed is, however, the atmosphere.[15] Its degradation spans the problems of acid deposition, global climate change and ozone depletion. The first, acid deposition, has had the most apparent environmental consequences in the form of acid rain. The second, ozone depletion, affects the upper atmosphere (stratosphere), which houses a thin layer of naturally occurring ozone that absorbs 99 per cent of the incoming ultraviolet solar radiation. Industrially produced chemicals, for example Chlorofluorocarbons (CFCs) diminish the ozone layer. In 1985, Antarctica's atmosphere was observed to have been punctured with an 'ozone hole', that is 40 per cent below average ozone levels, caused mainly by CFCs. The situation did not subsequently improve. Resultant increases in ultraviolet radiation are likely to have effects similar to those of carbon gases; but equally significantly, a 1 per cent reduction in the ozone layer could lead to a 10 per cent increase in human skin cancers.

The third, global climate change, is caused by the excessive emission of carbon dioxide that warms the lower atmosphere (troposphere). It is known that atmospheric concentrations of carbon dioxide have increased significantly over the last two centuries, mainly reflecting a tenfold increase in energy consumption during the twentieth century as well as the large scale cutting and burning of forests. While relatively small areas such as Scandinavia or Siberia may experience a somewhat longer growing season as a result, much larger tracts of land are destined to suffer

[14] See Victor et al. (1993).

[15] See Soroos (1991).

hotter and drier seasons and reduced production. Today, glacial ice is melting more rapidly and sea levels are rising due to thermal expansion, thus increasing the salinity of rivers and inundating highly populated areas. Bangladesh, for example is suffering from continual inundation of villages due to the close proximity of its numerous waterways to the sea. Various forms of damage occur on agriculture, forests, species, sea level, space cooling and heating, human amenity, life and morbidity, migration, construction, leisure, water supply and urban infrastructure, on an item by item basis.[16]

It is obvious that the targets for penalisation should be emissions of acid, CFCs and carbon into the atmosphere. A level of awareness, discussion and debate, if not a critical mass of consensus, already exists in the matter of targeting carbon emission. Appropriate policies at the global level, or policies coordinated at the national level by various nations, could help arrest atmospheric degradation and, at the same time, enable the generation of significant revenues for global use.

The policy conclusion that could be drawn from the fact that environmental degradation may lead to a reduced output for future generations is that, it is not enough for the present generation to bequeath pecuniary savings and presumed investment and consumption possibilities to posterity, i.e. it is also necessary to bequeath the natural habitat in a condition similar to that in which it was inherited from past generations. In order to do so, it is important to explore the possibilities of devising global tax mechanisms that could minimise environmental degradation and increase future production and consumption. The use of the revenue thus generated to mitigate global developmental concerns would comprise a double dividend.

## Appendix 1 Effect of Environmental Damage on Output

The world economy may be described as follows:

$$Y_t = C_t + I_t \tag{22.1}$$

$$I_t^0 = I_t\left(L_t,\ K_t,\ F_t^0\right) \tag{22.2}$$

$$C_t^0 = C_t\left(L_t,\ K_t,\ F_t^0\right) \tag{22.3}$$

$$C_{t+1} = f^c + C_t \tag{22.4}$$

$$I_{t+1} = f^i + I_t \tag{22.5}$$

$$L_t = \overline{L_t} \tag{22.6}$$

[16]OECD (1992) studied this. Cline (1992) took a cost- benefit approach for estimating such damage.

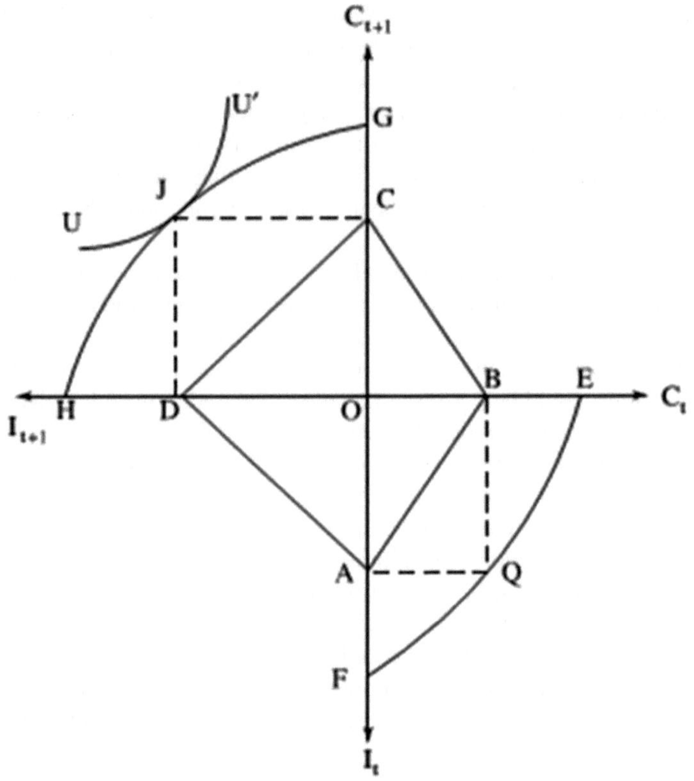


**Fig. 22.1** Unconstrained production–consumption. (Source: Shome (1996))

$$K_t = \overline{K_t} = I_{t-1} \tag{22.7}$$

$$F_t = F_t\left(f^c, f^i\right) \tag{22.8}$$

The world economy functions over two periods, present ($t$) and future ($t + 1$) with a global factor ($F$) that can constrain world production of consumption goods ($C$) and investment goods ($I$) by limiting the productivity of ordinary factors of production, labour ($L$) and capital ($K$). This is depicted in Eqs. 22.1, 22.2, and 22.3. In Fig. 22.1, the transformation curve EF in period $t$ is not limited by any constraints posed by $F$, and solely reflects the given endowments of labour and capital in Eqs. 22.6 and 22.7.

Assuming that the world is interested in leaving an adequate bequest, it prefers to consume OB, in period $t$. Then OA is the investment good produced.[17]

[17]OB plus OA yields $Y_1$ at normalized prices.

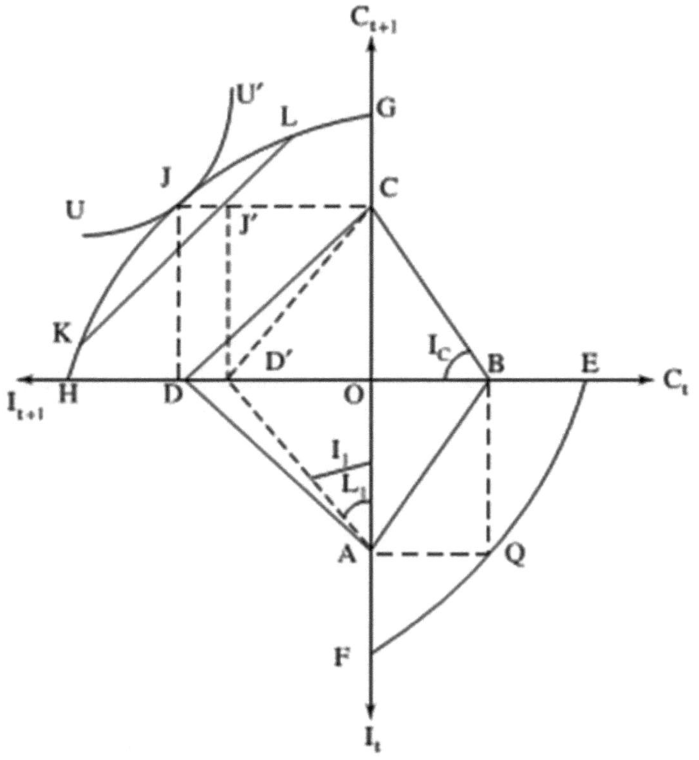


**Fig. 22.2** Lower production due to environmental degradation. (Source: Shome (1996))

Combined with $\overline{L}_{t+1}$, it yields the transformation curve GH in period $(t + 1)$, if unconstrained by $F$. The community indifference curve UU′ determines J as the equilibrium production–consumption combination.

Given Q and J, quadrilateral ABCD is the equilibrium production–consumption configuration for current and future generations.

The constraining influence of $F$ would appear, however, if the production of $C_t$ and $I_t$ ignored environmental factors. This would not show up in the production in period $t$ but would constrain production in period $(t + 1)$. This is depicted in Eqs. 22.4 and 22.5 which are simple specifications to facilitate the diagrammatic schemata. A more general specification could be Eqs. 22.9 and 22.10:

$$\left[I_t^0 > I_t^*/C_t^0 = C_t^*\right] \leftrightarrow F_t^0 > F_t^* \tag{22.9}$$

$$\left[C_t^0 > C_t^*/I_t^0 = I_t^*\right] \leftrightarrow F_t^0 > F_t^* \tag{22.10}$$

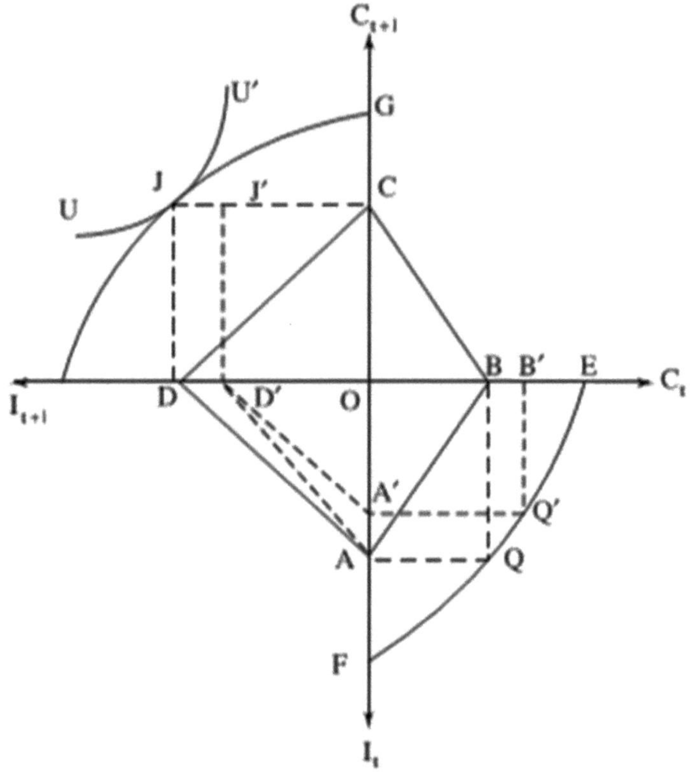


**Fig. 22.3** Consumption implication of environmental degradation. (Source: Shome (1996))

which indicate that the production of the investment goods or consumption goods will increase[18] (the production of the other remaining the same) if and only if, $F$, the constraining factor increases.[19]

Using the more restrictive formulation in Eqs. 22.9 and 22.10, Fig. 22.2 shows the impact of environmental degradation of period $(t + 1)$ production. Determined by $f^{c}$ and $f^{i}$, factor $F$ (see Eq. 22.8) constrains production in period $(t + 1)$ to J′ which lies within GH. As long as there is environmental degradation in period $t$, different combinations of $f^{c}$ and $f^{i}$ would constrain production in period $(t + 1)$ and comprise a binding constraint such as KL in period $(t + 1)$.

[18]The increase being referred to would be from a constrained equilibrium in period $(t + 1)$, such as J′ in Fig. 22.2.

[19]$F_t$ could be seen to work in a three-pronged manner. (1) A 'fixed endowment' of $F_t$ is determined by $f^c$ and $f^i$ which, in turn, are determined by the previous period's environmental policies; (2) a greater availability of $F_{t+1}$ implies that more $I_t$ can be brought into the production process as a factor of production, thus they are complimentary and (3) while $L_t$ and $K_t$ are substitutable in the production of $I_t$ and $C_t$, $F_t$ is not.

Thus, a reduced quadrilateral such as ABCD′ results if, for example in period *t*, the capital goods industry causes environmental degradation with detrimental consequences on its production in period (*t* + 1).

Figure 22.3 illustrates the backward implication of J′ for period *t* if factor *F* had not been depleted: more consumption good OB′ may as well have been consumed and less investment goods OA′ produced. The generation of period *t* unwittingly sacrificed consumption BB′ without receiving the anticipated results in period (*t* + 1).

To sum up: (1) the *F* constraint (environmental degradation) results in a reduced $Y_{t+1}$, (2) the maximum possible investment (and minimum consumption) need not be opted for in period *t* and (3) the reduced $Y_{t+1}$ results in factor unemployment in period (*t* + 1).

## References


Bell, Gerwin. 1995. User Charges. In *Policy Handbook*, ed. Parthasarathi Shome, 104–108. Washington, DC: IMF.

Bird, Richard M., and Barbara D. Miller. 1990. Taxes, User Charges, and the Urban Poor. In *Taxation in Developing Countries*, ed. Richard M. Bird and Oliver Oldman, 426–435. Baltimore: Johns Hopkins University Press.

Brown Weiss, Edith. 1993. Intergenerational Equity: Toward an International Legal Framework. In *Global Accord – Environmental Challenges and International Responses*, ed. Nazli Choucri, 333–353. Cambridge: The MIT Press.

Choucri, Nazli, and Robert C. North. 1993. Global Accord: Imperatives for the Twenty-first Century. In *Global Accord – Environmental Challenges and International Responses*, ed. Nazli Choucri, 477–507. Cambridge: The MIT Press.

Cline, William R. 1992. *The Economics of Global Warming*. Washington, DC: Institute for International Economics.

Davidian, Zaven N. 1994. *Economic Disparities Among Nations*. Calcutta: Oxford University Press.

Nellor, David C.L. 1995. Environmental Taxes. In *Policy Handbook*, ed. Parthasarathi Shome, 108–112. Washington, DC: IMF.

OECD. 1992. *Global Warming: The Benefits of Emission Abatement*. Paris: OECD.

Pigou, Arthur Cecil. 1920. *The Economics of Welfare*. Fourth Edition 1932 Reprinted in 2013. London: Palgrave Macmillan.

Richardson, Pearl. 1993. *The Growth of Federal User Charges*. Washington: Congressional Budget Office.

Rothenberg, Jerome. 1993. Economic Perspectives on Time Comparisons: Alternative Approaches to Time Comparisons. In *Global Accord – Environmental Challenges and International Responses*, ed. Nazli Choucri, 355–397. Cambridge: The MIT Press.

Shome, Parthasarathi. 1996. A 21st Century Global Carbon Tax. *Bulletin for International Bureau of Fiscal Documentation* 50 (11/12): 481–489.

Singh, Katar. 1994. *Managing Common Pool Resources*. Delhi: Oxford University Press.

Soroos, Marvin S. 1991. The Atmosphere as an International Common Property Resource. In *Global Policy Studies: International Interaction Toward Improving Public Policy*, ed. Stauart S. Nagel, 1888–1220. London: McMillan.

Victor, David G., Abram Chayes, and Eugene B. Skolnikoff. 1993. Pragmatic Approaches to Regime Building for Complex International Problems. In *Global Accord – Environmental Challenges and International Responses*, ed. Nazli Choucri, 453–474. Cambridge: The MIT Press.

# Indirect Taxation Prior to GST: India Case Study 23

## 23.1 Introduction

India has a long history of indirect taxes reflecting the tax assignment drawn out in the Indian constitution. Originally, it comprised sales taxes on commodities (goods) and a handful of listed services at the level of the states—with each state having its own regime—and excises at the manufacturing level at the level of the central government called Union, or central, excises. The excises were not selective and were imposed on all goods at different rates. Subsequently, it was realised that the system was beset with cascading and, in the 1980s, the central government introduced a modified VAT (MODVAT) on goods that allowed input tax credit (ITC) though not comprehensively. The MODVAT was subsequently called the central VAT (CENVAT).

Since these were confined exclusively to goods or commodities, in 1994 the central government—centre—introduced a tax on three selected services—insurance, telecommunications and stockbroking—at 5%. Gradually, more services were brought into the base, and the rate was gradually increased to 15% by 2017 (including a cess). Services as an overall category were not, however, mentioned in the taxes assigned to different levels of government in the national constitution, though a 'residual' category was assigned to the centre. Accordingly, the centre interpreted that category to include services.

During the same period, the states introduced their own VAT in 2005 based on deliberations in a committee of state-level finance ministers and a permanent invitee from the central government, with the central finance minister providing assurance and a holding hand in terms of financial compensation to the states for 3 years in the event of revenue loss after their VAT introduction. The state VAT slashed the number of tax rates of the earlier sales tax and introduced the same VAT base across all states with a few allowable exemptions.

After a decade of debate and preparation, India's scattered indirect tax system was brought under one umbrella entitled a Goods and Services Tax (GST) in 2017. The GST included goods and services and applied to both the centre and states. This was

 
P. Shome, *Taxation History, Theory, Law and Administration*, Springer Texts in Business and Economics, https://doi.org/10.1007/978-3-030-68214-9_23

an important move for a fiscally federal country to be able to introduce a comprehensive tax for both the centre and states. Other countries such as Argentina have not been able to do so. And Brazil which was the earliest to introduce such a tax in the mid-1960s has not been able to reform it as its base and rate structure have become increasingly fragmented through the ensuing decades.[1]

India's experience with indirect taxation prior to the introduction of GST comprises the subject matter of this chapter.

## 23.2 State-Level Sales Taxes

State sales taxes were levied on the intra-state sale of all commodities except newspaper, and a few services such as electricity, transportation including road and inland waterways and entertainment. There was also a tax on inter-state trade called the central sales tax (CST). Its rate was legislated by the centre but collected and revenue retained by states on exports made to other states. The CST rate increased from 1 to 4% over time as the states' revenue needs increased.

The evolution of the state sales taxes reflected their revenue needs without much recognition of the principles of taxation such as efficiency or simplicity. To add to the complexity, most states imposed a surcharge on their sales taxes. They also had a tax based on the turnover of traders whose marginal rate increased with the turnover of the dealer. Thus, there were the sales tax, surcharge and turnover tax. Some identified them through legislation; others simply lumped them under the rubric, additional tax. During certain periods, the tax was collected at multiple points along the supply chain though, by 1989–1990, most states were using a single point sales tax. Further, in some states, a tax on selected commodities such as sugarcane was levied on the purchaser—and thus called a purchase tax—because of the convenience of collection from large purchasers rather than from smaller, farmer suppliers.

The tax rates varied across states, from commodity to commodity, as well as with its intended end-use. Tax rates varied in the range 4–12%, and the number of rates between 7 and 25% depending on the state. The bases were narrow reflecting numerous exemptions and concessions, allowing tax deferral or use of unpaid tax as interest-free loan for region-specific, or commodity-specific, investment.

With a view to mitigating the impact of cascading caused by sales taxes, states gave some relief for taxes paid on inputs. Nevertheless, there was significant cascading left in the structure that carried with it the deleterious ramification of lost output. Similar was the effect of cascading from central excises. In 1989–1990, input taxes within central excises and state sales taxes accounted for more than 30%

[1]Arguments that France was the first is erroneous since it introduced the debit–credit principle in the calculation of tax for selected goods while Brazil introduced the tax on a comprehensive base; and it was a fiscal federal VAT comprising three levels—federal (central), state and municipal—of government. The fact that Brazil's VAT needs fundamental reform in current times is another matter; it reveals the wearing out of the VAT with age, and the difficulty in forging understandings, leave alone agreements, between the states on the one hand, and the centre, on the other.

of the effective tax rates for most commodities and 10% for state-level services. State sales taxes fared worse than central excises in input tax cascading.[2]

## 23.3 Other State-Level Taxes

**State-Level Excises:** The states taxed a few demerit goods and the centre some others. Thus, the states taxed consumable alcohol or liquor, and the centre taxed tobacco products. Most states' tax rates were high, buttressed by fees and fines, thus often rendering the higher than international rates. Some states even took over the wholesale distribution of liquor and undertook auctioning of vending rights to ensure that only liquor routed through formal channels was consumed.[3]

**Registration Fees:** These were, and continue to be, imposed by states as a service charge for the documentation and preservation of property documents. Rates were high, often close to 10%, often leading to litigation and evasion.

**Stamp Duty (Non-judicial Stamps):** It was, and continues to be, the tax paid on the purchase of property. The rates in the early era were very high, leading to an understatement of property value declared. Therefore, payment partially by cash for a property purchase became common practice. Consequently, some states began to lower stamp duty rates in recent times resulting in significant revenue gains. Further, the stamp duty, being in the nature of a tax on a transfer, possesses the elements of a cascading turnover tax. Ideally, the state VAT should have subsumed the stamp duty and allowed ITC for it. Unfortunately, that was not possible since most states did not agree to it. It was not possible to do even under the GST.

**Motor Vehicles Taxation (MVT):** It comprises a registration fee, permit and driving license, and has existed since 1940. The rates varied according to type of vehicle (motors, cabs, taxis, stage carriers) or laden weight. Permits of private carriers faced higher rates than those of public carriers. Some states used specific rates based on the vehicle's unladen weight or cubic capacity—while others had an ad valorem structure to avoid regressivity associated with specific rates.[4] In recent times, the MVT features as a lifetime tax as a practical measure.

**Tax on Passengers and Goods (PGT):** It was levied on passengers and goods carried by road or by inland waterways based on seating capacity. It was collected monthly at checkposts from tour operators. High administrative costs incurred in manning checkposts with the objective of controlling tax evasion increased the cost of tax collection.

Since the incidence of both MVT and PGT was on the same cohort of taxpayers, some states merged the two into a single tax. Some states levied an additional surcharge on MVT. The two taxes were similar to user charges and should have been ideally used for financing construction and maintenance of roads and

[2]See Aggarwal (1995).

[3]Government of India (1997).

[4]Physical attributes of a vehicle may not reflect the price.

waterways. However, they were not earmarked and the use of revenue was at the discretion of state-level policymakers. There was a subsumption under the GST when it came into being.

**Profession Tax:** The profession tax was a 'charge' on professions with a monetary ceiling of Rs. 2500. The ceiling was last fixed in 1989 through a constitutional amendment. Therefore, in effect, it became a miniscule tax in terms of revenue though it was always separated from any closeness with an income tax on the professions.

Profession tax, levied by the state government, continues to exist and is different in different states. Every state has its own laws and regulations to govern professional tax of that particular state. However, all the states do follow a slab system based on income to levy profession tax. A tax advisory group for the Tenth Plan recommended that the ceiling for profession tax should be increased to Rs. 5000. It said that it should be merged with the VAT (and, later GST) in the same way as the MVT. Nevertheless, the tax continues with a ceiling of Rs. 2500 to the present day.

The GST subsumed many indirect taxes on consumption and production at the level of both the centre and states including central excise duty, service tax, state VAT, CST, countervailing duty and special additional duty of customs, Octroi and entry tax, purchase tax,[5] luxury tax, and tax on lotteries, betting and gambling. That clearly reduced the fragmentation of indirect taxation. However, there are four state-level taxes that are excluded from GST: on petroleum products, electricity duty,[6] on alcohol for human consumption and stamp duty on immovable property. We shall address these taxes later in the chapter.

## 23.4 Central Sales Tax (CST)

In 1956, Parliament legislated the CST authorising the central government to levy a tax on inter-state sales, with the power to administer it delegated to the states, and retention of revenue with the state of origin of the sales (prior to its export to another state). Initially, the rate was 1%, then raised successively to 4%, for transactions between dealers registered for CST. It was collected by the exporter from the importer trader or dealer and transferred to the exporter state tax administration. If the importer dealer was not registered, the rate was double. The transaction was

[5]Octroi was a tax that imposed physical checks on transport vehicles prior to entering a municipal area. Entry Tax, a later version, was imposed based on financial accounts rather than physical checks though selected large municipalities including Mumbai had continued with the Octroi. The tax caused immense costs to the production–distribution chain. As already indicated, purchase tax on purchasers was collected in a few large agricultural states on their produce at the wholesale marketplace.

[6]The power ministry began deliberations on bringing electricity under GST, as a recent study it conducted showed that this would reduce per unit cost of power to generation, distribution and transmission companies by 17 paise per unit, leading to big savings for consumers. See Singh (2020). (Hundred paise equal one rupee).

conducted through a specified form entitled the C Form. The C Form was issued by the importing state to the importing registered dealers within the state. It was submitted to the exporting dealer in order that the importer could avail himself of CST paid to the exporter. The availability of C Form was often constrained, leading to consternation among honest taxpayers. For certain categories and tax rates, the C Form was not required.

There was a plethora of other conditions and forms associated with the type of trade. Since both sales tax and CST applied only when there was a sale, there was no tax applicable when goods moved from one state to another as a transfer between branches of the same business—on a 'consignment' basis. This was a source of tax evasion since an ordinary transfer could be classified as a branch transfer that would obviate paying CST in the exporting state. To plug this loophole, a constitutional amendment was passed to levy tax on consignments as well.

The CST converted the sales tax to an origin-based tax rather than a residence-based tax. Thus, the CST was not a consumption tax collected by the final consuming state. It constricted any possibility of a common market in India. Since the tax remained embedded in the prices of goods, it adversely affected the international competitiveness of exports. Inasmuch as the state administrations had to issue and monitor C Forms, the tax was an added burden on them.

The states maintained a vested interest in maintaining the CST since they collected some 20% of sales tax revenue from it and, in some exporting states, as high as 35%. It was not surprising that the CST could not be eliminated completely when states introduced the VAT but was reduced progressively. It was finally eliminated with the GST when the indirect tax structure became fully residence-based, or a tax on consumption. This meant that GST accrued to those states where a commodity or service is finally consumed. To ensure smooth flow of inter-state trade and tax collection thereof, a complex administrative mechanism was set up that shall be described in Chap. 24 which addresses the GST.

## 23.5 Union Excise Duties

### 23.5.1 Excise Structure Before MODVAT

There were a number of excise duties at the central level, levied on medium and large manufacturers. These comprised basic excise duty and a special excise duty which was a surcharge on the basic rate, until they were merged in 1993–1994. Additional excise duties in lieu of sales tax was levied and collected on textiles, tobacco and sugar, the revenue being transferred to the states. The general textile duties were earmarked for the development of markets for handlooms and power looms. Cesses were levied on a few commodities such as tea, coffee and sugar. These were earmarked for the development of their respective industries.

The excise structure was complex. There was a multiplicity of rates and rate changes were made annually. It was replete with exemptions, end-use concessions and other forms of incentives. They caused cascading due to the rates failing to keep up a relationship between output and input rates, and specified commodities were put under a presumptive 'proforma tax credit' (PTC) scheme.

Exemptions and tax concessions were notified throughout the year. Exemptions were granted for taxes paid on imported inputs or from specified domestic regions. Thus, the rates announced in the annual budgets effectively became ceiling rates. Effective duty rates were difficult to decipher. The entire structure lost rationale and became challenging to administer, relying on a rudimentary and hands-on approach, rather than on a modern, automated system.

### 23.5.2 Modified Value-Added Tax (MODVAT)

In 1986, the central government introduced MODVAT into the excise structure, the objective being to expand ITC across industries. It was done in a stepwise expansion, over the following years, in the number of goods it covered. ITC, now called MODVAT credit, could be taken against the tax manufacturers had collected on their outputs. Commodities other than textiles, petroleum products, tobacco products and plant and machinery were allowed MODVAT credit.

Small manufacturers in the metal industry were allowed MODVAT credit without production of documents to prove they had paid excise duty on inputs. However, it was allowed at specified rates and for certain inputs only, resulting in less than normally calculated ITC.[7] This option was extended from small units to all units after a month of the introduction of MODVAT.

To recall, the concept of the ITC mechanism is that a taxpayer has to pass on to the government the entire amount he has collected from his purchasers unless he can show the invoices for the amount of tax he has paid on his own input purchases. If he can show this, he needs to pay only the difference between debits (his tax collection) and credit (his own tax payments). Financial control mechanisms should suffice to keep the administration rolling, with selective audit of taxpayers. Nevertheless, dependence on physical control methods of administration (checking entry and exit at the factory gate) continued even in the mid-1990s. The objective apparently was the fear of revenue loss by the tax administration. Such continuing rudimentary practices of administration were analysed and revealed in a year-long research investigation.[8]

This carries important lessons for the administration of a VAT-like tax in its initial phase in that it may not be as easy to administer in emerging economies as it is usually made out to be by international tax experts. The reason is the likelihood of continuing tax evasion. Indeed, in areas of MODVAT administration where physical control had been replaced by financial control, the study found that serious lapses

[7]The scheme covered steel ingots and re-rollables, flat products of steel, unwrought aluminium, copper, lead and zinc and waste or scrap of aluminium, copper, lead and zinc.

[8]See Shome et al. (1997).

had occurred. Clearly, an overhauled VAT administration would be needed if India were to introduce a modern VAT in the future.

Administration problems arose from complex definitions of important concepts involved as a result of which, until 1994–1995, the end of the study period, a large number of challenges had arisen regarding admissibility of inputs for MODVAT credit. In the case of capital goods, for example, such controversies arose in 798 cases and, in the case of other inputs, there were 1501 cases. Together they accounted for 2299 cases or 40% of the total of 5840 cases. Questions regarding the admissibility of inputs were reflected, among other reasons, by the insertion of expressions such as 'used in manufacture' and 'used in relation to manufacture' in the MODVAT rules. While courts were generally of the view that both phrases should be taken in the same overall sense, clearly the latter definition was broader and continued to lead to more MODVAT credit claims, hence to litigation.

The audit system was found to be ununiform across regions. There appeared to be little difference in strategy between larger and smaller units. Some audits were function-based, some conducted on a geographical basis. The latter comprised auditing a group of factories in a particular area, the former to group visits to all factories relating to a particular set of commodities. Textiles would be covered by one group, metals by another, and so on. Despite its possibility for officers to develop expertise over a group of commodities that they audited, geographically based audit remained firmly anchored. These were just a few of the issues that persisted with the rudimentary MODVAT.

International experts have commented that a high percentage of administration staff should conduct audit rather than routine functions such as assessment. In countries where there was low tax evasion, the percentage of staff assigned to audit functions were reported to have reached 40%.[9] In India, the proportion was around 10% for customs and excise departments combined. In sum, at that point in time, many lessons were to be learnt before India could move forward to a comprehensive indirect tax structure in the future.

## 23.6 Value-Added Tax (VAT)

While the MODVAT was a central government phenomenon, the VAT was at the level of the states. Hence, it was a more complex process before it could be implemented with the majority of states on board. Few states that did not join at the beginning also joined in when they saw the revenue success of the VAT after the shift from their earlier fractured sales tax regimes.

[9]See Silvani (1992), p. 287.

### 23.6.1 Emergence of VAT

In a conference of finance ministers in December 1995, the central finance minister called upon the state-level finance ministers to study the ramifications of the prevailing distortive state sales taxes and the CST in adversely affecting business decision-making and production. States were known to outcompete one another by lowering sales tax rates to attract investment. To mitigate it, four-floor rates—by category of goods—had been agreed upon among themselves, but several negative features remained in the overall structure including the multiplicity of rates and exemptions. Therefore, there was a need for a VAT-like tax at the state level.

In December 1996, a task force comprising tax experts and state-level finance secretaries submitted a first report on phasing out the CST. It recommended a reduction of the CST rate from 4% to 2%, and further reductions based on certain preconditions. Subsequently, state chief ministers formed an 'empowered committee' of state finance ministers (EC-VAT) to consider the introduction of a VAT that would eliminate remaining lacunae in the improved sales tax.

In 2002, the central government, in a conference of EC (VAT), announced plans for the introduction of a VAT in all states from April 2003. They agreed on a minimum set of common features in every state's VAT legislation. A model VAT structure was circulated to all states. It was agreed that the CST would be phased out. However, the states postponed the implementation of VAT in the last minute, with impending general elections.[10]

### 23.6.2 Reasons for Not Introducing VAT in the First Round

To begin with, most states were not adequately prepared. Some states were hurrying through their VAT legislation in state assemblies even in the last week of March. Second, it was apprehended by dealers or traders that a VAT would increase their paperwork that appeared to be more complicated. Third, there was disagreement among states on several points. Thus, though the VAT was agreed to replace the sales tax and minor taxes such as the works contract tax, lease tax, turnover tax and luxury tax, it would fail to simplify comprehensively since some states did not agree to abolish Octroi, a distortionary tax on business entry into municipalities, and some states did not agree to merge taxes on selected services into the VAT. Fourth, most states were reluctant to subsume state-level excise duties into the VAT preferring, instead, to continue their prevailing structures with the objective to have separate, possibly politically motivated, control over them. Combined, it was agreed that the information chain across states would remain truncated, affecting the administration of a comprehensive VAT at the subnational level adversely.

Fifth, from the states' point of view, the fact that revenue gains would be uneven across states was a big obstacle, unless the centre came forward to compensate the

[10]The exception was the state of Haryana which went ahead with its own rudimentary VAT.

revenue losing states. Thus, the anticipated benefits did not match up to the lingering adverse political economy of VAT introduction at that point in time. Sixth, and not the least, traders apprehended that prices of certain products would rise, for example, medicines and drugs, due to an inevitable increase in their effective tax rates. There were demonstrations in many state capitals. In essence, there was a lack of consensus among all stakeholders—state policymakers and traders or dealers—for a VAT to be introduced at that point.

### 23.6.3 The Second Round in VAT Introduction

In January 2005, EC (VAT) completed a White Paper on VAT. It proposed rates of 4% and 12.5%, with a common base and exemption list and a pool of 40 exemptions for goods of local importance, from which each state could pick 10 exemptions. There was a peculiarity in that the lower rate of 4% covered capital goods and raw materials that, under the credit principle, would be credited out anyway. Therefore, it would have been better to reserve the lower rate for goods of consumption by lower-income deciles as is common global practice. Nevertheless, the uniformity attained in the VAT structure was superior to the sales tax structures that it replaced. The distortionary CST continued, however.

On 1 April 2005, the state-level VAT was introduced though opposition states did not join at first.[11] The experience from the VAT was salutary. Revenue growth from the VAT was 25% per annum in contrast to an average of 12.5% from the sales tax for 5 years prior to the VAT's introduction. The VAT was a good example of fiscal federal cooperation with the centre assuring a formula-based compensation for revenue loss incurred by states. It reflected their previous 3 best years' revenue (within the last 5 years) which was calculated at an average annual growth rate of 17.5%. The compensation would be given for 3 years, on a declining scale from 100% of revenue loss to nil. Rs. 5000 crores were allocated to a compensation fund. While most states experienced revenue gain, some large manufacturing states lost but were compensated from the fund, resulting in the centre's just exhausting the budgeted amount for compensation. In view of the nation-wide average revenue gain, eventually, all states introduced the VAT reflecting its revenue productivity.

An important cause of revenue expansion was, first, the extension of the taxpayer base to include traders and retailers. Earlier, under the sales tax, the practice in many states was merely to add a premium to the manufacturing value (based on the central excise) to derive a presumptive sales tax base. Second, many states that earlier applied rudimentary tax administration methods began to tax goods in a more careful manner using the invoice method for the first time, which expanded the effective tax base.

[11] States ruled by opposition parties such as the Bharatiya Janata Party (BJP), the Samajwadi Party (SP) and Dravida Munnetra Kazhagam (DMK) did not join at that time.

### 23.6.4 Phasing Out the CST

The next phase was a centre–state agreement to phase out the CST. Under this principle, the CST rate of 4% would decline by 1% per annum, reaching 0% by 1 April 2010, when a centre–state GST was planned to be introduced. While the process was initiated, the trajectory of reduction of CST stalled at 2%, reflecting different factors. First, states claimed that they were not being compensated for the revenue loss that they were suffering from CST reduction from 4% to 2%. They became increasingly vocal regarding the amount of compensation that they should receive for revenue loss from the lowering and eventual abolition of CST.

Second, states argued that the revenue loss from CST abolition would be a permanent one so that they expected the centre to work out a perennial compensation mechanism for that loss. The centre was unable to alleviate the states' concerns or work out a midway solution. The chairman of EC (VAT) declared publicly that there was a sense of distrust in the centre–state relationship. Centre–state fiscal federal relations appeared to have reached a nadir.

Third, if the CST were to be abolished, the prevailing mechanism based on filling out forms to administer and check the inter-state trade flow would be lost. Inter-state trade would then have to be tracked through a clearing house mechanism (explained in Chap. 24, Sect. 24.6). Without a robust, ICT software-based clearing house

**Table 23.1** Cascading in indirect tax structure

| Goods | Cascading | Services |
|---|---|---|
| *Manufacturing* | | |
| • CENVAT (Centre)<br>• ITC allowed within CENVAT[a] | • CENVAT<br>– Cascades within regionally dispersed firms<br>– ITC for capital goods given over 2 years | • Service tax (Centre)<br>• ITC allowed between CENVAT and service tax |
| *Wholesale (dealers)* | | |
| • Base includes CENVAT↓[b]<br>Cascading VAT (states) | • State-level VAT<br>– Cascades at three points (as shown in first column) | • ITC not allowed between state-level VAT and service tax |
| *Retail* | | |
| • ITC allowed within state-level VAT but not for services ↓<br>Cascading<br>• Inter-state trade is taxed by CST for which there is no ITC ↓<br>Cascading | | |

Source: Author's calculations

[a]However, ITC is allowed only within a unit, not within a firm across its different units situated in various jurisdictions

[b]↓ denotes that it leads to cascading

mechanism, the CST could not be abolished. Thus, much work remained to be done before abolishing the CST.

### 23.6.5 Cascading Under the VAT

Despite the forward step represented by the state-level VAT, considerable cascading remained in the indirect tax structure. Cascading continued also in the central excises. The points where cascading occurred are shown in the self-explanatory Table 23.1. While formal estimates were not available, using the occurrence of tax rates that could not be credited out in the process of production and distribution, calculations showed that the effective tax rate climbed by 20%. The battle to rid India's manufacturing and services sector from the adverse effects of cascading was not yet fully won. Over the years that followed, it was not too surprising perhaps that Indian manufacturing continued to suffer a significant decline in its share of GDP and lost much competitive edge in international markets.

## References


Aggarwal, Pawan K. 1995. *Incidence of Major Indirect Taxes in India*. New Delhi: NIPFP.

Government of India. 1997. *Tax Policy for the Ninth Five Year Plan (1997–98 to 2001–02)*. Report of the Working Group on Tax Policy. New Delhi: Centax Publications.

Shome, Parthasarathi, S. Mukhopadhyay, and Hasheem N. Saleem. 1997. MODVAT Administration. In *Value Added Tax in India: A Progress Report*, ed. Parthasarathi Shome. New Delhi: Centax Publications.

Silvani, Carlos A. 1992. Improving Tax Compliance. In *Improving Tax Administration in Developing Countries*, ed. Richard M. Bird and Milka Casanegra de Jantscher, 274–309. Washington, DC: IMF.

Singh, Sarita C. 2020. Government Begins Deliberations on Bringing Power Sector Under GST. *The Economics Times*, September 25.

# Goods and Services Tax (GST): India Case Study

# 24

## 24.1 Introduction

The task force on tax policy and administration for India's Tenth Five-Year Plan, 2001, in its report,[1] recommended a seamless tax on goods and services (GST) with parallel channels for the centre and states. The then finance minister mentioned the report in his 2002 Union Budget speech, indicating his intention to implement some of the report's recommendations. That was likely the earliest reference to a comprehensive GST in India's history of indirect taxation.

The subsequent finance minister announced, in his 2006 central budget speech, the intention of his government to introduce a GST.[2] He called for a comprehensive report which was submitted on 31 December 2007. It was co-authored by his representative, the permanent invitee to the state finance ministers' empowered committee (EC), together with a representative of that committee. Considerable work—research and policy oriented—followed between the centre and states for a proposed GST structure though agreement was slow in coming. The 13th Finance Commission also looked into the tax, forming a subcommittee that submitted a report on the GST in 2009. Thus, a range of governmental bodies, politicians and tax experts played crucial roles over one and a half decades in the formulation of India's GST.

On 20 December 2014, the then finance minister called GST the 'single biggest tax reform since Independence', in Parliament.[3] The chairman of a parliamentary select committee on GST played his role in 2015 in convincing his fellow

[1]It was presented to K C Pant, Deputy Chairman of the Planning Commission. The Chairman of the Planning Commission is always the Prime Minister though it is the Deputy Chairman who functions as the main executive and policymaker for this governmental institution that recommends structural economic policy to government. It formulates India's Five-Year Plans which stand apart from the finance minister's (Yashwant Sinha at that time) annual budgetary proposals for the fiscal budget.

[2]It was P. Chidambaram.

[3]It was Arun Jaitley.



P. Shome, *Taxation History, Theory, Law and Administration*, Springer Texts in Business and Economics, https://doi.org/10.1007/978-3-030-68214-9_24

parliamentarians on the efficacy of a GST.[4] However, conditions for an ideal GST were not yet met and it was not immediately introduced. Its eventual introduction was on 1 July 2017, when the national parliament and state assemblies ratified the GST bill, though lingering design faults were glossed over and made their presence felt in the structure of the new tax.

The GST structure turned out to be more complex than its ideal would require. In the end, it was a political compact of fiscal federalism among the centre and the states. Despite its flaws, few countries have achieved a fiscal federal value-added tax (VAT) or GST in this scale. Brazil introduced a conjoint VAT at three levels of government—central, state and municipal—in the mid-1960s, though today it has become fractured, narrow in base and is not managed well.[5] Canada also has a similar federal GST comprising the federal and provincial governments, but it is small compared to India or Brazil in terms of the number of taxpayers reflecting its small population, is highly computerised that utilises considerable financial resources, and enjoys the advantage of relatively little tax evasion. Australia is another country but there it is collected at the central level and then shared with the provinces. Thus, today India stands apart in having successfully introduced a GST simultaneously at central and state levels of government with an extensive scope of its base and nation-wide taxpayer base.

In that light, this chapter addresses a comprehensive list of aspects of the Indian GST. They include, on the policy side, a conceptual basis and ideal design, its revenue base, continuing cascading at certain points of the structure and needed corrections, and the role and functioning of the GST Council, the centre–state policymaking body. On the administration side, they include its success or lack to inculcate a customer focus, the management of GST on inter-state trade, the lack of much-needed software to auto-populate debit–credit links in the production chain, strategies to mitigate tax evasion and continuing incidence of litigation.

## 24.2 Concept and Structure of GST

As its name implies, a GST should cover all goods and services in its base and input tax credit (ITC) should be allowed seamlessly between all items in the base so that there are no items that are excluded from ITC. Second, it should be structured as a VAT such that cascading, or 'tax on tax', should be done away with. The higher are the number and extent of exemptions from the GST base, the more is the extent of cascading left in its structure. This is because an exemption means that an output is not taxed so that no credit can be taken on the tax paid on the inputs that went into its

[4]It was Yashwant Sinha again.

[5]Brazil's VAT was essentially one among the centre and states, the municipalities being assigned local services (ISS) without application of ITC. Also, the base of the state-level VAT (ICMS) was ample as a VAT should be while, at the central level (IPI), it was narrow and included a few industrial products.

production or distribution. The GST is sometimes criticised as exacerbating inflation that is generated through the build-up of product price through the tax-on-tax effect. Eliminating cascading would successfully address this important matter as well.

A third objective of a GST is to keep the number of tax rates as low as possible so that there is no significant mismatch between output and input rates. For example, if the output GST rate is lower than the input GST rate, then credit will be accumulated that cannot be taken against the output tax. And it becomes a difficult 'fitment' exercise to arrive at a menu of rates in a way that such anomalies are minimised.[6] As described below, there are continuing exercises to make necessary corrections since the GST's introduction with both good and bad effects of those interventions.

A fourth objective of GST was the creation of a common market through trade facilitation for the productive sector and enhancement of the ease of doing business. That should take precedence over the government's revenue enhancement at central and state government levels which is of course an objective as well.

Fifth, at the time of a GST or VAT's introduction, countries have attempted to clean up their earlier indirect tax systems. India's GST also subsumed many indirect taxes on consumption and production at the level of both the centre and states. They included central excise duty, service tax, state VAT, CST, Octroi and entry tax, purchase tax, luxury tax, tax on lotteries, betting and gambling, countervailing duty and special additional duty of customs. Thus, the GST clearly reduced the fragmentation of the indirect tax structure.

Table 24.1 presents a structure of how a fiscal federal GST should ideally have looked in India.

## 24.3 GST Base

The crux of a GST is to have a broad base that, in turn, enables a low tax rate to yield the same tax revenue. However, petroleum, alcoholic beverages and tobacco products, representing almost half the revenue yield, have been kept out of the GST base. Petroleum products contribute one-fourth to half of different states' revenues. To maintain their hold over this stream of revenue, the states have been opposed to including it in the GST base. Though the GST Council retains an enabling provision to tax petroleum, and the centre prefers to include petroleum in the base, states have been steadfast in their resistance to change their view. In addition, electricity duty and stamp duty on immovable property are also excluded from the GST base.

The question that arises is what portion of GDP is covered in the GST base. If one considers the exclusion of real estate from GST and all other inputs and exemptions, some estimates showed an exclusion of 60% of GDP from the GST base. If we ignore real estate, the figure could be between 40 and 50%. In any event, there is little doubt that about half of the GDP has been excluded. This implies that indirect

[6]Cnossen (2013) elaborated on several of these issues in preparation for the Indian GST.

**Table 24.1** Ideal GST framework

| Centre | | States |
|---|---|---|
| Central Goods and Services Tax (CGST) | Selected features | State Goods and Services Tax (SGST) |
| 1 general rate (1 lower rate could be accommodated) | | 1 general rate (1 lower rate could be accommodated) |
| • Broad base including petroleum, alcohol and tobacco<br>• Goods and services to be taxed at general rate<br>• A few low-income consumption items at lower rate<br>• Full ITC across multiple units of a firm | Parallel chains<br>→ No ITC between CGST and SGST<br>• Cascading removed from overall GST system<br>• No CST on inter-state trade<br>– Integrated Goods and Services Tax (IGST) to operate | • Broad base including petroleum, alcohol and tobacco<br>• Subsume smaller taxes<br>• Goods and services taxed at general rate<br>• A few low-income consumption items at lower rate<br>• Abolish CST<br>• Full ITC across states<br>• Monitor inter-state trade with computerised infrastructure<br>• Install clearing house (at central government level) for accounting and payments for inter-state trade (IGST) |

Source: Shome (2017)

taxes paid by this excluded portion will not be credited out in the supply chain and, instead, will be embedded multiple times as the production–distribution chain moves downstream. The ultimate outcome will be continuing distortions in price determination in the economy.[7]

Having a low proportion of GDP in the GST base also implies low revenue productivity even though the VAT or GST is known as a revenue productive tax. A measure of the GST's revenue productivity was observed in Latin America by this author where it has been referred to as the Shome VAT or GST productivity index.[8] To explain, if the general GST rate is X%, then if it is designed well, it should be able to yield ½X% of GDP in revenue. Chile and New Zealand both had an 18% VAT rate and collected approximately 9% of their GDP in revenue on a secular basis during the 1990s.

Most countries achieve 1/3X% of GDP or above without touching ½X%. Countries that linger below 1/3X% comprise examples of poor GST or VAT design and performance. In the United Kingdom, with a 17.5% VAT rate, VAT revenue hovers near 1/3 X% (or 6%) of GDP. The open secret of achieving high VAT or GST revenue productivity is to structure it in such a way that most commodities are at the general rate, there are not too many lower rates, exclusions and exemptions are few, zero-rated items are few—so that most goods and services are covered in the tax base—and tax administration has a customer focus so that tax compliance is enabled

[7]A detailed analysis of the GST base and exclusions from it is found in Srinivasan (2016).

[8]Modi (2009) refers to this.

and, last but not least, the taxpayer base is ample, can be steadily expanded, and mitigating tax evasion is achieved through strategic targeting rather than with a heavy hand.

## 24.4 Cascading Due to Exclusions

Petroleum and electricity are essential inputs in the supply—production and distribution—chain. By keeping these out, both upstream and downstream cascading occurs. This phenomenon can be explained as follows. First, there is a separated tax on petroleum in every state though not under GST. Therefore, the tax paid cannot be credited out by businesses who pay GST when they buy and use petroleum products. Second, petroleum being outside GST, petroleum companies themselves—since they are excluded from GST—do not get any credit for the GST that they are likely to have paid when purchasing their own inputs.

Thus, petroleum companies would tend to add in the tax they pay on their inputs into their product price. And businesses that purchase petroleum would then build in the tax they pay on their petroleum input into the sale price of their product. This could be viewed as double cascading. Also, the resultant high cost of petroleum products leads, in turn, to a high cost of production for several services and industries that receive no ITC on their petroleum use, with the inevitable impact of raising their prices as well.

Similar cascading occurs for other input commodities that are excluded from the GST. In effect, this continues the cascading through the production and distribution chain, with concomitant distortionary production decisions and, therefore, of the pricing of products. Those products that use more inputs that are excluded from GST must suffer a larger effect on their prices vis-à-vis those products that use less excluded inputs. The structure of relative prices that emerges from the anomaly will, in consequence, not reflect consumer preferences that should ideally have determined the relative prices of all products.

Regarding real estate, currently, the GST base only includes the cost of construction materials and services provided by architects and contractors. But land value is excluded; so stamp duty paid on real estate transactions cannot be set off. This generates cascading effects from the construction industry. Had real estate been comprehensively included in the GST base, those cascading effects would have been minimised. The reason for exclusion was the good revenue it generates directly for the states without the relative complications and transparency involved with the GST processes. To give a range, in Maharashtra—a populous and urbanised state—20% of its own revenue sources and, in Bihar—rural and with a lower per capita state GDP—12% of its own revenue, come from stamp duty.

## 24.5 Administrative Aspects

Large exclusions from the GST base limits the information that tax administrations at both central and state levels can gather to complete audit processes involving upstream to downstream production and distribution chains for these commodities. Therefore, it is important to bring them into the GST base. What countries do is to levy turnover-based excises and, in addition, impose the GST rate on them. That assures higher revenue from these products which is justified since tobacco and alcohol are considered to be demerit goods and petroleum is a non-renewable resource.[9]

The debate during the decade prior to the GST's introduction in India was for it to be structured along revenue-neutral lines. But there were bound to be winners and losers among the various players, for example, among the central and state tax administrations, among producers and dealers or traders, and among consumers. This was unavoidable to some extent but what is important is to install mechanisms to monitor against malpractice that could occur in particular during the early implementation phase. A monitoring cell to check if excessive prices are not being charged by retailers is commonplace in countries that introduce a GST or VAT. For example, in South Africa, such a cell played a crucial role in checking the immediate ramifications of its new VAT including keeping its inflation effect in check, so that prices actually fell as cascading was reduced significantly. A monitoring cell was not formally put in place in India.

From all the challenges that India's nascent GST is encountering (see Sects. 24.10 and 24.11 below), it becomes clear that it is not a simple tax, with an objective to provide a basic understanding of these topics. With the objective of providing a basic understanding of the GST in practice, the Indian Chartered Accountant Institute (ICAI) issued 11 handbooks on procedural aspects of this complex tax. A student interested in GST practice should peruse their content. They are entitled, Tax Deduction at Source (TDS) Provisions; Registration; Job Work; Casual Taxable Person; Invoicing; Reverse Charge; Annual Return; Refund; E-way Bill; Interest, Late Fee, and Penalties; Advance Ruling under GST.[10] They contain provisions under the law including notifications, circulars and orders up to 31 March 2020, issued by the government along with some frequently asked questions (FAQs).

## 24.6 Implications of Consumption Tax on Inter-state Trade Mechanism

The GST is designed to be a consumption-based tax. Therefore, for State Goods and Services Tax (SGST), a method has been found such that the revenue from inter-state trade goes to the state that imports and consumes rather than to the state that

[9]See Chap. 21, Sect. 21.9, and Chap. 22, Sect. 22.4, for details.

[10]See ICAI (2020).

produces and exports a good or service (as was the case under the CST). The producer/exporter in state A collects the revenue from the purchaser/dealer (from an importing state B) and passes that revenue to a clearing house operated by the central government from where it is transferred to the importer state's exchequer.[11]

The shared GST Network—GSTN—between the central government and states that works on this principle is a good feature of the GST. First, as a new feature in Indian taxation, the central government and states share the same platform. Second, the public and private sectors share the responsibility to deliver efficient processes that already exists in the income tax area since the design of the facility and the operational responsibility are shared with the private sector.[12] Teething problems do remain in that revenue intake deposited at the GSTN (in the central government's account) has to be correctly determined and distributed to all states.

## 24.7 GST Council: Centre–State Policymaking for GST[13]

GST-related policy is made on a continuing basis by a GST Council. It represents an example of successful fiscal federal cooperation.[14] Its composition comprises the central finance minister as chair, the central minister of state (deputy minister for revenue or finance) as a member and, at the level of states, the minister in charge of finance or taxation or any other minister nominated by each state government, as members. The centre has a one-third voting share and the states have two-third. The Council recommends changes in rates and bands, exemptions, thresholds, changes in the GST law, principles of levy, IGST apportionment among states, principles to govern the place of supply, and any other policy matter.

A dispute settlement authority that had been dropped from the originally proposed constitution amendment bill for the GST in 2011 was reinstated after the opposition parties in parliament refused to vote without its inclusion. The reasoning of the opposition was that, if each state had its own authority, the concept of a common market—the fountainhead of a federal GST—would be thwarted. A compromise was reached and the GST Council established a mechanism to adjudicate any dispute arising in the process of functioning of the GST. Since disputes can be between: (a) the centre versus one or more states; (b) the centre and some states versus one or more states; or (c) state versus state, the final position implies that there will be a standing mechanism to resolve various categories of disputes.

[11]An early description of the clearing house mechanism is found in Varsano (2000). A list of designated banks could also act as a clearing house but, for this arrangement, banks would have to be compensated as a service provider in particular if they are private sector banks.

[12]The government has contracted Infosys, an ICT major, for this purpose.

[13]The constitution, as amended, requires the GST Council to be constituted under article 279A of the Constitution. This was carried out by the President vide Notification dated 15 September 2016.

[14]See Poddar and Ahmad (2009).

In its immediate post-introduction phase, the GST Council has devoted significant time in making several rate changes. This mainly reflects inconsistencies in the initial fitment of rates between inputs and outputs as well as political pressures for other rate changes. It is hoped that, after correcting for rate anomalies, the Council will adhere to considering genuine policy improvements.

## 24.8 Government's Customer Focus

The government's attention to taxpayer welfare was evident in the initial phase of GST implementation. Between 1 July 2017 and 15 June 2018, there were 50 customer-focused communications addressed to tax officers from the chairman of the central board of indirect taxes and customs (CBIC), the main policymaking office for central level indirect taxation. They emphasised the following aspects:

- Officers were asked to get feedback from GST *sewa kendras* (service centres) through interactions with the trade to understand the pain points of taxpayers. Addressing grievances at the ground level, and attending to them on a real-time basis, were encouraged. Any issue requiring immediate attention was asked to be escalated up through video conferencing.
- GST outreach programmes, seminars, workshops for the trade and consumers were encouraged. Regional commissioners were asked to identify officers in need of training using a GST master class and ensure that they were equipped to handle queries from the trade. They were asked to file returns themselves in order to appreciate the nature of difficulties faced by taxpayers.
- A 'GST rates finder' mobile app featuring the rates for all goods and services, and reflecting notifications, was made available for download and use. When the GST Council reduced GST rates for certain items, the chairman immediately indicated that stakeholders needed to be updated on those decisions, wrote to industry leaders, and requested officers to ensure that the benefit of such reductions was passed on by suppliers to purchasers by way of commensurate reduction in prices.
- A GST practitioners' scheme was installed to assist taxpayers in comprehending their obligations and filing tax returns.
- On the customs side, an IGST refunds module on exports was successfully operationalised. A simple mechanism was improvised for immediate interim relief to exporters. A 'special refund fortnight' was organised from 31 May to 14 June 2018, for clearing pending GST refund applications that had been submitted on or before 30 April 2018. In a zonal office (Zone II) in Mumbai, the pendency of more than 100,000 drawback (refund) claims was successfully liquidated, reaching zero pendency within a month.
- The chairman asked that impeccable integrity be ensured while carrying out the assessment of taxpayers. Officers and staff across the country took an integrity pledge, with a continuation of assiduous reinforcing of the ideals of probity and integrity. The CBIC observed a 'vigilance awareness week' (against corruption) from 30 October to 4 November 2017.

Thus, customer focus was a recognisable focus during the GST's first year. Of course, its success depended on the extent to which it realistically influenced field officers and their operations. This experience could be a practice to be emulated by other countries while introducing or reforming their GST or VAT.

## 24.9 Critical Policy Corrections

A number of critical policy corrections have to be undertaken in the future by the GST Council.[15] Among them are:

- Removing continuing differentiation between goods and services.
- Reducing the number of rates and classifications. The voluminous list of the GST tariff structure reveals a possibility for a high incidence of litigation.
- Annulling an administrative requirement for inter-state dealers or traders to register in every state they trade in. For otherwise, such a registration requirement would go against the common market principle.
- Stepping back from a newly introduced rule which was not prevalent under the earlier state-level VAT. It allows a dealer or trader to be picked up for audit in any state making post-tax compliance onerous for taxpayers.
- Removing the rule that no ITC is to be given to an output supplier until the seller of input deposits the tax amount in the government's exchequer, thus shifting a government responsibility to the taxpayer (output producer). The impracticality of an input purchaser to ensure this is only too apparent.
- Removing a presumption of 'unjust enrichment'. This requires a producer not only to decrease the price of his product if the government has brought down its GST rate but also to prove that a refund has been made of any interim revenue he has already collected from the purchaser. Without proof that any gain in profit has been passed back to consumers, a national anti-profiteering authority or watchdog has been empowered to come down heavily on the producer.
  This is impossible to convincingly demonstrate in many cases. Indeed, the matter should be ideally addressed through a GST monitoring cell, already mentioned above, which had been included in the first GST draft but subsequently removed. By introducing such a cell, India would emulate many other countries and assume the correct technical and intellectual responsibility for GST implementation.
- Replacing the joint administrative powers of the centre and states over the same taxpayers even at low turnover levels. Currently, this comprises a prohibitive compliance burden on taxpayers who have to deal with tax administrations at both levels of government, as well as all the state-level administrations where he trades. In fact, taxpayers below a turnover level had been excluded by the centre under the earlier CENVAT and service tax. However, the GST regime lowered

[15] As of this writing. However, even if some of them are addressed, what is to be kept in mind is that such weaknesses are to be avoided while making initial policy.

the turnover thresholds, thereby putting an administrative burden on officers without the promise of much revenue gain, and making it punitive for small taxpayers to comply with the tax.

- Improving operations at inter-state checkpoints. Some states continue to check every incoming vehicle. This cuts into the administrative benefits from a GST, one of which is speed and ease of conducting business. A uniform checking model, based on spot checks, needs to be installed. This matter is not related to the Octroi or entry tax at the municipal level which were subsumed under the GST, but with the type of checking applied at the states' borders with other states. Of course, appropriate ICT-dependent mechanisms need to be installed to achieve success.
- Facilitating small taxpayers to pay tax rather than pushing them out of the formal economy or from productive activity altogether. So far, there have been sporadic accounts of small businesses having significant difficulty in paying taxes using complicated forms several times a year. The government has also attempted to simplify the process but much remains to smoothen the process further.
- Ensuring clarity from the central- and state-level authorities in order to maintain consistency. Designating a single nodal point to disseminate information about the application of the GST. There is evidence that multiple central ministries have issued complex and contradictory advisories. Inter-ministerial committees and regular meetings need to be put in place, and consistent and early responses to queries should become routine.

## 24.10 Tax Evasion of GST

While emphasising customer focus in the initial phase of GST implementation, the chairman of CBIC reminded officers to keep track of revenue collection. Any decline should be analysed and the reason(s) must be brought to the notice of more senior officers. There was a possibility of wrongful availment of ITC during the transition—as the system passed from the old to the new tax—that would affect revenue adversely. To counter it, continual monitoring and verification by formations of field officers would remain a major focus area of GST administration policy.

One possible error that was made was the existence of a cut-off date for a taxpayer's migration from the old to the new system. This did not play any ostensibly useful role. If a potential taxpayer was delayed in migrating, it did not mean that he should have been stopped from voluntarily entering, however late. Rather, keeping migration open, and steadily scaling up the penalty with the degree of lateness, would have made the transition more palatable especially to taxpayers who owned small and medium enterprises (MSMEs) since this group faced logistical challenges in migration.

### 24.10.1 Lack of Auto-populating Forms

As the GST unfolded, it became clear that there was a certain amount of tax evasion that persisted in particular sectors. This was enabled by slowness in the introduction of automated processes that form the backbone of a GST. The biggest lacuna of the administration was its inability to auto-populate linked information from one tax return form to another. Shorn of technical detail, essentially there are three GST forms that should be linked. Let us call them 1, 2 and 3.

The taxpayer has to report his sales in Form 1, each row showing one sale. The columns in the form comprise the taxpayer's GST number, detail of invoice issued, GST rate applicable, central GST value or amount and state GST value or amount. The total tax revenue collected by this taxpayer for the centre or states is obtained when the CGST or SGST column is aggregated.

Form 2 shows the taxpayer's purchases. Here, too, each row represents one purchase and the columns show the GST number, detail of invoice received, the rate of tax paid and the value of CGST and SGST paid. Aggregating CGST or SGST columns yields the value of CGST or SGST paid on purchases by the taxpayer. Importantly, this amount comprises the ITC that the taxpayer has the right to claim back.

Form 3 is the GST return (tax return for GST). The columns show the tax liability, which is the value of tax collected on sales minus the value of tax paid on purchases (ITC). Additional columns show how much of the tax is paid in the form of cash, and how much through accumulated credit (AC). AC is shown in an electronic ledger tracking how much tax is paid using cash and how much using ITC.

If output value is higher than input value as should usually be the case, one may expect that tax paid on inputs would be lower than the tax paid on output. But that is not always the case. It is not rare for ITC to get accumulated since the GST rate on output could be lower than on input, or ITC could be statutorily given over a period of years, or upon proof of documents—such as for exports—to the satisfaction of the administrator or ITC could be held up reflecting a lack of clarity in the determination of the correct classification of an imported input, or for various other reasons. Therefore, it is quite possible to pay GST in year two with both AC from year one and the remainder with cash available in year two.

The major continuing lacuna is that forms 1, 2 and 3 were intended to be electronically linked but are not. Form 3 should have been automatically (electronically) populated as soon as any information on purchases and sales was entered by a GST numbered taxpayer into form 1 or 2. There should ideally be no requirement or possibility for a taxpayer to enter information into form 3 independently. But that is what is not what is occurring despite the public–private partnership that is managing the ICT aspects currently and was supposed to have designed an electronic interconnectivity of the forms. The introduction of GST without this basic linked-framework is now rearing its head in tax evasion.

Essentially, GST without the innovation of linkages to ensure auto-population implies that it is not fundamentally different from India's earlier indirect tax structures. Similar modes of evasion continue under GST. One method of evasion is claiming huge amounts of tax payment through AC. Without field investigation, there is no way to find if the AC used to pay tax reflects the true picture. Indeed, many large corporations appear to be building up AC through which tax is being paid.[16] Some of it may certainly be legitimate, reflecting GST's structural deficiencies or delay in processing. But that is unlikely to be the entire story.

Another method of evasion is to show large and false turnover and, together with it, large input costs. This serves a triple purpose of satisfying shareholders, satisfying lenders for seeking bigger loans, as well as building up AC on paper, even though actual purchases (and sales) could be much lower. False AC limits GST revenue collection in cash, in turn constraining government expenditure disbursements and increasing the pressure on tax collectors to increase revenue collection in cash willy-nilly. This lead, in turn, to limiting legitimate ITC claimed by honest taxpayers.

Fake invoices also have been used by brokers who operate on behalf of company executives in particular sectors. Unbeknownst to the executives, such brokers are the ones who have made illicit profits through exploiting such businesses that they are supposed to serve. A relatively new bankruptcy code has been detrimental. It allows taxpayers to hide behind Section 13 on non-performing assets (NPAs). Once allowed, then tax liability under GST is set aside.

On the flip side, the frequent dropping and jamming of the GST website for uploading and other functions have challenged timely compliance by good taxpayers. Terminating GST registration when a supplier goes out of operation has also been known to be slow rather than being automatic, thus slowing the ease of doing business. Many other impediments continue against the good GST taxpayer.

### 24.10.2 E-way Bill (EWB) System

The electronic way bill (EWB) was another innovation whereby traders and transporters—in both inter- and intra-state transport—would carry an invoice whose number could be punched in by a tax officer, immediately revealing if the invoice belonged to a legitimate transaction. It was to be maintained also by the supplier and recipient, both registered and unregistered. It was to be introduced as a forward step to minimise tax evasion.

But its introduction had to be postponed several times reflecting logistical constraints. The CBIC chairman had requested chief commissioners (CCs), in consultation with their state commissioners, to decide the date of implementation of the EWB system for intra-state movement of goods within their state. It is understandable that, in a geographically large and highly populated country such as India, the EWB system would take longer to be applied to inter-state trade. However, the system has remained unapplied in both cases.

[16]As a Latin American finance minister once confessed to the author in frustration, 'Doctor, in my country, there are a lot of elephants hiding among the mice'.

A couple of explanations exist for the slowness in the introduction of the EWB. First, electronic portals do not work perfectly; they are often overloaded. It is not rare that the towers also do not work, often beginning to function back with a start. Under the circumstances, it should be contemplated how MSMEs with a low number of employees may be excluded from such an advanced ICT-based system for, otherwise, the GST could actually increase their compliance burden.

Second, the threshold for the requirement of carrying an EWB was set at an invoice of Rs 50,000,[17] a very low sum for practical administrative purposes. The validity period for an EWB is also shorter than it needs to be. From the time of its creation, it expires after just 1 day for a transportation distance of less than 100 km and an additional day for each extra 100 km. Given the uncertainty and unpredictability of road travel and inspection queues along national highways, the validity period for an EWB is unnecessarily low.

## 24.11 Minimising Litigation

An emerging problem is that of litigation over the place of supply (PoS) between states. A procedural improvement of a tax dispute online tracking system (TDOTS) helps in monitoring tax disputes and their resolution, but it does not reduce the number of litigations. The real problem is structural. The advance ruling authority (ARA) of different states has no jurisdiction over determining the place of supply. That is understandable since no single state should have the authority to determine the PoS since that would favour its own welfare over that of another state.

But even at the central level, the ARA has no jurisdiction over the matter though, ideally, it should resolve conflicting rulings among state ARAs. Therefore, there appears to be a good possibility of litigation piling up at the appellate tribunal level or courts. Unless this challenge is addressed quickly, the GST will be beset with comparable litigation problems of the earlier indirect taxation structure that it replaced.[18]

To conclude, ultimately, how GST fares will depend on the Indian taxpayer's attitude towards paying tax as well as the dexterity with which it is administered. Complementarity between the two is imperative. Policymakers should produce a consistent and stable tax rate structure; the public–private partnership (PPP) model for auto-populating forms should be achieved without delay; there should be a rethink on the applicability of the EWB system. The administration, on its part, should step back from the obstructive role of the anti-profiteering agency and, instead, facilitate refunds and deregistration, while fully eschewing any revenue objective for its own sake. Needless to say, the strictest action should be taken against tax evasion and corruption alike, and both taxpayer and tax officer should be

[17] Approximately 500 UK £.

[18] See Singh and Gupta (2019).

monitored on this count. If these concerns are successfully addressed, India should emerge with a modern, successful and globally acclaimed, fiscal federal GST.

## Appendix 1: Selected GST Administrative Aspects

Here we examine three GST aspects to buttress its administration that are identifiable due to their particular characteristics.[19] They comprise 3 of the 11 matters that the 11 ICAI handbooks cover.

### Reverse Charge Mechanism (RCM) Under GST

Normally, the supplier of goods or services collects tax from the purchaser and deposits the tax with the government. However, in the case of certain industries, the RCM is applied where chargeability gets reversed. It is the purchaser or recipient who is responsible for paying the tax on the supply of the goods or services, and it is he who is required to deposit the tax. The ICAI handbook covers the procedural aspects and legal provisions—rules, notifications, clarifications and orders—of RCM. In addition, registration requirements, time of supply under RCM, manner of invoicing, accounts and records to be maintained, payment of tax and ITC under RCM, consequences of failure—notice, interest and penalty, and FAQs to help taxpayers in understating issues related to RCM, are explained.

### Job Work Under GST

Section 2(68) of the CGST Act, 2017, stipulates that:

> job work means any treatment or process undertaken by a person on goods belonging to another registered person and the expression "job worker" shall be construed accordingly.

The exact meaning and examples of job work, its statutory provisions, procedure for supplying goods—delivery of inputs/semi-finished goods/capital goods—by a principal to a job worker, return of goods by a job worker, registration by a job worker, and ITC in case of job work, comprise the business arrangements. Special procedures to be followed, conditions and restrictions, specific contents required in the delivery of tax invoice ('challan'), transitional provisions for job work, and tax rates under job work, comprise this particular business category.

[19]See ICAI (2020), op. cit.

## Authority for Advance Ruling (AAR) for GST

An advance ruling (AR) helps advance planning of a taxpayer's business activity that is liable to GST. It brings certainty in his tax liability, since any AAR ruling given is binding on both government and the applicant. Further, it helps to avoid long and expensive litigation.

The aspects that are of essence here include the role and objective of an AR, provisions, definitions, scope of questions for which an AR can be sought; scope of AAR, the scope and powers of the appellate authority for advance ruling (AAAR), procedure to file at AAR or AAAR, orders of AAR, rectification, and the portal for filing for an AR.

## References


Cnossen, Sijbren. 2013. Preparing the way for a modern GST in India. *International Tax and Public Finance* 20 (4): 715–723.

ICAI. 2020. *Handbooks on GST*. New Delhi: Indian Chartered Accountant Institute (ICAI).

Modi, Arbind. 2009. Report of the Task Force on Goods and Services Tax. Thirteenth Finance Commission. Government of India. https://www.prsindia.org/uploads/media/Constitution%20122nd/Report%20of%20Task%20Force-%20GST.pdf. Accessed on 24 Ocboter 2020.

Poddar, Satya, and Ehtisham Ahmad. 2009. *GST Reform and Intergovernmental Considerations in India*. Working Paper No. 1/2009-DEA. Government of India. https://dea.gov.in/sites/default/files/GST%20Reforms%20and%20Intergovernmental%20Considerations%20in%20India.pdf. Accessed 24 October 2020.

Shome, Parthasarathi. 2017. *Goods and Services Tax*. Working Paper No. 227. Madras Institute of Development Studies (MIDS). https://www.mids.ac.in/doc/WP_227.pdf. Accessed 24 October 2020.

Singh, Rav P., and Vidushi Gupta. 2019. *Legislative Changes to Strengthen the GST Regime—Dispute Settlement*. Vidhi Centre for Legal Policy. https://vidhilegalpolicy.in/research/legislative-changes-to-strengthen-the-gst-regime/. Accessed 24 October 2020.

Srinivasan, Pagalthivarthi. 2016. Goods and Services Tax: Analysis, Findings and Suggestions. In *Insights into Evolving Issues of Taxation: Existing and Continuing Challenges*, ed. Parthasarathi Shome, 16–129. Gurugram: Wolters Kluwer.

Varsano, Ricardo. 2000. Subnational Taxation and the Treatment of Interstate Trade in Brazil: Problems and a Proposed Solution. In *Decentralisation and Accountability of the Public Sector*, ed. S.J. Burki and G. Perry. Washington, DC: World Bank.

# 25 Taxation of International Trade: Design and Experience

## 25.1 Introduction

As countries became economically increasingly integrated with a significant rise in international trade and finance, the traditional arguments of the 1950s and 1960s for protecting 'infant industries'[1] met with growing disfavour.[2] With the advent of the World Trade Organization (WTO), its member states reduced the levels of their customs tariffs. Indeed, there was an argument that the countries which experienced rapid growth in the 1980s and 1990s were those that reduced average tariffs the most. Examples offered were East Asian and South-East Asian economies.[3]

Similarly, exports of traditional commodities such as tea, coffee, rubber and minerals once yielded significant revenue from the export duties that were imposed on such commodities. In 1980, 67 countries imposed export duties; following the WTO, they would eventually come to abolish them reflecting the detrimental effects they had on the international competitiveness of their products. Only windfall gains from exports were taxed when their prices experienced sudden due to unanticipated global developments.

Greater international competition, which could be possible only with lower taxes on international trade, was perceived to improve economic links and transfer of technology and to result in improved products and diversification of output and exports. Protectionist policies would have the opposite effect. In this context, of course, recent policies of developed countries to reintroduce protective import duties have been challenging to the core the evolution of a rational global consensus on tax policy for international trade.

In this chapter, a range of issues regarding customs policy are addressed. They include selected conceptual issues together with the rationale and objectives of a

[1]Those industries that are nascent, not yet able to compete in international markets.

[2]See Shome (2001).

[3]See Krueger (2000).

 
P. Shome, *Taxation History, Theory, Law and Administration*, Springer Texts in Business and Economics, https://doi.org/10.1007/978-3-030-68214-9_25

customs regime, the role of the WTO in the reform of the structure of customs tariffs, expanded customs functions in recent years, revenue generation through customs tariffs in emerging economies, progressively reduced customs tariffs in the industrial sector and the diminishing role of customs as a revenue generator, changes in tariff structure in India, and anti-dumping duty on imports. Aspects of customs administration will be addressed in Chap. 36.

## 25.2 Costs of Protectionism

The rationale for imposing customs duties is couched in the need to protect domestic industry—typically infant industry—that needs to be sheltered from aggressive foreign competition that may occur before domestic units have had adequate time to catch up with foreign competition. Once the economy develops, the argument for the continuation of high customs tariffs cannot be easily maintained. Indeed, over the years, they have been scaled back in emerging economies such as India. The WTO has played a significant role in urging economies to become more competitive through scaling back of customs tariffs.

Early critics of the infant industry argument pointed out that: (1) protectionism assumes that governments can 'pick winners' to determine which industries to support; and (2) in reality, experience has revealed that the beneficiaries of protection tend to devote resources to rent-seeking activities aimed to maintain, if not extend, the existing protection. Yet, it is also true that the East Asian and South-East Asian economies that eschewed high customs tariffs in their early phase of development focused on select 'engine of growth' industries with a comparative advantage in production. In other words, these economies too opted for a policy of picking winners though not through high customs tariffs but, rather, through targeted domestic tax and economic policies. Thus, it seems that it is not the policy of picking winners that is good or bad. Rather, it is the ability to quickly compete in the world market for products that a country chooses to produce that becomes an indicator of the economy's potential to adapt and grow.

It is for this reason that there is universal acceptance today that taxes on international trade are harmful to economic growth. It is better to substitute them with an income tax on global income and a consumption tax on both imports and domestic consumption. Since such taxes are on final income or consumption, they are less distortive than customs duties that have narrow bases and, when levied also on capital goods and raw materials, they directly increase the cost of production.

Some developing countries tend to impose temporary surcharges on imports to meet short-run fiscal or external sector imbalances. Such taxes on imports that are levied at much higher rates than their domestic counterparts play an adverse role in economic growth in the medium to long run. Over time, exemptions creep into the customs tariff structure, rendering it voluminous, complex, difficult to interpret and, therefore, subject to corruption. In any event, if the prevalence of exemptions is high, it may be better to introduce a minimum tariff to capture all potential taxable commodities. This could be comparable to a minimum tax on corporate income that was addressed in Chap. 20.

There is one instance in which a tariff may be beneficial to a country. That is when the country has a monopsony or oligopsony, in import markets, that is, it is the sole or one of just a few, demanders of a product. For example, such a country can impose an import tariff on steel when it is a major buyer, if it calculates that the benefit to be gained from government revenue is higher than the costs of domestic price distortions and misallocation of resources that such a tariff might cause.[4]

High customs tariffs can be disguised as an anti-dumping measure against the exporting country to the detriment of world trade and welfare. This is a position that a country might exploit if it is able to exert influence in the world markets of their own imports reflecting, for example, giant shares that they import. Such protective customs duties on steel and other inputs have been used by the United States though they are, by and large, agreed to have been counterproductive in that anticipated gains in US production have failed to take place. The only solution, therefore, appears to be a shift up in the domestic productivity of the imported commodity.

Countries may also act as an oligopoly for a range of products they supply to the world market, for example, in sectors such as petroleum products, pharmaceuticals or weapons. They can once again improve their terms of trade with the rest of the world by pricing exports through collusion, to their advantage. These are experiences that tend to dampen the enthusiasm for free trade in some countries, though many country experiences have, by and large, demonstrated the benefits of free trade for economic growth and prosperity.

It has to be recognised that large trading economies have certain advantages that smaller ones do not. Experience indicates, for example, that economies of scale decrease average costs. Producers, whether from advanced or emerging economies, that have gained influence in international markets, tend to drive smaller suppliers out. This is what has occurred in China for a range of commodities, resulting in the phenomenal economic growth it has experienced since the 1990s.

A factor that is embedded in the consideration of protection is the extent of 'effective' protection as opposed to 'nominal' protection provided by the tariff structure. To the extent that tariffs apply to intermediate and capital goods, the domestic input prices increase, the value-added for the producer decreases, and the degree of protection diminishes.[5] The nominal level of customs duty on a product, in itself, does not reflect the extent of protection. If there is a customs duty on inputs and raw materials, then the 'effective' protection rate is the customs duty on the final good minus the customs duty on all imports. This is because the domestic producer of the final good has to pay customs duty on the inputs and raw materials and, to that

[4]See Subramanian et al. (1993).

[5]The effective protection rate is defined as the amount by which the value-added in a sector at domestic prices exceeds the value added in the sector at international prices, expressed as a percentage of the latter. Corden (1966) pointed out that the nominal customs duty may not indicate the effective protection rate.

extent, the protection of the final good actually diminishes. The higher are the tariffs on non-final goods, the wider is the expected divergence between nominal and effective protection, and the lower is the effective protection.

Yet many developing countries that have used customs duties with the objective of encouraging infant industry through protection have systematically also levied relatively high customs duties on intermediate and capital goods (presumably for revenue reasons or even to foster domestic activity in these sectors). In a sense, such policy brings them closer to the concept of neutrality in a trade regime—equal protection across industries of tradable goods—and away from the original intention of fostering leading sectors or engines of economic growth.[6]

In practice, trade reform has emphasised the need to lower average tariffs. Indeed, Chile introduced a low uniform tariff on all imports and removed all non-tariff barriers. The justification is based on the hypothesis that a low, broad-based tariff has a small economic cost, which is the value of the output forgone due to losses in economic efficiency. But it is not just that. It is also based on minimising the high administrative costs of a protection policy applied selectively to particular sectors or activities, and the likelihood of increased operations by special interest groups to work the system to their advantage.

If there is going to be customs tariffs, one view is that final goods should be taxed at higher rates than inputs. According to this view, tax-induced changes in the relative price of inputs can lead to the choice of inefficient technologies if more efficient technologies become costlier than less efficient technologies. Extending this argument, there should be an ordering in the customs tariff structure, with the highest rate for final consumption goods, a middle rate for intermediate goods, and the lowest rate for capital goods. But considerable information is required to construct such an optimal tariff structure that correctly reflects the nature of the use of imports in different industries and their elasticities of demand. Some economists have therefore felt that a policy of zero tariffs on all commodities possible to be used as inputs should be followed, in particular by those countries that have a high proportion of manufactured exports that use a range of inputs.

The case for a single tariff structure is strongest on both efficiency and administrative grounds, given all the shortcomings cited above in relation to alternative policies. Ultimately, that rate can be reduced even to zero when the tax system can rely solely on the domestic consumption base and income base for tax revenue, as in Hong Kong and Singapore.

[6]Across-the-board high tariffs are compatible with neutrality, though they would be distortive. Thus, neutrality is not an indicator of the efficiency loss from protection. Neither would such a regime provide much effective protection.

## 25.3 Customs in International Activities[7]

There are particular challenges that policymakers and officials encounter when designing customs tariffs and then implementing the customs code. The role of customs in international activities comprises two interrelated functions, reflecting (i) customs as an internationally linked institution and (ii) customs duty as being imposed on the imports of a country that are the exports of another. Accordingly, customs operations occur mainly at the geographical borders of a country.

### 25.3.1 Tariff Changes Through the WTO

The WTO is responsible for negotiating tariff rationalisation and reductions across the world while keeping track of customs activity in individual countries in case they go askew from commonly laid out international interests. It is its responsibility to protect other countries from high tariffs or anti-dumping duties imposed by any WTO member when there is no justification for them. It prevents trade wars arising from customs duty or quantitative restrictions on imports or exports. The WTO has had a strong positive impact on trade.[8]

Much of the global movement in the structure of customs tariffs reflects multilateral negotiations through the WTO which was established in 1995. The WTO and its predecessor organisation, the General Agreement on Trade and Tariffs (GATT), have made concerted efforts to push negotiations and consensus in global tariff reform.

The negotiations on reductions in tariffs on non-agricultural products are referred to as NAMA (non-agricultural market access) negotiations. NAMA refers to all products not covered by the Agreement on Agriculture.[9] In practice, it includes manufacturing products, fuels and mining products, fish and fish products, and forestry products. Over the years, NAMA products have accounted for almost 90% of the world merchandise exports.

In the first round of multilateral negotiations called the GATT rounds, 1947, tariffs were cut on a selective, product-by-product basis through requests and offers made between participants. However, subsequently, countries decided to use formulae to cut tariffs across-the-board. For example, during the 1964–1967 Kennedy Round proposed a linear cut formula and the 1973–1979 Tokyo Round proposed a one-third cut formula, though with several exceptions.

---

[7]While the value-added tax (VAT) levied on domestic consumption has been the subject of much analysis and comment, customs duty imposed on imports, mainly with the objective of providing protection to domestic production, has played a crucial role in an economy's growth and fulfilment of its revenue needs.

[8]For example, Subramanian and Wei (2007) pointed out that it amounted to about 120% of additional world trade or US$ 8 trillion in 2000 alone.

[9]Internationally, tariffs on agricultural products have been traditionally low.

During the 1986–1994 Uruguay Round, developing and developed participants negotiated tariff cuts using a variety of methods to reach an average reduction target comparable to that of the Tokyo Round. The Uruguay Round produced significant improvements in market access for NAMA products in developed country markets, as tariff averages were reduced from 6.3% to 3.8%. In the case of developing countries, the most important contribution was made in the form of new tariff bindings.[10] Binding coverage for NAMA products in developing countries increased from 21% to 73%, which increased the predictability of trade considerably.

In the 2001 Doha Declarations, country ministers agreed to launch tariff-cutting negotiations on all non-agricultural products. The aim was:

> to reduce or, as appropriate, eliminate tariffs, including the reduction or elimination of tariff peaks, high tariffs, and tariff escalation, as well as non-tariff barriers, in particular on products of export interest to developing countries.[11]

Another package was concluded on the Doha negotiations in Geneva in July 2008 that shaped the final agreement of a Doha Development Agenda that represented various interests. Modalities for NAMA and agriculture continued to be discussed in Geneva regarding the formulae to be used to cut tariffs and agricultural subsidies and to look at the next steps in concluding the Doha round of negotiations. Agreeing on modalities would determine the scale of reductions in tariffs on thousands of industrial and agricultural products and the future levels of farm subsidies in WTO member countries.

In a subsequent 2013 Bali package, ministers made a series of decisions aimed at streamlining trade, allowing developing countries more options for providing food security, boosting least-developed countries' trade and helping development more generally. The package included:

- Measures on trade facilitation to streamline customs procedures and minimise unnecessary border delays, delivering jobs and opportunities in times of unemployment and slow growth. Their impact was estimated to be up to $1 trillion per year for the global economy. The package would also deliver technical assistance for better integration of developing and least-developed countries (LDCs) into the global economy.
- Specific measures to improvements in duty-free/quota-free market access schemes for LDCs; simplified and more accessible rules of origin for their exports; improved market access for the services sector; and a push forward on incomplete negotiations for cotton.
- A mechanism for the review and strengthening of special and differential treatment provisions in WTO agreements.

[10]A tariff binding is a ceiling above which a WTO member cannot apply a tariff. However, it may be increased or withdrawn subject to compensation provided to the WTO members affected by such action.

[11]WTO (2001).

- Reform of export subsidies; provision for better implementation of tariff rate commitments; and provision for short-term as well as sustainable food security and food aid programmes.

The 2015 Nairobi package culminated in the adoption of a series of decisions on agriculture, cotton and issues related to LDCs. These included a commitment to abolish export subsidies for farm exports, which was hailed as the 'most significant outcome on agriculture' in the WTO's 20-year history. Exporters of information and communications technology (ICT) products agreed on a timetable for eliminating tariffs on 201 ICT products valued at over $1.3 trillion per year.

The trading world could be said to have changed significantly with the 2017 US administration. The United States has charted a new course of combative trade relationship with China and uneasy trade relations with Europe and even with emerging economies such as India, questioning their past trade arrangements and practices with the United States which were perceived as being unfavourable to US interests.[12] The United States also forced a renegotiation of the North American Free Trade Agreement (NAFTA) with Canada and Mexico. It blocked the appointment and reappointment of Appellate Body members at the WTO. Such steps have changed international relations in trade in a short span of time.

The age of discrete negotiations seems at an end. Scholars have commented that it has emboldened China with its expanding market size to chart its own course and rewrite global trade rules in favour of dependence of the world on Chinese manufacturing and, increasingly, services.[13] They have perceived the United States as causing a growing weakness in international institutions that could, otherwise, have helped provide meaningful constraints on China's unmitigated trade power. The role of the WTO over the last two decades in dispute settlement may no longer remain intact as states intervene unilaterally in pursuance of their individual interests. The flip side of this is that the American economic and free trade model may also lose its international dominance.

However, US unilateralism has also faced a backlash from China. It would not be surprising if other countries including a changed US administration prefer to return to appropriate multilateralism. However, state restraint would probably not be enough but public support and strengthening of the WTO may be essential.

Going forward, small yet robust steps could demonstrate the members' recommitment to multilateralism. One instance may be the European Commission's proposal to expand the Appellate Body member terms to 6–8 years without renewal (instead of 4 years, renewable once) to ensure continuity and for removal of any

[12]Some observers have, however, pointed to China's triumph over trade as propelled by policies of artificially low exchange rates so that its exports could enter international markets cheaply over a long period. Another issue was sophisticated technology that it obliged foreign investors to transfer at the end of a specified period of their operations in China. It has become clear, therefore, that international trade and customs policy have become more of a subject of international economic relations rather than of economics itself.

[13]See Brewster (2018).

vulnerability. In addition, WTO member countries could set up a system that would prevent any individual member (or a close ally) to shut down the dispute resolution system.

## 25.4 Expanded Customs Functions

As globalisation spread and tariff barriers to trade diminished, the typical customs department increasingly took on an expanded role to combat emerging international challenges of monitoring contraband, cutting out channels of money laundering, and eradicating international terrorism buttressed by modern developments in ICT, highly trained staff with increasingly common international principles, and broadened international cooperation among related departments.

Thus, today the operations of a customs department straddle a wide variety of objectives. First, it collects customs duty. Second, it collects some domestic taxes such as the GST or VAT on incoming imports which are taxes on domestic consumption. Tax is collected at the same rates as on the corresponding products from domestic sources since the tax should be the same for all consumers irrespective of source. In India, this is termed countervailing duty (CVD) in the sense that it countervails—or equivalises—domestic with foreign-sourced consumption items. The conceptual difference between customs tariffs and countervailing duty is that, while the customs tariff structure has been scaled back across the world to reflect international agreements and arrangements, the countervailing duty reflects the domestic consumption tax rate.

A third operational objective is the collection of statistics. For policymaking, it is important for any economy to keep account of the flow of goods and services to and from the economy in its international trade relations. Increasingly, trade classification has been finessed into multiple digits. To avoid tracking the import and export of goods and towards the objective of making the customs department exclusively an operational department, in some countries, this function has been passed to the official statistics department.

The more complex a customs tariff structure is—as is the case of India—or the higher tariff rates are—as was the case in India—the greater is the challenge on officers to impose and collect the right tariff on the imported good. Researchers have found that evasion increases proportionately faster than the rise in tariff rates.[14] Moral hazard can pose a problem if a section of the officers becomes unscrupulous. Leadership in the customs department is crucial in keeping this problem at bay. To combat it, many countries have simplified the tariff structure, the most extreme simplification being the case of Chile which has only a single tariff. Thus, if more revenue is needed, that rate is increased and, when revenue needs are less, the rate is scaled down.

[14]Mishra et al. (2008), by using the variation in tariff rates across time and products, identified 'a robust positive elasticity of evasion with respect to tariffs' (p. 1907).

## 25.5 Revenue Generation Through Customs Tariffs

Emerging economies, during their nascent period, depended heavily on customs duty not only to protect the infant industry but also as a source of revenue. The foreign trade sector of the economy has been traditionally a base that is easier to tax. This is due to the fact that 'administrative costs of monitoring, assessing, and collecting taxes on goods that go through a limited number of ports of entry are relatively low. Accordingly, many governments in developing countries rely heavily upon trade taxes (especially customs duties on imports) to generate revenues'.[15]

Nevertheless, there are limitations for revenue generation through customs duties in developing economies. First, revenue growth from customs tariffs reflects a country's industrial strategy. For example, as the economy increases its share of manufacturing in GDP, capital goods, intermediate goods and raw materials may need to be taxed at lower rates than final goods. This is because such goods are needed directly in the process of production. And there is no provision—because there is no rationale—for customs duty on intermediate goods to receive input tax credit. Thus, customs tariffs on such goods have to be lower. Further, as the share of manufacturing in GDP increases, the share of imports of intermediate goods vis-à-vis the imports of finished products would tend to increase. This would be the case especially if the growing manufacturing sector is significantly dependent on imported capital and intermediate goods. Thus, if the share of lower-rated to higher-rated imports goes up, that would reduce the growth rate of revenues from customs duties.

Second, if the manufacturing—private or public—sector expands while enjoying exemptions from import duties, as is likely to be the case under tax incentive provisions, the share of exempt imports in total imports also grows. Tax incentives play a role in increasing 'revenue expenditure'—a term used for the loss or sacrifice of revenue caused by tax incentives. Thus, as industrialisation progresses, the automatic growth in customs duty revenue tends to decline. Also, as countries promote export-oriented growth, more of the taxes on inputs—both domestic and imported—have to be refunded to export-oriented firms to enable exports to enter international markets competitively, that is, without any embedded taxes in their price.

Some countries follow 'duty drawback schemes' where tariffs are first payable upon importation of inputs and subsequently refunded after proof is provided that export has actually taken place. Refunds may be based on predetermined sector-wide input–output tables for exportable goods. And revenue erosion could occur if duty drawback rates are greater than the actual duty paid on the inputs. On the other hand, compliance burdens may be high, for example, to prove that exports have actually taken place.

Fourth, discretionary measures also tend to affect the import tax base. Sometimes, customs duty structures shift from ad valorem towards specific rates, in pursuit of

[15]See Mahdavi (2008), p. 610.

greater administrative simplicity. However, specific rates of customs duty tend to apply in a very limited number of goods, with only a few countries having taken this route. Also, as industries mature, the rates of nominal protection are frequently reduced over time as was mentioned above.

Fifth, it is not uncommon to use artificial exchange rates for import duty valuation purposes which further reduce potential revenue. There are, therefore, several factors that stand in the way of a naturally growing revenue trend from imports.

It is therefore seen in any cross-country comparison that, with economic development, the role of customs duty in revenue generation declines while other roles that have been mentioned earlier move forward even as domestic consumption taxes and income taxes assume the role of revenue drivers. The inverse relationship between the level of development and dependence on trade taxes as a source of revenue has been analysed by researchers.[16]

## 25.6 Changes in Tariff Structure in India

In the mid-1980s, tariff rates were high and the structures were complex. The government's 1985–1986 Long-Term Fiscal Policy (LTFP) document emphasised the need to reduce tariffs, apply fewer and more uniform rates, and reduce and eventually eliminate quantitative restrictions on imports. This was applied selectively by rationalising the rates for specific industries such as capital goods, drug intermediates and electronic goods.

However, contrary to the LTFP recommendations, tariffs continued to be raised for revenue reasons, the weighted average rate increasing from 38% in financial year (FY) 1980–1981 to 87% in 1989–1990. By 1990–1991, the tariff structure ranged from 0 to 400%. More than 10% of imports were subject to tariffs of 120% or more. Reflecting the influence of various special interest groups on tax policy, wide-ranging exemptions were granted outside the budgetary process, further complicating the system and rendering it ad hoc.

The reform of import duties began in earnest in 1991–1992 when all duties on non-agricultural goods above 150% were reduced to this level. This 'peak' rate was lowered over the next 4 years to 50%, and then to 40% in 1997–1998, 30% in 2002–2003, 25% in 2003–2004, 20% in 2004–2005, 15% in 2005–2006, 12.5% in 2006–2007 and finally to10% in 2007–2008. It is important to note that these reductions were not mandated by any WTO requirements as India's applied rates were considerably below the allowable, 'bound' rates. And the duty reductions were made even for unbound items.

The weighted average tariff rate of India in 2018 was 4.88%, down from 7.32% in 2015. But there have been recent reversals. These include increases in customs duty

[16]For example, using a panel of 80 developing and industrial countries between 1970 and 1998, Khattry and Mohan Rao (2002) confirm the inverse relationship. 'As countries become more developed their tax revenue/GDP ratio rises' (p. 1436).

on mobile phones from nil to 10% in July 2017, and to 15% in December 2017, with the objective of import substitution to support domestic production.

The 2018 central government budget witnessed a range of increases in customs duty on 40 categories of goods in the range of 33–100%. Diamonds and gemstones (excluding rough diamonds) suffered an increase from 2.5% to 5%, mobile phones from 15% to 20%, and their parts and accessories from 7.5–10% to 15%, smartwatches and wearable devices from 10% to 20%, accessories of motor vehicles, motor cars and motorcycles from 7.5–10% to 15%, and edible vegetable oils from 12.5–20% to 30–35%.[17]

In the 2020–2021 central government budget, India raised customs duties on 37 categories with the intention to provide a level playing field for domestic industry. Customs duties were raised on 10 additional items to generate additional revenues. And the government proposed to change the 1962 Customs Act, to give the government the power to ban the import or export of any goods, a power that was applicable earlier only to gold and silver. Customs duty was raised from 30% to 40% also on whey powder, cheese, butter, ghee and butter oil.[18]

The reversal in the journey towards free trade has been unilateral, reversing a quarter century of increasing openness, though it mirrors the pace recently set by the United States and China. Contrary to the expectation that such policies buttress domestic industry, they lead to higher cost and uncompetitive production in the economy as a whole as was learnt from four decades of protectionism until 1991. A tariff increase in any one industry affects firms in another industry and invites retaliatory action from trading partners. Tariffs changed after investments have been made are unlikely to depict India as investment-friendly.

## 25.7 Anti-dumping Duty on Imports

Anti-dumping duty is imposed by countries to protect their industries from unjustified competition that does not reflect market forces. It is leviable under Section 9A of the Customs Tariff Act, 1975, read with the rules which are framed under Section 9A (6). It is imposed and collected by customs. The customs department has to make the initial enquiry about the valuation of the imported goods. It has to be satisfied that the undervaluation, if so found, is a case of declaring less value in comparison with the same or similar products. If so, it becomes a case of dumping. Anti-dumping measures are allowed by the WTO and sometimes used by importing countries.

Dumping needs to be proved by demonstrating that the price declared is less than the cost of manufacturing in the country of origin. The role of customs is in assisting the commerce ministry through investigation and detection, to come to a conclusion as to whether any dumping has taken place and, if it has, how much of it is really to be compensated through an anti-dumping duty. This has to be determined by

[17]See Kaul (2020) and Bhattacharya (2018).

[18]See Kaul (2020) and Sally (2020).

investigations carried out by customs and the commerce ministry. After the determination, it is the role of customs to apply and implement the duty.

If the customs department uses the anti-dumping instrument within appropriate limits, the international economic and political relations are not disturbed. If there are too many anti-dumping cases where their imposition could be questioned or, merely allegations of dumping are made, then clearly international economic relations between the concerned countries suffer. Therefore, they have the potential to erode the benefits of globalised trade. Such examples are not rare, with countries pointing towards unfair use of anti-dumping duty by trading partners, for example, both India and the United States, and certainly, they are not the only ones. Taking one example, Indian steel has always found it difficult to export to the United States due to anti-dumping duty on some varieties of steel. Even Europe felt the impact of the barrier and seemed determined to take countermeasures against the US anti-dumping duty on steel.

A particular case that unfolded in the United States in the 2000s may be worth narrating. An amendment in US law—the October 2000 Byrd Amendment—was declared by the WTO to be illegal in January 2003. The amendment had allowed cash receipts from foreign exporters (to the United States) to be distributed to affected domestic industry, as protectionist and declared it as illegal. Subsequently, the law was repealed by the US Congress in October 2007 but, before the repeal, the law was used by the United States to collect cash from foreign exporters, for example, of shrimps. This action of the United States on the anti-dumping front had been to prevent the import of shrimps from China, Thailand, India, Brazil, Ecuador and Vietnam. The attempt to protect the domestic producer of shrimps from foreign competition did not succeed even after imposing 5–10% anti-dumping duty because exports from these countries nevertheless remained profitable for them.

Not satisfied with this, the Southern Shrimp Alliance representing US shrimpers and processors, wanted an upward review of the duty. Though looking into the books of accounts of hundreds of small exporters could not be feasible, yet they were asked to comply. And, if they did not reply or cooperate, they would have to pay nearly 50% anti-dumping duty. To avoid such a reprisal, the foreign exporters agreed to pay up to 2% of the value of the goods, which could be legally collected as settlement money and distributed to the Alliance.

Another example is a case of high anti-dumping duty levied by the United States against the import of Chinese tyres which were viewed as being dumped in the United States. That led to an angry reaction from China and it had to be settled by diplomatic efforts at the highest level. It must be said that the EU also uses avenues that may not always be so apparent but, instead, through non-tariff barriers such as environmental or labour conditions that tend to have similar adverse ramifications for exports from emerging and developing economies.

The use of the instrument of anti-dumping duty has become as widespread as globalisation itself. The attempt by the WTO to thwart protectionist tendencies could succeed only if greater power was to be given to it in order to make its findings immediately effective and not after 2 years or so as in the case of the Byrd

Amendment. The United States' use of anti-dumping duty or occasional reaping of returns from protectionism cannot be said to enhance the tenets of globalisation.

While anti-dumping duty is counter-positioned to globalisation, yet, its absence may allow domestic industry to suffer injury. Therefore, it is a matter of balance that has to be struck by customs and commerce departments when using the anti-dumping duty instrument against foreign imports.

## References

Bhattacharya, Ashok K. 2018. Budget Decision on Customs Duty Hike to Impact Imports of $85 bn in a Year. *Business Standard*, February 12.

Brewster, Rachel. 2018. The Trump Administration and the Future of the WTO. *Yale Journal of International Law Online*. Duke Law School Public Law & Legal Theory Series No. 2019–10. https://ssrn.com/abstract=3328929.

Corden, W.M. 1966. The Structure of a Tariff System and the Effective Protective Rate. *Journal of Political Economy* 74 (3): 221–237. https://doi.org/10.1086/259151.

Kaul, Vivek. 2020. The Dangers of India's Rising Tariff Walls. *Live Mint*, February 13.

Khattry, Barsha, and J. Mohan Rao. 2002. Fiscal Faux Pas?: An Analysis of the Revenue Implications of Trade Liberalization. *World Development* 30 (8): 1431–1444.

Krueger, Anne O. 2000. *The WTO as an International Organization*. Chicago: University of Chicago Press.

Mahdavi, Saeid. 2008. The Level and Composition of Tax Revenue in Developing Countries: Evidence from Unbalanced Panel Data. *International Review of Economics & Finance* 17 (4): 607–617.

Mishra, Prachi, Arvind Subramanian, and Petia Topalova. 2008. Tariffs, Enforcement, and Customs Evasion: Evidence from India. *Journal of Public Economics* 92 (10–11): 1907–1925.

Sally, Madhvi. 2020. Budget 2020: Change in Basic Customs Duties to Boost Make in India. *The Economic Times*, February 1.

Shome, Parthasarathi. 2001. Regional Trade Arrangements and SAARC. In *India and Economic Cooperation in South Asia*, ed. P. Shome. New Delhi: Indian Council for Research on International Economic Relations (ICRIER).

Subramanian, Arvind, and Shang-Jin Wei. 2007. The WTO Promotes Trade, Strongly But "Unevenly". *Journal of International Economics* 72 (1): 151–175.

Subramanian, Arvind, Ali Ibrahim, and Luis A. Torres-Castro. 1993. *Optimal Tariffs; Theory and Practice*. IMF Working Papers 1993/050. Washington, DC: IMF.

WTO. 2001. The Doha Declaration Explained. https://www.wto.org/english/tratop_e/dda_e/dohaexplained_e.htm. Accessed 26 October 2020.

# Unusual Taxes

# 26

## 26.1 Introduction

Countries occasionally introduce taxes to plug loopholes elsewhere in their tax systems and to enhance revenue generation. A tax on financial transactions has been contemplated at a global level though not successfully, but has been used in Latin America in different forms such as in Argentina and Brazil. Argentina removed it and Brazil kept it in the statutes at a zero rate. Subsequently, India too introduced a tax on bank withdrawals but then abolished it. The design, economic effects, revenue productivity and collection costs of this tax are analysed.

A tax on fringe benefits has been used in Australia and New Zealand. There is some justification for this tax when fringe benefits are not voluntarily reported as a part of the income tax base and tax paid on it. India introduced a well-designed tax on fringe benefits though its administration proved challenging. Hence it was removed. This chapter examines the conceptual basis of these taxes and takes up India as a case study.

## 26.2 Financial Transactions Tax (FTT)

In the late 1980s to mid-1990s, there was much discussion on Financial Transactions Tax (FTT) in the context of minimising swings in financial markets or as a revenue source of global proportions that could be earmarked for the alleviation of poverty. That discussion was not able to reach consensus, and a tax on financial transactions was never implemented at the global level.

A reconsideration of FTT emerged recently in the context of enhancing stability in global financial transactions in the face of general empathy, if not agreement, that some containment, through tax and non-tax instruments, for the intermittent upheavals in global financial markets was called for. This could be achieved through FTT, or some form of non-tax regulation, or both.



P. Shome, *Taxation History, Theory, Law and Administration*, Springer Texts in Business and Economics, https://doi.org/10.1007/978-3-030-68214-9_26

This section attempts to address both theoretical and practical considerations for the FTT. Most of the discussion centres on financial market issues, and how the functioning of financial markets drives the final views and outcomes over FTT. A central roadblock remains in that a clear understanding or explanation of the range of behaviours in financial markets remains incomplete or imprecise.

FTT proponents argue that technical and noise trading causes deleterious market volatility based on short-term destabilizing speculation and that FTT would contain this. And, on a global basis, its revenue productivity would be high. Further, the tax rates would need to be very small so that FTT would have only small adverse efficiency effects.

Opponents argue that FTT is inefficient since it would raise transaction costs and reduce market liquidity. It would also depress share prices, increase capital costs and decrease investment. If country tax rates are different, it could cause unwarranted capital flows. The final tax incidence between companies and their clients would depend on the strength of various responses or values of elasticities. And, if FTT were to raise significant amounts of revenue, then one cannot convincingly argue that efficiency costs would remain low.[1]

## 26.2.1 Theoretical Considerations

Keynes and the Keynesians, dormant in the 1980s to the early 2000s, manifested a resurrection in the late 2000s through fiscal stimuli across advanced, middle-income and emerging economies. This was to counter the fallout from a financial crisis of pandemic proportions essentially brought on by persistent unsustainable overconsumption and debt accumulation. But another corrective aspect that Keynes[2] had insightfully touched upon also came up for reconsideration. This is FTT. Following the Great Depression, he had commented that a 'transfer tax on all transactions' would be the 'most serviceable reform ... to mitigate ... speculation over enterprise'. However, he also cautioned that 'If ... investments were rendered illiquid, this might seriously impede new investment'. Herein lies the perspicacity with which Keynes saw the dual aspects. We attempt to review these competing positions that appear not to have been resolved to this day.

During the late 1970s and early 1980s, international capital flows were experiencing boundless economic growth. Some economists anticipated capital swings, indicating that they were to be expected with high economic growth.[3] To contain excessive shifts of funds with destabilising economic effects, they suggested a tax to buttress monetary policy. Such a tax never took effect, however. Indeed,

[1]Of course it could be argued that the sheer size of foreign exchange transactions would produce a lot of revenue even with a tiny tax that would cause minimal distortions. As is illustrated in this section, this argument continues to exist.

[2]See Keynes (1936/2006).

[3]See Tobin (1978).

until the late 1980s, the market efficiency assumption regarding the functioning of financial markets—reflected in dividend movements—did not change significantly. In this world, any rise in transaction costs would worsen market performance.

A post-mortem of the October 1987 stock market crash gave rise to an alternative view combining investor behaviour with rational expectations about returns on stocks, with investment behaviour of uninformed noise traders who invest while remaining oblivious of economic fundamentals and destabilise financial markets. This alternative view took the position that both types of investors complement each other so that no FTT was needed to control the noise traders. Indeed, an FTT would hamper the beneficial complementarity that existed in financial markets.[4]

Ensuing developments in global markets complicated real-life situations considerably. These situations have been examined and re-examined in various studies that have found the two types of behaviour as not being necessarily complementary. With these antecedents, we consider next some conceptual or theoretical perspectives of FTT from the recent literature that has emerged and provided evidence.

### 26.2.2 Prices and Transactions Volumes

There is evidence that transactions taxes cause a fall 'in asset prices in financial markets or, in exchange markets, an increase in the 'Bid-Ask spread'.[5] Old and new evidence reveals that they also cause a decline in the long-run number of transactions. Empirical studies have provided supporting evidence for this. For example, evidence based on early data from the London Stock Exchange indicated that share prices fell by 0.2 per cent and transactions volumes fell by 1.65 per cent for every 1 per cent increase in transactions costs.[6]

More recent evidence reveals for UK data that shares with the highest turnover rate effectively bear the highest tax on share transactions, and suffer the greatest price decrease in response to changes in FTT rates.[7] But does this imply that FTT

[4]Essentially, any tax would raise costs, so that the argument against tax metamorphosed not so much as a choice between different taxes but, rather, between tax and non-tax alternatives.

[5]Definitions from the website may be useful: http://www.investopedia.com/terms/b/bid.asp.

'Bid' is an offer made by an investor, a trader or a dealer to buy a security. The bid will stipulate both the price at which the buyer is willing to purchase the security and the quantity to be purchased. 'Ask' is the price a seller is willing to accept for a security, also known as the offer price. Along with the price, the ask quote will generally also stipulate the amount of the security willing to be sold at that price.

'Bid-Ask Spread' is the amount by which the ask price exceeds the bid. This is essentially the difference in price between the highest price that a buyer is willing to pay for an asset and the lowest price for which a seller is willing to sell it.

[6]See Jackson and O'Donnell (1985).

[7]See Bond et al. (2004). Note, however, that financial intermediaries are exempt from UK's Stamp Duty Land Tax (SDLT).

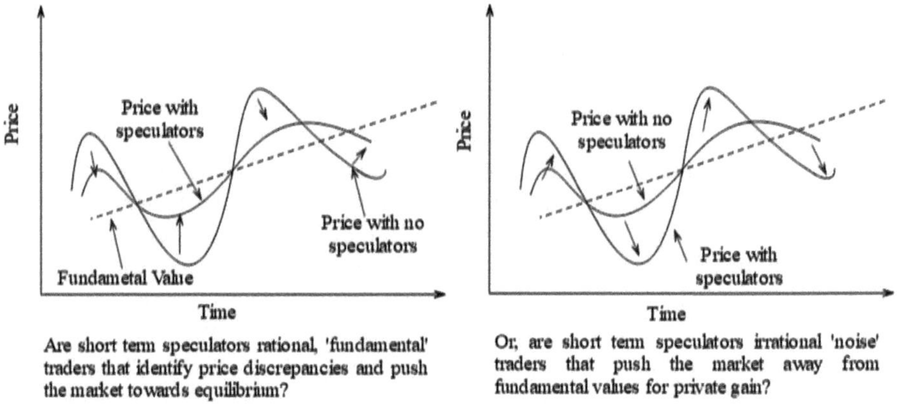


**Fig. 26.1** Theoretical impacts—volatility. (Source: Shome and Stotsky (1995))

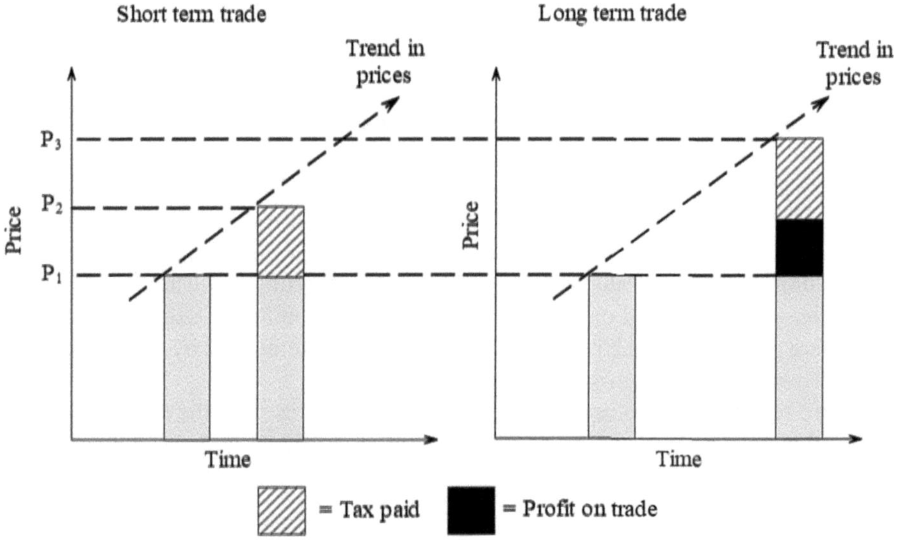


**Fig. 26.2** Differential impacts—profits. (Source: Shome and Stotsky (1995))

exacerbates volatility in contraposition to what we mentioned at the start—that proponents of FTT tend to argue that it would minimize volatility?

The crucial element in pinning down the impact of FTT would be an understanding of the underlying forces in a financial market. Two types of speculators typically operate in those markets: those who stabilize the market by their action and those who destabilize it. And since both behaviours are likely to be prevalent at the same time, and in the same market, it is difficult to separate the two. Figures 26.1 and 26.2 illustrate the market impact.

In Fig. 26.1, the left-hand figure illustrates when the presence of speculators can bring the trajectory of prices closer to the fundamental values that underlie the true market trend, while the right-hand figure illustrates when their presence moves prices away from the fundamental values. The old algorithm was that 'speculation is stabilizing'. Thus, on the left, when prices are high, speculators sell, so that prices decrease, the outcome being that speculation brings prices toward the fundamentals, that is speculation is stabilizing.

On the right, the opposite occurs. When prices are rising, speculators buy more under the expectation that prices will rise even more. This type of trader is said to trade often (too often perhaps), usually in a herd, and is a 'noise' trader who ignores market fundamentals. This is compounded by 'technical trading' which takes place on the basis of computer generated, price and trade volume information rather than on any analysis of fundamental or underlying economic data. The outcome is that prices are pushed further up, that is speculation becomes destabilizing. However, indeed it is the relative strengths of the two behaviours that determine the final outcome of whether market activity takes prices toward or away from fundamentals.

From here, it is but one step to see what an introduction of FTT might do. FTT would tend to increase transactions costs and subdue short-term speculation or the frequency of bids that are found to cause volatility. In this role, FTT would make marginal short-term trades less viable, thus reducing this type of speculation and, in turn, volatility. After the 1987 stock market crash, some economists[8] argued that FTT would reduce this type of noise trading by disproportionately curbing their behaviour. This hypothesis is illustrated in Fig. 26.2.

Both traders purchase the shares at $P_1$. However, the short-term trader sells the share more quickly at $P_2$. In that time there has not been a large enough gain for the transaction to be profitable, given the amount of FTT paid (gray portion).[9] However, if the share is held for longer, then the price rises to $P_3$ and an after-tax capital gain is made (black portion) to make the transaction profitable.[10] In essence, the FTT should dissuade a trader from selling early at $P_2$ in anticipation of making a capital gain in the longer term. He would sell at $P_3$ and make a capital gain. This is the crux of the argument of those who maintain that an FTT curbs short-term trading.

### 26.2.3 Volatility and FTT

However, we know that prices do not rise in mere straight lines—it may be that short-term traders spot short-term mispricing with gains to be made and, therefore, consistently trade with large gains.[11] This suggests that stock markets may be

[8]See Stiglitz (1989) and Summers and Summers (1989).

[9]Note that the trader makes no after-tax profit.

[10]The after-tax profit is shown by the black area. Note that, even though the tax paid is higher in the long term than in short-term case, nevertheless the trader makes a profit in the long term.

[11]See Farmer et al. (2004).

inherently volatile even without needing to introduce the long term–short term conflict.[12] It could be that the same trader maybe alternating between stabilizing and destabilizing behaviour in the same market at slightly different points in time, or in two markets at the same time. Unfortunately, these behaviours are not explained fully. Models of noise trading and technical trading are unable to provide explanations for these behaviours.

Government interventions such as FTT could be used if the market works imperfectly, because of short-term speculative behaviour that increases volatility in the market and for other participants.[13] As such, their private decisions do exert a negative externality that should be taxed. Indeed, FTT has been suggested or implemented internationally during periods of major financial disruption, for example in Argentina (2002), Brazil (1999) and Chile (1991).

### 26.2.4 Design and Economic Effects of FTT

Despite the possible stabilising role of FTT in a volatile financial market, it could have significant distortionary effects since it is levied upstream in the chain of production and distribution that could have adverse economic ramifications downstream. It typically takes the form of an excise levied on transactions in financial assets (in a domestic context) or on transactions involving currency conversions (in an international context). Its rate has to be very small since many financial markets operate on extremely small margins (in the order of 1 basis point for foreign exchange markets). However, small the FTT rate is, it would increase the cost of capital to firms which, in turn, would affect input choices, for example from equity towards debt. The increase in costs would reduce investment and subsequently GDP growth.

There are challenges in designing a truly uniform and robust FTT. First, a transaction tax applied at a uniform rate on all financial instruments would imply different effective tax rates depending on the maturities and holding periods of the assets.[14] Second, financial intermediaries pose another set of difficulties since they are not final players in a financial market. Third, another problem is that of foreign substitution: shifting the location of trade in financial assets to avoid taxes has been relatively easy even though there is increasing administrative action by tax authorities to combat this.

Fourth, derivatives which comprise an important component of financial markets pose complex challenges. They are derived from some other asset, index, event, value or condition (known as the underlying asset) and undergo constant innovation,

---

[12] A useful example is provided in Beinhocker (2007).

[13] See Palley (1999) and Wei and Kim (1999).

[14] This was why Tobin viewed long-term investment to bear little tax, while extremely short term (in seconds today) to carry a high tax, which would reduce the latter type of trade.

or transformation, into new forms of derivatives.[15] To design their taxation would not be straight forward. Would there have to be a different rule for each type of derivative (futures, options, swaps, financial spread bets or others, since their operational characteristics are quite distinct from one another)? For example, should an option be taxed if it is not exercised?[16] Further, many derivatives are not traded through exchanges; unless these are exempted, the collection cost of FTT would rise and the advantage of low FTT collection costs would diminish (see Sect. 26.2.5). Thus, any tax on the various components of the derivatives markets, leave alone financial markets as a whole, would face significant challenges if one recognises the reality of how these markets function in present times.[17] It is not entirely surprising that there has been no international consensus for implementing an FTT at the global level to collect revenue for a global objective.

### 26.2.5 Revenue Productivity and Collection Costs

In order to gauge the revenue potential of FTT, Fig. 26.3 illustrates the sheer scale of daily turnover values on global foreign exchange and equity markets, increasing from US$ 2.9 trillion in 2001 to US$ 9.3 trillion in 2010 and US$ 15.2 trillion in 2019. Of the total, derivatives represented US$ 8.3 trillion, traditional foreign exchange transactions over US$ 6.6 trillion and global equity markets US$ 360.5 billion in 2019. Therefore, one can perceive the temptation for generating revenues from this source—even a tiny cut of this huge amount would represent a very large global number.

Proponents of an FTT may also point towards its low collection and compliance costs. It can be collected using automated computerized systems at a low cost. For example, according to one study,[18] Her Majesty's Revenue and Customs (HMRC), the UK tax administration, spent £0.09 for every £100 of FTT collected, while the average collection cost for all taxes was £1.11, in 2000–2001. More recent data from HMRC show that it cost £4 billion to run HMRC in 2018–2019 against a £627.9 billion tax revenue generation. That is approximately £0.63 for every £1 of tax revenue collected. The cost reduction over the years could be explained partially by HMRC reducing baseline operating costs year-on-year, making £576 million in annual sustainable cost savings since 2015.[19]

---

[15]An example of a derivative is a futures contract, an agreement to exchange the underlying asset at a future date at a price specified today. Derivatives offer only a partial substitute for equities or foreign exchange, for example equity derivatives do not come with voting rights or dividend rights. Further, they can be used for both speculation and hedging of risks.

[16]Some options to buy at a later date are never used if the agreed price is above the market price.

[17]Nevertheless, the United Kingdom operates a stamp duty on trade in exchanges, and a stamp duty reserve tax on assessed tax bases in parallel. Moreover, policy trends are to create exchanges for certain over-the-counter (OTC) transactions and render them mandatory for trading.

[18]Hawkins and McCrae (2002).

[19]HMRC (2019).

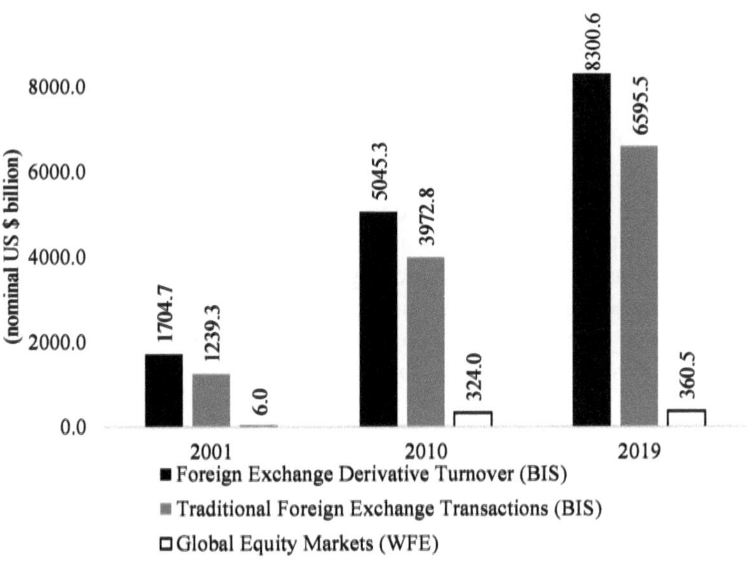


**Fig. 26.3** Financial transactions: daily global turnover. (Source: Bank of International Settlements (BIS) and World Federation of Exchanges (WFE))

### 26.2.6 Conclusions

Examples of actual use of FTT exist across the world, though they have tended to be temporary once their specific, momentary objectives are met. Hence, they seem to be disliked even by the policymakers who use them. Obviously, their deleterious efficiency ramifications are broadly accepted.

The design of a comprehensive, efficient and revenue productive FTT remains complex since it is difficult to define an appropriate base. Issues that challenge include, first, how to distinguish between short- and long-term elements so that only the former may be targeted by tax. Second, distinguishing debt and equity is not obvious since their separation is not seamless. Third, the treatment of derivatives remains a stumbling block; whether to tax the underlying value at a very low rate or, whether, and how, to tax 'call' and 'put' options instead.[20] Fourth, foreign substitutions would need special treatment reflecting, for example the occurrence of trading in US equities outside of the United States.

[20]Both types of options are between two parties—the writer and the buyer of the contract—used to manage risk on an underlying asset or commodity. In call options, the purchaser of the contract gets the right (but not the obligation) to buy the underlying asset from the writer of the contract at a fixed price set at the start of the contract. In put options, the purchaser of the contract gets the right (but not the obligation) to sell the underlying asset to the writer of the contract at a fixed price set at the start of the contract. In a variation, European call/put options have a single end date (or short period close to the end date) at which time the contract purchaser can decide to exercise the option (enforce the contract and buy/sell the underlying commodity), while American call/put options can be exercised at any time up to the termination date of the contract.

Nevertheless, in a volatile global financial environment, it is to be expected that an FTT would be used unilaterally by a country to protect itself from unwanted capital flows, or that multilateral attempts would be made by those countries nearest to financial turbulence. However, under such circumstances, non-tax institutions, rather than a tax, have been proposed, for example by the EU, for better coordination of national supervisory bodies and regulatory rules and even a common rule book. Regulations have the advantage of not burdening taxpayers and improving financial sector performance, for example through higher capital requirements for banks and financial intermediaries.[21]

Thus, between the two, the non-tax regulatory route has greater advantages than does FTT. If both instruments are to be used, a very small temporary, global FTT with clearly earmarked equity goals may be envisaged. For that, consensus building remains a major task, but that consensus may be building as more advanced economies surge towards unsustainable deficits and debt to which rating agencies are reacting adversely ever so strongly.

## 26.3 Banking Cash Transaction Tax

A financial transaction tax was introduced by Brazil at 0.038 per cent on an array of financial transactions, Argentina at 0.75 per cent, Colombia at 0.4 per cent, as well as Peru and a few other Latin American countries. All countries reported an increase in revenue collection after introduction. But its main benefit seems to be in the form of an enhanced flow of information for the tax administration. Brazil experienced a 40 per cent rise in tax assessment issued against taxpayers during the first nine months of 2004 as a result of the tax administration's new strategy of cross-checking taxpayers' records of the financial transactions tax (CPMF) with information provided by credit card companies and real estate brokers.[22] A 0.005 per cent capital gains withholding tax on stock sales in stock exchanges was also created to cross-check stock sales—which are exempted from CPMF—with taxpayers' returns.

With the same objective, in its annual 2005–2006 central fiscal budget, India introduced a withholding tax of 0.1 per cent on cash withdrawals from bank checking accounts in a single day totalling to more than Rs. 50,000 (approximately US$ 1,000 for individuals and Rs 10,00,000 (US$ 20,000) for others.[23] The finance minister said in his annual budget speech,

[21]It might increase financial costs but it has to be viewed in light of artificially low financial sector costs that made 'ninja'—no income, no job, no assets—loans possible prior to the 2008 global financial crisis. It would limit future costs on taxpayers who are now suddenly burdened with a formidable shift up in public debt whose impact is likely to fall significantly on future generations of taxpayers.

[22]See Soares da Silva (2004). In the first three quarters of 2004, assessments resulting from CPMF cross-checking totaled BRL 28 billion (US$ 9.63 billion, BRL 1 = US$ 0.344) a record since the CPMF began to be used as a tax audit instrument.

[23]Since then the rupee has depreciated to about Rs. 75 to US$ 1 (as on 6 August 2020).

> The National Common Minimum Program (NCMP) requires the government to introduce special schemes to unearth black money and assets. I am obliged to carry out the mandate, but without giving undeserved relief or amnesty. I am concerned about large cash transactions, especially withdrawals of cash, when there is no ostensible purpose to withdraw such large amounts of cash. These cash withdrawals leave no trail, and presumably become part of the black economy. Therefore, . . . I propose to levy a tax on withdrawal of cash . . . from banks at the rate of 0.1 per cent. (p 31)

A common form of money laundering takes place through false-account stock transactions and their subsequent channeling through multiple bank accounts, thereby legitimizing their existence without payment of tax. If Banking Cash Transaction Tax (BCTT) could be successfully used, the instrument could assist in tracking money laundering from source to destination. The tax met with popular opposition. It then came to stay in a scaled-back form with respect to its base. Despite its clipped wings, BCTT was withdrawn from April 2009 with the finance minister stating that 'the information is also being gathered through other instruments introduced in the last few years'.

## 26.4 Fringe Benefits Tax (FBT)

### 26.4.1 Introduction

Globally, employees seek, or are given, a part of their compensation in non-cash forms, which are commonly referred to as 'perquisites' or 'fringe benefits'.[24] Given that they are represent income, they should be taxed as income. However, taxation of fringe benefits is vexatious due to the conceptual problems relating to the definition of fringe benefits, allocation of collective benefits, valuation of benefits and likely impact on employee cash flow. These problems may be mitigated partially through government provided exemptions but, whatever portion is taxed suffers from under-valuation or low taxpayer compliance. The outcome is under-taxation of fringe benefits and, under that safety net, the individual income tax base is eroded by the practice of providing fringe benefits. Tax authorities have struggled to adopt various methods to prevent such tax base erosion. Such efforts are often unsuccessful due to powerful lobbies, if not political resistance.

### 26.4.2 Design and Justification of FBT

Fringe benefits comprising non-salary benefits may be cash or non-cash. Its taxation can be carried out in one, or a mix, of three ways. Most appropriately, it can be taxed

[24] Employers collaborate with employees to design tax efficient compensation packages by converting salary into a benefit at the cost of public revenues. Government, as an employer, also use such practices commonly, for example by providing under-valued housing, leave travel, schooling for children and so on.

at the hands of the employee through his individual income tax return, thereby requiring voluntary declaration by the taxpayer. Advanced economies use this method and tend to have stringent provisions to make it work. The second method is through disallowance from expenses under the corporate tax. If a company is declaring losses anyway, the disallowance would not be binding, however, and would not yield revenue. The third method is to have a positive list of fringe benefits and tax them at the hands of the employer at pre-specified presumptive rates. While the employer would be allowed to deduct all such expenses from his income tax, the more he deducts, the larger would be his tax base for the Fringe Benefits Tax (FBT).

As in the case of the FTT that was analysed in Sect. 26.2, the FBT is also a relatively new tax and not yet *a la mode*. Nevertheless, some have extolled its virtues. To quote,

> (An) .... obvious example of a technical rule that is unenforceable is one that allows business people to deduct the cost of business meals and entertainment. Allowing business people to deduct the cost of their business meals and entertainment makes absolutely no sense in terms of basic tax principles. Almost inevitably the personal value of a business meal, and in every case the personal value of a business entertainment expense, will equal its cost. The most basic tax principle is that taxpayers should not be allowed to deduct the cost of expenditures from which they derive personal value.
>
> But even if in some cases business people do not enjoy the business meal or entertainment that they inflicted on their clients, these expenses should still be non-deductible since they are impossible to verify. Who knows what business people talk about while enjoying a meal at a fancy restaurant? In Toronto, over 90 per cent of Blue Jays' (the city's National Baseball League team) season tickets are deducted as business expenses. It is impossible for the tax department to verify that these tickets were in fact used to take business clients to baseball games. Basically, for all so-called dual-purpose expenses, home–office expenses, education expenses, travel expenses, and automobile expenses, drafters should be ruthless in drafting enforceable bright-line tests for distinguishing between personal and business expenses and disallowing all of the rest.[25]

Australia and New Zealand are two advanced economies that were early introducers of the FBT. Following their experiences, India introduced an FBT though it was later abolished. The reason a recounting of India's FBT is important is that its experience with it—the good and the bad—remains an illustration of how best to approach it and where to avoid the pitfalls.

### 26.4.3 Indian Experience

Originally fringe benefits were taxed by a mix of criteria or methods though they suffered from under-declaration and under-taxation. They were the beneficiary employee-based method and the employer-based disallowance method. Under the beneficiary employee-based method, the value of the fringe benefits received by an employee was included in his salary and accordingly taxed in his hands. However,

[25]Brooks (2001), p. 23. Also see Burns and Krever (1998).

the valuation was based on imputation and was highly concessional relative to its market value. This method was supplemented by the employer-based disallowance method whereby expenditure on entertainment, advertisement in any souvenir, brochure, tract, pamphlet or the like published by a political party, provision of residential accommodation including guest house, travel by an employee or any related person (including hotel expenses or allowances paid in connection with such travelling) were either fully disallowed or partially allowed on a presumptive basis. Further, in the case of expenditure on travel and hotel, it entailed trip-wise determination of the fringe benefit. It was complex and onerous from both compliance and administration perspectives.

In 1983, the law was amended to provide that 20 per cent of the amount in excess of Rs. 1,20,000 (US $ 11,605.41)[26] spent in aggregate on advertisement, publicity, sales promotion, running and maintenance of aircraft and motor cars and payments made to hotels, would be disallowed in computing the taxable profits. However, these amendments were withdrawn in 1985 by the incoming government and the pre-1983 position was restored.

Officially, the disallowances including those in the pre-1983 regime were intended to discourage conspicuous expenditure in consonance with socialist economic policies. Therefore, trade and industry were constantly canvassing for removal of the artificial disallowances. It was argued that the expenditures were incurred for legitimate business purposes and the disallowances amounted to deviation from the principle of taxation of real income. However, the taxation did not change for the disallowances were, effectively, a method of taxing fringe benefits to employees.

In 1997, accepting the reasoning of industry, government eliminated all of these disallowances. Even if the disallowances were recognized as a method of taxing fringe benefits in the hands of the employer, in practice, this method resulted in large-scale litigation on account of ambiguity in defining the tax base. Further, the employer-based disallowance method was also claimed to be inequitable. The effective tax liability on loss-making and zero-tax companies was zero thereby discriminating against profit-making companies. Whatever be the reasoning for the disallowances, their elimination in 1997 seemed justified. Thenceforth, fringe benefits were subject to tax only by the beneficiary employee-based method which provided for concessional valuation of the benefits relative to their market value. The withdrawal resulted in significant erosion of the tax base, however.

In 2002, a comprehensive review of the taxation of perquisites in the hands of the employee was undertaken. Consequently, there was a significant increase in the imputed value of the benefits though it fell substantially short of the market value. Further, with a view to encouraging the popular acceptability of upward revisions, Section 192 of the Income-tax Act was amended to provide that the employer may,

[26]Average exchange rate was US$ 1 = Rs. 10.34 at that time.

at his option, pay the liability in respect of perquisites provided to the employees.[27] In spite of this, a large number of perquisites continued to remain outside the scope of taxation particularly those which were collectively enjoyed by employees.

The under-taxation of fringe benefits in India continued to increase as their market value increased. It became imperative to review the taxation of fringe benefits. In 2005, the beneficiary employee-based method of taxation of fringe benefits was supplemented by a mutually exclusive employer-based separate tax called 'fringe benefits tax' (FBT).

The FBT was introduced as a surrogate tax on fringe benefits provided by the employers with the objective of filling the gap in the existing scheme of taxation of fringe benefits. The challenge was to design the tax in a manner that would (1) substantially reduce compliance cost and administrative burden associated with identification of fringe benefits provided to employees, (2) reduce scope for evasion through disguising benefits as reimbursements or other miscellaneous expenses and (3) eliminate the need to distinguish genuine benefits from benefits that are consumed in the course of employment or that are a necessary condition of employment. Consequently, the tax base for FBT was innovatively designed to meet these challenges.

#### 26.4.3.1 Tax Base

The tax base for the purposes of FBT was the aggregate of two components, namely, (1) value of fringe benefits provided and (2) value of fringe benefits deemed to have been provided. The inclusion of the second component was conceptually a departure from the conventional definition of the tax base as reflected in the first component, and therefore, comprised an innovation in designing the tax base. Further, the tax base for FBT did not include perquisites in respect of which tax is paid under the beneficiary employee-based method.

The term 'value of fringe benefits provided' was defined to mean any consideration for employment provided by way of any privilege, service, facility or amenity, directly or indirectly, by an employer, whether by way of reimbursement or otherwise, to his employees (including former employees) during the financial year. It was further expanded to specifically include (a) any free or concessional tickets provided by the employer for private journeys of his employees or their family members and (b) any contribution by the employer to an approved superannuation fund for employees. This definition of the term 'value of fringe benefits provided' was all encompassing and generic in its scope so as to tax all genuine benefits to employees which are clearly identifiable as such.

[27] A recommendation that was made in 2002 came from a former Chairman of the Central Board of Direct Taxes (CBDT) advocated the introduction of an Australian type FBT as a separate levy. The then finance minister directed CBDT to examine this suggestion. However, CBDT argued that the Australian type FBT entailed high compliance cost and administrative burden. Accordingly, it recommended that the suggestion made by Pandey should be rejected, which was accepted by the finance minister. The FBT introduced later in 2005 overcame the problem of high compliance and administrative cost by resorting to a presumptive method for determining the tax base.

**Table 26.1** Purposes for which employer incurs expenditure or makes payment

| |
|---|
| (A). Entertainment |
| (B). Provision of hospitality of every kind to any person whether by way of food or beverages or in any other manner excluding food or beverages provided to the employees in the office or factory or non-transferable paid vouchers usable only at eating joints or outlets |
| (C). Conference excluding fees for participation by the employees in any conference |
| (D). Sales promotion including publicity excluding specified expenditure on advertisement |
| (E). Employee welfare excluding any expenditure or payment made to fulfil any statutory obligations or mitigate occupational hazards or provide first aid facilities in the hospital or dispensary of the employer |
| (F). Conveyance tour and travel (including foreign travel) |
| (G). Use of hotel boarding and lodging facilities |
| (H). Repair, running (including fuel), maintenance of motorcars and the amount of depreciation thereon |
| (I). Repair, running (including fuel), maintenance of aircrafts and the amount of depreciation thereon |
| (J). Use of telephone (including mobile phones) other than expenditure on leased telephone lines |
| (K). Maintenance of any accommodation in the nature of guest house other than accommodation used for training purposes |
| (L). Festival celebrations |
| (M). Use of health club and similar facilities |
| (N). Use of any other club facilities |
| (O). Gifts |
| (P). Scholarships |

Source: Government notifications

The term 'value of fringe benefits deemed to have been provided' was designed to provide that fringe benefits shall be deemed to have been provided by the employer if he has incurred any expense on, or made payment for, the purposes listed in Table 26.1. The quantification of the base on account of the deeming provision was based on a presumptive method applied to expenditure. The presumption was that 20 per cent of the expenditure incurred on items (A) to (K) and 50 per cent of the expenditure on items (L) to (P) in the table were incurred for providing fringe benefits to employees.[28] This presumption was considered irrebuttable.

The various items of expenditure were identified to prevent any abuse through misclassification, and were also based on field experience. They were often used to camouflage fringe benefits as if genuinely and exclusively incurred for the purposes for which they were booked in the accounts without any element of benefit to the employees either individually or collectively. The items of expenditure were used as a measure/indicator of fringe benefits (and not the subject of levy as alleged by critics). It sought to capture within its fold the perquisites disguised as reimbursements or other miscellaneous expenses.

[28]The Finance Bill, 2005, provided for much higher percentages. However, based on subsequent discussions with trade and industry representatives, the percentages were reduced to these levels.

It also intended to overcome the problem, as indicated earlier, of distinguishing genuine benefits from benefits that are consumed in the course of employment or that are a necessary condition of employment, and the problem of attributing all benefits individually to employees, particularly in cases where the benefit is collectively enjoyed. The prescribed items of expenditure were used as a measure (and not as the subject) of the levy. Therefore, FBT was not a tax on expenditure. The method had the virtue of simplicity, minimum disputes, low compliance cost and low administrative burden.

The FBT was payable by an employer who was a company; a firm; an association of persons or a body of individuals.[29] FBT was payable by the employer even if he was not liable to pay income tax on his total income. The rate of FBT was 30 per cent which was the maximum marginal rate of the individual income tax. It was not allowed as a deduction in computing the employer's income for the purposes of income tax. The law relating to FBT provided for a detailed mechanism for payment of tax, filing of tax return and assessment.

After the introduction of the 2005 central government budget, private sector corporations were critical of FBT with a view that the levy was unreasonable, complex and excessive and, on that basis, sought its withdrawal. It was argued that the levy was in the nature of an expenditure tax levied on legitimate business expenditure. However, this argument was flawed inasmuch as the supreme court had, as late as 2004, held that, in taxation matters, a levy was legitimate as long as the subject of the levy was within the competence of the national parliament or state legislatures even if any other indicator was used as a measure of the levy.

Therefore, the government refused to accept the demand for withdrawal but agreed to moderate the proposal by reducing the proportions of the various items of expenditure presumed to comprise fringe benefits. Upon enactment, a detailed circular, along with frequently asked questions, was released to address concerns raised during the public discourse. Simultaneously, a one-page tax return form was prescribed to facilitate compliance. These initiatives were intended to minimize the FBT's compliance cost and administrative burden. Nevertheless, the FBT could never leave criticism from the corporate sector behind.

## 26.5 Conclusions

Overall, the FBT was efficiency enhancing and it improved the equity of India's individual income tax. But it increased taxpayer compliance cost due to excessive record keeping requirements by the tax administration. The corporate sector, not having reconciled to the FBT, lobbied for its removal during subsequent pre-budget

[29]It excluded any fund, trust or institution that was eligible for exemption granted under certain sections of the Income-tax Act viz. cl (23C) of Section 10 or registered under Section 12AA; a local authority; or an artificial juridical person. An entity which did not have any employees based in India, was not liable to FBT. For example, a law firm, having only retainer relationship arrangements and no employees on its rolls, was not liable to FBT.

discussions. In 2009, in the aftermath of the global financial crisis and parliamentary elections, there was a general perception that the Indian economy was sliding and needed to be supported by appropriate incentives. The finance minister had changed even though the government was the same. It set aside the economics of FBT and took the political decision to withdraw it. Good economics was sacrificed at the altar of political constraints and administrative flaws. Consequently, India then opted to tax fringe benefits exclusively by the beneficiary employee-based method that regressed to the era of under-taxation of fringe benefits and erosion of the individual income tax base.

## References


Beinhocker, Eric D. 2007. *The Origin of Wealth: Evolution, Complexity and the Radical Remaking of Economics*. Boston: Harvard Business School Press.

Bond, Steve, Mike Hawkins, and Alexander Klemm. 2004. *Stamp Duty on Shares and its Effects on Prices*. Institute of Fiscal Studies WP04/11. http://www.ifs.org.uk/wps/wp0411.pdf.

Brooks, Neil. 2001. Key Issues in Income Tax: Challenges of Tax Administration and Compliance. *Tax Conference*. Asian Development Bank.

Burns, Lee, and Richard Krever. 1998. Individual Income Tax. In *Tax Law Design and Drafting*, ed. Victor Thuronyi, vol. 2. Washington, DC: International Monetary Fund.

Farmer, J. Doyne, Laszlo Gillemot, Fabrizio Lillo, Szabolcs Mike, and Anindya Sen. 2004. What Really Causes Large Price Changes? *Quantitative Finance* 4 (4): 383–397. https://doi.org/10.1080/14697680400008627.

Hawkins, Mike, and Julian McCrae. 2002. *Stamp Duty on Share Transactions: Is There a Case for Change?* Institute of Fiscal Studies, Commentary 89. http://www.ifs.org.uk/comms/comm89.pdf. Accessed 26 Oct 2020.

HMRC. 2019. *HMRC's Annual Report and Accounts 2018–19*. https://assets.publishing.service.gov.uk/government/uploads/system/uploads/attachment_data/file/824652/HMRC_Annual_Report_and_Accounts_2018-19__web_.pdf. Accessed 26 Oct 2020.

Jackson, P.D., and A.T. O'Donnell. 1985. *The Effects of Stamp Duty on Equity Transactions and Prices in the UK Stock Exchange*. Bank of England Discussion Paper No. 25. https://www.bankofengland.co.uk/-/media/boe/files/archive/discussion-paper/the-effects-of-stamp-duty-on-equity-transactions-and-prices.pdf. Accessed 26 Oct 2020.

Keynes, John Maynard. 1936/2006. *General Theory of Employment, Interest and Money*. Germany and India: Macmillan and Atlantic Publishers & Distributors (P) Limited.

Palley, Thomas I. 1999. Speculation and Tobin Tax: Why Sand in the Wheels can Increase Economic Efficiency. *Journal of Economics* 69 (2): 113–126. https://doi.org/10.1007/BF01232416.

Shome, Parthasarathi, and Janet Stotsky. 1995. *Financial Transactions Taxes*. Working Paper WP/95/77, International Monetary Fund. https://doi.org/10.5089/9781451849950.001. Accessed 26 Oct 2020.

Soares da Silva, D.R.R. 2004. Tax Assessments Soar as Brazil uses CPMF Information. *Tax Analysts*, December 2.

Stiglitz, Joseph E. 1989. Using Tax Policy to Curb Speculative Short-Term Trading. *Journal of Financial Service Research* 3: 101–115. https://core.ac.uk/download/pdf/161443799.pdf.

Summers, Lawrence H., and Victoria P. Summers. 1989. When Financial Markets Work Too Well: A Cautious Case for a Securities Transaction Tax. *Journal of Financial Services Research* 3: 261–286. https://doi.org/10.1007/BF00122806.

Tobin, James. 1978. A Proposal for International Monetary Reform. *Eastern Economic Journal* 4 (3–4): 153–159. https://web.holycross.edu/RePEc/eej/Archive/Volume4/V4N3_4P153_159.pdf.

Wei, Shang-Jin, and Jungshik Kim. 1999. *The Big Players in the Foreign Exchange Market: Do They Trade on Information or Noise?* CID Working Papers No. 5. Center for International Development, Harvard University. https://core.ac.uk/download/pdf/6720373.pdf. Accessed 26 Oct 2020.

# Part V

# International Taxation

# 27 Double Taxation Avoidance Agreements

## 27.1 Introduction

Taxation of productive factors in an economy—whether directly or indirectly—involves balancing national against international considerations. While national objectives are concerned with revenue, allocative efficiency and equity effects of taxation, such tax systems may have fundamental ramifications on the volume and allocation of productive resources internationally. This is because factor returns and the underlying tax bases straddle national boundaries. To deal with possible conflicts, adjustments to domestic taxation are needed. One set relating to direct taxation is represented by the residence and source principles. The analogous set for consumption taxes such as the VAT is the origin and destination principles.

In today's globalised world, cross-border transactions are increasing and becoming more complex. At the same time, domestic resource mobilisation has gained greater significance as governments are under pressure to generate additional revenues for various socio-economic programmes. Every country seeks to tax the income generated within its territory on the basis of one or more connecting factors such as the location of the source of income (source principle), residence of the taxable entity (residence principle) or presence of a permanent establishment (PE) in its territory for carrying out business activities which generate profits.

## 27.2 What Is Cross-Border Double Taxation?

For income taxation, the residence principle asserts that individuals are taxable in the country or tax jurisdiction in which they are resident regardless of the source of income. Tax laws provide the basis for determining the tax residence of individuals and other taxable entities. Establishing residence for non-natural persons is not always clear-cut, though it is increasingly tied to the location where the business activities are registered or where major management decisions are taken. The source principle asserts the prior, and even sole, claim of the country in which the income



P. Shome, *Taxation History, Theory, Law and Administration*, Springer Texts in Business and Economics, https://doi.org/10.1007/978-3-030-68214-9_27

arises to natural or legal persons, to tax such income without reference to other criteria.

A country chooses to emphasise one or the other of the aforesaid factors (source or residence) for exercising fiscal jurisdiction to tax the entity. Whether source or residence is chosen is not only to maximise its tax revenues but sometimes also reflecting the larger economic principles of trade and investment. In practice, countries have tended not to stay with the pure application of a single principle but to apply a mix—residence for nationals residing in the country and source for income earned within the country by non-residents or non-natural persons[1] or both. The nature of mixes has depended on a country's objectives regarding foreign investment, revenue, administrative capabilities and degree of co-operation with competing jurisdictions.

Double taxation might result as the same income of the same entity might become liable to taxation in different countries. For example, a particular income is taxed by Country A on the basis of 'Source of Income' and by Country B on the basis of 'Residence'. Moreover, situations may also arise when a person is a tax resident under the laws of both Country A and Country B and the same income is liable to tax under laws of both the countries on the basis of 'Residence'.

## 27.3 Elimination of Double Taxation

Double taxation of the same income gives rise to harsh consequences for taxpayers and impairs economic development. To avoid this anomalous and incongruous situation, there is a need for co-operation between countries and tax jurisdictions for the elimination of such economic double taxation. This inherent conflict is often resolved through tax treaties—or double taxation avoidance agreements (DTAAs)—initially contracted on a bilateral basis between developed countries with a rough balance in the exchange of their income flows.

Over time, however, the treaties have diverged on concepts, structures and operating rules, as many developing countries entered the field. Today, they cover complex and conflicting concerns of the contracting parties about sharing income taxing jurisdictions. They address concepts and definitions for tax purposes of a PE, tax treatment of dividends, interest, royalties and capital gains as well as an arrangement such as 'tax sparing', which allows any tax benefit accruing to a business in a capital importing source country to be spared from being recouped in a capital-exporting residence country.

The main objective of the DTAAs is not only to protect taxpayers from double taxation but also to encourage a free flow of international trade and investment. Such agreements also encourage the transfer of technology and personnel between nations and provide a reasonable level of legal and fiscal certainty to investors and traders.

[1]Non-natural persons include companies or body of persons that are treated as taxable entities under the domestic tax law.

The agreements also aim to prevent discrimination between taxpayers as well as set up a dispute resolution mechanism to arrive at an acceptable basis to share tax revenue between treaty partners in case of a tax dispute. They also provide a mechanism for information exchange and tax recovery in a cross-border situation.

In India, Article 73 of the constitution extends to the executive the powers to enter into treaties and implementation of treaties. The central government derives the power to enter into such treaties under Section 90 of the Income-tax Act, 1961. Section 90 has been brought into the statute to enable the executive to negotiate a DTAA and to implement it. This section empowers the central government to enter into an agreement with the government of any country outside India:

- For granting relief in respect of income on which income tax has been paid in both countries, or
- For the avoidance of double taxation of income, or
- For exchange of information for the prevention of evasion, or
- For recovery of income tax

Under Indian law, as in many countries, the taxpayer can either avail the benefit of bilateral agreements between the two countries or choose to be governed by the Indian tax laws, whichever is more beneficial to him. The General Anti-Avoidance Rule (GAAR) is, however, an exception to this general principle since GAAR has been deemed to supersede any international agreement.

## 27.4 Salient Features of DTAAs

DTAAs are important not only to provide certainty in international tax rules and allocation of taxation rights between participating countries but also to eliminate double taxation thereby promoting cross-border investment and trade. Over 3000 bilateral income tax treaties or DTAAs are currently in effect, and the number is growing. The majority of these treaties are based in large part on the United Nations Model Double Taxation Convention between Developed and Developing Countries 2017 (United Nations Model Convention[2]) and the Organization for Economic Co-operation and Development Model Tax Convention on Income and on Capital (OECD Model[3]).

The DTAA contains several articles laying down basic principles for the avoidance of double taxation and providing certainty to the taxpayers in cross-border situations. The salient features of a typical tax treaty between two treaty partners (contracting states) include:

[2]See United Nations (2017).

[3]See OECD (2019).

- **Scope**—DTAAs are generally applicable to persons (including an individual or company or any other taxable entity) resident of one or both the contracting states and does not apply to persons who are not residents of any of the contracting states.
- **Taxes Covered**—DTAAs mostly apply to taxes on income, though some treaties also include wealth or capital tax within their purview. Taxes include surcharge but do not include penalty or fine imposed relating to those taxes. Indirect taxes are not covered by the DTAAs, except for provisions of administrative assistance in certain cases.
- **Residence**—The DTAA provides steps for the determination of tax residence. It specifies that residence is determined as per domestic law depending on domicile, place of residence, place of management, any other criterion of similar nature. However, when an individual taxpayer is a resident of both contracting states as per their domestic laws, his residence is determined by a tie-breaker test based on factors such as permanent home, centre of vital interest, habitual abode and nationality. For other than individuals, residence is determined by the place of effective management in the case of dual residence.
- **PE**—The DTAA provides that business profits are taxable in the source state only when it has a PE, that is, a fixed place of business through which the business of an enterprise is carried on. The fixed place PE includes place of management, branch, office, factory, workshop, sales outlet, warehouse, farm, mine, quarry, oil, gas well or any other place of extraction of natural resources. Other forms of PE include construction PE, service PE and dependent agency PE. The concept of a fixed place PE is likely to undergo significant change in the context of tax challenges from the digitalisation of the economy.
- **Business Profits**—The business profits of an enterprise are taxed only by the country of residence of the enterprise. However, taxation by the source country is also allowed to the extent the profits are attributable to the PE of the enterprise situated therein. The expenses incurred for the business of the PE are deductible. Article 7 of the DTAA on business profits provides the broad principles for allocation of taxation rights of the PE between the contracting states. The profit allocation rules under Article 7 may undergo changes in the context of the Pillar One work on the tax challenges from the digitalisation of the economy.[4]
- **Dividend and Interest Income**—The DTAAs allocate the primary right for the taxation of dividend and interest income to the country of residence of the recipient. However, the taxation of such income is also allowed by the source country and is generally limited to a certain percentage (between 5 and 15%) under the DTAAs. If dividend or interest is connected with the PE in the source country, Article 7 on business profits applies and the taxation in such cases is on a net basis.

[4]See Chap. 31, Sects. 31.6, 31.7 and 31.8, for a discussion of Pillar One and Pillar Two on successful taxation of the digital economy.

- **Royalties and Fees for Technical Services**—The primary right of taxation of royalties and fees for technical services (FTS) under the DTAAs is allocated to the country of residence of the recipient. However, under some treaties source countries may also retain the limited right to withhold tax on such payments under certain conditions. If royalties or FTS are connected with the PE in the source country, Article 7 on business profits applies.
- **Capital Gains**—The DTAAs typically provide that capital gains arising out of alienation of immovable property is to be taxed in the country where the property is situated. Further, capital gains arising from alienation of shares of a company, the property of which consists principally of immovable property, may also be taxed in the country in which the immovable property is situated. Gains from the alienation of shares other than the above may be taxed in the country of residence of the alienator or the country of residence of the company whose shares are alienated, depending on the provisions of the relevant tax treaty.
- **Other Incomes**—Apart from the above-mentioned types of income, the tax treaties also cover the allocation of taxation rights between treaty partners for various other types of incomes arising from cross-border transactions such as income from immovable property, income from shipping and air transport, income from employment or pensions, income of artistes and sportspersons, income of professors, teachers and students and income from government service. The taxation rights of these incomes are also allocated between source or residence countries based on the provisions of relevant treaties. Typical examples of the source basis of taxation are income from immovable property that is taxed in the country in which the property is situated. The income of artists and sportspersons is taxed in the country where the activity generating income is performed. Examples of residence basis are income from shipping and air transport which is taxed in the country of residence of the enterprise carrying out such activities or income from pensions which are taxed in the country of the recipient.
- **Elimination of Double Taxation**—The DTAAs generally provide for one of the following two methods for elimination of double taxation:
  - **Exemption Method** under which the income earned in the country of source and taxed as such is fully exempt in the country of residence; or
  - **Credit Method** under which the total tax paid on a particular income in the country of source is allowed as a credit against any tax payable in the country of residence
- **Non-discrimination**—The DTAAs provide for non-discrimination between the nationals of two contracting states in the same circumstances whether or not the persons are residents of either of the contracting states. The non-discrimination article also applies to Stateless persons who are residents of either contracting states.
- **Dispute Resolution**—The DTAAs provide for an in-built mechanism for dispute resolution under the Mutual Agreement Procedure (MAP). Any person who considers that the actions of either or both of the contracting states result in taxation not in accordance with the provisions of this Convention may invoke MAP proceedings irrespective of the remedies provided by the domestic laws of

the contracting states. The competent authorities of the two contracting states are mandated under the treaty to endeavour to resolve the case by mutual agreement with a view to the avoidance of taxation, which is not in accordance with the Convention. One of the BEPS Action points (Action 14) was to make the dispute resolution mechanism under the tax treaties more effective.[5] The Multilateral Instrument (See Footnote 8) enhances treaty-related dispute resolution mechanisms and over 30 jurisdictions have decided to introduce, via the MLI, an arbitration procedure in their tax treaties.

- **Exchange of Information**—In addition to the allocation of taxation rights and elimination of double taxation, tax treaties also provide for administrative assistance through the exchange of information that is foreseeably relevant for the implementation of the provisions of tax treaties or the domestic laws concerning taxes covered by the treaties. The information exchanged is governed by strict confidentiality provisions and can be disclosed only to persons or authorities concerned with assessment, collection, enforcement, prosecution, appeals in respect of taxes covered by the relevant tax treaty and maybe only used for such purposes.
- **Assistance in Collection of Taxes**—DTAAs also provide the contracting states to lend assistance to each other in the collection of revenue claims, that is, the amount owed in respect of taxes imposed on behalf of either of the contracting states provided the taxation is not contrary to the Agreement. The tax treaties also provide for assistance in ensuring the collection of a revenue claim by taking measures of conservancy if the domestic laws of both the contracting states provide for such measures.
- **Limitation of Benefits (LoB)**—DTAAs have a specific provision to restrict treaty benefits to a resident of a contracting state in certain situations provided under the treaty. Thus, a benefit under a DTAA may not be granted in respect of an item of income if, having regard to all relevant facts and circumstances, it is reasonable to conclude that obtaining that benefit was one of the principal purposes of any arrangement or transaction that resulted directly or indirectly in that benefit (Principal Purpose Test). The benefit may, however, be granted if it is established that granting that benefit under the circumstances would be in accordance with the object and purpose of the relevant provisions of the DTAA. The drafting of the LoB article depends on how the treaty partners agree to implement their common intention, reflected in the preamble of the treaty to eliminate double taxation without creating opportunities for non-taxation or reduced taxation through tax evasion or avoidance, including through treaty shopping arrangements.

The above are salient features of a typical DTAA. However, the final provisions of each DTAA, including allocation of taxation rights for various kinds of income, may differ from one DTAA to another, based on the negotiations between the treaty

[5]See OECD (2015a) for BEPS Action 14.

partners which, among others, depend upon political, economic and trade relations between the contracting states.

## 27.5 Multilateral Instrument

The tax planning strategies that typically exploit gaps and mismatches in international tax rules to artificially shift profits to low or no-tax jurisdictions with little or no economic activity resulted in MNEs avoiding payment of due corporate taxes in countries where value was created or economic activities were performed. The G20 endorsed OECD project to tackle such tax base erosion and profit shifting (BEPS) recommended several tax treaty-related BEPS measures (under BEPS Actions 2, 6, 7 and 14) which required changes to the model conventions as well as bilateral tax treaties based on those model conventions.

The large number of bilateral treaties would have made the bilateral updates burdensome and time-consuming. Therefore, the Action 15 Report, 'Developing a Multilateral Instrument to Modify Bilateral Tax Treaties',[6] provided for an innovative approach of concluding a Multilateral Instrument to enable countries and tax jurisdictions to swiftly modify their bilateral tax treaties to implement tax treaty-related measures. This work finally culminated in the Multilateral Convention to Implement Tax Treaty Related Measures to Prevent Base Erosion and Profit Shifting ('the Multilateral Convention or MLI').[7]

The Multilateral Convention operates to modify tax treaties between two or more parties to the Convention, but does not function in the same way as an amending protocol to a single existing treaty, which would directly amend the text of a treaty, or 'Covered Tax Agreement'.[8] It, instead, is applied alongside existing tax treaties, modifying their application in order to implement the BEPS measures. The Multilateral Convention, therefore, enables all participating countries and tax jurisdictions to meet the treaty-related minimum standards, that is, the minimum standard for the prevention of treaty abuse under Action 6 and the minimum standard for the improvement of dispute resolution under Action 14, that were agreed as part of the final BEPS package.[9]

The Multilateral Convention that entered into force on 1 July 2018 now covers over 90 jurisdictions from all continents and all levels of development.[10] The signatories and parties that joined the MLI identified which of their existing tax treaties they wished to modify via the MLI and which of its provisions they wished

[6]See OECD (2015b).

[7]See OECD (2016).

[8]A Covered Tax Agreement is an agreement for avoidance of double taxation that is in force between Parties to the MLI and for which both Parties have made a Notification that they wish to modify the agreement using the MLI.

[9]See Chap. 30 for a full coverage of the BEPS Actions.

[10]See OECD (2020a) for elaboration for Multilateral Instrument.

to implement. The choices made by the parties through several notifications and reservations are reflected in their 'MLI Position'.[11] Once a tax treaty is listed by both the treaty partners, it becomes an agreement covered by the MLI and the effects of the MLI on a specific covered agreement are drawn from the 'matching' of its partners' choices. The current signatories and parties have listed over 2800 treaties, already leading up to over 1680 matched agreements. India has also provided its List of Reservations and Notifications at the Time of Signature of the MLI.[12]

The MLI is a flexible document and modifies tax treaties according to a jurisdiction's policy preferences with respect to the implementation of tax treaty-related BEPS measures. Reflecting this flexibility, jurisdictions may choose amongst alternative provisions in certain MLI articles, jurisdictions may choose to apply optional provisions such as that related to mandatory binding arbitration in the MAP article, and, in certain cases, jurisdictions may choose to reserve the right not to apply MLI provisions (i.e. opt out through a 'reservation'). For most countries, there is no legal requirement to prepare consolidated texts of the modified tax treaties. However, for the purposes of clarity, many governments are producing a consolidated text of their bilateral tax treaties for the guidance of practitioners and analysts. It could be said to comprise work in progress.

## References

OECD. 2015a. Making Dispute Resolution Mechanisms More Effective, Action 14 – 2015 Final Report. https://doi.org/10.1787/9789264241633-en. Accessed 13 October 2020.

———. 2015b. Developing a Multilateral Instrument to Modify Bilateral Tax Treaties, Action 15 – 2015 Final Report. https://doi.org/10.1787/9789264241688-en. Accessed 13 October 2020.

———. 2016. Multilateral Convention to Implement Tax Treaty Related Measures to Prevent BEPS. https://www.oecd.org/tax/treaties/multilateral-convention-to-implement-tax-treaty-related-measures-to-prevent-beps.htm. Accessed 13 October 2020.

———. 2017. India: Status of List of Reservations and Notifications at the Time of Signature. http://www.oecd.org/tax/treaties/beps-mli-position-india.pdf. Accessed 13 October 2020.

———. 2019. Model Tax Convention on Income and on Capital 2017 (Full Version). https://doi.org/10.1787/g2g972ee-en. Accessed 13 October 2020.

———. 2020a. Multilateral Instrument Information Brochure May 2020. https://www.oecd.org/tax/treaties/multilateral-instrument-BEPS-tax-treaty-information-brochure.pdf. Accessed 13 October 2020.

———. 2020b. Signatories and Parties to The Multilateral Convention to Implement Tax Treaty Related Measures to Prevent Base Erosion and Profit Shifting. http://www.oecd.org/tax/treaties/beps-mli-signatories-and-parties.pdf. Accessed 13 October 2020.

United Nations. 2017. United Nations Model Double Taxation Convention Between Developed and Developing Countries 2017. https://www.un.org/esa/ffd/wp-content/uploads/2018/05/MDT_2017.pdf. Accessed 13 October 2020.

[11] See OECD (2020b).

[12] See OECD (2017).

# Specific Anti-avoidance Rules (SAAR) 28

## 28.1 Introduction

Globalisation has resulted in greater multinational enterprise (MNE) operations. Emerging economy MNEs are also establishing or acquiring subsidiaries abroad. MNEs carry out complex international transactions involving intangibles and multi-tiered services. They tend to structure transactions such that intra-group prices—transfer pricing—are determined reflecting tax considerations. This includes shifting of profits from one jurisdiction to another in a way that their global tax contributions are minimised.

MNEs view such behaviour as 'tax efficiency'. Tax administrations view it as comprising artificial means to avoid tax worldwide, that may be strictly legal but unintended in the law. Therefore, they have introduced anti-avoidance measures in their tax laws to minimise the shifting of the tax base abroad by MNEs to low-tax jurisdictions.

Some rules against such 'tax planning' target specific identifiable means of tax avoidance and are, therefore, termed specific anti-avoidance rules (SAAR) for both domestic and international tax avoidance. Such rules attempt to contain tax avoidance through transfer pricing including excessive payments among related businesses for mutual international transactions, questionable sources of funds received as share capital or loans, transactions that strip out dividends or bonuses and artificial arrangements in transfers of movable property. This chapter surveys several anti-avoidance practices against which tax authorities have legislated SAAR instruments through law or subordinate law (rules).

Countries moved further on to legislating more widely or generally applicable anti-avoidance rules (hence GAAR). Chapter 29 will address country experiences with GAAR, including India.



P. Shome, *Taxation History, Theory, Law and Administration*, Springer Texts in Business and Economics, https://doi.org/10.1007/978-3-030-68214-9_28

## 28.2 Transfer Pricing

The tax treatment of branches and subsidiaries of MNEs has many facets. In general, attributable profits for tax purposes must adhere to arm's length conditions. But there are specific advantages and disadvantages of operating as a branch or subsidiary. For example, a corporation can usually deduct fully the losses incurred abroad by a branch against its home country tax liability. Further, a branch could repatriate after-tax profits to the parent company without further taxation, such as a withholding tax. Usually, parent companies can transfer property to a branch without incurring taxation in the home country. Tax incentives are often carried over to a branch but not to a subsidiary.

There are, however, many disadvantages of a branch operation. For example, a parent company cannot defer home country taxation on branch income that is not remitted to the home country. Host countries typically grant more generous tax options to subsidiaries than to branches, such as for loss carried forward or backward, or deductions, to limit transfer pricing abuses.

Transfer pricing (TP) refers to the setting of prices for transactions between associated enterprises. The requirement is that it be carried out at 'arm's length', that is, as if there is only a market relation between them. It is one of the most prevalent anti-avoidance measures used by tax administrations to protect their tax base. India introduced TP provisions in 2001.[1] It was amended in 2012 to apply TP rules to specified domestic transactions which were defined in a new section[2] of the Act.

### 28.2.1 Setting Arm's Length Price (ALP)

An arm's length price (ALP) is usually set following one of several available methods, an understanding of which is essential for TP analysis.[3]

#### 28.2.1.1 Cost Plus Method (CPM)

This rule prescribes that certain costs and adjustments be first determined. The direct and indirect costs of production incurred by the enterprise in respect of property transferred or services provided to an associated enterprise are determined. The amount of a normal gross profit mark-up to such costs (computed according to the same accounting norms) arising from the transfer, or provision of the same or similar property or services by the enterprise, or by an unrelated enterprise in a comparable uncontrolled transaction, is also determined.

[1]It came into effect from 1 April 2001, under Chapter X: Special Provisions Relating to Avoidance of Tax, Section 92 of the Income-tax Act and Rule 10A-10D of the Income-tax Rules.

[2]Section 92BA of the Act.

[3]See Singh (2020).

The normal gross profit mark-up is adjusted to take into account any differences between the international transaction and comparable uncontrolled transactions, that are seen to materially affect such profit mark-up in the open market.

The costs are increased by the adjusted profit mark-up. The sum so arrived at is taken to be the ALP in relation to the supply of the property or provision of services by the enterprise.

This method is applicable where some semi-finished goods are sold between related parties or in respect of joint facility agreements, and long-term buy and supply arrangements for the provision of services.

#### 28.2.1.2 Profit Split Method (PSM)

The combined net profit of the associated enterprises arising from an international transaction in which they are engaged is determined. Next, the relative contributions made by each of the associated enterprises to the earning of such combined net profit are evaluated on the basis of the functions performed, assets employed and risks assumed by each enterprise. Reliable external market data are used to arrive at how such a contribution would be evaluated by unrelated enterprises performing comparable functions in similar circumstances.

The combined net profit is then split among the enterprises in proportion to their relative contributions. The profit thus apportioned to the assessee is taken into account to arrive at the ALP in relation to the international transaction.

This method is applicable mainly in international transactions involving a transfer of selected intangibles (see below) or in multiple international transactions that are so interrelated that they cannot be evaluated individually for the purpose of determining the ALP of any one transaction.

#### 28.2.1.3 Transactional Net Margin Method (TNMM)

The net profit margin realised by an enterprise from an international transaction entered into with an associate enterprise is computed in relation to costs incurred or sales effected or assets employed by the enterprise. The net profit margin realised by the enterprise or by an unrelated enterprise from a comparable uncontrolled transaction is computed having regard to the same basis.

The net profit margin arising in comparable uncontrolled transactions is adjusted to take into account the differences, if any, between the international transaction and the comparable, uncontrolled transactions, or between the enterprises entering into such transactions, which could materially affect the amount of net profit margin in the open market. The net profit margin thus established is then taken into account to arrive at an ALP in relation to the international transaction.

The TNMM requires establishing a comparability level at a broad functional level. It requires comparison between the net margin derived from the operations of the uncontrolled parties and the net margin derived by an associated enterprise on a similar operation. Under this method, the net profit margin realised by an associated enterprise from an international transaction is computed in relation to a particular factor such as costs incurred, sales and assets utilised. The net profit margin earned by an associated enterprise is compared with the net profit margin of uncontrolled transactions to arrive at the ALP.

#### 28.2.1.4 Comparable Uncontrolled Price Method (CUP)

CUP is the price paid or charged for a property transferred or services provided in a comparable uncontrolled transaction and taken as the ALP in respect of the property transferred or services provided in an international transaction. Thus, CUP is, in effect, a comparison of prices charged for the property transferred or service provided in a controlled transaction to a price charged for property or services transferred in a comparable uncontrolled transaction. However, some adjustments are made as is explained in the case of RPM below.

#### 28.2.1.5 Resale Price Method (RPM)

In this method, a price is identified at which a property has been purchased or services obtained by a company from an unrelated enterprise. This is then used for a transaction with an associated enterprise. Some adjustments for gross profit margin, or expenses incurred in connection with the purchase, may need to be made in order to accommodate market facts. Different accounting practices may also have to be adjusted for. This price then comprises the ALP applicable when property is purchased or services are obtained from associated enterprises and the same are sold to unrelated enterprises.

### 28.2.2 Examination of Declared ALP

When an ALP is revealed by a taxpayer in his tax return, it is for the tax authorities to accept or disagree with it. The subsequent process to resolve the disagreement can be long and complex. The prevailing process in India is taken up to demonstrate the importance with which the tax authorities view TP as a means of tax avoidance. The process in India is comparable to those in most emerging economies, though the Indian approach is among the more complex and perhaps time-consuming.

Reflecting its importance, a TP matter can escalate to higher levels of the administration. The Assessment Officer (AO) who examines tax returns makes a judgement that there is a TP issue, that is, the reported ALP between related parties used in the tax return is incorrect and, therefore, the return needs further examination. If so, he refers the matter to a TP Officer (TPO) who is trained specially in TP matters. The TPO is authorised to carry out this task under a specific Section 92CA (3) of the Income-tax Act (ITA). In fact, if the transaction involving TP exceeds a certain amount, the rule stipulates that it is obligatory to refer it for examination by a TPO.

After completion of the TPO's determination of ALP, a higher official has to formally approve it. And very high transaction amounts are subjected to compulsory audit or scrutiny. The outcome is conveyed to the filer of the tax return in the form of a draft assessment order issued by the AO in conformity with the ALP determined by the TPO.

### 28.2.3 Appeal Mechanism

The determination of an ALP by the administration when it makes an adjustment to the declared ALP is a sensitive matter since it has important implications for the tax calculation of the taxpayer. Thus, a series of appeals has been made available to him. If the taxpayer does not agree with the assessment, he may file a first appeal against the TP adjustment before a tax commissioner who has been designated for appeals. Or, the taxpayer has the option to file an objection directly before a dispute resolution panel (DRP).

If not satisfied, the appeal can be taken to the next, judicial, level known as an Income Tax Appeals Tribunal (ITAT). Many tribunals, which are legal constructs, have a dedicated bench for TP with the objective of faster disposal of TP cases. An ITAT decision is not a final decision, however. Further appeals can be filed in any high court and, after that, to the supreme court. It is not surprising that the settlement of a single TP case can take years and that the number of pending disputes in India is among the highest in the world.

### 28.2.4 Advance Pricing Agreement (APA)

In order to reduce the incidence of disputes that arise after a taxpayer files a tax return and it is processed, India uses an APA scheme to infuse some predictability in ALP determination and reducing litigation. Under an APA, a taxpayer can enter into an agreement with the tax administration in respect of the ALP that may be used in a proposed transaction.

For this purpose, a competent authority (CA) has been designated in most countries from among senior tax administrators. They have been given the power to arrive at APAs. In India, taxpayers can seek and enter into unilateral, bilateral or multilateral APAs. While unilateral APAs provide tax certainty only in one country, bilateral or multilateral APAs are entered into after successful negotiations between the CAs of all the involved countries, thereby providing tax certainty in all participating countries. The APA mechanism is at a nascent stage in many emerging economies including India.

India does not publish information on the number of its APAs. However, some cross-country data are available from the OECD. It can be concluded that India has not had too many APAs compared to advanced economies. Since APAs make anticipation of tax more certain, it is important to complete as many APAs as possible in order to encourage investment and facilitate tax compliance.

### 28.2.5 Corporate Guarantee

Moving on from the determination of ALP, another tax behaviour is that of parent companies with respect to their newly formed subsidiaries in overseas territories. The latter are likely not to be able to obtain finance without a corporate guarantee from the former. Corporate guarantee is identified as an international transaction by the OECD and is accepted as such in most jurisdictions. What it implies is that, giving a guarantee by the parent amounts to the provision of benefits/services to the subsidiary for which an ALP needs to be determined.

In India, such a guarantee has been specifically mentioned in the definition of international transactions through an explanation in the law in 2012. And the explanation was brought in with retrospective application which hit certain taxpayers without anticipation.

### 28.2.6 Share Valuation

A taxpayer company may issue shares to their associated enterprises at values that are less than the market value or intrinsic value of those shares. The Indian tax law has defined capital financing as an international transaction through an Explanation to Section 92B of the ITA with effect from 1 April 2002. It implies that TP adjustments are permitted to include and determine the ALP for the issue of shares to an overseas associated enterprise.

A question remains, however, that if shares are issued at a price lower than the ALP, should the resultant benefit to the overseas entity be taxed in the hands of the domestic company issuing the shares, or should the difference be taxed as deemed income in the hands of the foreign associated enterprise. There is also a view that the difference should be subjected to capital gains in the hands of the foreign enterprise, and only at the time of alienation of such shares.

### 28.2.7 Interest on Outbound Loans

A taxpayer company may advance loans to a newly formed subsidiary or associated enterprise or related party in low tax or no tax jurisdictions at nil or low interest rates. There is no prevailing dearth of agreement that advancing of loan—interest-free or at lower than market rate—benefits the subsidiary. However, a dispute may arise regarding the quantification of the benefit.

In India, assessees usually benchmark the concerned interest rate on the London Inter-bank Offered Rate (LIBOR). LIBOR is applicable in the case of interbank lending where the banks have high credit ratings. It is applicable for high-value loans. Tax administrators may not agree with the use of LIBOR since the related subsidiary may have a low credit rating (on a standalone basis) reflecting that it is newly formed. Hence, it is unlikely that any such subsidiary could obtain the loans at a LIBOR rate.

The applicable rate in India, therefore, is searched and attempted to be set at the rate at which the lender company would have lent in the Indian market to a borrower having equivalent credit rating as that of the subsidiary. Alternatively, the starting point could be the rate at which the Indian taxpayer company itself borrows from the market. The ALP could then be determined as that rate adjusted by an appropriate factor.

### 28.2.8 Royalty

Royalty being an intellectual property, determining an ALP for royalty can be complex. Royalty is an amount that is paid by a domestic company for certain services for 'intangibles' that it receives from a foreign company abroad. Intangibles include patent, copyright, design or model, secret formula or process, trademark, trade name or for information concerning industrial, commercial or scientific experience.[4] In certain cases, companies appear to be paying for royalty even when there is no transfer of new technology. Therefore, royalty as well as the royalty rate may be considered to be tainted and the tax administration may choose to examine it.

There are available methods for rate determination. Application of the comparable uncontrolled price method (CUP) poses difficulty as identification of a closely comparable transaction between unrelated parties is challenging in the case of intangibles. The transactional net margin method (TNMM) uses net profit margin relative to an appropriate base such as costs, sales or assets of a comparable arm's length transaction. This method does not always give a reliable result as net margin (profit), and not price (royalty), is used as the base.

The Reserve Bank of India (RBI), India's central bank, permits royalty at the rate of 5% on domestic sales and 8% on exports under an automatic approval scheme. Accordingly, some TPOs use this as a benchmark.

### 28.2.9 Intra-group Services

Intra-group services in the form of management support fees, or cost allocations, are paid by a domestic taxpayer company to an overseas associated company. A tax administration may find it difficult to conclude whether any commensurate benefits have accrued to the domestic entity even as the domestic tax base gets eroded due to such payments.

These payments are often not taxable in the hands of the payee—the overseas associated enterprise—when they take the form of payments for services since that would be taxed abroad. However, a payout in the form of dividends from the domestic taxpayer to the overseas associated company would have been taxable.

Here again, determination of the correct valuation of such management fees through TNMM or CUP methods may be challenging and the tax administration would have to be careful to determine an acceptable via media.

[4]See Mantri (2015).

### 28.2.10 Safe Harbour Rules

'Safe Harbour' is defined to indicate circumstances in which the income tax authorities shall accept a TP declared by the taxpayer as long as it lies within a prescribed range stipulated by the tax authority. The objective is to reduce the number of TP audits and prolonged disputes. Some countries such as Brazil have legislated Safe Harbour Rules for many years. In India, they were introduced in 2009. Few companies opted for safe harbour since the ranges were considered unreflective of market realities. Accordingly, a government committee was formed and, in September 2013, it recommended sharpening the ranges for a list of eligible international transactions applicable to different sectors.[5] To provide an illustration of a set of safe harbours, they are shown in Table 28.1.

### 28.2.11 Controlled Foreign Company (CFC)

To prevent erosion of the domestic tax base through discouraging resident taxpayers from shifting income to low tax jurisdictions, the Indian Ministry of Finance configured a CFC regime in 2010 that was proposed in 2013. A CFC was defined as a foreign company: (i) which is a resident of a territory with a lower rate of taxation;[6] (ii) its shares are not traded on any recognised stock exchange of the territory of which it is a resident; (iii) it is controlled individually or collectively by one or more persons resident in India; and (iv) it is not engaged in any active trade or business.

Profits of a CFC are taxed by attributing it to resident shareholders, usually in proportion to their shareholding in the CFC.

For the purposes of the CFC rules, a company is deemed to be engaged in an active trade or business if and only if: (i) it actively participates in industrial, commercial or financial undertakings through employees or other personnel in the economic life of the territory of which it is resident for tax purposes; and (ii) less than 25% of the income of the company during the accounting period is passive in nature such as dividend, interest, income from house property, capital gains, annuity payment or royalty.

### 28.2.12 Thin Capitalisation (Thin Cap)

The Thin Cap rule usually applies when a company is 'thinly' capitalised, that is, its capital is made up of a much greater proportion of debt than equity. It is based on the

[5]Government of India (2012).

[6]'Territory with a lower rate of taxation' is defined as a country or territory in which the amount of tax paid under its law is less than one-half of the corresponding tax payable on those profits in the domestic jurisdiction, that is, India.

**Table 28.1** Safe Harbour for eligible transactions

| S. No. | International transaction | Circumstances |
|---|---|---|
| 1. | Provision of software development services other than contract R&D | The operating profit margin declared in relation to operating expense incurred is: 20% or more (where the total value of international transaction does not exceed Rs. 5 billion); and 22% or more (where the total value of international transaction exceeds Rs. 5 billion) |
| 2. | Provision of information technology-enabled services other than contract R&D | The operating profit margin declared in relation to operating expense incurred is: 20% or more (where the total value of international transaction does not exceed Rs. 5 billion); and 22% or more (where the total value of international transaction exceeds Rs. 5 billion) |
| 3. | Provision of knowledge process outsourcing services other than contract R&D | The operating profit margin declared in relation to operating expense is 25% or more |
| 4. | Advancing of intra-group loan to wholly owned subsidiary where the amount of loan does not exceed Rs. 500 million | The Interest rate declared in relation to the international transaction is equal to or greater than the base rate of the State Bank of India (SBI) as on 30th June of the relevant previous year plus 150 basis points |
| 5. | Advancing of intra-group loans to wholly owned subsidiary where the amount of loan exceeds Rs. 500 million | The Interest rate declared in relation to the international transaction is equal to or greater than the base rate of SBI as on 30th June of the relevant previous year plus 300 basis points |
| 6. | Providing explicit corporate guarantee to wholly owned subsidiary where the amount guaranteed does not exceed Rs. 1 billion | The commission or fee declared in relation to the international transaction is at the rate of 2% or more per annum on the amount guaranteed |
| 7. | Providing explicit corporate guarantee to wholly owned subsidiary where the amount guaranteed exceeds Rs. 1 billion and the credit rating of the associated enterprise, done by an agency registered with the SEBI is of the adequate to the highest safety | The commission or fee declared in relation to the international transaction is at the rate of 1.75% or more per annum on the amount guaranteed. |
| 8. | Provision of specified contract research and development services wholly or partly relating to software development | The operating profit margin declared in relation to operating expense incurred is 30% or more |
| 9. | Provision of contract research and development services wholly or partly relating to generic pharmaceutical drugs | The operating profit margin declared in relation to operating expense incurred is 29% or more |

(continued)

**Table 28.1** (continued)

| S. No. | International transaction | Circumstances |
|---|---|---|
| 10. | Manufacture and export of core auto components | The operating profit margin declared in relation to operating expense is 12% or more |
| 11. | Manufacture and export of non-core auto components | The operating profit margin declared in relation to operating expense is 8.5% or more |

Source: Government of India (2012), op. cit.

policy assumption that such excessive debt funding would not occur between unrelated or independent parties.

Thin Cap legislation is aimed at restricting the deduction on account of interest on the borrowing between related parties where normal market forces do not operate. Including Thin Cap rules in the tax statute is a measure used by several tax administrations to protect the tax base, though India did not include it in its SAAR list. Instead, it became part of its GAAR law in 2017.

Broadly, Thin Cap legislation in various countries can be categorised as: (i) the fixed debt to equity approach, where interest payment is accepted—no cap applied—if the debt/equity ratio is up to a certain level (say 2:1); beyond the threshold, interest cap becomes applicable; (ii) earnings stripping approach, in which deduction is denied for interest payable to related parties if net interest expenses exceed a specific threshold (say 50%) of the taxable income of the company; and (iii) arm's length or independent banker's approach, which takes into account how much capital the enterprise could have borrowed from an independent banker at the time of the borrowing. The legislation may give the option to employ one, or, a selection of approaches to ensure that no thin capitalisation has taken place in the eyes of the tax administration.

## 28.3 Additional Considerations in the Indian SAAR[7]

### 28.3.1 Capital Gains Tax on Transfer of Shares

Some of India's treaties such as with Mauritius, Singapore and Cyprus provided that, if a shareholder in those countries whose shares were in an Indian company, made profits on disposing of the shares, the profits therefrom would be taxed where the seller was resident, that is, in Mauritius or Singapore or Cyprus. This was despite the fact that the company was Indian and was situated in India.

This was considered by the Indian tax authorities to be a specific avenue for tax avoidance leading to revenue leakage for India. Accordingly, the treaties were amended such that capital gains are now taxed reflecting where the company is

[7]Bhattacharya (2020) explains more SAAR examples in considerable detail. See Chap. 7.

situated hence, in this case, in India. Thus, taxation moved from residence (of taxpayer) to origin (of taxable profits) basis.

### 28.3.2 Taxation of Net Value of Share Buyback

A dividend distribution tax (DDT) was introduced in 1997 in India to simplify the taxation of income from dividends (see Chap. 17, Sect. 17.4). In fact, that income accrued to dividend recipients and, therefore, should have been taxed at the level of individual income tax earners. Since that was not easy to collect due to low declarations, the government replaced it by taxation at the hands of corporations at the point of distribution of the dividends. It was also easy to administer since DDT was collected from a much lower number of taxpayers—corporations—rather than from individual taxpayers.

The DDT was being avoided as companies began to interpret the dividend distribution or payment as consideration for buyback of shares, which happened to be exempt from DDT. Though buyback of shares was subject to capital gain tax, treaties protected the beneficiaries from paying the tax in India. A new provision was introduced in 2013 to counter this tax avoidance route by levying a tax on the buyback. Its base was designed to be the value of the buyback minus the value received by the company at the time of issuing the shares. Further, no treaty benefits are associated with this taxable base.

However, tax experts and advisers may conclude that this action by the government was an indirect means of denying treaty benefits to a taxpayer. Thus,

> Such matters in international taxation are, therefore, not settled and come up in the judiciary for final resolution. A technical effect of such a mode of taxation would be to sterilize tax treaties. It will then be a question of tax morality for the government and also a question whether bypassing the reach of treaties this way betrays a Directive Principle of State Policy in the Constitution of India,[8] where the state endeavours to foster respect for international treaty obligations.[9]

Clearly, the tax administration and the taxpayer may have genuine differences in the way they view a particular matter in the area of tax avoidance.

### 28.3.3 Place of Effective Management (POEM)

Companies were considered to be resident in India if they were incorporated in India or their place of management and control was wholly in India. The law was changed from Assessment Year (AY) 2017–2018. The phrase 'management' was changed to 'effective management', that is, where key management decisions necessary for the

[8]Constitution of India, Article 51(c).

[9]See Bhattacharya (2020).

conduct of the entity are in substance made. Before the change, even if a company effectively controlled and managed it from India, it could nevertheless be incorporated in a low-tax jurisdiction, indicating that it had done so due to the availability of advanced information and communication technology in the low-tax jurisdiction. By claiming that it is a resident of that jurisdiction, it could escape residence-based taxation in India. Instead, if a company held even one meeting outside of India, it would not be a tax resident. This route was not possible to use after the change.

India's change followed the practices prevalent in countries that had already introduced the POEM principle to determine tax residency. It is also recognised by the OECD which has defined POEM as the place where key management and commercial decisions that are necessary for the conduct of the entity's business as a whole are, in substance, made.

Subsequently, it was clarified by the Indian tax administration, however, that the location of senior management would determine the location of effective management, rather than that of the board of directors. Thus, even if the latter made the major decisions from abroad, a company could end up being a tax resident of India if its senior management resided in India. Therefore, experts have raised questions whether this would not lead to lower foreign investment and India would not suffer the deleterious ramifications thereof.[10]

## 28.4 Taxation of Indirect Transfers

'Indirect transfers' refers to income arising from the transfer of shares between foreign companies of underlying assets in India. Its taxation is another method adopted by the tax administration to protect the tax base. The conceptual issue is that of how taxing rights should be allocated between the country where the underlying asset is situated, and those located abroad and involved in the transaction itself.

Taxability of indirect transfers in India has been the subject of debate during the recent past with the tax authorities inserting Explanations in Sections 2 and 9 of the ITA to 'clarify' terms such as 'property', 'transfer', 'through' and 'situated in India' for the taxation of indirect transfers. The following clarifications, among others, were made through Finance Act 2012 with retrospective effect from 1 April 1962: (i) in the ITA, income accruing or arising, whether directly or indirectly, through the transfer of capital asset situated in India, is deemed to accrue or arise in India. And (ii) an asset being any share or interest in a company or entity registered or incorporated outside India shall be deemed to be situated in India, if the share or interest derives, directly or indirectly, its value *substantially* from the assets located in India. 'Substantially' is not defined in the ITA (see Sect. 28.4.1.4).

[10]See Bhattacharya (2020) and Sekar (2016).

### 28.4.1 Vodafone Versus Government of India (GOI)

The case of Vodafone versus GOI is an important case of taxation of an indirect transfer. An indirect transfer of assets located in India occurred when the capital gain arising to Hutchison (HTL, a Hong Kong company) was transferred through CGP (a Cayman Islands company) to Vodafone (VIH, a Dutch company). They were all outside the territorial tax jurisdiction of India since all of them were incorporated abroad, and despite the fact that the capital assets reflecting the shares were situated in India.

Accordingly, Vodafone took the position that India had no right to tax the capital gain and did not withhold tax from Hutchison. This was despite an intimation from the Indian tax authorities to Vodafone of probable future taxation of capital gains enjoyed by Hutchison. Reflecting that Hutchison had no remaining assets in India, the Indian tax authorities claimed a tax of US$ 2.6 billion from Vodafone. The procedures that followed through stages of the judiciary culminated in the supreme court ruling in favour of Vodafone in 2012 which, therefore, considered the outcome a 'settled' matter.

The judgement thrust GOI to immediately introduce legislation on indirect transfers with retrospective application that took back applicability to 1962, the beginning of implementation of the Income-tax Act.[11] The language and scope of the amendments countered the supreme court judgement line for line, thus obviating the supreme court's decision. It also stipulated new reporting requirements (see Appendix 1). It led to apprehensions about the certainty, predictability and stability of Indian tax law, and created universal adverse reactions in the global investor community. Investors viewed the amendments made applicable dating back to more than 50 years as causing tax uncertainty that could dig into the past. Any tax understanding forged today could be altered tomorrow through new and unanticipated legislation by the authorities. That would impact on investment decisions already made and, commensurately, projects undertaken yesterday.

An argument regarding deleterious ramifications for economic growth and development can be elaborated simply through the lack of viability of a business model in those circumstances. When a business considers an investment, it takes a decision reflecting its attitude towards risk—averse, neutral or preferer—and its assessment of the prevailing laws on labour, investment, tax or trade. If these are amended in the future and, as long as the changes are applied prospectively, the risk model can be redesigned for any future investment.

If, however, a law is changed retrospectively, its impact on business decisions already made and implemented has to be unexpected and adverse. Resultantly, the business outcomes get vitiated. For example, if unanticipated taxes have to be paid in significant amounts at a time in the future, then the earlier cost, income and profit calculations are rendered baseless. This leads to what could be termed 'impossibility to perform' in an environment of 'uncertainty' rather than only 'risk-taking'.

[11]ITA dates back to 1961 and was made applicable from 1962.

There is little doubt that the ramifications of the changes made in the ITA were deleterious to business investment. The implications of changes made in the definitions of 'capital asset',[12] 'transfer'[13] and 'rule of accrual'[14] are examined below. The new definitions reveal that their scope being amplified, it was not merely the revenue addition on Vodafone, but the taxability of gains made through indirect transfers was amplified retrospectively.

#### 28.4.1.1 Capital Asset

The definition of 'property' or capital asset was amended. It would include any rights in or, in relation to, an Indian company. These would include, rights of management or control, or any other rights whatsoever. If a shareholder holds say a 10% stake in a company, it may be presumed that, with it, he possesses some management right. It is this right to management which the amendment clarifies to be an asset, over and above the investment asset the shareholder holds.

Say the shareholder holds a 10% stake in the company. Now there is an issue of a preferential share to another investor. As a result, the stake held by the first shareholder declines from 10% to 5%. Since the stake is a separate asset from the shareholding as defined by the amendment, the first shareholder may be viewed as having transferred a 5% stake to the second shareholder, despite the fact that the company did not consult him regarding the preferential share issue. He could be seen as being chargeable to capital gains tax on the amount that he charges in the transaction.

#### 28.4.1.2 Transfer

The term 'transfer' was defined to mean disposing of, or parting with, an asset or any interest therein; or creating any interest in any asset (including involuntarily). The main requirement would be that there has to be a transfer of rights in the taxable territory, no matter that such transfer of rights arose from a transfer of shares of a company registered outside India.

Interpreting the above, the transfer of rights goes beyond shares but include, for instance in the case of an insolvent company, the transfer of management rights to creditors. Technically, this could be interpreted to be a taxable transfer.

#### 28.4.1.3 Accrual of Gains

An explanation was provided on the place of accrual of incomes, indicating that an asset or capital asset being any share or interest in a company or entity registered or incorporated outside India shall be deemed to be situated in India if the share or interest derives value substantially from assets located in India. The tax profession is familiar with the taxability of a share transfer. India's extended reach beyond shares and companies to 'entity' and 'other interests' that could cover interests in

[12]Income-tax Act, 1961, Section 2(14).

[13]Id., Section 2(47).

[14]Id., Section 9.

partnership firms or other conglomerates and ownership interests expands taxability in unknown dimensions that is likely to lead to future litigation.

#### 28.4.1.4 'Substantial' Presence

It was clarified that an asset being any share or interest in a company or entity registered or incorporated outside India shall be deemed to be situated in India, if the share or interest derives, directly or indirectly, its value 'substantially' from assets located in India.

'Substantially' is not defined in the Income-tax Act. However, a government group working on a direct tax code in 2010 suggested a 50% threshold of global assets to be located in India for taxation of income from an indirect transfer in India.

A continuing effort at a direct tax code in 2013 provided for a reduced threshold to 20% of global assets to be located in India as sufficient for taxation of income from an indirect transfer in India. The argument of the government was that the 50% threshold was too high and could result in situations where a company had 33.33% assets in three countries and would not get taxed anywhere.

#### 28.4.1.5 Participatory Note (PN) and Foreign Portfolio Investors (FPIs)

An exemption or transfer of small shareholdings (up to 5%) outside India was introduced to exclude small Participatory Note (PN) holders from the ambit of indirect transfer taxation. PNs are financial instruments issued by SEBI-registered[15] foreign institutional investors (FII) to their overseas investors.[16] All dividends or capital gains from the underlying shares go exclusively to those investors.

On 21 December 2016, the Central Board of Direct Taxes (CBDT) comprising the most senior officials of the income tax department issued a clarification on the scope of the indirect transfer provisions that sought to extend taxation to FPIs. This would have taxed small profits made by funds with equities in India. However, following pressures, CDBT in a press release on 17 January 2017, held back the circular on the taxation of indirect transfer of shares.

### 28.4.2 Multilateral Efforts

The UN Committee of Experts on International Cooperation in Tax Matters has been looking into the feasibility, through its UN Model Tax Convention (MTC), of imposing an Offshore Indirect Transfer Tax (OIT) by source jurisdictions within the tax treaty framework. In its meeting held on 7 October 2020, the committee

[15]Securities and Exchange Board of India.

[16]Essentially, PNs are offshore derivative instruments (ODI) that have Indian stocks as their underlying assets. It allows a foreign investor to buy stocks listed on Indian exchanges without being registered with any authorities in India but, rather, through an intermediary agent. For example, India-based registered brokerages issue PNs to foreign agents that take up India-based securities on behalf of those investors. See Jaiswal (2019).

approved the release of draft changes to the Commentary accompanying the UN MTC.

Three changes proposed included: (i) modification to limit residuary capital gains tax entitlement of resident states; (ii) a treaty clause (within the capital gains provision) to permit source taxation of gains from certain OITs along with an explanation of the scope of the proposed clause; and (iii) a treaty article to permit source countries to tax gains from the direct transfer of: (a) derivatives and securities issued by resident companies; and (b) rights granted under laws of the source state which are used or exercised exclusively in the source state, such as telecommunication licences and mining rights. These are anticipated to be discussed in future committee discussions.[17]

The Indian tax administration has been holding a view that tax on OITs is within its entitlement and has been contesting a similar view before the supreme court against Sanofi Pasteur. It could be viewed as an attempt by Indian tax authorities to renegotiate treaties for claiming entitlement to tax OITs, and to push its agenda on treaty override via multilateral agency avenues.

## 28.5 Conclusions

No doubt TP is an involved matter in the area of international taxation. What should be noted is that TP adjustments are to be used to curb tax avoidance but should not be used as a revenue-generating tool by any tax administration. Thus, ideally, TP is a 'minimising' instrument with respect to tax avoidance and not a 'maximising' instrument for revenue generation.

In practice, reflecting its number of TP adjustments, India makes many times more adjustments than is the prevailing international norm. While the outcome is a huge volume and value of demands by international standards, available evidence suggests that actual collection does not come close to the demands raised.

Tax administrations should reduce the number of TP audits by developing a mechanism for the identification of high-risk TP cases. The accompanying approach should be to make the dispute prevention and resolution mechanisms more robust and dependable.

Capacity building and specialisation are important in the area of international taxation and TP in particular in view of the recent introduction of GAAR. In emerging economies, therefore, increased support to TPOs through international databases like Capital IQ, Moody's, Bloomberg, Reuters, Royalty Stat and others as well as installation of dedicated research teams including economists who can carry out analysis on industry-specific data is much needed.

Retrospective application of tax laws not only causes apprehensions about the certainty, predictability and stability of tax laws but also the impossibility of

[17] See United Nations (2020).

performance. Retrospectivity should, therefore, be resorted to in the rarest of rare cases after comprehensive stakeholder consultation.

## Appendix 1: Government of India Committee Views, Added Reporting Requirements and Final Outcome of Arbitration

Government of India's (GOI) legislation through Finance Act 2012 making the law on indirect transfers applicable retrospectively that followed the supreme court's judgement on Vodafone versus GOI, attracted universal adverse reaction in the global investor community.

### Views of GOI Committee

It could be said that, reflecting international reaction to the 2012 legislation, GOI was obliged to set up an expert committee in July 2012 to look into the issues related to the taxation of indirect transfers. It submitted its recommendations in October. The committee's views reflected international practice. It reviewed the practice of retrospectivity elsewhere. Countries such as the United States and United Kingdom have allowed some retrospective application, nevertheless for finite periods of time. European countries such as Sweden on the other hand have eschewed the principle. There is no particular reason why India should select one or the other, except that India's stage of economic development and the commensurate need for foreign investment are strongly linked to eradicating uncertainty facing businesses in their tax compliance-related business decisions.

Accordingly, the committee's view was that retrospectivity tests the strength of the full force of applicability in future cases by shifting focus to the past. Besides, an 'impossibility of performance' is likely to be caused for taxpayers because of the absence of knowledge of the future ramifications of prevailing taxation laws that could be changed tomorrow with effect from yesterday.

The committee recommended that retrospective application of tax law should occur in exceptional or rarest of rare cases and with particular objectives such as: (i) to correct apparent mistakes/anomalies in the statute; (ii) to apply to matters that are genuinely clarificatory in nature, i.e. to remove technical defects, particularly in procedure, which have vitiated the substantive law; or (iii) to 'protect' the tax base from highly abusive tax planning schemes that have the main purpose of avoiding tax, without economic substance, but not to 'expand' the tax base.

Moreover, retrospective application of a tax law should occur only after exhaustive and transparent consultations with stakeholders who would be affected. The government finally made statements indicating they would not apply new taxes retrospectively.

The committee's recommendations were under consideration of the government for a long time. The matter of removing retrospectivity in taxation remains unattended in India's ITA even though the current government has assured the business community that it would not apply tax laws retrospectively.

Yet the Vodafone case was not withdrawn and put through international arbitration. This reflects the GOI position that Vodafone had been cautioned that a tax may be applied at a future date when the transaction with Hutchison had occurred, but it also reflects GOI's unwillingness to treat the matter as having been 'settled'. This position necessarily rejects the 2012 view taken by the supreme court, leave alone subsequently by the expert committee.

## Reporting Obligation

Subsequent to the 2012 legislation, other aspects made the application of the law more draconian. A 2016 amendment made it obligatory for an Indian company (which contributed to the value of shares that were being indirectly transferred abroad) to report the transaction irrespective of the level above it (in the overall company structure) at which the indirect transfer was taking place. Figure 28.1 explains a few outcomes that are possible.

Say A Co holds B Co. B Co holds C Co. A, B and C are all outside India. C Co holds D Co which is in India.

Shareholders of A Co transfer A Co's shares to a purchaser. In that case, D Co will have the obligation to report the transaction in India through Income Tax Form 49D, if A Co is liable to tax in India. Thus, D Co has to be fully aware, informed and compliant with providing information to the Indian tax authorities regarding its related companies abroad.

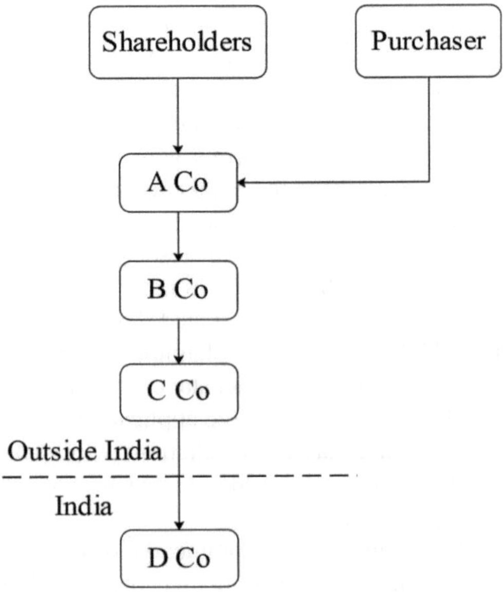


**Fig. 28.1** Structure of related companies. (Source: Bhattacharya (2020))

It does not stop there. Take the example of an indirect transfer involved in an internal restructuring, which is not exempted from taxation in India. Say A Co transfers shares of B Co to a fellow subsidiary (A1 Co which is not in the chain, and not in India). It will be as much a taxable transfer from B Co to A Co, because B Co's shares ultimately derive value from India. Thus, the 2016 amendment renders any internal restructuring involving any indirect transfer more costly for compliance, and likely to lead to added litigation.[18]

## Recent Developments

In a surprise move, in November 2019, the supreme court issued a verdict that subjected Vodafone to a heavy penalty and a large amount in back-tax payments. Vodafone threatened to abandon its operations in India unless a significant tax discount was provided to assist it in cushioning its high losses from this newest imposition. Nevertheless, GOI lost to Vodafone in the arbitration at the international court in The Hague in September 2020.

## References


Bhattacharya, Saurav. 2018. Since Vodafone . . . – An Analysis of Developments in the Taxation of Indirect Transfers. *Asia-Pacific Tax Bulletin* 24 (1) https://www.ibfd.org/sites/ibfd.org/files/content/marketing/Journal_Previews/APTB/Asia-Pacific-Tax-Bulletin-2018-1.html. Accessed 29 September 2020.

———. 2020. Legislative Over-Activism as Cause of Business Uncertainty. In *International Taxation in the Digital Era*, ed. Parthasarathi Shome, 105–133. Gurugram: OakBridge Publishing Pvt. Ltd.

Government of India. 2012. *A Committee on Taxation of Development Centres and the IT Sector*. New Delhi: Ministry of Finance.

Jaiswal, Anand Kumar. 2019. Base Erosion and Profit Shifting (BEPS). Study of the Impact of BEPS on Income Tax Collections, 29–90. https://shodhganga.inflibnet.ac.in/bitstream/10603/287728/6/10%20chapter-3.pdf. Accessed 30 September 2020.

Mantri, Deepak. 2015. Royalty Payments and Transfer Pricing Issues. TaxGuru. https://taxguru.in/income-tax/royalty-payments-transfer-pricing-issues.html. Accessed 30 September 2020.

Sekar, Kunisi R. 2016. Place of Effective Management (PoEM). In *Insights into Evolving Issues of Taxation: Existing and Continuing Challenges*, ed. Parthasarathi Shome, 296–330. Gurugram: Wolters Kluwer.

Singh, Deepak P. 2020. Calculation of Arm's Length Price-Section 92C of Income Tax Act, 1961. TaxGuru. https://taxguru.in/income-tax/calculation-arms-length-pricesection-92c-income-tax-act-1961.html. Accessed 30 September 2020.

United Nations. 2020. Capital Gains on Offshore Indirect Transfers. Note by the Subcommittee on the UN Model Tax Convention between Developed and Developing Countries. https://www.un.org/development/desa/financing/sites/www.un.org.development.desa.financing/files/2020-10/CRP36%20for%2021st%20session%20-%20Capital%20gains%20on%20OIT%207OCT20.pdf. Accessed 7 October 2020.


[18]See Bhattacharya (2018) for many examples including the Sanofi Aventis case, Genpact–General Electric litigation, Genpact–Bain Capital litigation, and Cairn cases.

# General Anti-avoidance Rules (GAAR) 29

## 29.1 Introduction

Tax avoidance began to be targeted through a widely applicable instrument that came under the rubric, general anti-avoidance rules (GAAR). While each SAAR targets a single tax avoidance behaviour, GAAR is designed to target a broad spectrum of tax avoidance. The popularity of GAAR increased with growing disappointment among policymaking authorities regarding low tax contributions by services sector multinational enterprises (MNEs), particularly in the e-commerce sector, during the global economic crisis of 2008–2009 when revenue needs for public expenditure were at an all-time high. This feeling redoubled as SAARs were considered insufficient to capture tax avoidance comprehensively.

GAAR enables wider scrutiny of intra-group MNE structures that are considered unacceptable. Cross-country GAAR legislation is found in a number of jurisdictions. This chapter reviews examples of GAAR across countries ranging from advanced economies such as Australia, the European Union (EU), the United Kingdom (UK) and the United States (US) to the emerging economies of Brazil, China and South Africa. A case study of India is included, that explores the core tensions—between the justifiable elements and the overzealousness of the tax authorities—in the emergence of the Indian GAAR originally introduced in 2012, then put in abeyance, and finally legislated in 2017, with effect from Assessment Year (AY) 2018–2019.[1]

[1]In India, an assessment year refers to the year after the financial year during which tax assessment is undertaken by the tax administration.



P. Shome, *Taxation History, Theory, Law and Administration*, Springer Texts in Business and Economics, https://doi.org/10.1007/978-3-030-68214-9_29

## 29.2 GAAR Characteristics in Advanced Economies

### 29.2.1 An Early, Broad-Spectrum GAAR

Among the early countries was Australia, which introduced GAAR in 1981. It has 'operated as an effective means to challenge arrangements that are deemed to be entered into with an impermissible Australian motivation'.[2] Subsequently, in 2013, the GAAR corrected 'technical deficiencies' as pointed out in federal court rulings during 2010–2011,[3] to emphasise the 'dominant purpose test' that would be applied to check if a 'scheme achieves a tax benefit in conjunction with a broader economic benefit for the taxpayer involved',[4] and if that was the sole or dominant purpose. If the lesser tax outcome 'would', or 'might reasonably be expected'[5] not to have occurred in the absence of the scheme, then GAAR could take effect.

### 29.2.2 A Late Entry, Narrowly Focused GAAR

As opposed to Australia, the UK,

> for many years . . . has been an outlier in a world of statutory GAARs. Despite having played a role in the enactment of GAAR's in some of its former colonies, it did not legislate GAAR for itself. In addition, for a long time the judicial approach to statutory interpretation in tax cases was a somewhat literal one.[6]

The GAAR that was ultimately introduced in 2013 eschewed the word 'avoidance' and replaced it with 'abuse'. Freedman explains that the word 'avoidance in the extended sense is almost impossible to define so as to give a viable operational rule. The UK GAAR, therefore, covers a defined area of egregious abuse and not everything that might be described as avoidance in recent popular discourse'.[7] This draws attention since the United Kingdom is ostensibly the only country that has defined avoidance narrowly enough to confine itself to abusive, contrived and artificial arrangements, not leaving any room for 'roving enquiries' in a so-called 'broad-spectrum GAAR' that is otherwise explicably popular among several global tax administrations.

The UK approach has also been described by others as well. Thus,

> [t]here may be tax avoidance arrangements that are challenged by HMRC using other parts of the tax code, but if they are not abusive, they are not within the scope of the GAAR . . . . It

[2]See PwC (2016), p. 2.

[3]See PwC, op. cit., p. 2.

[4]See PwC, op. cit., p. 5.

[5]See PwC, op. cit., p. 5.

[6]See Freedman (2016).

[7]See PwC, op. cit., p. 4.

> is narrower in scope than India's, which relates to misuse and abuse. In essence, the outcome of the UK's consultation process has been to opt for a model that will be applied to exceptional cases where there is clear evidence of an extremely aggressive arrangement to escape tax.[8]

It may be concluded that the authorities had in mind the protection of legitimate investors and the economic growth process of the UK economy when they limited the scope of the initial 2013 legislation on GAAR.

Subsequently, however, that scope broadened, perhaps inevitably. In the March 2016 Finance Bill, new measures included GAAR penalties, and the ability of HMRC to take 'provisional counteraction' measures and issue 'binding notices' to taxpayers who enter a tax arrangement equivalent to one against which a counteraction notice exists. The measures also stipulated a penalty at 60% of the counteracted advantage.[9]

### 29.2.3 Absence of Any GAAR

The United States has no GAAR. Rather, common law has given rise to doctrines—primarily economic substance and business purpose—that could lead to denial of tax benefits. The application of the doctrines has intensified somewhat with outcomes supporting the government. Thus, in effect, the GAAR approach exists without its usual procedural safeguards.

Anti-avoidance is, of course, addressed in domestic legislation, mainly on 'thin capitalization (earnings stripping), expatriation tax, transfer pricing, substance over form, step transaction, economic substance, limitation on hybrid entities, anti-conduit regulations, and Foreign Account Tax Compliance Act (FATCA) rules'.[10] Anti-avoidance rules also exist in bilateral treaties comprising 'beneficial ownership, limitation on benefits (LOB), and limitation on residents'.[11] A mainstay of commentaries has been whether, with such comprehensive anti-avoidance characteristics in its tax law, a statutory GAAR is essential or appropriate.

Japan may also be categorised in the group of countries with no statutory GAAR. While the absence of a GAAR has been critiqued among some commentators, others have emphasised that not having a GAAR should not be confused with slowness with actions against attempts by MNEs to erode the tax base and shift profits (BEPS). This group strongly disagrees with the view that 'academic debate on tax avoidance in Japan is "lagging"'.[12] There is, however, general agreement that a GAAR, inasmuch as it would not suffer from a limitation in scope of application, would confirm and clarify case law doctrines and interpretations.

---

[8]See Ved and Kenkre (2018), p. 256.

[9]See PwC, op. cit., p. 17.

[10]See Avi-Yonah and Halibi (2012), p. 3.

[11]See Avi-Yonah and Halibi, op. cit., p.3.

[12]See Nagato (2017), p. 35.

## 29.3 GAARs in Emerging Economies

Since the revival of the Group of 20 (G20) and BRICS, it has been common to group Brazil, China, India and South Africa (excluding Russia) together in academic investigations to compare their experiences and to project their trajectories to economic growth. Interestingly, the microcosm of GAAR is one area where the dissimilarities in country experiences is quite stark, revealing the error of putting them in the same basket for policy purposes even where it is perceived that their interests may lie close to one another.

### 29.3.1 Brazil

Brazil has no statutory GAAR even though, among the four, it is the country with the longest independent experience in taxation.[13] For example, it was the first country to introduce a comprehensive VAT in the mid-1960s. Nevertheless, despite two decades of attempting to legislate a GAAR by the federal tax authorities, Brazil has not been successful since 'there is no unanimous interpretation of the current existing rules'.[14]

Of course, the existing concepts have been applied to some tax planning cases. In identifying artificial transactions and arrangements, tax authorities may file a 'deficiency claim' if there is evidence of 'malice, fraud or...of wholly artificial transactions'.[15] To fortify it, in 2001, the following paragraph was added in Article 116 of the Tax Code:

> The tax authority may disregard transactions or contracts made with the purpose of dissimulating the occurrence of a taxable event or the nature of any element related to such taxable event, according to procedures to be established by the law of the competent federative entity.[16]

While this came closer to a GAAR orientation than before, it nevertheless led to disagreements over whether the paragraph had altered the sense of earlier practice in an effective way, other than to pave the way for the tax authorities to introduce, as and when necessary, 'rules to establish a specific procedure to disregard a wholly artificial arrangement'. Others further argued that, if there were no intentions to move forward decisively towards a GAAR like instrument, the paragraph should not have been added at all.

The embedded 'taxpayer-friendly principle of free enterprise ... has been in conflict with the federal government's design .... This gave rise to a type of GAAR ... to re-characterise for tax purposes a transaction entered into solely for

[13]See Derzi et al. (2017).

[14]See Rubinstein and Vettori (2016).

[15]See Rubinstein and Vettori, op. cit.

[16]See Rubinstein and Vettori, op. cit.

tax purposes'.[17] This allows re-characterisation towards taxation of a transaction entered into solely for tax purposes. Nevertheless, Brazil could be said to have stayed away from a statutory GAAR. Attempts in 2002 by the tax authority to form sharpened rules were thwarted by congress (parliament) reflecting 'the high unpopularity of such rules among taxpayers and scholars alike'.[18] Nevertheless, the actual outcome of such a reticence seems to have been rather the opposite, for '[t]o avoid entering into the GAAR discussion, authorities usually classify the planning structures as wholly artificial arrangements'.[19]

At the same time, Brazil was one of the leaders in the advent of safe harbour rules among emerging economies, having worked on it from the early 1990s to achieve simplification and minimise the likelihood of litigation. It reveals, to no small extent, a continuous attempt not to overlook economic productivity and growth resulting from private sector activity in favour of its revenue potential for government.[20] Those who have pointed towards the so-called lags in sharpening the tax law of Brazil tend to mix this with the incidence of corruption at high levels. Dissecting the matter should reveal that the two should primarily be quite independent matters though one could argue in favour of an extraneous link between the two.

### 29.3.2 China

A GAAR became effective from 1 January 2008, in China, for arrangements without reasonable commercial purpose, and resulting in elimination, reduction or deferral of taxable income. A primary focus has been to raise issue with 'indirect transfer of Chinese companies by non-residents through the disposal of interposed offshore companies (so-called "offshore indirect equity transfers")',[21] a matter of paramount importance in recent Indian taxation history as well.[22] In 2009, a circular specified that GAAR may be invoked to look into intermediate holding companies to re-characterise any gain from the disposal of a Chinese sourced asset, and apply a withholding tax.

China's GAAR does not focus on indirect transfers alone but applies it using rules delineated in December 2014. It is of importance that a tax avoidance scheme is one,

[17]See Derzi et al., op. cit.

[18]See Rubinstein and Vettori, op. cit.

[19]See Rubinstein and Vettori, op. cit.

[20]The marginal productivity of public sector activity is likely to be below that of the private sector, a matter that is often ignored when considering the tax revenue potential from the productive activity of a private enterprise.

[21]See PwC, op. cit., p. 7.

[22]In India, the matter became controversial between the judiciary and the executive branch of government, resulting in a government committee, chaired by Parthasarathi Shome, to be formed in 2012. Its view was that indirect transfers should not be taxed on retrospective basis, as the executive had attempted to do in contraposition to a Supreme Court verdict in a case between the Indian government and Vodafone. See Government of India (2012a).

the sole or main purpose of which is to obtain a tax benefit. Thus, it stands apart from India's first attempt at defining it as 'one of main purposes of which', etc. China also specifies that a tax benefit may be by the tax rules, but economic substance would determine taxability. Both these purpose test and substance test are assessed to determine if a tax avoidance scheme exists. The use and application of GAAR is believed to comprise an instrument of last resort, and taken up only if the application of SAAR cannot eliminate the undue tax benefit.

In February 2015, following the introduction of specified GAAR rules, China widened the scope of offshore indirect equity transfers to include 'transactions involving either the transfer of immovable property in China or the transfer of assets held under (an) establishment and place in China by a foreign company via an offshore transfer of a foreign intermediate holding company'.[23]

The Chinese GAAR has been applied cautiously and, mainly, has been used to examine only cross-border arrangements, in the context of offshore indirect equity transfers. Nevertheless, two issues have emerged that may expand the GAAR's application in the future. First, Chinese local authorities have questioned offshore indirect transfers. Though there is no domestic legal provision for it at the local level, the central authorities may begin to recognise its validity. Second, the advent of BEPS and China's participation in it could make China re-examine its use of GAAR in the backdrop of tightening of rules in the multilateral context.

### 29.3.3 South Africa

Introduced in 2006, the South African GAAR focuses on checking the commercial substance test against the 'sole or main purpose to obtain a tax benefit'.[24] Note that it is not 'main or one of the main purposes'. There are three tainted elements mentioned as 'abnormality, lack of commercial substance, and misuse or abuse of tax provisions of the same Act', leading to 'any avoidance, postponement or reduction of any liability for tax'.[25]

It is interesting that South Africa which should be keen to attract investment has, instead, legislated a relatively harsh, statutory GAAR. Its GAAR specifies that:

- The Commissioner may determine the tax consequences under this Act of any impermissible avoidance arrangement for any party by
- Disregarding, combining or re-characterising any steps or parts of the (arrangement)
- Disregarding any accommodating or tax-indifferent party or treat such parties and any other party as one and the same person

[23]See PwC, op. cit., p. 8.

[24]See Ved and Kenkre, op. cit., p. 267. See also Government of India (2012b) report on GAAR.

[25]See Ved and Kenkre, op. cit., p. 267.

- Deeming persons who are connected persons in relation to each other to be one and the same for the purpose of determining the tax treatment of any amount
- Reallocating any gross income, receipt or accrual of a capital nature, expenditure on rebate amongst the parties
- Re-characterising any gross income, receipt or accrual of a capital nature or expenditure, or
- Treating the impermissible avoidance arrangement as if it had not been entered into or carried out, or in such manner as in the circumstances of the case the commissioner deems appropriate for the prevention or diminution of the relevant tax benefit.[26]

South Africa also applies various SAARs such as a broad definition of connected persons for natural persons, trusts, members of any partnership, companies and closed companies. Connected persons appear to resemble a 'related party', but is more complex, with multiple thresholds for each category of connected persons.[27] Thus, a tour of selected country experiences appears to indicate that there is not much uniformity in the global experience.

## 29.4 Harmonisation

If taxes across international borders were generally 'harmonised', there would be little need for tax treaties. At another level, however, tax competition through market pressure may be desirable because it would exert a downward pressure on taxes and possibly on greater efficiency in the allocation and use of global public resources. But tax competition could also have inter-country spillover effects destabilising the macroeconomy that, in turn, could interfere with the efficient functioning of global trade and capital markets. Thus, tax harmonisation does play a salutary role in supporting locational neutrality and inter-jurisdictional equity.

Some harmonisation has been attempted internationally with respect to GAAR. For example, in July 2016, the EU attempted it through an Anti-Tax Avoidance Directive (ATAD) to reduce tax avoidance in its internal market.[28] ATAD imposed a legally binding obligation on EU member states to incorporate selected recommendations that took the form of BEPS Actions[29] in the areas of controlled foreign company (CFC) rules (see Chap. 30, Sect. 30.2.3), limits on excessive interest deductions, and others.

Scholars believe that this 'has secured a certain uniformity in countries implementing measures across the EU. In addition, ATAD has also set out a GAAR and exit tax provisions, which further strengthen the EU's baseline

[26]South African GAAR, Section 80B. See Ved and Kenkre, op. cit., pp. 267–268.

[27]See Ved and Kenkre, op. cit., p. 268.

[28]See Cédelle (2016).

[29]The topic of tax base erosion and profit shifting (BEPS) comprises Chap. 30.

protection of tax revenues'.[30] It should not be forgotten, however, that the EU is a group of, by and large, homogeneously thinking European economies with a strong executive that plays the role of rule setting, implementation and refereeing among its members. Thus, the EU experience could be considered unique in the larger global context that comprises diverse advanced and emerging economies.

To conclude, what is generally observed is relatively little cohesion in the GAAR laws across countries. Some have opted for statutory GAARs, some of which have sharp aspects to it such as South Africa, unrestricted by concerns of economic growth. Others have introduced a GAAR slowly if not reluctantly while being observant to a GAAR's probable deleterious growth effects, such as China and the United Kingdom. Yet others have eschewed a formal GAAR using SAARs to address tax avoidance, such as Brazil, Japan and the United States. Thus, the cross-country experience with GAAR is veritably diverse and is unlikely to be reined in with much uniformity in the foreseeable future.

## 29.5 Indian GAAR Experience

### 29.5.1 Introduction, Revision and Reintroduction

India spent quite a few years formulating, legislating, re-examining and reintroducing its GAAR. The law was found to be harsh to begin with and, after scrutiny by a government-appointed expert committee, it was toned down, and reintroduced at a later date. Nevertheless, the tax authorities appear to have reattempted to reinstate some of the stringency, the main lesson to learn from which is that tax authorities in general, and in India as well, are not in the habit of a broad perspective of placing taxation in the context of the overall economy or its growth, but primarily, if not exclusively, on the production of tax revenue. This outcome tends to be exacerbated if the structure and administrative rules covering the bureaucracy assign little accountability for actions taken—this of course differs from country to country.

The development of the Indian GAAR can be said to have appeared from 2009 when an initial draft of a comprehensive direct tax code was put up by the government for open consultation. At that early stage, GAAR was proposed to be applied where a taxpayer entered into an arrangement, the 'main purpose' of which was to obtain a tax benefit, and such arrangement:

- Was entered into or carried on in a manner not normally employed for bona-fide business purposes, or
- Was not at arm's length, or
- Abused the provisions of the DTC, or
- Lacked economic substance

[30] See Cedelle, op. cit., p. 1.

Further, on invoking GAAR, an assessing officer (AO) may determine the tax consequences for the taxpayer by disregarding the arrangement.

After consultation within the tax department and with stakeholders, the draft was modified and placed for further consultation in 2010. The GAAR elements went through more stringent modifications and GAAR (though not the entire draft direct tax code) was enacted in 2012, to be applied from 2013. In many ways, this first attempt to introduce GAAR resembled South Africa's stringent version rather closely. But it faced severe opposition from taxpayers emanating from certain changes made in the draft including:

- Replacing 'main purpose' with 'purposes'
- A fear that GAAR would not necessarily be applied uniformly by tax officers
- A belief that there was a lack of awareness among tax officers who had the responsibility to invoke such an advanced tax instrument, and
- Lack of proper sensitisation of both domestic and foreign investors to whom the rules would apply

There were several SAAR elements already in the income tax law and, being specific, provided certainty to taxpayers while GAAR, being general in nature, was prone to be widely interpreted without adequate experience or comprehensive guidance to the implementing officers. Indeed, even transfer pricing clauses (comprising a SAAR as was seen in Chap. 28) were used so frequently that the number of adjustments and associated litigation instances numbered far higher than in any other comparable country.

Since GAAR was generally intended for deterrence of abusive practices of creating corporate structures for the main purpose of avoiding tax, administrators would need to be guided regarding the manner in which it was to be applied for which significant preparation time was needed. Instead, GAAR, in the way it was formulated and introduced as draft law was understandably feared and objected to by the taxpayer.

Those considerations led the Indian Government to set up an independent expert committee in July 2012, with this author as its chairman, to re-examine the proposed GAAR provisions and make appropriate modifications prior to the introduction of GAAR. The formal terms of reference (ToR) were elaborated in great detail by the government in revisiting a complex tax issue with the intention to reconsult and re-examine every element embedded in the matter.

The committee recommended drastic changes in both the approach of GAAR and its application, together with a deferment of implementation to 1 April 2016. Consequently, several modifications to the legislation and accompanying rules were incorporated. In the event, in the central government's 2016–2017 annual budget, the finance minister announced the implementation of GAAR from 1 April 2017.

### 29.5.2 Acceptance of Committee Recommendations

It is of some relevance to recount how the government altered its position in acceptance of the committee's recommendations. Among those accepted were the following:

- GAAR should be applicable only to arrangements that have the main purpose (and not one of the main purposes) of obtaining a tax benefit.
- Factors such as the period for which the arrangement exists; the fact of payment of taxes, directly or indirectly, under the arrangement; and the fact that an exit route (including the transfer of any activity or business or operations) is provided by the arrangement, are relevant but may not be sufficient to prove commercial substance. This condition was important in that they had been specifically denied in the first version.
- A requirement of detailed reasoning by the assessing officer in the show-cause notice to the taxpayer may be prescribed in the rules.
- Time limits for actions by various authorities and statutory forms for making reference by income tax authorities should be prescribed.
- While determining the tax consequences of an impermissible avoidance arrangement, it should be ensured that the same income is not taxed twice in the hands of the same taxpayer in the same year or in different assessment years.
- GAAR should not apply to a foreign institutional investor (FII) that chooses not to take any benefit under a Double Taxation Avoidance Agreement (DTAA) entered into by India and subjects itself to tax in accordance with domestic law provisions.
- A monetary threshold of Indian Rs. 30 million (Rs.100 = UK £1 approximately) for tax benefit to a taxpayer in a year should be provided for the applicability of GAAR provisions.
- The tax audit report may be amended to include reporting of tax avoidance schemes above the threshold of tax benefit of Rs. 30 million.
- Where only a part of the arrangement is impermissible, the tax consequences of an 'impermissible avoidance arrangement' should be limited to that portion of the arrangement (accepted in 2017).

### 29.5.3 Setting Aside Committee Recommendations

Having acceded to several of the committee recommendations as listed above, in 2017, the Central Board of Direct Taxes (CBDT) indicated that, 'GAAR is with respect to an arrangement or part of the arrangement and therefore a limit of Rs. 30 million cannot be read in respect of a single taxpayer only'.[31]

---

[31] CBDT (2017).

Further, some recommendations of the committee were not immediately accepted by the government. These included the following:

- GAAR should be applicable only in cases of abusive, contrived and artificial arrangements.
- Where anti-avoidance rules are provided in a tax treaty in the form of limitation of benefit (as in the Singapore treaty) etc., the GAAR provisions should not apply overriding the treaty.
- GAAR should not be invoked in intra-group transactions that may result in a tax benefit to one person but overall tax revenue is not affected either by actual loss of revenue or deferral of revenue.
- The GAAR provisions should be subject to an overarching principle that tax mitigation should be distinguished from tax avoidance before invoking GAAR.

An illustrative list of tax mitigation, or a negative list for the purposes of invoking GAAR, was provided by the committee but neither recognised by the government nor included in the teaching syllabus of the National Academy of Direct Taxes (NADT).

### 29.5.4 Presumption of Purpose

What is of significance is the nature of thought, if not presumption and, therefore, preoccupation, among some country tax authorities in populating their GAAR structures and rules. This is revealed in the original definition in India of the presumption of purpose that was subsequently set aside as an outcome of the committee's recommendations.

The government's two above-mentioned discussion papers both contained a provision that an arrangement that results in any tax benefit 'shall be presumed' to have been entered into for the main purpose of obtaining the tax benefit, unless the taxpayer proves otherwise. This provision was also introduced in Finance Bill 2012, Section 96(2), but was later dropped and not brought into the Income-tax Act (ITA). It was also removed in the government's further modified discussion paper of 2013, which resulted from the recommendations of the committee.[32]

A press release issued by the government dated 14 January 2013, clarified that GAAR would be applicable even where a part of the arrangement was considered an impermissible avoidance arrangement, but the tax consequence would not apply to the whole arrangement but would be restricted to that part. Further, Finance Act 2013 raised the expectation that the GAAR law would be supplemented by

[32]Though the GAAR elements were taken into account, a draft DTC prepared in 2013, and approved by all line ministries, was never presented to Cabinet. One explanation could be impending parliamentary elections a few months later which could be considered to be not too propitious a time for any government to propose a new tax code.

subordinate legislation or rules, though there was good reason for it to have been incorporated in the principal legislation and thus be subject to legislative scrutiny.[33]

## 29.6 Tax Efficiency, Avoidance and Evasion

There are some important matters of concern pertaining to tax authorities everywhere. There is always a possibility for them to mingle issues relating to tax mitigation—or what is sometimes referred to in the tax profession as tax efficiency—with tax avoidance in the application of GAAR. In so doing, they tend to be oblivious of the important impact that their actions can have on the functioning of the business sector and on its consequences on economic growth. This is a matter that should be raised and discussed rather than remaining untouched due to the power that tax administrations hold as an institution.

The optimal or desired behaviour of a tax administration can be perceived through differentiating among different taxpayer behaviours towards tax compliance. First, tax mitigation results from a taxpayer using a fiscal incentive available to him in the tax legislation by submitting to the conditions and economic consequences that the particular tax legislation entails. An example would be a special economic zone where a taxpayer sets up his establishment, or avails a backward area linked tax incentive, or uses provisions for accelerated depreciation, or one among various alternatives offered under the income tax regime of a particular country. Several emerging economies such as Brazil, India and China offer such incentives. Tax authorities should not spend staff resources on raising issues with such legal provisions offered by the government.

Second, tax avoidance is different from tax mitigation. While both are strictly within the tax law, tax avoidance arises from the application of the law in a manner that goes against the intention of the law. While there is an overall understanding of what it might comprise, different tax authorities explain it differently. Thus, tax avoidance involves the legal exploitation of tax laws to a taxpayer's own advantage. While strictly legal, it takes advantage of selected provisions by identifying alternatives, one of which results in less tax than another though the outcome does not reflect the intention of the tax law. It is designed solely for obtaining a tax advantage without a backdrop of economic content.

The upshot is that, while a taxpayer may consider it his right to arrange as low a tax payment as possible as long as it is strictly legal, tax authorities may consider some strictly legal inter-corporate or intra-corporate business structures to be artificial and unacceptable if they are perceived not to reflect the intention of the law. Instead, they are viewed as eroding the tax base unnaturally and reducing the effective rate of tax.

Third, tax evasion is a behaviour that is unlawful, occurring from illegality, suppression, misrepresentation and fraud. Clearly, it is illegal and impermissible.

[33] Ved and Kenkre, op. cit., p. 408.

When the three behaviours are kept in mind, respective actions to be taken by tax authorities should become clear. First, tax mitigation has to be allowed and should not be confused with tax avoidance. Some tax administrations reveal a tendency to focus unduly on tax mitigation characteristics within tax law, which is easy to identify from tax returns themselves. But this practice should be strictly eschewed and tax officers should be redirected to detect and take counter-measures against tax avoidance instead.

Tax evasion, on the other hand, has to be eradicated. Suspected tax evasion calls for the application of strict tax administration instruments including search and seizure. However, there could be a tendency towards heavy use of these measures on the basis of suspicion rather than proof. Such means should be used cautiously and sparingly. Of course, incarceration is called for in the case of identified tax evaders, as is the likely outcome in most advanced economies. For this to materialise, the justice system should be unbiased and rapid, a feature more often than not absent in emerging economies.

This leaves tax avoidance, which is the most obfuscated and thus difficult for tax authorities to contend with. Professionals—lawyers, accountants, advisers—tend to design tax avoidance structures, calculating tax payments or defending clients when called out by the authorities. This happens only because tax avoidance is not illegal even though the authorities question it, leaving wide room sometimes for argumentation against, or in favour of, the taxpayer. Therefore, tax avoidance tends to lead to a high incidence of litigation, as indeed has happened in some countries such as Brazil and India.

## 29.7 Conclusions

The increasing incidence of legislating GAAR has had the objective of enabling tax authorities to address tax avoidance more aggressively. And, perhaps for the very reason that tax avoidance is difficult to pin down, once it is identified in the assessment of tax authorities, there has been a proclivity to come down heavily on it, in turn, to the detriment of potential investment and growth. Thus, it is important for national policymakers in particular in emerging economies to keep any overenthusiasm of tax administrators in this regard in check.

This chapter found variations in national practices in GAAR legislation and practices. Some have enacted specific laws while others have not, instead taking up tax avoidance on a case-by-case basis. Some use rules cautiously, applying them only in egregious cases of avoidance or abuse, while others have tended to enact laws that are more stringent and are applicable more widely. While citing selected country examples, the chapter used the Indian experience as a case study in the conceptual development and formulation of legislation of GAAR in some detail.

## References


Avi-Yonah, Reuven S., and Oz Halibi. 2012. *US Treaty Anti-Avoidance Rules: An Overview and Assessment*. Law and Economics Working Papers No. 45. https://repository.law.umich.edu/law_econ_current/art45/.

Cédelle, Anzhela. 2016. The EU Anti-Tax Avoidance Directive: A UK Perspective. *The British Tax Review*: 490–507.

Central Board of Direct Taxes (CBDT). 2017. *Clarifications on Implementation of GAAR Provisions Under the Income Tax Act, 1961*. Circular No. 7. https://www.incometaxindia.gov.in/communications/circular/circular7_2017.pdf. Accessed 30 Oct 2020.

Derzi, Misabel Abreu Machado, André Mendes Moreira, and Fernando Daniel de Moura Fonseca. 2017. Income Taxation in Brazil: A Comparative Law Approach. In *Taxation and Development—A Comparative Study*, ed. Karen B. Brown, 77–93. Washington, DC: Springer.

Freedman, Judith. 2016. *General Anti-Avoidance Rules (GAARs)—A Key Element of Tax Systems in the Post-BEPS Tax World?* Legal Research Paper Series, University of Oxford. https://ssrn.com/abstract=2769554 or https://doi.org/10.2139/ssrn.2769554.

Government of India. 2012a. *Expert Committee Report on Retrospective Amendments Relating to Indirect Transfers*. New Delhi: Ministry of Finance.

———. 2012b. *Expert Committee on General Anti-Avoidance Rules (GAAR)*. New Delhi: Ministry of Finance.

Nagato, Takayuki. 2017. GAAR and the Rule of Law in Japan. *Public Policy Review* 13(1): 35–70. https://ssrn.com/abstract=3393022.

PwC. 2016. *Recent Global Developments in General Anti-Avoidance Rules*. https://www.pwc.com/gx/en/tax/newsletters/tax-controversy-dispute-resolution/assets/pwc-TCDR%20Insights-GAAR-recent-developments.pdf. Accessed 30 Oct 2020.

Rubinstein, Flavio, and Gustave G. Vettori. 2016. Closing the Brazilian Tax Gap: Public Shaming, Transparency and Mandatory Disclosure as Means of Dealing with Tax Delinquencies, Tax Evasion and Tax Planning. *Finance and Capital Markets* (formerly *Derivatives & Financial Instruments*) 18 (1). https://www.ibfd.org/IBFD-Products/Journal-Articles/Derivatives-and-Financial-Instruments/collections/dfi/html/dfi_2016_01_br_1.html.

Ved, Uday, and Akshay Kenkre. 2018. *General Anti-Avoidance Rules (GAAR)—Establishing Substance over Form*. New Delhi: Bloomsbury.

# Tax Base Erosion and Profit Shifting (BEPS) 30

## 30.1 Introduction

In the wake of the 2008–2009 global financial and economic crisis, the Group of 20 (G20) nations became concerned about very low tax payments globally by select multinational enterprises (MNEs). It came to be widely accepted that, using a process of eroding the tax base by shifting profits (BEPS) among parent companies, branches and subsidiaries across national boundaries, they were able to slash their global tax contribution as a proportion of their global pre-tax profits by locating profits in low tax jurisdictions.

Such tax avoidance was found especially in the newly emerging service sector in particular in e-commerce that had not yet come under the adequate scrutiny of domestic tax administrations. That would have required well-advanced administrative acumen to comprehend and track the way MNEs structure their business models for which meaningful international co-operation on the exchange of information would also be essential. These did not exist in a significant way. Accordingly, the Organisation of Economic Cooperation and Development (OECD) seized the moment of international concern over tax avoidance and obtained the endorsement of the G20 to undertake appropriate studies and suggest comprehensive measures to address the perceived egregious tax avoidance practised by MNEs.[1]

Though such MNE structures were legal in terms of the strict letter of the law, tax administrations increasingly viewed such practices as unreflective of the intention of the law. In the rush for corrective measures, however, governments were quick to conclude that inappropriate tax behaviour of MNEs was endemic. Tax avoidance was not viewed as a phenomenon pertaining to selected sectors or individual enterprises but, rather, perceived to be a phenomenon afflicting the global MNE sector as a whole.

[1]See Baker (2016), Chap. 3.



P. Shome, *Taxation History, Theory, Law and Administration*, Springer Texts in Business and Economics, https://doi.org/10.1007/978-3-030-68214-9_30

The G20 included the BEPS objective in its February 2013 communique in Mexico. This was followed by the G20 and OECD adopting, in September 2013, 15 Action Plans to address the BEPS challenge. Subsequently, 15 Actions in 13 final reports were released by the OECD at a G20 meeting in Lima, Peru, in October 2015. The report on Action 1 on digital economy taxation called for further work, with a report to be delivered by 2020. Reflecting the sector's recent emergence and expansion, and the controversies involved, developments in the taxation of the digital economy are covered separately in Chap. 31.

In July 2020, the OECD released its first stocktaking exercise of whether signatory countries were meeting the minimum standards that they had signed on to for being a part of the BEPS process.[2] In particular, data on over 1100 measures taken by more than 110 jurisdictions were shared publicly by the OECD. It found that countries were collaborating and sharing best practices regarding fiscal policy and tax administration. Reflecting on the information collected, the report assessed how the standards could be improved for countering BEPS practices.

Thus, the G20 moved on from its early macroeconomic agenda initiated at the appearance of the 2008–2009 global crisis, through a global development agenda as the global financial crisis came to be controlled, and took up a new agenda to address international tax avoidance.[3] To mitigate concerns of emerging economies that the OECD analysis would be relevant exclusively for advanced economies, Brazil and India were included by the OECD as members of a steering committee for BEPS.[4]

This chapter takes up the 15 Actions recommended in the 2015 reports on BEPS. It examines how they have addressed the international tax avoidance problem, whether they have been successful and what the overall reactions of countries participating in the BEPS process have been.

## 30.2 The BEPS Actions

Even prior to the BEPS project, there were allocation norms for how tax revenue collected from enterprises associated with MNEs was to be distributed among different jurisdictions. Indeed, the allocation issue went through different discussions and resultant norms over the last century. They comprised the subject

[2]See OECD (2020).

[3]See Shome (2014, 2015, and 2016) for a comprehensive review of each of these aspects carried out by a group of researchers.

[4]See Baistrocchi (2021). He argues that the global economy's centre of gravity and, accordingly, of international taxation, are shifting. A global economic power shift from the West to the East is manifest with 50% of global GDP coming from emerging global economies. Commensurately, since the emergence of the international tax regime (ITR) in the early twentieth century, its evolution has been associated with two global power shifts in the ITR: first, a power shift from the United Kingdom to the United States in the 1930s and then, an emerging power shift from the United States to China beginning in the early twenty-first century. It may be added that Brazil and India are playing an increasing role in this shift.

matter of Article 9 of the OECD Model and Article 9 of the UN Model, usually termed the Model Tax Convention.[5] The OECD Model was a guidance for countries to conclude bilateral tax treaties and assisted in limiting tax-related barriers to international trade and investment. It also buttressed business activity by promoting transparency while helping to minimise tax evasion and avoidance.[6]

The OECD BEPS Action Plan of July 2013 revived the matter in a visible manner as the G20 provided support for the modernisation of those norms. The BEPS Action Plan got converted, in its October 2015 report, to 15 Actions in the form of concrete steps to tackle the problem of BEPS. Actions 8, 9 and 10 continued existing work on substantive transfer pricing (TP) rules and Action 13 focused on TP documentation. Action 1 was to address challenges with the taxation of the digital economy. Actions 2, 3, 4, 5, 6 and 7 targeted non-TP aspects of BEPS. Other Actions dealt with additional aspects. Action 11 concerned the collection of data to provide evidence of the impact of BEPS. Action 12 proposed the introduction of systems of disclosure of tax avoidance schemes and was based upon the implementation of such arrangements in a number of OECD countries, particularly the United Kingdom. It was not specifically targeted at BEPS.[7]

Action 14 was concerned with tackling long-running problems with dispute resolution under tax treaties and was a recognition of the probable increase in the number of cross-border disputes resulting from the BEPS changes. Action 15 was concerned with the ultimate implementation of some of the BEPS Actions as a consolidated multilateral instrument (MLI).[8]

The 2017 edition of the OECD Model consolidated the treaty-related measures under BEPS Action 2 to neutralise the effects of hybrid mismatch arrangements, Action 6 to prevent the granting of treaty benefits in inappropriate circumstances, Action 7 to prevent the artificial avoidance of permanent establishment (PE) status and Action 14 to make dispute resolution more effective.

Below we will familiarise ourselves with the various BEPS Actions. Further, since several Actions are subsumed into the MLI Action 15, when we discuss each Action, we shall also refer to the MLI's coverage of, and reference to, that Action.

---

[5]See Baistrocchi (2020), 'The allocation norm regarding the profits of associated enterprises, now encapsulated in Article 9, of the OECD Model and the UN Model, has found itself in the midst of a creeping, spiral evolution since the beginning of the twentieth century: from standards to rules, and then back to standards. The spiral trajectory of the allocation norm can be divided into 60 core stages representing, in turn, the rise, decline and fall of each of its three sequential eras (standards–rules–standards) over a period of 109 years running from 1908 to 2017'. (p. 1) By 'spiral', the author implies the direction of the trajectory that may be gleaned.

[6]Since its publication in 1977, updates were released in 1992, 1994, 1995, 1997, 1998, 2000, 2003, 2005, 2008, 2010, 2014 and 2017.

[7]The Actions could also be viewed from other perspectives. For example, Actions 4, 7, 8, 9 and 10 were aimed at protecting the tax base associated with how value created by MNEs could be taxed without letting them erode that tax base.

[8]Many authors have examined them. See, in particular, Baker (2016).

This way, the student should find a one-to-one correspondence between an Action and its coverage, if any, in the MLI.

### 30.2.1 Action 1: Addressing Tax Challenges of the Digital Economy

Many MNEs that drew the attention of policymakers for paying very low tax on their overseas income were involved with the digital economy. Being a new means of conducting global business that did not exist even 50 years back, its rapidly expanding operations took authorities the world over by surprise while their potential tax base continued to erode for decades.

Following this cue, Action 1 dealt with the tax challenges of the digital economy. It perceived that the tax base should be shifted from where its value is created to where its value is consumed. Thus, it would evolve a scheme of taxation based on the digital footprint in the state where the consumption of products and services occurs.

However, the OECD's recommendations in the Action 1 report turned out to be weak, reflecting issues raised by the United States, thus pushing analysis and final recommendations to a future date. Recently, countries such as France, India and the United Kingdom have begun to tax the digital economy unilaterally for fear of continued base erosion of a potential tax base. However, since then, the United States began to contest such decisions, in particular, that of France. As indicated above, Chap. 31 is dedicated to digital economy taxation where we shall take up a panoply of issues that have emerged up to the current point in time.

### 30.2.2 Action 2: Addressing 'Hybrid Mismatch Arrangements'

Two or more jurisdictions may examine a tax matter and conclude differently for tax purposes and, therefore, tax the same base in different ways. This is known as a hybrid mismatch and may result in double non-taxation, that is, no taxation of the taxable base in any jurisdiction.

Many examples exist. One comprises debt instruments convertible into shares. These may be viewed by one jurisdiction as debt (on which interest is payable) and by another jurisdiction as equity (on which the return is in the form of dividends). If it is interest, the quantum of interest would be tax-deductible thus reducing the tax base. If it is equity, then the returns would be taxed as income. Another example is stock lending. This may be viewed either as a disposal, or not as a disposal, of the underlying asset. If not considered as a disposal, there would be no capital gains tax on it. If it is considered to be a disposal, tax would be imposed.

MNEs can pick and choose among the legal options available in competing jurisdictions to minimise tax contribution. Such hybrid arrangements that have been present in prevailing MNE structures have resulted in low effective tax rates. While MNEs may view it as 'tax efficiency', tax authorities may view it as egregious tax avoidance not intended in the law, and thus confront it through legislation or rules.

Though countries could pass domestic law to oblige MNEs to elect beforehand how they preferred an entity to be taxed—known as 'check-the-box' legislation in the United States—most countries have not taken such a route. Action 2 proposed methods to address hybrid mismatch arrangements by domestic law changes as well as by changing provisions in tax treaties. That would enable jurisdictions to agree beforehand on the tax treatment of MNE business structures.

Thus, Action 2 called for the development of 'model treaty provisions and recommendations regarding the design of domestic rules to neutralise the effects of hybrid instruments and entities'. Drawing the attention of domestic rules to model treaty provisions would consolidate efforts to achieve positive outcomes for containing tax base erosion.

#### 30.2.2.1 Do Hybrid Mismatch Arrangements Protect Taxpayers?

The recommendations from Action 2 appear in the MLI in the form of several Articles.

**MLI Part II Article 3: Transparent Entities**

- Income derived from an MNE business structure operating in two jurisdictions that is considered to be fiscally transparent by both tax authorities who are party to a Covered Tax Agreement (CTA),[9] shall be considered income only in the residence jurisdiction of the MNE.
- This would eliminate double taxation, hence accommodate the interests of the taxpayer MNE.[10]
- However, the protection is not guaranteed. For example, several countries including India have 'reserved the rights', that is, refrained from agreement to Article 3 in its entirety.

**MLI Part II Article 4: Dual Resident Entities**

- It could so happen that an MNE is deemed to be a resident of more than one jurisdiction. Then the parties to the CTA must determine by mutual agreement which jurisdiction the person is a resident of for the purposes of the CTA. The decision must be made giving regard to the person's place of effective management (POEM), the place where the entity is incorporated, or otherwise constituted, and any other relevant factors. The POEM aspect was covered in Chap. 28, Sect. 28.3.3.
- If no agreement exists between the CTA jurisdictions, then the MNE is not entitled to any relief or exemption from payment of tax. Therefore, the MNE is not protected unless a mutual agreement procedure (MAP) has been agreed upon on the matter. The MAP aspect is covered below in Sect. 30.2.14.1.

[9]The OECD uses this term for what is commonly known as double taxation avoidance agreements (DTAA). See Chap. 27.

[10]However, this protection does not necessarily extend to a tax exemption or deduction provision, thus limiting how much advantage an MNE can derive from the protection.

Each country, say A, can make an entry on its position. A lists those of its CTAs that contain provisions not subject to reservations under Article 4. If all jurisdictions to a particular CTA also list the same provision, then A's CTA provision is to be replaced by the provision of MLI Article 4(1). All countries of course follow the same approach.

#### MLI Part II Article 5: Other Methods for Elimination of Double Taxation

Different methods are to be employed to ensure the elimination of double non-taxation and double taxation:

- A provision in a CTA exempting tax on an income of a resident in a jurisdiction A to eliminate double taxation shall not apply if the jurisdiction B has also applied the same exemption provision on the same income.
- A provision in a CTA exempting tax on an income of a resident in a jurisdiction A to eliminate double taxation because the income is treated as a dividend in A shall not apply if that same income gives rise to a deduction in the income of a resident of the other jurisdiction B.
- When a resident of one jurisdiction A derives income or owns capital which may be taxed in jurisdiction B, then A will allow a tax deduction on the income equal to the income tax paid by the resident, or allow a tax deduction on the capital equal to the capital gains tax paid by the resident, in jurisdiction B.

Some countries including India have reserved the rights to Article 5 in its entirety. Thus, countries have expressed their individual preferences and have preserved their final say on many matters. This variation is somewhat of a challenge to the MLI. However, it is important to keep in mind that the entire list of BEPS recommendations is voluntary. Nevertheless, over time, considerable pressure has grown for countries to fall in line, of course keeping in mind domestic policy realities.

### 30.2.2.2 July 2020 OECD Report

Since the release of the Action 2 recommendations, a number of countries adopted rules to address hybrid and branch mismatches such as Australia, Costa Rica and New Zealand or made changes to their existing hybrid regimes, such as Mexico and the United Kingdom. Hybrid rules were introduced as part of the 2017 U.S. Tax Cuts and Jobs Act and through the Anti-Tax Avoidance Directive II (ATAD) adopted by the EU to implement anti-hybrid rules consistent with Action 2 by 2020. As part of the common approach to addressing hybrid mismatches, work continues among members to share practical examples of these structures, to enable them to confront such structures through consistent, comprehensive and coherent outcomes from the application of the new rules.

### 30.2.3 Action 3: Controlled Foreign Company (CFC) Rules[11]

A CFC is defined as a foreign company that is either directly or indirectly controlled by a resident taxpayer. It is now recognised that CFC rules improve the taxation of certain categories of MNE income in the jurisdiction of the parent company by countering such offshore structures that result in no or indefinite deferral of taxation. In such instances, effective CFC rules can reduce the incentive to shift profits from the parent jurisdiction into a low-tax jurisdiction. In July 2020, the OECD recommended best practices in the design of CFC rules for countries to get back such lost tax base.[12]

Jurisdictions apply a variety of criteria to extend the taxability of CFCs in the domestic jurisdiction. These include the extent of voting rights held by resident taxpayers or shareholder value held by resident taxpayers. Some jurisdictions use tests on the basis of how much activity it carries out in the foreign jurisdiction. Of the 49 jurisdictions that had CFC rules in 2019, 11 had no substantial activity tests in place. Or CFC designation may be determined by a taxation test, that is, if the foreign company does not pay tax in its jurisdiction of residence. Such criteria determine if a foreign company is to be considered a CFC that is to be taxed by the domestic jurisdiction.

The next question is what incomes of a CFC are to be taxed. Jurisdictions vary in the taxability of CFC income. Some apply CFC rules to any type of income, while others apply them to only passive income (income from interest, rental property, dividends, royalties or capital gains).

CFC rules are now in place in all EU countries by virtue of its ATAD I Directive. Furthermore, consistent with the recommendations set out in the BEPS Action 3 report, the United States enacted, as part of its 2017 U.S. Tax Cuts and Jobs Act, a minimum tax on the foreign income of CFCs. It provides a useful example of a minimum tax envisaged in Pillar 2.

### 30.2.4 Action 4: Limitation on Interest Deductions

Intra-group financial payments are often used by MNEs to reduce their tax burden. Entities in low tax jurisdictions are over-capitalised while thin capitalisation is employed in entities in high tax jurisdictions. Intra-group financial payments such as interest expenses, financial and performance guarantees, derivatives and captive insurance arrangements have lowered the tax base in countries where economic activities are actually carried out.

[11]See Chap. 28, Sect. 28.2.11, for the concept and operations of CFCs.

[12]The BEPS project calls for the development of a co-ordinated set of rules to address ongoing risks from structures that allow MNEs to shift profit to jurisdictions where they are subject to no or very low taxation. This objective has particular relevance for CFCs.

There is growing recognition, therefore, that tax planning leads to structures that build in loans internally within a group that leads to significant base erosion. To counter it, the tax base on account of value created through economic activity carried on in a state was recommended to be protected against base erosion through Action 4.

The report on Action 4 recommended limiting the deductibility of interest to protect the tax base, in line with legislation already applied in some countries. It limits the deductibility of interest expense and other financial payments, establishing rules that link an entity's net interest deductions to its level of economic activity within the jurisdiction, using taxable earnings before interest, taxes, depreciation and amortisation (termed EBITDA).

Action 4 established three main elements:

- A fixed ratio rule based on a benchmark net interest/EBITDA ratio
- A group ratio rule allowing an entity to deduct more interest expense based on the position of its worldwide group
- Targeted rules to address specific risks not addressed by the general rule

OECD's July 2020 report elaborated that:

> By 2019, 90 OECD/G20 Inclusive Framework[13] members had indicated that interest limitation rules were in place, and in a variety of forms. The most common type was thin cap rules (43 jurisdictions),[14] followed by earnings stripping rules (33), rules of a general nature or not specified (9), rules of another type (4) and, finally, safe harbour rules (1).
>
> Thin cap rules disallow tax deductibility of internal interest payments if the amount of debt passes a permissible threshold, where the threshold is based on debt-to-equity or debt-to-assets ratios, though the former criterion is more commonly used by jurisdictions. The ratio values range from 0.3:1 in Brazil (that is, interest payments are fully deductible only if the indebtedness of the Brazilian borrowing does not exceed 30% of the borrower's net equity) to 6:1 in Switzerland (for finance companies). Ratios of 2:1, 3:1 and 4:1 are also found.
>
> Earnings stripping rules restrict tax deductibility of interest if the ratio of interest to earnings exceeds a certain threshold. While Action 4 recommended the use of EBITDA as the measure of earnings in the denominator, it also allowed for the flexibility to introduce rules based on earnings before interest and taxes (EBIT). There are other interest limitation rules, such as interest caps that do not depend on a ratio or make reference to other ratios, such as the rule in Denmark that applies the ratio of interest to tax value of total assets.

---

[13]Following the delivery of the 2015 BEPS package, the G20 asked that a broader range of countries be engaged in the implementation of the measures. Accordingly, the OECD/G20 Inclusive Framework (IF) on BEPS was established in June 2016. It brought all interested and committed countries and jurisdictions together in the OECD's Committee on Fiscal Affairs and its subsidiary bodies. The IF undertakes peer reviews of implementation of the BEPS minimum standards and works to complete standard setting to address BEPS issues. Other international organisations and regional tax bodies are also involved in IF's work. It also consults business and civil society on its various work streams. More than 135 members work on an equal footing to adapt international tax rules for the present era. See OECD (2018).

[14]See Chap. 28, Sect. 28.2.12, for definitions.

Among the 33 jurisdictions with earnings stripping rules, the most commonly referenced ratio was interest-to-EBITDA (30 jurisdictions), with ratio values ranging from 10% in Romania to 30% which was, the most common ratio (24 jurisdictions).[15]

### 30.2.5 Action 5: Harmful Tax Practices

Action 5 targets special tax regimes offered by particular countries or 'tax havens' that may be identified as harmful tax practices. It comprises a continuation of earlier work of the OECD that underlined the need to identify the existence of substance as a way of identifying whether tax practices were harmful or not. The Action 5 report focuses on patent box regimes (regimes that impose a lower tax rate than the general rate on income from intellectual property).

Action 5 highlights the so-called 'substance test', linking the accrual of intellectual property (IP) rights and associated income, and the right of taxation thereof, to where research and development (R&D) take place, making jurisdictional taxability a more transparent phenomenon than before. This supports the emerging economy viewpoint to the extent that they host R&D of MNEs.

In its July 2020 report, the OECD indicated that, since 2016, over 285 regimes were reviewed to ensure that there was substance associated with the activities they were intended to attract, and virtually all harmful preferential regimes had been amended or abolished. Further, over 30,000 exchanges of information on rulings, covering over 18,000 rulings, took place, thereby ensuring greater transparency of the arrangements between tax administrations and taxpayers. Post 2020, Action 5 country positions could be subjected to a peer review process.

#### 30.2.5.1 Preferential Tax Regimes

The Forum on Harmful Tax Practices (FHTP) initiated a review of preferential tax regimes as far back as 1998. Presently, some 300 regimes have been reviewed over 70 jurisdictions, including both IP and non-IP regimes. The Action 5 minimum standard requires that there be substantial business activities in the jurisdiction offering preferential tax regimes. For this to be achieved, a 'nexus' criterion is utilised[16] for IP regimes, and a 'substantial activities' requirement is applicable to non-IP regimes. Using these criteria, tax benefits are granted where the core activities behind the income earned are undertaken.[17] Furthermore, such preferential regimes cannot have harmful features that are lacking in transparency, could unfairly

---

[15]See OECD (2020), op. cit., pp. 12–13.

[16]The 'nexus approach' was developed in the context of IP regimes. It allows a taxpayer to benefit from an IP regime only to the extent that a taxpayer incurred qualifying R&D expenditures that resulted in IP income.

[17]Core income-generating activities must be conducted with a specified minimum number of full-time qualified employees. In addition, there must be a minimum amount of operating expenditure associated with such activities.

impact the tax base of other jurisdictions, or do not possess the ability to be subject to the exchange of information with other jurisdictions.

#### 30.2.5.2 Exchange of Information on Tax Rulings

The spontaneous exchange of information on tax rulings has been an important element of Action 5. As of date, 30,000 exchanges have occurred connected to 18,000 rulings. The exchanges have provided information to tax administrations to be used in conducting risk assessments against BEPS, and enhanced transparency in the tax rulings practices of over 100 countries. Also, as MNEs become more aware of the transparency that the exchange of information generates, there is some anticipation that they will step back from tax base depletion through BEPS practices.

Taking up the case of India, for decades, it has had to battle the menace of black money and unaccounted assets hidden in overseas jurisdictions. A substantial amount of information is now being received automatically from foreign authorities under the exchange of information provisions of India's tax treaties. It is India's sovereign obligation to ensure that the financial account information received under the tax treaties and agreements is kept confidential and used only in accordance with the terms of the treaties and agreements including the Foreign Account Tax Compliance Act (FATCA)[18] and the reporting system designed under the BEPS project's[19] Common Reporting Standards (CRS).[20]

India also looks at the Information Security Framework in place in the Income Tax Department for safeguarding and safekeeping of the data. Confidentiality assessments are to be carried out in the future by the Global Forum on Transparency and Exchange of Information of Tax Purposes (Global Forum) including the outcomes thereof.

There is a clear need for appropriate mechanisms for the use of the exchanged data to guard against any disclosure not permitted under the provisions of the treaties and agreements intentionally or by accident or negligence. Otherwise, it is recognised that it will adversely affect a country's ability to receive information in the future and jeopardise its government's resolve to fight the menace of tax evasion through offshore channels.

### 30.2.6 Action 6: Prevention of Tax Treaty Abuse

Tax treaty abuse by a taxable entity can occur in two ways:

---

[18]FATCA was passed by the United States in 2010 as part of the Hiring Incentives to Restore Employment (HIRE) Act. It requires foreign financial Institutions and selected non-financial foreign entities to report on the foreign assets held by their U.S. account holders or be subject to withholding on payments. The HIRE Act also contained legislation requiring U.S. persons to report, depending on the value, their foreign financial accounts and foreign assets. See Chap. 29, Sect. 29.2.3.

[19]Action 12, Mandatory disclosure Rules. See Sect. 30.2.12.

[20]See Manohar (2020).

- When a taxable person tries to circumvent limitations provided by the treaty itself, for example, through treaty shopping
- When a taxable person tries to circumvent the provisions of domestic law by using treaty benefits

Action 6 points to treaty abuse as an important source of BEPS concerns. It has accordingly been designated as a minimum standard among steps to be taken by signatories to BEPS Actions. Thus, it is among the mandatory provisions in MLI Articles 6 and 7.

Action 6 explains that the problem has to be alleviated through a general anti-avoidance rule in treaties and, with that purpose, proposes the Principal Purpose Test (PPT) and Simplified Limitation on Benefit (SLOB) in the MLI.

#### 30.2.6.1 MLI Part III Article 6

Entitled, Purpose of a Covered Tax Agreement (CTA), MLI Article 6(1) asks that the following preambular text be added to a CTA:

> Intending to eliminate double taxation with respect to the taxes covered by this agreement without creating opportunities for non-taxation or reduced taxation through tax evasion or avoidance (including through treaty-shopping arrangements aimed at obtaining reliefs provided in this agreement for the indirect benefit of residents of third jurisdictions).

It is required that this text be included in place of, or in the absence of, any preambular language in a CTA referring to an intent to eliminate double taxation. As it is a minimum standard, the only reservation allowed is if there already exists preambular language describing the intent to eliminate double taxation without creating an opportunity for tax evasion or avoidance. MLI Article 6(3) provides the option of an addition to the preambular text:

> Desiring to further develop their economic relationship and to enhance their co-operation in tax matters.

Being optional, it is applicable only if all parties to a CTA choose to apply it.

The Indian position document is silent on Article 6. As a minimum standard the provision in Article 6(1)—mandatory inclusion of preambular text—can therefore be taken as automatically applicable.

#### 30.2.6.2 MLI Part III Article 7

Referring to a minimum standard for the prevention of treaty abuse, it offers three options to fulfil the mandatory obligation of Action 6.

**Option 1. Principal Purpose Test (PPT)**

- A benefit under the CTA will not be granted if it is reasonable to conclude that obtaining that benefit was one of the principal purposes of any arrangement or transaction that resulted directly or indirectly in that benefit.[21]
- The benefit may yet be granted if, on the request of the person and, after relevant facts and circumstances are taken into consideration, it is determined that the benefit would have been granted in the absence of the transaction under scrutiny.

**Option 2. Simplified Limitation on Benefit Clause (SLOB) Supplemented by the PPT**

- CTA benefits will be limited to only CTA provisions that provide the following:
  - If a person is the resident of more than one party to a CTA, then the provision determines which party the person will be considered a resident of, for the purposes of the provision.
  - If initial adjustments are made by other parties to an enterprise of one party, to the tax amount on associated enterprises, and the CTA provides for corresponding adjustments.
  - Residents are allowed to request tax authorities of a party to a CTA to consider tax cases not in accordance with the CTA.
  - Unless the resident is designated to be a qualified person as determined by Article 7(9).
  - Benefits will also be entitled:

    When a resident with an 'active conduct of business' in one jurisdiction to a CTA, derives an income in the other jurisdiction which is incidental to that business (regardless of whether the resident is a qualified person) (Article 7(10)).

    When an unqualified resident owns at least 75% of the beneficial interests of the resident, on at least half of the days of any 12-month period (including the time when the benefit would otherwise be accorded) (Article 11).

    At the discretion of a tax authority, for a resident not entitled to the above benefits, if such resident can demonstrate that its principal purpose was not to attain such benefit from the CTA.[22]

[21] As was pointed out in Chap. 29, Sect. 29.5.1, the Indian GAAR restricts the condition to 'the principal purpose' rather than to 'one of the principal purposes'. Thus, the Indian GAAR is more beneficial on this point to the taxpayer than is the OECD's PPT.

[22] While the PPT is automatically applicable as a minimum standard, the SLOB is only applicable if all parties to a CTA opt for the same.

**Option 3. Detailed LOB Clause**

- The MLI does not include a detailed LOB provision. This is because a detailed LOB requires substantial bilateral customisation, which would be challenging in the context of a multilateral instrument.[23]
- Only parties wishing to adopt a detailed LOB provision are permitted to reserve Article 7 in its entirety. A detailed LOB must be combined with either rules to address conduit financing structures or a PPT (Article 7(15) (a)).

India has opted for the PPT provision for nearly 40 CTAs and the SLOB provision for about 10 CTAs. India has also introduced a GAAR in its domestic law, as have several other countries. What then is the role of BEPS Action 6 on treaty abuse? The answer is that, at a minimum, BEPS Action 6 provides a sounding board against domestic GAAR provisions.

#### 30.2.6.3 July 2020 OECD Report

According to the report, a 2019 peer review indicated that, by 30 June 2020, 94 countries had begun to update their bilateral treaty network and were implementing the Action 6 minimum standard, using the MLI as the instrument for it. However, this was limited by the fact that a large number of jurisdictions had not ratified the MLI at that point. Many such jurisdictions had expressed interest in signing the MLI and, if all waiting agreements[24] became CTAs, the figure could rise dramatically.

Another point to bear in mind is that the peer review process does not measure whether the implementation of the minimum standard has actually reduced treaty shopping in practice since BEPS implementation began. A review of Action 6 will be carried out in the forthcoming biennium.

### 30.2.7 Action 7: Preventing the Artificial Avoidance of Permanent Establishment (PE) Status

There is widespread recognition that particular aspects of the definition of PE were out of date and had become subject of manipulation by MNEs to reduce their tax contribution in treaty countries. Action 7 proposes amending the definition of PE in tax treaties (that could be extended to domestic law).

The usual definition of a PE, through exclusion, allows an entity resident in a jurisdiction A to carry out substantial economic activity in another state B without being legally required to pay any tax in the latter state B.

The amended definition would align the taxation to value creation to economic activities being carried on in the state of economic activity to capture a wider tax

[23] An elaboration is given in the Explanatory Statement to the MLI.

[24] A 'waiting agreement' is an agreement that has been listed under the MLI by only one of the treaty partners and is therefore waiting for the other partner to sign the MLI to create a match.

base internationally. In the above example, the entity would possibly be required to pay tax in B. This aspect, therefore, also enhances confidence in the MLI in moving towards source-based taxation.

#### 30.2.7.1 MLI Part IV Article 12 Artificial Avoidance of PE Status Through Commissionnaire Arrangements and Similar Strategies

Action 7 looks to address the artificial avoidance of PE status through commissionnaire arrangements.

A commissionnaire arrangement is defined as 'an arrangement through which a (taxable) person sells products in a given state (jurisdiction) in its own name but on behalf of a foreign enterprise that is the owner of these products. Through such an arrangement, a foreign enterprise is able to sell its products in a state without having a PE to which such sales may be attributed for tax purposes'.

If allowed to operate within such an arrangement, the taxable person concluding the sale does not get taxed on the profits as it does not own the products, but only on the remuneration that it receives for its services, usually in the form of a commission.

Therefore, Article 12 provides that an MNE will be deemed to have a PE in a jurisdiction of a CTA if any taxable entity on behalf of the MNE habitually concludes contracts:

- In the name of the MNE; or
- For the transfer of ownership, or the right to use property owned, by the MNE; or
- For the provision of services by that MNE

unless these activities are deemed not to constitute a PE by the CTA concerned. However, an exclusion applies in that the conditions of establishing a PE discussed above shall not apply if the taxable entity acting on behalf of the MNE does so as an independent agent and in the ordinary course of that business. Nonetheless, that exclusion does not apply if such an entity acts exclusively or almost exclusively on behalf of one or more MNEs to which it is closely related.

India has provided a list of provisions contained in its CTAs describing the condition for establishing a PE. Article 12 provisions will apply in place of those listed provisions.

#### 30.2.7.2 MLI Part IV Article 13 Artificial Avoidance of PE Status Through the Specific Activity Exemptions

Article 13 provides two options or the option not to choose either.

**Option 1**

- Notwithstanding CTA provisions defining a PE under the MLI, the term PE shall not include:
  - The activities deemed not to constitute a PE under the CTA
    Whether or not, under the CTA, that exception from PE status is contingent on the activity being of a preparatory or auxiliary character
    If such activity is indeed of a preparatory or auxiliary character

- The maintenance of a fixed place of business solely for the purpose of carrying on, for the MNE, any activity not described in (a)
  - If such activity is of a preparatory or auxiliary character
- The maintenance of a fixed place of business solely for any combination of activities mentioned in (a) and (b)
  - If the overall activity of the fixed place of business is of a preparatory or auxiliary character

**Option 2**

- Notwithstanding CTA provisions defining PE under the MLI, the term PE shall not include:
  - The activities deemed not to constitute a PE under the CTA
    - Whether or not, under the CTA, that exception from PE status is contingent on the activity being of a preparatory or auxiliary character
    - Except to the extent that the relevant provision of the CTA provides explicitly that a specific activity shall be deemed not to constitute a PE provided that the activity is of a preparatory or auxiliary character
  - The maintenance of a fixed place of business solely for the purpose of carrying on, for the enterprise, any activity not described in (a), provided that this activity is of a preparatory or auxiliary character
  - The maintenance of a fixed place of business solely for any combination of activities mentioned in (a) and (b), provided that the overall activity of the fixed place of business resulting from this combination is of a preparatory or auxiliary characterIndia has selected Option 1 to apply to its CTAs. It has provided a list of CTAs containing similar provisions with the corresponding Article and paragraph number. Option 1 will only apply to CTAs listed by India if the other parties to the CTA also choose the same option.

### 30.2.8 Action 8: Intangibles

Actions 8–10 deal with an essential orientation which is to align taxation to where there is 'value creation'. The focus is on cross-border transactions involving capital, both financial and 'intangibles' such as goodwill or reputation.[25] The idea is to ensure that a legal owner of intangibles will become less relevant while activities performed within the intangibles cycle of development, enhancement, maintenance, protection and exploitation will become more relevant.

The 2015 work on these Actions resulted in expanded guidance in Chap. VI of the OECD's already existing Transfer Pricing Guidelines on an approach for tax

[25]Intangibles are by definition mobile and they are often hard to value. Misallocation of the profits generated by valuable intangibles has contributed to BEPS.

administrations to ensure appropriate pricing of hard-to-value intangibles (HTVI) due to information asymmetry. In 2018, additional guidance was added as an annex to Chap. VI.

In 2019, a process was begun by gathering information from over 30 jurisdictions on their legislation and practices related to the HTVI approach. This reflects the attempts of many countries, including India, to move in this direction. Therefore, the MLI's contribution in this aspect is noteworthy for, until recently, advanced and emerging economies clearly disagreed on this issue for most productive activity.[26]

### 30.2.9 Action 9: Risks and Capital

Action 9 could be said to go deeper into the relationship between risk-taking and intangibles, safeguarding that they are not dissociated from revenue rewards. Reflecting that risk-taking is more often than not attributed to advanced economies, the OECD protects the latter's interest in this matter. This Action also narrows down on how TP principles may be used to achieve the objective of preventing BEPS, for example, using interest deductibility.

### 30.2.10 Action 10: High-Risk Transactions

Action 10 focuses on other high-risk areas, including the scope for addressing profit allocations resulting from transactions that are not commercially rational. TP methods may be used in a way that, in the absence of alignment with value-creation, result in diverting profits from the most economically important activities of an MNE group to various payments among them, such as management fees and head office expenses, that successfully erode the tax base.

### 30.2.11 Action 11: BEPS Data Analysis

The Action 11 report on measuring and monitoring BEPS highlighted the lack of good data on corporate taxation. This limited the measurement of the fiscal and economic effects of tax avoidance or the impact of the implementation of BEPS measures as had been agreed as a part of the BEPS project. Methodologies were accordingly recommended to collect and analyse data to meet those objectives.

On that basis, new and enhanced datasets and analytical tools were being developed to improve the quality and expand the range of information available to analyse BEPS. A corporate tax statistics (CTS) database was launched in January

[26]As we shall see in Chap. 31 on the taxation of the digital economy, that the United States, however, continues to stand apart with its disagreement with taxation rights being confined to jurisdictions with value creation.

2019 which was assembling appropriate data to assist in the analysis of BEPS and for the study of corporate tax policy. The OECD's existing datasets were also being consolidated within CTS. The 2020 edition[27] of the database contains the following data categories:

- Corporate tax revenues
- Statutory corporate income tax (CIT) rates
- Corporate effective tax rates
- Tax incentives related to research and development (R&D)
- Anonymised and aggregated statistics collected through country-by-country (CbC) reports
- Intellectual property regimes
- CFC rules
- Interest limitation rules

Thus, over time, such statistics should provide valuable information on the location of the largest MNEs' taxes, income and business activities.

### 30.2.12 Action 12: Mandatory Disclosure Rules

In the interest of transparency, Action 12 recommended rules to require taxpayers and advisors to disclose aggressive tax planning arrangements. A balance between the early disclosures of aggressive tax planning schemes while avoiding placing an undue compliance burden on taxpayers was the selected approach.

With that in mind, reflecting the Action 12 report, a Model Mandatory Disclosure Rules for Common Reporting Standard—Avoidance Arrangements and Opaque Offshore Structures (i.e. structures where the beneficial owners are disguised) was approved and published by the OECD in early 2018. It is expected that the rules should have a deterrent effect against the design, marketing and use of aggressive tax planning arrangements.

The OECD reported that, since 2018, over 30 jurisdictions had decided to implement mandatory disclosure rules. At the EU level, the model rules were incorporated into its Directive on Administrative Cooperation in Tax Matters and were expected to become effective in the course of 2020.

[27] CTS released on 7 July 2020, provides aggregated information on the global tax and economic activities of nearly 4000 MNE groups headquartered in 26 jurisdictions and operating across more than 100 jurisdictions worldwide.

### 30.2.13 Action 13: Country-by-Country Reporting

One impact of the BEPS project has been that MNEs operating in multiple jurisdictions will have to meet the tax compliance requirements of each of the jurisdictions in which they operate. The annual submittal requirements for a consolidated MNE group with a revenue threshold of EUR 750 million, are:

- A 'master file' containing information relevant for all MNE group members, providing a high-level overview of their global business operations, transfer pricing policies and global allocation of income and economic activity. The master file is to be made available to all relevant country tax administrations
- A 'local file' containing detailed information on all relevant material on inter-company transactions in each country to be provided to such country's tax administration
- A CbC report containing certain information relating to the global allocation of the MNE group's income and taxes paid, together with certain indicators of the location of economic activity within the MNE group

The understanding is that the master file, local file and CbC report should be reviewed and updated annually.

An increasing cynicism of the BEPS project from businesses and researchers comprises the possible overreach of the proposed new documentation requirements on MNE costs and, effectively, its ramifications for productivity and economic growth.

An important distinction has to be made between what is good for tax authorities and what is good for well-performing MNE taxpayers. The information reporting requirement in Action 13 is demanding on the MNEs operating in emerging economies where their operations may be small compared with their global operations. There is a limit to the extent and detail imposed on MNEs in reporting their macro- and micro-data on turnover, income and taxes without hampering their operational flexibility, if not productivity.[28]

Action 13 may have empowered tax administrations beyond what is needed for transparency or equity in cross-country MNE tax contribution. For example, a big challenge would be when companies within a group operate in a decentralised manner and/or follow different TP methodologies for similar businesses.

#### 30.2.13.1 July 2020 OECD Report

The OECD's July 2020 report perceives the matter differently. It indicates that the initial CbC reports were made in June 2018. As of May 2020, there were more than 2500 bilateral relationships established for the exchange of CbC reports under the Convention for Mutual Administrative Assistance in Tax Matters, under bilateral double tax conventions and tax information exchange agreements.

[28] See Baker (2016) for a development of this argument.

The OECD reported that, in total, over three quarters of the participating countries introduced or were in the process of introducing a CbC reporting obligation, including all G20 countries. The first release of aggregated CbC statistics for 2016 became available in July 2020 for 26 countries, covering nearly 4000 MNE groups. A full review of Action 13 was being conducted during 2020.

A Forum on Tax Administration (FTA) was said to have undertaken a number of initiatives to support tax administrations in using CbC reports and prevent its misuse. These include:

- CbC reports risk assessment workshops
- Handbook on the effective use of CbC reports in tax risk assessment
- International compliance assurance programme (ICAP)
- Comparative risk assessment initiative (CoRA)
- Tax risk evaluation and assurance tool (TREAT) and tax risk assessment questionnaire (TRAQ)

Initiatives to support MNE groups and jurisdictions in preparing and using CbC reports and to improve the quality of data in CbC reports comprise:

- Information on the implementation of CbC reporting by OECD/G20
- Guidance on the interpretation of Action 13
- Common errors in the preparation of CbC reports

#### 30.2.13.2 Impact on Economic Growth

Despite the positive actions taken by the OECD, many serious questions arise, most importantly, even from the tax administration side, do emerging economies of Africa and Asia such as South Africa and India have the financial or manpower resources to conduct annual examinations of the data as envisaged and, even if so, what would be the justification for spending competing administrative resources in such a manner.

MNEs have been productive in technology, in supply and in raising living standards globally. Their tax performance should be segmented into good and bad performers. There are likely to be good taxpayers even among those who fall above the high threshold that BEPS Action 13 has stipulated for the three-step reporting of their global operations. Unless this is recognised and separate treatment is worked out for them, it may be expected that Action 13 would be scaled back in future deliberations. It would reflect that the collapse in global growth was the motivator for the G20's BEPS initiative while revenue decline was only its outcome. It can only be hoped that, ultimately, despite the enthusiasm of tax administrators—and the OECD is heavily represented by ex-tax administrators or those on loan—mechanisms to generate tax revenue at the cost of economic growth will fail to receive sympathetic ears from global policymakers.

### 30.2.14 Action 14: Dispute Resolution

Action 14 recognises that countering BEPS must include actions that ensure certainty and predictability for business. It identifies mutual agreement procedure (MAP) as an essential complement to BEPS and therefore is a minimum standard. The minimum standard also includes easy access to procedures for the taxpayer and timely resolution. These standards are evident in Article 16 of the MLI.

#### 30.2.14.1 MLI Part V Article 16: Mutual Agreement Procedure (MAP)

A person aggrieved by the taxation in any of the parties to a CTA due to the provisions of the CTA may approach the competent authority (CA)[29] in either of the jurisdictions even if a remedy is available through the domestic law of the jurisdiction where the person is aggrieved. Parties to the CTA must present the case within 3 years of the objection being raised by the person. Associated details comprise:

- If such objection appears justified and the jurisdiction is unable to reach a satisfactory solution, the competent authorities of the parties to the CTA must aim through mutual agreement to resolve the case with a view to avoiding taxation not in accordance with the CTA.
- Agreements reached will be implemented notwithstanding any time limit in domestic law.
- Parties to a CTA must endeavour to resolve difficulties and doubts in the CTA through mutual agreement. They may also consult for double taxation outside the purview of the CTA.
- Article 16 pertains to a minimum standard. Hence, parties are allowed to make reservations to this Article only according to the directions provided within the Article.

India has reserved the right to the first part of the first provision, thereby disallowing aggrieved persons to approach the CA of any party to the CTA as per Article 16(5)(a). India took this position, as permitted by the MLI, that it intended to meet the minimum standard by allowing the resident of the jurisdiction, aggrieved by a provision of the CTA, to approach the CA of that particular jurisdiction (instead of either jurisdiction). And, in the case of provisions based on nationality, residents would be allowed to approach the CA of the jurisdiction where the national belonged. Finally, India has explained its position that if a CTA contains (or does not contain) provisions similar to those in Article 16, then the matter would be resolved within (or longer than) 3 years.

[29]See the role of CA in Chap. 28, Sect. 28.2.4.

#### 30.2.14.2 July 2020 OECD Report

The MAP is critical to ensuring that tax disputes are resolved in a timely, effective and efficient manner. Eighty-two participating members had been peer reviewed and 46 members qualified for deferral, with another nine-pending deferral. The peer review led to a significant increase in the number of closed MAP cases in most jurisdictions under review, and an increasing number of jurisdictions introduced or updated comprehensive MAP guidance to provide taxpayers with clear rules and guidelines on MAP. Results from a second phase of the peer reviews also demonstrated that jurisdictions were able to reduce the amount of time needed to close MAP cases.

Consideration was being given through a MAP Forum to three aspects comprising the minimum standard, reporting of MAP statistics, and the assessment methodology, in particular, what changes, if any, should be made to these three components of Action 14.

### 30.2.15 Action 15: Multilateral Instrument (MLI)

As already explained, Action 15 envisages the formulation of the MLI, also called the Convention (2015 Final Report), drawn up to comprise the preceding 14 BEPS Actions. The structure of MLI contains Articles, as they were referred to in the preceding discussion, that comprise provisions pertaining to corresponding subjects of the different BEPS Actions.

For India, the MLI represents a major commitment in the implementation of its international taxation convictions, even as challenges in advancing international taxation perspectives had already been emerging in its domestic law and treaty aspects. In this sense, the MLI could be seen as a cross-check or sounding board for most countries.

#### 30.2.15.1 July 2020 OECD Report

The MLI was finalised in 2016 and signed on 7 June 2017 by 76 jurisdictions. The entry into effect of the MLI provisions underlines the international political commitment to a multilateral approach to fighting BEPS and translating commitments into concrete measures. Currently, the MLI covers 94 jurisdictions of which 49 have ratified it. This approach is more beneficial for governments than bilaterally renegotiating the 3500 tax treaties currently in force.

Thus, treaties will reflect aspects relating not only to treaty shopping but also to hybrid mismatch arrangements and PEs, as well as strengthen provisions to resolve treaty disputes. As of May 2020, the MLI had already modified about 300 agreements across the worldwide network of tax agreements, and this number is expected to go up rapidly as more signatories ratify the MLI.

#### 30.2.15.2 Critique of MLI

Some authors have, however, questioned the role of the MLI at least in the context of developing economies. To quote:

There are three points of contention that could derail the delicate negotiations on the multilateral treaty. First, there continues to be a strong opinion among developing countries that the arm's length TP method adopted under the Actions is not going to prevent BEPS. In addition, the CbC reporting rules do not appear to have the kind of wide impact as initially envisaged. It appears now that it would be difficult for developing countries to obtain comprehensive financial information from the home jurisdictions of MNEs on their international commercial operations.[30] To this extent, the multilateral treaty cannot reflect the primary concerns of the developing countries.

Second, the OECD would like the multilateral treaty to include binding arbitration under the MAP procedure. While a more efficient dispute resolution system would be welcomed by developed countries, developing countries such as India are wary of it.[31] Third, there is no provision in the multilateral treaty on creating a permanent institutional framework that would be able to amend bilateral treaties in the future and would continue to develop appropriate policy responses to combat global tax avoidance. The stakes are high: if the multilateral treaty fails to gather momentum or provides only for a limited intervention in current international tax law, a historical opportunity to reshape global tax rules would have been lost.

Developing countries, including India, must make more of an effort to use the multilateral treaty negotiations to advance their perspective in return for some concrete measures to improve investor confidence in their tax systems. The multilateral initiative has been in the background of the OECD BEPS initiative, and it is up to India and nations that share India's concerns to seize the moment and try to catalyse further possible change.... Both developed and developing countries would like a more efficient response to international tax avoidance. India must utilise this opportunity of shared interests to actively seek a change to the current multilateral efforts in international taxation.[32]

Other authors have raised issue with the relevance of BEPS norms for emerging economies, placing the blame at the altar of advanced economies. To quote:

The MNE tax avoidance problem could be linked primarily to those MNEs with headquarters in the US. An accepted method to check BEPS would be the use of the controlled foreign company (CFC) instrument across the developed world that allowed a tax authority to reassign foreign subsidiary income from source to residence location. In the 1990s, the US changed its rules and allowed such related foreign companies to be de-linked from their US parent by 'ticking the box'—a set of lose criteria—resulting in a lack of relationship for tax purposes.

...an existing globally accepted manner of appropriately taxing MNEs essentially crumbled after this. Low and declining corporate tax rates at a global level, as well as binding rulings confirming low effective tax in a range of European countries ensured that MNEs across the board faced advantages in legally lowering their tax contributions. These combined to yield single digit effective tax rates to many MNEs.[33]

Despite reservations, there is, however, a recognition of the role of BEPS in setting international norms. Thus:

---

[30]See Ryding (2015).

[31]One reason for the wariness of the Indian tax administration is the high cost of international arbitration.

[32]See Nuggehalli (2016), pp. 193–94.

[33]See Baker, as described in Shome (2016), p. 6.

> . . .any workable international regime on tax law must be concerned with managing information on global tax payers, making policy choices that are agreed upon widely in the international arena, and implementing efficiently the agreed global norms in each of the member country's tax regimes. It is rare for all three conditions to come together at the same time. The OECD has managed to obtain that broad consensus under the auspices of the G20 countries, towards a workable global order in international taxation.[34]

India, and several emerging economies, had steadfastly argued well before BEPS that tax revenue must justly accrue in source jurisdictions where value added was created in the international supply chain of a commodity or service. Advanced economies by and large ignored this stance, their position being, revenue should accrue where risk taking and management decisions were made and where capital resided. However, with the collapse in advanced economy revenue with the onset of the 2008 global crisis, they began to realise the potential revenue benefits of applying the source principle as India did.

Interestingly, there is a relevant question that arises when a country is both capital exporting and capital importing. Taking one country example:

> South Africa is a member of the G20 and has OECD Observer status. Both the G20 and OECD were instrumental in driving the recent international tax regime changes, with reference, for example, to the BEPS Project. Like many of the BRICS countries, South Africa is, in its region, both a capital importer and capital exporter. This position places the BRICS in a unique position with respect to the implementation of the BEPS proposals, MLI and other initiatives.[35]

Some observers have raised a further pertinent issue that it may be somewhat fallacious that taxing by the source principle would assist all developing countries. Therefore,

> Emerging economies that are significant source countries would gain from BEPS recommendations since the definition of source has been widened.... But (it) would not help the many countries with more rudimentary economies whose sources of earnings continue to be limited by their lack of tangible capital or intellectual know-how. The BEPS arrangements would thus be beneficial to a handful of emerging economies rather than to the bulk of developing countries.[36]

## 30.3 Conclusions

The upshot of the analysis presented in this chapter is that international norms proposed by BEPS Actions may not always serve the interests of all emerging economies. At the same time, there is little alternative but for the international community to move forward in tandem to allay double non-taxation on the part of

[34] See Nuggehalli (2016), op. cit., p. 192.

[35] West (2017).

[36] Dwarkasing, as described in Shome (2016), p. 5.

the MNEs but keeping in mind not to affect worldwide economic growth adversely in their attempt to eradicate tax avoidance. The different—good and bad—tax behaviours across the MNE community must also be kept on the anvil as the BEPS project progresses and it becomes feasible for tax authorities to collaborate with the objective of fine-tuning different reporting and scrutiny requirements reflecting differences in MNE behaviours.

## References

Baistrocchi, Eduardo. 2020. Article 9: Associated Enterprises-Global Tax Treaty Commentaries. Department of Law, London School of Economics.

———. 2021. The International Tax Regime and Global Power Shifts. *Virginia Tax Review* 40 (2), Winter.

Baker, Philip. 2016. BEPS: Emergence of International Tax Law and Future Direction. In *Base Erosion and Profit Shifting (BEPS): The Global Taxation Agenda*, ed. Parthasarathi Shome, 51–70. Gurugram: Wolters Kluwer.

Dwarkasing, Ramon. 2016. The Mercantilist Paradigm: History and Basis of BEPS. In *Base Erosion and Profit Shifting (BEPS): The Global Taxation Agenda*, ed. Parthasarathi Shome, 171–197. Gurugram: Wolters Kluwer.

Manohar, Navneet. 2020. Automatic Exchange of Information-Confidentiality and Appropriate Use of the Data. *Taxalogue* 1 (3): 60–67.

Nuggehalli, Nigam. 2016. Multilateralism in the BEPS Initiative: Pros and Cons. In *Base Erosion and Profit Shifting (BEPS): The Global Taxation Agenda*, ed. Parthasarathi Shome, 31–50. Gurugram: Wolters Kluwer.

OECD. 2018. Tax Challenges Arising from Digitalisation – Interim Report 2018, Inclusive Framework on BEPS. OECD/G20 BEPS Project. https://www.oecd.org/tax/tax-challenges-arising-from-digitalisation-interimreport-9789264293083-en.htm. Accessed 30 October 2020.

———. 2020. OECD/G20 Inclusive Framework on BEPS-Progress report July 2019 – July 2020. OECD/G20 BEPS Project. http://www.oecd.org/tax/beps/oecd-g20-inclusive-framework-on-beps-progress-report-july-2019-july-2020.pdf. Accessed 30 October 2020.

Ryding, Tove. 2015. An Assessment of the G20/ OECD BEPS Outcomes: Failing to Reach Its Objectives. European Network on Debt and Development (EURODAD). https://www.eurodad.org/bepsfacts. Accessed 30 October 2020.

Shome, Parthasarathi, ed. 2014. *The G20 Macroeconomic Agenda: India and the Emerging Economies*. New Delhi: Cambridge University Press.

———, ed. 2015. *The G20 Development Agenda: An Indian Perspective*. New Delhi: Cambridge University Press.

———, ed. 2016. *Base Erosion and Profit Shifting (BEPS): The Global Taxation Agenda*. Gurugram: Wolters Kluwer.

West, Craig. 2017. Status Quo of International Tax Reform in South Africa: Implementation of BEPS and CRS and the Influence on Domestic Law Amendment. https://doi.org/10.2139/ssrn.3009193. Accessed 30 October 2020.

# Taxation of Digital Economy 31

## 31.1 Introduction

The emergence of digitalisation of significant and growing segments of economic activity has been posing challenges due to its lack of physical presence in taxing jurisdictions despite its instantaneous global reach. It has sent national and international taxation communities into a flurry without a multilateral solution so far. The issue, therefore, deserves particular attention and is the subject matter of this chapter.

The OECD's 2013 BEPS Action Plan as well as the October 2015 Action 1 Final Report on the digital economy[1] observed that digitalisation exacerbated BEPS issues and raised a series of broader tax challenges related to how taxing rights on income generated from cross-border activities in the digital age should be allocated among jurisdictions. Suggestions for addressing associated 'nexus, data and characterisation' issues were identified, but there was no agreement or recommendation in the Action 1 report. The G20 asked that OECD's multilateral Inclusive Framework (IF)[2] of more than 100 countries deliver a consensus-based solution to the tax challenges of the digital economy by 2020.

In March 2017, the G20 asked the IF, working through its Task Force on the Digital Economy, for an Interim Report.[3] This was delivered in 2018. It analysed new and changing business models and possible implications for the international tax system (in particular nexus and profit allocation rules). However, it repeated the conclusion of the Action 1 report that ring-fencing the digital economy for taxation purposes would be well-nigh impossible. Nevertheless, the IF remained committed to continue working on a consensus-based solution by 2020.

[1] See OECD (2015).

[2] See Chap.30, Sect. 30.2.4, and Chap. 30, Footnote 13, for a description of IF.

[3] See OECD (2018), op. cit.



P. Shome, *Taxation History, Theory, Law and Administration*, Springer Texts in Business and Economics, https://doi.org/10.1007/978-3-030-68214-9_31

The IF released a Policy Note[4] in January 2019 that grouped proposals into two pillars—one on nexus and profit allocation (Pillar One) and one on ensuring a minimum level of taxation (Pillar Two). A Programme of Work (PoW)[5] was agreed in May 2019 to move the work forward. For Pillar One, the proposals of the IF could not generate consensus. Nevertheless, the OECD developed a 'Unified Approach' (UA) that attempted to build on the commonalities identified in the PoW, releasing it for public comment in October 2019.[6] A public consultation was held also on Pillar Two in December 2019.

In January 2020, the IF reiterated its commitment to the two-pillar approach.[7] Building on the UA, it included a note entitled, 'Outline of the Architecture of a Unified Approach on Pillar One'. An updated PoW identified 11 building blocks for further work towards a solution. A progress note on Pillar Two was also agreed upon. An IF meeting was to occur in October 2020 towards the agreement of a package. Unfortunately, in mid-October 2020, the OECD issued a statement essentially indicating that the work had stalled and that it was deferring the discussions for an IF on Pillar One discussions.[8]

In August, the United Nations released an alternative framework for taxing the digital economy though it did not generate immediate traction.

It may be surmised from the unfolding of these events how sensitive the taxation of digital services has become internationally, and why countries are taking unilateral steps to tax it.[9] In order to fully understand what has given rise to such complexity in multilateral discussions and the failure to arrive at any agreement to develop international norms for the taxation of the digital economy, it is essential to comprehend the digital economy first. Accordingly, this chapter relates the operational nature of the digital economy and tracks its technical characteristics to assess the challenges encountered in arriving at a multilateral consensus regarding how to tax it.

---

[4]See OECD (2019a).

[5]See OECD (2019b).

[6]See OECD (2019d). Note that the Inclusive Framework Secretariat Proposal for a 'Unified Approach' under Pillar One focuses on 'consumer-facing businesses', which would cover highly digitalised and profitable business models that interact with consumers. It proposes a new nexus, distinct and separate from the existing concept of the PE, which would ensure a company is taxable in a jurisdiction where its sales exceed a certain threshold even if it is not physically present in that market.

[7]See OECD (2020).

[8]See Butani and Jain (2020). They have pointed out that taking the UN Model route may provide a solution in the final analysis.

[9]Indeed, with some cohesion, it is not impossible to tax the digital economy. For example, the OECD's 2017 International VAT/GST Guidelines included principles and mechanisms for collecting VAT on cross-border sales of digital products. Implementing such standards, EU members raised EUR 14.8 billion during the first 4 years of implementation (2015–2019).

## 31.2 Nature of Digital Economy

Advances in Information and communication technology (ICT) has transformed the means of doing global and domestic business, altering familiar supply chains of businesses and modifying, or changing altogether, the manner of procuring and distributing goods and services. It has ushered 'invisible' players who did not exist earlier. The OECD's 2018 interim report indicated that technological advances in Web 2.0 technology were most dramatically introduced and experienced by companies such as Facebook, Uber and Amazon using data aggregation as their main tool. But little remuneration was received in exchange by the original data owners—the users. What appeared to make the situation glaring was that such companies demonstrated minimal or no economic presence in the countries from where they sourced the data.[10]

Web 3.0 technology moves some remuneration to the source. It allows users to own their data and monetise it by selling it to the companies for use with user consent, leading to the creation of data market places. This should, in turn, enable tax jurisdictions to identify the sale of data at its source. Among OECD members, however, it has been difficult to garner consensus to fully shift taxation to source (Pillar One), even though a minimum tax contribution by MNEs (Pillar Two) has become less controversial. This mainly reflects the US position which perceives itself as a major loser if taxation moves from residence to source basis. It has introduced a minimum tax, however.

To fully understand the current state and future direction of digital economy taxation, reflecting its relative recent emergence as a sector, it is worthwhile to familiarise ourselves with its characteristics and functioning. Following that, the formidable challenges associated with its taxation will be addressed.

### 31.2.1 Internet of Things

The ability to connect any smart device to a network of networks has enabled an 'Internet of Things'. The term refers to a series of components of equal importance including machine-to-machine communication, cloud computing, big data analysis, sensors and actuators, the combination of which leads to further developments in machine learning and remote control. The number of devices connected to the Internet is expanding rapidly, but it is miniscule in terms of potential.[11] As increasing numbers of connected devices are developed and sold, machine-to-machine

[10]See Sekar (2018).

[11]Some early figures of Cisco, an American technology conglomerate showed between 10 and 15 billion devices connected to the Internet, a figure that represented less than 1% of potential connection (Evan 2012). In the OECD area alone, the figure was estimated to rise from 5.8 billion by 2017 and to 14 billion by 2022 (OECD 2013).

communication should expand and improve the ability and efficiency of businesses to collect and analyse data.

### 31.2.2 Other Developments

Selected examples are as follows:

- Virtual Currencies: These are digital units of exchange that are not yet backed by government-issued legal tender, though China has announced its intention to do so. They can be used in online games to purchase in-game assets and services. In some cases, they can be exchanged for real currencies or used to purchase real goods and services, through exchanges that may be operated by the game creators or by third parties. Other virtual currencies also exist, for example, 'cryptocurrencies', including 'Bitcoins'. They rely on peer-to-peer verification to secure and verify transactions. Some private operators are accepting payment in Bitcoins.
- Advanced Robotics: These are robots that are making manufacturing more efficient and productive through the use of automated factories. MNEs can take advantage of lower labour costs and move back to where their customers are.
- Three-Dimensional (3D) Printing: This also brings manufacturing closer to the customer, with direct interaction with them to design product features. Manufacturing could gradually move away from mass production to customised products and more experimentation.

## 31.3 Digital Economy and Business Models

The digital economy uses electronic commerce (e-commerce) which has been defined by the OECD as,

> the sale or purchase of goods or services, conducted over computer networks by methods specifically designed for the purpose of receiving or placing of orders. The goods or services are ordered by those methods, but the payment and the ultimate delivery of the goods or service do not have to be conducted online. An e-commerce transaction can be between enterprises, households, individuals, governments, and other public or private organisations.[12]

E-commerce has enabled new business models. To cite a few:

- The online retailer model allows goods to be sold on online platforms for a placement fee or a commission. Examples are Amazon, Zalando and Alibaba.

[12]See OECD (2011).

- In the social media model, network owners rely on advertising revenues by delivering targeted marketing messages to consumers. Examples are Facebook, XING and Qzone.
- The subscription model platforms charge a subscription fee for continued access to a digital service (e.g. music or videos). Examples are Netflix and Spotify.
- In the collaborative platform model, digital platforms connect spare capacity and demand and enable individuals to share 'access' to assets rather than own them outright. Platforms charge a fixed or variable fee on each transaction. Examples are Airbnb, BlaBlaCar and Didi Chuxing.

Some business models used in e-commerce are described below.

### 31.3.1 Business-to-Business (B2B) Model

The B2B model involves transactions of one business with another, accounting for the majority of e-commerce. First, it represents the conversion of traditional business to online. But it also includes the provision of goods or services in: (a) logistics services such as transportation, warehousing, and distribution; (b) application services offering deployment, hosting and management of packaged software from a central facility; (c) outsourcing of support functions for e-commerce, such as web-hosting, security and customer care solutions; (d) auction solutions services for the operation and maintenance of real-time auctions via the Internet; (e) content management services, for the facilitation of website content management and delivery; and (f) web-based commerce enablers that provide automated online purchasing capabilities.

### 31.3.2 Business-to-Consumer (B2C) Model

B2C was an early form of e-commerce in which a business sells to a consumer but not as a business consumer. B2C categories include: (a) 'pureplay' online vendors with no physical stores or offline presence; (b) 'click-and-mortar' businesses that supplement existing consumer-facing business with online sales; and (c) manufacturers that use online business to allow customers to order and customise directly. The sales of B2C can be tangible (such as a hard copy CD of music) or intangible (the same in an electronic format).

Through digitisation of information, including text, sound and visual images, an increasing number of goods and services can be delivered digitally to customers irrespective of physical distance. It shortens the supply chain by eliminating wholesalers, distributors, retailers or other intermediaries, cutting out impediments to market entry, slashing costs of retail shops and replacing them with a website. It enhances the efficiency of operation by increasing consumer access to information, thus reducing search costs and subsequent transaction costs.

### 31.3.3 Consumer-to-Consumer (C2C) Model

C2C is becoming increasingly common. Businesses can be intermediaries, helping consumers to sell or rent residential property, cars, motorcycles and other personal property. Their information is uploaded on the website from where transactions take place. The businesses may or may not charge the consumer for their services, reflecting their use of commercial advertising or similar sources.

C2C comes in various forms including: (a) auctions facilitated at a portal allowing online bidding on the items being sold; (b) peer-to-peer systems allowing sharing of files among users; and (c) classified ads portals providing an interactive, online marketplace allowing negotiation between buyers and sellers.

It is not surprising that e-commerce has widened the reach of smaller businesses, enabling them to reach markets that would not have been otherwise possible to reach. Thus, the number of firms using e-commerce has increased rapidly in recent times.

## 31.4 Taxation of Digital Economy

Challenges associated with the taxation of the digital economy in the context of its new business models may be listed as:

- Identification of significant economic and digital presence
- Avoiding the creation of permanent establishment (PE) status
- Attribution of profits to PE or a significant economic presence
- Application of transfer pricing (TP) to new business models
- Collection of tax

Tax treaties allocate the right to tax profits if a PE or business connection/nexus is established, though royalties have no such prerequisite. There is a significant difference in the rate of tax levied—40% for business income and 10% on royalty, in the case of India. Thus, disputes arise, for example, over the characterisation of income from subscription fee, whether it is business income or royalty. Tax authorities tend to characterise it as business income to maximise tax liability while businesses attempt to minimise it by characterising it as royalty. Further, given that a PE has a geographical connection, it does not fit well into the digital landscape which cuts across geographies. Since a digital enterprise may not require personnel to be placed locally, arm's length price (ALP) based on functions performed, remains a challenge for PE type calculations.

### 31.4.1 Applying Principles

In an early report,[13] the OECD set out a list of principles that should apply to the taxation of e-commerce that essentially re-emphasised the traditional principles of taxation in general. They included neutrality (between the taxation of e-commerce and conventional forms of commerce); low costs of implementation and compliance; certainty and simplicity: tax rules should be simple and taxpayers should be able to anticipate the tax consequences of a transaction; effectiveness and fairness: taxation should yield the right amount of tax while being cognizant of the laxity or severity of measures against tax evasion and avoidance; and flexibility: the tax system ensures to keep pace with technological and commercial developments.[14]

### 31.4.2 Isolating Digital Economy

Though the applicable principles for digital economy taxation were specified to be similar to the economy as a whole, from the start one consideration that assumed some importance was whether the digital economy should be segmented from the rest of the economy. The BEPS Action Plan concluded that segmenting the digital economy from the rest of the economy was difficult. Nevertheless, rules under domestic that are meant primarily to tax profits arising from traditional routes of business may not suffice to tax the digital economy comprehensively as is being proved in international dispute settlement in the taxation of the digital economy. A recent example from July 2020 is a case that the EU lost against Ireland, one of its own members, for perceived insufficiency in the taxation of Apple. Therefore, there may be little choice but to ensure that rules for taxing the profits from the digital economy are segmented from rules for taxing profits from the traditional economy. This is despite the increasing acceptance that the digital economy cannot be easily ringfenced from the rest of the economy.

### 31.4.3 Direct Tax

With respect to direct taxes, challenges relate to the allocation of taxing rights between source and residence jurisdictions, and whether the existing paradigm used to determine where economic activities are carried out and value is created for tax purposes continues to deliver appropriate results. These challenges are classified into three broad categories:

[13]See OECD (2001).

[14]See OECD (2015) op. cit., p. 17.

- Nexus: Whether the current rules to determine nexus with a jurisdiction for tax purposes are appropriate?
- Data: The issues of how to attribute value created from the generation of data through digital products and services, and of how to characterise for tax purposes a person or entity's supply of data in a transaction (e.g. as a free supply of a good, as a barter transaction or in some other way). Further, the value of the platform to existing users is enhanced as new users join and contribute, may raise other challenges.
- Characterisation: New digital products or means of delivering services create uncertainties in relation to the proper characterisation of payments made in the context of new business models, particularly in relation to cloud computing.

Together, the broader tax challenges raised relate directly to the operation and interaction between the rules for determining nexus and the allocation of profit.

### 31.4.4 Indirect Tax

The digital economy has magnified the capability of private consumers to shop online and the capability of businesses to sell to consumers around the world without the need to be present in the consumer's country. This often results in no VAT being levied on cross-border low-value parcels or on services provided. This has adverse effects on VAT revenues and on the level playing field between resident and non-resident vendors.

A consumption tax such as VAT or GST is an indirect tax. Though it is the businesses that collect it, they do so as an agent of government. It is not intended to be borne finally by businesses but by the final consumer. Collection in the context of the digital economy is challenging due to many identification issues over and above the usual, high compliance costs of collection, completing numerous tax returns, waiting for refunds and being subject to audit and scrutiny. Thus, the burden on businesses could turn out to be heavy.

VAT or GST on cross-border trade of goods is collected at the customs border, and exports are zero-rated. However, taxing services provided cross-border, mainly Electronically Supplied Services (ESS), is a challenge since they can escape tax more easily. Business models of ESS are still evolving; therefore, they are quite dynamic, for example, 'order to fulfilment' services, such as ticketing services, software downloads, radio and TV broadcasting and telecom. There is a hybrid category 'online order with offline fulfilment', such as online retail and hotel booking. They possess complex structures that are layered with multiple service providers.

Considerations of B2B (both parties are GST registered) or B2C (customers unregistered) pose different issues. If a business (B) is also unregistered, it would be taxable as customer (C). 'Peer to peer' includes one-off or pre-owned product sales where both parties are unregistered. The actual basis of collection depends on whether the supplier is located in the jurisdiction or not. It demonstrates the complexity of indirect taxation negating the usual depiction of its simplicity vis-à-vis direct tax, as revealed by several court decisions in different countries. A case against Uber was decided in its favour since the service provided by Uber was found to be an integral part of the principal service of providing transportation, hence could not be included as e-commerce.

Procedural principles on collection have been analysed by the World Customs Organization (WCO) in a 2016–2017 study. They included advance electronic data and risk management, facilitation and simplification of procedures for low-value supply, simplified return and refund processes, revenue collection based on pre-importation data, development of common terms, definitions and mechanisms to measure cross-border e-commerce, amongst others. Based on these principles, a common legislative framework was recommended in 2018 through WCO's E-commerce Framework Standards.

### 31.4.5 Options Proposed by OECD in its Action 1 Report

In 2014 itself, the OECD unveiled the concept of a permanent 'virtual' establishment (PVE) in a report. An MNE would be designated as a PVE if the level of sales in a jurisdiction reached a certain level. Thus, profits from the MNE attributable to the PVE would be taxed by the source jurisdiction. In effect, a healthy customer base, with a continuous and commercially significant business activity of a non-resident enterprise should suffice to entitle a source jurisdiction with the right to tax profits arising in (or from) that jurisdiction. This matches the source principle of taxation. However, at that stage, the OECD indicated that the discussion had been included 'only for the sake of completeness'. Hence the concept did not receive backing.

The OECD BEPS Action 1 pointed towards important elements to address direct taxation of digitised businesses. They may be considered options under consideration.

#### 31.4.5.1 Modifying the Rules of Exemption from Permanent Establishment Status

One intent of the BEPS strategy on digital economy taxation is to have rules for allocation of profits for different jurisdictions as business conducted through the digital economy spans across regions. The Action 1 report suggested that, if the exemption available in Article 5 of the OECD Model Convention relating to preparatory and auxiliary services in connection to the PE is made unavailable, it would be a forward step. However, eliminating the exemption for all enterprises whose core business would also be eliminated would affect business conducted through traditional methods; therefore, a distinction between core and non-core business activities may be appropriate, with precise rules framed for the purpose. As each country seeks to tax profits based on sourcing principles, it would become essential that rules distinguishing core from non-core be made clear.

#### 31.4.5.2 Creating New Nexus Rules Based on Significant Digital Presence

An enterprise engaged in certain 'fully dematerialised digital activities' would have a PE if it maintained a 'significant digital presence' in the economy of another country. The present rules on PE specify the creation of a PE through physical presence. The Action 1 report suggested a number of tests to determine the creation of a permanent 'virtual' establishment (PVE) based on criteria including the extent of fully dematerialised goods or services under remotely provided B2C, the significance of payments by clients in the country for the provision of digital goods or services as part of the enterprise's core business, and if an existing branch of the enterprise in the country offers marketing and consulting functions strongly related to the core business of the enterprise.

These would need modifications in Article 5 and Article 7 of the OECD Model Convention. Care should be taken not to make changes that extend or dilute rules relating to traditional businesses. It could be better, therefore, not to change Article 5 or Article 7, but to introduce a new article relating to PE and attribution of profits for the digital economy.

#### 31.4.5.3 Virtual PE

Some options were provided for the creation of a virtual PE for the digital economy. They included:

- A 'virtual fixed place of business PE' that would create a PE when the enterprise maintains a website on a server of another enterprise located in a jurisdiction and carries on business through that website
- A 'virtual agency PE', which would apply when contracts are habitually concluded on behalf of an enterprise with persons located in the jurisdiction through technological means, rather than through a person
- An 'on-site business presence PE', which would look at the economic presence of an enterprise within a jurisdiction where the foreign enterprise provides on-site services or other business interfaces at the customer's location

Again, in the context of a digital economy, the attribution of profits under Article 7 would be critical. If the concept of virtual PE is introduced, eliminating preparatory and auxiliary services altogether from Article 5 should not prevail as indicated above.

#### 31.4.5.4 Withholding Tax (WHT) on Digital Transactions

Imposing a final WHT was considered for certain payments made by residents of a country for digital goods or services provided by a foreign e-commerce provider. This would bring PEs with no physical presence within the tax base. It would eliminate any subjective test on a PE and subjective assessment of attribution of profits.

The WHT could be used as a means of tax collection only in cases where a primary liability to tax exists on the foreign e-commerce provider. In practical terms, the challenge would be that, since most payments are made through credit cards or online credit, ensuring compliance would be difficult. Financial institutions involved with such payments would have to become a part of the implementation. Further, the WHT on digital transactions would have to be extended into the foreign tax credit allowed under the tax treaties.

India has introduced an Equalisation Levy (EL) through Finance Act, 2016. It provides for the imposition of a 6% levy on the amount received by a non-resident taxpayer not having a PE in India for providing specified services. Its objective is to equalise the tax burden on a non-resident, providing digital services and operating in the Indian market and their domestic competitors.

Specified services, defined under Section 164(i) are, 'online advertisement, any provision for digital advertising space or any other facility or service for the purpose of online advertisement and includes any other services as notified by Central Government'. Currently, no service has been notified by the government, and hence, the scope of the levy is limited only to advertisement services.[15] However, it has acquired a dubious reputation, the argument being that, after the introduction of the GST, the EL should not exist independently. An adverse consequence of the EL is double taxation since it is not deductible against the income tax. Several tax experts in India are currently analysing the problem to recommend possible ways to tax the digital economy in meaningful ways.[16]

Another question that has arisen is regarding the merit of a data localisation requirement by the Reserve Bank, India's central bank, mandating payment systems operators in India to store data only in India. Its objective may be to provide protection to customers but it also converts these businesses to PEs and brings them within the ambit of Indian taxation.

The United States views the EL and other prevailing digital economy taxes as ring-fencing the digital economy. In 2019, the Office of the U.S. Trade Representative (USTR) initiated an investigation into a 3% digital services tax (DST) adopted by France on revenue generated from providing certain digital services to, or targeted at, persons in France. On completion, the USTR concluded that the DST was unreasonable, unfair and discriminatory towards U.S. commerce. The French DST was applied to revenue rather than to income, hence inconsistent with accepted principles of international tax policy. Further, it was retroactive and extraterritorial in application. It was held to discriminate against U.S. companies.

The USTR found that the DST was especially discriminatory against digital companies based in the United States, such as Google, Facebook, Amazon and Apple. The USTR proposed 100% ad valorem duties on certain French products including French cheese and wine. The imposition of the duty is currently on hold as the two countries have arrived at a temporary truce until the end of 2020 in view of OECD efforts to arrive at a global consensus on the taxation of the digital economy.

[15]See Kumar and Agarwal (2020).

[16]See Gupta et al. (2020).

In June 2020, USTR extended its investigation to other countries. It issued a notice of initiation of an investigation into DSTs which have been adopted or are under consideration in Austria, Brazil, the Czech Republic, the European Union, India, Indonesia, Italy, Spain, Turkey and the United Kingdom. In January 2021, USTR found that India, Italy and Turkey also discriminated against U. S. tech firms. The future course of this tax and its variants elsewhere in the world, therefore, remain uncertain, awaiting the OECD's recommendations and the willingness of members, in particular the United States, to accept them.[17]

## 31.5 OECD's 2019 Reports[18]

As suggested by some countries, the OECD explored potential changes to the nexus and profit allocation rules for the digital economy in a February–March report. Three proposals attempted to apply a global approach to the determination of profit, the objective continuing to comprise the recognition of value created by a business's activity or participation in user or market jurisdictions that is not recognised in the current framework for allocating profits. Therefore, they focussed on the extent of user participation and the place of marketing of intangibles.

### 31.5.1 User Participation Proposal

The activities and participation of users that contribute to the creation of a brand to establish market power are recognised as value creation and aligned with profit allocation. Typical business models are social media platforms, search engines and online marketplaces. For businesses that have more traditional relationships with customers, there would be no change in the profit allocation or nexus rules.

Due to the difficulties in using traditional TP methods for determining the amount of profit that should be allocated to a user jurisdiction, a non-routine or residual profit split approach was suggested.[19] However, significant challenges exist in calculating non-routine profit across an MNE group or even for an individual business line. Therefore, some practical solutions were proposed.

### 31.5.2 Marketing Intangibles Proposal

Unlike the user participation proposal, this proposal would not be restricted to highly digitalised businesses, but given a wide scope in situations where an MNE group can 'reach into' a jurisdiction, either remotely or through a limited local presence, to

[17] See Choudhury and Dey (2020).

[18] See OECD (2019c).

[19] See Chap. 28, Sect. 28.2.1, for an explanation of various approaches.

develop a user or customer base and other marketing intangibles. It portrays a link between marketing intangibles and the market jurisdiction. It would modify TP and treaty rules to require marketing intangibles and risks associated with such intangibles to be allocated to the market jurisdiction. Thus, tax would occur even in the absence of a traditional taxable presence.

Current profit allocation and nexus rules would be modified to require that the non-routine or residual income be allocated to the market jurisdiction. All other income, such as income from R&D and routine functions would be allocated according to existing profit allocation principles since they are perceived to already reflect allocation as per value creation. Given its wide scope, there is little doubt that there would be some uncertainty of double taxation with two jurisdictions claiming tax on the same income. Therefore, this approach should come with a strong dispute resolution component.

### 31.5.3 Significant Economic Presence Proposal

A taxable presence in a jurisdiction would arise when a non-resident enterprise has a significant economic presence (SEP) implying evidence of a purposeful and sustained interaction with the jurisdiction via digital technology. Revenue generated will not, however, be a sufficient indicator to establish nexus but would need to be combined with other factors including the existence of a user base, high volume of digital content derived from the jurisdiction, billing and collection in the local form of payment, website in a local language, after-sales service or repairs and maintenance, or sustained marketing and sales promotion activities, online or otherwise, to attract customers.

Action 1 Report's fractional apportionment method could be used and the tax base could be determined by applying the MNE group's global profit rate to the revenue (sales) generated in a particular jurisdiction. In addition, where users meaningfully contribute to the value creation process, users would also be taken into account in apportioning income.

## 31.6 Revised Nexus and Profit Allocation Rules[20]

Soon after its February–March 2019 report, the OECD issued a Programme of Work (PoW) in May 2019 to develop a consensus on digital economy taxation. This work is ongoing. It has two 'Pillars'. Pillar One focusses on the allocation of taxing rights among countries and seeks to undertake a coherent and concurrent review of the profit allocation and nexus rules. The United States continues to have issues with it because it would reallocate taxing rights which it perceives as vexatious to its interests. Pillar Two recommends a minimum tax on the digital economy to be

[20]See OECD (2019b).

introduced by all jurisdictions. At present, there is more agreement on Pillar Two than on Pillar One. The United States is more at ease with it.

The three proposals under Pillar One—user participation, marketing intangibles and significant economic presence—were reviewed in Sect. 31.5. The associated PoW include finding solutions for the technical issues that were also mentioned.

### 31.6.1 New Profit Allocation Rules

The new taxing right requires a method to quantify the amount of profit reallocated to market jurisdictions, and a method to determine how that profit should be allocated among the market jurisdictions entitled to tax under the new taxing right. The PoW would explore issues and options in connection with new profit allocation rules. These issues and options are expected to include:

1. The development of conceptually underpinned methods for determining the amount of profit and loss subject to the new taxing right, consistent with the principle of avoiding double taxation
2. The use of simplification measures where appropriate to limit the burden of the new rules on tax administrations and taxpayers alike
3. An assessment of the administrability of the features of any proposal, taking into consideration capacity and resource constraints

### 31.6.2 New Nexus Rules

The PoW would explore the development of a concept of remote taxable presence (i.e. a taxable presence without traditional physical presence) and a new set of standards for identifying when such a remote taxable presence exists:

- The PoW would also consider a new concept of taxable income sourced in (i.e. derived from) a jurisdiction. This taxing right would generally not be constrained by physical presence requirements.
- Developing a new non-physical presence nexus rule to allow market jurisdictions to tax the measure of profits allocated to them under the new profit allocation rules would require an evaluation of the relative merits of alternative approaches, including:
  - Amendments to the definition of a 'permanent establishment' (PE) in Article 5 of the OECD Model Convention, and potential ensuing changes to Article 7 of the OECD Model Convention
  - Development of a standalone rule establishing a new and separate nexus, either through a new taxable presence or a concept of source

## 31.7 OECD's January 2020 Report

In yet another attempt on revitalisation, a January 2020 report proposed a 'Unified Approach' on Pillar One for negotiating a consensus-based solution to be agreed by mid-2020 buttressed by a revised PoW for Pillar One (revised PoW). It replaced the May 2019 PoW and defined the remaining work that needed to be accomplished in 2020. It was expected that Pillar One options would: (A) result in a formulaic allocation of profit rather than being based on physical presence; or (B) use a fixed remuneration based on the ALP for defined baseline distribution and marketing functions that take place in the market jurisdiction; or (C) be applicable where in-country functions exceed the baseline activity compensated under (B). Unlike (A), options (B) and (C) would not create any new taxing rights, rather, would be based on existing profit allocation rules (including the reliance on physical presence), and reflect efforts to improve the practical application of the ALP. The formula-based approach (with no connection to ALP) would be applied only in option (A). Tax experts have expressed views that, reflecting various checks and balances of thresholds, and mandatory acceptance of any arbitration that may come about, the likely revenue outcomes would not be ample.[21]

If the technical details had been worked out, key policy features of a consensus-based solution to Pillar One issues were expected in July 2020, with a report by the end of 2020. Instead, the OECD announced a deferral of consensus through the IF framework.

> The reason for OECD's inability to garner consensus is pedestaled on its underlying objective to achieve a consensus under the 'unified approach', which is perhaps predicated on a one-size-fits-all approach and is, therefore, fundamentally at odds with the inherent attributes of the digital industry, besides being seen as going against the interest of emerging consumer markets. (This) will ignite pangs for unilateral measures. Whereas it means a source of tax revenues for nations....it also means uncertainty and risk of dual taxation, given that such efforts are not coordinated between nations.[22]

## 31.8 A UN Proposal—Tax Treatment of Payments for Digital Services

The UN proposed an optional UN model tax treaty provision in August 2020, for granting additional taxing rights to countries where an automated digital services provider's customers are located.[23] The tax base would include payments for services provided on the internet or an electronic network requiring minimal

[21] See Avi-Yonah (2020).

[22] See Butani and Jain (2020), op. cit.

[23] See Martin (2020).

human involvement from the service provider.[24] The tax base would also include the sale or other alienation of user data would also be covered by the new tax.

Drawn up by an ad hoc drafting group, the UN varies from the OECD's IF unified approach to Pillar One, though both the OECD and the UN have, as their objective, the granting of greater taxing rights to source countries. The draft proposes to add a new Article 12B to the UN Model Double Taxation Convention between Developed and Developing Countries, requiring an MNE group to pay taxes on payments for automated digital services under one of two approaches.

The two routes for source countries to tax cross-border payments for automated digital services would comprise (1) a 'gross-based tax' at a rate agreed upon by the two treaty parties; and (2) a net income-based tax using an apportionment formula. An MNE would choose either route.

The UN net income formula apportions 30% of net income from automated digital services to countries where sales revenues arise. This is broader than the OECD because it does not have the size, profitability or local revenue thresholds that are in OECD's Pillar One. It is also more straightforward to determine taxable income in the source country without any thresholds.

The UN gross-based tax option also stands apart from the OECD Pillar One. The UN highlights problems that a gross-based tax could lead to. These include (1) a foreign digital services provider could raise customer prices in the source country, (2) it could deter investment due to foreign tax credit limits, and (3) it could imply a high effective tax rate on net income.

After the deferral of the OECD IF option, the UN proposal may nevertheless face challenges in winning the support of the United States inasmuch as the US treasury secretary (finance minister) having expressed doubts over any proposal that focuses exclusively on digital businesses. Thus, discussion and debate over taxation of the digital economy is likely to continue.

## 31.9 Conclusions

The OECD has correctly claimed that there has been a historic level of participation from more than 135 members of the OECD/G20 IF, all of which work on an equal footing in a continuous effort to adapt the international tax rules for the twenty-first century. The BEPS Action Plan, followed by Actions, had as their objectives of a new recognition of substance and an augmentation of transparency in cross-country international taxation. Nevertheless, more remains to be done in light of the OECD's announcement of deferral of discussions for an inclusive framework on Pillar One discussions. Gaining the full confidence of emerging economies to ensure that their interests are safeguarded will take more time.

[24]Activities covered would include online advertising services, online intermediation platform services; social media services, digital content services; cloud computing services, and standardised online teaching services.

The UN too has come into the picture with its own proposal under the aegis of the UN Committee of Tax Experts. Those discussions are attempting to find a solution within an existing bilateral treaty-based framework, sharing the taxing rights with the host states where the digital service providers create value and earn revenue. India supports this approach as will many emerging economies that should benefit from source-based taxation of the digital economy. The future course of taxation of the digital economy with multilateral guidance and norms is yet to be determined.

## References


Avi-Yonah, Rueven S. 2020. Lecture, UTDT Global Tax Talks 2020. Universidad Torcuato Di Tella (UTDT). https://www.utdt.edu/ver_contenido.php?id_contenido=20347&id_item_menu=32584. Accessed 26 August 2020.

Butani, Mukesh, and Tarun Jain. 2020. Digital Taxes: If Multilateral Fails, Look for Bilateral Solutions. *Financial Express*, October 21.

Choudhury, Asim, and Aesa Dey. 2020. Indian Equalization Levy Under U.S. Scrutiny—What Comes Next? *Bloomberg*. https://news.bloombergtax.com/daily-tax-report-international/insight-indian-equalization-levy-under-u-s-scrutiny-what-comes-next. Accessed 26 August 2020.

Evan, Dave. 2012. *The Internet of Everything: How More Relevant and Valuable Connections Will Change the World*. Cisco Internet Business Solutions Group. https://www.cisco.com/c/dam/global/en_my/assets/ciscoinnovate/pdfs/IoE.pdf. Accessed 26 August 2020.

Gupta, Vidushi, Vinti Agarwal, Mukesh Butani, and Sumeir Ahuja. 2020. *Removing Roadblocks in Taxing Business Income in the Digital Era: Building Global Consensus for an Equitable Solution*. Vidhi Centre for Legal policy and BMR Legal Advocates. https://vidhilegalpolicy.in/wp-content/uploads/2020/06/20200620_-Digital-Economy-report-VIDHI-and-BMR.pdf. Accessed 26 August 2020.

Kumar, Alok P., and Vinti Agarwal. 2020. Challenges in the Design of Digital Taxation in India. In *International taxation in the Digital Era*, ed. Parthasarathi Shome, 23–37. Gurugram: OakBridge Publishing Pvt. Ltd.

Martin, Julie. 2020. UN Committee Proposes New Model Treaty Provision Altering Taxation of Automated Digital Services. *MNE Tax*. https://mnetax.com/un-committee-proposes-new-model-treaty-provision-altering-taxation-of-automated-digital-services-39609. Accessed 26 August 2020.

OECD. 2001. Taxation and Electronic Commerce: Implementing the Ottawa Taxation Framework Conditions. https://doi.org/10.1787/9789264189799-en. Accessed 26 August 2020.

———. 2011. OECD Guide to Measuring the Information Society 2011. https://doi.org/10.1787/9789264113541-en. Accessed 26 August 2020.

———. 2013. OECD Communications Outlook. https://doi.org/10.1787/comms_outlook-2013-en. Accessed 26 August 2020.

———. 2015. *Addressing the Tax Challenges of the Digital Economy, Action 1 – 2015 Final Report*. OECD/G20 Base Erosion and Profit Shifting (BEPS) Project. https://doi.org/10.1787/9789264241046-en. Accessed 26 August 2020.

———. 2017. International VAT/GST Guidelines. http://www.oecd.org/tax/consumption/international-vat-gst-guidelines-9789264271401-en.htm. Accessed 26 August 2020.

———. 2018. *Tax Challenges Arising from Digitalisation – Interim Report 2018, Inclusive Framework on BEPS*. OECD/G20 BEPS Project. https://www.oecd.org/tax/tax-challenges-arising-from-digitalisation-interimreport-9789264293083-en.htm. Accessed 26 August 2020.

———. 2019a. *Addressing the Tax Challenges of the Digital Economy-Policy Note*. OECD/G20 Inclusive Framework on BEPS. https://www.oecd.org/tax/beps/policy-note-beps-inclusive-frameworkaddressing-tax-challenges digitalisation.pdf. Accessed 28 August 2020.

———. 2019b. *Programme of Work to Develop a Consensus Solution to the Tax Challenges Arising from the Digitalisation of the Economy*. OECD/G20 Inclusive Framework on BEPS. https://www.oecd.org/tax/beps/programme-of-work-to-develop-a-consensus-solution-to-the-tax-challenges-arising-from-the-digitalisation-of-the-economy.pdf. Accessed 28 August 2020.

———. 2019c. *Addressing the Tax Challenges of the Digitalisation of the Economy*. Public Consultation Document, 13 February–6 March. https://www.oecd.org/tax/beps/public-consultation-document-addressing-the-tax-challenges-of-the-digitalisation-of-the-economy.pdf. Accessed 28 August 2020.

———. 2019d. *Secretariat Proposal for a "Unified Approach" Under Pillar One*. Public Consultation Document, 9 October–12 November. https://www.oecd.org/tax/beps/public-consultation-document-secretariat-proposal-unified-approach-pillar-one.pdf. Accessed 28 August 2020.

———. 2020. *Statement by the OECD/G20 Inclusive Framework on BEPS on the Two-Pillar Approach to Address the Tax Challenges Arising from the Digitalisation of the Economy – January 2020*. OECD/G20 Inclusive Framework on BEPS. https://www.oecd.org/tax/beps/statement-by-the-oecd-g20-inclusive-framework-on-beps-january-2020.pdf. Accessed 28 August 2020.

Sekar, Kunisi R. 2018. Taxation of Digital Economy-Challenges and Response. In *Challenges in Domestic and International Taxation: Emerging Indian Experience*, ed. P. Shome, 77–145. Gurugram: OakBridge Publishing Pvt. Ltd.

# Part VI

# Tax Administration

# Structure, Customers and People 32

## 32.1 Introduction

For any tax administration, defining its objectives or targets is a good starting point. This is done through a vision statement. Senior management may articulate their vision through broad statements about increasing staff productivity, increasing customer satisfaction, minimising tax gaps and articulating a revenue strategy. For example, should a young tax administration focus on developing traditional tools for enhancing revenue, rather than sharpening precision instruments for lowering tax evasion? The answer to that has been given as follows:

> The best tax administration is not simply one that collects the most revenue. How that revenue is raised ... effect on equity ... and ... economic welfare may be equally important.[1]

Additionally, the vision of the tax administration needs to be interpreted in practical terms, representing the organisation's priorities as well as for those working within the organisation. A menu of specific, measurable objectives and key performance indicators (KPIs) needs to be in place for the different branches of the administration. These must not only reflect the day-to-day work and needs of the employees but also specify the likely consequences for over- or underperformance.[2]

Accordingly, this chapter focuses on a tax administration's integrated structure, customers and people or staff. It elaborates on governance, management, information generation, customer focus, taxpayer services, dedicated staff for services delivery, e-access to customers, e-filing, pre-filled tax returns, administrative effectiveness and customer surveys, erroneous objectives, tax gap as an appropriate criterion, cutting off any nexus between tax officer and taxpayer, preventive and punitive vigilance and cross-country advances.

---

[1] See Bird and de Jantscher (1992). See also Silvani and Baer (1997).

[2] See Crandall (2010).

 
P. Shome, *Taxation History, Theory, Law and Administration*, Springer Texts in Business and Economics, https://doi.org/10.1007/978-3-030-68214-9_32

## 32.2 Structure and Governance

### 32.2.1 Functional Directorates and Information Generation

A modern tax administration that places taxpayers, or customers, at the centre of its activities needs to structure its departments along functional lines. For example, taxes affecting businesses should be grouped separately from those for individuals. Within the business category, rather than separating corporate tax (CT) from GST, it is more rational to bring these two taxes together for administrative purposes since many commonalities exist between them. They include exchange of information and cross-verification and the fact that, for most businesses, these two taxes represent the most important of their revenue contribution. If a distinction has to be made, it is better to distinguish large businesses from small and medium enterprises (SMEs). These advantages cannot be reaped if they are separated into non-intersecting operational departments.

Similarly, maintaining close links between high-income individuals and capital gains taxes (CGT) would benefit the administration while simple-tax individuals, with only wages and interest as sources of income, could be treated under a separate function. Similarly, small businesses that have low incomes and low turnover and sales are better administered under one umbrella for ampliation of information on them.

Overall, fostering linkages enables the flow of complementary information and knowledge across tax or geographic boundaries. Downstream data analysis should, in turn, support the formulation of strategic objectives and action. For example, it could point to which customer categories should be monitored and which treated with a light touch, whether customer response vehicles such as contact centres could be cut back or revamped, whether there is a need for any one industry, say construction, to be treated differently, and others.

On the other hand, some tax officers at the field level have brought to notice that the advantages gained earlier from computerised data have tended to get reduced due to the emergence of policy decisions to accommodate the end-customer. This has resulted in a tendency to scale back on information required on tax return forms such that the possibility of subsequent tax analysis also gets truncated. The formulation of future tax policy suffers. This danger should be kept in mind rather than being glossed over in a rush to simplify procedures merely with customer convenience in mind. In other words, achieving the right balance between customer focus and protection of administration efficacy is the essence of a good vision and strategy of a tax administration.

Keeping the above-mentioned considerations in mind, a desirable functional structure is shown in Fig. 32.1.

Figure 32.1 highlights the bare essentials of the point being made. It differentiates tax divisions from functional divisions. It shows business taxes—CT and VAT—in one column, which is then divided between large businesses and small and medium enterprises (SMEs). Individual or personal income tax (PIT) and CGT appear in one column and are then divided between complex individuals (with many sources of

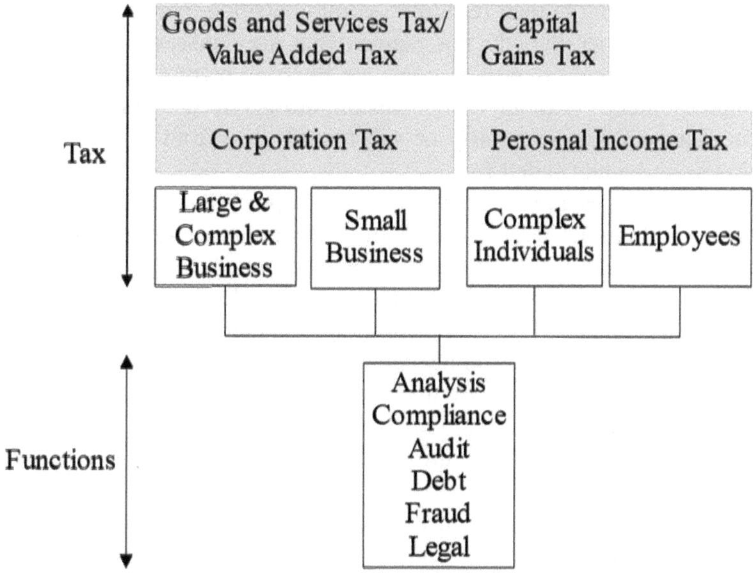


**Fig. 32.1** Functional structure. (Source: Shome (2012))

income) and employees (with salaries alone, or salaries plus interest). Under these two major tax divisions are grouped various functions such as analysis, compliance, audit, debt, fraud and legal matters. The administration structure could be set up in a way that the various 'tax' departments could 'buy' services from 'functional' departments by apportioning their internally allocated resources. This is the way some advanced tax administrations have set up their structures.

### 32.2.2 Management

With the above overall organisational structure, the next question is what its management set-up should be. The deepest lacunae are found in this area. At the core could be a flawed recruitment process. The rules and regulations that determine recruitment practices are a key element in the induction and maintenance of a dynamic staff structure.

On the one hand, private sector tax professionals tend to voice the need for skilful counterparts with whom they can interface. On the other hand, a part of the private sector tax advisory community—tax advisors—may market tax avoidance schemes that are likely to be strictly within the law but often eschew the spirit or principle behind it. To tackle the challenge successfully, astute tax professionals must be represented in the top layer of a tax administration. Other officials may focus on management including human resources, communication, budget control or understanding the customer that do not demand tax specialisation at the top level.[3] Experience reveals that tax professionals are likely to be represented insufficiently in top management. Without this inclusion, however, it is unlikely that a tax administration can systematically, or successfully, confront the private advisory profession as and when called for.

It is crucial to establish, maintain and support links among the different participating professions in the organisation of a tax administration that would foster understanding across all areas of the administration and at all levels. It is preferable for all senior leaders and decision-makers to have at least some knowledge of tax systems, tax structures and tax administration to understand the full dimensions of any strategy they formulate or policy action they take. Some tax administrations in advanced and emerging economies alike have to bear the burden of top management with no tax experience. Such administrations suffer from low work productivity since performance criteria to measure the quality of work tend to move away from the context of taxation.

In terms of linking top management to lower levels, while drawing up a strategy or vision statement remains important from a management perspective, its mere script would not safeguard implementation nor filter down to field offices that are generally manned by tax inspectors trained in the details of tax law and procedures. Hence, a meaningful link from the organisation's vision architects down to the level of field operations is crucial.

Figure 32.2 presents an example of the management of a tax administration comprising a governing board, a tax council, a large taxpayer unit, an independent evaluation office and commissioners for field functions. Functions such as dispute management, taxpayer services, research and analysis and others would be required to converge with the suggested structure below.

The primary goal of a tax administration management ought not to be to meet merely revenue targets but to maximise compliance and minimise the 'tax gap', defined as the difference between potential tax revenue and actual collection. All good tax administrations build their compliance strategies on the foundation of sound risk management around the promotion of voluntary compliance by moving its environment towards the compliant end of the taxpayer spectrum.

Compliance is enhanced by segmenting taxpayers according to their inclinations to pay tax. Tax administrations need to move beyond the premise that a taxpayer is naturally inclined to evade or avoid paying tax. It is necessary to recognise that individuals and businesses have a complex set of motivations that are strongly affected by the actions of the tax administration itself, the tax system's legal framework, as well as societal norms and economic incentives.

Amongst these motivations is often a social duty to 'do the right thing'—to pay tax legitimately, albeit with the occasional error. A tax administration needs a legal

[3]Each of these aspects is a good one if contained within limits. The problem is when they are assigned excessive resources to the detriment of fields requiring tax specialisation.

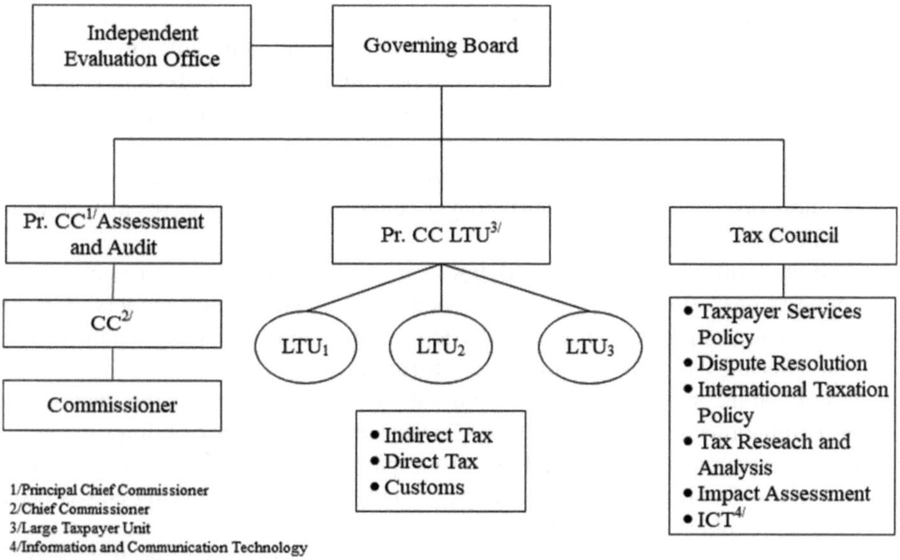


**Fig. 32.2** Management structure (see Appendix for additional figures that elaborate some of the verticals). Note: An ideal structure of the Governing Board appears in self-explanatory Fig. 32.3. (Source: Restructured from TARC (2014), First Report, Chap. III)

and applied framework to reward positive behaviour and differentiate between honest mistakes and aggressive avoidance or evasion. This will encourage voluntary compliance, thereby reducing costs to the administration. For taxpayers inclined towards compliance, taxpayer assistance is an important tool. For taxpayers disinclined towards compliance, the response has to be effective enforcement and deterrence. Specialised technological and human capabilities and suitable structures and processes to deploy enforcement tools effectively are essential elements of such a strategy.

The proposed management structure reflects such a strategy. As tax administrations move to acquire greater autonomy, a high-level board operates as the main policy-making body reporting to the minister of finance. Such bodies commonly have the mandate for oversight of the administration, providing it guidance and advice and approving its strategic priorities and plans. Key stakeholder interests, such as the government, industry and taxpayers should be represented in the composition of these bodies. Such boards, however, should not deal with the day-to-day operational aspects of the administration that are left to directors general at the next level of seniority.

### 32.2.3 Fully Integrated Tax Administration

Many modern tax administrations have, over the last few years, moved towards a fully integrated tax administration. This approach to organising work allows more standardisation for work processes across taxes, payments arrangements for taxpayers, and consolidation and use of information and communications technology (ICT) processes, all contributing to improving operational efficiency. A fully integrated tax administration would usually possess the following characteristics:

- CT, GST or VAT, selective excises and customs duties are clubbed together as business taxes to provide better taxpayer convenience to businesses as well as to ensure better taxpayer compliance.
- Staff and officers are organised under a vertical comprising principal chief commissioner (PCC), chief commissioner (CC) and commissioners (C), by functional groupings such as registration, information processing, audit, collection, appeals, and they generally work across taxes.
- Individual income tax also comes under the PCC vertical who is the final arbiter of its functions, though the CC and C's bear important responsibilities thereof.
- Large taxpayers above a threshold of tax payment or pre-tax profits should be separately classified into a large taxpayer unit (LTU), also working across taxes (See self-explanatory Fig. 32.4).
- Function-wise responsibilities including tax research and analysis, ICT, impact assessment of policy change, dispute resolution and prevention, international taxation policy, taxpayer services are included under an overall rubric of a tax council.
- An independent evaluation office reports directly to the governing board and may have access to the minister of finance (See self-explanatory Appendix Fig. 32.5).

This framework may be viewed along the lines depicted in self-explanatory Fig. 32.3, its main emphasis being that direct and indirect taxes are in a single consolidated structure, the separation of large business taxpayers for their convenience and for careful monitoring by the administration under one vertical, all regular functions beginning from the filing of returns and ending with audit and assessment and collection from small businesses and all individual taxpayers under a second vertical and, under a third vertical, all support functions including research and analysis, disputes, ICT and related matters as shown.

An effort more than fifty countries have made is to achieve a greater degree of integration between the direct tax and indirect tax silos of the tax administration through large taxpayer units (LTUs). This has helped to promote the sharing of data and to build a common framework for the delivery of services to large taxpayers. This is especially useful in those few countries that continue to separate direct tax and indirect tax operations so that essential information exchange can be carried out through LTUs. For taxpayers as well, being able to access and use a single-window system for their tax activities is usually beneficial. Some countries remain to catch up with this approach. LTUs in India, for example, need to be transformed into an operational large taxpayer unit as shown in self-explanatory Fig. 32.4. There is a need to close the gap with international practice and provide greater autonomy to its LTUs with an appropriate accountability and governance framework for them.

In sum, the establishment of LTUs is an effective initial step for improving tax administration. It should be made up of the best trained and less corruptible officers that are able to monitor tax collection from large taxpayers who, although not large in number, account for the major part, sometimes as high as 80–90 percent of tax revenue from CT, GST or VAT and selective excises.[4] At the same time, officers positioned in an LTU should be open-minded and professional enough to be able to put the best foot forward for enhancing the good reputation of their tax administration with top taxpayers.

Typically, most countries tend to have a simplified structure for small taxpayers. For instance, in the structure of a GST or VAT, there are two thresholds. Those taxpayers who fall below the first (lower) threshold, do not need to register; those who fall below the second (upper) threshold, need to register, but pay GST or VAT on a 'compounded' or turnover basis, that is, not on the basis of detailed accounts that would have given them the opportunity to participate in the debit–credit mechanism. And those above the second threshold, being in the organised sector, have to abide by conditions of accounts maintenance and are subject to audit, scrutiny and other aspects of administrative review. Such layered structures exist in most countries for the taxpayer and administrative convenience, but since they tend to modify the objective of the original tax structure in terms of the efficiency of the country's resource allocation among economic sectors, policy analysts are not particularly fond of them.

## 32.3 Customer Focus

Tax administration should begin with a customer focus. India's 2014–2015 tax administration reform commission (TARC) report,[5] rook this view and begins with a chapter on customer focus, thus revealing it as the most desirable primary focus of any tax administration. This is because a key element of the strategy for any modern tax administration has to be the customer taxpayer, where a 'customer' refers to any individual, business or agent who has a relationship with the tax administration while 'focus' refers to the wide range of activities designed to improve his experiences with the tax administration.

Reflecting an increased demand for better services by taxpayers, tax administrations increasingly recognise their obligation to offer quality services to them. With this in mind, some advanced economy tax administrations consult taxpayers regularly in groups of taxpayer categories and size and refer to taxpayers as 'stakeholders' in the functioning of a tax administration. The interaction between

[4]Tanzi and Pellechio (1995).

[5]It was a full-fledged commission rather than a committee and, in a cross-country comparison, is arguably the longest such report on tax administration in recent years.

the two is continually monitored to ensure customer focus, transparency, convenience and even a friendly approach adopted by selected administrations.[6]

Such an approach also has the potential to increase tax revenue. Perhaps taxpayers are more likely to comply voluntarily when tax administrations adopt a service-oriented approach towards them. Educating and assisting taxpayers help them meet their obligations more easily. Cross-country experience has revealed the great importance of taxpayer education in the implementation of a new tax such as the VAT or GST[7] or the introduction of electronic income tax payment in emerging economies in recent years. Taxpayer services, therefore, need to be taken as an integral and continuing part of the functions of a responsible and responsive tax administration. Taxpayers must receive clear and concise information describing what is taxable, when taxes apply and how to calculate their tax liabilities. Forms and procedures for calculating and paying taxes should be as simple as possible without sacrificing data needed for subsequent analysis.

Given this, the cost to administer taxpayers who take full advantage of the opportunity to self-assess their tax liabilities (see Chap. 33, Sect. 33.8) and accurately follow instructions and procedures for paying these liabilities, should also be low.

Indeed, the service delivery and enforcement tasks are linked. Although voluntary compliance is to be emphasised, complex tax laws skew the feasibility of proper compliance. It is, therefore, crucial to provide services to the taxpayer right from the beginning of his engagement with the administration to the end of the process. This will minimise disputes between the taxpayer and tax administration. For that, an administration, with specialised staff having the correct professional skills and attitudes, and with a service orientation, is required and has to remain a primary goal of the management's vision and strategy.

### 32.3.1 Components of Taxpayer Services

Many tax administrations set up effective programmes for taxpayer services, which include:

- Services related to the simplification of procedures to facilitate voluntary compliance.
- Easing the information flow on tax obligations through better website design or a cooperative approach from call centres, reducing the cost of uncertainty by

[6]This could be done through industry forums, meetings with account managers of major taxpayers, public consultation for proposed changes or independent reviews of the tax system. The two-way communication channels help improve perceptions of the tax administration and in finding effective solutions.

[7]See Tanzi and Pellechio (1995), op. cit.

providing clarity on tax obligations in advance for large, complex transactions, and decreasing the costs of understanding the tax system by explanatory sessions.
- Providing taxpayers with relevant and appropriate information to prepare tax returns and after filing returns.
- Facilitation of tax payment through online filing and payment.
- Manning a phone-based functional customer communication centre (CCC) with tax advisors who can respond to queries regarding the above-listed matters on a real-time basis. Several CCCs located in different regions, rather than only the capital cities, may be needed.

In sum, lowering the effective cost for compliance will make more people follow the rules (Table 32.1).

At the same time, the possibility of egregious tax avoidance and tax evasion cannot be simply set aside. A functioning, 'risk-based' approach to tax returns can play an important role in identifying tax avoidance and evasion schemes quickly, providing certainty as quickly as possible to the taxpayer and reinforcing positive customer behaviours. Essentially this is an approach in which a skilled tax professional quickly reviews returns, for example, for a business and rates them according to how much risk they pose to the tax administration.

**Table 32.1** Categories of various taxpayer services

| Service category | Description | Examples of services | Characteristics |
|---|---|---|---|
| Information | Information services and products which are one-way communication and do not result in a change in the account status. | • Education<br>• Publications (paper and web)<br>• Campaigns<br>• Mass distribution of different types of information<br>• Instructions | • Timing volume: partly predictable<br>• Size volume: flexible, can be influenced, revenue body initiate<br>• Standardisation/automation: possible in many cases |
| Interaction | Two-way communication, which in itself does not result in any change in account status. | • Enquiry<br>• Audit<br>• Guidance<br>• Debt collection | • Timing volume: partly predictable<br>• Size volume: flexible, can be influenced<br>• Standardisation/automation: difficult |
| Transaction | Activity or services that result in a change in the account status or account information. | • Filing of tax returns, VAT, etc.<br>• Payment/refund | • Timing volume: very predictable<br>• Size volume: can be influenced to a very small degree<br>• Standardisation/automation: great potential |

Source: OECD, May 2007 as reported in TARC (2014), First Report, Chap. II

Rating is based on the structure of the business's tax affairs that need to be analysed to conclude on its approach to paying tax. In the United Kingdom, for example, each large business service (LBS),[8] demarcated by a sector, has a sector specialist who is familiar with the specific industry under the LBS and is usually brought in from the private sector. A business with a low-risk score then receives fewer demands for information, audits and a generally more positive approach to the relationship. A business with a high-risk score draws more attention to detail and receives more invasive demands for information. This helps incentivise voluntary compliance and tax transparency whilst effectively cautioning those businesses that push the boundaries between tax planning and aggressive avoidance or evasion.

### 32.3.2 Dedicated Organisation and Staff for Delivery

Some administrations have segmented inquiries by taxpayers by size of taxpayers or by industry groupings. New and start-up businesses may have a separate inquiry service set up for specific service, including education, programmes to ensure correct compliance on their part and so on.

Newly trained staff may also be separated for taxpayer services. Their evaluation may be carried out to check whether the training has helped customer focus to emerge as a distinct application. The Chilean tax administration has adopted the training and evaluation approach. For placement of trained staff for taxpayer services, the Japanese tax administration considers the suitability of staff based on their ability, aptitude, past performance and personal circumstances, to increase overall efficiency in delivering taxpayer services.

### 32.3.3 E-access to Customers

Taxpayer service delivery may be based on a 'maturity model'. It comprises four stages in e-service delivery with increasing maturity in a number of dimensions such as from static content to dynamic content, publishing to interaction, generic dialogue to individualised dialogue, simple transactions to complex transactions, the inclusion of authenticated transactions, partly-automated processes to fully-automated online processes, agency-aligned delivery to citizen-centric delivery, and agency-aligned services to cross-agency services.

The first stage is a website that publishes information about services. The second stage allows users to browse, explore and interact with that data and

[8]Usually, an LBS is demarcated as a sector or a cluster of sectors such as telecom, oil and gas, banking, insurance and others.

information. The third stage allows taxpayers to transact on the tax administration's website with real-time responses to queries. The fourth stage facilitates the transaction process by allowing data-sharing and requires prior user-approval or consent in a legal framework. It is common to find that moving from stage three to stage four is challenging.

### 32.3.4 E-filing

Modern ICT methods are being used for tax collection and assessment processes that can reduce compliance costs and administrative costs for the tax administration. For example, the electronic filing of tax returns that provide built-in tax calculations is helpful. Indeed e-filing has been made mandatory in several jurisdictions, being more common for CT than for PIT. Most GST or VAT returns are also being e-filed. Brazil has 98% of its taxpayers filing electronically. India is attempting to rapidly increase the ratio of e-filers in the overall taxpayer net by intensifying its ICT orientation in the processing of tax returns.

### 32.3.5 Pre-filled Tax Returns

Pre-filled tax returns for PIT have been made feasible due to ICT advances. The tax administration pre-fills them based on information available to them. Instead of adopting an approach of using third party reports to detect unreported income, these reports are used in a pre-filling context to inform taxpayers of the information they need to fill in to meet their return filing obligations. In several North European countries and the United Kingdom, this is done by way of a pre-filled tax return that is sent to each taxpayer. This assists taxpayers early in the process rather than under an enforcement tool after the event. It has also helped reduce the administrative burden.

### 32.3.6 Evaluation of Success of E-services

The most commonly used criteria for evaluation are timeliness of specific services provided to taxpayers, quality of services delivered and taxpayer satisfaction as established via customer survey responses, trends in the adoption rate of specific services and tax administration cost reduction.

The importance of timeliness is paramount. As the taxpayer service programme progresses through the maturity model, the time expended reduces commensurately. Most tax administrations have fixed timelines for the delivery of taxpayer services. Once a tax administration has established its timelines, it communicates them to all its stakeholders and puts in place suitable mechanisms to deliver services in a fixed time period.

### 32.3.7 Customer Surveys

Surveys are carried out to assess customer needs channelled through customer relationship managers (CRMs) for the taxpayers.[9] Through such an arrangement, they cater to each taxpayer's needs individually. The data collected from surveys are subjected to data mining techniques through simulation centres—an in-house usability lab that allows the administration to understand the root causes of service demands.

The Singapore tax administration has a taxpayer feedback channel on tax policies, processes, services and initiatives. A biennial taxpayer survey reaches out to various taxpayer segments to understand and meet taxpayers' needs and expectations in a changing economic and business environment. The US tax administration conducts periodic surveys to measure the pre-filling and filing burden of individual taxpayers. The sample design ensures (1) a sufficient number of respondents within and across strata, (2) reliability of estimates and (3) facilitates comparisons between a current year survey and that of the previous year.

Transparency through published annual reports and official statistics is crucial. At the same time, tax administrations need to be aware of their access to confidential and personal information and of the need to protect the confidentiality of such information.

### 32.3.8 Whole-of-Government Approach

Several countries require a single registration for individuals and businesses, the registration number used for all purposes by all branches of government. This makes it easier for a taxpayer to comply. This is because common processes and services across different government agencies are shared through the use of ICT to achieve benefits of scale and reduce duplication of filing requirements. On the administration side, it improves inter-agency collaboration while moving away from a 'silo' approach to administration.

[9]The UK tax administration, for example, has put in place CRMs for each of its approximately 700 largest UK businesses. CRM is a well-known concept to the private sector today, for example, in banking.

### 32.3.9 Taxpayers' Rights and Complaints

Recognition of the rights of a taxpayer is an emerging trend. The Netherlands has codified these rights in the tax law. India's tax charter has also been put into law in 2020. It is an opportunity to build trust between the taxpayer and administration with a potential for practical protection for taxpayers by making tax law predictable and compliable. Others such as Australia, India, Ireland, New Zealand, Singapore and South Africa have taxpayer charters that are essentially tax administration documents.

Some tax administrations have special institutional arrangements to deal with taxpayers' complaints. Dedicated bodies like the Ombudsman in Australia, Canada, the United Kingdom, Brazil, South Africa and tax mediators in Belgium and France look into tax-related complaints. These bodies are independent of the tax administration. In many countries, they have been set up under a specific law. The primary purpose of the Ombudsman is to ensure that taxpayers have an opportunity to raise issues when they feel they have been treated in an unfair manner. India too has set up an office of the Ombudsman at different places. However, taxpayers may remain doubtful to file formal complaints for fear of retaliation, whether unfounded or not, from the tax administration.

An accountability framework is required to ensure that responses to taxpayers are delivered accurately, consistently and promptly without any compromise to the standards and quality of service delivery. If taxpayers remain dissatisfied with the framework, improvements would be needed for better performance and greater accountability to be able to move steadily towards taxpayer satisfaction.

The United States has a tax advocate service (TAS), an independent organisation within the tax administration that attempts to ensure that taxpayers are aware and understand their rights, thereby ensuring fair and just treatment. It guides them through complex processes involved in resolving tax problems. It makes recommendations to help prevent future problems. A taxpayer can approach the TAS at any stage when he is unable to resolve a problem caused by little response to his queries from the tax authorities, or if he faces financial difficulties or imminent threat of adverse action. The TAS provides services including assigning a lawyer to assist him.

India's initial step in 2010 was the introduction of a Citizen's Charter by the Central Board of Direct Taxes (CBDT) in the form of administrative guidelines. The charter included a service delivery standard, expectations from taxpayers and a grievance redressal mechanism. However, it failed to protect taxpayers as it does not have any legislative backing.[10]

In 2014, TARC[11] pointed to

[10] See Girish (2020).

[11] TARC (2014), First Report, p. 26.

an urgent need to revisit the present citizen's charter to make it more meaningful and customer focused. The citizen's charter should be renamed the taxpayers' charter to focus on all categories of taxpayers.

The tax administration system underwent several changes in the area of digitisation of procedures to ensure easier taxpayer compliance, complemented by circulars and notifications issued for protecting the interests of taxpayers as regards demands from the tax administration. However, those measures did not prove effective.

Most recently, India's finance minister announced yet another Taxpayers' Charter in the central government's 2020 budget. Entitled, 'Transparent Taxation—Honouring the Honest', it was unveiled effective 13 August 2020. The new aspect was that it has legislative backing through an insertion of Section 119A in the Income-tax Act. The CBDT has mandated the adoption of the taxpayers' charter. Other countries that have adopted the Taxpayers' Charter as part of the statute are Belgium, Brazil, Chile, Italy, the United States, Kenya and Mexico.

In conclusion, the obligations of a tax administration to enforce the law, and meeting legitimate expectations of taxpayers based on a charter, are a difficult balance to achieve.[12] A successful charter should create a trust-based relationship between taxpayers and the tax authorities and reduce harassment of taxpayers who are given legislative rights. It is also important to protect the interest of the tax administration for the successful implementation of the charter. Thus, the quality and implementation of orders, instructions, directions and guidance issued by the tax administration and the ability of taxpayers to abide by them determine the success of a charter.

## 32.4 People Function[13]

### 32.4.1 Recruitment

Advanced economy tax administrations use this term to refer to the tax administration staff. Rather than thinking of them as staff, they should be considered as people whose welfare should comprise an intrinsic objective of the administration and its management. Alternatively, it may be referred to as human resources. While few administrations have the autonomy to depart from public service pay structures, several governments increasingly allow some autonomy to their tax administrations in hiring numbers and types of people with the requisite skills and qualifications, and in the nature of contracts. Lateral entry through open recruitment into the tax administration is usually allowed, especially at senior management levels. However, practices are circumscribed by the overall budgetary allocations received. Few

[12]See Butani and Shah (2020).

[13]See TARC (2014), op. cit., Chap. IV, and Shome (2012), Chap. 2.

countries adhere to any strict service or cadre structure such as one that India maintains, breaking from international norms as they have developed in recent years.

Brazil caters to professionalised recruitment at the top level. Its revenue secretary (deputy minister in charge of taxation) is not a member of congress (parliament), but is usually a career technocrat from the centre or a state and selected on the basis of experience in financial or fiscal matters. This, in fact, is a model that matches that of the United States and the rest of the Americas. Nominees for such high-level positions are examined and confirmed by congress's lower and upper houses. This is to ensure and safeguard professional—rather than exclusively administrative—knowledge and competence in public sector analysis and decision-making.

Other senior positions in the US government have also been filled from a pool of professionals from both the public and private sectors after testing and confirmation by congress. This generally ensures that tasks and operations are carried out by specialists who can deal confidently with the private sector positioned across the table. It is not that mistakes or partisanship in appointments do not occur in such a system but they are less damaging than the routine, usually seniority-based, positioning of administrators in professional public sector jobs without adequate knowledge of the subject.

### 32.4.2 Training and Specialisation

People concerns include the development of a human resources management strategy, policies, systems and procedures to protect people while achieving the tax administration's objectives. Australia completed a job profiling exercise to categorise all staff positions, the objective being to identify jobs, streamline recruitment for those jobs and implement robust work levels standards for each job. Many tax administrations conduct assessments of their current and future needs for skills and capability and instal structured training and professional development. Their career advancement schemes tend to be merit-based and performance-linked, often with weightage given to specific areas of training and acquisition of higher professional qualifications.

Most tax administrations adopt policies that promote the growth of specialisation and allow their personnel to advance in their chosen areas of specialisation, without limiting their tenures in any one field to short periods. Training includes commercial awareness, risk management and financial management. In South Africa, for example, staff are exposed to commercial awareness through dialogue with large corporations and participation in commercial forums reflecting a network approach that lends an appreciation of the economic climate for businesses. Tax administrations also partner with educational bodies including universities across the globe for training purposes, closely linked to the higher objective of increasing organisational capability.

### 32.4.3 Staff Assessment

The performance of staff should be measured as an ongoing process of ascertaining the quality of their performance and provide information and feedback relative to the goals of the organisation and its programmes. In turn, this enables the identification of areas that require corrective steps to improve performance. Performance assessment or measurement should be discussed with individual staff. Some administrations do not reveal staff assessment or grade. This is an erroneous policy. Some tax administrations have initiated 360° assessments for staff performance. This involves appraisals of staff not only by superiors but also by peers and subordinates.

Staff also should be allowed to react. Occasional staff surveys should attempt to gauge staff satisfaction and engagement with the system. Australia's above-mentioned job profiling exercise was also meant to deepen conversations between management and staff on performance and training requirements. The Finnish tax administration carries out a regular job satisfaction survey, and responses are discussed individually with staff members. It has helped the Finnish tax administration to improve job satisfaction over time. The Singapore tax administration receives staff feedback biannually, helping to identify how to improve the staff workplace. The US tax administration conducts annual employee surveys to obtain feedback on a wide range of workplace issues. The United Kingdom also conducts staff surveys regularly. The culture of surveys demonstrates that human resources encouragement is a key requirement for a successful tax administration.

## 32.5 Administration Effectiveness

The quality of performance of the tax administration directly affects the business climate and cost competitiveness of industry on the one hand and the ability of the government to raise revenues fairly on the other. A tax administration involves a large number of knowledge workers, working together to administer fairly the tax policies to an expanding base of taxpayers. Its mission should be to use tax policy and its administration not only to promote a culture of voluntary compliance and revenue collection but also to be cautious not to obstruct but, rather, to facilitate economic growth.

### 32.5.1 Erroneous Criteria

A poorly performing tax administration, beset with arbitrariness, constrains the growth of the economy. The effectiveness of a tax administration should be measured using meaningful tools that do not lead to flawed conclusions. For instance, a tax administration's expenditure as a percentage of revenue collection would decline if tax revenue increased as a result of higher tax rates, without any change in the tax administration's efforts. The number of taxpayers penalised, or the amounts collected from fines, are often proposed as alternative performance indicators, but these can also be misleading.

Evasion cases detected may increase as enforcement effort intensifies. Thus, higher expenditure on evasion control by a tax administration may reveal more evasion though, what effect it has on the quantum of actual—detected plus undetected—tax evasion has to be deciphered through proper analysis. Effectiveness indicators, therefore, have to be drawn up carefully when linked to such quantitative indicators and interpreted intelligently.

The general perception among taxpayers persists that the tax administration is focused on only one dimension—that of revenue generation. This perception emerges if there is a high incidence of roving enquiries, unwillingness to close assessments or lengthy duration of litigation despite the subject matter having been lost by the administration in earlier cases. In such an environment, an underlying revenue target may be endemic with a systemic emphasis on performance assessment, promotion and lucrative transfer posts reflecting an officer's success with revenue generation, irrespective of how that revenue is collected. Taxpayer confidence in such a tax administration will be non-existent.

### 32.5.2 Tax Gap: A Better Criterion

In the United Kingdom, revenue is not specified as an objective of the tax administration; the focus, rather, is on minimisation of the 'tax gap'. Attention is on whether tax evasion is minimised rather than on how much revenue is collected. This has direct implications for minimising tax avoidance and evasion, as well as moral hazard and the prevalence of graft in collection methods. On the contrary, a pure revenue maximisation objective results in twisting the taxpayer's arm during revenue shortages and in relaxing the grip—and hence a rise in leakages from both taxpayer and tax collector—during periods of plenty.

### 32.5.3 Cutting Off Nexus

Too much exposure to the tax administration fails to protect taxpayer rights or ensure transparency, tending instead to perpetuate an unhealthy relationship in a situation in which there should be no relationship at all. The practice of linking a taxpayer to a tax officer through a 'file' system, wherever it still exists, should be discontinued. In most advanced economies such as the United Kingdom, such a possibility would not occur since each tax function pertaining to an individual taxpayer would be administered by a different tax officer wearing a particular functional hat.

In August 2020, the Indian finance minister floated the concept of a faceless assessment system that replaced the phrase 'e-assessment'.[14] An e-assessment centre may issue a notice to the assessee but will have to specify the issues for selection of his case for assessment; and the assessee will have 15 days to respond. The case will be assigned by the national e-assessment centre, through an automated allocation system, to any regional e-assessment centre. The regional centre may request and obtain further information on the taxpayer file from the national centre and seek technical assistance from a technical unit or a verification unit through the national centre which will redirect that request. Once the report is obtained, it will forward it to the regional assessment centre. The intention is apparently to cut off direct links not only between taxpayer and tax officer, but also within departments and, instead, to channel interdepartmental communication only through an automated national department.

It is too early to tell how this will be taken by tax officers and taxpayers alike since there are inconveniences attached to both. From a practical point of view, it is to be seen how an assessment file from a major metropolitan city could be assigned and completed successfully in an office in a small tax office across the country. Nevertheless, if it can be implemented successfully, it would comprise good reform since it would cut out the many webs of nexus that exist today.

## 32.6 Preventive and Punitive Vigilance

Vigilance is a term that is sometimes used to keep vigil on the officers, that is, on their corporate and social behaviour as well as on corruption. It comprises (1) preventive vigilance that deters the occurrence of moral lapses or unacceptable conduct and (2) punitive vigilance that comprises punishment for such conduct. Experience reveals that punishment against corruption must be quick and decisive, such as immediate suspension followed by final punishment. Administrations that introduce too many checks and balances have not been able to rid themselves of this malaise. Without the unquestionable integrity of top management, corruption is likely to continue.

## 32.7 Cross-country Advances

African nations such as Kenya, Rwanda, South Africa and Tanzania have been focusing on modern aspects of tax administration, judiciously utilising international experiences from the IMF, UK's DFID, Denmark's DANIDA[15] and other providers of technical assistance. Asian nations such as Bangladesh, Cambodia, Nepal and

[14] See Government of India (2020).

[15] International Monetary Fund (IMF), UK Department for International Development (DFID) and Danish International Development Agency (DANIDA).

Thailand have also done so, though India has by and large not interacted with the international community in this fashion. This is not to say that there is no networking at all. Participation in select international forums such as the Customs Cooperation Council has resulted in the standardisation of customs tariffs and valuation, and at the OECD in a steering committee on emerging international taxation issues has led to sharing of ideas.

Many tax administrations have opted for introducing LTU's or, as in the case of the United Kingdom, have restructured tax administration targeted towards large businesses in major economic sectors as already mentioned. This has allowed offering single-window service to large taxpayers while providing synergies to the tax administration for all taxes a large business pays through cross-checks and joint audits. A few countries such as India have introduced LTUs but have been unable to comprehensively serve both direct and indirect tax branches of the administration through LTUs.

## 32.8 Conclusions

Certain norms have developed globally in how to structure a successful tax administration. It is agreed today that the best structure is along functional lines. It is also necessary to consider what taxes are paid by groups of taxpayers in both direct and indirect taxes and to enable taxpayers to pay them as well as to carry out other compliance responsibilities through one window. It is important for a tax administration to treat taxpayers in the best way possible while clamping down on tax evasion. Tax officers should also be given independence to deal with taxpayers while corruption should be dealt with briskly.

It is imperative for tax officers to be able to specialise in a particular branch of tax administration function or policy and to adhere to it with advancement. This is needed for the tax administration to be able to handle highly knowledgeable private-sector tax advisers across the table with their own matching knowledge. This can happen only if the top management of a tax administration comprises professionals who themselves know tax as a subject rather than being recruited at senior levels from a purely management background. If these guidelines are adhered to, a successful tax administration will be the outcome.

# Appendix

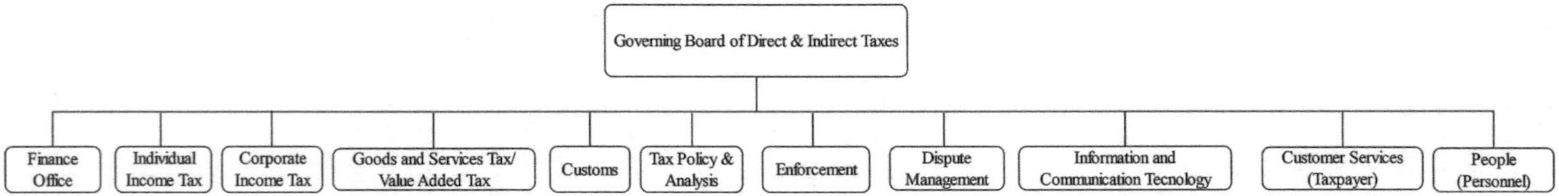


**Fig. 32.3** Structure of tax administration. (Source: Restructured from TARC (2014), First Report, Chap. III)

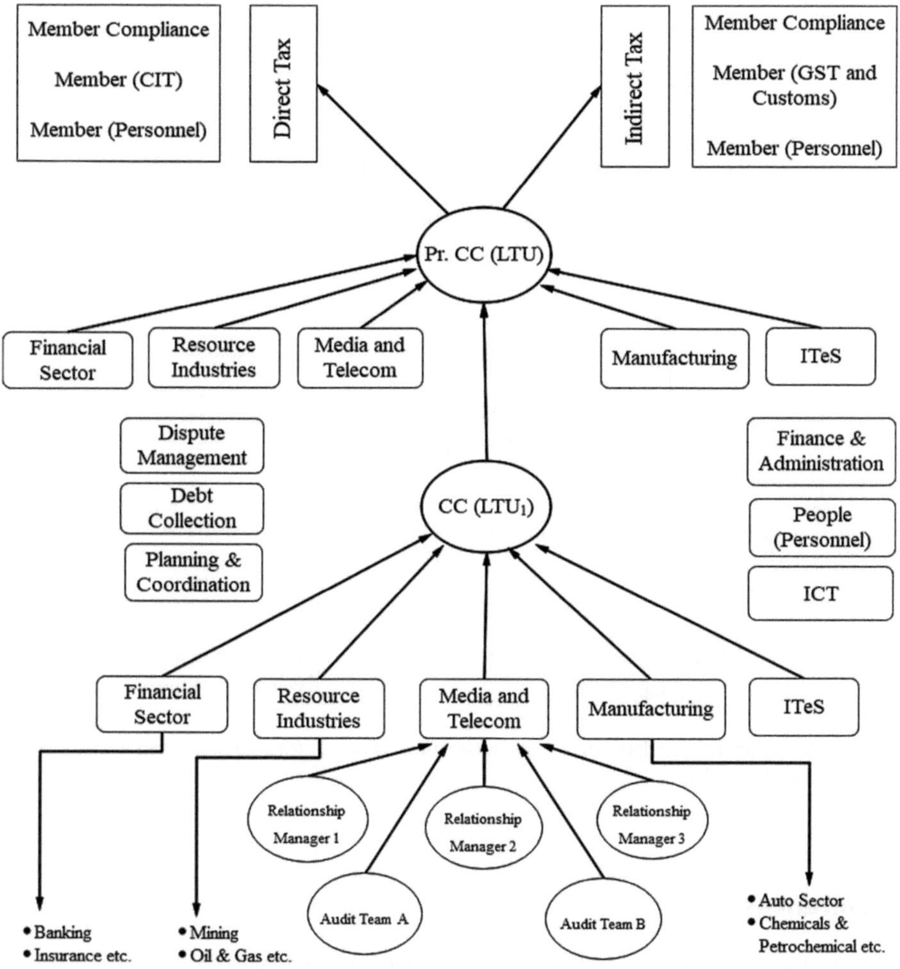


**Fig. 32.4** Large Taxpayer Unit (LTU). Same structure would apply to $LTU_2$ and $LTU_3$ depicted in text Fig. 32.2. (Source: Restructured from TARC (2014), First Report, Chap. III). *CC* Chief Commissioner, *CIT* Corporate Income Tax, *GST* Goods and Services Tax; *ICT* Information and Communication Technology, *ITeS* Information Technology Enabled Services, *LTU* Large Taxpayer Unit

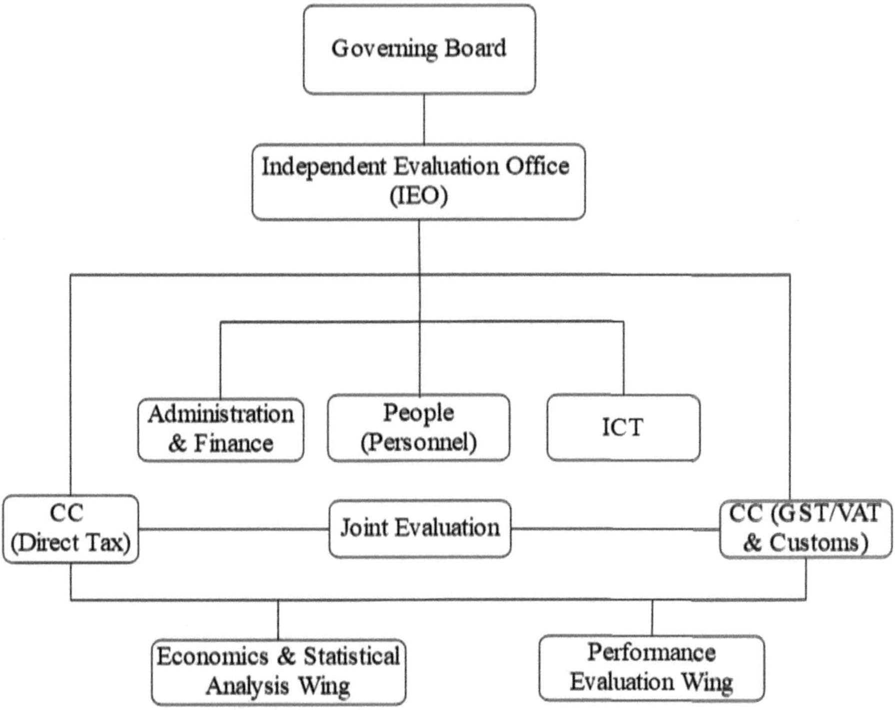


**Fig. 32.5** Structure of independent evaluation office. (Source: Restructured from TARC (2014), First Report, Chap. III)

## References

Bird, Richard Miller, and Milka Casanegra de Jantscher, eds. 1992. *Improving Tax Administration in Developing Countries*. Washington DC: International Monetary Fund (IMF).

Butani, Mukesh, and Shreyash Shah. 2020. Taxpayer Charter: A Roadmap for Mutual Trust and Respect. *Financial Express*, August 21.

Crandall, William Joseph. 2010. *Revenue Administration: Performance Measurement in Tax Administration*. Technical Notes and Manuals No. 2010/11. https://www.imf.org/en/Publications/TNM/Issues/2016/12/31/Revenue-Administration-Performance-Measurement-in-Tax-Administration-23956. Accessed 17 November 2020.

Girish, K.R. 2020. Taxpayers' Charter—Cure to Long-drawn Concerns? *Taxsutra*. https://www.taxsutra.com/experts/column?sid=1594. Accessed 30 August 2020.

Government of India. 2020. *Income-Tax*. The Gazette of India: Extraordinary, Notification No. 61/2020 [F.No.370149/154/2019-TPL]/SO 1746(E). https://www.incometaxindia.gov.in/communications/notification/notification_61_2020.pdf. Accessed 30 August 2020.

Shome, Parthasarathi. 2012. *Tax Shastra: Administrative Reforms in India, United Kingdom and Brazil*. New Delhi: Business Standard Books.

Silvani, Carlos, and Katherine Baer. 1997. *Designing a Tax Administration Reform Strategy: Experiences and Guidelines*. Working Paper No. WP/97/30. https://www.imf.org/en/Publications/WP/Issues/2016/12/30/Designing-a-Tax-Administration-Reform-Strategy-Experiences-and-Guidelines-2134. Accessed 30 August 2020.

Tanzi, Vito, and Anthony Pellechio. 1995. *The Reform of Tax Administration*. IMF Working Paper No. WP/95/22. https://www.elibrary.imf.org/doc/IMF001/07242-9781451843941/07242-9781451843941/Other_formats/Source_PDF/07242-9781455256402.pdf. Accessed 8 September 2020.

Tax Administration Reform Commission (TARC). 2014. *Tax Administration Reform in India: Spirit, Purpose and Empowerment (First Report)*. New Delhi: Government of India.

# 33 Key Administration Processes

## 33.1 Introduction

A tax administration has some core functions. They include taxpayer registration, tax payments, filing tax returns for both direct and indirect taxes. They include, among others, taxpayer identification, registration and payment arrangements, audit and scrutiny and, in association, developing risk-based audit selection and protocols, training and placement of audit staff on the basis of competency and specialisation in carrying out audit and scrutiny, and combined audit of direct and indirect taxes such as income tax and GST or VAT.

Core functions also include the application of tax deducted at source (TDS), carrying out refunds and foreign tax credit in a timely manner, installing self-assessment requirements and procedures thereof, and using tax recovery when needed to minimise delinquency or eliminate stopfilers. What emerges is that processes can become quite complicated unless simplicity for ease of compliance and administrative convenience are preserved and nurtured as a strategy and an objective to be achieved. This chapter elaborates on those core functions of a tax administration.

## 33.2 Taxpayer Registration

Taxpayer identification and registration are the first-contact functions of a tax administration vis-à-vis a taxpayer. The tax administration in every country requires the allotment of a taxpayer identification number (TIN) or permanent account number (PAN)[1] to a taxpayer if his income, or that of any other person for whom he is assessable to tax during a financial year, exceeds the maximum amount not

[1]In India it is termed PAN. See TARC (2014), First Report. Also see Asian Development Bank (2018).



P. Shome, *Taxation History, Theory, Law and Administration*, Springer Texts in Business and Economics, https://doi.org/10.1007/978-3-030-68214-9_33

chargeable to income tax.[2] A TIN is also compulsorily required for charitable trusts. TIN is required to be quoted by a person in all his returns, correspondence with the tax administration, and invoices for the payment of any sum due under the tax law, whether income tax or Goods and Services Tax (GST), as well as for bank transactions, property transactions, and so on.[3]

Issuance of TIN requires details of correct name, father's name and date of birth, but many countries require more information such as address to ensure follow-up if needed. Any change of address should be immediately reported; otherwise, the continuance of a wrong address could hamper correspondence between the tax administration and the taxpayer.

Some countries follow a system of territoriality in which an assessment officer (AO) is assigned jurisdiction over a particular taxpayer. India followed such a system that was considered inefficient, for example, the same AO would continue to deal with his 'file' even though the taxpayer may have moved. And since the system required his appearance before the AO whenever called to do so, the system suffered from a great deal of impracticality. Requests by a taxpayer to move his file to a location had become a monumental task that could take years to accomplish. In August 2020, the Indian government introduced a framework of 'faceless assessment' delinking an AO from any taxpayer.

A one-time registration is enabled through the adoption of TIN into a common business identification number (CBIN) by other government departments such as GST, selected excises, customs and pension and provident fund organisations. From the government's point of view, this makes the identification of a taxpayer convenient and quick, as in Australia and the United States. However, this is not an easy task since many government departments have to come together to make the consolidation possible. Quoting TIN in all transaction documents should be required by law. This would enable comparisons of data and information across departments, including the verification of identity and location of the business, bank account details, nature of business undertaken, list of company directorships and others.

## 33.3 Tax Payments

Tax administrations are increasingly computerising tax payments through tax identification network systems that enable taxpayers to make tax payments through a net-banking facility. Usually, the taxpayer's bank processes the transaction online by debiting his bank account with the tax amount and generates a printable acknowledgement indicating an invoice identification number. Many tax administrations

[2]Usually, for tax purposes, a person is defined as an individual, a joint family, a company or corporation, a partnership firm, an association of persons, a local authority or an artificial juridical person.

[3]There should be a mechanism to revoke TIN on the death of a TIN holder or on the closure of a business. Otherwise it can lead to a pool of infructuous TINs.

have already legislated e-payments of major direct and indirect taxes for taxpayers above a stipulated threshold.

There are, however, some intrinsic challenges for the efficient functioning of fledgling e-systems. For example, an employer or service purchaser from a taxpayer may be obligated by the government to withhold tax while making any payment. But this may not get correctly reflected in the taxpayer's account with the government. This is likely to lead to denial of credit for taxes already paid for no fault of the taxpayer. There may also be differences between the data seen on the taxpayer's screen and that seen by the AO who may consequently deny tax credit. This, in turn, could lead to considerable delay in receiving refund due to the taxpayer from the government. With the expansion of the number of payment gateways,[4] mismatches could be more easily traced.

## 33.4 Filing Tax Returns

Tax returns are filed several times a year by a taxpayer as required by the government for different taxes. Many tax administrations use returns to collect customer feedback on important elements such as ease of filing, time taken to file and cost of compliance. Information so collected is used to improve customer service, as elaborated in Chap. 32.

Three steps may be identified for the tax return process. First, when filed, it undergoes routine assessment or a checking of correctness of the entries on the return and other such routine information. The ICT system crosschecks any tax TDS already made by employers or purchasers from the taxpayer, incomes reported by employers and contractors, interest earned from banks and financial institutions and other sources on the government's list. If no error is found, the ICT system refunds any tax due to the taxpayer.

The second step enables a taxpayer to be picked for a more detailed audit that may require the submission of supporting documents by him. A third step may be an even more detailed scrutiny. If not satisfied, the tax administration may call for an investigation in an extreme case of suspected tax evasion which is illegal. And the worst case is one of contraband, smuggling and so on.

### 33.4.1 Direct Taxes

**Single Return** If there is a wealth tax, in that case, income and wealth taxes should have a single return and be processed together in a computerised, central processing centre (CPC). The CPC should be set up using the latest available ICT and preferably

[4]A payment gateway is an e-commerce application for a service provider that authorises credit card payments for e-businesses, online retailers, bricks and clicks, or traditional brick and mortar. It is the equivalent of a physical point of sale terminal located in most retail outlets.

as a joint public–private sector project. Both compliance and audit of income tax and wealth tax would substantially improve.

Even after its wealth tax was abolished, India has continued to require the submission of wealth data in its income tax returns. Whether this is a legitimate premise for gathering taxpayer information remains doubtful. Some experts have advised the reintroduction of a wealth tax in which case, of course, asking for data on both income and wealth in the same return would be legitimate.

**Accompaniments and Frequency of Returns** Filing corporate income tax returns is mandated on an annual basis, though advanced tax payments are also usually required. Returns are filed together with relevant tax audit reports and certificates for the deductions and exemptions claimed in the tax return. Returns are usually required to be signed by the managing director (MD) or, in the absence of the MD, by a director. Some countries allow the chief financial officer (CFO) of a business to sign a tax return instead of only the MD in order to simplify and facilitate tax compliance.

**Litigation Disclosures in The Return** Some experts feel that a return should be accompanied by a short report on ongoing litigation, if any, between the tax administration and the taxpayer, indicating the factual and legal position as perceived by the taxpayer. Emerging economies generally do not have such requirements, though India's tax administration reform commission (TARC) recommended it in its 2014–2015 report. The intention behind such a document is for taxpayers to be protected from any allegation of non-disclosure, suppression or escapement of income though, on the other hand, it could lead to a taxpayer's confidential or sensitive information to be revealed to the tax administration in contradiction to his self-interest.

**Eschewing a Jurisdiction** In advanced economy tax administrations, usually, there is no territorial jurisdiction. Since data can be sought through an e-system, and uploaded by the taxpayer, his personal presence for hearings in tax cases should not be needed except in very complex cases. If required, video conferencing can be used to hear the views of taxpayers or their representatives. These should be recorded for future reference if needed.

### 33.4.2 Indirect Taxes

**Centralised Processing** Tax departments should adopt centralised processing of tax returns and TDS returns, enabling speedy processing and issuing of refunds without delay. Many emerging economies including India have introduced centralised processing in their GST or VAT. The challenge arises in 'auto-populating' an output tax return with an input tax return. As a taxpayer A enters his TIN on the output return, the information on his input tax paid should get automatically filled, with the information flowing from manufacturer B or trader C from whom A had bought his inputs.

The automaticity would occur because B and C would be required to have submitted A's TIN number when they had submitted their tax returns. The fool-proof characteristics of a GST or VAT can occur only when such an automatic and automated process is in place. However, some countries including India have not been able to instal an auto-population feature in their ICT framework thus far. In that case, time-consuming, manual cross-checks slow down administrative processing and taxpayer refunds.

**Jurisdiction Free Returns** Many tax administrations in emerging economies require monthly or quarterly filing of returns for each of a taxpayer's registered premises with the geographically jurisdictional office. In India, it is likewise though large businesses registered under the Large Taxpayer Unit (LTU) may file returns for all premises with the LTU. With India's new federal GST that covers both central and state governments, a major compliance challenge for a taxpayer is that he may be picked up for assessment and audit by any state-level administration where he conducts business.

**Credit Matching and e-Invoicing** Nevertheless, tax evasion may appear as a compliance risk to the tax administration in particular where a taxpayer may avail input tax credit without paying tax on an input. This problem appears in advanced economies as well, though with a greater incidence in emerging and developing economies. Only detection systems based on advanced ICT can address the problem adequately. Ideally, a tax administration should issue all invoices from an e-portal that is compatible with the invoicing systems of companies. But this has not been achieved comprehensively in most emerging economies.

## 33.5 Audit and Scrutiny

Audit and scrutiny refer to a tax administration's process of examining a taxpayer file. They are crucial functions because they are administrative verticals that are responsible for detecting errors, avoidance and evasion, if any, of taxpayers. As such they are considered a specialised aspect of tax administration.

### 33.5.1 Developing Specialisation

It is important for tax officers to develop specialisation and domain knowledge of economic sectors to be able to carry out effective audits.[5] In advanced tax administrations, industry experts and outside specialists in areas such as international accounting standards and accounting fraud recognition provide valuable inputs. This enables audit and scrutiny assessment to be based on knowledge, analysis and intelligence.

In the absence of a balanced approach supported by specialised professionals, it is likely that roving enquiries, high pitched assessments and unreasonable demands from taxpayers may become routine practice unless strictly controlled by

[5]See Chap. 32, Sect. 32.4.2, for details on specialisation.

administration management. Hence, the practice of a transaction-based approach to data gathering and examination thereof should be replaced by a systems-based one to facilitate timely and transparent data gathering and analysis for audit purposes.

### 33.5.2 Developing Audit Protocols

Internationally, many countries categorise audits reflecting the detail with which it has to be conducted. The categories include in-depth comprehensive audit, less-detailed desk audit, and specific audit, among others. The aspects covered are determined through risk assessment information. India has made some progress towards issue-based audits and scrutiny, though desk audits continue to prevail.

Recently, the Indian government announced a faceless assessment scheme that promises to cut off any nexus between tax officers and taxpayers[6] as mentioned in Chap. 32, Sect. 32.5.3. But what if the taxpayer fails to comply? This is addressed in some detail in the government announcement.

Essentially, an AO will not be able to summon a taxpayer to his office. If the tax administration, on the recommendation of an AO, issues a notice, the taxpayer would have the right to 'show cause' within a date and time specified in the notice, as to why the assessment in his case should not be undertaken to the best of its judgement. Otherwise, he should file his response with asked-for details. His file is then transmitted to a national e-assessment centre (NEC). NEC may take a view on the file or, as needed, send it to one of several regional e-assessment centres (REC). When a view emerges, the AO will be informed. The latter will inform the taxpayer of the final finding regarding income declared, or sum payable, or sum refundable. The AO will also send a copy of the draft order to the NEC.

In the faceless assessment model, various checks and balances are built in to ensure impartiality in the taxpayer's treatment reflecting the number of departments that will get involved in the process. Several opportunities will also be given to the taxpayer to reply with questions or information-based responses. After completion of the assessment, the NEC will transfer all electronic records of the case to the original AO having jurisdiction over the case for any future action.

The crucial element in the process will be that the taxpayer would not come to know who the officers have been in assessing his file or in which tax office they may be located. The taxpayer would not be required to appear either personally or through any authorised representative in connection with any proceedings during the assessment at the NEC or REC that would have been involved in the process. If the chief commissioner approves a personal hearing, it must be conducted only through video conferencing or any ICT application software. The tax administration will establish suitable facilities for video conferencing.

If it becomes a successful process, it will represent a major advance for the Indian tax administration. Rolling out ICT-based processes has posed major challenges,

[6]Government of India (2020).

however, in the implementation of GST as described above. Whether this particular assessment process in income tax will be successful, only actual experience will reveal. What is clear is that the administration is making efforts to modernise tax administration.

### 33.5.3 Combined Audit of Taxes

Indirect tax administration may be organised separately for GST and customs. Nevertheless, taxpayer compliance benefits from joint audit of the two as most of the tax functions are repeated for them. For example, export verification for input tax credit is applicable to customs but also to GST or VAT. Requiring taxpayers to undergo two audits, even though the business and financial records on which the taxes are assessed are the same, is unjustifiably overburdening a taxpayer. The audit commissionerates should undertake integrated audits covering GST and customs together. Most countries also have onsite post clearance customs audit in the case of accredited clients. These could be conveniently used for GST audit as well, as the records and books to be verified are common to both taxes.

As an advanced step, joint audit can be extended to both direct taxes and indirect taxes. There would be co-ordinated action for income tax, GST or VAT, and customs. In a joint audit, a single audit team with competencies in individual taxes would conduct a taxpayer examination, in particular for large taxpayers. A joint audit is likely to result in more streamlined fact-finding, quicker issue resolution and more effective compliance. These advances should shorten examination processes and reduce costs for both tax administrations and taxpayers.

### 33.5.4 Training and Placement of Audit Staff

The proportion of staff deployed for audit operations should be sufficiently high and appropriately trained, considering the importance of this function. Audit capabilities should be enhanced by identifying the required competencies and providing training accordingly. Different competencies may be identified in different areas of compliance verification and segments of taxpayers. Given limited staff resources, the number of staff in routine assessment functions may have to be cut back in light of it getting increasingly computerised through ICT systems. Audit staff should be retained for a sufficiently long assignment to develop and apply field competence for detecting non-compliance. They should be accountable and responsible for audits undertaken by them.

### 33.5.5 Risk-Based Scrutiny and Audit Selection

An audit should begin with a risk-based collection of information and data from external and internal sources. The ICT system should be efficient with no conflicting data. Therefore, prior data cleansing is needed. Typically, risk profiling should include:

- Identifying and evaluating risk by using a range of financial and tax-specific indicators, and knowledge of a taxpayer's activities and transactions from third party sources.
- Comparing the accounting results with the tax results reported by the taxpayer with those of his market peers falling within a class of industry. The analysis should identify across-the-board patterns, trends and risks, and specific cases in which tax results appear to be inconsistent with accounting performance.
- Matching information relating to taxpayer's transactions, including in respect of investments and expenditure, available from other departments and agencies, own intelligence and publicly available information such as stock exchange reporting and news reports.
- Utilising information provided by local field formations other than the main audit team.
- Posting relevant information about a taxpayer, or taxpayers with related transactions, litigation history, and dispute analysis may be considered in extreme cases. And
- Ascertaining the potential quantum of under-reported income through appropriate analysis.

A tax administration should not disclose any information regarding its audit selection strategy and the number of taxpayers to be audited in a given period of time.[7] However, it should be followed as a dictum that, if a tax return is compliant with an acceptable risk score, that return does not need to be picked up for audit or scrutiny.

### 33.5.6 Documentation Requirement

For audit, on the taxpayer's side, he is obliged to maintain appropriate documentation. Often, a list of transactions has to be submitted with a tax return while details of those transactions have to be retained and preserved. If, during audit, documentation is not provided, the taxpayer is likely to face a variety of penalties. Adequate documentation is characterised by (1) the timely manner in which details are prepared and submitted to tax authorities upon their request; and (2) the sufficiency of the details demonstrating the taxpayer's compliance.

Excessively detailed and stringent documentation requirements could increase compliance costs and become burdensome to the taxpayer. The tax administration should, therefore, frame any documentation requirement keeping in view that such documentation should be reasonable. In extreme cases, the tax administration is

[7]See Tanzi and Pellechio (1995).

known to have entered office premises and carted off lorries full of documents from a taxpayer's office, sometimes including trade secrets and business plans. A taxpayer should be protected by law that ensures transparent reasons as to why such action may be necessary and in what form the documents should be returned to him.

## 33.6 Tax Deducted at Source

Tax deducted at source (TDS) and tax collected at source (TCS)—or withholding taxes—are practices that governments have passed on to the responsibility to private corporations and businesses. Currently, no tax administration exists that does not utilise it. It is a way of capturing revenue at the moment an income is earned or a transaction is carried out, respectively representing 'pay as you earn' and 'collect as it is being earned'. Governments have justified this practice since withholding an amount of tax from payments of income or expenditure made to taxpayers by employers or contractors significantly reduces, if not eliminates, chances of understating income. This reflects the trail TDS and TCS create for any subsequent audit. Also, administrations do not have to wait for the end of the year to receive revenue; instead, remittances, as incomes are earned during a year, ensure a regular revenue flow that buttresses treasury management.

Specific deduction and compliance rules are laid out for the tax deductor. To begin, he has to furnish a certificate of withholding to the person from whom tax is deducted. In an automated system, any error on the deductor's part may require him to submit the entire return afresh. The process of uploading an entire file for one or two corrections may be cumbersome and disproportionate to the gravity of the error. Thus, there are fixed costs that a deductor has to bear for carrying out a function that should actually rest on the tax administration. Therefore, some compensation for deductors is justified. It could be a small commission or deduction as business expenses from taxable income. Very few countries provide for such compensation, however.

## 33.7 Refunds and Foreign Tax Credit

### 33.7.1 Refunds

A grievance that is not uncommon among emerging economy individuals and businesses is the slow speed with which their tax refunds are received from the tax administration even when directed by appellate or court orders. It has been found that, in a few countries, delaying refunds tends to be used as a tool to augment tax collections. In turn, it adversely affects the cash flow of businesses, especially small taxpayers. It also discourages 'fence-sitters' who cannot decide whether to register and come into the tax net. Therefore, the issuance of refunds should follow strict timelines.

Refunds should carry the designated and applicable interest without exception, and non-payment or under-payment of interest by the government is an unacceptable administrative limitation. For transparency, refunds should be disbursed through an ICT based system, which should calculate the interest due. The EU encourages the filing for refunds via the internet and disbursement within a fixed time limit.[8]

Delay results in real-time problems, for example, in the case of exporters. An exporter faces a number of issues imposed by the tax administration including filing online refund claims against which physical examination may be demanded, detailed documentation that were already provided when the export actually took place, or a long time taken for refund processing. If they do not receive timely refunds, their business models get jeopardised reflecting the manner in which global international trade functions with little accommodation for delays in financial transactions. One way to alleviate the problem of waiting for ITC refunds is to allow a set-off of accumulated ITC against tax liability on domestic supplies.

### 33.7.2 Foreign Tax Credit (FTC)

Double tax avoidance agreements (DTAAs) provide methods to remove or reduce juridical double taxation by allocating taxing rights between residence and source countries on various categories of income, by eliminating or limiting source country taxation or by requiring a residence country to grant relief for source country taxation through a credit or exemption mechanism. This is provided for in the income tax acts of most countries.[9] Of course, detailed rules are provided for FTC in the tax law. Unless such rules clearly specify the compliance requirements, there remains the possibility of disputes and litigation. A country may also provide for unilateral relief from double taxation of income arising from another country with which it has not concluded a DTAA.

Differences in the definition of the fiscal year among trading countries may lead to conflicts. The United States uses a calendar year; India uses 1 April to 31 March; the United Kingdom uses 6 April to 5 April. Taxpayers in India tend to face challenges in claiming FTC for taxes paid in the United States between January and March as those taxes are accounted for in a different fiscal year. FTC rules that address such differences may appear insignificant to formulate, but they bring relief to taxpayers affected adversely by unmatched financial years. Customer facilitation must be kept in mind, in particular, where exports that are closely related to economic growth are concerned.

[8]Directive 2008/09/EC.

[9]DTAAs are not expected to provide rules on the computation and operation of the credit.

## 33.8 Self-Assessment

In the final analysis, taxation is a vital element in the relationship between citizens and the state. An ordinarily benign relationship based on a common set of values serves a larger social purpose. Many tax administrations are building trust-based systems as part of their strategic policy framework with a conviction that the more productive way to achieve genuine acceptance of, and adherence to, tax law and rules is not through the exclusive reliance on sanctions and legal coercion but through strategies that appeal to a law-abiding citizen.

At the same time, self-assessment has to be facilitated with the help of clear instructions, simple procedures and sufficient encouragement to taxpayers to calculate and pay their tax liabilities on their own. With self-assessment, high ratios of taxpayers per tax official can be achieved, and it could become a basic principle guiding tax administration practice. Accordingly, the global trend in tax governance is towards self-assessment, with the promotion of voluntary compliance comprising the keystone of a tax administration's strategy.

Self-assessment implies a fundamental shift in the relationship between the state and the taxpayer. It implies a tacit compact based on trust in each other and shared responsibility for ensuring compliance with the country's tax laws. In broad terms, the responsibility of the taxpayer is to exercise diligence in the payment of taxes correctly and that of the tax administration to create conditions in which the taxpayer is enabled to do so. This way, his rights are protected and his confidence as a taxpayer is built. Sanctions would be applied if that trust is broken by the taxpayer and he violates the law.

The shared responsibility between a taxpayer and the state is an inevitable consequence of growing complexity in the business and taxation world. It reflects the scale of challenges faced by a tax administration that cannot be met by a predominantly sanctions based regime and, instead, rests on an 'enhanced relationship' between taxpayers and the tax administration in which the latter develops a commercial awareness of the business world that is reflected in strategy and action.

## 33.9 Delinquency, Stopfilers and Tax Recovery

While self-assessment is the signature of an advanced tax administration, any tax administration also has to confront stopfilers and delinquent taxpayers for which adequate resources have to be allocated. Detecting them is the first task though it must be based on

> a system of tax returns processing and accounting that quickly and accurately records taxpayers' transactions with the tax administration and identifies stopfilers and delinquent taxpayers. Whether this system is based on manual ledgers, computers, or other means depends on many factors, including the customary business practices and relative costs of labor and capital, in a specific country. The nature of the system is not as important as the

fact that it constitutes an efficient system for processing returns and detecting noncompliance.[10]

After identification of a delinquent or stopfiler, tax recovery has to follow. Recovery represents the collection of tax in cases where taxpayers have not paid due tax. It can comprise an important function of a tax administration. Recovery, like audit, should use a risk profile of the taxpayer in default, that should ideally be ready at the time of creation of a tax demand related to an earlier assessment. It should be culled from a prior segmentation exercise based on size, sector, past behaviour and unexpected discrepancies from similar taxpayers in his group. Information including tax debts and outstanding tax returns, as well as assets data could also be needed.

This approach has helped monitor and improve taxpayer revenue behaviour while also indicating to the tax administration that neither too little nor too much revenue should be targeted or expected from him. Taxpayers identified as least compliant have to be subjected to more watchful methods of recovery as against those who are more compliant so that timely intimation may suffice.

Some tax demands may not be recoverable if a taxpayer goes bankrupt or indigent. Then the system should allow speedy write-offs so that the focus can shift to cases in which the chances of recovery are high. However, due diligence needs to be applied before writing off a pending demand.

Finally, if there is information on illegal activity including hoarding of cash and jewellery in lockers accumulated with tax evasion, the tax administration may have to carry out clandestine inquiry and undertake an unannounced raid of such premises for comprehensive search and seizure, albeit on the basis of a legal warrant. Such an instrument should be used only when no other recourse is possible but in countries with an incidence of high tax evasion, it cannot be entirely eschewed. Interestingly, while advanced country tax administrations shy away from search and seizure, once found, incarceration is not unknown. In emerging economies, on the other hand, search and seizure may be more readily used—perhaps more as a threat—than initiating processes that may end in incarceration. Clearly, the former route is more equitable for the taxpayer population as a whole.

## 33.10 Conclusions

To conclude, processes that are integrated in a tax administration are involved and, with growing complexities in the business world, pose increasing challenges to both tax administrators as well as taxpayers. In any event, customer focus should remain the administration's crucial concern and every attempt should be made not to deviate from this central theme. It is judicious, therefore, for a tax administration to adopt a benign approach in facilitating tax compliance while complementing it with strict and quick action when tax evasion is identified.

[10] See Tanzi and Pellechio (1995), op. cit., p. 12.

## References

Asian Development Bank (ADB). 2018. A Comparative Analysis of Tax Administration in Asia and the Pacific. https://doi.org/10.22617/TCS189264. Accessed 8 September 2020.

Government of India. 2020. *Income-Tax*. The Gazette of India: Extraordinary, Notification No. 61/2020 [F.No.370149/154/2019-TPL]/SO 1746(E). https://www.incometaxindia.gov.in/communications/notification/notification_61_2020.pdf. Accessed 30 August 2020.

Tanzi, Vito, and Anthony Pellechio. 1995. *The Reform of Tax Administration*. IMF Working Paper No. WP/95/22. https://www.elibrary.imf.org/doc/IMF001/07242-9781451843941/07242-9781451843941/Other_formats/Source_PDF/07242-9781455256402.pdf. Accessed 8 September 2020.

Tax Administration Reform Commission (TARC). 2014. *Tax Administration Reform in India: Spirit, Purpose and Empowerment (First Report)*. New Delhi: Government of India.

# 34 Dispute Management

## 34.1 Introduction

The dispute management function should commence from policies and measures to prevent or minimize disputes to their efficient and satisfactory resolution. Advanced tax administrations have a dedicated organization for dispute management that functions with independence so that a taxpayer has confidence in the administration's objectivity and fairness. It should ensure that avoidable disputes are not generated and only exceptionally, cases escalate to litigation. Operating procedures should be transparent and made available to taxpayers. Tax administrations may issue binding technical guidance to ensure clarity and consistency in interpretation and application of law and to enhance taxpayer understanding of it.

Pre-dispute consultation and pre-filing support together with high-quality show cause notices and tax demands are complementary instruments. Advance ruling and mutual agreement procedures (MAP) prevent disputes. Alternative dispute resolution (ADR) methods are employed to resolve tax disputes out of court including settlement commissions and arbitration mechanisms. They should incorporate administrative and appellate level functions. For success, dispute resolution requires officers with relevant knowledge, expertise and maturity. Assigned officers should receive adequate induction and on-the-job training in the principles of law and jurisprudence, principles of statutory interpretation, theory of precedents and principles of evidence.[1] These aspects comprise the subject matter of this chapter.

[1] See TARC (2014), First Report, Chap. V, for a detailed treatment of dispute management.



P. Shome, *Taxation History, Theory, Law and Administration*, Springer Texts in Business and Economics, https://doi.org/10.1007/978-3-030-68214-9_34

## 34.2 Dispute Prevention

### 34.2.1 Clarity in Law and Procedures

Effective communication is fundamental to dispute prevention. A fair number of disputes arise due to the ambiguity and imprecision in laws, rules and regulations that need to be addressed at the drafting stage. Drafting should ensure proper language of the tax provisions, consistent with the legislative intent. The process should include adequate consultation with stakeholders at the drafting stage of the law. Once completed, the draft law should be placed in the public domain to encourage taxpayers to comment and identify potential areas of ambiguity that could lead to tax disputes. The views of stakeholders should be evaluated appropriately and accepted where helpful.

A standard operating procedure should be followed during the framing of tax laws, rules and regulations.[2]

- Initiation: The rationale for the proposed law, regulation or change in regulation should be given, and an impact analysis or cost-benefit analysis both in relation to the taxpayer and the tax administration should be undertaken before a decision is made to frame it.
- Statement of objects and reasons: A clear and detailed statement of objects and reasons including how the proposed law or regulation would achieve it, should accompany any new law or regulation or amendment to a regulation.
- Drafting: The language of the law or regulation should use plain language, and be clear and precise. A general taxonomy of terms and expressions common to various tax and regulatory legislation should be listed to underline clarity and consistency.
- Public consultation: All proposed laws and regulations should be put up on the website of the tax administration for comments, and a summary of the comments and their consideration should be published. A summary of the cost-benefit analysis should accompany publication of the law or regulation.[3]

### 34.2.2 Timely Intervention to Clarify Contentious Matters

It is important to clarify contentious matter through interpretative statements to remove confusion. This has been known to prevent disputes in particular in direct tax areas such as GAAR, SAAR including transfer pricing, taxation of the indirect transfer of capital assets, Advance Pricing Agreements (APAs) (See Chap. 28, Sect. 28.2.4) and, for indirect taxes, on taxation of software-related transactions, transactions relating to intellectual property rights, scope of the definition of

[2]See Government of India (2013).

[3]See Chap. 14, Sect. 14.4, for details on framing the language of law.

'goods' and 'service' where the two are distinguished in a VAT or GST regime, identification of establishments of service provider and service recipients, among others.

Reflecting the complexity of emerging international taxation issues, it is essential that subject matter experts are involved in the development of such instructions. This will enhance the possibility of checking potential conflicts with international agreements including tax treaties, tax information exchange agreements, guidance by agencies such as the OECD, UN and others.

### 34.2.3 Advance Ruling and Advance Pricing Agreements

Many countries have channels to issue interpretative statements or clarifications of various provisions of tax law, on the request of the taxpayer. The Authority for Advance Ruling (AAR)[4] and APA are two such channels in India the likes of which are prevalent in many countries. They provide taxpayers authoritative guidance on various provisions of tax law that have the potential to create disputes.

The AAR issues binding rulings within 6 months (90 days in the case of the AAR dealing in indirect taxes) of receiving the application. Rulings are binding on the taxpayer and the tax administration. Nevertheless, India allows appeals to be made to a high court or, under special leave of appeal, to its supreme court.

The APA provides for an agreement between the taxpayer and tax administration to fix the prices of future related party transactions, covered by international transfer pricing (TP) rules. In some countries, it is extended to cover domestic TP cases. Its rules and provisions should match those of the AAR.

A set of preliminary guidelines released by the tax administration indicates the availability of multiple approaches to an APA programme, viz., unilateral, bilateral and multilateral. APAs can be executed for a continuing international transaction, or for a proposed international transaction. The outcome of a signed APA is binding on the taxpayer and the tax administration. The taxpayer, however, should have the option of withdrawing from the process before the APA is executed.

For successful acceptance by MNEs and successful implementation of APAs, there are certain preconditions:

- APAs have to explicitly provide for confidentiality of taxpayer information that is shared with the competent authority (CA) for APAs, in particular sensitive data on business processes and strategy including classified information pertaining to foreign associated enterprises that, sometimes, a business may be required to share.
- APAs are based on critical assumptions regarding a business and any change in detail may require appropriate revisions in an APA. It must, therefore, be provided for as to what circumstances would lead to such change.

[4]Under Article 226 and Article 136 of the constitution, respectively.

- A tax treaty has to contain an enabling provision for a corresponding adjustment as indicated under Article 9(2) of the OECD-UN Model Convention. Otherwise, there will be a fundamental hurdle for MNEs to approach the CAs of the two jurisdictions in which it is operating and he is attempting to avoid being double taxed.

The APA regime in India, introduced in 2012, was designed to reflect global best practices and was intended to provide certainty to MNEs operating in India. The APA process is divided into four distinct phases to meet the stages that were described above—pre-filing meeting, filing APA application, preliminary processing of APA application and negotiation and finalization.

### 34.2.4 Pre-Dispute Consultation

A collaborative approach could provide a pre-dispute solution at the pre-notice stage through an open dialogue where both parties can articulate and discuss their respective positions on the matter at hand. If a common view emerges on the facts, a mutually agreed upon legal position could result. If taken up in the proper spirit, it could eliminate many potential disputes. The others would have to follow the legal route.

Tax officers should not possess the freedom for coercive action for recovery during the consultation process. An officer issuing a notice should be the one engaging in the consultation, open to a full consideration of the taxpayer's viewpoint. His objective should be to find common ground to the extent possible before reverting to formulating his position document. At the conclusion of this process, the proceedings should be recorded and signed by both parties. A notice or draft assessment order should be issued only in respect of unresolved issues. The points on which there is agreement should not be contested by either party.

### 34.2.5 Pre-Filing Support to Taxpayers

Non-resident taxpayers and certain specified categories of resident taxpayers can usually file applications to obtain binding rulings on income tax issues or issues under indirect tax laws arising out of a transaction or proposed transaction. In order to ascertain the tax liability a priori, there should be an adequate mechanism to provide pre-filing support to taxpayers to help them plan their business and avoid disputes.

### 34.2.6 Quality of Show-Cause Notices and Demands

The starting point of a formal dispute is the show-cause notice (SCN) in the case of indirect taxes and demands for direct taxes.[5] Their quality plays an important role in the nature of the outcome of the dispute. Therefore, they must meet quality parameters of clarity and transparency to meet the tests of legality and fairness. The factual basis of the allegations made and the correct invocation of relevant legal provisions are essential. Standardized processes should be followed in both direct and indirect taxes to ensure consistency across all demands and show cause notices across all taxes.

## 34.3 Taxpayer Dispute Resolution Centre

Countries should consider setting up dispute resolution centres to provide a single point of contact to guide taxpayers on whether they should opt for the early dispute resolution (EDR) channel or the ADR channel. A Taxpayer Dispute Resolution Centre (TDRC) would communicate with the taxpayer and narrow down the issues in a dispute, as to whether it involves a question of fact, a question of law, or a mixed question of law and fact. A taxpayer should ideally avail the EDR facility if the disputes are small with simple rectification possible.

The ADR channel, on the other hand, comprises conciliation and arbitration. Ideally, disputes involving simple questions of fact should be referred for conciliation while those involving a mixed question of law and fact should be referred for arbitration. Substantial questions of law, however, would not be fit for resolution through these methods and TDRC should advise the taxpayer to opt for litigation for the resolution of such disputes.

After the taxpayer moves to EDR or ADR and gets his issues resolved, the tax demand can be prepared and communicated by the TDRC to the taxpayer. The tax demand would crystallize at this point. If the taxpayer is dissatisfied with the resolution from the EDR or the conciliation process in the ADR, he can decide to object to it and a formal process of litigation can be initiated thereafter. Arbitral awards are final and binding and cannot be appealed against. A possible structure for dispute management is shown in Appendix Fig. 34.1.

## 34.4 Alternate Dispute Resolution Mechanisms

Most jurisdictions currently deploy alternate mechanisms to mitigate potential disputes. These include APAs already seen above, settlement commissions, and mutual agreement procedure (MAP).

[5] They may be termed differently in different countries.

### 34.4.1 Settlement Commission

A settlement commission (SC) gives a taxpayer an opportunity to disclose undisclosed income and settle his cases. A taxpayer can approach it when his case is pending before an AO, and make a 'full and true' disclosure of relevant particulars and pay tax accordingly. The idea is to attract the taxpayer to 'come clean'. The key motivator for taxpayers to approach the SC is if it possesses the power to grant immunity from penalties and prosecution.

Though SCs are conceptualised as a problem-solving tool, they may not be fully successful if the tax law is not fully clear, with interpretative issues embedded in its provisions. There may be operational constraints as well that could, however, be alleviated. Thus,

- If a taxpayer cannot approach the SC once his case gets 'time-barred' or concluded upon by the AO, then he cannot take advantage of the process once he enters the appeal stage. Whether this policy fully reflects the intention of problem-solving has to be carefully pondered by the tax administration before introducing too many constraints.
- If a SC reaches a conclusion on questions of facts and the law, that should not be challenged except under rare circumstances, such as on grounds of validity of the manner in which it conducted the proceedings.
- Indeed, if the SC is suggested as a body that is independent of the tax administration, then the latter should not be reviewing the SC orders as if to monitor them since integrity among SC members must be assumed. If there is any question, then the very continuance of the SC should be examined.
- For approaching the SC, a taxpayer may be typically asked to make a full and true disclosure of any additional income that may not have been disclosed to the AO. This should not be interpreted as malafide on the basis of its being declared, and no additions in demand should be made by the investigative wing of the tax administration without giving sufficient opportunity to the taxpayer to rebut them. Otherwise, it could lead to litigation, thus defeating the purpose of reaching a solution.

In India, SCs have been set up in several cities with the principal bench in New Delhi and three additional benches at Chennai, Kolkata and Mumbai. It consists of one Chairman and two Members in the principal bench in New Delhi, and one Vice Chairman and two Members in each of the three additional benches.[6] The functioning of SCs has come under question from time to time reflecting a lack of confidence in SC conclusions or an emergence of the very issues listed above. Nevertheless, they have survived such challenges and the institution is well grounded at present.

[6]See Butani (2016), pp. 42–43.

### 34.4.2 Mutual Agreement Procedure

The Mutual Agreement Procedure (MAP)[7] framework is provided in Article 25 of the UN Double Taxation Convention and OECD Tax Convention on Income and Capital. Article 25 of tax treaties set out two areas in which the two contracting states endeavour to resolve their differences by using MAP:

- Cases in which a taxpayer considers that the acts of one or both of the contracting states result or will result in taxation not in accordance with the provisions of the treaty (covered in paragraphs 1 and 2 of Article 25).
- Cases in which there are difficulties or doubts as to the interpretation or application of the treaty (covered in paragraph 3 of Article 25).[8]

Thus, essentially, the MAP allows CAs of states having a bilateral tax treaty, to resolve disputes, difficulties or doubts arising in relation to the interpretation or application of the treaty that may otherwise result in taxation not in accordance with the tax treaties. And it qualifies the taxpayer to access MAP where a dispute may arise notwithstanding remedies available under domestic law. Most Indian tax treaties are negotiated on the UN model and ordinarily contain Article 25 on MAP procedure. Hence the MAP is viewed as a familiar procedure in international law practice.

### 34.4.3 Arbitration

Traditionally, therefore, tax authorities attempt to resolve any tax treaty disputes through amicable settlement amongst themselves through the MAP, without involvement from third parties such as arbitrators or mediators. However, in recent years, due to globalisation and the commensurate proliferation of tax treaties,[9] the number of tax disputes has also increased. With that, their complexity and revenue consideration have also escalated. Despite the transfer of staff resources to international taxation matters, MAP cases tend to take up longer time and exceed the capacity of many tax administrations, in particular, in emerging economies that have globalised. Sometimes disputes remain unresolved.

In such an environment the OECD has put arbitration on the table—though it has hardly been tried in practice—including it in BEPS Action 15 on the multilateral instrument (MLI).[10] Arbitration has also appeared in the EU Directive on dispute

[7]See Chap. 30, Sect. 30.2.14, for MAP as an essential complement to BEPS and, therefore, a minimum standard for BEPS signatory jurisdictions.

[8]See Butani (2016), op. cit., p. 45.

[9]See Baistrocchi (2020) on the spread of tax treaties over the past century.

[10]See Chap. 30, Sect. 30.2.15, for a detailed analysis on the MLI.

resolution in international tax matters. These have 'created a new momentum'[11] with arbitration. Arbitration has developed into an accepted legal alternative to litigation whereby the parties to a dispute agree to submit their respective positions to a neutral third party—the arbitrator—for resolution. It is now up to tax authorities if they can accustom themselves to the use of arbitration as a tool for resolving tax disputes.

In India, an Arbitration and Conciliation Act was passed in 1996 that applies to statutory or non-statutory, institutionally administered or ad hoc arbitrations. It includes domestic and international commercial arbitration and, based on a 1980 UN Trade Law Conciliation, it also covers enforcement of foreign award and conciliation. Though its objective was to diminish the need for court intervention in arbitration, experts have commented that arbitration in India remains ad hoc, expensive, and long drawn, thus resulting in excessive court intervention.[12]

Subsequently, a law commission reviewed and recommended comprehensive reform measures for arbitration, and an amendment was passed by parliament in 2015. The changes it introduced included (1) an increase in e-communication, (2) a prescribed maximum of ninety days for arbitral proceedings to begin after any order of an interim measure, (3) appointment of the arbitrator by the supreme court or a high court instead of their chief justices, (4) a maximum of 60 days, from date of notice served to the opposite party, for the application for appointment of the arbitrator, (5) passing the award within twelve months, with extensions possible for six months at the end of which the arbitrator's mandate terminates unless time is extended by the court, (6) provision for a fast track, (7) enablement to exercise jurisdiction over international commercial arbitration even if the place of arbitration is outside India provided such award is enforceable and recognised under the India's arbitration law and (8) an arbitral award made in a country to which India is a party, to be treated as a foreign award.

## 34.5 Conclusions

To conclude, a good law may be placed in an emerging economy tax administration for alternate dispute resolution. For it to be effective, however, tax administration practices must be able to convey confidence in the taxpayer. Experience has revealed that this may not always be the case and that application of tax law and implementation of tax administration principles may not reflect the written law. For example, disputes are likely to arise mainly in large enterprises that come under large taxpayer units (LTUs) and it is imperative that LTUs function efficiently and to the taxpayer's satisfaction that the system is equitable. Tax administrations especially in emerging economies must ensure that preventable shortcomings are overcome. Then the number of disputes will reduce to begin with, and conclusions from alternate dispute mechanisms will be quicker and more reliable.

[11]See Mooij (2019).

[12]See Butani (2016), op. cit., p. 113, and pp. 116–117.

## Appendix: How to Structure Dispute Management

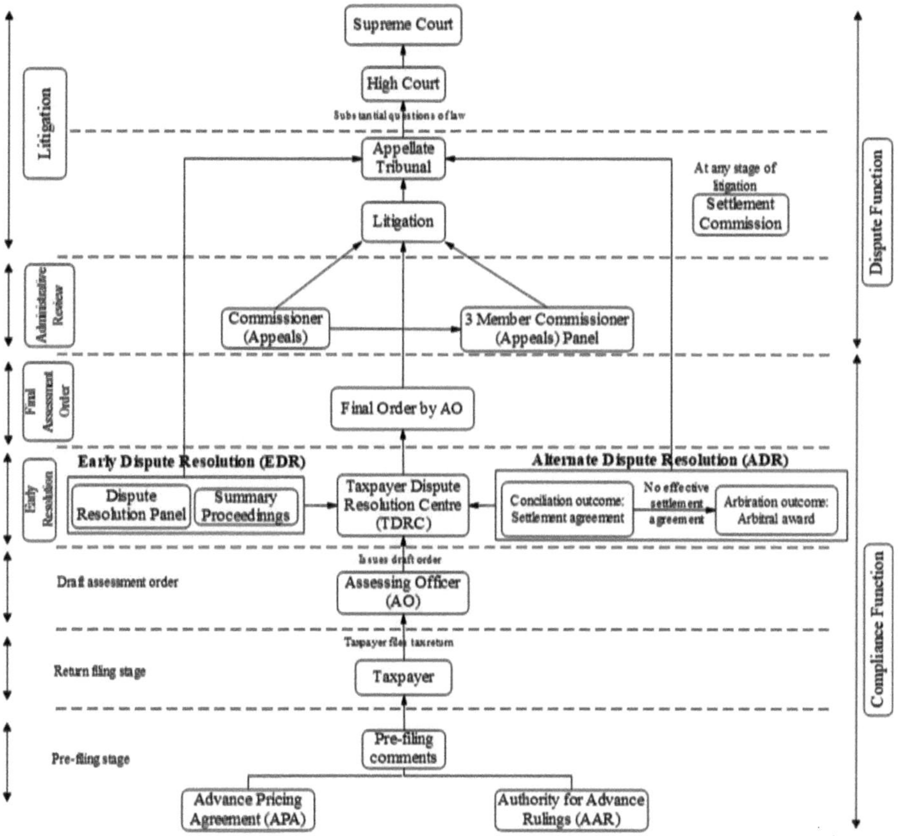


**Fig. 34.1** Dispute management structure. (Source: Restructured from TARC (2014), First Report, Chap. V)

## References

Baistrocchi, Eduardo. 2020. *Article 9: Associated Enterprises-Global Tax Treaty Commentaries*. Department of Law, London School of Economics.

Butani, Mukesh. 2016. *Tax Dispute Resolution: Challenges and Opportunities for India*. Gurgaon: Indian Council for Research on International Economic Relations (ICRIER) and Lexis Nexis.

Government of India. 2013. *Handbook on Adoption of Governance Enhancing and Non-Legislative Elements of The Draft Indian Financial Code*. https://dea.gov.in/sites/default/files/Handbook_GovEnhanc_fslrc_2.pdf. Accessed 10 Sept 2020.

Mooij, Hans. 2019. Tax Treaty Arbitration. *Arbitration International* 35 (2): 195–219. https://doi.org/10.1093/arbint/aiy004.

Tax Administration Reform Commission (TARC). 2014. *Tax Administration Reform in India: Spirit, Purpose and Empowerment (First Report)*. New Delhi: Government of India.

# 35 Technology and Research

## 35.1 Introduction

The starting point for any analysis of a tax administration is the revenue performance it is associated with. A cross-country analysis of tax–GDP ratios, for example, usually gives rise to some interesting queries. How different are their economies? Are differences in their economies the explanation for the differences in their revenue performance? How important are the differences in the way they organise and manage their tax administrations? How deeply do their tax structures—for example, tax incentives—erode the tax base? To what degree do they use information and communications technology (ICT) to facilitate tax compliance and enhance revenue performance?

Rapid growth in the use of ICT has been a global phenomenon. Most countries introduce an array of administrative measures to buttress policy measures and encourage voluntary taxpayer compliance through the means of ICT. One example is the rapidity with which the Tax Identification Number (TIN) or Permanent Account Numbers (PAN) of taxpayers has been issued and revised in cases where required.[1] Electronic filing has been implemented for an increasing number of taxpayers in emerging economies and has progressed rapidly for both corporate and individual taxpayers.[2]

To facilitate compliance, administrations organise fairs where taxpayers are helped to fill out and file electronic tax returns. They have also invested resources in simplifying return forms and procedures while depending more on information submitted through e-returns, rather than requiring submittal of statutory hard copy records. ICT has also reduced the processing costs of tax returns. Together, such

[1]India made rapid advancements in introducing ICT towards the integration of processes in its tax administration. See Shome (2006).

[2]Indeed the use of ICT should not be perceived in the narrow context of tax administration alone, but in the broader context of public sector reforms and the government's overall ICT strategy. See Engelschalk et al. (2000).



P. Shome, *Taxation History, Theory, Law and Administration*, Springer Texts in Business and Economics, https://doi.org/10.1007/978-3-030-68214-9_35

administrative measures have contributed in no small way to a surge in tax revenue experienced in recent years. Those administrations that have lagged behind in simplification and the use of ICT have suffered taxpayer dissatisfaction and higher tax evasion.

Of course, there are risks posed by the use of IT by tax administrations. These include data security risks and problems with large-scale public procurement. These risks have to be actively managed by tax administrations and the sharing of experience of best practices across jurisdictions should assist in moving it forward.

In sum, ICT has allowed the transformation of data and information to knowledge that, in turn, has enhanced a tax administration's operational efficiency and analytical capacity. Thus, it has helped improve tax policy structures based on appropriate methods of revenue analysis and projections, as well as internal decision-making by management on a variety of key performance indicators, including a reduction in compliance costs, improvements in taxpayer segmentation and profiling, containment of tax debt of taxpayers and impact of customer contact on compliance. Analyses based on ICT use have led to strategies to enhance compliance of an array of taxes including income tax, GST or VAT, selective excises and customs.[3] This chapter focuses on ICT and its impact on tax analysis and governance.

## 35.2 Revenue Forecasting

### 35.2.1 Macro Economy and Tax Administration

The macroeconomy of a country effectively influences tax policy and administration. Thus, if the administration builds in the economic principles and a regular assessment of the macroeconomy into its decision-making processes, it will benefit from a clearer understanding of revenue collection trends and the tax gap between potential and actual collection of tax revenue.

As an economy flourishes, there may be an increase in the number of applications to register businesses, to apply for tax incentives or more tax deductions at source (TDS) to be applied by employers for employees. During an economic slump, TDS would tend to get curtailed though new, small, service-oriented businesses may begin to register as self-employment increases. Benefits for the unemployed, if any, may also increase and these may be administered through the tax system. In turn, each such changing phenomenon could have a strong impact on the workload of the tax administration. There is a rate of natural attrition of tax administration staff. If its workload increases without sufficient revision in emoluments, attrition will increase or there will be an increase in moral hazard. Both have to be considered by a tax administration seriously.

[3]See Shome (2012), Chap. 4, for analytical methodologies developed in the United Kingdom. Examples are provided of methods that could be utilised to improve the analytical base of a modern tax administration.

Ideally, revenue projections should be made on the basis of sectoral GDP, consumption, fixed investment, net trade, unemployment, inflation including asset prices, stock market index, housing projections and so on. Once the tax research and analysis division under the tax council (see Fig. 32.2) makes those projections, the tax administration can use the information for its own projections of revenue and tax debt from all taxes, and of the direct and indirect tax gaps.

However, it is important for a tax administration's governing board to also take cognizance of economic projections by independent forecasters and not rely exclusively on projections by its own analytical wing. A good place to begin would be to take the average of well-regarded independent forecasters (excluding outliers) and compare it with that of its own. If the two sets of projections are not similar, then necessary adjustments should be made for the tax bases which an administration can reliably use for its projections. Sometimes there are pressures from a minister's officials on a tax administration to scale up a revenue objective. Such differences between a ministry of finance and the tax administration are best not aired in public. On the other hand, no pressure from the former should be accepted by the latter to use unrealistic base projections that might translate into unjustifiably large estimates of collectible revenue, tax gap reduction objectives, and in turn, translate into unjustifiable pressure on taxpayers.

### 35.2.2 Approaches to Revenue Forecasting

Forecast of tax revenue is crucial for constructing a government's annual budget. The closer its revenue projection is to subsequent revenue collection, the better could the government's expenditure match the budgeted amount without exacerbating public debt. A revenue forecast generates confidence if it transparently reveals the assumed tax base and rates, historic and projected revenue trends, methodology of the analysis, and data used. Some human judgement is always employed but different stakeholders[4] should participate in arriving at a particular forecast. Credible estimates lead to better accountability to taxpayers. This is unlikely to be achieved through revenue augmentation by pressuring taxpayers to pay more tax during the final months of a fiscal year or by stopping refunds or stalling input tax credit owed to them. Such stop-gap measures are likely to adversely affect the credibility of a tax administration with taxpayers in particular if such practices persist over the medium term.

[4]In India, for example, appropriate stakeholders would be the budget division and the economic division in the Department of Economic Affairs of the Ministry of Finance, that function independently of the tax administration.

### 35.2.3 Revenue Forecasting Methods

Nascent tax administrations may use a basic estimation model for revenue projections in which tax revenue, *T*, is expressed as a function of *b*, its broad tax base, *t*, the average tax rate that is applied on it, and *c*, a derived or assumed rate of compliance. Each tax can be independently estimated since the tax rate, tax base and compliance rate are likely to vary across different taxes.

However, a tax administration should attempt to develop more complex revenue forecasting models that are more accurate in their projections. Some emerging economies, including India, despite advanced ICT characteristics, have been slow in this process. Ideally, a tax administration should strive to set up a Computable General Equilibrium (CGE) model that possesses the ability to estimate the impact of tax measures under consideration on major macroeconomic variables. It would also indicate the revenue gap between projections and actual collections when the function of collections has terminated. If appropriately designed, such a model should be able to project revenue over the country's annual business cycles and indicate how wide the revenue gap is likely to be.[5]

To take an example, CGE modelling could be used to examine the effects of selective excise taxes. During an economic recession, the importance of traditional revenue sources temporarily recedes and indirect taxes become an easy revenue source. Yet the negative economic effects of such taxes in the form of the 'dead-weight loss' (DL) they create may be high.[6] The CGE model is applied to estimate their revenue impacts in the backdrop of their DL. The analysis reveals that DL is different for different excise taxes. Economists have argued that taxing intermediate products creates a double distortion in terms of both production and consumption decisions while a consumption tax would tax—and therefore distort—relative prices only at the consumption level. Further, the more upstream a tax is applied, the larger is the number of times the tax cascades in subsequent downstream stages.[7] Therefore, the final price gets all the more distorted. This is only one example of the type of detailed analysis that can be carried out through CGE models.

The United Kingdom's CGE model has revealed that duties on alcohol and tobacco, air passenger duty, vehicle excise duty, insurance premium tax and fuel duty have an ascending order of economic distortion that they create. Alcohol and tobacco duties are least distortive since these are close to the point of final consumption even if collected at the factory gate. However, a tax on petroleum products tends to fall near the upstream supply chain as could a tax on business insurance. Therefore, they are more distortionary. This analysis is carried out by simple exercises on the CGE model by estimating how adversely GDP would be affected by raising the same amount of revenue, say £1 billion, from each tax. The more

[5]See TARC (2015), Fourth Report, Chap. XIII.

[6]See Chap. 8, Sect. 8.3, for a discussion of excess burden or deadweight loss of a tax.

[7]See Diamond and Mirrlees (1971).

distortion a particular tax causes, the greater is the decline in GDP, initially, as well as in its future trajectory. Accordingly, their impact on revenue would vary as well.

## 35.3 Regulatory Impact Assessment

### 35.3.1 What Is Impact Assessment?

A summary of a cost–benefit analysis and supporting evidence should be published following the initiation of a public consultation or the introduction of a new tax policy. This is known as a Regulatory Impact Assessment (RIA). The RIA measures the administrative burden of a policy change on the customer (taxpayer) as well as on the tax administration. The methodology used to assess the revenue impact of the change should also be published. As a result, various aspects of tax policy design should be subjected to minute analytical exercises, followed by discussions among appropriate policy directorates in a tax administration.

The burden should be modelled using a Standard Cost Model (SCM) that was originally pioneered in the Netherlands and Denmark and adopted by the United Kingdom in 2005.[8] Its methodology comprises: (i) breaking down individual pieces of information required for the tax return to be filled; (ii) identifying the population of businesses that need to produce that information; and (iii) specifying the time required to complete the obligation. Whilst populating the database is relatively costly and prone to some error, it offers a valuable way to capture and model changes in the administrative burdens placed on businesses due to a tax change.

Therefore, data availability and its understanding are an important component of an impact assessment. An assessment of techniques provides an assessment of the data required that is facilitated through a systematic and functional approach to data collection. Context analysis should be carried out so as to understand and analyse the universe of analytical techniques available, which ones are to be employed, the expected quality of data to be collected, the estimated cost of collection, the predicted non-response rates, the expected level of errors and the length of time for data collection.

Prior to the actual annual budget presentation, a pre-budget review (PBR) is a good practice that enables mid-year policy changes. This could include an assessment of the behavioural response for a proposed tax that might be expected from businesses. It could also present modifications that may be contemplated in the methodology for quantifying the effects of the proposed changes so that academia could take it up and point to any errors well before the final changes in tax policy are presented in the government's annual budget. Advanced country tax administrations

[8]KPMG (2006), a tax advisory company, estimated the administrative burden on businesses at £5.1 billion. It covered 28 different regimes where the greatest burdens resided (HMRC website). Cnossen (1994) provides a comprehensive review of the issues of compliance cost for the taxpayer as well as administrative cost, albeit for the particular case of VAT.

tend to follow such a process so that, when a tax policy change is finally introduced, taxpayers are already familiar with its workings and what is expected from them for successful tax compliance.

### 35.3.2 Administrative Burden Versus Compliance Cost

It is important to distinguish the administrative burden (AB) from the compliance cost (CC). AB typically represents the financial cost of administrative activities directly related to implementing a tax measure by both the taxpayer and the tax administration. CC, on the other hand, also includes other cost aspects such as non-business costs, costs of uncertainty associated with the tax, or of a tax measure's complexity, psychological costs, effects of a tax change on a business's cash flow or operational convenience, as well as transitional costs.

AB could be conceptually defined as:

$$\text{AB} = \text{price} * \text{quantity}$$

where

price = (time needed * tariff or wage rate) + fixed costs (such as stamps for affixing new prices); and

quantity = number of businesses * frequency

Through this process of calculation, AB not only assesses the impact of the tax change but also identifies the high-cost areas, thus indicating which expenses could perhaps be reduced. In emerging and advanced tax administrations alike, AB for small and medium enterprises has to be kept in mind when introducing tax changes.

Regarding CC, though the goal has to be evidence-based decision-making, there is no single CC model that fits all situations. With this in mind, CC has to be calculated, to the extent possible, by using surveys, cost–benefit analysis, and business impact tests and other available information relevant to a particular case. The choice of method should reflect tax administration staff capacity, resource availability and data availability. Aggregation of impact may be difficult as the impact is sometimes measured by different indicators and scales. Costs and benefits—quantitative and qualitative—nevertheless should be assessed. In practice, CC, except for AB, tends to be ignored mainly because it is difficult to measure such costs. AB is a narrower tool and can be used to assess the main drivers of the tax burden.

Tax administrations sometimes consider the timing of the process of greater concern than the methodology itself. If the process starts late, it would be difficult to include its outcomes in the policymaking process. Alternatives can be formulated only when it is timely, not when discussions are too advanced. While ex-ante analysis is a necessary step in impact assessment, ex-post reviews of impact have a positive impact on the overall quality of ex-ante analysis. Ex-post reviews of impact assessments impart dynamism to ex-ante analysis as they could reveal systemic errors in methodologies used, and help in correcting them. Lessons could be fed back into impact assessment guidelines.

### 35.3.3 Institutional Arrangements and Training

Different countries have adopted different institutional frameworks for impact assessment, some preferring a centralised structure while others preferring a decentralised framework. A centralised approach relies on an oversight body for regulatory reform located at the centre of the administration or ministry. Some OECD countries have a central body that is tasked with the impact assessment process to ensure, from their viewpoint, higher consistency, credibility and quality. On the other hand, a decentralised institutional framework also has merit in that it does not rely on a specific oversight body, instead, relying on co-ordination between different entities to achieve desired policy objectives.

Staff training is essential to familiarise officers with the scope of, and the work involved in, impact assessment, and their obligations thereof, with the objective of buttressing the quality of impact assessments. The training programmes could be run on two tracks—one for the research and analysis, and impact assessment divisions under the tax council (see Fig. 32.2), and the other for analysis and compliance divisions of various tax and taxpayer categories and LTU sectors (see Fig. 32.1). While the former will need to be well versed in the methodologies and algorithms of impact assessment, the latter would focus on the development and application of consultation mechanisms. The two would have to interface during training and, of course, later in the formulation of strategy and dialogue on impact assessment with stakeholders.

## 35.4 Information and Communications Technology (ICT)

### 35.4.1 Introduction

The role of ICT is central to the efficient running of a tax administration. It plays a crucial part in administrative processes and in analysis that supports policymaking and implementation. ICT offers two direct benefits to modern tax administrations:

- Increased operational productivity by enabling tax administrations to store vast amounts of data in a single electronic database and reduce storage costs. It also facilitates faster and cheaper filing of returns and makes for better co-ordination between the administrative offices by enabling automated services and greater geographical mobility of information.
- New routes of communication between a tax administration and taxpayers through many forms such as online guidance, e-filing or automated telephony systems. It thus provides a greater range of access to taxpayers.

The pace of development in ICT means that new opportunities are consistently arising. To take just a couple of examples at the forefront, questions and opportunities arise over whether better guidance could be written collaboratively by employing corporate social responsibility (CSR) practices with tech giants, or could information be spread more effectively using podcasts.

### 35.4.2 Risks and Challenges

On a cautionary note, ICT exposes a tax administration to risks generated by the procurement and use of systems. Even advanced tax administrations have suffered embarrassing exposures of taxpayer data due to errors in transmittal or cracks in data protection. Therefore, systems need to be actively managed to avoid disruption to an administration's ICT operations and services.

A key difficulty is the procuring of ICT services in the first place. The onerous requirements of the public sector tendering system often result in a lack of competition among ICT companies that are large enough to fulfil a government contract of the size needed by many tax administrations. Also, there is an element of non-transferable risk whereby governments are held responsible for the failure of a private company to fulfil an ICT contract. At the same time, there is a need for flexibility in contracts to enable future innovations in the rapidly developing ICT market to be incorporated as and when needed. Such factors could result in high prices irrespective of the existence of an element of competition in the ICT market.

Security of data and information is a major risk. Tax administrations receive a vast array of information on individuals from bank details to addresses. Modern ICT enables this information to be held in a single database. If anyone should gain wrongful access to this kind of information, then it opens up the possibility of fraudulent activity. Additionally, it is necessary to ensure that the database is suitably backed up so that data recovery arrangements are in place and there is no loss of data or business continuity.

Finally, a heavy reliance on ICT could exclude sectors of society such as the small business sector or senior citizens; the administration must provide support for those segments of society that are not quite comfortable with the use of modern technology. Nevertheless, despite the risks that have been highlighted, it would be hard to argue that the costs of ICT outweigh the benefits. The practical case studies provided below demonstrate how the benefits of adopting modern IT are numerous while the risks can be managed.

Though there are some associated risks, different tax administrations have outsourced the installation of both hardware as well as the processing of tax returns in India. Some countries have chosen strategic partners to meet the full range of their ICT requirements such as the Her Majesty's Revenue and Customs (HMRC) in the United Kingdom. Others have set up specialised organisations to service their needs such as Federal Data Processing Service (SERPRO) in Brazil. However, irrespective of the choices they make, all modern tax administrations maintain a strong ICT in-house skill set. This is clearly an acknowledgment of the strategic importance they attach to the ICT function.

## 35.5 Predictive Analysis

Predictive analysis is used to detect taxpayer behaviour specific to non-compliance, tax avoidance, tax evasion and tax fraud. Its common parlance, 'analytics', is a data-driven approach that relies on information and knowledge contained within the data storage of a tax administration. Unlike simple analysis, analytics is the discipline of using statistics in combination with computer programming to gain insights contained in large quantities of data and undertaking actions based on those insights.

Analytics uses historical and current data to predict future events and operates on the basis of using data on a very large scale. It is suited to understanding, using and communicating complex data. Apart from statistical and econometric techniques, analytics transforms data into usable knowledge by finding complex and hidden patterns that are not otherwise easily apparent. It uses linear and nonlinear mathematical programming algorithms, advanced 'neural' systems (or 'deep learning'), which can identify complex patterns from large data sets to predict the probability that an individual will exhibit certain behaviours that could be of great value in identifying risks for tax evasion.

In the final analysis, analytics enhances taxpayer profiling and segmentation, tracking taxpayer behaviour as well as the administration's business processes. It identifies non-compliance, provides support for effective risk management, enables sectoral and industry-wise trend analysis of tax collections, explains the tax gap, improves recovery of arrears or tax debt collection and provides predictive support for intelligence and fraud detection. Best practices in advanced tax administrations today comprise analytics as a centrepiece in their risk detection strategies. The United Kingdom uses analytics to achieve effectiveness in its larger risk management strategy.

## 35.6 Research for Tax Governance

### 35.6.1 Introduction

Research in tax governance requires a multidisciplinary approach involving economics, accounting, finance, law, management, behavioural science, ICT and statistics. Only then can the research be useful in helping design new approaches to expand the tax base and increase tax revenue. Governance research also includes taxpayer convenience or customer welfare. Such research needs to be meticulously designed, implemented and executed so that the output is relevant and usable to the tax administration. It requires an organisational framework, finance, staff, the development of linkages for collaboration—an internal governmental mechanism or with outside agencies—and the building of skills needed to evaluate outputs to assess their practical utility. Research cannot be a one-off exercise; it has to be embedded in the tax administration so that there is two-way movement, top-down as well as bottom-up, among and within various verticals to build an ecosystem for undertaking meaningful research.

### 35.6.2 Areas of Research

Key areas of research that may be undertaken include how to reduce tax exemptions, deductions or other incentives, effects of tax on investment and research and development, taxing natural resources, taxation of the insurance sector and expansion of the taxpayer base. In addition, research on issues of governance should include compliance tracking, identifying the rich and wealthy, measuring voluntary compliance, identifying audit/scrutiny risk elements, impact analysis, taxpayer surveys; issues in trade and customs, taxing hard-to-tax sectors, performance management, fairness in tax disputes and leakages due to corruption in tax administration.

### 35.6.3 External Research Collaboration

Most advanced tax administrations access and engage with a broad base of external research organisations as research partners for short-term or long-term research projects. This is in addition to in-house research on topics that need to be worked on only within the tax administration. The value of using external research institutions comes from the possibility of accessing professional knowledge and research techniques. This, when combined with the tax officer's familiarity with data and its interpretation, results in a high quality of tax analysis and outcomes for the tax administration.

However, for such collaborative research to be successful, a well-articulated system to manage such alliances needs to be put in place. The tax administration has to clarify that collaboration with external research organisations is intended on a long-term basis for a broad list of topics requiring external assistance and support. This will also require making encrypted data available in the form of anonymous taxpayer data. Data could be housed in an accessible data lab or data bank for use by external researchers.

Collaboration with external research organisations will need to include a framework for dissemination of research results, as external researchers and academics will be interested in sharing research results and getting them published in refereed accredited journals. Partnership and collaboration with external research organisations will not only be useful to the tax administration but will also be of advantage to external research organisations since their research experience with a government department should give them wider research opportunities and funding.[9]

### 35.6.4 Dissemination, Human Resources and Allocation of Funds for Research

The tax administration should conduct quarterly seminars and annual conferences to showcase its ongoing and final research output. Such conferences and seminars should provide officers an opportunity to interact with tax experts from the private sector, academia as well as multilateral organisations.

People working and involved in research should have university-level education in the field of economics, psychology, statistics, management, or law, with adequate experience in public policy formulation. But this in no way suggests that those with other educational specialisms cannot carry out or produce research work. In fact, their inputs should also be of considerable value given the multidimensional nature of what should comprise a tax administration's research interests. It is also the case that officers often acquire the requisite knowledge while on the job; they can also be engaged in research work if they have proven ability to do so.

If a tax administration appoints a chief economist, he should play an important role in identifying, guiding, monitoring and evaluating research topics. He should have to provide quality assurance of the tax administration's analytical work. He should be responsible for examining the evidence, using analytical input and presenting the outcomes of analysis to support the formulation of tax policy and buttress internal administrative decisions. There should be intense training of officers involved in research on research methodologies and data analysis, either in-house or at reputed research institutions.

Officers may be deputed to attend research seminars or courses, whether in the country or abroad. Adequate funds will need to be allocated for this purpose to ensure that it is done on a regular basis. To give adequate emphasis and focus to research in tax administration, sufficient funds should be provided in the budget under a separate head. To sustain the focus and to establish continuity, no re-appropriation of funds should be allowed from the research vertical.

## 35.7 Expanding the Base

Research has a role to play in certain administrative areas, for example, in expanding the taxpayer base. There are constraints to expanding the taxpayer base. First, the administrative resources required for such a task are likely to be higher than what is feasible from a government's available resources. Second, administrative resource

[9]See Shome (2012), Chap. 4, Sect. 4.1.12, for country experiences on external research collaboration.

expansion is often carried out as a response to political economy pressures rather than as part of a medium-term efficiency-enhancing strategy. To give an example, a significant increase in excise and customs inspectors to administer India's Special Economic Zones (SEZ)—a colossal tax incentive scheme introduced in 2006—tended to constrain or even pre-empt enhancements in other needed areas for modernising tax administration. This kind of policy can potentially reduce resource allocation in one area of operations to benefit another. Thus, a potential increase in the taxpayer base that could be envisaged by appropriately directing the enhanced use of ICT, had to be left unrealised.

Studies have shown that excluding taxpayers from an already operational tax base could have deleterious effects. The issue of an appropriate threshold for the inclusion of small taxpayers has been studied by those in favour of, and against, having a high threshold. The danger of excluding small taxpayers has been studied in some detail over the years in the form of potential revenue that may be lost while, at the same time, limiting the stake of small taxpayers in civil society by excluding them from tax participation or contribution.[10]

Others have provided a toolkit to facilitate small business compliance, focusing on incentives for micro- and small enterprise formalisation.[11] In many developing countries the business sector can be dominated by corner shops and small businesses who cannot all be excluded from participating in the tax net. While earlier eschewing the potential role of the small taxpayer, the International Monetary Fund's (IMF) Fiscal Affairs Department subsequently endorsed the benefit of making administrative efforts to include them in the tax net. Most technical assistance in the area of tax administration increasingly takes note of this issue.

Broadening and widening of the tax base and taxpayer base should comprise a strategic objective for a tax administration. Major contributors to the low tax base are a large cash economy comprising mainly the unorganised sector, high net worth individuals, and small businesses. An important factor that influences the attitude towards tax payment is the perception that the tax system is complicated and not taxpayer-friendly. Other factors include a multitude of tax exemptions and incentives, slack enforcement and a poor tax climate characterised by inadequate customer focus and absence of trust between the administration and the taxpayer, leading to a negative tax culture with weak awareness of compliance responsibilities.

To address this, various measures have to be taken including the simplification of laws and procedures, extension of the scope of presumptive taxation and tax deduction at source, creation of a separate cell for high net worth individuals in the compliance vertical, carrying out surveys based on lifestyle, expenditures made, and sectoral growth trends, structured information sharing and matching, data mining and developing an analytics tool. The supportive role of research is quintessential in all these functions.

---

[10]See Shome (2002).

[11]See Engelschalk (2007).

Thus, a strategy to expand the taxpayer base will require the tax administration to adopt and sustain a high multidisciplinary analytical and technological capability buttressed by the research vertical. It should be leveraged by co-operative and joint working between all branches—direct and indirect taxes—of the administration. They also need to be accompanied by the creation of a conducive environment for voluntary compliance, mutual trust and improved organisational ethos in tax administration. Needless to say, strong political will is a must for these measures, which may affect high net worth individuals, to result in positive outcomes. In the end, expansion of the taxpayer base remains one of the most challenging aspects that any tax administration, in particular in emerging and developing countries, faces.

## 35.8 Compliance Management

For taxes to be complied with, taxpayers need to understand their obligations under different tax laws. Compliance is the extent to which a taxpayer meets these obligations. If taxpayers fail to meet them, they could be considered non-compliant. Non-compliance is a result of the actions of taxpayers themselves, caused by ignorance, carelessness or deliberate action (evasion) or inaction (non-filing), or due to inherent weaknesses in the tax administration. Compliance management traditionally includes a structure for the systematic identification, assessment, ranking and treatment of tax compliance risks (for example, failure to register, failure to properly report tax liabilities and pay the taxes due on time).

While audit remains a fundamental and necessary approach to addressing non-compliance, this cannot be the only action—based solely on verification and enforcement—against non-compliance since it is not a guarantor of success. Therefore, there has been a transition from the enforcement dominated approach to a more holistic compliance management philosophy that comprises customer focus, self-assessment and voluntary compliance.[12] Of course, no strategy can eschew risk assessment and taxpayer segmentation to assess the diversity of taxpayers' compliance behaviours, so that the right strategic balance for compliance management can be struck.[13]

In conclusion, activities related to compliance management should not be seen in a disjointed fashion. It is a continuum ranging from taxpayer services to enforcement. For compliance management to be successful it needs to be supported by effective governance, risk management and robust performance management based on measurement and continuous monitoring of both lead and lag indicators.[14] People or staff are the most important element in this and the administration needs to adopt policies that are conducive to building a meritocracy, focusing on building and sustaining the required competencies and sustaining a highly motivated workforce.

[12]See Chap. 32, Sect. 32.3, and Chap. 33, Sect. 33.8.

[13]See Chap. 33, Sect. 33.5.5.

[14]As delineated in TARC (2014), First Report, Chap. IV, Sect. IV.3.d.

## 35.9 Information Exchange

### 35.9.1 Introduction

The adoption of ICT by tax administrations has helped in the collection, management and analysis of large volumes of data and information. Perhaps due to the flood of data, tax administrations tend to find it daunting to handle all the data that are collected. Data can be unreliable as they may not be accurately sourced, complete, relevant or integrated. Different agencies generating data or information do so for different purposes and uses but they can still be useful to a tax administration. Therefore, a mechanism should be instituted to encourage inter-agency partnerships and co-ordination to assure data quality, relevance and exchange.

Data-driven tax administrations are able to transcend organisational boundaries and successfully leverage the sourcing of data from different agencies. They share a common vision and commitment and work across the boundaries of different agencies to achieve it. Such a whole-of-government approach implies responding to one another's needs. It ensures the accuracy and credibility of data since it is known across agencies that erroneous data would expose inefficiency in collection and processing. Countries have adopted various collaborative mechanisms for such inter-agency exchange of data and information. These exchanges are generally mandated by law in the form of statutes. Various inter-agency partnership agreements, memoranda of understanding (MoUs), statements of practice, and standard protocols supplement laws to ensure the exchange of data or information. Tax administrations, as a result, have been able to reduce the time and cost of collecting the data afresh.

### 35.9.2 Common Framework

The basic principles of the common framework are: (i) collection of quality data or information, (ii) storage of the data or information for quick retrieval, (iii) use or reuse of data or information from a source, (iv) institution of multilayered authorisations, (v) promotion of a culture of mutual trust, openness and willingness to share between the collaborating organisations, with rights and responsibilities, and (vi) generation of information to support decision-making. Thus, the framework promotes 'one data, many users', with a common taxonomy, format and metadata. It enables and facilitates the reuse of data, thereby reducing the time and cost of the data collection process.

### 35.9.3 Common Taxonomy and Standard

For data exchange between different organisations possibly with disconnected data and information that do not necessarily have tax as their primary work, for example, the central bank, security exchange, directorate of foreign trade, or registrar of companies or banks, the key requirement is a common taxonomy, standardisation of data description, data context and data sharing. Common taxonomy-based data exchange enables better reporting and analysis across involved organisations.

All stakeholders should be based on a common platform where they bring their data catalogue, scoping of data, data availability and periodicity of data exchange. A common identification number (CBIN)[15] creates a common platform and standard. A periodic evaluation of the database must be carried out to check that a CBIN has remained valid and continues to provide a common standard and platform.

### 35.9.4 Third-Party Information

Several advanced tax administrations have MoUs with agencies supplying third party information. They establish common standards and taxonomy for such transactions and set up a mechanism that ensures that such information is exchanged on a regular basis on a digital platform in a seamless manner. CDs and external drives should be avoided when exchanging data as evidenced by poor experiences in some advanced tax administrations.

For data or information exchanged through Service Level Agreements (SLAs), a contact person has to be named through whom a request may be directed. Any change of person has to be informed across the board on a real-time basis so that stakeholders are not misdirected. A concern remains in third party information exchange regarding the maintenance of confidentiality of data exchanged. This is because, essentially, no blame can be laid if there is an erroneous release or use of one organisation's data by another.

## 35.10 Data Storage, Usage and Security

The consolidation of multiple data warehouses and other operational data stores housing multiple sets of data and information is an optimal approach to provide a single view of the inflow and outflow of data or information. An integrated data warehouse also enables cross-function examination and analysis.

The most critical aspect of establishing a data analytics infrastructure is to establish a mechanism to process and structure massive data so that it is ready for analysis. Therefore, it will be imperative for all collaborating agencies to evaluate the quality of data available for meaningful analysis.

Unauthorised access or use of data has to be prevented through safeguarding processes for exchange including security-related protocol of the data and information shared, with clearly articulated access and sharing rights. For reasons of security and confidentiality, data cannot be open to everybody in the organisation. Access should reflect matching of job responsibility with the nature of information. Access

[15] See Chap. 33, Sect. 33.2.

controls are needed in the data warehouses using personnel clearances and layered authorisations. Adopting best practices around data security is a must for maintaining data integrity and privacy, preventing fraudulent use, at the same time allowing seamless and efficient use of data and information.

## 35.11 Conclusions

The use of ICT to facilitate and improve tax compliance and enhance revenue performance is well established. This is witnessed through the widespread and growing its use across tax administrations globally. ICT buttresses tax administration in various ways through the enablement of research in a number of areas. Thus, ICT has helped improve tax policy structures through appropriate revenue modelling, analysis and projections. ICT use has improved voluntary taxpayer compliance, simplified tax return forms and facilitated tax participation. It has improved and sped up the many internal processes that a tax administration must comply with. It has helped construct taxpayer profiles and identified tax evasion including through international information exchange. ICT has, therefore, become an intrinsic component part of an efficient tax administration.

There are of course some risks involved with the increasing use of ICT that include data security risks and problems with large-scale public procurement that have to be actively managed by tax administrations. International knowledge sharing in the ICT field is extremely important and is routinely rendered through multilateral technical assistance.

## References

Cnossen, Sijbren. 1994. Administrative and Compliance Costs of the VAT: A Review of the Evidence. *Tax Notes* 63: 1609–1626.

Diamond, Peter, and James A. Mirrlees. 1971. Optimal Taxation and Public Production: Production Efficiency. *American Economic Review* 61 (1): 8–27.

Engelschalk, Michael, Samia Melhem, and Dana Weist. 2000. Computerizing Tax and Customs Administrations. PREM Notes no. 44, Public Sector. http://documents.worldbank.org/curated/en/543371468298748508/Computerizing-tax-and-customs-administrations. Accessed 18 September 2020.

Engelschalk, Michael. 2007. Designing a Tax System for Micro and Small Businesses: Guide for Practitioners. International Finance Corporation, World Bank Group. http://documents1.worldbank.org/curated/en/980291468158071984/pdf/424350TaxSystem01PUBLIC1.pdf. Accessed 5 November 2020.

KPMG. 2006. *Administrative Burdens – HMRC Measurement Project.* Report by Tax Area, Part 24: Tax Credits. https://webarchive.nationalarchives.gov.uk/20070607050215/http://www.hmrc.gov.uk/better-regulation/part24.pdf. Accessed on 18 September 2020.

Shome, Parthasarathi. 2002. Value Added Tax: Structure and Administration. In *India's Fiscal Matters*, 154–178. New Delhi: Oxford University Press.

———. 2006. Reforms in Tax Administration: Customs. Skoch Group. http://skoch.in/index.php?option=com_content&view=article&id=668:reforms-in-tax-administration-customs&catid=67:bfsi. Accessed 18 September 2020.

———. 2012. *Tax Shastra: Administrative Reforms in India, United Kingdom and Brazil.* New Delhi: Business Standard Books.

Tax Administration Reform Commission (TARC). 2014. *Tax Administration Reform in India: Spirit, Purpose and Empowerment (First Report).* New Delhi: Government of India.

———. 2015. *Tax Administration Reform in India: Spirit, Purpose and Empowerment (Fourth Report).* New Delhi: Government of India.

# Customs Administration

# 36

## 36.1 Introduction

Customs administration fits into an overall tax administration structure in terms of customer focus, structure, people or personnel, and strategy. Yet there are certain functions that are specific to a customs administration in its domestic activities and, in particular, its international liaison aspects. Though customs should provide seamless service rather than becoming an impediment to international economic relations through bureaucratic approaches, and computerisation (ICT) is playing an increasing role in customs processes, there are growing complexities faced by border agencies in trade facilitation challenged by security, money laundering and smuggling with the spread of globalisation. The World Customs Organization (WCO) plays a role in bringing administrations closer in enhancing international economic relations. Specialised skills, competencies, tools and processes are needed, supported by adequate resources, to achieve a world-class customs administration.

Customs administrations have had to respond to these challenges by redefining their roles, reorienting their strategies and altering the traditional control paradigm that had served them well in earlier, more uncomplicated times. They have had to build newer technological, human and organisational capabilities and adopt governance practices congruent with modern standards to both effectively deal with risks as well as meet growing client expectations for higher service standards. In the process, the best practice customs administrations have radically transformed their structures and business processes, taking advantage of the opportunities the rapid advance of technology offers. This chapter focuses primarily on those functions that comprise unique challenges in a customs administration.[1]

[1]See TARC (2014), Second Report, Chap. VIII, for an elaboration of these aspects.



P. Shome, *Taxation History, Theory, Law and Administration*, Springer Texts in Business and Economics, https://doi.org/10.1007/978-3-030-68214-9_36

## 36.2 Customer Orientation

### 36.2.1 Customs Clearance Process

Despite the need for strong risk management, risk in itself should not be allowed to stymy seamless cargo movement through ports and airports. A rigid 'gatekeeper' approach is not a good administrative tool since it has proved to encourage rent-seeking. Instead, enlarged capacity in post-clearance audit should ensure that the smooth flow of goods does not succumb to security failures. Comprehensive digitisation of processes, dematerialisation of documents and advance filing of cargo documents are increasingly the mode used to ensure speed efficiency. High quality of data and documents management close the loop. Thus, highly skilled and expert staff are crucial for post-clearance audit the results from which have to be fed back into risk management. They should be placed in a directorate of valuation carrying out the task.

Customs administrations are advancing their technology platform in the form of the newest techniques such as the 'internet of things' (IOT) that would enable real-time tracking of the movement and clearance of goods through the supply chain, typically through container freight stations and inland container depots with the objective of eliminating more costly and error-prone paper-based processes. Non-intrusive inspection methods such as container scanners and X-ray scanners have to be introduced despite high initial costs. A directorate of procurement and contract management should be established that could also engage with industry and technical institutions to keep its knowledge current.

### 36.2.2 Trade Facilitation

The objective of trade facilitation is to simplify and harmonise trade procedures through rationalising them, to expedite the release and clearance of goods under import, export and transit. That should also reduce the transaction costs of traders and result in greater transparency and predictability of processes.

Stakeholder involvement is essential to gain a better understanding of their needs and concerns. The trade facilitation function should be located with customer focus and taxpayer services in mind (see Chap. 32, Sect. 32.3). A trade facilitation committee containing officials and stakeholders should be empowered to review the facilitation performance of customs and suggest measures for improvement. The committee should have local chapters where customs exist, to resolve local issues.

In countries where private agents play an important role to interact with the customs administration on behalf of their industry clients, there may be some self-interest on the agents' part not to have procedures simplified. Therefore, direct stakeholder involvement of business and industry is essential to achieve meaningful trade facilitation. The customs administration should be proactive with outreach programmes in co-operation with chambers of commerce and industry in this effort. The facilitation committees should also play a part in such programmes.

## 36.3 Risk Management

### 36.3.1 Types of Risk and Mitigation

Customs should establish a specialised risk management division (RMD) that examines all aspects of risk that customs have to address. For example, container selection for inspection of imports and exports comprise one type of risk. Identification of individuals involved poses another type of risk. Criminal activity could be involved. Border control on the water and in air comprises other types of risk. An Information and Communications Technology (ICT)-based passenger information system (PIS) for air transport, incorporating modern identity management, can mitigate those risks. It is not unknown that, reflecting the secrecy involved, sometimes communication may fall in between the cracks which must be studiously avoided. Countries such as Australia, New Zealand and the United States have adopted a national approach to risk management based on research, evidence and action.

### 36.3.2 Anti-smuggling and Enforcement

The work of collecting customs duty and checking for contraband are important tasks assigned to a customs administration. In prevailing times, customs offenses have superseded those related to mere customs duty evasion in many countries, having escalated to money laundering, narcotics, terrorism and narco-terrorism. Simply put, a rationally structured and effective customs organisation is needed for containing the manifestations and occurrence of international terrorism.

Countering trade-based money laundering (TBML) is an emerging phenomenon internationally as it poses an increasing threat to an economy's trade and payments system.[2] Over the last two decades, money laundering and drugs trafficking have been assigned to customs organisations, tasks that were assigned earlier exclusively to security departments. In particular, curbing money laundering is a deeply challenging additional task assigned to customs departments. Money laundering is 'a global phenomenon and international challenge. It is a financial crime that often involves a complex series of transactions and numerous financial institutions across foreign jurisdictions'.[3] It is the cross-border aspect through which the role of customs departments has emerged.

TBML represents mis-invoicing of imports and exports of a country. For example, if imports are undervalued, it implies that actually more cash has been paid than is shown on the import invoice. This results in money being sent out from the country without being accounted for. Similarly, if exports are undervalued, it implies that in reality, more cash must be coming into the country than is being revealed on

[2]See report of Asia Pacific Group on Money Laundering (2012).

[3]See Buchanan (2004), p. 115.

the export invoice. Apart from money laundering, trade mis-invoicing could enable traders to avail of more tax incentives under certain circumstances. It has many such adverse effects.

There is a clear role of customs at the borders with neighbouring countries. For India, the borders with Pakistan, Bangladesh, Nepal and Myanmar are important not only in respect of the military but also in respect of cross-border smuggling. Among advanced economies of the EU, the smuggling of demerit goods such as cigarettes and alcoholic beverages across borders poses a challenge if these items are taxed more highly domestically than across the borders. Sometimes the same bill of lading may be used several times across borders by vehicles, and customs checks play an important role in keeping such practices to a minimum.

Modern tax administrations such as that of the United Kingdom have sharpened their instruments for risk detection through intelligence that continually identifies and contains smuggling and fraud. A well-known instance is what has been called 'carousel fraud' that may take different forms. One is for buyers and sellers to collude. Sellers collect tax at lower than stipulated rates but do not pass it on to the exchequer. Thus, the benefit is effectively shared between seller and buyer through collusion. It was originally detected by customs in the export–import circle; hence the name of the term. This is the kind of role that customs officers have to take on even in advanced economies. Inevitably, this has occurred as their role in collecting revenue from customs has receded with the lowering or abolition of customs tariffs.[4]

For meeting various common objectives, co-operation among customs departments across the globe has intensified over the years. Key factors associated with a low incidence of money laundering have been found to include high internet penetration rates among authorities, connections through international networks, the effectiveness of financial and taxation systems to identify illicit transfer activities and the efficiency of legal systems to resolve cases and bring perpetrators to justice.[5]

Nevertheless, while revenue dependence from customs is a thing of the past in advanced economies, developing economies continue to depend on it through import duties and export duties on commodity exports over which they have international market influence. In such countries, the customs administration tends to examine any undervaluation of imports with a keen eye to prevent revenue leakage, and over-valuation of exports to prevent deceitful availing of export benefits. Ideally, this should be matched with careful matching of customs data with financial flow data of concerned businesses. A directorate of revenue intelligence (DRI) should be set up that co-ordinates with other concerned units such as a risk management division, a financial intelligence unit (FIU), a directorate of enforcement and even the central bank that usually has units to check on the use of foreign exchange in the economy.

As national and international economic and financial crimes proliferate and become more sophisticated, the need for ICT support for intelligence and

---

[4]Shome (2012), p. 18 and p. 60, has dealt in some detail with carousel fraud.

[5]Vaithilingam and Nair (2009) explored these and associated aspects in a study of 88 countries.

investigation also grows. This is one area where the appropriate use of data analytics and computer forensics can play a crucial role in identifying such crimes. Customs officers should be encouraged to specialise in those areas over and above action-oriented activity along coasts and borders that are often popular among younger officers. Specialised training facilities have to be created for such training. India, for example, has established centres of excellence with such training in mind.

### 36.3.3 Infringement of Intellectual Property Rights

The 1994 Agreement on Trade-Related Aspects of Intellectual Property Rights (TRIPS Agreement) has ushered in an era of monitoring intellectual property rights (IPR) through customs which has to increasingly take into account the incidence of counterfeit currency that vitiates the functioning of an economy, and counterfeit goods that threaten health and safety. Counterfeit drugs cause deaths in a number of developing countries as reported by the World Health Organization (WHO) developing countries. Weak enforcement of IPR in such countries enables fake pharmaceuticals to enter their boundaries jeopardising their own citizens. To effectively tackle IPR violations, customs administrations must invest resources in capacity building through training, as well as establish close links with industry that can assist in providing useful third-party information.

### 36.3.4 Terror Challenge

In the prevailing era, the challenge from terror is possibly the newest high risk on the horizon of every customs administration. The World Customs Organization (WCO)[6] Council adopted a Framework of Standards to Secure and Facilitate Global Trade (SAFE FoS) in 2005 to tackle the terror challenge. Many WCO members subsequently began the process of implementing SAFE provisions along four core principles:

- Harmonise advance electronic cargo information on inbound, outbound and transit shipments
- Apply a consistent risk management approach to address security threats
- Use non-intrusive detection equipment even for high-risk containers and cargo
- Provide benefits to businesses that meet a minimum of supply chain security standards and best practices

Thus, the SAFE FoS is based on the twin pillars of customs-to-customs network and customs-to-business partnership that directly addresses the good practices of a customs administration.

---

[6]See Sect. 36.7, for details.

## 36.4 Benefits of Computerisation in Customs Processes in India

'Prudent management of ICT is a means to reap benefits that impact positively on the effectiveness of all customs operations, and hence the improvement of national finances'.[7] In India, two systems integrators have been set up in recent years to achieve connectivity of all offices across the country, thereby sharpening customs administration and improving taxpayer services. First, the customs' electronic data interchange (EDI) allows online assessment of import and export documents. Documents, after being filed, are assessed by the customs department more easily than before. It enables remote control between the customs department and the customs agent so that the latter does not have to be physically present in the customs department. ICT also connects the customs department with the Reserve Bank of India (RBI), India's central bank, other banks and custodians such as the Port Trust. The EDI now covers 85–90% of India's international trade.

Second, the customs department introduced an e-commerce gateway or Indian Customs and Central Excise Electronic Commerce (ICEGATE) in 2004. Currently, it enables e-filing of import or export goods declarations, filing of manifests by airlines and shipping agents and exchange of data between customs and agencies such as the directorate general of foreign trade (DGFT). Thus, declarations and filing, all go through an electronic channel.

There have been other advances. Thus, third, clearance of customs drawbacks and refunds were speeded up through a risk management system so that the total time for clearance has been diminished to a fraction of what it was a few years back. The risk management techniques identify suspect cargo on a random basis. Today in a world that requires enhanced security, there may be a need to revisit such a highly selective system, though the customs authorities should look for methods to be able to retain the essential elements of the risk management system that helped reduce processing time significantly.

Fourth, enhanced computerisation is leading to the production of more meaningful statistics and data management so that both on the customs and domestic—GST and excises—side, the type of data that are generated, can be utilised more usefully for policymaking and administrative improvements.

A national data centre comprises an electronic hardware storage database and facilities management and is linked through a wide area network (WAN) and local area networks (LAN) in offices across the country. This has enabled a build-up of profiles of assessees and an information database of returns of units that pay tax above a certain threshold. Increasingly more units are covered over time under the electronic filing system.

Fifth, electronic registration of assessees has been introduced through several registration facilities including in Bengaluru, Chennai, Delhi, Kolkata and Mumbai. A digital certifying authority enables electronic transactions using digital signatures.

[7] See Lewis (2009), p. 3.

Looking ahead, the future of the customs department in India lies in further deepening of ICT following international norms. The benefits of a robust and healthy customs service through rapidly increasing the use of ICT are continually conveyed to officers. The best way to complement the process is to continue with intensive training workshops to visualise for officers the benefits of ICT. There must also be a concerted effort in reducing moral hazard by minimising the interface between officers and customs agents, with continuing comparative reports on how other emerging economies are proceeding on this issue.

## 36.5 International Co-operation

Customs international co-operation enables the exchange of information on customs aspects such as export and import declaration data, and trader-related and valuation-related information. Bilateral intelligence co-operation occurs through customs mutual administrative agreements (CMAAs) that improve security and facilitation. Customs co-operation also provides training and technical assistance to build capacity and familiarisation of new instruments and tools of analysis and detection.

The international work of customs should be designated to a department that would deal with key international departments, ministries, organisations and stakeholders. The directorate should be empowered to provide technical assistance when requested in a recognised field of the administration's expertise. The Indian customs administration, through its National Academy of Customs, Indirect Taxes and Narcotics (NACIN), that has grown into a high-quality institution, and the Directorate of Valuation provide technical assistance in areas such as drug law enforcement and the use of valuation databases, among others.

## 36.6 Customs' Balancing Role in International Economic Relations

Smoother relations in customs formalities and reasonable restrictions in the clearance of goods and persons foster a good political economy. Unduly tight control or delay in clearance of goods at the point of import or export leads to strains in international relations, both economic and political, apart from the usually discussed rise in business costs. All international commercial transactions are enforced at the border by customs. The commerce department of a government designs the policies on licensing, quantitative restrictions and subsidy to import or export; but such policies are implemented by customs at the point of import and export. Thus, trade facilitation by a customs administration is a significant consideration in promoting good economic and political relations between two countries, and its absence may prove to be a big impediment in those relations.

### 36.6.1 High Tariffs Cause Poor Relations

A high or low customs tariff structure not only has an impact on revenue but it is also an issue in fostering comfortable or tense international economic relations. By raising the customs duty structure very high, imports from any country can be effectively blocked. Sometimes it is directed against cheap imports of selected goods from some country against which the indigenous industry cannot compete, which may go well beyond the infant industry argument. Duty on cars in India had been high to protect the domestic automobile industry. In particular, second-hand cars were protected with high duty in addition to their receiving protection through licence requirements. High duty on agricultural goods in India also made agricultural imports unprofitable. And the limit imposed by the World Trade Organization (WTO) in this respect was high enough so that it enabled India to keep its duty rates within that limit. At one stage there was the case of high customs duty on shoes imported by the United States which made export by other countries to the United States impracticable. Thus, countries continue to create tariff barriers to protect selected domestic industries of particular interest to policymakers. Invariably these lead to counter-pressures from exporting countries thereby affecting trade relations adversely.

### 36.6.2 Interpretation of Licence Requirements

The role of promoting good international relations can be understood more from what adverse impact customs activities could have on international relations. An account is given by an ex-customs officer of India of how the relations between India and Bangladesh came under stress some years back due to the action of customs at the border. It was a religious occasion in Bangladesh when the consumption of onion goes up significantly. Last-minute supply of many truckloads of onion from India was held up by customs at the India–Bangladesh border due to non-compliance with some customs formalities by onion exporters at the Indian end. It created almost a crisis across the border and led to frantic telephone calls by the diplomatic staff from the High Commission of Bangladesh. Last-minute intervention by the senior-most customs officer in Kolkata prevented a crisis and saved the day from precipitating both an economic and a political situation between the two neighbours.

Unduly harsh customs interpretation of licence requirements or regulations had also upset jute trade with Bangladesh. There was an instance when, for apparently insignificant violation of licence given for the purpose of import of raw jute, whole shiploads of raw jute consignments were held up by the customs. It was only after a timely intervention by higher authorities that such consignments were released. Thus, overtly strict positions by customs on smaller matters should be reconsidered from a realistic perspective for, otherwise, international economic relations would certainly suffer. Customs has to rise to this responsibility over and above attending to its routine tasks and calls of duty.

### 36.6.3 Customs and International Treaties

The interplay between customs and an international treaty can be seen both as a theoretical premise and in practice. In theory, it is important because, at the stage of negotiation of the treaty, the role of customs is to help arrive at desirable rates of duty due to their probable favourable impact on the economy, in comparison with existing rates. At the execution stage, the role of customs is perhaps even greater because it has to ensure that the intention of the treaty is achieved in implementation.

Yet, caution needs to be taken. In the implementation of India–Nepal treaties where passage-through is allowed, for example, it is incumbent on customs to ensure that the goods intended for Nepal do not flow back for sale in India.[8] However, it has been noticed that Nepal's imports are of a kind that are unlikely to be needed in Nepal. For example, an instance arose in which enormous amounts of zip fasteners and machinery were imported which could not be absorbed in Nepal in practical terms. It is the duty of customs to maintain a balance between surveillance and maintenance of friendly relations with an important neighbour in both geopolitical and sociopolitical terms. No excessive counter-measure can be taken that might tilt the balance in an unwarranted direction. Thus, the nuanced role expected of customs in enforcing international treaties with a fine balance cannot be exaggerated.

## 36.7 World Customs Organization (WCO)

The WCO is an independent intergovernmental body whose mission is to enhance the effectiveness and efficiency of member customs administrations. The WCO was originally established as the Customs Co-operation Council (CCC) in 1952. The CCC adopted the name World Customs Organization in 1994 in order to reflect its transition to a truly global intergovernmental institution. It has two wings, valuation and classification. It is headquartered in Brussels. With its worldwide membership, the WCO is recognised as the voice of the global customs community. It is particularly noted for its work in areas covering the development of international conventions, instruments and tools on topics such as commodity classification, valuation, rules of origin, collection of customs revenues, international trade facilitation, customs enforcement activities and combating counterfeiting in support of IPR.

The WCO's objective is the attainment of the highest possible degree of harmony and uniformity in nomenclature, valuation and rules. Its Harmonized System for the Description and Coding of Goods (HS) is based on rules that have been developed for classification, headings and subheadings. It comprises a nomenclature for goods and administers the technical aspects of the WTO agreements on customs valuation and rules of origin. Today the same nomenclature for goods and the same system of

[8]Nepal, being a land locked country, has the right to import via India and there are treaties to enforce this right.

valuation of goods are followed all over the world as almost all countries have joined the WCO.

> The HS 2007 contains 380 notes and 56 sub-heading notes which are valid worldwide, and the EC has added 98 additional notes within a combined nomenclature (CN) and the Common Customs Tariff (CCT). The 534 notes that accompany the 1221 HS-headings, 5052 HS-sub-headings and 9720 CN-sub-headings are proof of the complexity of the rules of the CCT which contains more than 16,500 legal rules for the classification of goods.[9]

This micro-information has to be meticulously noted and entered, a task that is often assigned to the customs department.

Trade has become smoother since the nomenclature of goods has made the basis of trade clearer. For example, if an item is described as 5402 20 10 in the invoice of the manufacturing country, wherever it is sold anywhere in the world, it will be taken as a synthetic filament yarn of terylene or dacron. There is no need to test the goods chemically unless the customs have any specific information to the effect that the goods have been misdeclared. This has made customs clearance, maintenance of statistics and related customs activities transparent and seamless.

## 36.8 European Customs Union (ECU)

The ECU, as a part of the European Union (EU), performs the job of smooth customs regulations within the EU. Its focus is on trade relations within the EU and in the global economic community in general. That the EU has a separate organisation within its fold exclusively for the purpose of customs activities, underlines the importance that European countries assign to customs policy and its application in international trade.

## 36.9 Capacity Building

### 36.9.1 Multilateral Efforts

The WCO has initiated capacity building for WCO members through the so-called Columbus Programme introduced in January 2006. Its aim is to implement the SAFE FoS, and other WCO conventions and instruments, as well as best practices in the area of customs administration. It is a three-phase programme to deliver a standardised approach to developing solutions tailored to a country's reality. It incorporates links to WCO instruments, tools and best practices including organisational development, customs capacity diagnostics, leadership and management, orientation for decision-makers, risk management and integrity. All WCO members can benefit from this comprehensive programme in the quest to achieve

[9]See Weerth (2008), p. 111.

harmonisation with other member countries in the rising challenges of customs administration.

### 36.9.2 Domestic Policies

Capacity building requires long-term action consisting of multi-year plans for building, sustaining and renewing the developed capacities. Chapter 32, Sect. 32.4 addressed the people function extensively, identifying weaknesses and outlining the course for improvement. Those issues carry over to the customs area as well. Training courses should incorporate upgraded curricula and use ICT tools including e-training and webinars. Adequate allocation of financial resources has to be a part of such capacity building.

In a competency-based approach, having the right people in the right jobs with the right skills can be the secret of the organisation's success. This calls for the specialisation of officers who, after comprehensive training in a specialised field, should be allowed to stay on in a highly specialised job rather than getting transferred routinely after every 2 or 3 years. This is also an important element of the people function.

## 36.10 Customs Administration and Exports

If duties on exports and on their inputs are high, the post-tax cost of those goods is high and exports become uncompetitive. Duty drawback assumes importance in such cases. These are usually designed by the commerce department in consonance with the customs department and implemented by the latter. Achieving appropriate design, including the removal of embedded taxes from exports, as well as implementation, are major tasks in ensuring export competitiveness. Reflecting the complexity of a well-functioning duty drawback system, some developing country environments have not been fully cognizant of the need to provide duty drawback or offset for GST or VAT against exports.

In recently emerging economies such as Myanmar, it has been found that[10] as the country opens up to international norms and practices, tariff structures may not yet be set up so that exports are given an input tax credit. Though customs tariffs on import components of exports are theoretically given drawback, unless the manufacturing unit is fully export-oriented, businesses may remain unable to receive drawback for the portion that is exported. This partially reflects the lack of a formula based on which drawback can be given and partially poor administration practices. In turn, it gives rise to tensions among the domestic business community against their international competitors or invitees who operate in new Special Economic Zones (SEZs) with full facility of customs duty drawback and input tax credit and

[10] See Myanmar taxation report by Shome and Chaudhury (2012).

offset of commercial taxes paid.[11] Thus, poor design and administrative practices at customs can have adverse ramifications on industry and trade. If that is the case, corrective policies to mitigate discrepancies have to be put in place as early as possible.

## 36.11 Conclusions

To conclude, while customs administration reflects operational aspects that are typical of the domestic side of a tax administration, it also plays a crucial role in the stability of international trade and finance. Its role has moved on from mere collection of customs and export duty to managing smuggling, money laundering and international terror that bear upon the smooth and safe functioning of the prevailing global economy. For such an increasingly complex role, a well-designed customs administration incorporating specialisation in the responsibilities of officers, and buttressed by an advanced ICT system, is a must.

Reflecting such international aspects, multilateral organisations including the WTO and WCO, dealing with customs structures based on globally recognised codes and co-ordinated implementation strategies, are playing increasingly visible roles. They provide guidance for limiting tariff dispersions and controlling disputes. Several multilateral organisations also provide technical assistance for the development of specialised skills, competencies and ICT knowledge with the objective of countries being able to achieve world-class customs administration levels.

Customs administrations have tended to respond by redefining their roles, reorienting their strategies and altering traditional approaches by moving towards international norms. They are increasingly using cutting edge ICT, incorporating human and organisational capabilities and adopting reformed governance practices to meet growing client expectations for higher service standards.

## References

Asia Pacific Group on Money Laundering. 2012. *Money Laundering Vulnerabilities of Free Trade Zone.* 2010 Financial Action Task Force. APG Typology Report on Trade Based Money Laundering.

Buchanan, Bonnie. 2004. Money Laundering – A Global Obstacle. *Research in International Business and Finance* 18 (1): 115–127.

Lewis, Gareth. 2009. The Impact of ICT on Customs. *World Customs Journal* 3 (1): 3–25.

Shome, Parthasarathi. 2012. *Tax Shastra: Administrative Reforms in India, United Kingdom and Brazil.* New Delhi: Business Standard Books.

Shome, Parthasarathi, and Hafiz Chaudhury. 2012. *Myanmar: Fundamental Tax Reform.* Washington DC: International Tax and Investment Centre (ITIC).

[11] Myanmar did not yet have a VAT but a commercial tax against which offset was given for tax paid on goods though not for tax on services.

Tax Administration Reform Commission (TARC). 2014. *Tax Administration Reform in India: Spirit, Purpose and Empowerment, Second Report.* New Delhi: Government of India.

Vaithilingam, Santha, and Mahendhiran Nair. 2009. Mapping Global Money Laundering Trends: Lessons for Pace Setters. *Research in International Business and Finance* 23 (1): 18–30.

Weerth, Carsten. 2008. HS 2007: Notes of the Tariff Nomenclature and the Additional Notes of the EC. *World Customs Journal* 2 (1): 111–115.

# Part VII

# Ideal Tax Design

# A Good Tax System: A Rapid Review 37

## 37.1 Tax Policy, Tax Revenue and Tax Reform

The justification for taxes lies in a government's need for resources to carry out its essential functions while keeping in mind various costs associated with taxation. These costs reflect the direct cost of tax collection as well as its probable deleterious effects on the efficiency of an economy's allocation of resources and the possibility that it could have high compliance costs or result in inequity among taxpayers. Nevertheless, to reduce the fiscal deficit, before curtailing expenditures, governments often tend to identify new tax measures. This is possible because, within fiscal policy, a tax revenue increase, though its underlying processes may be complex, is generally easier to implement than the politically more difficult task of cutting public expenditure. This is especially so as increasing proportions of the expenditure budget reflect debt service of government and administrative costs that are impossible or difficult to cut back. These factors explain country authorities' heavy focus on taxation measures.

The challenge has become more real in recent years as economies have been forced to grapple with increasing public expenditure demands leading from crises of economic destabilisation such as during an Asian economic crisis during 1997–1998, a global financial and economic crisis during 2008–2010 and an exogenous pandemic in 2020 that is likely to continue into 2021 and has resulted in formidable declines in global economic growth or even contraction of some economies. The need to raise tax revenue is clear; yet raising it when unemployment is rising and incomes are falling in every economic sector becomes a double-edged knife. Therefore, the challenges to tax policy and tax administration cannot be overemphasised and they are anticipated to grow in the decades to follow.

The fascination with tax revenue increase is understandable in cases where governments undertake reform. Reform usually comes after a downward slide in tax revenue attributable to a prevailing cumbersome tax structure that they wish to correct. Country experiences reveal that most countries that carried out tax reform with the stated objectives of improving the efficiency, equity, neutrality and

 
P. Shome, *Taxation History, Theory, Law and Administration*, Springer Texts in Business and Economics, https://doi.org/10.1007/978-3-030-68214-9_37

administrative simplicity of their tax systems also experienced a perceptible increase in their tax revenue to GDP ratios. Thus, even though tax reform need not necessarily be declared to have a direct revenue objective, in effect, this seems to have been commonly the case.

The conceptual basis and principles of taxation were examined and applied to various taxes including taxes on individual and corporate incomes. We elaborated on offshoots of the corporate income tax that use alternate tax bases such as taxes on cash flow and presumptive and minimum taxes on some definition of net worth or gross assets that are contemplated for surer revenue collection or greater conceptual simplicity. The problem with such taxes, however, often lies in their narrow bases or their possibly inequitable effects.

We examined pertinent design and policy issues for taxes on consumption such as the GST and VAT, and on production such as selective excises. Many countries have reformed their consumption tax structures with a simpler and more rational base such as value added of goods and services supplied, and crediting out any taxes paid on inputs, thus eliminating double taxation or cascading. We also examined taxes on international trade such as customs and export duties that have undergone major tariff reforms in recent years, bringing down tariff rates and providing a positive impulse to globalisation.

Subsequently, we addressed the essential task of drafting good tax law and the role of a fair yet firm tax administration that are important areas in their own right. We examined in some detail the emergence of international taxation as an emerging concern regarding effective non-taxation of multinational enterprises (MNEs). This has arisen from their structuring their tax affairs by using provisions accessible through tax treaties and loopholes in domestic law, to pay less than a percent or even half a percent of their global profits as tax revenue globally. And we looked at the history of taxation using India as a case study, citing from its history what modern economies have to avoid in their extraction of tax revenue from the otherwise willing taxpayer.

## 37.2 A Rapid Review

After the sojourn we have undertaken in this textbook, we are now ready to sum up what may be thought of as a good tax system, that is, one that is economically rational and easy to understand and administer. Such a system's focus should be on major revenue sources with simple structures while eschewing small taxes and minimising exemptions and incentives. The short review undertaken here is not exhaustive; rather, it should be considered as a checklist for the most essential elements of what we have learnt and what comprise the minimum considerations of a good tax system.

### 37.2.1 Principles of Taxation

- Minimise the efficiency costs of resource allocation, including the detrimental inter-temporal effects of taxation that have emerged through new analyses.
- Maintain, and possibly enhance, equity through the tax system.
- Support stabilisation of the economy through appropriate progressivity in, and built-in elasticity of, the tax system.
- Be aware of the adequacy of revenue, though this should not be the sole or primary purpose of the tax system.
- Ensure simplicity of the overall structure so that it is easy for officials to administer and for taxpayers to comply with.

### 37.2.2 Tax Structure

- Shorn of all superstructure, at the central government level, the tax system should comprise a single-rated GST or VAT, three or four selective excises, a single-rated customs tariff, and a zero-export duty.
- There should be one to three individual income tax rates, a payroll tax on wages to finance a pension system that may be complemented by an option to save for retirement through provident fund of individual accounts.
- The best is a single rated corporate income tax and an environmental tax on businesses. In case of the existence of tax incentives, this should be countered with a minimum tax based on a wider base than that of the corporate income tax.
- The tax system should eschew small taxes, such as estate duty (at death), bequests or gift tax, or select one that provides a rationale suitable for that society. At times of a national emergency or international crisis, a short-term tax such as a very small tax on all financial transactions has been contemplated though not with much success.
- At the subnational level, tax systems should include a GST or VAT at the state or provincial government level and a property tax and user charges at the local government level. Tax assignment to different levels of government is elaborated in Sect. 37.2.12.

### 37.2.3 Tax Law

#### 37.2.3.1 Separation of Powers

- Democracies practice a separation of powers among the legislature, executive and judicial branches of government. Lawmaking is carried out by the legislature, implementation of law is undertaken by the executive or administrative branch, and judicial consideration and pronouncements on the application of law and resolution of litigation are the responsibility of the judiciary.
- The separation of powers among the branches—legislative, executive, judiciary—is practised in India. Its evolution can be tracked over centuries.

- The separation tends to become unclear in non-democratic forms of government. This reflects a major deficiency in the constitutional setup of such systems.

#### 37.2.3.2 Tax Assignment in the Constitution

- A country's constitution assigns the responsibility of collection and allocation of revenue of different taxes to several levels—central or federal, state or provincial, local or municipal—of government.
- A mix of the definitions of taxpayer, taxable event, tax base, tax rates, and rules of administration may, or may not, be specified in the constitution.
- While upper levels of government can usually borrow, it is unusual for a constitution to allow lower levels of government to borrow. Yet bonds issued by municipalities in the United States provide an example of local governments successfully financing and undertaking economic infrastructure projects.
- Revenue assignment of taxes to lower levels of government has not necessarily led to their determined effort to generate revenue, particularly in developing countries. Thus, grants and revenue sharing from central government taxes have played an important role in financing lower-level governments.

#### 37.2.3.3 Tax Legislation

- In the writing of tax law, one aspect that has assumed importance is the purpose of the legislation. Thus, any treatise on the principles of tax law provides references to case law to provide justification for a position being taken on a particular point.
- The introduction of tax law can face various practical obstacles through lobbyists or because of internal political pressures. Thus, through successive administrations, India has been unable to introduce a new Direct Tax Code, though a GST law was introduced in 2017 in somewhat of a hurry after more than a decade of deliberations and drafting of draft laws. The common perception has been that, as a result, it suffers from faulty design.
- Thus, 'tax is often seen as an ephemeral area: as a part of law devoid of principle and subject to the whims of politicians'.[1]

#### 37.2.3.4 Law and Subordinate Law

- Implementation of tax law usually rests with the executive branch and, accordingly, its first interpretation as well. It, therefore, issues subordinate law or rules and regulations, and circulars including for clarifications of law. Subordinate law should explain rather than conflict with statutory law, however.
- Courts are the final arbiter of tax law and adjudicate disputes between the tax administration and the taxpayer. However, judicial interpretation may vary regarding whether an interpretative issue even exists, or in ascertaining the legislative intent of a law. Some judiciaries use more, others less, legislative history, in concluding on a point.

---

[1]Lee (2013), p. 13.

#### 37.2.3.5 Drafting Tax Law

- In the case of tax law, factual considerations such as organisation of sections, the type of language to be used to ensure comprehensibility without sacrificing necessary detail, and effectiveness in conveying the proper message to taxpayers and tax officers alike, combine to indicate the quality of the law.
- In drafting tax law, the drafter has to be aware of the policy behind the law and subordinate law so that the purpose of the law is conveyed through the law itself.
- It is the drafter's responsibility to see that there is no ambiguity between the law and subordinate law. The certainty that the absence of ambiguity produces ensures the effectiveness of the law combined with subordinate law.
- It is the responsibility of the legislator to determine what goes into law and what goes into subordinate law. While a law has the force of legislative backing, rules usually do not and, therefore, must possess the quality of absolute clarity if it has to minimise the possibility of litigation.
- Subordinate law protects the main law from becoming too cumbersome. The drafter has to achieve sufficiency in the law and, at the same time, convey the importance and gravity of rules almost in the same light.
- Usually, there are so many definitions in a tax law that modern tax law tends to place definitions in a special section at the end. Short definitions may be put in footnotes which facilitates cross-referencing. However, there is no hard and fast rule in approaching this separation.
- Brevity, consistency and organisation remain paramount objectives to be achieved in drafting tax law:
  - Brevity is a quality of good drafting. A short tax statute is likely to be frequently referred to for popular use in contrast to a tome meant to be picked up by only a few.
  - The structure of sentences has to be simple and consistent in the use of number, voice, punctuation, parentheses, phrases and footnotes.
  - The organisation must be also simple in section headings, and the way they are numbered and sequenced. If there are volumes, they must be rationally distributed.
- There is a caveat. No justifiable complexity should be sacrificed of course.

### 37.2.4 Taxing Income and Expenditure

- Both income and expenditure may be taxed, though they may be seen as two sides of a macroeconomic identity so that a student of taxation may ask: why tax both?
- For practical reasons, both are considered independent revenue sources and, from an administrative viewpoint, the income tax and VAT could be used jointly to enhance cross-verification and reduce tax planning by straying taxpayers.

## 37.2.5 Income Tax: Individual and Corporate

### 37.2.5.1 Basic Design

- The definition of income for tax purposes should be comprehensive: consumption plus net wealth accumulation.
- The personal and corporate income taxes should be ideally integrated; otherwise, there is likely to be some double taxation between the two.
- Capital gains and income should be distinguished since a change in value is different from the flow of income. For example, exchange rate effects are gains, not income.
- The measurement of income, of progressivity and of valuation have posed, and continue to pose, challenges in tax systems.
- Correct valuation methods of assets and liabilities have to be specified. It has to be kept in mind that varying specifications of loss carry-over may affect risk-taking and investment differently.
- Interest and dividends pose problems. The former is deductible, but the latter is not (or only partially); thus, there is a bias towards debt financing and thin capitalisation from full interest deductibility. Some tax systems have accordingly limited its full extent.

### 37.2.5.2 Financial Sector Deductibility

- The tax deductibility of provisioning for bad loans has become important in the post-financial crisis era. However, there has to be a ceiling for provisioning that is allowable for tax purposes.
- Deduction should be allowed for the costs of services relating to an investment. Such costs may be lumped with the cost of the investment itself but have to be separated to minimise any understatement of income.
- Insurance premiums represent both a payment for services and a deposit for investment; separating the two could be difficult but has to be carried out for tax purposes.

### 37.2.5.3 Globalisation and Income Tax

- Globalisation has spread rapidly. For example, 85–90% of trade—exports and imports—of US parent MNEs are made to and from their foreign affiliates.
- Transfer pricing rules attempt to limit an MNE's strategy to distribute prices and costs across subsidiaries to minimise tax liability.
- Arm's length transactions require parent companies and subsidiaries to set prices for internal transactions as if there was no mutual relationship between them.
- The form of establishment chosen—branches and subsidiaries—selected usually reflects competing criteria.
- The advantages of a branch are:
  - The losses of a branch are deductible in computing home-country tax liability.
  - A parent company can transfer property to a branch without tax liability in the home country.

  - A branch can repatriate after-tax profits to the parent company without further taxation, such as a withholding tax.
  - Tax incentives are applicable to a branch, but not to a subsidiary.
- The advantages of a subsidiary are:
  - The parent company cannot defer home-country taxation of branch income, whether or not it is remitted to the home country.
  - To limit tax avoidance, host countries give less generous tax options to branches than to subsidiaries (such as loss carry-overs and deductions).

#### 37.2.5.4 Source Versus Residence Principle

- Countries have used the source principle of taxation for non-residents and the residence principle for persons residing within the country. Variations in treatment among countries imply the likelihood of double taxation of MNEs.
- Double taxation avoidance agreements (DTAAs) or bilateral tax treaties to limit double taxation between country tax authorities grew over the past decades including among emerging economies. But, as their number has grown, MNEs learnt to find loopholes in them and thereby to minimise their overall global tax contribution while adhering to the literal interpretation of tax law.
- Resultantly, at the behest of the G-20 group of countries, the Organisation of Economic Cooperation and Development (OECD) took up a project to minimise tax base erosion and profit shifting (BEPS) that MNEs use across international boundaries to minimise their global tax contributions.

### 37.2.6 Tax Structure and Foreign Direct Investment (FDI)

- Globalisation translates to increased opportunities for cross-border investment. This has resulted in a unilateral scaling back of corporate tax rates across the globalised world as competition for FDI has grown.
- For an investor, if non-tax factors such as labour markets and provision of infrastructure are similar across countries, then tax factors assume importance.
- If tax factors are indeed significant, their relative transparency, simplicity, stability and certainty become important.
- Tax relief may enhance the attractiveness of the host country if it is able to offset additional business costs of a particular location.
- For a country, FDI yields a stream of benefits, such as host-country tax revenue from increased employment and capital stock as well as the transfer of advanced technology, but FDI also has a stream of static costs, such as the revenue forgone from tax incentives.
- The predominant view remains that tax incentives are distortive and lead to tax planning and to short—rather than long—term investment. If non-tax factors characteristics of an economy are of high quality, providing tax incentives would not be necessary.

### 37.2.7 Alternative Corporate Tax Bases to Reduce Complexity

#### 37.2.7.1 Cash-Flow Tax

- It taxes the difference between the sales and purchases of a company. There are some variants of this concept.
- It succeeds in avoiding grappling with the definition of economic depreciation, measuring capital gains, valuing inventories and adjusting for inflation.
- It eliminates the bias towards debt financing.
- No country has introduced a cash-flow tax since it fails to follow the underlying tenets of taxation based on economic income; also, it would drastically reduce the tax base and, therefore, need a high tax rate to maintain revenue adequacy.

#### 37.2.7.2 Minimum Alternate Tax (MAT)

- Advanced and emerging economies have used some variant of the concept of MAT.
- A MAT attempts to restore revenue adequacy based on an alternate, expanded tax base.
- It enhances equity by reducing tax avoidance by profit-making 'zero tax companies'.
- It improves efficiency since the MAT necessitates low-yielding business activities to shift resources to higher-yielding economic activities.
- The advantage of designing a MAT that uses gross assets as a base is that it is easy to define and administer. To illustrate, if a taxpayer is assumed to earn a 6% return on gross assets and the corporate tax rate is 35%, the equivalent MAT rate is 2.1% ($35 \times 6/100$) on gross assets.
- Alternate bases such as net worth is more complex and erode the base.
- A MAT can become the tax expected to be paid in the long run if it allows sufficiently long periods of loss carry-overs against which the MAT could be adjusted.

### 37.2.8 Financial Transaction Tax (FTT)

- A tax on financial transactions such as bank debits should, at best, be a temporary revenue-raising measure. After Argentina and Brazil, many smaller Latin American countries introduced a tax on bank debits. Brazil continues to maintain it in its tax statute but has reduced its rate to zero. India introduced its own version in 2006 but subsequently removed it in 2009.
- The prevailing expert view is that an FTT has the potential to distort financial sector functioning and drive some transactions underground. Thus, if it is at all used, it should be used with a specific objective and only as a short-term measure.
- Recently it appears that the FTT, together with a global tax on carbon emissions, has come into view as a possible financing instrument against global climate change but it is likely to face stiff opposition from powerful country authorities.

### 37.2.9 Payroll Tax

- The payroll tax is earmarked for social insurance—social security, health, unemployment and disability. Its basis is an intergenerational social contract, termed pay-as-you-go (PAYG).
- An alternative is an individual account-based, fully funded (FF) provision that provides a retirement pension to participants.
- The tax is imposed on wage income; employers also have to contribute. The incidence of the payroll tax, however, is mainly on labour since the amount collected from employers is likely to be passed on to employees. Thus, it is said to be regressive.
- Its characteristic structure puts a ceiling on contributions and it is therefore doubly regressive since it has no incidence above a certain income. In this sense, it is not a transfer from the rich to the poor.
- Slowly growing developed economies with ageing populations face problems with a build-up of liability under a PAYG system. Yet they use this principle, while faster-growing labour-rich developing countries tend to use an FF system, mainly to contain the financial costs of a typical PAYG system that has a wider coverage and set of objectives.

### 37.2.10 Taxation of Non-renewable Resources

- Royalties should be based on the difference between the commodity price at the mine or well-head and the cost of extraction. If companies cannot pay this, the resource should remain unexploited.
- Expenditures that yield income over many periods have to be capitalised and appropriately matched.
- The involvement of MNEs requires careful watch to limit any bias towards debt. Good transfer pricing rules are necessary, and they should be enforced to ensure that transactions are at arm's length. Contract negotiations with MNEs can be a major lacuna for developing countries.
- A cash-flow type tax has been recommended to supplement royalties. The government would receive revenue only after the investor makes a threshold return on the project; thus, the government would share in the profit. The fear that the tax will scare away investment is not well founded since investment decisions at the margin would remain unaffected.

### 37.2.11 Taxes on Production and Consumption

#### 37.2.11.1 Consumption Taxes

- The retail sales tax (RST) and the GST or VAT should be equivalent if the GST or VAT is correctly designed. The RST is difficult to apply in developing countries because it is collected only at the stage of retail sales while the same amount of revenue is collected over the entire chain of production and distribution from the GST or VAT. Thus, if the retail stage is missed then the RST does not yield any revenue from the commodity concerned. But if any stage is missed, then revenue from only that stage is lost in the case of GST or VAT. Therefore, the latter are likely to yield more revenue than the RST on the same tax base.

- The GST or VAT eliminates 'cascading' or 'tax on tax' since credit is given on input taxes paid along the supply chain. Theoretically, even an RST should not suffer from cascading unless some inputs are taxed as retail sales for which no credit is given.
- The GST or VAT is not an easy tax: it needs time to prepare, and its structure affects its success and the rate of evasion. The broader the tax base covering goods and services, the lower is the evasion.
- Country experience reveals that tax evasion is lower with a GST or VAT than with the income tax.
- The consumption of services should be included in the GST or VAT base, to begin with in the form of an exhaustive list of services which are to be taxed (positive list) and, later, in the form of a negative list that identifies only those services that are to be excluded from the base.

#### 37.2.11.2 Production Taxes

- Selective excises are levied on a few commodities over and above the GST or VAT and are levied on depletable and non-renewable resources such as petroleum products, demerit goods such as consumable alcohol and tobacco products, and luxuries such as fur, yachts, and sports cars.
- The tax rates are preferred to be ad valorem or percentage rates since the revenue yield is not lost with inflation. On the other hand, specific rates, in currency units per unit of production, yield less revenue in real terms during times of inflation but are more convenient to collect, for example, in terms of the number of cigarette boxes or crates of liquor.
- If possible, the design should be ad valorem, that is, based on a percentage but practicality, such as in developing countries, may dictate the inclusion of specific rates as well.
- Most countries use a combination of ad valorem and specific rates.

#### 37.2.11.3 Environment Taxes

- Environment taxes are essential as global pollution has triggered climate change that scientists claim is likely to cause the destruction of the planet in a few centuries or earlier.
- Yet few countries impose them adequately due to its cost implications since the tax rate must be set to 'internalise' costs that are not ordinarily perceivable in the market. For example, the cost of pollution caused by the emission of smoke from a factory must be included in a product's market price, and tax revenue extracted from the resultant higher market price.

- Important developed countries remain unconvinced of the need for environmental taxes. Only global action can address the issue of global environmental or carbon tax comprehensively.

#### 37.2.11.4 International Trade Taxes

- The consensus view is that a graduated customs tariff structure is good—the highest rate on final goods, a middle rate on intermediate goods, and the lowest rate on capital goods.
- A uniform customs tariff, however, is better to maintain a simple overall customs tariff structure, since a graduated structure is difficult to work out correctly without knowing the exact nature of final, intermediate and capital goods in any system of production.
- Advanced economies had achieved almost a zero-tariff structure until, over the last 5 years, geopolitical tensions have witnessed the reintroduction of tariff rates on the imports from rival trading countries. The overall consensus is that movement in such a direction has been detrimental to global trade and economic growth.

### 37.2.12 Taxation in a Decentralised Economy

#### 37.2.12.1 Essential Concepts

- Tax assignment means where tax revenue rights from a particular tax lie at different levels of government as per a country's constitution.
- Usually, the central government is assigned the income tax, customs tariffs, GST or VAT, and selected excises. States may also be assigned a GST or VAT to run in parallel with that of the central government. This is the case, for example, in Brazil, Canada and India.
- States in the United States are allowed by its constitution to 'piggyback' on the central government's income tax, but this is not common in other countries.
- Revenue-sharing refers to how tax revenue is shared among different levels of government reflecting recommendations of a country's appointed body such as a finance commission.
- Analysis has revealed that vertical imbalance among higher to lower levels of government is not necessarily harmful. Expenditure responsibility at the lower levels of government can be beneficial, but balancing the fiscal sector should remain the central government's responsibility. This implies that revenue-sharing should be accordingly increased from central to state or provincial governments, in order to maintain fiscal balance across levels of government.

#### 37.2.12.2 Local Governments

- Local governments should tax immobile bases—the property tax is best. The base should be simple, for example, sale price, and not esoteric concepts such as fair market value.

- The tax rate should be low, 0.5–0.7%. This explains the United States' success in mobilising resources with the tax.
- Developing countries impose higher rates fearing that the correct bases of properties are not revealed for property taxation. Experience has shown, however, that this does not lead to greater revenue generation.
- Developing countries' lament that there is a constraint posed by the lack of a cadastral survey is sometimes exaggerated. Municipalities in such countries have adopted innovative methods of calculations of location blocs on which the same tax is imposed. This has ensured revenue productivity.
- Local governments also utilise user charges since they can be collected immediately, that is, at the point of using a public service. This supports the maintenance and improvements in such services such as that of roads and parks.

#### 37.2.12.3 Country Experiences

- Brazil and Canada introduced a state-level VAT to limit cascading. India was a relative latecomer.
- The United States uses an RST at the state level. Each state has its own structure. Some states eschew the tax and depend on revenue from other sources such as petroleum in Texas and the insurance sector in Delaware.
- India has a GST. It is a federal tax comprising bother central and state governments. The GST being a consumption tax, the concern is how to transfer the revenue collected in the producing state to the consuming state for every product.
- The producing state puts the revenue collected from an importer in another state into a clearing house operated by the central government. It is the latter's responsibility to distribute revenue collected from a producing state to the appropriate importing state. Sophisticated ICT algorithms work to ensure success in this operation.
- Other federal countries such as Argentina have attempted to introduce a federal VAT or GST but it has proven too challenging so far for the central governments and provinces to arrive at an agreement.
- The health of a consolidated fiscal arrangement, encompassing all levels of government, has to be monitored by the central government, and adequate safeguards must be put in place for it to function efficiently.

#### 37.2.12.4 Finance Commission

- India's experience reveals that this quinquennial constitutional body has been a stable institution that has determined the rules for revenue sharing by the central government with state governments as well as the rules for interstate revenue distribution every 5 years.
- Such a body should be temporary and should not be made into a permanent institution lest it should turn into a bureaucracy.
- Countries such as Argentina and Brazil that do not have a stable framework such as India's finance commission have perennially suffered from instability in their revenue-sharing arrangements.

## 37.3 Role of Tax Administration

### 37.3.1 Guiding Principles

The guiding principles in designing a good tax administration comprise a simple tax structure pari passu with clear and transparent tax and accounting laws. This facilitates tax administration and reduces compliance costs faced by taxpayers that, in turn, encourages voluntary compliance on their part. On the operations side, tax collection processes, rationally differentiating the treatment of taxpayers by size, identifying key bottlenecks in taxpayer registration, tax returns and processing of payments, detection of stop-filers and delinquent taxpayers, a selective audit system with a rational penalty structure, complimented by taxpayer service and publicity, are its nuts and bolts. The overall structure of a tax administration, with the processing of tax aspects of large taxpayers under one umbrella, is crucial. Staff or people management with the objective of inculcating a cadre of professional personnel is imperative for efficient implementation.[2]

### 37.3.2 Service Delivery

It is not a surprise that a tax administration is an institution that requires constant alertness and willingness to reform its accountability, cost-effectiveness and, increasingly in a modernising context, the quality of its service delivery, over and above its objective of revenue productivity. Some countries have developed the practice of subjecting their tax administration structure to occasional external examination to facilitate and introduce corrective measures.

### 37.3.3 Customer Focus

The widespread international view is that taxpayer services with a 'customer focus' must be designed to improve the experience of taxpayers with the tax administration and to decrease the cost of taxpayer compliance. Ease of following the rules can come from reducing uncertainty in tax laws and providing clarity on tax obligations. Opening two-way communication channels between the tax departments and customers is another aspect of the strategy. This part addresses tax administration aspects and provides evidence on cross-country practices.

[2]See Silvani and Baer (1997).

### 37.3.4 Structure and Management

#### 37.3.4.1 Unified Management

No tax administration reform can be complete without examining its structure and management. While there is no unique model of the structure and management of a tax administration, cross-country patterns have emerged. The clear movement is towards a common organisation for direct taxes and indirect taxes. Another area of synergy is organising a tax administration on a functional basis instead of on the basis of territorial jurisdictions. A unified management structure could be achieved based on data integration, a common delivery structure for the benefit of taxpayers, and the training of officers and staff reflecting benchmarked parameters.

#### 37.3.4.2 Specialisation in Skills

A tax administration must allow its officers to specialise in skills. Otherwise, they would suffer from a lack of deep understanding of complex emerging issues or to interface with highly specialised private sector tax intermediaries and taxpayers. These skills do not come with only theoretical exposure but while working on the subject for a minimum of 4–5 years. International experience reveals even periods as long as a decade during which an officer is encouraged to specialise. Specialisation is required in the minutiae of audit functions, international taxation, dispute management and taxpayer services. Other specialised functions include tax research and analysis, and information and communications technology (ICT) management.

#### 37.3.4.3 People Function

Globally, the 'people' function has become increasingly nuanced. It refers to the guidance and welfare of activities, responsibilities and behaviour of administration staff. Training, including e-training, is an essential component but it also includes practices that have become common in modern tax administrations such as mentoring, transparent performance evaluation methods and the ability to deal with customers as needed.

### 37.3.5 Dispute Management

Dispute management and resolution have become a quintessential element of any tax administration as tax laws have become increasingly complex. The dispute management structure should be a separate vertical function so that the tax collection functions do not influence the resolution of disputes. Countries such as Ireland and the Netherlands, for example, have stepped back from an adversarial approach to disputes and transformed it into one that is collaborative and solution-oriented. They have had significant improvements in efficiency in dispute resolution and revenue collection. Modernisation includes the inclusion of alternative dispute resolution mechanisms through arbitration. This may require legislative change. In addition, regular interpretative statements by the tax administration's management have to be issued to avoid disputes that could otherwise arise due to ambiguity and imprecision in laws, rules and regulations.

### 37.3.6 Internal Processes

The organisation and practice of internal processes—such as filing methods and deadlines, assessment rules and periods, scrutiny and audit, investigation comprise an integral part of a good tax administration, though they may be perceived as ordinary or regular functions. Crucial aspects are the need for in-depth research and analysis including the modelling of taxpayer behaviour, revenue forecasting and policy impact assessment. The penetration of ICT in tax departments forms the backbone of improved service delivery. It could be achieved through a private sector special purpose vehicle (SPV) such as SERPRO of Brazil, or through a public–private model such as in India.

## 37.4 Lessons from History

- Evidence reveals the visage that taxation took over the course of human history. This textbook took India as a case study and found that taxation took on an extractive role that impinged upon the peasantry and merchant class, providing important lessons for what not to do in designing and implementing modern taxation.
- Prehistoric ancient texts of India formulated several guidelines on governance and in fact cautioned against mindless imposition on the subjects of a ruler. Evidence in some texts also suggests that inviting foreign intervention may be justified for the removal of a ruler for reasons of poor governance.
- Moving forward in time, various kingdoms and empires that ruled India from the later part of the second millennium to the mid-second millennium—mainly representing Buddhist and Brahminic kingdoms—reveal land-based taxation from crops, some selected excises in areas that had considerable trade, and tolls on highroads. But there is little evidence of overburdening of the taxpayer though authors have occasionally linked emigration to abandonment of land and assets due to excessive taxation.
- The Mughal era that followed roughly between the mid-fifteenth to the mid-eighteenth century demonstrates sophisticated measurement of land, fertility of soil and crop yield that translated into differentiated tax rates across the vast reaches of the empire. There was a religion-based tax that was occasionally imposed by some emperors on subjects on account of their being Hindu.
- The British era from the mid-eighteenth to the mid-twentieth century was one of extreme extraction from every available tax base, though mainly based on land. Several authors have given detailed accounts of the impoverishment of an earlier productive nation. Interestingly, even during periods of famine, revenue was not only extracted but maintained and this was reported in the British parliament as

matters deserving commendation. Hindu aristocrats were appointed to collect revenue failing which their land was transferred to competing land managers.

- Impoverishment and accompanying inability to pay tax led the British rulers also to use firepower to bring Indian subjects under subjugation. Taxation played a unique role in India's independence movement when leaders used salt, which was not allowed to be collected by Indians without paying tax. Salt became an object that was collected from seashores without paying tax in western and eastern India. The imprisonments that followed comprised only one of many extreme acts by the rulers that led to India's independence in 1947.
- India introduced its voluminous constitution detailing, among intricate constitutional aspects, rules of tax assignment. On that basis, it introduced a well-delineated Income-tax Act in 1961 applicable from 1962 at the central level. It introduced many indirect taxes including a range of state-level sales taxes and central-level selective excises as per its constitution. Most of the indirect taxes were transformed into a centre–state GST in 2017 complemented by selective excises.
- Modern India has gone through many trials and tribulations in reforming its tax system and tax administration though all indications are that there have been persistent attempts to do so. That process will continue as it must in all emerging and advanced economies alike.

## References

Lee, Natalie. 2013. *Revenue Law: Principles and Practice*. 31st ed. Haywards Heath: Bloomsbury.

Silvani, Carlos, and Katherine Baer. 1997. Designing a Tax Administration Reform Strategy: Experiences and Guidelines. Working Paper No. WP/97/30. https://www.imf.org/en/Publications/WP/Issues/2016/12/30/Designing-a-Tax-Administration-Reform-Strategy-Experiences-and-Guidelines-2134. Accessed 30 August 2020.

MIX
Papier aus verantwortungsvollen Quellen
Paper from responsible sources
FSC® C105338

If you have any concerns about our products,
you can contact us on
**ProductSafety@springernature.com**

In case Publisher is established outside the EU,
the EU authorized representative is:
**Springer Nature Customer Service Center GmbH**
**Europaplatz 3, 69115 Heidelberg, Germany**

Printed by Libri Plureos GmbH
in Hamburg, Germany